The Urban Question

for Katherine

The Urban Question

A Marxist Approach

Manuel Castells

Translated by Alan Sheridan

The MIT Press
Cambridge, Massachusetts

First MIT Press paperback edition, 1979
First MIT Press edition, 1977
Authorized translation from the French
La Question urbaine
published by François Maspero 1972; second edition 1976
© François Maspero 1972; 1976
Part V first published by Edward Arnold (Publishers) Ltd. 1977
© Manuel Castells 1977.
This translated edition first published in 1977 by
Edward Arnold (Publishers) Ltd.,
25 Hill Street, London W1X 8LL,
as number one in the Social Change
Series, David Harvey and Brian
Robson, general editors.
English translation by Alan Sheridan
© Alan Sheridan 1977.

ISBN 0-262-53035-X (paper)
ISBN 0-262-03063-2 (hard)
Library of Congress Catalog Card Number 77—75345

The original manuscript was prepared with the help of the Centre d'Etude des
Mouvements Sociaux, and particularly of Mme Colette Didier.

Contents

Preface to the English-language edition

All intellectual work is highly dependent, whether one wishes or not, on the social context in which it is produced. That is why the translation of a work poses not only problems of a linguistic order, but obstacles of a cultural order. When a book written in 1970—71 in a French context reaches an intellectual field as different as that produced by the English-speaking tradition, it may be useful to add a few remarks which, by explaining at the outset the specificity of the approach, might help to situate it more clearly.

The fundamental aim of this book is to develop new tools of research while criticizing the traditional categories with which the social sciences, technocracy and the mass media have usually conceived urban problems. The criticism aims at being as rigorous as possible: that is why, on the one hand, it is based on an examination of the urban sociological literature of several countries in relation to different themes and, on the other hand, it tries to deconstruct the mechanisms by which these categories displace questions and distort our vision of reality, in terms of socially dominant interests.

It is perhaps this dimension of epistemological criticism, which underlies this book, that makes it relatively difficult, particularly for an empiricist intellectual tradition. And yet it is not a question of remaining in the speculative sphere. On the contrary, this work may be regarded as the reaction of one researcher to a large number of unanswered questions that have emerged in the course of a first phase of empirical research that tried to go straight to the facts. Experience has shown that such an approach became the prisoner of intellectual frameworks that had distorting effects at the level of the research operations themselves. For example, to consider space as a physical given and not as a certain historically-constituted social relation, is not a neutral point of departure: it links us with the organicist and mechanistic perspective which presupposes the determination of social behaviour by reactions to a particular physical environment.

What was needed, then, was a critical revision of the traditions of the urban social sciences in order to detect the distorting ideological mechanisms and to reread in a new light the empirical discoveries made. On this basis and on the basis of the new problems emerging from social practice, questions could be asked that could later be translated, theoretically and empirically, into research terms.

Now, questions of the type that we wished to ask did arise, governed by social practice. Indeed, any social science that is not a new metaphysics must establish for itself such a relation with reality. What is not acceptable, however, is that social practice should directly determine one's treatment of these questions. Between the questions and the answers there must be a relatively autonomous mediation: the work of scientific research. But this research, fruitful as it may be, must be inspired by a background of real life. In the world today, urban problems mean the urban crisis, accelerated urbanization, the ideologies of the environment, the increasing intervention of the state, the contradictory efforts of urban planning, popular revolts, neighbourhood organizations, urban politics.

These are the questions that we were concerned with. These are the questions with which this book tried to deal, initially by setting out in search of conceptual tools that would be adequate to such a problematic. For, from the moment one abandons the moralistic or integrationist preoccupations of the old urban sociology or the technocratic perspective of the new urban political science, one must also find new tools of intellectual work.

We looked for these tools, mainly, in the Marxist tradition. Why there? Because we had to answer questions linked to topics such as social classes, change, struggle, revolt, contradiction, conflict, politics. These terms and themes refer us back to a sociological theory the heart of which is the analysis of society as a structure of the class struggle. But this theoretical preference (or venture) poses particularly difficult problems for urban analysis. For here the Marxist tradition is practically non-existent and the development of theory must be linked to the historical recognition of the new problems posed by everyday experience.

This is the task I have set myself and this book represents a beginning. In order to carry it through in the long term, I have accepted from the outset the unequal development of and the concomitant tension between the theoretical schemata proposed and the observations of practice. From time to time, I have attempted a certain fusion of the two levels by means of empirical research, producing at the same time partial knowledge of urban contradictions, a rectification of theoretical schemata and methodological experience.

On the theoretical plane, I have proposed an adaptation of Marxist concepts to the urban sphere, using in particular the reading of Marx given by the French philosopher Louis Althusser. In this respect this book, too, derives from the intellectual context in which it was produced. The development of my research has shown that certain discussions around the concepts employed were superfluous and that the degree of formalism in my construction was useless at the actual research level. The reader will find elements of rectification in the Afterword 1975 at the end of the book.

But such rectifications do not change fundamentally the general theoretical perspective of the application of Marxism to urbanization, for the excesses of the Althusserian language do not undermine the relevance of the concepts advanced and of the theoretical laws based on the Marxist tradition and on the practical experience that has nourished this theory. Certainly Marxism has not solved all the theoretical problems that are constantly being posed: it is not a schema, but a perspective. This means that one is committed to developing it unceasingly, proposing new concepts, rectifying laws that prove to be incorrect, using it as a *tool* instead of repeating it as a *dogma*. That is why the only justification of the propositions advanced in this book is the fruitfulness of the empirical research that they gave rise to. I have tried to present a few concrete examples, in particular in the domain of urban politics, in order to put the concepts into practice. Certainly the tools were still too crude and the results are only partial. But the difficulties of overthrowing a whole traditional perspective, proposing a new theory as an extension of Marxist thought, and translating it into empirical research with a high degree of rigour, are too numerous for one to be able to overcome them in the short term. The main thing is not so much to prove a point from the outset as to give rise to a dynamic that gradually opens up a new field of research that responds to the questions that are now being put to us by increasingly explosive urban contradictions.

That is why, in the Afterword 1975 published in this edition, I have presented a number of references to empirical research: some of these, which implement my concepts, are my own; others, though not a direct application of my theoretical schema, have transformed the style of urban research, the questions asked and the investigations carried out, in an intellectual movement that is

adjusting urban sociology to the society in which we are living.
There are, however, still a great many problems, especially from
the point of view of the methodological rigour of the research
carried out in this perspective, and this derives from a double
obstacle: 1. The intrinsic difficulty of translating into terms of
empirical research such complex questions as those with which
Marxist theory is concerned; 2. The technological under-development of the social sciences in France, and the concomitant absence
of a *milieu* of research that is as concerned about rigour as it is,
rightly, preoccupied with the problem of the relevance of research.
Accordingly, the gradual development of an intellectual exchange
and debate between the European Marxist tradition and the current
of English-speaking research may be extremely fruitful for both
sides, on the condition that the cultural barriers can be overcome
and the exchange is not limited to institutional and academic links.
It is a question of exchanging experience not only of articulating
resources.

For in the world society in which we are living, class conflicts,
in the urban domain as elsewhere, are a challenge to our commitment and to our imagination everywhere. That is why it is increasingly necessary to oppose to the International of technocratic
experts a new International of 'social scientists' who, coming from
fairly diverse political and intellectual horizons, meet in the con-
viction that cities are made *by people* and with the determination
that they should be made *for people*.

Madison, Wisconsin
June 1975

Epistemological Introduction

This book was born out of astonishment.

At a time when the waves of the anti-imperialist struggle are sweeping across the world, when movements of revolt are bursting out at the very heart of advanced capitalism, when the revival of working-class action is creating a new political situation in Europe, 'urban problems' are becoming an essential element in the policies of governments, in the concerns of the mass media and, consequently, in the everyday life of a large section of the population.

At first sight, the ideological character of such a profound shift of interest — expressing in the terms of an imbalance between technology and environment certain consequences of the existing social contradictions — leaves little doubt as to the need to emerge, theoretically and politically, from this labyrinth of mirrors. But, although it is easy enough to agree as to the broad outlines of such a situation (unless politico-ideological interests are working in the opposite direction), this does not solve the difficulties encountered in social practice. On the contrary, all the problems begin at this point, that is to say, at the point where an attempt is made to *supersede* (and not to *ignore*) the ideology that underlies the 'urban question'.

For, although it is true that 'urbanistic thinking' in its different versions, of which the ideology of the environment seems to be the most advanced, is above all the prerogative of the technocracy and of the ruling strata in general, its effects are to be felt in the working-class movement and, still more, in the currents of cultural and political revolt that are developing in the industrial capitalist societies. Thus, in addition to the hold the various state organs have over the problems associated with the environment, we are witnessing increasing political intervention in the urban neighbourhoods, in public amenities, transport, etc. and, at the same time, the charging of the spheres of 'consumption' and 'everyday life' with political action and ideological confrontation. Now, very often, this shift of objectives and practices takes place without any change in the thematic register — that is to say, while remaining within the 'urban' problematic. It follows that an elucidation of the 'urban question' is becoming urgent, not only as a means of demystifying the ideology of the dominant classes, but as a tool of reflection for the political tendencies which, confronted by new social problems, oscillate between the dogmatism of general formulations and the apprehension of these questions in the (inverted) terms of the dominant ideology.

Indeed, it is not simply a question of exposing this ideology, for it is the symptom of a certain intensely experienced, but still inadequately identified, problematic; and if it proves to be socially effective, it is because it is offered as the interpretation of phenomena that have acquired an ever greater importance in advanced capitalism and because Marxist theory, which only poses the problems raised by social and political practice, has not yet proved capable of analysing them in a sufficiently specific way.

In fact, the two aspects of the problem are one. For, once the contours of the ideological discourse on 'the urban' have been established, the supersession of this discourse cannot proceed simply by means of a denunciation; it requires a theoretical analysis of the questions of the social practice it connotes. Or, in other words, an ideological misunderstanding/recognition can be superseded, and therefore interpreted, only by a theoretical analysis; this is the only way of avoiding the twin dangers encountered by any theoretical practice:

1. A right-wing (but apparently left-wing) deviation, which consists in recognizing these new problems, but doing so in the terms of the urbanistic ideology, moving away from a Marxist analysis and giving them a theoretical — and political — priority over economic determination and the class struggle.

2. A left-wing deviation, which denies the emergence of new forms of social contradiction in the capitalist societies, confining all discussion of the urban to a purely ideological sphere, while exhausting itself in intellectual acrobatics to reduce the increasing diversity of the forms of class opposition to a direct opposition between capital and labour.

Such an undertaking requires the use of certain theoretical tools in order to transform, through a process of labour, a raw material, both theoretical and ideological, and to obtain a product (which always remains provisional), in which the theoretico-ideological field is modified in the direction of a development of its theoretical elements. The process becomes more complicated in so far as, for us, there is production of knowledge, in the strict sense of the term, only in connection with the analysis of a concrete situation. This means that the product of research is, at least, twofold: there is the effect of specific knowledge of the situation studied, and there is the knowledge of this situation, obtained with the help of more general theoretical tools, linked with the general context of historical materialism. The fact that they make a given situation intelligible is demonstrated by the material realization (or experimentation) of the theoretical laws advanced; in becoming more specific, these laws develop, at the same time, the theoretical field of Marxism and, by the same token, increase its efficacy in social practice.

If this seems to be the general schema of theoretical work, its application to the 'urban question' comes up against certain particular difficulties. Indeed, 'the raw material' of this work, which is made up of three elements (ideological representations, knowledge already acquired, the specificity of the concrete situations studied), is characterized by the almost total predominance of the ideological elements, a very great difficulty in the precise empirical mapping of 'urban problems' (precisely because it is a question of an ideological delimitation) and the virtual non-existence of elements of already acquired knowledge in this field, in so far as Marxism has approached it only marginally (Engels on housing) or in a historicist perspective (Marx in *The German Ideology*), or has seen in it no more than a mere transcription of political relations. The 'social sciences' for their part, owing to their close links with the explicative ideologies of social evolution, are particularly poor in analyses of the question and of the strategic role played by these ideologies in the mechanisms of social integration.

This situation explains the slow and difficult work that has to be undertaken in matching the general concepts of historical materialism with situations and processes very different from those that were the basis for the production of these concepts. However, we are trying to extend their scope without any change of perspective, for the production of new concepts must take place in the development of fundamental theses, without which there can be no deployment of a theoretical structure, but merely a juxtaposition of 'intermediary hypotheses'. There is nothing dogmatic about this method of work, in so far as attachment to a particular perspective does not derive from some sort of fidelity to principles, but from the 'nature of things' (that is to say, from the objective laws of human history).

Having said this, the paucity of properly theoretical work on the

problems connoted by urban ideology obliges us to take as fundamental raw material, on the one hand, the mass of 'research'
accumulated by 'urban sociology' and, on the other hand, a whole
series of situations and processes identified as 'urban' in social practice.

As far as urban sociology is concerned, it, in fact, constitutes the
'scientific foundation' (not the social source) of a great number of
ideological discourses that merely enlarge, combine and adapt
theses and data accumulated by researchers. Furthermore, even
though this field is heavily dominated by ideology, there appear
here and there analyses, descriptions, observations of concrete
situations that can help us to track down in a specific way themes
dealt with in this tradition, and questions perceived as urban in the
spontaneous sociology of subjects.

This sociology, like all 'specific' sociologies, is, above all, quanti-
tatively and qualitatively, Anglo-Saxon and, more precisely,
American. This is the reason, and the only one, why the American
and British references in this work are so important. This is reinforced by the fact that, very often, 'French', 'Italian, 'Latin
American', even 'Polish' or 'Soviet' sociologies are little more than
bad copies of the empirical research and 'theoretical' themes of
American sociology.

On the other hand, I have tried to diversify, as far as my own
limitations allowed me, the historical situations that serve as a concrete mapping for the emergence of this problematic, in order to
circumscribe more completely the various types of urban ideology
and to locate the different regions of the underlying social structure.

It goes without saying that I do not claim to have arrived at a
reformulation of the ideological problematic from which I set out
and, still less, therefore, to have carried out true concrete analyses
leading to knowledge. This book merely communicates certain
experiences of work in this direction, with the aim of producing a
dynamic of research rather than establishing a demonstration,
which is in any case unrealizable at the present theoretical conjuncture. The point at which I have arrived is quite simply the belief
that any new theoretical position that is not anchored in concrete
analyses is redundant. In trying to escape formalism and theoreti-
cism, I have tried to systematize my experiences, so that they may
be superseded in the only way in which they can be: in theoretical
and political practice.

Such an attempt has come up against very serious problems of
communication. How is one to express a theoretical *intention* on
the basis of material that is above all ideological and which bears
on inadequately identified social processes? I have tried to limit the

difficulties in two ways: on the one hand, by systematically envisa-
ging the possible effect on research practice of taking these analyses
and propositions as a starting point, rather than by aiming at the
coherence and correctness of the text itself; on the other hand, by
using as the means of expressing a theoretical content, sketches of
concrete analyses that are not in fact concrete analyses. Thus this
is indeed, then, a properly theoretical work, that is to say, one
bearing on the production of tools of knowledge, and not on the
production of knowledge relative to concrete situations. But the
way of expressing the mediations necessary in order to arrive at the
theoretical experiences proposed has consisted in examining this or
that historical situation while trying to transform our understanding
of it with the help of advanced theoretical instruments or, too, in
showing the contradiction between the observations at one's disposal and the ideological discourses that were juxtaposed with
them.

This procedure has the advantage of making the problematic
concrete, but it involves two serious drawbacks that I would like
to point out:

1. It might be thought that the present book is a collection of
concrete researches, whereas, apart from a few exceptions, it offers
only the beginnings of a theoretical transformation of empirical
raw material, the necessary minimum to indicate the direction the
work might take; indeed, how could we claim to analyse so rapidly
so great a number of theoretical problems and historical situations?
The only possible point of the effort expended is to reveal, through
a diversity of themes and situations, the emergence of the same
problematic throughout its articulations.

2. One might also see here the concrete illustration of a theoretical system, complete and offered as a model, whereas the production of knowledge does not proceed from the establishment of a
system, but through the creation of a series of theoretical tools
that are never validated by their coherence, but by their fruitfulness in the analysis of concrete situations.

This, then, is the difficulty inherent in this project: on the one
hand, it aims at deducing theoretical tools of observation from concrete situations (situations that I have observed myself, or that
have been dealt with by sociological ideology), and, on the other
hand, it is only one moment in a process that must, at another conjuncture, reverse the approach, setting out from these theoretical
tools to know situations.

The importance accorded to the tactical problems of theoretical
work (essential, if one wishes to struggle at one and the same time
against both formalism and empiricism, while avoiding the voluntarist

project of establishing 'the foundation of science') is directly
reflected in the organization of the work. The first part recognizes
the historical terrain, in order to give a relatively precise content
to the theme approached. I then try to establish the contours of
ideological discourse on 'the urban', which is supposed to be a delimitation of a field of 'theoretical knowledge' and social practice.
In trying to break open this ideological envelope and to reinterpret
the concrete questions it contains, the analyses of the structure of
urban space offer a first theoretical formulation of the question as
a whole, but they show, at the same time, the impossibility of a
theory that is not centred on the articulation of the 'urban question' with political processes, that is to say, relative to the state
apparatus and the class struggle. This book opens, therefore, with a
discussion, theoretical and historical, of 'urban politics'. An illustration of the interaction between urban structure and urban
politics is shown through the study of the process of the urban
crisis in the US.

Such a conclusion makes it necessary to introduce a remark
whose concrete consequences are enormous: there is no purely
theoretical possibility of resolving (or superseding) the contradictions that are at the base of the urban question; this supersession
can come only from social practice, that is to say, from political
practice. But, in order for such practice to be correct and not blind,
it is necessary to make explicit theoretically the questions thus
approached, developing and specifying the perspectives of historical
materialism. The social conditions for the emergence of such a reformulation are extremely complex, but, in any case, one may be
sure that they require a point of departure that is historically
bound up with the working-class movement and its practice. This
excludes all the 'avant-gardist' claims of any 'individual theory';
but it does not deny the usefulness of certain work of reflection,
documentation and inquiry, in as much as such work forms part of
a theoretico-practical approach to the urban question, so urgent
today in political practice.

1 The Historical Process
of Urbanization

Every form of matter has a history or, rather, it is its history.
This proposition does not solve the problem of the knowledge of a
given reality; on the contrary, it poses that problem. For, to read
this history, to discover the laws of its structuring and transformation, one must break down, by theoretical analysis, what is given
in a practical synthesis. However, it is useful to fix the historical
contours of a phenomenon before undertaking an investigation of
it. Or, in other words, it seems more prudent to undertake this
search on the basis of a false theoretical innocence, taking a look,
in order to discover the conceptual problems that arise whenever
one tries — in vain — to apprehend the 'concrete'. It is in this sense
that a study of the history of the process of urbanization would
seem to be the best approach to the urban question, for it brings us
to the heart of the problematic of the development of societies,
and shows us, at the same time, an ideologically determined conceptual imprecision.

But, although it is clear that the process of the formation of
cities is the basis of the urban networks and conditions the social
organization of space, one remains too often at the level of an overall presentation, without any specification of a rate of demographic
increase, linking in the same ideological discourse the evolution of
the spatial forms of a society and the diffusion of a cultural model
on the basis of a political domination.

Analyses of the process of urbanization are situated, generally
speaking, in an evolutionist theoretical perspective, according to
which each social formation is produced, without break, by a
duplication of the elements of the preceding social formation. The
forms of spatial settlement are therefore one of the most visible
expressions of these modifications (Lampard, 1955, 90−104;
Wooley, 1957; Handlin and Burchard, 1963). This evolution of
spatial forms has even been used to classify the stages of universal
history (Mumford, 1956; 1961). In fact, rather than establishing

the criteria of periodization, it is absolutely necessary to study the production of spatial forms on the basis of the underlying social structure.

To explain the social process that underlies the organization of space is not simply a matter of situating the urban phenomenon in its context. A sociological problematic of urbanization must regard it as a process of organization and development and, consequently, set out from the relation between productive forces, social classes and cultural forms (including space). Such a research project cannot proceed solely in the abstract; it must, with the help of its conceptual tools, explain particular historical situations, in sufficient number to reveal the lines of force of the phenomenon studied, the organization of space.

However, the ideologico-theoretical confusion existing in this field forces us to make an initial mapping of our object, both in conceptual terms and in terms of historical reality. This work is in no sense academic and is presented, on the contrary, as a technically indispensible operation if we are to avoid evolutionist connotations and approach, in all clarity, a particular field of our experience.

I

The Urban Phenomenon: Conceptual Delimitations and Historical Realities

In the jungle of subtle definitions that sociologists have provided us with, it is possible to distinguish very clearly two extremely distinct senses of the term *urbanization*. (Eldridge, 1956; Popenoe, 1969.)

1. The spatial concentration of a population on the basis of certain limits of dimension and density (Bogue and Hauser, 1963; Davis, 1965);

2. The diffusion of the system of values, attitudes and behaviour called 'urban culture'. (Bergel, 1955; Anderson, 1959—60, 68; Friedmann, 1953; Sirjamaki, 1961; Boskoff, 1962; Gist and Fava, 1964.)

For a discussion of the problematic of 'urban culture', the reader is referred to Part II. (See Wirth, 1938.) But the essence of my conclusion is the following: we are concerned here with the cultural system characteristic of capitalist industrial society.

Furthermore, and following the same line of thought, one assimilates urbanization and industrialization, making an equivalence of the two processes at the level of the choice of the indicators used (Meadows, 1967), in order to construct the corresponding dichotomies, rural/urban and agricultural/industrial employment. (Sorokin and Zimmerman, 1929.)

In fact, the culturalist tendency in the analysis of urbanization presupposes the correspondence between a certain technical type of production (essentially defined by industrial activity), a system of values ('modernism') and a specific form of spatial organization, the city, whose distinctive features are a certain size and a certain density.

That this correspondence is not obvious may be seen in a simple analytical account of the great pre-industrial urban centres such as that carried out by Sjoberg (1960). Some authors (e.g. Reismann,

1964) remain consistent by refusing to use the term 'city' to designate those forms of settlement, thus making explicit the confusion of the 'urban' problematic and a given socio-cultural organization.

This link between spatial form and cultural content may possibly serve as a hypothesis (which I shall examine in detail in the following pages), but it cannot constitute an element in the definition of urbanization, for the theoretical response would be already contained in the terms in which the problem was posed.

If one is to keep to this distinction, leaving until later the establishment of the theoretical and empirical relations between the two forms, spatial and cultural, one may take, to begin with, the definition of H. T. Eldridge (1956, 338), who characterizes urbanization as a process of population concentration at two levels: 1. the proliferation of points of concentration; 2. the increase in size of each of these points.

Urban would then designate a particular form of the occupation of space by a population, namely, the urban centre resulting from a high concentration and relatively high density, with, as its predictable correlate, greater functional and social differentiation. Granted, but when one wishes to use this 'theoretical' definition directly in a concrete analysis, the difficulties begin. On the basis of which levels of dimension and density can a spatial unit be regarded as urban? What, in practice, are the theoretical and empirical foundations of each of the criteria?

Pierre George (1964, 7—20) has exposed clearly enough the insurmountable contradictions of statistical empiricism in the delimitation of the concept of the urban. Indeed, if the number of inhabitants, corrected by the structure of the active population and administrative divisions, seems to be the most common criterion, the thresholds used vary enormously, the indicators of the different activities are dependent on the individual type of society and, lastly, the same quantities take on an entirely different meaning according to the productive and social structures that determine the organization of space. (Beaujeu-Garnier and Chabot, 1963, 35.) Thus the United States Census (1961) takes the threshold of 2500 inhabitants as the criterion of an urban district, but also adds the urban areas strongly linked to a regional metropolitan centre. On the other hand, the European Conference of Statistics at Prague takes 10 000 inhabitants as its criterion, correcting it by the distribution of the active population in the different sectors.

In fact, the most flexible formula consists in classifying the spatial units of each country according to several dimensions and several levels and in establishing between them theoretically significant empirical relations. More concretely, one might distinguish the quantitative importance of the urban areas (10 000 inhabitants, 20 000, 100 000, 1 000 000, etc.), their functional hierarchy (nature of activities, situation in the chain of interdependences), their administrative importance, then, combining several of these characteristics, one might arrive at different types of spatial occupation.

The rural/urban dichotomy then loses all meaning, for one might equally well distinguish between urban and metropolitan, and, above all, cease to think in terms of a continuous movement from one pole to the other and establish a system of relations between the different historically given spatial forms. (Ledrut, 1967.)

What emerges from these observations is that it is not by seeking academic definitions or criteria of administrative practice that one will achieve a valid delimitation of one's concepts; on the contrary, it is the rapid analysis of a number of historically established relations between space and society that will enable us to give an objective basis to our study.

Archaeological research has shown that the first settled urban areas with a high density of population (Mesopotamia, about 3500 BC; Egypt, 3000 BC; China and India, 3000–2500 BC) (Mumford, 1961; McAdams, 1966; Lampard, 1965) appeared at the end of the Neolithic Age, where the state of technology and the social and natural conditions of labour enabled cultivators to produce more than they needed to subsist. From that time onwards, a system of division and distribution of the product developed, as the expression and deployment of a technical capacity and of a level of social organization. The cities were the residential form adopted by those members of society whose direct presence at the places of agricultural production was not necessary. That is to say, these cities could exist only on the basis of the surplus produced by working the land. They were religious, administrative and political centres, the spatial expression of a social complexity determined by the process of appropriation and reinvestment of the product of labour. It is thus, then, a new social system, but one that is not separate from the rural one, nor posterior to it, for they are both closely linked at the heart of the same process of production of social forms, even if, from the point of view of these forms themselves, we are presented with two different situations. (Sjoberg, 1960, 27–31; Braddwood and Willey, 1962.)

Let us take, for example, V. Gordon Childe's (1950) synthesis of the criteria which, according to existing empirical knowledge, characterized the first urban areas: the existence of non-productive specialists working full time (priests, functionaries, 'service workers'); a population of sufficient size and density; a specific art;

the use of writing and arithmetical figures; scientific work; a system of taxation that concentrates the surplus of production; a state apparatus; public architecture; external trade; the existence of social classes.

These observations, based on abundant documentation, are of manifest interest, despite a classificatory procedure reminiscent of that of Borges's celebrated Chinese encyclopedia. But reading these data in terms of theory, it becomes clear enough that the city is the geographical locus in which is established the politico-administrative superstructure of a society that has reached that point of technical and social development (natural and cultural) at which there is a differentiation of the product in the simple and the extended reproduction of labour power, culminating in a system of distribution and exchange, which presupposes the existence of: 1. a system of social classes; 2. a political system permitting both the functioning of the social ensemble and the domination of one class; 3. an institutional system of investment, in particular with regard to culture and technology; 4. a system of external exchange. (Mumford, 1956.)

Even this cursory analysis shows the 'urban phenomenon' articulated with the structure of a society. The same approach may be taken up (and lead to a different result in terms of content) in relation to the various historical forms of spatial organization. Although it is not possible in a few sentences to sum up the human history of space, we can, for analytical purposes, make a few remarks on the possible reading of certain significant urban types.

Thus the imperial cities of the earliest historical times, in particular Rome, combined the characteristics mentioned above with commercial and administrative functions deriving from the concentration, in the same urban area, of a power exercised, by conquest, over a vast territory. Similarly, the Roman penetration of other civilizations took the form of urban colonization – a support both for the administrative functions and for mercantile exploitation. The city is not, therefore, a locus of production, but of administration and domination, bound up with the social primacy of the political-administrative apparatus. (Mumford, 1961.)

It is logical, therefore, that the fall of the Roman Empire in the West brought with it the almost total disappearance of the socio-spatial forms of the city for, the central politico-administrative functions having been replaced by the local domination of the feudal lords, there was no other social reason for maintaining the cities other than the divisions of the ecclesiastical administration or the colonization and defence of the frontier regions (for example, in Catalonia or East Prussia). (Pirenne, 1927.)

The medieval city revived as a consequence of a new social dynamic within the preceding social structure. More concretely, it was created by the union of a pre-existing fortress, around which a nucleus of living quarters and services had been organized, and a market, especially after the opening up of the new commercial routes by the Crusades. On this foundation were organized the politico-administrative institutions proper to the city, which gave it an internal coherence and greater autonomy. It is this political specificity of the city that makes it a world in itself and defines its frontiers as a social system. The best analysis of this phenomenon is that of Max Weber (1947). The ideology of belonging to the city, which lasted into advanced industrial society, finds its historical foundation in this kind of situation.

Although this politico-administrative autonomy was common to most of the cities that developed in the early Middle Ages, the concrete social and spatial forms of these cities were strictly dependent on the conjuncture of the new social relations that had appeared as a result of transformations in the system of distribution of the product. In opposition to the feudal power, a mercantile class had formed which, breaking up the vertical system of distribution of the product, established horizontal links by acting as an intermediary, superseded the subsistence economy and accumulated sufficient autonomy to be capable of investing in manufactures. (See the extraordinary account in Pizzorno, 1962.)

Since the medieval city represents the emancipation of the mercantile bourgeoisie in its struggle to free itself from feudalism and the central power, its evolution will vary greatly according to the links forged between the bourgeoisie and the nobility. Thus, where these links were close, relations between the city and the surrounding territory, dependent on the feudal lords, was organized in a complementary way. Conversely, the conflict of these classes led to urban isolation.

From a different standpoint, the contiguity or geographical separation between the two classes affected the culture of the cities, especially in the spheres of consumption and investment: the integration of the nobility into the bourgeoisie enabled the former to organize the urban system of values according to the aristocratic model, whereas, when the bourgeoisie was left to itself, exposed to the hostility of the surrounding territory, the community of citizens created new values, in particular those relating to thrift and investment; socially isolated and cut off from supplies from the near-by countryside, their survival depended on their financial and manufacturing capacity.

One might also analyse the evolution of the urban system of each country in terms of the triangular relations between bourgeoisie, nobility and monarchy. For example, the underdevelopment of the Spanish commercial cities compared with the Italian or German cities during the sixteenth and seventeenth centuries can be explained by their role as 'transmission belt' between the crown and the American trade, contrasting with the role played by the Italian and German cities, which were highly autonomous in relation to the emperor and princes, with whom they formed only temporary alliances.

The development of industrial capitalism, contrary to an all too widespread naive view, did not bring about a strengthening of the city, but its virtual disappearance as an institutional and relatively autonomous social system, organized around specific objectives. In fact, the constitution of commodities as a basic cog of the economic system, the technical and social division of labour, the diversification of economic and social interests over a larger space, the homogenization of the institutional system, brought about an explosion of the conjunction of a spatial form, the city, with a sphere of social domination by a specific class, the bourgeoisie. Urban diffusion is precisely balanced by the loss of the city's ecological and cultural particularism. The process of urbanization and the autonomy of the 'urban' cultural model are thus revealed as paradoxically contradictory processes. (Lefebvre, 1968; 1970.)

The urbanization bound up with the first industrial revolution, and accompanying the development of the capitalist mode of production, is a process of organizing space based on two sets of fundamental facts. (Labasse, 1966.)

1. The *prior* decomposition of the agrarian social structures and the emigration of the population towards the already existing urban areas, providing the labour force essential to industrialization.

2. The passage from a domestic economy to a small-scale manufacturing economy, then to a large-scale manufacturing economy, which meant, at the same time, a concentration of manpower, the creation of a market and the constitution of an industrial milieu.

The towns attracted industry because of these two essential factors (manpower and market) and industry, in its turn, developed new kinds of employment and gave rise to the need for services.

But the reverse process is also important: where functional elements were present, in particular raw materials and means of transport, industry colonized and gave rise to urbanization.

In both cases, the dominant element was industry, which entirely organized the urban landscape. Yet this domination was not a technological fact; it was the expression of the capitalistic logic that lay at the base of industrialization. 'Urban disorder' was not in fact disorder at all; it represented the spatial organization created by the market, and derived from the absence of social control of the industrial activity. Technological rationality and the primacy of profit led, on the one hand, to the effacement of any essential difference between the towns and to the fusion of cultural types in the overall characteristics of capitalist industrial civilization and, on the other hand, to the development of functional specialization and the social division of labour in space, with a hierarchy between the different urban areas and a process of cumulative growth deriving from the play of external economies. (See George, 1950.)

Lastly, the present problematic of urbanization revolves around three fundamental facts and one burning question:

1. The acceleration of the rhythm of urbanization throughout the world (see Table 1).

2. The concentration of this urban growth in the so-called 'under-developed' regions, without the corresponding economic growth that had accompanied the first urbanization in the industrialized capitalist countries (see Table 2).

3. The appearance of new urban forms and, in particular, the great metropolises (see Table 3).

4. The relation between the urban phenomenon and new forms of social articulation springing from the capitalist mode of production and tending to supersede it.

These problems are clearly posed, though no clearly defined research methods are indicated, in Greer *et al.* (1968). My research is an attempt to pose these problems theoretically, on the basis of certain definitions that can now be proposed and on the basis of the few historical remarks that I have just made.

1. The term *urbanization* refers both to the constitution of specific spatial forms of human societies characterized by the significant concentration of activities and populations in a limited space and to the existence and diffusion of a particular cultural system, the urban culture. This confusion is ideological and is intended: (*a*) To establish a correspondence between ecological forms and a cultural content. (*b*) To suggest an ideology of the production of social values on the basis of a 'natural' phenomenon of social densification and heterogeneity (see Chapter 2).

2. The notion of *urban* (as opposed to *rural*) belongs to the ideological dichotomy of traditional society/modern society and refers to a certain social and functional heterogeneity, without being able to define it in any other way than by its relative distance from modern society. However, the distinction between town and country poses the problem of the differentiation of the spatial forms of social organization. But this differentiation may be

Table 1
Situation and projections of the urban phenomenon
in the world (1920–1960 and 1960–80) – in millions (estimation)

Geographical regions and occupation of space	1920 (est.)	1940 (est.)	1960 (est.)	1980 (proj.)	Absolute growth 1920–60	1960–80
World total						
Total population	*1 860*	*2 298*	*2 994*	*4 269*	*1 134*	*1 275*
Rural and small towns	1 607	1 871	2 242	2 909	635	667
Urban	253	427	752	1 360	499	608
(Large towns)	(96)	(175)	(351)	(725)	(255)	(374)
Europe (without USSR)						
Total population	*324*	*379*	*425*	*479*	*101*	*54*
Rural and small towns	220	239	251	244	31	7
Urban	104	140	174	235	70	61
(Large towns)	(44)	(61)	(73)	(99)	(29)	(26)
North America						
Total population	*116*	*144*	*198*	*262*	*82*	*64*
Rural and small towns	72	80	86	101	14	15
Urban	44	64	112	161	68	49
(Large towns)	(22)	(30)	(72)	(111)	(50)	(39)
East Asia						
Total population	*553*	*636*	*794*	*1 038*	*241*	*244*
Rural and small towns	514	554	634	742	120	108
Urban	39	82	160	296	121	136
(Large towns)	(15)	(34)	(86)	(155)	(71)	(69)
South Asia						
Total population	*470*	*610*	*858*	*1 366*	*388*	*508*
Rural and small towns	443	560	742	1 079	299	337
Urban	27	50	116	287	89	171
(Large towns)	(5)	(13)	(42)	(149)	(37)	(107)
Soviet Union						
Total population	*155*	*195*	*214*	*278*	*59*	*64*
Rural and small towns	139	148	136	150	3	14
Urban	16	47	78	128	62	50
(Large towns)	(2)	(14)	(27)	(56)	(25)	(29)
Latin America						
Total population	*90*	*130*	*213*	*374*	*123*	*161*
Rural and small towns	77	105	145	222	68	77
Urban	13	25	68	152	55	84
(Large towns)	(5)	(12)	(35)	(100)	(30)	(65)
Africa						
Total population	*143*	*192*	*276*	*449*	*133*	*173*
Rural and small towns	136	178	240	360	104	120
Urban	7	14	36	89	29	54
(Large towns)	(1)	(3)	(11)	(47)	(10)	(36)
Oceania						
Total population	*9*	*12*	*16*	*23*	*7*	*7*
Rural and small towns	6	7	8	11	2	3
Urban	3	5	8	11	5	3
(Large towns)	(2)	(2)	(5)	(8)	(3)	(3)

Source: *Population Division, United Nations Bureau of Social Affairs.*

Table 2
*Evolution of urbanization according to levels
of development (in millions)*

	1920 (est.)	1940 (est.)	1960 (est.)	1980 (proj.)	Absolute growth 1920–60	1960–80
Occupation of space				World total		
Total population	*1 860*	*2 298*	*2 994*	*4 269*	*1 134*	*1 275*
Rural, small towns	1 607	1 871	2 242	2 909	635	667
Urban	253	427	752	1 360	499	608
(Large towns)	(96)	(175)	(351)	(725)	(255)	(374)
			Developed regions			
Total population	*672*	*821*	*977*	*1 189*	*305*	*212*
Rural, small towns	487	530	544	566	57	22
Urban	185	291	433	623	248	190
(Large towns)	(80)	(134)	(212)	(327)	(132)	(115)
			Underdeveloped regions			
Total population	*1 188*	*1 476*	*2 017*	*3 080*	*829*	*1 063*
Rural, small towns	I 120	1 341	1 698	2 343	578	645
Urban	68	135	319	737	251	418
(Large towns)	(16)	(41)	(139)	(398)	(123)	(259)
	Underdeveloped regions as percentage of whole world					
Total population	*64*	*64*	*67*	*72*	*73*	*83*
Rural, small towns	70	72	76	81	91	97
Urban	27	32	42	54	50	69
(Large towns)	(16)	(24)	(40)	(55)	(48)	(69)

Source: *Population Division, United Nations Bureau of Social Affairs.*

reduced neither to a dichotomy nor to a continuous evolution, as natural evolutionism, incapable of understanding these spatial forms as products of a structure and of social processes, supposes. Indeed, the impossibility of finding an empirical criterion for the definition of the urban is merely the expression of theoretical imprecision. This imprecision is ideologically necessary in order to connote, through a material organization, the myth of modernity.

3. Consequently, in anticipation of a properly theoretical discussion of this problem, I shall discuss the theme of the *social production of spatial forms* rather than speak of urbanization. Within this problematic, the ideological notion of urbanization refers to a process by which a significantly large proportion of the population of a society is concentrated on a certain space, in which are constituted urban areas that are functionally and socially independent from an internal point of view and are in a relation of hierarchized articulation (urban network).

4. The analysis of urbanization is closely linked with the problematic of *development*, which is also a term that we ought to define.

Table 3
Growth of large urban areas in the world 1920–1960
(general estimates of population, in thousands)

City	1920	1930	1940	1950	1960
World total	30 294	48 660	66 364	84 923	141 156
Europe (total)	*16 051*	*18 337*	*18 675*	*18 016*	*18 605*
London	7 236	8 127	8 275	8 366	8 190
Paris	4 965	5 885	6 050	6 300	7 140
Berlin	3 850	4 325	4 350	3 350	3 275
North America (total)	*10 075*	*13 300*	*17 300*	*26 950*	*33 875*
New York	7 125	9 350	10 600	12 350	14 150
Los Angeles	(750) a	(1 800) a	2 500	4 025	6 525
Chicago	2 950	3 950	4 200	4 950	6 000
Philadelphia	(2 025) a	(2 350) a	(2 475) a	2 950	3 650
Detroit	(1 100) a	(1 825) a	(2 050) a	2 675	3 550
East Asia (total)	*4 168*	*11 773*	*15 789*	*16 487*	*40 806*
Tokyo	4 168	6 064	8 558	8 182	13 534
Shanghai	(2 000) a	3 100	3 750	5 250	8 500
Osaka	(1 889) a	2 609	3 481	3 055	5 158
Peking	(1 000) a	(1 350) a	(1 750) a	(2 100) a	5 000
Tientsin	(800) a	(1 000) a	(1 500) a	(1 900) a	3 500
Hongkong	(550) a	(700) a	(1 500) a	(1 925) a	2 614
Shenyang	..... b	(700) a	(1 150) a	(1 700) a	2 500
South Asia (total)	.....	.....	*3 400*	*7 220*	*12 700*
Calcutta	(1 820) a	(2 055) a	3 400	4 490	5 810
Bombay	(1 275) a	(1 300) a	(1 660) a	2 730	4 040
Djakarta	..... b	(525) a	(1 000) a	(1 750) a	2 850
Soviet Union (total)	.....	*2 500*	*7 700*	*4 250*	*9 550*
Moscow	(1 120) a	2 500	4 350	4 250	6 150
Leningrad	(740) a	(2 000) a ,	3 350	(2 250) a	3 400
Latin America (total)	.....	*2 750*	*3 500*	*12 000*	*22 300*
Buenos Aires	(2 275) a	2 750	3 500	5 150	6 775
Mexico City	(835) a	(1 435) a	(2 175) a	3 800	6 450
Rio de Janeiro	(1 325) a	(1 675) a	(2 150) a	3 050	4 700
São Paulo	(600) a	(900) a	(1 425) a	(2 450) a	4 375
Africa (total)	.....	.....	.....	.....	*3 320*
Cairo	(875) a	(1 150) a	(1 525) a	(2 350) a	3 320

(a) Towns below 2 500 000 are not included in the totals.
(b) Smaller than 500 000.
Source: *Population Division, United Nations Bureau of Social Affairs.*

The notion of development creates the same confusion by referring both to a level (technological, economic) and to a process (qualitative transformation of social structures, permitting an increase of the potential of the productive forces). This confusion corresponds to an ideological function, namely, the function that presents structural transformations as simply an accumulative movement of the technological and material resources of a society. From this point of view, therefore, there would seem to exist different levels and a slow but inevitable evolution that organizes the passage, when there is an excess of resources, to the higher level.

5. The problem evoked by the notion of development is that of the transformation of the social structure on which a society is based in such a way as to free a capacity for gradual accumulation (the investment/consumption ratio).

6. If the notion of development is situated in relation to the articulation of the structures of a given social formation, it cannot be analysed without reference to the articulation of a set of social formations (on the so-called 'international' scale). For this, we need a second concept: that of *dependence*, characterizing asymmetrical relations between social formations of such a kind that the structural organization of one of them has no logic outside its position in the general system.

7. These points enable us to substitute for the ideological problematic (which connotes the relation between national technological evolution and the evolution towards the culture of modern societies) the following theoretical questions: *what is the process of social production of the spatial forms of a society* and, conversely, *what are the relations between the space constituted and the structural transformations of a society, within an intersocietal ensemble characterized by relations of dependence?*

2

The Formation of the Metropolitan Regions in Industrial Capitalist Societies

In analysing the principles of production of a new spatial form, the metropolitan region, what we are dealing with is the problematic of the organization of space in the advanced capitalist societies. However, it would be better to limit ourselves to this precise point, for we are dealing with the essential culmination of the overall process and an innovation in urban forms.

The most complete set of world statistical data is that prepared long ago by International Urban Research (1959). But what is at issue is something more than an increase in the size and density of the existing urban areas. The most widely accepted definitions (Blumenfeld, 1965; Mckenzie, 1933; Boskoff, 1962; Ardigo, 1967; Whyte, 1958; Wilson, 1968) and the criteria of statistical delimitation take no account of this qualitative change and might, in fact, be applied to any pre-metropolitan large town. What distinguishes this new form from the preceding ones is not only its size (which is the consequence of its internal structure), but the diffusion in space of activities, functions and groups, and their interdependence as a result of a largely independent social dynamic of geographical interconnection.

Within such a space, one finds a whole range of activities – production (including agricultural production), consumption (in the broad sense: the reproduction of labour power), exchange and administration. Certain of these activities are concentrated in one or several zones of the region (for example, the head offices of certain companies or industrial activities). Others, on the other hand, are distributed throughout the whole of the region with variable densities (housing, everyday amenities). The internal organization of the metropolis involves a hierarchized interdependence of the different activities. For example, industry brings together in space certain technologically homogeneous or complementary units, although it disperses others, which nevertheless belong to the same firm. Commerce concentrates 'scarce' products and organizes the mass distribution of everyday consumption. Lastly, the fluctuations of the system of circulation express the internal movements determined by the differential location of the activities: they are like a phantom of the metropolitan structure (see Part III).

This spatial form is the direct product of a specific social structure. (For the best synthesis on the subject of the metropolitan region see Bollens and Schmandt (1965). See also Eldredge (1967) and Hall (1966).) After indicating the general lines of the process of the production of space, I shall try to propose a few elements for the concrete analysis of two particularly exemplary historical processes of 'metropolitanization': the United States and the Paris region.

I Technology, society and the metropolitan region

Technological progress is very often regarded as the basis of the metropolis. In spite of all the detailed information I shall bring to bear on this point, the role played by technology in the transformation of urban forms is indisputable. This influence is exercised both through the introduction of new activities of production and consumption and by the almost total elimination of the obstacle *space*, thanks to an enormous development of the means of communication. At the stage of the second industrial revolution, the generalization of electrical energy and the use of the tramway system permitted a widening of the urban concentrations of manpower around ever larger units of industrial production. Public transport ensured the integration of the different zones and activities of the metropolis, distributing the internal flows according to a bearable time/space relation. The motor-car contributed to urban dispersion, with enormous zones of individual housing extending throughout the region and linked by through roads to the different functional sectors. The daily transportation of staple consumer products also favoured such mobility: without the daily distribution by truck of the agricultural produce harvested or stored in the region, no great metropolis could survive. (Gillmore, 1953; Schnore, 1961.) The concentration of company head offices in certain sectors and the hierarchized decentralization of the centres of production and distribution were made possible by the transmission of information by telegraph, radio and telex. (See Vernon, 1962; Labasse, 1966.) Lastly, the development of aerial navigation was a fundamental factor in strengthening the interdependence of the different metropolitan regions.

If, on the one hand, thanks to changes in the means of communication, technological progress made possible the evolution of urban forms towards the regional system of interdependences, on the other hand, it directly reinforced this evolution by means of the transformations brought about in fundamental social activities, in particular in the sphere of production. (See Isard, 1956.) Industry is increasingly freed from factors of rigid spatial location, such as raw materials or specific markets, (Florence, 1953; Luttrell, 1962; Survey Research Center, 1950; Boulet and Boulakia, 1965) whereas it is, on the other hand, increasingly dependent on skilled manpower and the technological and industrial environment, through the chains of functional relations already established. Industry seeks above all to be integrated into the urban system, rather than located in relation to the functional elements (raw materials, resources, outlets), which determined its location in the first phase (see Part III). (Castells, 1969.)

At the same time, the increasing importance of administration and information, and the interconnection of these two activities in the urban environment has reversed the relations between industry and city, making the first increasingly dependent on the complex of relations brought about by the second. Furthermore, technological evolution (in particular, the development of nuclear energy and the leading role of electronics and chemistry) favours the spatial regrouping of activities, reinforcing the links internal to the 'technological environment' and increasingly loosening dependence on the physical environment. It follows from this that development is taking place on the basis of the existing urban-industrial nuclei and that activity is concentrated in the networks of interdependences thus organized. (Rémy, 1966.)

Lastly, changes in the construction industry have also made possible the concentration of functions, in particular functions of administration and exchange, in a limited space, accessible to all the districts of the metropolis, thanks to the construction of tall buildings. (Gottman, 1967.) Prefabrication has been the basis of construction in series of individual houses and thus of the phenomenon of residential diffusion.

However, the metropolitan region is not the necessary result of mere technological progress. For 'technology', far from constituting a simple factor, is one element in the ensemble of productive forces, which are themselves, above all, a social relation and therefore also involve a cultural mode of using the means of labour. This link between space and technology is thus the most immediate material link in the fundamental connection between the ensemble of a given social structure and this new urban form. Urban dispersal and the formation of metropolitan regions are closely bound up with the social type of advanced capitalism ideologically designated by the term 'mass society'.

In fact, the monopolistic concentration of capital and the technico-social evolution towards the organization of very large units of production are at the root of the spatial decentralization of functionally linked establishments. The existence of large commercial firms, together with the standardization of products and prices, makes possible both the diffusion of housing and provisioning at shopping centres, which can be easily reached by means of a rapid communications system.

On the other hand, the uniformity imposed on an increasing mass of the population (wage-earners), as far as their position in the relations of production is concerned, is accompanied by a diversification of levels and a hierarchization within this social category – which spatially leads to a veritable segregation in terms of status, separates and 'marks off' the different residential sectors, spreading out over a vast territory, which has become the locus of a symbolic deployment.

The ideological integration of the working class into the dominant ideology goes side by side with the separation experienced between work activity, residential activity and 'leisure' activity, a separation that underlies the functional zoning of the metropolis. The high value placed on the nuclear family, the importance of the mass media and the domination of the individualist ideology all encourage an atomization of relations and a fragmentation of interests in accordance with particular strategies, which, at the spatial level, is expressed by the dispersal of individual dwellings, whether in the isolation of the suburban house or in the solitude of a block of flats.

Lastly, the increasing concentration of political power and the formation of a technocracy that ensures the long-term interests of the system gradually eliminate local particularisms and tend, through 'urban planning', to treat the problems of the functioning of the ensemble on the basis of a division into significant spatial units, that is to say, based on the networks of interdependences of the productive system. Now, this helps to regulate the rhythm of the urban machine within that unit of real functioning which constitutes the metropolitan region. (Ledrut, 1967; 1968.)

As a central form of the organization of space of advanced capitalism, the metropolitan region reduces the importance of the physical environment in the determination of the system of functional and social relations, abolishes the distinction between rural

and urban, and places in the forefront of the space/society dynamic
the historical conjuncture of the social relations that constitute its
basis.

II The metropolitan system in the United States

North America, a territory exposed to colonization, has from the
outset linked industrialization and urbanization, even from the first
administrative and commercial settlements on the northeast coast.

Since the concentrations of population did not depend on a pre-
existing network but on the new productive activities, there
occurred both a scattering of small communities developing areas
of fallow land and a rapid increase of urban areas based on industrial activities, with a gradual movement towards the centralization
of administration and management. (Green, 1965; McKelvey, 1963.)

This urban growth was entirely determined by economic development and was characterized by two basic features:

1. A particularly high rate, a consequence both of the low rate
of initial urbanization and of the massive influx of immigrants
drawn by the jobs created by accelerated industrialization.

2. The predominance of the metropolitan region as the spatial
form of this urban growth. This phenomenon of 'metropolitanization' was due to a very rapid rate of economic growth, its concentration over a few points of the North American territory, the
vastness of this territory, the preponderance of the United States
in the world economy and, lastly, the influx of immigrants (foreign
and rural) into the already constituted urban centres. (Glaab,
1966.)

Although it is true that the diffusion of private transport, which
quickly outstripped the railways, contributed greatly to this urban
explosion, it seems fairly clear that the motor-car was the socially
conditioned technological response (in the form of its individual
use) to a need for transport caused by the vertiginous distances
between the first places of settlement (see Table 4):

If, as I have said, what characterizes a metropolis is the influence
it exerts, in functional, economic and social terms, over the given
territory, (McKenzie, 1933; Hawley, 1956) then this implies that a
metropolis is integrated into an urban network (or articulation of
regional systems), within which it constitutes one of the strong
points, dominating and administering other units, and being itself
under the control of a unit of regulation at a higher level.

A classic study by Donald J. Bogue (1950) of the sixty-seven
most important metropolitan areas in 1940 shows the economic
and functional interdependence between the central cities and the

Table 4
Development of transportation by road and rail
United States, 1900—1950

Year	Railways (miles)	Freeways (miles)	Locomotives	Motor vehicles
1900	193 348	128 500	37 663	8 000
1910	240 293	204 000	60 019	468 500
1920	252 845	369 000	68 942	9 239 161
1930	249 052	694 000	60 189	26 531 999
1940	223 670	1 367 000	44 333	32 035 424
1950	223 779	1 714 000	42 951	48 566 984

Source: *US Bureau of Census, Historical Statistics of the United States.*

surrounding territory. From the results of this research one observes that:

1. The density of the population tends to decrease when the relative distance to the city centre increases.

2. The city centres are more specialized than the periphery in the operations of retail commerce.

3. The monetary value of the activities is higher in the city centre.

4. Industry tends to be concentrated between the city centre and a limit of twenty-five miles, and the value of the products manufactured decreases with the distance.

5. Lastly, a metropolis is defined by the extent of its economic domination — as far as its dispositions and circuits of distribution meet no decisive interference from another metropolis.

The difficulty is precisely in circumscribing the influence of a metropolis in so exclusive a way, whereas Hawley (1950) has shown very clearly the different possible levels of this influence, also on the basis of American data:

Primary influence: daily movements between centre and periphery, including above all commuting and shopping (direct contacts).

Secondary influence: indirect contacts of a more or less daily kind (telephone calls, listening to the radio, circulation of newspapers, etc.).

Tertiary influence: including vast, spatially discontinuous areas (even at world level: finance, publishing, information, etc.).

This perspective naturally leads to a consideration of the ensemble of American spatial organization as a specialized, differentiated and hierarchized system, with points of concentration and various spheres of domination and influence, according to the territories and characteristics of the metropolises. Duncan (1960) has tried to establish empirically the existence of such an open urban system, on the basis of an analysis of fifty-six American metropolises of over 300 000 inhabitants. This leads him to the following typology which, supporting in a way the works of Alexandersson (1956), sums up fairly precisely the urban profile of the United States on the basis of a combination of financial, commercial and industrial concentration and of the degree of specialization in a productive activity.

1. *National metropolises*, basically defined by financial, administrative and information activities and a world-wide sphere of influence: New York, Chicago, Los Angeles, Philadelphia and Detroit.

2. *Regional metropolises*, whose economic domination and use of resources are exercised above all over the surrounding territory: San Francisco, Kansas City, Minneapolis-St Paul.

3. *Sub-metropolitan regional capitals*: their administrative functions are exercised over a limited region, within the area of influence of a metropolis. This is the case for Houston, New Orleans, and Louisville.

4. *Diversified industrial centres with metropolitan functions*, but which are above all defined by the importance of their productive activities: Boston, Pittsburgh, St Louis.

5. *Diversified industrial centres with weak metropolitan functions*, practically speaking, within the network of an external metropolis: Baltimore, Milwaukee, Albany.

6. *Specialized industrial centres*: Providence (textiles), Rochester (photographic equipment), Akron (rubber), etc.

7. *Particular types*: Washington DC (capital), San Diego, San Antonio (military installations), Miami (tourism), etc.

Such a dynamic leads to the constitution of a new spatial form, the metropolitan area, whose ultimate expression is what has come to be called the *megalopolis*, an articulated assemblage of several areas within the same functional and social unit. (Gottmann, 1961.) The 37 000 000 people (1960), who live and work along the northeast coast, from New Hampshire to Virginia, along a strip 600 miles long and 30 to 100 miles wide, do not form an uninterrupted urban web, but rather a sytem of relations that contains rural zones, forests and tourist spots, points of industrial concentration, zones of high urban density, extremely extended suburbs traversed by a complex network of intra- and inter-urban roads.

In effect, the population is concentrated in a little over 20% of the surface of the megalopolis; this shows very clearly that it is not a question of generalized urbanization, but of a diffusion of the habitat and of activities according to a logic that depends little on contiguity and is closely bound up with economic functioning and, particularly, with administrative activities.

The existence of the megalopolis is due to its function at a higher level in the American urban network — a fact that results in turn from its historical priority in the urbanization process. But, unlike the situation experienced in Europe, this primacy does not tend to be reinforced, but to be diminished, by the dynamism of new nuclei of economic growth, such as California or Texas.

Such a process of production, determined by economic growth in the context of a capitalism as aggressive as that of the United States, explains the internal structure of this new spatial form, the megalopolis (for further details, see Part III, *The Urban Structure*):

First, within each metropolis (Boston, New York, Philadelphia, Washington):

A concentration of tertiary activities in the business centre, industrial activities in the inner urban belt and dispersal of individual housing in the free surrounding terrain.

A physical deterioration of the city centre, a flight of the middle classes towards the suburbs, and an occupation of the central space by the new immigrants, in particular by the ethnic minorities, victims of discrimination on the housing market.

The location of industry increasingly independent of the city, tending to recreate functional nuclei near road junctions.

The total lack of correspondence between the administrative divisions and the units of life and work.

Secondly, as far as the links established between the metropolises are concerned, leading to the existence of the megalopolis (Wilson, 1968):

Relations are forged by successive concatenations of different functions.

However, there is no clearly defined hierarchy of functions within the megalopolis: the various centres are not conjoined with one another: they form rather a multiform network whose organs of transmission are situated largely outside the megalopolis.

The production of knowledge and information becomes essential for the activity of the megalopolis as a whole. The university complex of Boston or the world of publishing and journalism in New York, have a vital importance for this concentration and tend to organize their sphere of intervention. The regional channels for the dissemination of information seem to play a considerable role in the orientations of the development tendencies of the territory.

The extremely complex communications network is an essential instrument for the realization of such a diffusion.

The megalopolis results, therefore, from the interdependent,

28 *The Historical Process of Urbanization*

weakly hierarchized tangle, arising from the concentration within
the territory of the original American urbanization, of the administrative functions and an essential part of the productive activities
of the metropolitan system of the United States. It expresses the
domination of the law of the market in the occupation of land and
reveals both the technological and social concentration of the
means of production and the atomized form of consumption,
through the dispersal of housing and amenities in space.

III The production of the spatial structure of the Paris region

The dynamics of the production process of the Paris region, as a
spatial form, may be discovered from the system of relations established between Paris and the whole of France in the movement of
capitalist industrialization, on the basis of the politico-administrative centralization consolidated under the *Ancien Régime*. (Chevalier, 1950; Lavedan, 1960.)

We know that the acceleration of the urban growth of Paris, in
relative as well as absolute terms, is bound up with industrialization
and, more concretely, with two periods: the sudden economic
take-off of the years 1850—1870, and the prosperity that followed
World War I. Thus the Paris urban area represented 2·5% of the
French population at the beginning of the nineteenth century,
5·2% in 1861, 10% in 1901, 16·5% in 1962, 18·6% in 1968. The
introduction of industry having been achieved on the basis of a
strategy of profit, the attraction exerted by Paris derives from the
combined presence of a very extensive market, a potential work
force already *in situ* and a privileged situation on a transportation
network whose radiality (still further reinforced today) expressed
the social organization dominated by the state apparatus. (Bastié,
1964.) From a certain level onwards, the industrial milieu thus
created developed of itself and gave rise to new jobs, which further
increased the market and strengthened the administrative functions
of both the private and public sectors. To the state administration
were added the growing mass of management, administrative and
information services of the great industrial and commercial organizations, the universities and the cultural and scientific institutions.
(George and Randet, 1964.)

The new phase of urbanization is characterized by a predominance of the tertiary as motive force of this growth. If the viscosity
of the already constituted industrial milieu acted as a brake on a
technically possible decentralization, the Paris concentration is
further explained by the importance of the problems of administration and information, the growing specialization of Paris in this

domain and the reorganization of the French urban network, as a hierarchized system of transmission of instructions, distribution of services and communication of information. Thus, the 'counter-balanced' metropolises were created on the basis of work carried out on the French urban structure that took as its criterion of hier-archization the capacity of the 'upper tertiary' of each urban area (unusual services, administrations of a certain size, etc.), rather than their potential dynamic in terms of economic development. (Hautreux *et al.* 1963.)

In this new mode of urban growth, Paris benefited again from the sheer weight of its established position and from the fact that it was easier to continue a movement that had already been begun long since. An administrative, political and cultural capital trans-formed into a centre of administration for capitalist businesses and a centre for the distribution of information and services for the whole country, it became still further strengthened in the internal organization of this administration and set up new organizations necessary both to the development of the world of information and research and to the gradual integration of the French decision-mak-ing centres into the world network. (Chombard de Lauwe, 1952; 1965.)

Thus, with regard to the data for 1962, although the Paris urban area contains 16·5% of the French and 21% of the active population, the concentration is greater in the tertiary and 'quaternary' sectors: 25% of the civil servants, 30% of the tertiary jobs, 64% of the head offices of companies, 82% of the turnover of the great companies, 95% of the share quotations on the Bourse, 33% of the students, 60% of the artists, 83% of the weekly papers, etc. (Bastié, 1964.)

The economic, political and cultural predominance of Paris over the whole of France and over each of the other urban areas taken separately is such that one may clearly regard the whole of France as the Paris 'hinterland' and find the key to the arrangement of the territory in the internal processes of the Paris network. (Leron, 1970; Joly, 1970; Rochefort *et al.* 1970.) There is no need to em-bark on a description: a few significant tables are enough to remind the reader of the phenomenon (see Tables 5, 6, 7).

Apart from these widely known facts, the essential thing is to remember, in accordance with what has been said above, the social logic of such an 'imbalance', and to show the determination, through this process, of the spatial form of the Paris region as a metropolitan region with specific characteristics.

The spatial unit thus delimited is above all an economic and functional ensemble, comprising, in 1968, 12 000 sq km and 9 240 000 inhabitants. This unit is constituted by daily relations

Table 5
Comparative distribution of the active French population
between the Paris region and the provinces

Year	Paris region	France	PR France
1936	2 974 000	18 889 000	15·7%
1954	3 514 000	18 570 000	18·9%
1962	3 893 000	18 558 000	20·9%
1968	4 300 830	20 005 620	21·5%

Source: Leron, *op. cit.*, 1970, table 2.

Table 6
Wage disparities in France
AVERAGE ANNUAL WAGE — 1966

	Total	Men	Women
Paris region	14 492	17 114	10 643
Champagne	9 780	10 901	6 820
Picardie	9 923	11 069	6 638
Haute-Normandie	10 777	12 123	7 041
Centre	9 469	10 573	6 625
Nord	10 130	11 280	6 417
Lorraine	10 174	11 148	6 490
Alsace	10 343	11 611	6 947
Franche-Comté	10 083	11 234	6 952
Basse-Normandie	9 375	10 313	6 603
Pays de la Loire	9 259	10 121	6 687
Bretagne	9 268	10 121	6 644
Limousin	8 694	9 518	6 471
Auvergne	9 565	10 407	7 187
Poitou-Charentes	8 965	9 872	6 323
Aquitaine	9 746	10 899	6 856
Midi-Pyrénées	9 438	10 345	6 581
Bourgogne	9 569	15 525	6 681
Rhône-Alpes	10 925	12 274	7 429
Languedoc	9 391	10 294	6 564
Provence-Côte d'Azur	10 979	12 009	7 632
France as a whole	11 344	12 600	8 079

Source: *Statistiques et indicateurs des régions françaises*, 1969.

between, on the one hand, the centre of the urban area (in which are concentrated the tertiary activities bound up with the administration of the whole of France, the amenities and essential services of the Paris urban area and an urban belt in which are located the most important industrial zones) and, on the other hand, a suburban belt and a zone of attraction (along the transportation routes) in which are spread out housing estates which, for the most part,

Table 7
Economic power of the French urban areas, 1962
(Index: number of wage-earners employed in company
headquarters in an urban area after subtracting those
who, while working in the urban area, are employed by
outside companies — selected data.)

Urban areas	Number of wage-earners
Paris	+1 277 877
Mulhouse	+ 18 827
Metz	+ 16 832
Saint-Etienne	+ 9 729
Clermont-Ferrand	+ 3 910
Aix-en-Provence	− 139
Lyon	− 10 674
Marseille	− 13 126
Bordeaux	− 23 964
Lille	− 21 547
Roubaix	− 4 765
Toulouse	− 18 556
Thionville	− 42 403

Source: Paul Le Fillatre, *Etudes et Conjoncture*, INSEE, Paris, 1964.

have not found a place near the nucleus of activity from which the urban growth took place (see Table 8). (INSEE, 1961; Delegation générale, 1963.)

To this basic relation must be added a few essential features: the existence, beyond the Paris residential complex, of a rural-urban zone, with strong points of urbanization (the secondary urban areas of the Paris region: Melun, Fontainebleau, Meaux, Montereau, Mantes, etc.) characterized by an extremely close relation with the whole of the region, such that most of its economic activity is directed towards feeding the population of this region or towards carrying out industrial and tertiary operations with daily links to Paris locations. Thus at the level of the spatial unit, the distinction between rural and urban is abolished, despite the persistence of agricultural activity and the diversity of the residential *milieux*. (For the data on which my examination is based see Beaujeu-Garnier and Bastié, 1967, and especially pp 447–553 concerning agriculture.)

In so far as centrifugal tendencies exist movements tangential to the urban centre, and even the reinforcement of the industrial activity of the periphery, take place, but these do nothing to counteract the functional division of the region.

This unit of functioning is expressed, however, in a technological division and a social differentiation of the regional space, both in terms of activity and amenities and in terms of population. By

Table 8

Job/active population ratio by socio-occupational category and geographical zone, Paris region, 1968

Geographical zone	Paris		Urban belt (Seine)		Urban belt (Seine-et-Oise)		Suburban belt		Zone of attraction	
Category	J−AP	J/AP	J−AP	J/AP	J−AP	J/AP	J−AP	J/AP	J−AP	J/AP
Craftsmen, small tradesmen	+ 8 400	1·08	− 5 920	0·94	− 2 340	0·91	− 2 940	0·88	− 1 120	0·90
Industrialists. Liberal professions	+ 4 680	1·08	− 3 260	0·88	− 1 360	0·78	− 1 720	0·69	− 180	0·92
Upper management	+ 46 540	1·38	− 23 460	0·72	− 15 340	0·47	− 14 260	0·35	− 280	1·04
Middle management	+ 95 620	1·51	− 41 020	0·77	− 24 280	0·54	− 30 600	0·36	− 3 540	0·78
Office workers	+ 200 160	1·72	− 107 880	0·56	− 37 060	0·41	− 44 520	0·25	− 9 720	0·56
Shop assistants	+ 44 120	1·27	− 25 700	0·74	− 7 620	0·69	− 10 180	0·36	− 1 900	0·77
Army	+ 9 110	1·45	− 12 300	0·46	− 2 060	0·71	− 5 140	0·54	− 80	0·97
Foremen, skilled workers	+ 87 580	1·43	+ 9 940	0·97	− 28 260	0·62	− 44 040	0·43	− 10 900	0·70
Semi-skilled and unskilled workers	+ 48 820	1·25	− 10 280	1·04	− 22 020	0·68	− 30 800	0·54	− 7 960	0·78
Agricultural workers and domestic staff	+ 3 340	1·04	− 2 780	0·93	− 120	0·99	− 1 300	0·90	− 400	0·96
Others	− 1 120	0·51	− 1 020	0·31	− 380	0·05	− 280	0·07	− 40	0·50
Total	+ 547 280	1·39	− 223 000	0·84	− 141 240	0·62	− 185 780	0·46	− 34 860	0·77

Building and Public works	+ 35 360	1·56	− 9 640	0·90	− 8 460	0·71	− 12 960	0·67	− 5 620	0·66
Engineering industries	+ 19 600	1·12	+ 56 080	1·19	− 36 260	0·56	− 37 380	0·34	− 3 400	0·90
Other processing industries	+ 105 820	1·47	− 40 620	0·83	− 24 620	0·56	− 32 440	0·41	− 8 640	0·62
Transport	+ 45 480	1·64	− 11 520	0·95	− 12 860	0·34	− 18 620	0·34	− 4 600	0·52
Retail commerce	+ 42 940	1·33	− 23 380	0·79	− 7 700	0·74	− 9 700	0·63	− 3 060	0·74
Other commerce and equivalent	+ 129 440	1·62	− 73 480	0·53	− 25 260	0·36	− 24 500	0·28	− 6 260	0·50
Private services	+ 73 700	1·27	− 45 300	0·71	− 11 280	0·76	− 16 040	0·57	− 1 940	0·84
Public services	+ 99 440	1·53	− 69 480	0·61	− 11 120	0·79	− 30 400	0·46	+ 200	1·01
Other activities and undeclared activities	− 4 500	0·95	− 5 660	0·87	− 3 680	0·77	− 3 740	0·75	− 1 540	0·87
Total	+ 547 280	1·39	−223 000	0·84	−141 240	0·62	−185 780	0·46	− 34 860	0·77
Men	+ 298 640	1·39	− 88 220	0·89	− 93 820	0·60	−125 260	0·45	− 21 780	0·78
Women	+ 248 640	1·38	−134 780	0·75	− 47 420	0·65	− 60 580	0·47	− 13 080	0·74
Married women	+ 152 240	1·52	− 83 480	0·74	− 27 660	0·64	− 37 180	0·46	− 7 520	0·74
Total	+ 547 280	1·39	−223 000	0·84	−141 240	0·62	−185 780	0·46	− 34 860	0·77

technological division, I mean the separation in space of the different functions of an urban ensemble, namely, the productive activities (industry), the activities of administration and dissemination of information, activities involving the exchange of goods and services (commerce and leisure), activities concerned with housing and amenities, activities of circulation between the different spheres. It is clear that this separation is not an absolute one, but one of tendency, in terms of the predominance of one activity over a space (except, perhaps, in perspective, in certain Parisian *arrondissements*, the 9th and 8th, which have been gradually occupied by offices).

This division breaks up, by a process of generalization, the existence of the quarter as an urban unit, for, if the quarter has any meaning, it is precisely through the juxtaposition in one space of an ensemble of functions that render it relatively autonomous (see Part II). (Coing, 1966.) It is certainly in this sectorial specialization and the reconstitution of structural links in the urban area as a whole that the fundamental criterion of a metropolitan region is to be found, and not in the impressionistic notion of spatial dispersal, which is merely a blind description of the phenomenon. A very crude appreciation of this ecological division may be obtained by comparing the relative importance of each activity in the land occupation of the three belts of the extended urban area (see Table 9).

However, Paris *intra-muros* is much more diversified in itself although it presents an enormous specialization in the activities of administration and information when compared with the whole of the region (see Beaujeu-Garnier and Bastié, 1967, maps 81—1, 82—1 and 82—2).

The logic of this distribution in no way follows the metaphysical rationality of the urbanists' 'zoning', but expresses the social structure of advanced capitalism, articulated with the conditions of historical development of French society. Thus the presence of the administrative processes in the city centre responds to the need to constitute a concentrated business milieu, in so far as this entails setting up head offices for companies and for the central administration of the state, which alone are capable of bearing the costs of occupying buildings in the heart of Paris, even though these buildings are being emptied of their tenants and the owners have an interest in developing them for these administrative services, as is the case with bourgeois housing (9th, 8th, 16th, 7th *arrondissements*), or in redeveloping them and setting up offices in them when the deterioration of the immediate environment no longer corresponds to the status expected (especially the 1st, 2nd and

13th *arrondissements*). (Prefecture de Paris, 1968.) The difficulty of situating offices in the suburbs also derives from the symbolic role of a good address (hence the attempts to create new peripheric symbols, e.g. *La Défense*) and from the interdependences existing at the higher level of the milieux of administration and information.

The location of industry in Paris was organized on three lines, according to the technological, economic and financial characteristics of the companies: the large productive units were set up along the axes of transport and in sites favourable to the functioning of the factory (space, water, energy), mainly in the bends of the Seine and Marne and around the canals of the North of France; the small commercial firms or firms working on a market of local consumption followed the already formed industrial and urban milieux very closely, with little room for manoeuvre; lastly, a new tendency has recently emerged among the most advanced companies whereby an attempt is made to re-establish new modern industrial milieux on socially valued spaces, for example, around the southern suburbs (see Part III, Chap. 9, Section IA). (Castells, 1967).

Lastly, the type of habitat and location of amenities (Dumazedier and Imbert, 1967) not only corresponds to social segregation but, from the point of view of technological division, it is bound up with the social determination of the production of housing. More concretely, on the basis of the old nucleus, reshaped by Hausmann in order to provide the bourgeoisie with adequate accommodation, the diffusion of the habitat over the whole of the region was the result of three great tendencies: 1. the explosion of the surburbs, with the unorganized construction of *pavillons* (small, detached houses) between 1918 and 1930, under the auspices of the Ribot Loucheur laws, leading to the occupation of 65% of the inhabited surface (in 1962) by 18% of the population, itself deprived of the most elementary amenities; 2. the almost total cessation of building in Paris between 1932 and 1954, causing a deterioration in existing buildings, price rises and an increase in the pressure of demand; 3. largely as a result of the situation caused by the previous phase, the accelerated development of a building programme for public housing in the suburbs, in the form of '*grands ensembles*' (high-rise housing estates) or 'dormitory-towns', a high proportion belonging to the public sector, conceived as an urgent response to social pressure. (Bastié, 1964; Beaujeu-Garnier and Bastié, 1967.)

There are direct relations between the logic of this location and the form of the habitat on the one hand, and, on the other, the social struggles subjacent to the process of the reproduction of labour power: the individualization of working-class housing in the inter-war years (an attempt at social integration by means of

ownership without amenities); an economic crisis and the subordination of social needs to the needs of economic accumulation during
reconstruction; the need to do something about the strangling
bottle-neck that housing had become with the increase in growth
after 1954. The individualization movement is bound up with
urban dispersal; the building of the '*grands ensembles*' corresponds
to the concentration of housing outside the urban network; in both
cases, the absence of elementary commercial and socio-cultural
amenities (Cornuau *et al.* 1965) is explained by the character of a
housing policy conceived almost as a form of social welfare.

As far as the *social differentiation* of regional space is concerned,
the opposition between a working-class East Paris and a West inhabited by the higher social strata has been a classic observation
since Chevalier, reinforced by the conquest of the 16th *arrondissement* by the bourgeoisie and, at the present time, by the new
'urban reconquest' of historic Paris, under cover of urban renewal,
by the liberal professions and technocrats. (Beaujeu-Garnier, 1967;
see also Part IV.) Curiously enough, this social segregation has spilt
over into the adjacent suburban area following the same geographical sectors. The typology of the *communes* of the suburban areas
close to Paris, drawn up by the IAURP on the basis of a factor
analysis, (Taisne-Plantevin, 1966) shows a profound contrast in the
whole set of indicators of standard of living and social status between the West and the South, with their high level, and the East
and North, with their significantly lower level.

Within each sector and each *commune* there are further distinctions, which impress social stratification upon space and add to it
new disparities in the sphere of public amenities, given the discrimination that operates in the choice of these amenities. Thus
the inquiries carried out by the Centre d'Études de Groupes Sociaux
have shown to what extent the attraction of Paris for the inhabitants of the suburbs is motivated above all by the lack of commercial and cultural amenities in the suburbs, whereas the residents
demand a level of consumption comparable on every level.
(Cornuau *et al.*, 1965; CEGS, 1964–65.) Furthermore, this lack of
amenities implies the need to travel to obtain a whole range of
services, while, of course, working-class mobility is much less, because workers own fewer cars on average and enjoy a less diversified system of social relations. (Retel, 1965; Lamy, 1967.)

Lastly, the transport network, in so far as it must ensure exchange and communications between the different functional and
social sectors thus constituted, is doubly determined, for it is
entirely dependent on the disposition of the elements to be related.
Whereas the placing of the transport network is very often regarded

Table 9
Land occupation in the extended urban area
(not including Paris)

Type of occupation	First urban belt (collective dwelling)		Second urban belt (mixed dwelling)		Suburban belt	
	Hectares	%	Hectares	%	Hectares	%
Total area	10 455	100	54 210	100	70 229	100
Habitat	5 396	51·5	27 295	60·5	18 594	26·5
Industry and ware- housing	2 724	26	3 080	6	754	1
Large amenities (secondary schools, universities, hospitals, airports, railways, etc.)	977	9·5	2 827	5	4 558	6·5
Green spaces	312	3	9 856	18	13 625	19.5
Agricultural land Various activities (rivers, sand pits, roads; railways)	1 046	10	11 152	20·5	32 698	46·5
Total population	1 298 062		2 417 384		840 751	

Source: C. Delprat et J. Lallemant, *L'Occupation du sol dans l'agglomeration parisienne,* IAURP, 1964, p. 22.

as the cause of the axes of growth, it is good to recall that, for example, the motorways were constructed, a century after the railways, according to a parallel orientation and in the same chronological order (west, south, north, east). Indeed, although technological progress in transport made possible the diffusion of populations and activities, and these populations and activities were concentrated within reach of the axes of transport, the density and orientation of the network were a function of the system of interdependences described above. (Beaujeu-Garnier and Bastié, 1967, 357 ff.)

The structure of the Paris region expresses, therefore, the same processes that have already caused the Paris/provinces asymmetry, with the special feature that it is based on the role of Paris as a centre of administration and decision and on the total predominance of the productive units of the Paris region. The concrete consequences are: 1. specialization and concentration, in the heart of the urban area, of a *business centre* whose dimensions are explicable only on a national or international scale; 2. an industrial concentration of such an order that it has given rise to a vast agglomeration of housing and services, organized and differentiated technologically and socially; 3. a self-sustaining movement of urban concentration, bound up with both the attraction for new companies of the external economies of the urban area and the development of the services necessary to the life of such an ensemble.

The logic of the spatial organization of the Paris region derives, therefore, from its character as the higher level of an urban structure with a tertiary base, formed on a national territory shaped by capitalist industrialization and characterized by very great concentration around the administrative capital.

3

Urbanization, Development and Dependence

I The acceleration of urban growth in the dependent societies of the capitalist system

The increasing attention accorded, in sociological literature, to the analysis of the process of urbanization is largely motivated by the practical, that is to say political, importance of urban evolution in those regions to which has been applied the equivocal term 'under-developed'.

More concretely, if the populations of North America and Europe represented, in 1950, 6·7% and 15·7%, respectively, of the world population, these proportions will, in the year 2000 be 5% and 9·1%. On the other hand, Asia (without the USSR) which, in 1950, comprised 23% of the human species, will, in the year 2000 comprise 61·8%. If one relates this evolution with the economico-political structure on a world scale, and, more concretely, with the decline in the standard of living (Kuan-I-Chen, 1960) in the regions with the greatest demographic growth, and with the gradual political mobilization of the working masses, one can understand the sudden interest that western sociologists have discovered in both the problem of birth control and the process of urbanization.

Indeed, if demographic growth is high, that of the urban population is spectacular and the spatial forms it assumes are profoundly expressive of and charged with political significance. To determine their meaning, in relation to the place they occupy and the role they play in the social structure, seems to be the common objective of analyses that go beyond mere description. (Breese, 1969; Greer *et al.* 1968; Meadows and Mizuchi, 1969; Frank *et al.* 1969.)

At first sight, urbanization and economic development seem to be linked. In a piece of technically very competent research, Brian J. L. Berry (1962) has made a factor analysis that links, for ninety-five countries, forty-three indices of economic development, chosen around two dimensions: technological and economic progress on the one hand, demographic characteristics on the other. The two dimensions have a negative correlation, that is to say, the higher the economic and technological level, the lower the demographic growth. On the basis of this analysis, Berry has constructed a scale of development in which one places different countries on a single dimension and studies the link between this scale and the indicator of urbanization (percentage of the population living in towns of over 20 000 inhabitants). The result is a positive correlation between level of economic development and degree of urbanization.

Parallel with this, a now classic analysis by Gibbs and Martin (1962; see also Kahl, 1959) formulates a series of propositions empirically verified for forty-five countries, showing the dependence of the level of urbanization on industrial diversification (indicator of the division of labour), technological development and the plurality of the societies' external exchanges. The higher these variables, the higher, too, is the percentage of the population in the metropolitan zones.

However, if such research observes a historically given co-variation between the technico-economic level and the level of urbanization, it does not provide an explanation of the process and above all it runs counter to another equally important observation, that of the acceleration of urban growth in the 'underdeveloped' regions, at a higher rate than that of the urban take-off of the industrialized countries, without the concomitant economic growth. It is this phenomenon that we must try to explain, by providing ourselves with the theoretical means of posing the problem in non-tautological terms.

Indeed, one interpretation, as frequent as it is erroneous, that derives from the empirical observations to which I have just referred, considers urbanization as a mechanical consequence of economic growth and, in particular, of industrialization. The present rate of urbanization in the 'underdeveloped' countries is then explained by the initial stage of the process in which they find themselves. Development, therefore, appears to be a path already traced that societies follow in so far as they manifest a spirit of enterprise. (Rostov, 1960.)

The available statistical data enable us to reject such a proposition categorically. The urbanization in progress in the 'underdeveloped' regions is not a replica of the process experienced by the industrialized countries. At the same level of urban population reached by the 'underdeveloped' countries, the level of industrialization of the 'developed' countries was much higher. (Davis and Golden, 1954.) The rate of growth of Indian towns in the twentieth

century is not very different from that of European towns in the
second half of the nineteenth century, but if one fixes an approximate level of urbanization for India and for several western countries, the composition of the active population is extremely
different (see Table 10).

The phenomenon illustrated by these figures is known as *over-
urbanization* − a term that connotes the idea of a level of urbanization higher than that which can 'normally' be attained, given the
level of industrialization. Over-urbanization appears as an obstacle
to development, in so far as it immobilizes resources in the form of
non-productive investments, necessary to the creation and organization of services indispensable to great concentrations of population,
whereas these concentrations do not justify themselves as centres
of production. (Hauser, 1961.) Furthermore, the concentration on
the same space of a population with a low standard of living and a
high rate of unemployment is regarded as threatening, since it
creates conditions favourable to 'extremist' political propaganda!
(Hoselitz, 1957.) From this analysis may be deduced the distinction between 'generating' or 'parasitical' cities, according to
whether they encourage or impede economic growth. (Hoselitz,
1953.)

Although this situation is highly significant and must be regarded
as the point of departure for our reflection, it becomes incomprehensible when analysed in terms of 'over-urbanization', which
applies in a quite ethnocentric way the schema of economic growth
of the advanced capitalist countries to other social forms in an
entirely different conjuncture. N. V. Sovani (1964) has reacted

Table 10
Active population and level of urbanization

Country	Year	% A.P. in agriculture	% A.P. industry	% A.P. services	% urban (+ 20 000 inhab.)
Austria	1890	43	30	27	12·0
Ireland	1851	47	34	19	8·7
France	1856	53	29	19	10·7
Norway	1890	55	22	23	13·8
Sweden	1890	62	22	16	10·8
Switzerland	1888	33	45	22	13·2
Portugal	1890	65	19	16	8·0
Hungary	1900	59	17	24	10·6
Average country		52·1	27·3	20·6	11·0
India	1951	70·6	10·7	18·7	11·9

Source: Bert F. Hoselitz, The role of urbanization in economic development. Some
International comparisons in Roy Turner (editor) *India's Urban Future*, University of
California Press, 1962, pp. 157−82.

brilliantly against such a perspective by showing, on the basis of the same data as used by Davis and Golden (1954), the real complexity of the process.

In fact, in the first place, the correlation between urbanization and industrialization is not linear. If, instead of calculating it globally for all countries, as Davis and Golden do, one separates these countries into two groups according to their level of development, the correlation between urbanization and continuous industrialization has to be raised for the 'underdeveloped' countries (r = ·85), but considerably diminished for the 'developed' countries (r = ·39), in 1950. But if the calculation for the 'developed countries' is made for 1891, instead of 1950, the connection becomes strong once again (r = ·84). That is to say, in a feebly urbanized society, the impact of initial industrialization is much more considerable.

Furthermore, the notion of over-urbanization was worked out by Davis in a comparison between Asia and four western countries in their take-off phase: the United States, France, Germany and Canada. But if the comparison had been made with Switzerland or Sweden, one would not have found appreciable differences in the urbanization/industrialization ratio between these two countries in their take-off phase and the Asiatic countries of today.

Lastly, over-urbanization is a source of non-productive expenditure only if one manages to prove that the capital invested in public services should have been employed in a more directly productive way. Now, we know that the principal characteristic of 'underdevelopment', in addition to a lack of resources, is the impossibility of a social organization capable of concentrating and directing existing means towards the development of the collectivity.

If industrial employment in the 'underdeveloped' cities is not very important, what, then, is the activity of this increasing mass of urban population? In the active urban population of India, in 1951, 25% worked in industry, 14% in agriculture, 6% in transport, 20% in commerce and 35% in 'various services', whereas in Germany, in 1882, at a similar level of urbanization, 52·8% of the urban population were employed in industry. This uprooted and changing population, unemployed, a 'reserve army' for a non-existing industry, is the foundation of urban growth. This is an essential initial fact that requires explanation.

Other particularly significant facts emphasize the specifity of this process of urbanization, without any possible historical equivalence: 1. concentration in large urban areas, without integration into an urban network, which necessitates a clear distinction between the super-urban areas of the 'underdeveloped' countries and the metropolitan regions of the industrialized countries, which are instruments of economic articulation at the level of space. Some authors have recourse to the highly symptomatic subterfuge of calling these areas 'premature metropolises' (Bose, 1965); 2. the absence of a continuum in the urban hierarchy; 3. the social and cultural distance between the urban areas and the rural communities; 4. the ecological juxtaposition of two cities: the native city and the western city, in the urban areas that have been inherited from colonialism. (George, 1950.)

II Dependent urbanization

The situation thus described becomes intelligible only through an analysis of the process of its formation. The study of urbanization in the 'underdeveloped' regions must be integrated into an over-all analysis of 'underdevelopment'. Now, it is clear that this term, which refers to a question of *levels* of growth, is equivocal, in so far as it designates one of the parts of a complex structure, in relation to the process of development. (For the theoretical perspectives see Cardoso, 1968; for economic analysis, Baran, 1954; for international mechanisms, Emmanuel, 1969; Amin, 1970.) It is not a question of different sequences of a single development, but of forms of expansion of a given historical structure, the advanced capitalist system, in which different social formations fulfill various functions and present characteristics corresponding to these functions and to their form of articulation. (Jalee, 1969.) I would agree with Charles Bettelheim (1967, chapter 3), that, rather than speak of underdeveloped countries it would be better to describe them as 'exploited and dominated, with a deformed economy'.

These effects are produced by the differential roles of these countries in a structure which spills over institutional frontiers and is organized around a principal axis of domination and dependence in relation to development. (Cardoso and Faletto, 1970.) That is to say, although all societies are interdependent, their relations are asymmetrical. It is not a question of reviving the caricature of an 'imperialism' responsible for all ills, but of determining rigorously the true extent of such an imperialism. From an analytical point of view, the main thing is not the political subordination of the 'underdeveloped' countries to the imperialist metropolises (which is no more than the consequence of a structural dependence), but the expression of this dependence in the internal organization of the societies in question and, more concretely, in the articulation of the system of production and class relations. (See the important work of Poulantzas, 1968.)

A society is dependent when the articulation of its social structure, at the economic, political and ideological level, expresses asymmetrical relations with another social formation that occupies, in relation to the first, a situation of power. By a situation of power I mean the fact that the organization of class relations in the dependent societies expresses the form of social supremacy adopted by the class in power in the dominant society.

To deal with 'underdevelopment' is equivalent, therefore, to analysing the development/dependence dialectic, that is to say, to studying the penetration of one social structure by another. This implies:

1. An analysis of the pre-existing social structure in the dependent society;

2. An analysis of the social structure of the dominant society;

3. An analysis of their mode of articulation, that is to say, of the type of domination.

The process of urbanization becomes, therefore, the expression of this social dynamic at the level of space, that is to say, of the penetration by the capitalist mode of production historically formed in the western countries, of the remainder of the existing social formations at different technological, economic and social levels, from extremely complex cultures like those of China or India to organizations with a tribal basis, particularly vigorous in central Africa.

The types of domination historically given are three in number. They may co-exist, but they always involve a preponderance of one over the others.

1. *Colonial domination*, with, as its essential objectives, the direct administration of an intensive exploitation of resources and the affirmation of political sovereignty.

2. *Capitalist-commercial domination*, through the terms of exchange, procuring for itself raw materials below their value and opening up new markets for manufactured products at prices higher than their value.

3. *Imperialist industrial and financial domination*, through speculative investments and the creation of local industries which tend to control the movement of substitution of imports, following a strategy of profit adopted by the international trusts throughout the world market.

Dependent urbanization reveals, in its forms and in its rhythms, the concrete articulation of these economic and political relations.

Before undergoing penetration by external social formations the cities, where cities already existed, played an essentially political and administrative role, (Norton and Ginsburg, 1965) controlling the surplus of agricultural production and the supply of services for the dominant class. The town/country opposition which certain authors interpret naively, as if the spatial forms could be equated with social agents (e.g. Keyfitz, 1965) manifests the specificity of class relations, which may range from certain variants of feudalism (Japan) to the bureaucratic forms of exploitation known as 'Asiatic despotism', with, in between, situations of more complex origin, such as the caste system in India. The religious function is combined with the administrative role and often gives rise to settlement. On the other hand, commerce has only a secondary influence and is located much more in time (fairs and markets) than in space.

Upon this weak urban structure, of which the only important developments were the administrative cities of Japan and China, the system of domination is organized, at the spatial level, in two essential variants:

1. *The colonial-type settlement*, characterized by a function that is above all administrative, and the organization of 'reserved' urban districts which reproduce the cities of the mother country. This variant, the best illustration of which is provided by the Spanish cities of America, presents few changes in relation to the function of the cities previously existing within the rural civilizations. However, the new domination is expressed by the increase in number and size of these cities, by their internal design, predetermined according to a standardized colonial plan, and by their much closer relations with the home country than with the surrounding territory.

2. The second fundamental variant is the *business centre* directly linked to the home country, a place of call on the trade routes (it is, therefore, almost always a port) and itself a commercial centre in relation to the zones of the interior. We are dealing with 'gateway' cities (Pizzorno, 1962), the urban form of a trade economy, the beginning of a close conjunction between the local trading bureaucracy and the imperialist businessmen and their protective apparatus. The classic illustration is given by the cities created by the British along the commercial route to India. But one finds equally clear examples in the Portuguese settlements in Brazil and in Africa and the Dutch settlements in southeast Asia.

As the capitalist mode of production developed in the West, and as the process of industrialization accelerated, its effects were felt in the spatial organization and the demographic structure of the dominated societies. But we must clear up at once an ambiguity that is very common in the specialist literature: it is not a question of the impact of *industry* on urbanization, for in the beginning the establishment of industry was rare and not very significant, but of the impact of the western *process of industrialization* through a relation of specific dependence. Industrialization might, for example, have an impact on the urban growth of a country without an appreciable modification of the proportion of manpower employed in the secondary sphere through the increase in production of an industrial branch in the home country, based on a raw material obtained in the dependent country.

Thus, a relation must be established, between dominant industrialization and dependent urbanization on the one hand; and, on the other, between urbanization and the growth, in the country, of technologically modern manufacturing activities.

On the basis of this exposition of the social structures subjacent to the process of urbanization, we may advance certain explanatory hypotheses concerning the fundamental data presented above:

1. The accelerated growth of the urban areas is due to two factors: (a) an increase in the rate of natural growth, both urban and rural; (b) rural-urban migration.

The first factor is above all a consequence of the decline in the death rate, caused by the sudden diffusion of medical progress. The birth rate is also raised by the age structure of the population, which is particularly young, as is normal in a situation of demographic explosion.

But the essential phenomenon that determines urban growth is that of migration. The rush towards the towns is, in general, regarded much more as the result of a rural *push* than of an urban *pull*, that is to say, much more as a decomposition of rural society than as an expression of the dynamism of urban society. The problem is to know why, with the penetration of one social formation by another, a migratory movement is triggered off, whereas the possibilities of urban employment are well below the dimensions of the migration and the prospects with regard to living standards are very limited.

In effect, if urban *per capita* income, despite its low level, is generally higher than rural income, the capacity for real consumption declines rapidly in the towns, in that the direct consumption of agricultural produce becomes rare, and a whole series of new items is added to the budget (transport in particular), quite apart from the superfluous consumption induced by a developing market economy.

It is a question, then, not so much of an economic balance-sheet at the individual level as of the decomposition of the rural social structure. Great emphasis has often been laid on the role of new western cultural values and on the attraction exerted by the new types of urban consumption diffused by the mass media. Although these changes in attitude express the reorganization of the personality in a new situation, they cannot be regarded as a motive force of the process, unless one accepts the liberal ideological postulate of the individual as the essential historical agent. What, then, is this new social situation? It is a general crisis of the economic system of the previous social formation. For it is impossible, after a certain phase has been reached in the process of social penetration, for two different commercial systems to function alongside each other, or for the economy of direct exchange to develop at the same time as the market economy. With the exception of geographically and culturally isolated regions, the whole of the productive system is reorganized according to the interests of the dominant society. It is logical that, under these conditions, the internal economic system should be 'inarticulated' or deformed. But this 'incoherence' is only the result of a perfectly coherent economic network, if one examines the social structure as a whole (dominant society and dependent society).

If the demographic pressure on cultivated land causes the standard of living to deteriorate, thus causing emigration, this is not only because of a sporadic and non-integrated irruption of new health services but, above all, because the system of land ownership and land use is based on an exploitation that is extensive and under-productive, but more than adequate to the interests of the landlord himself. (Barraclough, 1968.) Now, this system forms part of the class relations of the dominated society and these are determined by its relation of dependence within the structure as a whole.

If the familial system declines as a basic economic institution, this is due, very often, to the existence of casual employment in the intensive, seasonal production of an agricultural material closely linked to the fluctuations of the world market. Once broken, the circuit of traditional agricultural production cannot be re-established when a fall in international prices brings unemployment. (Baran, 1953.)

Thus there is no shortage of examples. But the essential fact is to perceive the close link between the urban processes and the social structure and to break with the ideological schema of a dualistic rural/urban, agricultural/industrial, traditional/modern society. For, if this schema corresponds to a certain social reality in its forms of relation and in cultural expressions, this reality is quite simply the reflection of a single structure, in which the effects at one pole are produced by the particular and determined mode of its articulation with the other pole.

2. Dependent urbanization causes a super-concentration in the

urban areas (primate cities), a considerable estrangement between these urban areas and the rest of the country and a break in, or the non-existence of, an urban network of functional interdependences in space. (Linsky, 1965.)

We have already seen that this incoherence is, partly, the result of the close link between the first urban centres and the mother-country. But there is another very important reason: the refloating of the medium-sized towns, their integration in an urban hierarchy, appears to require a policy of thrust with regard to smaller units of production, not directly viable in terms of their capital/product ratio, but justified by the creation of jobs and the social dynamism achieved. Now, this presupposes industrial planning, an employment policy and administrative regionalization. And it is obvious that, even when a bureaucracy is set up overtly dedicated to these objectives, the situation of dependence in relation to the dynamic of the system as a whole precludes any effective realization. (Hoselitz, 1957.) Moreover, since the migration towards the towns does not correspond to a demand for manpower, but to an attempt to find a viable life in a more diversified milieu, the process can only be cumulative and unbalanced.

3. Lastly, we can now understand the inter-ecological structure of the large urban areas, which are quite different from the western metropolitan regions. They are characterized by the juxtaposition, with the primary urban population, of an increasing mass of un-employed, with no precise function in the urban society, but who have broken their links with the rural society. It is entirely ideo-logical to call *marginality* what is a situation of tension between two interpenetrating social structures. Since the migration towards the towns is the product of the breakdown of the rural structures, it is normal that it should not be absorbed by the productive urban system and that, consequently, the migrants are integrated only very partially into the social system. But this does not mean that these groups are 'outside', 'at the edge' of society, as if 'society' were the equivalent of an historically situated institutional system. Their mode of articulation is specific, but this very specificity is a characteristic, not a pathological, feature unless one chooses to play the doctor for the established order.

Let us summarize the theoretical orientations with which we should approach the problem. The analysis of urbanization in dependent social formations may be carried out by considering the matrix of the relations among four fundamental processes:

1. The political history of the social formation in which the city (or urban system) is situated and, in particular, the degree of auto-nomy of the bureaucratic stratum in relation to external interests.

2. The type of agrarian society in which the process of urbanization develops. More concretely, the spatial forms will differ according to whether the agrarian structure is feudal or tribal, according to whether its breakdown is more or less advanced, and according to the greater or lesser harmony of interests between the urban and rural dominant groups.

3. The type of dependency relation maintained and, in particular, the concrete articulation of the three types of domination — colonial, commercial and industrial.

4. The autonomous impact of the industrialization proper to the dependent society. For example, in the case of a local industry, the type of industry will have specific effects on the type of housing and, in particular, on the socio-cultural milieu formed by the conjuncture of industries and housing. This is the case with the Latin American industrial urban areas dominated by the presence of manufacturing or mines. But sometimes one can also detect in the process of urbanization derived from industrial growth, the influence of a national bourgeoisie and proletariat, the dynamics of whose contradictory relations leaves its mark on space.

At such a level of complexity, it is no longer possible to make general statements and, even for a simple statement of perspectives, we must address ourselves to an analysis of concrete situations.

III Development and dependence in the process of urbanization in Latin America

Is Latin America a typical example of 'over-urbanization'? Or is it an intermediary situation between 'development' and 'under-development'? Or the co-existence of self-sustaining growth and the gradual 'marginalization' of an important part of the population? (Dorselaer and Gregory, 1962.)

The blossoming of 'sociological' myths concerning Latin American societies is such that particular prudence and precision are required in the organization of data and the formulation of hypotheses. Fortunately, there are three excellent syntheses available (Morse, 1965; Miro, 1964; Durand and Pelaez, 1965). See also OEA, 1970 and *Espaces et Sociétés*, 1971.

First, it is useful to recall that, if Latin America possesses a theoretically significant individuality, apart from enormous internal differences and some resemblances to other 'third-world' regions, this is precisely because the societies that compose it present a certain similarity in the structuring of their situation of dependence. The social formations existing in Latin America before

the colonialist penetration of the Spanish and Portuguese were
practically destroyed and, in any case, socially disintegrated during
the conquest. (Frank, 1968; Morse, 1962.) It is, therefore, within
a situation of dependence that new societies arose, presenting
scarcely any peculiarities relating to the previous social structure,
as was the case in Asia. The subsequent evolution of the ensemble
and its gradual internal diversification result from the different
regional articulations of the metropolis, and from the reorganization of the power relations between the dominant countries: the
replacement of the Spanish domination first by the British and
then by the American. The 'privileged' politico-economic relations
between Latin America and the United States reinforce a certain
identity of problems and constitute the warp of the social forms
in the process of transformation. (Frank, 1968; Petras and Zeitlin,
1968.)

Urbanization in Latin America, as a social process, may be understood on the basis of the historical and regional specification of the
general schema of the analysis of dependent urbanization. (See
Quijano, 1967.)

The available data indicate a high level of urbanization and an
ever accelerated rate of urban growth (see Tables 11 and 12). If
one takes as a criterion of urban population the threshold of
100 000 inhabitants, the rate of urbanization of Latin America in
1960 (27·4%) is almost equal to that of Europe (29·6%) and the
rate of 'metropolitanization' (population of cities of over a million
inhabitants) is higher (14·7% for Latin America as against 12·5%
for Europe — according to Homer Hoyt).

As Tables 11 and 12 show, the internal disparities are very great
and the situation of Central America has few points in common
with that of South America. We can begin to understand this more
clearly if we compare the very different results within the same
structure. The Latin American 'urban explosion' is largely the consequence of the demographic explosion, but the ecological distribution of this growth is highly significant. The rate, already high as
far as the population as a whole is concerned, is much higher in the
cities (see Table 12). This process occurs not only in all the Latin
American countries, but also within each province: the cities concentrate the demographic growth of the surrounding region, attrac-
ting the excess rural population. (Smith, 1964.)

The acceleration of urban growth usually takes the form of an
imbalance in the urban network of each country, since it is concentrated in the dominant urban area, almost always a capital.
More recently, however, this tendency appears to have declined:
in any case, it is a question of a relative diminution of the gap

between the cities, while no decline is taking place in absolute terms (see Table 13). In fact, with the exception of Colombia and, to a lesser degree, Brazil and Ecuador, Latin American societies are characterized by a macrocephalic urban system, dominated by the principal urban area. In 1950, in 16 countries out of 21, the first urban area was at least 3·7 times larger than the second and comprised a decisive proportion of the population (see Table 14). (Morse, 1965, 17; Browning, 1958.)

This being so, the fact that remains at the centre of the problematic is the observation, for Latin America, of a disparity between a high level and high rate of urbanization and a level and rate of industrialization markedly lower than those of other equally urbanized regions. Furthermore, within Latin America, although the most urbanized countries are also the most industrialized, there is no direct correspondence between the rates of the two processes within each country.

Although, for Latin America as a whole, the urban population (urban areas of over 2000 inhabitants) rose from 29·5% in 1925 to 46·1% in 1960, the percentage of the active population employed in manufacturing remained practically stable: from 13·7% in 1925 to 13·4% in 1960. (Cardoso, 1968, 74.)

At first sight, then, there is a disparity between industrialization and urbanization. But things are more complicated, for this analysis rests on a statistical artefact: the fusion, under the overall term 'Latin America', of very different social conjunctures. For example, a factor analysis carried out by G. A. D. Soares (1966), on data concerning Brazil and Venezuela, shows a common variance of 64% between urbanization and industrialization, even if the author concludes the non-identity of the two variables.

Furthermore, the proportion of the active population employed in industry is by no means the best indicator of industrialization, for it conceals an essential phenomenon: the modernization of the manufacturing sector and the increase of productivity. (Furtado, 1965.) Although, from 1925 to 1960, the active population employed in manufacturing remained stable, in fact, it fell from 10·2% to 6·8% in the craft sector and more than doubled (from 3·5% to 7·5%) in the modern industrial sectors.

In order to estimate the possible relation between the real increase of industrial production and the rate of urbanization, I have drawn up a list of eleven countries, for which we have relevant data, according to these two criteria (see Table 15).

With the exception of Panama, whose high rate of urbanization without industrialization may be understood without difficulty, the symmetry of the position occupied by countries in relation to

Table 11
Urban population and total population, Latin America,
by country, 1960, 1970, 1980

	Total population* (thousands)			Urban population** (thousands and percentage of total population)					
	1960	1970	1980	1960	%	1970	%	1980	%
Argentina	20 010	24 352	28 218	14 758	73·7	19 208	78·8	23 415	82·9
Barbados	232	270	285	11	4·7	?		?	
Bolivia	3 696	4 658	6 006	1 104	29·8	1 682	35·4	2 520	41·9
Brazil	70 327	93 244	124 003	28 292	40·2	44 430	47·6	67 317	54·2
Colombia	17 485	22 160	31 366	8 987	51·3	12 785	57·6	20 927	66·7
Costa Rica	1 336	1 798	2 650	428	32·0	604	33·5	968	36·5
Cuba	6 819	8 341	10 075	3 553	52·1	4 450	53·3	5 440	53·9
Chile	7 374	9 760	12 214	4 705	63·8	6 886	70·4	9 205	75·3
Dominican Republic	3 047	4 348	6 197	3 943	28·8	1 603	36·8	2 815	45·4
Ecuador	4 476	6 028	8 440	1 700	137·9	2 756	45·7	4 563	54·0
Salvador	2 511	3 441	4 904	804	32·0	1 305	37·9	2 259	46·0
Guatemala	4 204	5 179	6 913	1 242	28·9	1 593	30·7	2 342	33·8
Guyana	560	739	974						
Haïti	4 138	5 229	6 838	517	12·3	907	17·3	1 684	24·6
Honduras	1 885	2 583	3 661	405	21·3	716	27·7	1 280	34·9
Jamaica	1 610	2 003	2 490						
Mexico	34 923	50 718	71 387	18 858	53·9	31 588	62·2	49 313	69·0
Nicaragua	1 536	2 021	2 818	4 808	35·8	808	39·9	1 338	47·4
Panama	1 076	1 463	2 003	550	42·3	733	50·1	1 142	57·0
Paraguay	1 819	2 419	3 456	456	31·0	872	36·0	1 494	43·2
Peru	(1961)							49·2	10 791	50·2
	9 907	13 586	18 527	564	39·8	6 690			
Trinidad-Tobago	834	1 085	1 348	878	40·0				
Uruguay	(1963)								
	2 593	2 889	3 251	334	76·5	2 308	79·8	2 721	83·6
Venezuela	7 524	10 755	14 979	1 984	63·9	7 737	71·9	11 807	78·8

Source: Departamento de Asuntos Sociales, Secretaria General de OEA Washington DC, 1970.
* estimate   ** towns of 2000 inhabitants and over.

the two indicators is fairly striking, which seems to go against the asynchrony of the two processes.

What is certain and essential is that the impact of industrialization on the urban forms does not take place through an increase of *industrial employment*, and that, consequently, the social content of this urbanization is very different from that of the advanced capitalist countries.

In fact, as Anibal Quijano (1967) shows, the relation that links Latin American urbanization to industrialization is not a technological relation caused by the establishment of localized industry, but an effect of the characteristics of the industry of the country,

Table 12
Rates of urbanization in Latin America

| Country | Period | Annual rate of population growth | | | Rate of urbanization $r = 100 \frac{(u) - (t)}{100 + (t)}$ |
		Total (t)	Urban (u)	Rural	
Costa Rica	1927–50	2·3	2·9	2·2	0·6
	1950–63	4·0	4·5	3·8	0·5
Dominican Republic	1920–35	3·4	8·5	3·1	4·9
	1935–50	2·4	5·5	2·2	3·0
	1950–60	3·5	9·0	2·6	5·3
Salvador	1930–50	1·3	3·1	1·1	1·8
	1950–61	2·8	5·8	2·3	2·9
Cuba	1919–31	2·7	3·8	2·3	1·1
	1931–43	1·6	2·5	1·2	0·9
	1943–53	2·1	3·7	1·3	1·6
Honduras	1940–50	2·2	3·3	2·1	1·1
	1950–61	3·0	8·1	2·5	5·0
Jamaica	1921–43	1·7	3·9	1·4	2·2
	1943–60	1·5	4·0	0·9	2·5
Mexico	1940–50	2·7	5·6	2·0	2·8
	1950–60	3·1	5·2	2·3	2·1
Nicaragua	1950–63	2·6	5·9	1·9	3·2
Panama	1930–40	2·9	4·5	2·4	1·5
	1940–50	2·6	2·6	2·6	0·1
	1950–60	2·9	5·1	2·0	2·1
Puerto Rico	1920–30	1·7	6·2	1·2	4·4
	1930–40	1·9	4·9	1·4	2·9
	1940–50	1·7	5·5	0·6	3·7
	1950–60	0·6	1·0	0·5	0·3
Argentina	1947–60	1·8	3·2	0·3	1·3
Brazil	1920–40	1·5	3·0	1·3	1·5
	1940–50	2·4	5·3	1·7	2·9
	1950–60	3·1	6·5	2·1	3·3
Chile	1920–30	1·4	2·9	0·7	1·5
	1930–40	1·6	2·8	1·0	1·2
	1940–52	1·4	2·8	0·5	1·4
	1952–60	2·8	5·9	0·2	3·1
Colombia	1938–51	2·2	6·7	1·3	4·4
Ecuador	1950–62	3·0	6·6	2·0	3·5
Peru	1940–61	2·2	5·7	2·3	3·4
Venezuela	1936–41	2·7	5·0	0·9	2·2
	1941–50	3·0	9·7	1·3	6·5
	1950–61	4·0	8·1	1·4	3·9

Source: United Nations

and of the services, in so far as they exercise an economic function in the wider system as a whole.

Change in the structure of employment in Latin America has been much less determined by the process of industrialization than by the integration of part of the agricultural population into the

Table 13
Urban growth in Latin America according to the size of the urban area

Annual growth rate according to the size of towns (inhabitants)

Country	Period between censuses	Total 20 000 +	20 000 – 99 999	100 000 and over	Larger towns
Costa Rica	1927–50	3·0	–	–	3·0
	1950–63	4·6	–	–	4·6
Cuba	1931–43	2·1	1·9	1·7	2·4
	1943–53	3·2	3·9	3·4	2·6
Dominican Republic	1935–50	4·6	2·8	–	6·3
	1950–60	6·1	4·2	–	7·3
Salvador	1930–50	2·2	1·3	–	3·0
	1950–61	4·0	3·6	–	4·3
Honduras	1940–50	3·4	1·8	–	4·4
	1950–60	6·5	7·6	–	5·9
Mexico	1940–50	.....	.....	4·9	5·6
	1950–60	.....	.....	5·3	4·9
Panama	1940–50	2·8	2·2	–	3·0
	1950–60	4·4	2·1	–	5·2
Puerto Rico	1940–50	5·1	3·1	–	6·6
	1950–60	1·3	0·2	–	1·9
Brazil	1940–50	.....	.....	4·4	4·6
	1950–60	5·2	6·4	5·5	3·9
Chile	1940–52	2·6	2·7	1·4	3·1
	1952–60	4·4	5·1	3·0	4·2
Colombia	1938–51	5·7	5·0	6·1	6·2
	1951–64	.....	.....	.....	6·7
Ecuador	1950–62	.....	.....	.....	5·2
	1940–61	4·6	4·6	3·7	4·9
Peru	1941–50	7·6	7·1	7·2	8·3
Venezuela	1950–61	6·5	6·5	6·2	6·8

Source: United Nations.

tertiary sector (services) (see Table 16). (Cardoso, 1968, 74.)

Under the misleading term 'services' are grouped mainly three kinds of activities: commerce, administration and, in particular, 'various services'. It is easy to imagine how real or concealed unemployment takes the guise of a travelling salesman or an 'odd-job man' according to circumstances and, very often, according to the modes of consumption of the dominant class. The importance of the *services* sector in Latin America exceeds or equals that of the same sector in the United States and goes well beyond that in Europe (see Table 17). Furthermore, as Richard Morse (1965) has said, the Latin American and American tertiary sectors have nothing in common. In the first case, it is mainly a question of small commerce and travelling salesmen, servants, unskilled and temporary labour — a disguised form of unemployment. The most drama-

Table 14
The primacy of the great metropolises in Latin America, 1950

Metropolitan Areas	Year	Percentage of metropolitan population out of total population	Number of times greater than the country's second largest urban area
Montevideo	1954	32·7	17·0
Asuncion	1950	15·4	12·9
San José	1950	19·7	10·5
Buenos Aires	1947	29·7	8·9
Guatemala City	1950	10·6	8·2
Havana	1953	21·4	7·4
Lima	1955	12·4	7·3
Mexico City	1950	11·5	7·2
Port-au-Prince	1950	6·0	6·4
Santiago	1952	22·4	4·4
Tegucigalpa	1950	7·3	4·2
La Paz	1950	11·5	4·1
San Salvador	1950	11·9	4·0
Managua	1950	13·3	3·9
Santo Domingo	1950	11·2	3·7
San Juan	1950	23·9	3·7
Panama City	1950	23·9	3·1
Caracas	1950	15·7	2·9
Bogota	1951	6·2	2·0
Guayaquil	1950	8·3	1·3
Rio de Janeiro	1950	5·9	1·2

Source: Harley L. Browning, Recent Trends in Latin American Urbanization, *The Annals*, March 1958, pp. 111–126, table 3.

tic example is perhaps the division of labour between the inhabitants of the *favelas* and of the *barriadas*, who deliver manure and 'specialize' in the collection of certain objects and materials.

Even if the theme may lead to moralizing digressions, two aspects of the situation are worth remembering: 1. on the one hand, non-integration in productive activities and, consequently, an extremely low standard of living for the mass of migrants and the recently urbanized generations; 2. on the other hand, given the absence of any social cover for individual needs, an increase in the number of deteriorated urban zones, shortages of amenities either in the unhealthy quarters of the old city or in the shantytowns built on the edges of the city by the new arrivals.

Do these people constitute a marginal group? 20% of the population of Lima (1964), 16% at Rio (1964), 30% at Caracas (1958), 10% at Buenos Aires, 25% at Mexico City (1952), etc. Most studies carried out on this subject show that it is in no case a question of districts of 'social disorganization', but that, on the contrary, the internal cohesion of these groups is greater than in the rest of the

Table 15
Scale of classification of countries according to their rate of industrial growth (industrial products) and their rate of urban growth. (Latin America, countries selected according to data available.)

Country	Rate of industrial growth 1950—60	Industrial rank	Urban rank	Urban growth rate 1950—60
Brazil	1·78	1	2	5·2
Venezuela	1·70	2	1	6·3
* Peru	1·54	3	9 (?)	3·5
Nicaragua	1·42	5	3	4·9
Costa Rica	1·26	6	7	4·0
Chile	1·18	7	8	3·7
Ecuador	1·17	8	5	4·6
Salvador	1·04	9	10	3·3
Paraguay	0·88	10	11	2·8
Panama	0·78	11	6	4·1
Mexico	1·48	4	4	4·7

(*) The only important distortion in relation to the hypotheses is that of Peru. The explanation for this is simple: the non-existence of data for the period 1950—1960. Consequently, while the industrial product is calculated for 1950—1960, the urban growth was calculated on the basis of the comparison 1940—1960, whereas there was an enormous qualitative change during the 1950s. We were unable to make a statistical correction that possessed adequate guarantees, in view of the lack of data. If it had been possible to do so, Peru would probably occupy second place in the scale of urban growth, as can be seen in an inter-city comparison I made between Peru and Brazil and from the remarks made on this point by Jacqueline Weisslitz in the study quoted (1971).

Source: Cardoso, 1968; Miro, 1964; CEPAL, 1963.

Table 16
Latin America: Active population by economic sector

DISTRIBUTION OF THE ACTIVE POPULATION BY SECTOR

	1945		1960		Change between 1945—1960	
	Total	%	Total	%	Total	%
Agriculture	26 780 000	56·8	32 620 000	47·2	+ 5 840 000	− 9·6
Mines	560 000	1·2	520 000	0·9	− 40 000	−0·3
Primary	27 340 000	58·0	33 140 000	48·1	+ 5 800 000	− 9·9
Construction	1 500 000	3·2	2 800 000	4·1	+ 1 300 000	+ 0·8
Manufacture	6 500 000	13·8	9 900 000	14·3	+ 3 400 000	+ 0·5
Secondary	8 000 000	17·0	12 700 000	18·4	+ 4 700 000	+ 1·3
Tertiary	11 830 000	25·0	23 200 000	33·5	+ 11 370 000	+ 8·5
Total	47 170 000	100·0	89 100 000	100·0	+ 22 020 000	0·0

Source: Desal, *Marginalidad en America Latina. Un ensayo de Diagnostico.*

Table 17
Importance of the services sector in the active population.
Latin America and selected countries
(tertiary/secondary ratio)

Venezuela	2·08	Malaya	2·82
Cuba	2·00	India	2·17
Haïti	1·56	USA	1·48
Argentina	1·51	Canada	1·31
Mexico	1·48	France	1·15
Bolivia	1·40	Spain	1·09
Brazil	1·27	Italy	0·96
Paraguay	1·18	Germany (FGR)	0·85

Source: R. Morse, 1965.

urban area and even takes the form of locally-based organizations. On the other hand, the objectives of the groups structured in this way often do not coincide with socially accepted ends, that is to say, in the final analysis, with the interests of the dominant class. We must not, therefore, fall into the paradox of speaking of marginality where a more appropriate term would be contradiction. (Weisslitz, 1969.)

Latin American urbanization is characterized, then, by the following features: an urban population unrelated to the productive level of the system; an absence of a direct relation between industrial employment and urbanization, but a link between industrial production and urban growth; a strong imbalance in the urban network in favour of one predominating urban area; increasing acceleration of the process of urbanization; a lack of jobs and services for the new urban masses and, consequently, a reinforcement of the ecological segregation of the social classes and a polarization of the system of stratification as far as consumption is concerned.

Must we conclude, then, with the United Nations seminar on urbanization in Latin America, (Hauser, 1961) that such a process is parasitical and advocate an economic policy centred on basic industry rather than the satisfaction of needs in terms of social amenities? Indeed, such an industry, centred more on natural resources than on concentrations of possible buyers, might encourage the 'continentalization' of the economy, reorganize the urban network inherited from colonialism and orientate the rural migration towards more productive activities. Such a policy would be preferable to the measures adopted so far, which tend to reinforce the concentration of the population and to pour resources down a drain of non-productive urban areas. (Hauser, 1961, 88–90.) Posed in this way, the question is excessively abstract, in so far as it confronts a technical rationality with a social process. There can be no policy of urbanization without an understanding of the meaning of the social process that determines it. And this social process expresses the form of the society/space ratio according to the specific articulation of the Latin American countries within the overall structure to which they belong.

The history of the economic and social development of Latin America and, consequently, of its relation to space is the history of the different types and forms of dependence that have been organized, successively, in societies. What makes the problem complex is that, in a concrete social situation, the urban conjuncture expresses not only the dependence relation of the moment, but the survivals of other systems of dependence and their mode of articulation.

It is a matter, therefore, of stating briefly and concretely how the theoretical schema presented here organizes and explains the characteristic features of the urban history of Latin America.

(*Important observation*: it is not at all a question of explaining the 'present' by the 'past', but of showing the organization of the different social structures that merge at the level of a concrete social reality. Allusion to history is a convenient way of avoiding a translation into analytical variables of the processes under discussion. It is obvious that concrete research going beyond the general schema of analysis presented here would begin by carrying out this specification.)

A. The bases of the present urban structure largely reflect the type of domination under which the Latin American societies were formed, that is to say, the Spanish and Portuguese colonization.

The Spanish colonial cities in Latin America fulfilled two essential functions: 1. the administration of the conquered territories, in order to exploit their resources for the Crown and to reinforce a political domination by means of settlement; 2. commerce with the surrounding geographical area, but above all with the home country. Depending on the concrete forms of colonization, one or other of the two functions predominated. In general, the Spanish cities were mainly concerned with government, corresponding to the mercantilist policy of the Castile Crown, whereas the Portuguese settlements in Brazil were centred much more on the profitability of the exchange of products and the intensive exploitation in the regions near the ports. (Aravena, 1968.)

Two fundamental consequences result from this as far as the process of urbanization is concerned:

1. The cities were directly linked to the metropolis and scarcely went beyond the limits of the surrounding region in their communications and functional dependences. This explains the weak-

ness of the urban network in Latin America and the type of urban settlement, far removed from the natural resources of the interior of the continent. J. P. Cole (1965) has made a calculation, weighted in relation to the urban centres of the territorial administrative units, which makes it possible to divide the spatial area into three belts progressively distant from the coast. The results are very revealing: in 1950, 86·5% of the population of South America was concentrated in the coastal belt, which comprises only 50% of the surface.

2. The urban functions of a vast region are concentrated in the nucleus of the initial settlement, thus laying the foundation for the primacy of one great urban area. The city and its territory establish close and asymmetrical relations: the city administers and consumes what the countryside produces.

B. The substitution for political dependence on Spain of a commercial dependence on other European powers, in particular Great Britain, from the eighteenth century onwards and above all after independence, affected the situation already obtaining, but without modifying its main outlines in any qualitative way. On the other hand, from the quantitative viewpoint, the commercial activity and the extension of productive activities brought about by the widening of the market are the foundation of a strong demographic and urban growth (see Table 18).

On the basis of the complete introduction of the whole of the continent into the sphere of the world market, under British hegemony, there began the systematic exploitation of the resources of the primary sector demanded by the new industrial economies and, parallel with this, the creation of the network of services and transport necessary to these activities. The most direct consequence of this situation for urbanization was the regional diversification of

Table 18
Evolution of the population in Latin America (1570–1950)

Year	Population (in millions)
1570	10·2
1650	11·4
1750	11·1
1800	18·9
1825	23·1
1850	33·0
1900	63·0
1950	160·0

Source: Rosenblat, Carr-Saunders, in Angel Rosenblat, *La Población indígena en América Latina,* Buenos Aires, 1954.

production. Thus, the Argentine and Uruguay, founded on the
extraordinary expansion of cattle rearing (Condé and Gallo, 1967)
and on the fusion of interests between the mercantile bourgeoisie
of Buenos Aires and the landowners of the interior, experienced
high economic growth, with a concentration of all the tertiary
functions in the capital, already a privileged place as an exporting
port.

A parallel phenomenon can be shown in Chile, with a spectacular take-off based on mining and supported on the solid foundation of the bureaucratic machine left to the nascent bourgeoisie by
Portales. (Pinto, 1962.)

On the other hand, the countries of the interior and those north
of the Andes, in particular Peru, remained almost on the fringe of
the new economic structure — societies dominated by the land-
owning oligarchy and reduced, in their urban system, to municipal
collectivities inherited from Spanish colonialism. (Quijano, 1967.)

In Central America, however, the articulation of the imperialist
system took the form of plantation economy with urban functions
practically reduced to port activities and the maintenance of order.
This explains a level of urbanization much lower than that of the
rest of the continent, with the exception of Cuba, where the long
duration of Spanish domination maintained the power of the
administrative apparatus in the urban centres.

C. On the basis of this spatial organization, the process of Latin
American industrialization marks the urban forms differentially, in
terms both of rate and of level. Thus the first phase of industrialization, whether almost exclusively on the basis of foreign capital
(the Argentine, Uruguay, Chile), or on the basis of the mobilization of the national bourgeoisie using populist movements (Mexico,
Brazil), played a limited role, closely dependent on external trade.
Consequently, although it accelerated the disintegration of rural
society, it scarcely changed the urban functions (perhaps with the
exception of Buenos Aires).

On the other hand, after the slump of 1929, the collapse of the
mechanisms of the world market and the new situation created in
class relations encouraged a restriction on imports and created
industries centred on local consumption. (Halperin, 1968.) Given
the characteristics of these industries — low capitalization and an
immediate need of profitability — their introduction depended
closely on urban manpower and, above all, on the potential market
of the great urban areas. Even this limited industrialization gave
rise to an excessive expansion of 'services', for this was an opportunity of partially absorbing a whole mass of more or less unemployed people.

After World War II foreign, particularly American, investment found an outlet for surplus capital in the development of this local industry; it was also a question of opening up new markets. (Frank, 1968.) The process was accelerated in those countries where a basis already existed (the Argentine, Chile and, above all, Mexico and Brazil) and it rose rapidly in other countries that had hitherto been limited to primary production, such as Peru and Colombia, where the changes during the last fifteen years have been spectacular.

The cities thus became to some extent industrial centres and, furthermore, suffered the second impact of their new dependence through the mass of services introduced and through the further destruction of the old agricultural and artisanal forms of production. Let us try to look at the course of this process in detail.

It seems likely that the expansion of the labour market and the increasing ability to carry out public investment introduced by industrialization brought about a raising of the standard of living and the realization of certain public amenities. But the breakdown of the agrarian structure (produced by the persistence of the system of traditional land-ownership in new economic conditions) and the limits of this industrialization (subordinate to the expansion of solvent demand) accentuated the imbalance between town and country and led to the accelerated concentration of the population in the principal urban areas. (Graciarena, 1967.)

The decisive factor in urban growth in Latin America is undoubtedly rural-urban migration. The UNESCO seminar on this problem managed to establish, after comparing different sources of data, a similar rate of demographic growth for the towns and the country. Consequently, although the growth of the urban population is much higher, this is because only 50% of it is due to natural growth whereas the other 50% comes from rural migration. (Hauser, 1961; Solari, 1968, 40.)

Emigration is a social act and not the mechanical consequence of economic imbalance. The analysis of it, essential to the study of urbanization, requires an effort towards specific theorization calling for research in depth, beyond the scope of this book. (Touraine, 1961.)

But we can, without going into the internal logic of the process, indicate the structural conditions that increase its importance and lead to a very high rate of urbanization. (Weisslitz, 1968.)

One indisputable fact is the enormous inequality of means and standards of living between the towns and the countryside. The data presented on this subject by the Secretariat of CEPAL in *El Desarrollo de America Latina en la postguerra* (1963) are quite unequivocal (see also Solari, 1968), whether consumption is considered at the individual or at the collective level. This same discrepancy is to be found in the negative balance sheet of migration: the scope of the movement created goes well beyond the capacity for absorption of the new productive system (see Table 19).

Table 19
*Urbanization and social stratification
in Latin America, 1950 (percentages)*

	Rural population		Urban population	
Country	Persons employed in agriculture (15+)	Middle and upper strata	Middle and upper strata	Persons living in towns of 20 000 inhabitants or more
Central America				
Haïti	83	3	2	5
Honduras	83	4	4	7
Guatemala	68	8	6	11
Salvador	62	10	9	13
Costa Rica	54	12	14	18
Panama	48	15	16	22
Cuba	41	22	21	37
South America				
Bolivia	70	8	7	20
Brazil	58	15	13	20
Colombia	54	22	12	32
Paraguay	54	14	12	15
Ecuador	53	10	10	18
Venezuela	53	18	16	31
Chile	30	22	21	45
Argentina	25	36	28	48

Source: *Algunos aspectos salientes del desarrollo social de America Latina* (OEA 1962) p. 144; G. Germani, Estrategia para estimular la movilidad social. *Aspectos sociales del desarrollo economico de America Latina*, UNESCO, 1962, vol. 1, p. 252.

However, inequality of living conditions does not explain the massive transfer of populations, unless one holds with the ideological affirmation of a *homo economicus* solely determined by individual economic rationality. Underlying the phenomenon of migration there is, above all, the disorganization of rural society. This disorganization cannot be explained by 'the diffusion of urban values'; the simplistic hypothesis that sees a major fact in the penetration of rural society by the mass media forgets that information theory sets out from a certain correspondence between the code of the emitter and the code of the receiver in relation to a message. That is to say, the messages are perceived and selected according to the cultural system of the agent, himself determined by his place in the social structure.

Consequently, if in certain rural zones there is 'urban diffusion', this is due to the fact that the structural bases of the new situation have disorganized the traditional cultural systems. At a purely infra-structural level, we can say that the essential determinant of the breakdown of agrarian society is a contradiction between the accelerated increase of the population, a consequence of the recent fall in the mortality rate, and the maintenance of non-productive forms of land-ownership. (Barraclough, 1968.)

Now, the maintenance of these forms is part of the same social process as urban industrialization, through the fusion of interest, in the last resort, of the respective dominant classes. It is not, therefore, a question of a simple imbalance of levels, but of the differential impact of industrialization in rural and urban societies, decreasing and increasing respectively their productive capacity, while exchanges between the two sectors are made easier.

Lastly, the influx of population into the urban centres profoundly transforms the ecological forms, but affects only very relatively the non-productive activities. The CEPAL report (1963) shows, indeed, a very marked tendency of artisanal industry and commerce to create jobs that are not very productive, thus impeding the progress of productivity by the use of abundant, cheap manpower. Similarly, the administrative organisms give rise to variable systems of clientèle that correspond not to a real increase in activity, but to the development of networks of personal influence.

Urbanization in Latin America is not the expression of a process of 'modernization', but the manifestation, at the level of socio-spatial relations, of the accentuation of the social contradictions inherent in its mode of development — a development determined by a specific dependence within the monopolistic capitalist system.

4

Mode of Production and Process of Urbanization: Remarks on the Urban Phenomenon in the Socialist Countries

So far I have spoken of urbanization in a capitalist society, be it in the dominant or in the dependent countries. This characterization does not derive from an ideological option. It is the consequence of a theoretical point of departure: the hypothesis that the relation between society and space (for that is what urbanization is) is a function of the specific organization of modes of production that coexist historically (with a predominance of one over the others) in a concrete social formation, and of the internal structure of each of these modes of production. (Althusser, 1968; Balibar, 1970.)

On this basis, designating a society as capitalist, then specifying the precise conjuncture and the stage of capitalism that is revealed in it, enables me to organize my analysis theoretically.

But the reverse is not true: to designate a social formation as 'socialist' does not elucidate its relation to space and, very often, it tends to divert research, which takes refuge in a series of ideological dichotomies tending to present the obverse side of the capitalist logic, instead of showing the real processes that are developing in the new social forms.

The reason for this difference in the analytical capacity of the two categories appears fairly clear: whereas the theory of the capitalist mode of production has been elaborated, partly at least (especially as far as his own economic region is concerned) by Marx, in *Capital*, the theory of the socialist mode of production exists only in an embryonic state. Although Bettelheim (1967) has taken some steps towards an analysis of socialist economics, it seems to me that the theoretical nucleus for the analysis of the new social forms will have to be sought in the work of Mao Tse-Tung. (See also Balibar 1970). In these transitional forms, the category 'socialism' plays, therefore, the role of ideal type towards which one tends rather than that of an instrument of analysis of the social structure. Now, the theory of these 'transitional forms' does not exist in a finished form either and there can be no question here of approaching such a problem.

However, we can try to show a few peculiarities at the level of the space/society relationship, in such a way as to present observed elements towards a new logic of social structuring, typical of 'post-capitalist' social formations.

In any case, it seems clear that in these 'transitional social formations', private ownership of the means of production disappears as a structural element. The market is no longer the economic regulator and therefore it ceases to influence urbanization directly. The principal factor of social organization is the state and, through the state, the party in power. This displacement of the dominant system (the political taking the place of the economic) does not settle the question of the organization of social classes and their relation in space and, more precisely, it does not determine according to whose interests the process of urbanization is directed, for the relations between the social classes, the state and the party is closely dependent on the respective historical conjuncture.

But it is this primacy of the *political* and its independence of the economy that must characterize the process of urbanization in a socialist country. Furthermore, this primacy will produce a different content of spatial forms according to the political line in operation. I will formulate the hypothesis, therefore, that socialist urbanization is characterized by the decisive weight of the political line of the party, in the organization of the relation to space, possibly changing the relation to the economic or to the technological, such as can be seen in capitalist urbanization. A positive response to this hypothesis would put us on the path of mapping the dominant social level in the 'transitional forms'. I shall only be able to suggest a perspective on the basis of limited and extremely summary data. In view of the fact that on this problem I am merely asking questions, I limit my references here to fundamental works, on the basis of which further research into first-hand data may be undertaken. (Sorlin, 1964; George, 1962, Konstantinov, 1960; Chambre, 1959; Svetlichnyi, 1967; and the publications of the Foreign Language Publishing House, Moscow.)

In the Soviet Union, where 84·5% of the population was estimated to be rural in 1913, the economic policy intended to create the bases of socialism advocated accelerated industrialization, in particular the development of heavy industry. In concrete terms, this means strengthening the industrial basis already existing in the cities and developing the resources of the new regions, through a veritable *industrial colonization*. Hence the creation of new urban zones and a fairly high general rate of urbanization. On the other hand, since the revolution had been the achievement of the urban proletariat, intense propaganda was developed among the peasants to attract them towards the towns, where they would be able to participate more directly in the political process and in the building of a revolutionary society. It is a fact of fundamental importance that the Bolshevik Revolution was an almost exclusively proletarian and urban revolution in an overwhelmingly rural country.

However, despite the tendency of the policy of the CPSU to develop urbanization, the difficulties of the first decade — the struggle to the death between the old and the new orders — gave rise to an almost contrary process, for the urban masses emigrated towards the countryside in search of the means of subsistence. The total disorganization of the economy and the famine that followed made the growth of the towns entirely dependent on the capacity of the country to feed them, and on the system of transport and distribution necessary for exchange. This explains that the rate of urban population (15·5%) in 1913) should have fallen to 14% in 1920, rising slowly afterwards (16% in 1923, 17% in 1930).

But once the new political system was safely established, the line of the CPSU was imposed and the acceleration of urbanization was a result of the party's two great aims: industrialization on the one hand and the social restructuring of the countryside through agricultural collectivization on the other. Between 1930 and 1933, coinciding with the struggle against the *kulaks*, the proportion of urban dwellers rose suddenly from 17 to 23% and, in 1938, to 32%.

Despite the development of new urban zones east of the Volga, encouraged by industrialization and the exploitation of mining and energy sources, most of the urban growth took place in the already existing cities. It was inevitable that an economy at grips with the construction of an industrial infra-structure should have great difficulty in satisfying the urban needs that had suddenly appeared. The housing crisis reached very serious proportions: if, in 1927—28, the urban population enjoyed on average only 5·9 square metres of housing space per person, in 1940 this space fell to 4·09 square metres. (Chambre, 1965.) However, this crisis was conjunctural and, as the economy improved, a whole series of measures were put into effect with a view to: 1. redistributing the population over the whole territory and limiting the growth of the great urban centres; 2. investing in the construction of housing and organizing the corresponding public services.

In the first phase, therefore, Soviet urbanization presented certain features similar to those of the capitalist countries in their phase of industrial-urban take-off, with this difference, that the

working-class population did not experience unemployment
(Sorlin, 1964) and that, even if the standard of living was extremely
low, the urban organism proved capable of assimilating the rate of
growth.

But once this first phase was past, the organization of space
tended to become effectively the expression of the policy
implemented. Thus industrial diversification and the urban colonization of vast territories, in particular Western Siberia and Kazakh-
stan, did in fact get results. After the war, it was decided to slow
down concentration in the cities. Although it was impossible to
maintain the ceiling of 5 million inhabitants in Moscow (it had
8 500 000 in 1963), urban expansion took place mainly in the
medium-sized towns and the new centres of the colonized regions
(over six hundred new towns). Thus, whereas between 1926 and
1939, Moscow, Leningrad and Kharkov doubled their population,
between 1939 and 1959, towns of less than 200 000 inhabitants
increased by 84%; those between 200 000 inhabitants and 300 000,
by 63%; those between 500 000 and 1 000 000 by 48% and
Moscow by 20%.

On the question of housing, the public programmes were carried
out with a view to building the greatest possible quantity of apartments, without concern for quality, sometimes with unfortunate
consequences: between 1959 and 1962, 12% of the new apartments
were declared uninhabitable. But an enormous effort was made:
between 1954 and 1964, 17 million urban dwellings and 6 million
rural houses were built. The average surface area per person rose
from 4·09 square metres in 1940 to 7·2 square metres in 1954 and
9·09 square metres in 1961. Although the decisive factor in this
success was the amount of money invested in housing, progress in
the production of pre-fabricated elements made a very high construction rate possible.

The new political orientation that resulted from the Twentieth
Congress, which placed the accent on consumption, on measures
towards decentralizing the economic administration and on the
reinforcing of social integration by non-political means led to
attempts at urbanistic creation. In fact, the plans of the 1920s for
the revolution in urbanism were buried under the urgencies of the
first period. (Kopp, 1967.) On the other hand, in recent years,
'modernist' initiatives have emerged in the urban sphere with, for
example, the creation of a scientific township in Siberia or of
'micro-rayons' in the Moscow suburbs. (Hall, 1966; *L'homme et la
ville*, 1960.)

The micro-rayon is a unit of some 15 000 people, composed of
buildings of four or five stories, provided with educational

amenities, public services, leisure centres and protected by a green belt. A residential complex, it is linked to one or more centres of activity by public transport. In conception, it is very similar to the New Towns in Britain, with this essential difference that it is expressly dependent on a centre of production. The micro-rayon reflects the new relation to space defined, implicitly, by the political line of the present Soviet leaders: integration and emphasis on consumption.

At the same time, in connection with the new economic policy of preferential investment in agriculture, the 'agro-towns' project was launched to overcome the differences between town and country. However, in so far as these differences are rooted in the economic subordination of agriculture to industry, and in so far as the re-establishment of a balance between the two sectors is an economico-social rather than a spatial process, these rare experiments in agro-towns, which soon came to an end, never went beyond the stage of centres of public amenities in rural zones, or, in the best cases, strong points of agricultural colonization.

If there is any fusion of rural and urban, it is rather at the level of the Soviet metropolitan region of the kind described by Pchelintsev (1966). How close is this to Gottmann's Megalopolis? It would be over-hasty to conclude that there is an identity of spatial forms, with the same technological level and a different mode of production, on the basis of a simple observation of formal similarities. For we must take the following facts into account: 1. the capitalist mode of production is still present, although dominated *for the moment*, in Soviet society; 2. although the 'urban problems' are close to those of the Americans in nominal terms, their social meaning, their technological function and, above all, their solution are essentially different; 3. research remains to be done, beyond the forms, to reveal the differential urban structure of each situation — that which necessitates the articulation of this particular urban structure with the social structure.

The remarks that follow aim to explore this course by dealing with a non-capitalist mode of production at another level of economic and technological development. Indeed, an analysis of China and of Cuba will prove most significant: 'underdeveloped' according to static, taxonomic criteria, these countries have experienced a process of urbanization very different from that of the capitalist countries at the same level of 'development'. Furthermore, although the relation to space expresses, as in the Soviet Union, the primacy of politics, the specific content of the spatial organization is different, since the political lines are not identical in each case.

It is important to remember that the Chinese revolution, although directed by a workers' party, relied primarily on the masses of poor peasants and, after the strategic about-face proposed by Mao Tse-Tung, adopted the military and political tactics of encircling the towns by the countryside. The Chinese cities, in particular Shanghai and Canton, were inherited from colonialism — they were the headquarters of the administrative bureaucracies, of the representatives of foreign interests and the armies of occupation. The industrial proletariat was relatively small. It is obvious, therefore, that the political bases of the People's Republic, after the seizure of power in 1949, were much more secure in the countryside where, in 1950, 90% of the population lived. (Guillermaz, 1967; Ullmann, 1961; Wu-Yuan-Li, 1967.)

The first years, however, saw the emergence of an urbanization movement in so far as the industrial take-off and the reorganization of services required an increased labour force (see Table 20). It should be observed, however: 1. that the urban population statistics are over-estimated on account of the extension of the administrative frontiers of the urban areas and the annexation of semi-rural zones; 2. that, in any case, urban growth was due essentially to the natural growth of the population much more than to migration (the reverse of what occurred in the under-developed capitalist countries). (Ullmann, 1961; Guillermaz, 1967; Pressat, 1958; Orleans, 1959.)

But it was above all after 1957 that the reversal of the classic link between economic development and urbanization took place. Two reasons determined this new spatial policy:

1. The priority given to agriculture and the desire to rely on one's own forces, following the motto of Mao Tse-Tung: let agriculture be the base and industry the dominant factor. (Peking Revolutionary Committee, 1969; Kin-Ki, 1966.)

2. The Hsia-Fang movement, which tended to shift millions of intellectual workers to rural labour in order to check the right-wing deviations that had appeared during the implementation of the so-called 'Hundred Flowers' policy. This attempt was, in the opinion of foreign observers, a complete success, which managed to limit urban growth to that of the natural rate for each town (Orleans, 1966; *Pekin Information*, 1969) or even to reduce it: in 1963, 20 million rural migrants were returned to the countryside. (Lewis, 1966.)

This movement had very serious repercussions on the Chinese urban structure, for it made it possible, for example in Peking, to free enormous areas of office space, which were converted into housing: 260 000 square metres in 1958 and 100 000 square

Table 20

The evolution of the urban population in China, 1949–1957

Year	Total	Urban		Rural	
		No.	%	No.	%
1957	642 000	92 000	14·3	550 000	85·7
1956	627 800	89 150	14·2	538 650	85·8
1955	614 650	82 850	13·5	531 800	86·5
1954	601 720	81 550	13·6	520 170	86·4
1953	587 960	77 670	13·2	510 290	86·8
1952	574 820	71 630	12·5	503 190	87·5
1951	563 000	66 320	11·8	496 680	88·2
1950	551 960	61 690	11·1	490 270	88·9
1949	541 670	57 650	10·6	484 020	89·4

Source: China's Population from 1949 to 1956. *T'ung-chi kung-tso* (Statistical Bulletin), no. 11, June 14, 1957; translated in ECMM, no. 91; July 22, 1957, pp. 23–25.
1957: Wang Kuang-wei, How to Organize Agricultural Labor, *Chi-hua ching-chi* (Planned Economy) no. 8, 1957, pp. 6–9, translated in ECMM, no. 100, September, 23, 1957, pp. 11–14.

metres in 1959 (which is very important if one remembers that from 1949 to 1956 the total housing built in Peking occupied only 3 660 000 square metres). (Howe, 1968.) One has only to think of the shifting of populations away from the city centre to set up offices in the capitalist societies, and the differences in the use of space become quite obvious.

One may note five fundamental features that explain this maintenance of 'ruralization' in Chinese society, compared with the Russian experience:

1. The Chinese revolution developed and, in the main, took root among the peasant masses. Later collectivization was always based on long-term political education campaigns. (Bernstein, 1967.)

2. The Chinese Communist Party considers that agriculture is the foundation of economic development, although it also proposes to construct an industry capable of activating this development. (Chi-Ming How, 1968; *Pekin Information*, 1969.)

3. Political mobilization is regarded as an essential element of the productive system. It depends on the integration into the system of all the regions, and not on the creation of a few 'poles of development'. (Abaydoulla, 1966.)

4. Given the political and military leadership of China, the geographical dispersal of the population, by eliminating the distinction between strong and weak points, was a decisive factor in the People's War.

5. Above all, from the cultural revolution onwards, the effective negation of the principle of the social division of labour resulted

not only in a massive migration from the towns to the countryside, but in a continuous exchange of productive tasks among people and places. (*Pekin Information*, 1969; *La Chine en Construction*, 1966; Tchen Ta Louen, 1968; Perkins, 1967.)

However, in certain sectors or activities, a policy of creating urban forms has been launched in order to develop a productive capacity or in order to structure the social organization. An excellent example of the first case is the dynamism of the construction of the industrial complex of Wu-Han, which grew from 1 100 000 inhabitants in 1949 to 2 500 000 in 1967 (the projection followed a carefully drawn-up plan of urbanism). (Lagneau, 1959.) On the other hand, the people's communes have been an achievement rich in experience, despite the set-backs of their early days. (Salaff, 1967.)

The political determination of the process of urbanization, in China, was manifested recently during the cultural revolution. In its first phase, when the Red Guards opposed the urban bureaucracies, there occurred a massive influx into the towns, where most of the struggle was taking place. Later, when it was a question of reorganizing production and opening up new political and economic horizons, not only did the Red Guards return to their original regions, but there were also many movements towards the zones of colonization.

Certain of these characteristics are also present in the recent political process in Cuba. The determination of the revolutionary government to eliminate the supremacy of Havana (the centre of the counter-revolution), to develop settlement in the rural zones, to extend the population network over the whole territory, is explained both by the social bases of the movement (the poor peasants), the clearly agricultural options of the economy, the preparations for a possible guerrilla struggle and the desire to limit social differences. (Garcia Vasquez, 1968; Segré, 1970; Garnier, 1973.)

The examples of China and Cuba show clearly that accelerated, uncontrolled urbanization is not a necessary evolution determined by the level of development, and indicate how a new structuring of the productive forces and of the relations of production transforms the logic of the organization of space.

All the historical observations that have been formulated cannot take the place of explanation. On the contrary, through them, it is possible to identify the problematic connoted by urbanization, without being in any sense in a position to treat it theoretically. To do this, there is no other way than that of concrete research, drawing out the signification of each social situation, on the basis of its specificity. This is the opposite of a macro-historical overview, which can serve no other purpose than reconnaissance of the terrain of work, of the raw material to be transformed if we are to arrive at knowledge. For this research is in turn dependent on the elaboration of theoretical tools that make it possible to go beyond particular descriptions, while positing the conditions for the discovery (forever incomplete) of the laws that link space and society.

II The Urban Ideology

Is the city a source of creation or decline?

Is the urban lifestyle an expression of civilization? Is the environmental context a determining factor in social relations? One might well deduce as much from the most common formulations about urban questions: high-rise housing estates alienate, the city centre animates, the green spaces relax, the large city is the domain of anonymity, the neighbourhood gives identity, slums produce crime, the new towns create social peace, etc.

If there has been an accelerated development of the urban thematic, this is due, very largely, to its imprecision, which makes it possible to group together under this heading a whole mass of questions felt, but not understood, whose identification (as 'urban') makes them less disturbing: one can dismiss them as the natural misdeeds of the environment.

In the parlance of the technocrats, the 'city' takes the place of explanation, through evidence, of the cultural transformations that one fails to (or cannot) grasp and control. The transition from a 'rural culture' to an 'urban culture', with all its implications of 'modernity' and resistance to change, establishes the (ideological) framework of the problems of adaptation to new social forms. Society being conceived as a unity, and this society evolving through the transformation of the values on which it is based, nothing remained but to find a quasi-natural cause (technology plus city) for this evolution, in order to establish oneself in the pure administration of a classless society (or one naturally and necessarily divided into classes, which amounts to the same thing) and at grips with the discontinuities and obstructions imposed upon it by its own internal rhythm of development.

The urban ideology is that specific ideology that sees the modes and forms of social organization as characteristic of a phase of the evolution of society, closely linked to the technico-natural conditions of human existence and, ultimately, to its environment. It is this ideology that, in the final analysis, has very largely made possible a 'science of the urban', understood as theoretical space defined by the specificity of its object. Indeed, as soon as one thinks one is in the presence of a specific form of social organization — *urban society* — the study of its characteristics and of its laws becomes a major task for the social sciences and its analysis may even govern a study of particular spheres of reality within this specific form. The history of 'urban sociology' shows the close link between the development of this 'discipline' and the culturalist perspective that sustains it.

The consequence of this double status of urban ideology is that although, *qua ideology,* one may analyse it and explain it on the basis of the effects it produces, *qua theoretical ideology* (producing effects not only in social relations, but also in theoretical practice), one must learn to recognize it in its different versions, through its most rigorous expressions, those that give it its 'legitimacy', while at the same time knowing that these are not its social source.

For, like all theoretical ideology, it has a history, which we will trace briefly in order to bring out and discuss its essential themes.

5

The Myth of Urban Culture

When one speaks of 'urban society', what is at issue is never the
mere observation of a spatial form. 'Urban society' is defined above
all by a certain culture, *urban culture,* in the anthropological sense
of the term; that is to say, a certain system of values, norms and
social relations possessing a historical specificity and its own logic
of organization and transformation. This being the case, the quali-
fying term 'urban', stuck to the cultural form thus defined, is not
innocent. It is surely a case, as I have indicated above (see Part I),
of connoting the hypothesis of the production of culture by nature
or, to put it another way, of the specific system of social relations
(urban culture) by a given ecological context (the city). (Castells,
1969.)

Such a construction is directly linked to the evolutionist—
functionalist thinking of the German sociological school, from
Tönnies to Spengler, by way of Simmel. Indeed, the theoretical
model of 'urban society' was worked out above all in opposition
to 'rural society' by analysing the passage of the second to the first
in the terms used by Tönnies, as the evolution of a *community
form* to an *associative form,* characterized above all by a segmentation of roles, a multiplicity of loyalties and a primacy of secondary
social relations (through specific associations) over primary social
relations (direct personal contacts based on affective affinity).
(Mann, 1965.)

In extending this reflection, Simmel (whose influence on 'American sociology' is growing) managed to propose a veritable ideal type
of urban civilization, defined above all in psycho-sociological terms:
on the basis of the (somewhat Durkheimian) idea of a crisis of
personality — subjected to an excess of psychological stimulation by
the extreme complexity of the big cities — Simmel deduced the
need for a process of fragmentation of activities, and a strong

limitation of the commitment of the individual in his different roles as the only possible defence against a general imbalance resulting from the multiplicity of contradictory impulses. Among the consequences that such a process brings about in the social organization, Simmel indicates the formation of a market economy and the development of the great bureaucratic organizations, instruments adequate to the rationalization and depersonalization demanded by urban complexity. On this basis, the circle closes upon itself and the 'metropolitan' human type, centred on its individuality and always free in relation to itself, may be understood. (Simmel, 1950.)

Now although, in the work of Simmel, there remains an ambiguity between a metropolitan civilization conceived as a possible source of social imbalance and a new type of personality that adapts to it by exacerbating his individual freedom, in the prophecies of Spengler the first aspect becomes overtly dominant and urban culture is linked to the last phase of the cycle of civilizations in which, every link of solidarity having been broken, the whole of society must destroy itself in war. But what is interesting in Spengler is the direct links he establishes, first, between the ecological form and the 'spirit' of each stage of civilization and, secondly, between 'urban culture' and 'western culture', which seems to have been manifested, above all in this part of the world, by virtue of the development of urbanization. (Spengler, 1928.) We know that Toynbee took these theses as his basis when proposing, quite simply, an assimilation between the terms 'urbanization' and 'westernization'. Spengler's formulation has, no doubt, the advantage of clarity; that is to say, he carries the consequences of the culturist perspective to their logical conclusion, by grounding the historical stages in a 'spirit' and linking its dynamics to a sort of natural, undifferentiated evolution. Max Weber's *The City* (1905) which, in fact, formed part of *Wirtschaft und Gesellschaft,* has sometimes been interpreted as one of the first formulations of the thesis of urban culture. In fact, in so far as he strongly specifies the economic and political conditions of this administrative autonomy which, according to him, characterizes the city, I think that it is rather a question of a historical localization of the urban, opposed to the evolutionist thesis of the culturalist current, for which urbanization and modernization are equivalent phenomena.

All these themes were taken up again with a good deal of force by the culturalists of the Chicago School, on the basis of the direct influence undergone by Park, the founder of the school, during his studies in Germany. This was how urban sociology, as a science of the new forms of social life appearing in the great metropolises, came about. For Park, it is a question, above all, of using the city, and particularly the astonishing city that Chicago was in the 1920s, as a *social laboratory*, as a place from which questions would emerge, rather than as a source of explanation of the phenomena observed. (Park, 1925.)

On the other hand, the propositions of his most brilliant disciple, Louis Wirth, are really an attempt to define the characteristic features of an urban culture and to explain its process of production on the basis of the content of the particular ecological form constituted by the city. In all probability, it is the most serious theoretical attempt ever made, within sociology, to establish a theoretical object (and, consequently, a domain of research) specific to urban sociology. Its echoes, thirty-three years later, still dominate discussion. This has induced me, for once, to attempt a succinct, but faithful, exposition of his point of view, in order to define the theoretical themes of 'urban culture' through the most serious of its thinkers.

For Wirth, (1938; 1964) the characteristic fact of modern times is a concentration of the human species in gigantic urban areas from which civilization radiates. Faced with the importance of the phenomenon, it is urgent that we establish a sociological theory of the city which, on the one hand, goes beyond simple geographical criteria and, on the other hand, does not reduce it to the expression of an economic process, for example, industrialization or capitalism. To say 'sociology', for Wirth, is equivalent to centring one's attention on human beings and on the characteristics of their relations. Given this, the whole problematic is based on a definition and a question. A sociological definition of the city: 'A permanent localization, relatively large and dense, of socially heterogeneous individuals.' A question: What are the new forms of social life that are produced by these three essential characteristics of *dimension, density* and *heterogeneity* of the human urban areas?

It is these causal relations between urban characteristics and cultural forms that Wirth tries to stress. Firstly, to take the *dimension* of a city: the bigger it is, the wider its spectrum of individual variation and, also, the greater its social differentiation; this determines the loosening of community ties, which are replaced by the mechanisms of formal control and by social competition. On the other hand, the multiplication of interactions produces the segmentation of social relations and gives rise to the 'schizoid' character of the urban personality. The distinctive features of such a system of behaviour are therefore: anonymity, superficiality, the transitory character of urban social relations, *anomie,* lack of participation. This situation has consequences for the economic process and for the political system: on the one hand, the fragmentation and utilitarianism of urban relations leads to the functional specialization of activity, the division of labour and the market economy; on the other hand, since direct communication is no longer possible, the interests of individuals are defended only by representation.

Secondly, *density* reinforces internal differentiation, for, paradoxically, the closer one is physically the more distant social contacts are, from the moment when it becomes necessary to commit oneself only partially in each of one's loyalties. There is, therefore, a juxtaposition without mixture of different social milieux, which leads to the relativism and secularization of urban society (an indifference to everything that is not directly linked to the objectives proper to each individual). Lastly, cohabitation without the possibility of real expansion leads to individual savagery (in order to avoid social control) and, consequently, to aggressiveness.

The *social heterogeneity* of the urban milieu makes possible the fluidity of the class system and the high rate of social mobility explains why membership of groups is not stable, but linked to the transitory position of each individual: there is, therefore, a predominance of *association* (based on the rational affinity of the interests of each individual) over *community* as defined by membership of a class or possession of a status. This social heterogeneity is also in keeping with the diversification of the market economy and a political life based on mass movements.

Lastly, the diversification of activities and urban milieux causes considerable disorganization of the personality, which explains the growth of crime, suicide, corruption and madness in the great metropolises.

On the basis of the perspectives thus described, the city is given a specific cultural content and becomes the explicative variable of this content. And urban culture is offered as a way of life.

In essence these theses concerning urban culture in the strict sense constitute only variations on Wirth's propositions. However, they have been used as an instrument of an evolutionist interpretation of human history, through the theory developed by Redfield (1941; 1947) of the *folk—urban continuum*, which has had an enormous influence in the sociology of development. (See also Miner, 1952; Redfield and Singer, 1954.)

Indeed, Redfield takes up the rural/urban dichotomy and situates it in a perspective of ecologico—cultural evolution, identifying traditional/modern and folk/urban. With this difference that, setting out from an anthropological tradition, he conceives of urban society in relation to a previous characterization of *folk* society: it is a question of a society 'small, isolated, non-literate, and homogeneous, with a strong sense of group solidarity. Such a system is

what we mean in saying that the folk society is characterized by a
"culture".' Behaviour is 'conventional, custom fixes the rights and
duties of individuals and knowledge is not critically examined or
objectively and systematically formulated . . . behaviour is personal,
not impersonal . . . traditional, spontaneous and uncritical.' The
kinship system, with its relations and institutions, is derived directly
from the categories of experience and the unit of action is the
familial group. The sacred dominates the secular; the economy is
much more a factor of status than a market element.'

The *urban type* is defined by symmetrical opposition to the set
of factors enumerated above. It is centred, therefore, on social
disorganization, individualization and secularization. The evolution
from one pole to the other occurs almost naturally, through the
increase in social heterogeneity and possibilities for interaction, as
the society grows; furthermore, the loss of isolation, caused by the
contact with another society and/or another culture, considerably
accelerates the process. Since this construction is ideal—typical, no
society corresponds to it fully, but every society is placed some-
where along this continuum, so that the different features cited are
present in various proportions according to the degree of social
evolution. This would indicate that these characteristics define the
central axis of the problematic of society and that, consequently,
the gradual densification of a collectivity, with the social complexity
it gives rise to, is, then, the natural motive force of historical evolution, which is expressed materially through the forms of the occupation of space.

It is in this sense that Oscar Lewis's criticisms of Redfield's thesis,
showing that the 'folk' community, which had served him as his
first terrain of observation, was torn by internal conflicts and
accorded an important place to mercantile relations, are somewhat
ill-founded (despite their verve), for the theory of the *folk—urban
continuum* is intended as a means of defining the essential elements
of a problematic of social change, rather than of describing a reality.
(Lewis, 1953, 121—34.)

On the other hand, Dewey's fundamental critique (1960) constitutes a more radical attack on this perspective by indicating that,
although there are, obviously, differences between town and
country, they are only the empirical expression of a series of processes that produce, at the same time, a whole series of specific
effects at other levels of the social structure. In other words, there
is a concomitant variation between the evolution of ecological
forms and cultural and social forms, without it being any the more
possible to affirm that this co-variation is systematic, let alone that
the second are produced by the first. This may be proved by the

fact that there may be a diffusion of 'urban culture' in the country, without any blurring of the difference of ecological forms between the two. We must, therefore, keep the descriptive character of the 'folk–urban continuum' thesis, rather than treat it as a general theory of the evolution of societies.

This critique of Dewey's is one of the few, in the literature, that go to the root of the problem for, in general, the debate on urban culture, as formulated by Wirth and Redfield, has revolved around the purely empirical problem of establishing the historical existence or non-existence of such a system, and around discussion of the anti-urban prejudices of the Chicago School, but without going beyond the problematic of the culturalist terrain in which it had been defined. Thus, authors such as Scott Greer (1962) or Dhooge, (1961) indicate the importance of the new forms of social solidarity in modern societies and in the great metropolises by exposing the romantic prejudices of the Chicago School, who were incapable of conceiving the functioning of a society other than in the form of community integration which, of course, had to be restricted to primitive and relatively undifferentiated societies. In reopening the debate, other sociologists have tried to revive Wirth's theses, either on a theoretical plane, as Anderson has done, (1962) or by 'verifying' them empirically for the umpteenth time, as Guterman has tried to do, to mention one of the most recent examples. (1969.)

More serious are the objections raised in relation to possible causal connections between the spatial forms of the city and the characteristic social content of 'urban culture'. At a very empirical level, Reiss showed, long ago, the statistical independence (in the American cities) of 'urban culture' in relation to the size and density of the population. (Duncan and Reiss, 1956.) Again, in an extensive inquiry, Duncan found no correlation between the size of the population, on the one hand and, on the other, income, age-groups, mobility, schooling, family size, membership of ethnic groups, active population – all the factors that ought to specify an 'urban' content. (Duncan and Reiss, 1956.) Again, Sjoberg's great historical inquiry (1965) into the pre-industrial cities shows how completely different in social and cultural content are these 'cities' and the 'cities' of the early period of capitalist industrialization or of the present metropolitan regions. Ledrut has described in detail and shown in its specificity the different historical types of urban forms, with extremely different social and cultural contents, which are not located on a continuum, for they are spatial and social expressions qualitatively different from one another. (Ledrut, 1968, Ch. 1.)

Must we, then, with Max Weber (1905) or Leonard Riessman, (1964) reserve the term *city* for certain definite types of spatial organization, above all in cultural terms (the cities of the Renaissance or 'modern', that is to say, advanced capitalist, cities)? Perhaps, but then one slips into a purely cultural definition of the urban, outside any spatial specificity. Now, it is this fusion—confusion between the connotation of a certain ecological form and the assignment of a specific cultural content that is at the root of the whole problematic of urban culture. One has only to examine the characteristics proposed by Wirth to understand that what is called 'urban culture' certainly corresponds to a certain historical reality: the mode of social organization linked to capitalist industrialization, in particular in its competitive phase. It is not to be defined, therefore, solely in opposition to *rural* but by a specific content proper to it, above all at a time when generalized urbanization and the interpenetration of town and country make their empirical distinction difficult.

A detailed analysis of each of the features that characterize it would show without difficulty the causal link, at successive levels, between the structural matrix characteristic of the capitalist mode of production and the effect produced on this or that sphere of behaviour. For èxample, the celebrated 'fragmentation of roles', which is the foundation of 'urban' social complexity is directly determined by the status of the 'free worker', which Marx showed to be necessary to assuring maximum profitability in the use of labour force. The predominance of 'secondary' relations over 'primary' and the accelerated individualization of relations also express this economic and political need of the new mode of production to constitute as 'free and equal citizens' the respective supports of the means of production and of the labour force. (Poulantzas, 1968, 299ff.) And so on, though we cannot develop here a complete system of determination of cultural forms in our societies, the purpose of my remarks being simply to treat this social content other than by an analysis in terms of *urban.* However, a major objection might be raised against this interpretation of urban culture. Since the Soviet, non-capitalist, cities present similar features to those of the capitalist societies, are we not confronted by a type of behaviour bound up with the urban ecological form? The question may be answered on two levels: in fact, if we understand by capitalism the legal private ownership of the means of production, this character is not enough to ground the specificity of a cultural system. But, in fact, I am using the term 'capitalism' in the sense used by Marx in *Capital*: the particular matrix of the various systems at the basis of a society (economic, political, ideological). However, even in this vulgar definition of capitalism, the resemblance of the cultural types seems to be due, not to the existence of the same ecological form, but to the social and technological complexity that underlies the heterogeneity and concentration of the populations. It would seem to be a question rather of an 'industrial culture'. The technological fact of industrialization would thus appear to be the major element determining the evolution of the social forms. In this case, we would be coming close to the theses about 'industrial societies'.

But, on the other hand, if we hold to a scientific definition of capitalism, we can affirm that in historically given societies where studies have been made of the transformation of social relations, the articulation of the dominant mode of production called capitalism may account for the appearance of such a system of relations and of a new ecological form.

The observation of similar behaviour patterns in societies in which one may presume that the capitalist mode of production is not dominant, does not invalidate the previous discovery, for we must reject the crude capitalism/socialism dichotomy as a theoretical instrument. At the same time, this raises a question and calls for research that should have as its objective: 1. to determine whether, in fact, the real and not only the formal content of these behaviour patterns is the same; 2. to see what is the concrete articulation of the different modes of production in Soviet society, for, indisputably, the capitalist mode of production is present there, even if it is no longer dominant; 3. to establish the contours of the new post-capitalist mode of production, for, although the scientific theory of the capitalist mode of production has been partially elaborated (in *Capital*), there is no equivalent for the socialist mode of production; 4. to elaborate a theory of the links between the concrete articulation of the various modes of production in Soviet society and the systems of behaviour (see Part I).

It is obvious that, in such a situation, the problematic of urban culture would no longer be relevant. However, in the absence of any such research, we can say, intuitively: that there are similar technological determinants, which may lead to similarities of behaviour; that this is reinforced by the active presence of capitalist structural elements; that formal similarities in behaviour have meaning only when related to the social structure to which they belong. For to reason otherwise would lead us to the logical conclusion that all societies are one because everyone eats or sleeps more or less regularly.

This being the case, why not accept the term 'urban culture' for the system of behaviour bound up with capitalist society? Because, as I have indicated, such an appellation suggests that these cultural forms have been produced by the particular ecological form known

as the city. Now, one has only to reflect for a moment to realize
the absurdity of a theory of social change based on the growing
complexification of human collectivities simply as a result of
demographic growth. In effect, there has never been, there can never
be, in the evolution of societies, a phenomenon apprehensible solely
in some such physical terms as, for example, 'size'. Any development in the dimensions and differentiation of a social group is itself the product and the expression of a social structure and of its
laws of transformation.

Consequently, the mere description of the process does not
inform us as to the technico-social complex (for example, the
productive forces and the relations of production) at work in the
transformation. There is, therefore, a simultaneous and concomitant production of social forms in their different dimensions and,
in particular, in their spatial and cultural dimensions. One may
pose the problem of their interaction, but one cannot set out from
the proposition that one of the forms produces the other. The theses
on urban culture were developed in an empiricist perspective,
according to which the context of social production was taken to
be its source.

Another problem, our problem, is to discover the place and the
laws of articulation of this 'context', that is to say, of the spatial
forms, in the social structure as a whole. But, in order to deal with
this question, we must first break up the globality of this urban
society understood as a true culmination of history in modernity.
For, if it is true that, in order to identify them, new phenomena
have been named according to their place of origin, the fact remains
that 'urban culture', as it is presented, is neither a concept nor a
theory. It is, strictly speaking, a myth, since it recounts, ideologically, the history of the human species. Consequently, the writings
on 'urban society' which are based directly on this myth, provide
the key-words of an ideology of modernity, assimilated, in an
ethnocentric way, to the social forms of liberal capitalism.

In a 'vulgarized' form, if one may put it in this way, these
writings have had and still have an enormous influence on the
ideology of development and on the 'spontaneous sociology' of the
technocrats. On the one hand, it is in the terms of a passage from
'traditional' society to 'modern' society (Lerner, 1958) that one
transposes the problematic of the 'folk—urban continuum' into an
analysis of the relations internal to the imperialist system (see
Part I, Chap. 3, Section II).

On the other hand, 'urban culture' is behind a whole series of
discourses that take the place of an analysis of social evolution in
the thinking of the western ruling élites and which, therefore, are

largely communicated through the mass media and form part of the everyday ideological atmosphere. Thus, for example, the Commissariat Général au Plan (1970), in a series of studies on cities published as preparation for the sixth French Plan, devoted a small volume to 'urban society' that constitutes a veritable anthology of this problematic.

Setting out from the affirmation that 'every city is the locus of a culture', the document tries to enunciate the conditions for realizing ideal models, conceptions of city-society, while taking into account the 'constraints of the economy'. This is highly characteristic of a certain technocratic humanism: the city (which is simply society) is made up of the free initiatives of individuals and groups, which are limited, but not determined, by a problem of means. And urbanism then becomes the rationality of the possible, trying to link the means at one's disposal and the great objectives one sets oneself.

For the urban phenomenon is 'the expression of the system of values current in the culture proper to a place and a time', which explains that 'the more a society is conscious of the objectives it pursues . . . the more its cities are typed'. Lastly, on the basis of such a social organization, one finds the ecological factors that have long been advanced by the classics of urban culturalism: 'The basis of urban society lies in the grouping of a collectivity of a certain size and density, which implies a more or less rigorous division of activities and functions and makes necessary exchanges between the sub-groups endowed with a status that is proper to them: to be differentiated is to be linked' (p. 21). Here we find a whole theory of the production of social, spatial and cultural forms, simply on the basis of an organic phenomenon of growth — as if it were a question of a sort of upwards, linear movement of matter towards spirit.

Now, although it is clear that there are cultural specificities in the different social milieux, it is just as obvious that the cleavage no longer passes through the town/country distinction, and the explanation of each mode of life requires that one should articulate it in a social structure taken as a whole, instead of keeping to the purely empirical correlation between a cultural content and its spatial seat. For our object is quite simply the analysis of the process of the social production of the systems of representation and communication or, to put it another way, of the ideological superstructure.

If these theses on 'urban society' are so widespread, this is precisely because they permit one the short cut of studying the emergence of ideological forms on the basis of social contradictions and class division. Society is thus unified and develops in an organic way, producing universal types, formerly opposed by way of being unsynchronized but never, within any given social structure, opposed by way of contradiction. This, of course, in no way prevents one from commiserating with the alienation of this 'unified Man', at grips with the natural and technological constraints that impede the full development of his creativity. The city — regarded both as the complex expression of its social organization and as the milieu determined by fairly rigid technological constraints — thus becomes, in turn, a focus of creation and the locus of oppression by the technico-natural forces brought into being. The social efficacity of this ideology derives from the fact that it describes the everyday problems experienced by people, while offering an interpretation of them in terms of natural evolution, from which the division into antagonistic classes is absent. This has a certain concrete force and gives the reassuring impression of an integrated society, united in facing up to its 'common problems'.

6

From Urban Society to Urban Revolution

> *Long before me, bourgeois historians had described the historical development of this class struggle and bourgeois economists had expressed its economic anatomy. What I did that was new was: 1. to show that the existence of classes is bound up only with stages of historical development determined by production; 2. that the class struggle leads necessarily to the dictatorship of the proletariat; 3. that this dictatorship itself constitutes only a transition towards the abolition of all classes and a classless society.*
>
> (Karl Marx, letter to Weidemeyer, 1852)

The urban ideology has deep social roots. It is not confined to academic tradition or to the milieux of official urbanism. It is, above all, in people's heads. It even penetrates to the thoughts of those who set out from a critical reflection on the social forms of urbanization. And it is there that it does the most damage, for it abandons the integrating, communal, conformist tone, and becomes a discourse on contradictions — on urban contradictions. Now, this shift leaves intact the theoretical problems that have just been raised, while adding new, much more serious, *political* problems. Such flexibility of tone shows very well the ideological character of the theme of urban society, which may be 'left-wing' or 'right-wing' according to preference, without in any way changing the positive or negative feeling one invests in it, while recognizing urban society as a specific historical type with well-defined characteristics and even as the culmination of human evolution.

The most striking expression of this 'left-wing' version of the ideological thesis on urban society is no doubt the urbanistic thinking of one of the greatest theoreticians of contemporary Marxism, Henri Lefebvre. Such intellectual power applied to the urban problematic ought to produce decisive results in this sphere, not only in terms of influence, but also by opening up new approaches, detecting new problems, proposing new hypotheses. However, in the end, the problematic engulfs the thinker and, having set out from a *Marxist analysis of the urban phenomenon,* he comes closer and closer, through a rather curious intellectual evolution, to an *urbanistic theorization of the Marxist problematic.* Thus, for example, after defining the emerging society as urban, he declares that the revolution too, the new revolution, is logically *urban.*

In what sense? Let me try to explain in detail, for we are confronted here by a complex body of thought, full of subtleties and theoretico—political modulations that are impossible to grasp as a coherent whole. Nevertheless, if one looks attentively, beyond its open, asystemic character, there is a nucleus of propositions around which the central axes of the analysis are ordered. Let me sum up briefly and as faithfully as possible what this nucleus is, so that we may discuss in concrete terms its principal implications for a study of urbanization and, indirectly, for Marxism.

Despite the diversity and extent of Lefebvre's thinking (which is no doubt the profoundest intellectual effort that has been made towards understanding the urban problems *of the present day*), we have, in 1971, three texts to help us to grasp it: a collection of his writings on the problem, which includes the most important texts up to 1969, *Du rural à l'urbain* (which I shall refer to as *DRU*) (Lefebvre, 1970.); a short polemical work, *Le droit à la ville,* (*DV*) (1968); and, above all, the first general discussion of the question in *La révolution urbaine,* (*RU*) (1970); lastly, a short piece, *La ville et l'urbain,* (*VU*) (1971), which sums up very clearly the principal theses. (I shall continue to specify my textual references even if this seems over-scrupulous.)

Lefebvre's urbanistic exposition is 'constructed on a hypothesis, according to which the crisis of urban reality is the most important, more central than any other' (*VU*, 3).

This crisis, which has always existed in a latent stage, has been masked, impeded, one might say, by other urgent problems, especially during the period of industrialization: on the one hand, by the 'housing question' and, on the other, by industrial organization and overall planning. But, ultimately, this thematic must increasingly gain recognition, because 'the development of society is conceivable only in urban life, through the realization of urban society' (*DV*, 158).

But what is this 'urban society'? The term designates 'the tendency, the orientation, the potentiality, rather than an accomplished fact'; it stems both from the complete urbanization of society and from the development of industrialization (one might also call it 'post-industrial society') (*RU*, 8, 9).

This is a central point of the analysis: urban society (whose social content defines urbanization as a process rather than the reverse) is produced by a historical process that Lefebvre conceives as a model of dialectical sequence. In effect, human history is defined by the overlapping succession of three eras, fields or continents: the *agrarian*, the *industrial*, the *urban*. The political city of the first phase gives place to the mercantile city, which is itself swept away by the movement of industrialization, which negates the city; but, at the end of the process, generalized urbanization, created by industry, reconstitutes the city at a higher level: thus the urban supersedes the city that contains it in seed form, but without being able to bring it to flower; on the other hand, the reign of the urban enables it to become both cause and instrument (*RU*, 25).

In this evolution, there are two critical phases; the first is the subordination of agriculture to industry; the second, which we see today, is the subordination of industry to urbanization; it is this conjuncture that gives meaning to the expression 'urban revolution', conceived as 'the ensemble of transformations undergone by contemporary society, in order to pass from the period in which questions of growth and industrialization predominate, to the period in which the urban problematic will decisively triumph, in which the search for solutions and modalities proper to *urban society* will become of prime importance' (*RU*, 13).

But what is significant is that these fields, or stages, in human history (what Marxists called modes of production) are not defined by (spatial) forms or techniques (agriculture, industry); they are, above all, 'modes of thought, action, life' (*RU*, 47). Thus the evolution becomes more clear if one associates each era with its properly social content:

Need   — Rural
Work   — Industrial
Pleasure   — Urban (*RU*, 47)

The urban, the new era of mankind (*RU*, 52), seems to represent, then, deliverance from the determinisms and constraints of earlier stages (*RU*, 43). It is nothing less than the culmination of history, a post-history. In the Marxist tradition, one would call this 'communism'. A veritable *episteme* of a final period (our own period, it seems, forms the hinge between the two ages), the urban is realized and expressed above all by a new humanism, a concrete humanism, defined in the type of *urban man* 'for whom and by whom the city and his own everyday life in the city becomes work, appropriation, use-value' (*DV*, 163 — see, for the development of the whole problematic in terms of historical transformation, *RU*, 13, 25, 43, 47, 52, 58, 62, 80, 99, 100, etc.).

It is clear that this analysis refers to a historical type of society, urban society, defined by a precise cultural content ('a mode of life, action'), as was the case for the thesis on urban culture or on urban—modern society, even if the content differs. In fact, the essential, in each case, is the identification of a form, the urban, with a content (for some, competitive capitalist society; for others 'modern technocratic' society; for Lefebvre, the reign of freedom and the new humanism).

At an initial level of criticism, one might challenge Lefebvre's libertarian and abstract conceptions of the reign of post-historical or communist society, in which one perceives no concrete process of constructing new social relations through the revolutionary transformation of different economic, political, ideological agencies by means of the class struggle and, therefore, of the dictatorship of the proletariat. But this debate would merely, for the most part, reproduce the theoretical argument that has been advanced, for over a century, by Marxists against anarchists, a debate in which the history of the working-class movement has decided much more than a rigorous demonstration would have done. Having no pretension to adding anything new of great importance to a polemic that has largely been superseded by practical politics (spontaneism always destroying itself by its theoretical inability to direct the real processes), I have nothing to say to the resumption of millenarist utopias in Lefebvre's thinking. He is perfectly free, if he so wishes, to call 'urban' the utopian society in which there would no longer be any repression of the free impulses of desire (*RU*, 235), and also to call urban the still inadequately identified cultural transformations that are emerging in the imperialist metropolises.

But the whole problem is here: the term 'urban' (as in 'urban culture') is not an innocent one; it suggests the hypothesis of a production of social content (the urban) by a trans-historical form (the city) and, beyond this, it expresses a whole general conception of the production of social relations, that is to say, in fact, a theory of social change, a *theory of revolution*. For 'the urban' is not only a libertarian utopia; it has a relatively precise content in Lefebvre's thinking: it is a question of centrality or, rather, of simultaneity, of concentration (*RU*, 159, 164, 174; *VU*, 5). In urban space, what is characteristic is that 'something is always happening' (*RU,* 174); it is the place in which the ephemeral dominates, beyond repression. But this 'urban', which is therefore nothing more than emancipated creative spontaneity, is produced, not by space or by time, but by a form which, being neither object nor subject, is defined above all by the dialectic of centrality, or of its negation (segregation, dispersal, periphery — RU, 164).

What we have here is something very close to Wirth's thesis concerning the way social relations are produced. It is density, the warmth of concentration that, by increasing action and communication, encourage at one and the same time a free flowering, the unexpected, pleasure, sociability and desire. In order to be able to justify this mechanism of sociability (which is connected directly to organicism), Lefebvre must advance a mechanistic hypothesis that is quite unjustifiable: the hypothesis according to which 'social relations are revealed in the negation of distance' (RU, 159). And that is what the essence of the urban is in the last resort. For the city creates nothing, but, by centralizing creations, it enables them to flower. However, Lefebvre is aware of the excessively crude character of the thesis according to which mere spatial concentration makes possible the flowering of new relations, as if there were no social and institutional organization outside the arrangement of space. This is why he adds the condition: *providing this concentration is free of all repression;* this is what he calls *the right to the city.* But the introduction of this corrective destroys any causal relation between the form (the city) and human creation (the urban), for if it is possible to have repressive cities and freedoms without place (u-topias), this means that the social determinations of this inactivity, the production of the conditions of emergence of spontaneity, pass elsewhere than through forms — through a political practice, for example. What meaning, then, can the formulation of the problem of freedom in terms of the urban have!

One might add many remarks on the theoretical and historical error of the supposed determination of content by form (a structuralist hypothesis if ever there was one), by observing, to begin with, that it is a question, at most, of a correlation that still requires to be theorized, by linking it to an analysis of the social structure as a whole. And this correlation may even prove to be empirically false. Thus, when Lefebvre speaks of generalized urbanization, including Cuba and China, he is quite simply ignorant of the statistical and historical data of the processes he describes, particularly in the case of China, where urban growth has been limited to the natural growth of the towns (without peasant immigration) and where, on the contrary, one is witnessing a permanent and massive shift towards the countryside, reinforced by the constitution of the people's communes, as forms that integrate town and country. Although the absence of information about the Chinese, Cuban, Vietnamese experiences does not warrant overly affirmative conclusions, we know enough to reject once and for all the notion of the generalization of the urban as the only form, characteristic both of capitalism and socialism. Since, for Lefebvre, the urban is a 'productive force', one is directed toward a transcending of the theory of the modes of production, which is reduced to the ranks of 'Marxist dogmatism' (*RU*, 220), and to its replacement by a dialectic of forms, as explanation of the historical process.

Thus, for example, the class struggle still appears to be regarded as the motive force of history. But what class struggle? It would seem that, for Lefebvre, the urban struggle (understood both as relating to a space and as expressing a project of freedom) has played a determining role in social contradictions, even in the working-class struggle. Thus, for example, the Commune becomes a 'revolutionary urban practice', in which the 'workers, chased from the centre to the periphery, once again took the road back to this centre occupied by the bourgeoisie'. And Lefebvre wonders 'how and why the Commune has not been conceived as an *urban revolution,* but as revolution carried out by the industrial proletariat and directed at industrialization, which does not correspond to the historical truth' (*RU*, 148, 149). The opposition between forms without precise structural content (industry, the urban) makes it possible to maintain, by playing on words, that a proletarian revolution must be aimed at industrialization, whereas an urban revolution is centred on the city. The fact that, for Lefebvre, the state must also be a form (always repressive, regardless of its class content) permits this confusion for, political power being the central issue in any revolutionary process, suppressing it condemns one to an interminable opposition of every possible form of the class struggle (industrial, urban, agrarian, cultural), and renders an analysis of the social contradictions on which it is grounded unnecessary.

Such a perspective, if carried to its logical conclusion, even leads to politically dangerous consequences that seem to me to be alien to Lefebvre's thinking, although fairly close to what he actually says. Thus, for example, when the analysis of the process of urbanization enables him to declare that 'the vision or conception of the class struggle on a world scale seems today to be superseded. The revolutionary capacity of the peasants is not increasing; it seems even to be on the decline, although unevenly' (*RU*, 152), and the blindness of the working-class movement is contrasted with the clear-sightedness, on this theme, of science fiction (*RU*, 152). Or again, when he proposes to replace by urban praxis an industrial praxis which is now over. This is an elegant way of speaking of the end of the proletariat (*RU*, 184) and leads to the attempt actually to ground a new political strategy not on the basis of the structures of domination, but on the alienation of everyday life.

It is even suggested that the working class no longer has political weight, because it has nothing to offer in terms of urbanism (*RU*, 245). However, it remains an essential agent, but one whose actions are given meaning from the outside. A return to Leninism? Not at all! What might illuminate the options of the working class is well known: it is philosophy and art (*DV*, 163). At the intersection of these two, then, urbanistic thought plays a strategic role and may be regarded as a veritable avant-garde, capable of orientating the revolution towards new social conditions (the urban revolution) (*RU*, 215).

Although such statements rise towards metaphilosophical regions, far from the modest scope of the researcher, or even, quite simply, of people at grips with 'urban problems', one might, still, wonder what they teach us that is new or original about the urban question in the strict use of the term — about space and/or what is institutionally called the urban. And it is here that one becomes fully aware of the profoundly ideological character of Lefebvre's theses, that is to say, of their social rather than theoretical implication.

Indeed, space, in the last resort, occupies a relatively modest and subordinate place in the whole analysis. The city, according to a famous and on the whole correct formula, projects on the terrain a whole society, with its superstructures, its economic base and its social relations (*DRU*, 147). But when it comes to specifying these relations or showing the articulation between the social and spatial problematics, the second is perceived rather as a mere occasion of deploying the first. For space is 'the result of a history that must be conceived as the work of social *agents* or *actors, collective subjects,* operating by successive thrusts . . . . From their interactions, their strategies, their successes and defeats, result the qualities and "properties" of urban space' (*RU*, 171). If this thesis means that society creates space, everything still remains to be explained in terms of a mode of specific determination. But it goes much further: it indicates that space, like the whole of society, is the ever-original work of that freedom of creation that is the attribute of Man, and the spontaneous expression of his desire. It is only by accepting this absolute of Lefebvrian humanism (a matter of philosophy or religion) that the analysis might be pursued in this direction: it would always be dependent on its metaphysical foundation.

This spontaneism of social action and the dependence of space upon it becomes still more clear if one refers to the synchronic analysis that Lefebvre has made of urban space (*RU*, 129). His keystone is the distinction between three levels: the global or state level; the mixed level or level of 'urban organization'; the private level or the 'habitat level'. Now, what characterizes urbanization in the second critical phase of history is that the global level depends on the mixed level and that the mixed level tends to depend on the 'inhabiting'. This means, in concrete terms, that it is the inhabiting, *everyday life*, that produces space. Now, such independence of the everyday implies that one refuses to conceive it as the pure expression of general social determinations. It is the expression of human initiative, and this initiative (that is to say, the projects of subjects) is therefore the productive source of space and of urban organization. Thus one arrives at the following paradox: whereas one makes urban practice the centre of social transformations, space and urban structure are pure transparent expressions of the intervention of social actors. Another proof of the use of the term urban to express above all a cultural content (the free work). But one also arrives, at the same time, at this much more serious conclusion, that the whole perspective has no specific answer to give to the theoretical problems posed by the social determination of space and urban organization.

This being the case, 'urban practice', understood as a practice of transformation of everyday life, comes up against a number of 'obstacles' in terms of institutionalized class domination. Thus Lefebvre is led to pose the problem of urbanism as one of ideological coherence and as the repressive-regulatory intervention of the state apparatus. This is the critical side of Lefebvre's thinking, always accurate, brilliant, knowing how to detect new sources of contradictions. A large part of the social resonance of Lefebvre's urbanistic work derives from the political role played by an implacable critique of the system of official urbanism — a critique that one can only approve and pursue in the direction that Lefebvre has had the courage to open up.

But even this critique is experienced as the problematic of alienation, as opposition on the part of urban spontaneity to the order of urbanism, as a struggle of the everyday against the state, independent of (or above) the class content and specific conjuncture of social relations. That 'everydayness', that is to say, social life, governed above all by the rhythms of the ideological, may be the expression of new forms of contradiction in social practice, there can be no doubt. But that it should be the source, rather than the expression, of complex class relations determined, in the last resort, by economic relations, is a reversal of the materialist problematic and sets out from 'men' rather than from their social and technological relations of production and domination.

Nevertheless, Lefebvre has seen, on the one hand, the emergence of new contradictions in the cultural and ideological sphere and, on the other hand, he has linked the urban question to the process of the extended reproduction of labour power. In doing so, he has opened up what is perhaps a crucial direction in the study of 'the urban'. But he has closed it immediately afterwards by falling into the trap that he himself denounced, that is to say, by treating in terms of the urban (and therefore attaching them to a theory of social forms) the social processes that are connoted ideologically by urbanistic thinking. Now, in order to supersede this ideological treatment of the problem, it was necessary:

1. To treat space and the urban separately, that is to say, to treat the process of collective consumption at its different levels.

2. To proceed to the analysis of the social determination of these processes, in particular explaining the new forms of intervention of the state apparatuses in this domain.

3. To study the organization of space as a chapter of social morphology as Lefebvre proposes, while establishing the specificity of such a form, but without treating it as a new motive force of history.

4. Lastly, and above all, to explain the social bases of the ideological link between the problematic of space and that of the reproduction of labour power ('everydayness', to use Lefebvre's term).

Now, in elaborating a new theory of social utopia (or, to put it another way, of the end of history), Lefebvre has found in the urban form a 'material' support (a *place*) to which to attach the process of production of new social relations (the urban) through the interaction of creative capacities. Thus his analyses and perspectives, which have opened up new paths in this domain, are lost in the flood of a metaphilosophy of history, which takes the place of theoretical discourse and tries to convey the political spontaneism and the cultural revolt that are being manifested in the imperialist metropolises. This new urban ideology may thus serve noble causes (it is not always completely certain that spontaneism is one of them) while masking fundamental phenomena that theoretical practice still finds difficult to grasp.

The theoretical path opened up and closed by Lefebvre has been taken up in an extremely relevant way by the '*Utopie*' group, led by Hubert Tonka, which defines the urban problematic as 'the problematic of the mode of reproduction of the mode of production'. (Utopie, 1970.) But, quite unlike Lefebvre, these researchers do not make the 'urban', conceived as 'everydayness', the axis of social development, nor the cultural culmination of history. On the contrary, centring their analysis on capitalist society, they set out from a study of production and of the realization of surplus value in order to understand the extension of its logic to the world of consumption, an extension itself derived from the development of the productive forces and of the class struggle.

Rather than replace the 'industrial' problematic by the 'urban' problematic, they take the reverse direction, making the problems of the city entirely dependent on the forms and rhythms of class relations and, more particularly, on the political struggle: 'The so-called problems of the city are simply the most refined expression of class antagonisms and of class domination, which, historically, produced the development of civilizations.' 'Urbanization', as a policy of state power, is taken in the sense of 'civility', that is to say, as having the essential aim of resolving class contradictions. However, such an analysis seems to me, on the one hand, utterly to conceal a certain specificity of articulation between space and society and, on the other hand, to underestimate the interventions bearing on other spheres than political class relations, for example, attempts of a reform—integration kind, or the regulation of the economic, etc. It is true, however, that in the final analysis, all social intervention remains marked by its class content, although one must specify its mediations.

The few analyses made by *Utopie* have not been followed up in concrete research, given the essentially critical and political—cultural perspective that the group gives itself — in which it deserves all the support and encouragement of those who, in one way or another, are against the established 'urban order'. However, they reflect the essential problems to be treated, even if they do not embark on the long road of theoretical mediations to be traversed. But if a fruitful perspective is to be opened up, it will be done by placing oneself in opposition to the culturalist and spontaneist theses; that is to say, by approaching the analysis of new aspects of the capitalist mode of production through the development of new and adequate theoretical tools, which specify, without contradicting them, the fundamental elements of historical materialism.

The urban ideology would thus be superseded and the theme of urban culture, in its different versions, would be regarded as a myth rather than as a specific social process. However, if 'the city' or 'the urban' cannot be a social source of systems of values considered as a whole, would not certain types of organization of space or certain 'urban units' have a specific effect on social practices? Would there be 'urban sub-cultures'? And what would be their relation to the social structure?

7

The Urban Sub-cultures

The relation between a certain type of habitat and specific modes of behaviour is a classic theme of urban sociology. It is precisely at this level that the 'constructors' try to find a use for sociological reflection in their search for formulas that make it possible to express architectural volume or urbanistic space in terms of sociability. The manipulation of social life through the arrangement of the environment is a dream sufficiently linked to the utopists and technocrats to give rise to an ever growing mass of research, aimed at verifying a correlation, empirically observed in another context.

But this relation between context and life-style also occurs spontaneously in the representations of individuals and groups. Everyday reactions are full of associations, derived from a particular experience, according to which one quarter corresponds to a working-class mode of life, another is 'bourgeois', X new town is 'soulless', while the small town Z has kept its charm. Beyond social images aroused by the urban zones — the analysis of which forms part, strictly speaking, of the ideological representations in relation to the living context (see Part III) — we are presented with the following practical and theoretical question: is there a relation, and which relation, between the ecological context and the cultural system?

Now, the analysis of urban sub-cultures has usually come up against a confused amalgam of several research objectives. Cultural monographs of a residential community, usually trying to 'test' the emergence of a system of 'urban values' have alternated with attempts to link certain behaviour patterns and attitudes to a given ecological context.

That is why a discussion of the whole of the problematic requires a prior distinction between the various questions that are entangled here, the answers to which, theoretical and empirical, are very

different. Fortunately, there is available in this field an extraordinary analysis which, after reviewing most of the important
contributions made by American and British specialists up to 1968,
clears the ground by uncovering a few fundamental theoretical
distinctions. (Keller, 1968; see also Popenoe, 1963.) Keller indicates,
quite rightly, that it is a question of two series of non-equivalent
questions:

1. The existence of a system of specific behaviour patterns in
relation to local social life, in particular, in relation to neighbours.
This system of neighbouring involves at least two distinct dimensions: activities relative to neighbouring (mutual aid, mutual loan-
ing, visits, advice, etc.) and social relations in the strict sense
(namely, the ratio between relations of friendship, of family, of
neighbourhood, participation in association and centres of interest,
etc.). All these behaviour patterns express the cultural definition
of the role neighbour; this role varies in intensity and intimacy,
according to the dimensions and cultural norms interiorized by the
different social groups.

2. The existence of a particular ecological unit (quarter, neighbourhood, etc.) with sufficiently well-defined frontiers to produce a
socially significant demarcation. In fact, the very problem of the
existence of such urban units within urban areas, brings us back
immediately to the criteria for dividing up space (economic, geographical, functional, in terms of perception or the 'feeling of
belonging', etc.).

To these two questions must be added the strictly sociological
problem of the relation between each type of ecological unit, defined according to certain criteria, and each mode of cultural
behaviour. The relation, from the theoretical point of view, may be
regarded in both senses, for the determination of behaviour by a
context may be reversed through the influence that social practices
may have on the constitution of space. The problematic of the
urban social *milieux* thus poses, at least, these four series of
questions, which I shall try to deal with by referring to the major
tendencies, not always mutually consistent, that have emerged in
research. After this *ordered* theoretical reading, a provisional
meaning may be attributed to the mass of empirical results in such
a way as to synthesize (or to reprise) the formulation of the problem.

1. Is there an 'urban' behaviour pattern characterizing social life
in the residual units?

This is, in fact, a resumption of the theme of urban culture at the
specific level of the residential unit. Thus, if the city as a whole

may be summed up by a single cultural feature, there would be a type of 'urban' behaviour characterized by superficiality of contacts and the importance of secondary relations: this is what Guterman, in a recent study, tried to deduce from the negative correlation he finds between the size of the urban area and the degree of intimacy and friendship observed in social relations. (Guterman, 1969.) However, the matter is more subtle, for the translation from urban culture to residential unit is not done directly by reproducing, at the lowest level, the general urban type. It is a case of new formulas of social relations adapted to the residential milieux of the great urban areas. For, from the moment one could observe that the 'city' was not the equivalent of 'social integration', it was patently necessary to discover the new forms through which the system of social relations is developed in the situation of generalized urbanization.

The cultural typology suggested by functionalist sociology is thus placed on two axes: on the one hand, the opposition between 'local' and 'cosmopolitan' expresses the general trend towards a segmentation of roles, and of domination in secondary relations (Dobriner, 1958.); on the other hand, the 'local' pole is divided between a type of 'modern' behaviour and 'traditional' behaviour, the second being constituted by the turning in of a residential community upon itself, a strong internal concensus and a strong line of cleavage in relation to the outside, whereas the first is characterized by an open sociability, but one limited in its commitment, since it co-exists with a multiplicity of relations outside the residential community.

It is probably the research of Willmott and Young (1960) of the Institute of Community Studies in London that has best isolated the two types of cultural behaviour by analysing successively an old working-class quarter in East London and a new, middle-class suburb. In the latter, life is centred primarily on the home, with the woman who remains in the house and the man who, outside work, spends most of his time in domestic activities: gardening, doing odd jobs, helping with household tasks. But the home is not everything; a new form of sociability is developing through local organizations, brief visits to neighbours, going to the pub and social gatherings, according to a well defined rhythm. On the other hand, in the old working-class district, sociability does not need to be institutionalized; the networks of mutual aid are entirely open and the extended family, the central pivot of intimate relations, establishes communication between the elements of different generations.

The two modes of behaviour have been shown to correspond, on the one hand, to the new suburban housing and to the districts of the old town centre; on the other hand, to the way of life of the middle class and that of the working class. But, in any case, they are offered as a sequence, as a progressive passage from one to the other. Especially as the suburban residential community is not opposed to the preponderance of secondary relations and group membership at the level of society as a whole; on the contrary, they reinforce each other. Thus, for example, the classic research of M. Axelrod on Detroit shows both the persistence of primary relations of sociability and the concomitant variation of participation in social relations and organized associations. (Axelrod, 1956.)

This type of behaviour, in so far as its 'discovery' is bound up with studies of the new residential milieux of the American suburbs, has made possible the emergence of new theses concerning the advent of a cultural form that seems to some extent to have superseded the urban type. The suburban way of life, of which so much has been said, (Fava, 1956) is characterized by a veritable system of values, in particular, by the overwhelming importance of family values (in the sense of the nuclear family), a certain intensity of neighbourhood relations (usually polite, but distant), the constant search for an affirmation of social status and profoundly conformist behaviour. Thus, after dubbing the distinctive features of behaviour bound up with the competitive phase of capitalism 'urban culture', we are now asked to call 'suburban culture' the norms of the 'consumer society', individualized and turned in upon its stratified comfort, bound up with the monopolistic phase and the standardization of social life.

Now, the first point to establish seems to be the supposed generality of this new mode of social life that extends the urban, by a process of renewal, outside the context of the city. Whereas, just as the cities presented historically a diversity of cultural contents, the 'suburbs' and the residential units display an astonishing variety of modes of behaviour depending on their social structure. Thus, for example, to take only a minimum of studies that might serve as landmarks, Greer and Orleans, in their inquiry into St Louis, revealed a very high degree of simultaneous local and political participation and established important differences of attitude between the residential units, showing that they depended on the differential structure of the possibilities they offered. (Greer and Orleans, 1962.)

In a particularly brilliant study of a working-class suburb in California, Bennet M. Berger (1960) sets out to demolish the myth of 'suburban culture'. His principal empirical discoveries are the following: weak residential mobility, given the economic constraints to which the inhabitants are subjected; a persistence of interest in

national politics; on the other hand, weak participation in associations; great poverty of informal social relations; the dominant role
of television, a turning in upon the home, little going out, etc. Such
a picture, in contradiction with the model of active local participation, leads him to conclude that the mode of life proposed as suburban is, in fact, the model of behaviour of the middle class and that
the suburbs do not have a social specificity, only an ecological one.
Wendell Bell (1969), through a review of the literature, also shows
the diversity of cultural relations in terms of the social characteristics
of the residential milieux.

Things become more obvious if one leaves the American cultural
context where the myth was forged. Ferrarotti's (1970) important
study of the *borgate* of Rome presents a completely different pano-
rama of life in the suburbs. Thus, in *Borgata Alessandrina,* despite
the rural origin of the inhabitants, there are practically no social
relations on the local plane and, by savagely opposing any threat
of promiscuity, the family becomes the sole point of support,
completely cut off from the surrounding milieu. The terms are
reversed, on the other hand, in the system of relations observed by
Gutkind (1966) in the outskirts of Kampala (Uganda): while
integrated into urban life, a strong local community exists where
everyday life is concerned, and networks of families, friends and
neighbours profoundly interpenetrate one another.

In France, observations tend, despite various divergences, to
confirm the thesis of the non-existence of a 'suburban' model of
behaviour beside an 'urban' model centred on the *quartier* as such.

Thus, although the interesting inquiry by Gabrielle Sautter
(1963) into a new district at Pontoise (in the Paris region) depicts
a local lower-middle class sociability very close to that of the
American 'suburb', Retel (1965) concludes his inquiry into social
relations in the Paris suburbs by declaring that 'urban social life,
after passing through a phase of territorial structuring, will find a
new lease of life in a strictly sociological structuring of urban
groups among themselves', given the poverty of social relations of a
local kind. Ledrut (1968, 37), in his research into the *grands
ensembles* (high-rise housing estates) of Toulouse finds a 'fairly
good social climate', frequent visits between neighbours and easy,
though superficial, relations. Furthermore, he shows that such a
situation does not come about by chance: it stems from the non-
isolation and social heterogeneity of the milieu for, according to
his hypothesis, 'the isolation of a residential collectivity, of high
density, and feeble differentiation, is the determining condition of
the most intense social pressure and the sharpest tensions'. Now,
such a perspective goes beyond a mere observation of the existence

or non-existence of a model of behaviour defined by the residential milieu, and is orientated towards the search for differential conditions of relation between these two terms.

Similarly, when Chombart de Lauwe (1965, 67) approaches the cultural problematic of the *quartier*, also proposed by some researchers as specific communities of life, he links it to the urban ensemble, considering the *quartier* as an 'elementary unit' of this ensemble, with economic and geographical limits and particular urban and social functions. This means that the 'culture of the *quartier*', together with 'suburban culture' sometimes offered as particular cultural models, expresses a certain conception of the space/culture relation and that there is no possible urban problematic without previous examination of the ecological foundations of such behaviour.

2. Are there specific urban units?

Although it is obvious that there is a fractional differentiation of urban space linked to the social division of labour, it is much less clear that there are residential units ecologically marked off in such a way that they make it possible to break up an urban area into sub-ensembles possessing real specificity. Now, the existence of such ecological units seems a prior condition of the question as to whether certain spaces determine a certain form of behaviour. Indeed, how could one pose the problem, if there were no real differentiation of residential space?

The tradition of urban ecology tried to define the conditions of existence, within the city, of 'natural areas' which, in the classic definition of Paul Hatt (1946, 423–7), were made up of two elements: 1. a spatial unit, limited by natural frontiers within which one finds a homogeneous population with a system of specific values; 2. a spatial unit inhabited by a population structured by internal symbolic relations. There is, therefore, a *link* between ecological frontiers and social characteristics at the very level of the definition of the urban unit.

Such a link between the spatial context and social practice is at the root of the historical typology drawn up by Ledrut in order to differentiate the various forms of territorial collectivity. (Ledrut, 1967; see also Frankenberg, 1966.) Drawing up a sort of continuum in terms of the increasing complexity of society, Ledrut distinguishes between:

The village, fairly homogenous, with weak internal differentiation, in which the essential spatial relations involve circulation around centres of activity.

The neighbourhood, defined above all on the basis of residence and of the networks of mutual help and personal contacts that are created in it.

The small town (bourg), a grouping of residences with which an activity is associated and which constitutes, in the strict sense of the term, a community, that is to say, 'the spatial, concrete extension that represents the living sphere of the life of each individual', in which one finds, for example, common collective amenities and in which space is on a pedestrian scale.

The quarter, which has a double delimitation: it is provided with public amenities, accessible to the pedestrian; but, in addition, it is constituted around a sub-culture and represents a significant break in the social structure, being capable of reaching even a certain institutionalization in terms of local autonomy.

Lastly, *the city* is posited as a gathering at a higher level of individuals or groups, whereas the *megalopolis* presupposes a spreading of the primary units, foreshadowing, perhaps, a restructuring of local life on other bases.

Now, what is disturbing, even in a categorization as elaborated as that of Ledrut, is the constant repetition of this link between a certain space and a certain culture that seems to be given through an empirically mappable type of territorial collectivity. Now Ledrut himself, after defining the conditions of emergence of these quarters, (1968, 148) observes that they are practically non-existent in the Toulouse urban area (1968, 275) and concludes, in another work, that social life is polarized around two extremes, the city and one's residence, with scarcely any possibility of survival for 'intermediary groups' in modern society. (Ledrut, 1967.)

Similarly, the pioneering inquiry of Ruth Glass (1948), which tries to begin by delimiting the ecological frontiers of the neighbourhood units, establishes thirty-six economico—sociographical neighbourhood units for the town studied, but these units prove (with five exceptions) not to coincide with the social use of space. We may, in effect, divide an urban space into as many units as we wish, with the help of a whole battery of criteria. But each division bears an implicit proposition and, consequently, the social specificity of such sub-ensembles is not itself given. In the case of the Glass inquiry, it is very interesting to observe the specificity of the five sectors in which ecological and social specificities do overlap: they are the poor, isolated and socially very homogeneous zones. Since then, Suzanne Keller (1968) has tried to demonstrate the interesting hypothesis that since what reinforces the residential community seems to be precisely its weak capacity for general social initiative, there would seem to be an inverse correlation between local sociability, forming part of a system of generalized interaction, and the existence of a strong cultural specificity bound up with an ecological zone. Similarly, the feeling of attachment to the quarter seems to reflect a general attitude in relation to living conditions, rather than to the characteristics of the surrounding context.

If one then considers whether the polemic is borne out by the properly ecological specificity of the new suburban housing estates, one obtains similar results. Thus, for example, Walter T. Martin's (1958) study of the ecology of the suburbs in the United States distinguishes between the characteristics proper to these residential zones and those that are derived from them. Now, all those belonging to the first group are ecological truisms: location outside the city centre, the importance of commuting, smaller size and less density; but, still more, the derived factors (the predominance of young couples with children, the 'middle-class' level, a certain social homogeneity) derive rather from selective migration, which is fundamental to the constitution of these zones. They are, then, 'displaced segments' of the social structure, rather than local collectivities structuring themselves in relation to a certain use of space.

Identical discoveries are to be found in the abundant literature on the American suburbs, especially in the classic studies by Dobriner (1958) and Taueber (1964).

In France, Paul Clerc's (1967) inquiry into the *grands ensembles* has resulted in showing (astonishingly in view of the social image one generally has of them) a fairly minimal difference between the socio-economic composition of the *grands ensembles* and the urban areas adjacent to them (except for the proportion of 'employers', which is very low in the *grands ensembles, and that of middle management, which is very high). Should we conclude that the *grands ensembles* have no social significance? This would be over hasty, for the fact of concentrating on a limited space the average profile of an urban area — a profile that extends, in reality, through a wide differentiation — is in itself a significant situation. And, furthermore, as Chamboredon and Lemaire (1970) have shown, it would be necessary to differentiate the upper stratum of the population, which is in a process of renewal — the *grands ensembles* being a step in its social progress — from that which permanently remains there and thus constitutes the social base of the milieu of relation. But this goes beyond the question of the ecological specificity of the *grands ensembles* and draws them into a certain social process that still remains to be defined.

This is why one remains sceptical when Chombart de Lauwe (1965) defines the quarters as elementary units of social life 'that reveal themselves to the attentive observer', and which are expressed in 'the behaviour of the inhabitants, their turn of phrase'. These quarters, which, for Chombart de Lauwe, seem to be structured around both socio-economic amenities and meeting-places (above all cafés), are not ecologically given, urban districts, the basis of the urban area, linked together like the parts of a puzzle, but, as the same author observes, (1963, 33) 'they really exist only in the sectors in which the standard of living is fairly low'; they are produced, in fact, by a certain situation, and the community spirit of the quarter seems to be the result of a certain combination of social life, work life and situation with regard to the relations of production and consumption, both linked through a certain space, rather in the way that Henri Coing (1966) retraces the image of a Parisian quarter demolished by urban renewal.

Henceforth the empiricist debate concerning the existence or non-existence of quarters in modern society, or the possible emergence of new social links in the suburban housing estates, quite simply has no meaning, put in these terms: one does not discover 'quarters' as one sees a river, one constructs them; one maps the processes that culminate in the structuring or de-structuring of the social groups in their 'inhabiting' (*habiter*), that is to say, one integrates in the processes the role played by the 'spatial context', which amounts therefore to denying space as 'context', and incorporating it as an element in a certain social practice.

This is what Henri Lefebvre did when, after analysing the community ideology that is at the base of the 'quarter, the natural unit of social life', he proposed to study, not the ossified socio-ecological forms (which are, by definition, inapprehensible), but the tendencies of the urban units, their inertia, their explosion, their reorganization, in a word, the practice of 'inhabiting', rather than the ecology of the habitat. (Lefebvre, 1967.) The ideology of the quarter consists precisely in treating the forms of social life as natural phenomena linked to a context.

Thus, just as 'urban' or 'suburban' culture refers constantly to a spatial specificity, without naming it, the theme of residential units (quarters, suburbs, etc.) has meaning only through the implicit link that is made between an ecological context and a cultural content. The direct link between social and spatial variables seems, therefore, to be at the centre of the whole problematic of urban sub-cultures.

3. Is there a production of the social by a specific spatial environment?

In coming down from the heights of the philosophy of history to social research the theses of urban culture become operational; they try to show the link between certain modes of behaviour and the ecological context in which, according to the culturalist hypotheses, they are grounded. This type of research has a long history and continues to be a privileged tool of 'explanation by co-variation', a veritable safeguard of the good conscience of the 'empirical sociologist'.

It is all the more interesting to sketch the analysis of this perspective in that, on the one hand, it expresses in all its purity the relation of causality postulated between space and culture and that, on the other hand, it serves as a scientific (because observed) foundation for the most general theoretical constructions.

Thus, for example, the classic research by Farris and Dunham (1939) into the ecology of deviance, in Chicago, tried to verify Wirth's theses as to the unbalancing character of the urban milieu, by showing the gradual diminution in the rate of mental illness as one moved further away from the centre of the urban area. Now, this famous study, taken up and extended later to other spheres by dozens of researchers (for example, by Marshall Clinard (1960) to the analysis of criminal behaviour) was based on statistics relating to the public hospitals — which immediately invalidates the observation for if, in the city centre, the socio-economic level of the population causes it to become concentrated in the public hospitals, in the middle-class suburbs, there is a diversification, with a high proportion of patients in private clinics, thus diminishing the rate of illness for the sector. Furthermore, in relation to 'criminal behaviour', research like that of Boggs (1964) has shown the close relationship between the attitude to dominant norms and social categories, at the root of ecological co-variations.

If one turns to the level of housing, the determination of behaviour by the habitat is even more uncertain. Of course, the standard of the housing, the overcrowding that one has to put up with, are socially significant, but, again, it is not a question of a social relation, for, according to Chombart de Lauwe's perceptive summing up in the now classic inquiry into the question, (1960, 77) 'it appears that the critical attitude with regard to housing refers more to the way in which this housing is distributed than to the architectural aspect of it'.

Furthermore, the way of inhabiting (and therefore the behaviour that should normally undergo the influence of the habitat most directly) is highly differentiated according to the social groups, in each of the new residential units studied by Chombart and his team. Does this mean that the disposition of the housing has no influence on the way of life? Not at all! The relation between habitat and inhabiting operates via a complex link between the specific social characteristics of the inhabitant and the symbolic and functional content of the housing, which takes us far away from any attempt to explain a sub-culture in terms of a form of habitat.

This being the case, if ecological determinism, in its most elementary forms, has been generally superseded, urban culturalism has been strengthened by a series of studies proposing a certain spatial environment as explanatory of a specific social ambiance, whether in the production of a 'traditional' community in the quarters of the old urban nuclei or of a new way of life (the 'suburbanism' of the Americans and British) in the suburban housing estates.

One of the best expressions of this perspective is, for example, the technically impeccable research carried out by Sylvia F. Fava (1958) into the system of neighbour relations in three different contexts (a central quarter of New York, the outskirts of the same city and a local suburb). After observing seven variables that ought to have explained the differences of behaviour (sex, age, civil status, educational level, length of residence, origin, size of the community of origin), the inquiry reveals the increasing importance of neighbour relations, according to the classic 'middle-class' model, as the spatial context moves out towards the suburbs. Hence one deduces the opposition between two cultural models ('urban' and 'suburban').

Obviously, one could cite many other inquiries that lead to quite opposite results: for example, Ross's (1965) study of two residential zones, central and peripheral, of the same city of New York, in which differences of life-style are linked above all to the internal cleavages in each zone, according to social characteristics and age groups.

But the problem is not to come down on one side or other: this diversity of situations certainly corresponds to an ensemble of social processes at work, whose concrete combinations lead to different modes of behaviour. This is what Wilmott and Young (1960) tried to grasp in their comparative studies of a London working-class quarter and a middle-class suburb. They concluded by establishing a continuum, moving from a model of community relations to a polite but superficial sociability, with, at one extreme the workers of the working-class quarter and, at the other, the middle-class of the suburb and, between them, the workers of this same suburb.

But this interaction between the two types of determinants is not equivalent to recognizing a specificity of the spatial context as such, for the fact of living in a residential unit in which a social group is in the majority may be expressed sociologically as the existence of a social sub-culture, linked to the dominant group and not to the spatial context, which, if taken as a system of cultural reference, affects the behaviour of the minority group. (Bell and Forge, 1956.) The influence of the variables of social affiliation, with the related phenomena of condensation, distribution and interaction seem ultimately determinant. Both Ledrut's inquiry, already mentioned, into the Toulouse *grands ensembles* and Whyte's (1956) observations on the residential suburb of Park Forest in the Chicago area, show the essential role of social homogeneity if a certain type of behaviour is to develop, directly linked to the social characteristics of the residents. Once this behaviour occurs, spatial concentration may come into play, reinforcing the established system of relations.

In another context, an interesting study by Ion Dragan (1970) of the new district of Crisana, in the Rumanian town of Slatina, reveals the profound differentiation of a system of behaviour according to social categories within the same housing estate and, in particular, establishes the link between the importance of neighbour relations and the immediately rural origin of the migrants. This supports yet again the thesis of the cultural specificity of the social groups and contradicts the link between these neighbour relations and the suburban way of life (for they are practised to a far less degree by the 'suburbanites' of urban extraction).

This predetermination of behaviour by social groups, themselves a function of the place occupied in the social structure, is found again in analyses of 'district life' as many investigations in Europe and the United States show. (See for America, Beskers, 1962; for England, Pahl, 1970; for France, Castells, 1968.) Among other examples, one striking illustration of the differentiation of social life within the same urban context is the recording made by C. L. Mayerson (1965) of the everyday life of two boys, living a few yards from one another in the centre of New York, one of whom is Puerto Rican and the other the son of well-off, middle-class parents.

Even when a residential zone is strongly defined from the eco-logical point of view, as in the case of the 'marginal' communities established on the periphery of the Latin American cities (some-times in the city centre, as in Rio), the social differentiation explodes the cultural norms into so many segments. There too, to take only one example, the CIDU inquiry into the enormous 'marginal sector' of Manuel Rodriguez, in Santiago, Chile, shows that 'each of the sub-populations — differentiated above all in terms of resources and occupation — reveal different standards of living, a different set of values and various degrees of social participation' (Munizaga and Bourdon, 1970, 31). Furthermore, the working-class strata are those that show greater cohesion and a higher level of mobilization, social and political, contrary to the supposed law that links local participation to a 'middle-class' model of behaviour.

This does not mean that the concentration of certain social characteristics in a given space has no effect and that there cannot be any link between a certain ecological site and cultural specificity. The North American slums and ghettos are a concrete manifestation of the importance of the organization of a certain space in reinforcing a system of behaviour. (Suttles, 1968.) But for such effects to be manifested, there must, first of all, be the social production of a certain cultural autonomy, and this production depends on the place occupied in the relations of production, the institutional system and the system of social stratification. Besides, the way in which the ecology accentuates the cultural effects produced is also radically determined; in the case of the American slums, for example, racial discrimination is twofold, it is manifested, on the one hand, by the distribution of 'subjects' in the social structure and, on the other, by the distribution of housing and amenities in space. Their high cultural specificity results, therefore, from this correspondence and from the meaning it assumes in the sphere of social relations, through the conditions of the particular organization of the class struggle in the United States.

Similarly, the classic inquiries that try to demonstrate the link between residential proximity and choice of marriage partner ended by isolating a certain effect of spatial proximity (in so far as it increases the probability of interaction), but within a cultural definition of couples, itself determined by membership of different social milieux. (Katz and Hill, 1958.) Maurice Imbert's inquiry (1965), which shows how spatial distancing in relation to cultural centres reinforces the social differentiation determined by the socio-professional category, education and family situation, arrives at similar conclusions.

Although spatial forms may accentuate or deflect certain systems of behaviour, through the interaction of the social elements that constitute them, they have no independent effect, and, consequently, there is no systematic link between different urban contexts and ways of life. Whenever a link of this order is observed, it is the starting-point for research rather than an explanatory argument. Specific urban milieux must, therefore, be understood as social products, and the space/society link must be established as a problematic, as an object of research rather than as an interpretative axis of the diversity of social life, contrary to an ancient tradition in urban sociology. (See the work of the Chicago School, esp. Burgess and Bogue, 1964.)

4. Is there production of specific residential milieux by the values of social groups?

In so far as research has shown the secondary role played by the ecological context in the determination of cultural systems, a reversal of the terms of the problem has taken place, and a strong intellectual tendency seems to be directed towards considering residential milieux as a specification of the norms and values emitted by the preponderant social group in each context. Thus, once again, there seem to be 'urban sub-cultures', but their specificity seems to derive from the fact that each racial group chooses and produces a certain space in accordance with its type of behaviour.

In their conclusion on the celebrated problematic of the new American 'suburban culture' Gist and Fava (1964) consider that it does in fact exist and that it expresses a profound reorganization in the system of values of American society, evolving from an individualistic, puritan, Protestant ethic towards a profoundly hedonistic, 'social' ethic, based on sociability. The suburbs, inhabited by these new strata of the middle class, the bearers of the values of 'consumer society' would seem, therefore, to be the *locus* of expression most suited to a particular life-style.

Wendell Bell (1958) goes further, for he sees the ecological form of the suburbs as directly dependent on the new values of these middle strata. These independent values seem to be of three kinds: the importance of family life, a professional career governed by regular upwards mobility, an interest in consumption. Suburbs, both on the symbolic plane and in terms of instrumentality, offer adequate conditions for the realization of these modes of behaviour. In which case, it is not at all surprising that this new culture should be suburban.

This perspective was developed much more vigorously by Melvin and Carolyn Webber (1967), who analyse the different relations to space implied by the values of the intellectual élite on the one hand and of the working-class on the other. In the first case, the openness to the world that may be enjoyed by the élite favours a 'cosmopolitan' type of relation to time and space, which determines high residential mobility and a habitat that opens on to a multiplicity of relations. On the other hand, for the working class, the impossibility of predicting the future and the need to define oneself always here and now enforce a certain 'localism' and the concentration of the residential community around particularly secure primary links. The different types of residential milieux are, therefore, the direct ecological expression of the particular orientations of each of the groups.

In a very different context, the excellent inquiry by Mario Gaviria and his team into the outlying quarter of Gran San Blas, in Madrid, (Gaviria *et al.*, 1968) even manages to show how the structuring and functioning of a new town of 52,000 inhabitants are directly determined by the underlying concept of social relations (in this precise case, the urban paternalism of the Falangist unions). As the research report observes, 'the conception of an entirely working-class quarter, socially differentiated in space — it is situated close to the industrial zones — a quarter in which all the streets bear the names of trades and jobs, which is inhabited mainly by workers, in which all the public buildings are constructed according to the plans of the unions and in which there was an architectural competition to erect a monument in honour of 'the producer slain in the war' — such a conception is full of sociological significance. (It must be remembered that the unions in question are the fascist unions, the only ones having legal existence in Spain. The war referred to is, of course, the Spanish Civil War.)

It reflects, in physical terms, a society divided into classes and spatially deliberately differentiated: industrial zones, union housing, working-class population, 'monument to the producer'. It is a form of urbanistic development that 'runs the risk of proving full of surprises' (p. 104).

Gran San Blas obviously represents an extreme case, in so far as residential space is seldom shaped in so direct a way by an overall social conception. Furthermore, one might say that it expresses a specific social relation: that of the direct domination of inhabiting (working-class inhabiting) by a bureaucratic institution possessed of full powers over the habitat. And even in this case, if the residential space presents a certain social coherence in its configuration, the residential milieu that has been constituted in it does not seem to adjust without difficulty to the social appropriation that was envisaged. This residential milieu results rather from the encounter, not always a harmonious one, between the projected environment (linked to a certain policy with regard to the habitat) and the social practice of the inhabitants.

And, in reality, it is the necessary dislocation between the system of the production of space and the system of the production of values and the link between the two in social practice that makes quite impossible the relevance of hypotheses concerning the constitution of the residential milieux as mere projections of the values of each group. In effect, society is not the pure expression of cultures as such, but a more or less contradictory articulation of interests and therefore of social agents, which never present themselves simply as themselves but always, at the same time, in relation to something else. Nor is residential space a page on which the imprint of social values is laid. It is, on the one hand, historically constituted, and on the other, articulated within the social structure as a whole – and not only with the ideological instance.

Consequently, when there is a precise correspondence between the values of a group and the residential community, as a social and ecological unit, it is a question, once again, of a specific social relation, which is not given in the mere internal characteristics of the group, but expresses a social process that must then be established.

Nor can 'urban sub-cultures' be regarded as the production of an ecologico-social context by cultural values specific to a group, fraction or social class. When they exist in their specificity, they represent a certain situation whose significance is always discoverable by analysis.

Furthermore, rather than discovering the existence or demonstrating the non-existence of localized types of social relations, we should lay bare the processes of articulation between the urban units and the system of producing social representations and practices. This seems to be the theoretical space connoted by the problematic of the residential sub-cultures.

Many of the observations and arguments advanced in the course of this chapter may have seemed elementary and no more than common sense. This is all the more reason to cling to them and to recall: 1. that there is no cultural system linked to a given form of spatial organization; 2. that the social history of humanity is not determined by the type of development of the territorial collectivities; 3. that the spatial environment is not the root of a specificity of behaviour and representation.

In fact, a pious silence on such digressions would have underestimated the power and influence of the urban ideology, its power of evoking everyday life, its ability to name the phenomena in terms of the experience of each individual and to replace explanation. Urban sociology was founded on these themes, cultural analyses of development derive their support from them, the discourses of moralists and politicians are inspired by them (using a wide gamut of registers), the theoreticians of the 'cultural revolution' of the western petty bourgeoisie patch up the myth in order to give a 'material base' to their theses on the mutation of our societies. Lastly, the treatment of the fundamental problem, of the relation between 'the urban' and the ideological system, required the foregoing theoretical delimitation of so confused a terrain.

Having identified the theoretical question to which the

problematic of the 'urban sub-culture' refers, we have scarcely progressed in its treatment, for the study of the articulation of the ideological instance within the specificity of the urban units leaves the essence of the difficulty vague. In effect, although the ideological level, despite all its difficulties, may be relatively recognized and defined in theoretical terms, what exactly is one talking about when one refers to 'urban units'? The relation between 'ideology' and 'urban' (and, therefore, between 'ideology' and 'space') cannot be studied without a previous analysis in depth of the social content of 'the urban', that is to say, without an analysis of urban structure.

III The Urban Structure

8

The Debate on the Theory of Space

To consider the city as the projection of society on space is both an indispensable starting point and too elementary an approach. For, although one must go beyond the empiricism of geographical description, one runs the very great risk of imagining space as a white page on which the actions of groups and institutions are inscribed, without encountering any other obstacle than the trace of past generations. This is tantamount to conceiving of nature as entirely fashioned by culture, whereas the whole social problematic is born in the indissoluble union of these two terms, through the dialectical process by which a particular biological species (particular because divided into classes), 'man', transforms himself and transforms his environment in his struggle for life and for the differential appropriation of the product of his labour.

Space is a material product, in relation with other material elements — among others, men, who themselves enter into particular social relations, which give to space (and to the other elements of the combination) a form, a function, a social signification. It is not, therefore, a mere occasion for the deployment of the social structure, but a concrete expression of each historical ensemble in which a society is specified. It is a question, then, of establishing, in the same way as for any other real object, the structural and conjunctural laws that govern its existence and transformation, and the specificity of its articulation with the other elements of a historical reality.

This means that there is no theory of space that is not an integral part of a general social theory, even an implicit one.

Urban space is structured, that is to say, it is not organized randomly, and the social processes at work in it express, in specifying them, the determinisms of each type and of each period of social organization. On the basis of this evidence, which, however, has far-reaching implications, the study of urban structure must be carried out on two levels: we must, on the one hand, use these tools in a discontinuous succession of particular analyses of historically given phenomena. Such a study has been attempted by several theoretical schools — and the abundance of research material is evidence of their efforts. Thus, the theoretical effort of the Chicago School still dominates the apprehension of urban organization, in the literature and in practice, whether through a resumption of its classic themes or through the criticisms and reactions it has provoked. (Park *et al.*, 1925; Theodorson, 1961.) Indeed, most of the theoretical alternatives proposed, which have this tradition as their frame of reference, merely give an inverted image, without redefining the actual terms of the question.

It is impossible to approach an analysis of the organization of space without a discussion, however cursory, of this tradition of research. Not in order to provide a history of ideas, but in order to examine the theoretical efficacity of the propositions advanced and the work carried out. For the formulation of Burgess's (1925) celebrated theory on the evolution of urban areas by concentric zones brings a smile too easily to the lips, because of its ethnocentric ingenuousness, whereas it does account for a certain process of urban development, historically situated in socio-economic conditions that Quinn (1940) has described in great detail: a certain degree of ethnic and social heterogeneity; an industrial—commercial economic base; private property; commerce; economic organizations functionally specialized and spatially differentiated; an effective system of transport, without too much irregularity; a central urban nucleus with high property values.

It is a question, therefore, of the evolution of an urban area of rapid growth, dominated by capitalist industrialization entirely governed by the logic of profit, on the basis of a pre-existing urban nucleus with little symbolic weight and weakly constituted from the social and architectural points of view. Thus, in the Chicago studied by Burgess, the occupation of the urban centre (zone I) by the head offices of companies and administrative centres (in a strategic place as regards accessibility and the social density of the city) proceeds from the social domination of the companies and the strategic importance of their directional centres concentrated within a highly organized milieu. Zones II and III, which correspond to the invasion of the old urban space by industry and the housing necessary for the workers employed, are the result, on the one hand, of the enormous advantages represented for industry by the first period of its grafting on to the urban tissue and, on the other hand, of the social possibility of domination and even of the destruction of the urban context by the introduction of industry. Zone IV, the residential area of the upper classes, is the consequence of the urban deterioration thus produced, and the expression of social distance, manifested in the creation of a new residential space beyond the city, which is abandoned to the functional. Lastly, Zone V, comprising the residential and productive satellites still not integrated into the urban area, expresses the city's gradual domination of its hinterland, through economic concentration and functional specialization. (Mann, 1965.)

The rendering explicit of the basic conditions makes it possible to understand how the same model of urbanization could have accounted for the growth of a certain number of American cities (See for example Bowers, 1939; Anderson and Egeland, 1961; O'Brien, 1941.) and, in part, of European cities, as Chombart de Lauwe (1950) has shown in Paris or McElrath (1962) in Rome, while introducing this very important modification: the existence of privileged housing for the upper classes in the city centre, a space charged with symbolic links and places of cultural consumption.

On the other hand, when basic conditions change qualitatively, the claim of Burgess's model to universality collapses of itself. This is the case with Gist's (1957) classic study of the ecology of Bangalore, for example, which shows the explosion of the centre and the spatial interpenetration of activities and populations. Still more interesting is Schnore's (1965) analysis of the spatial organization of about sixty Latin American cities, which arrives at the conclusion that there are two principal urban forms: the 'traditional' model, a historic centre, surrounded by working-class suburbs, which serves as a seat for the upper strata and for the administrative functions — and the model of industrial growth, which partly reproduces the fundamental features of development by zones.

Better still, Chicago itself, in the mid-nineteenth century, and the great European cities before industrialization, structured their space in a hierarchized way around the original centre. Similarly, certain cities in the south of the United States depart considerably, in their configuration, from the norms of a spatial organization dominated by the law of the market, in so far as their social composition gives a larger place to the remains of the traditional agrarian oligarchy. (Gilmore, 1944.)

The attempts to modify the theory of zones do not represent a substantial shift of problematic and are subject, therefore, to the same criticism, requiring a specification of the historical conditions of their validity. Thus, the sectorial distinctions proposed by Hoyt (1939) try to adapt the model to the situations in which, owing to the particular history of a zone, one finds social rigidity. A particular stratum, introduced into a sector, colonizes the whole of an area radially from the inside outwards, without transforming it *en bloc* into a new belt. But the ecological movement and its functional determination remain the same.

On the other hand, the theory of multiple nuclei (Harris and Ullman, 1945), which tries to combine the development by belts and the functional division of the city, considering the spatial deployment of each function as a series of separate processes, extends to some extent the initial propositions of the Chicago School in the analysis of the new metropolitan regions, whose complexity goes beyond the summary framework of the Burgess model. It is certain that, despite this effort, the metropolitan region completely refutes the classic formulation, as is shown in the concrete and important analyses presented by Gottman (1961) for the northeast coast of the United States, or by Vernon (1960) for New York.

The example of the theory of urban growth developed by the Chicago School illustrates the limits of research as defined by its concrete formulation rather than by its principles of analysis. Now, in fact, all the work of Burgess, McKenzie, Wirth, etc., uses a series of notions whose scope goes beyond an individual study and on which, in fact, much work is still based. It is this effort to construct a true theory of space, so infrequent in a field swept alternately by empiricism and futuristic prophecy, which explains the persistence of conceptions directly linked to evolutionist organicisms of the oldest kind.

Indeed, underlying the spatial analyses there is a general theory of social organization, which one sees as directed by two essential principles.[1]

1. *The principle of interdependence between individuals,* based on their complementary differences (symbiotic relationships) and their supplementary similarities (commensal relationships).

2. *The principle of central function:* in any system of relation with an environment, coordination is ensured by the mediation of a small number of central functions. The position of each individual in relation to this function determines his position in the system and his relations of dominance. (Hawley, 1950.)

Given the immediate (vulgar?) materialism of this theoretical perspective, the problems of the relation to space will be a terrain eminently suited to its development in research, for society is understood, above all, as a community, this community being

---

[1] For this discussion I have had the benefit of valuable help from L. de Laberbis, professor at the University of Montreal and former pupil of A. Hawley.

defined as 'a system of relations between functionally differentiated parts, which is localized territorially'. (Hawley, 1963.)

Urban organization is then explained by an ensemble of processes that shape, distribute and relate 'ecological units', namely, any spatial expression that presents a certain specificity in relation to its immediate environment (housing, factories, offices, etc.). The principal ecological processes are: (McKenzie, 1926) *concentration* — namely, an increase in the density of a population in a certain space at a certain moment; *centralization*, or the functional specialization of an activity or network of activities in the same space, with its hierarchized articulation over the whole regional territory; centralization, with its corollary, *decentralization*, underlies the processes of mobility of the urban structure and, consequently, the functions of *circulation*, in the broad sense; *segregation* refers to the process by which the social content of space becomes homogeneous within a unit and is strongly differentiated in relation to external units, in general according to social distance, derived from the system of stratification; lastly, *invasion-succession* explains the movement by which a new population (or activity) takes root in a previously occupied space, having been either rejected by its previous site, or integrated into it or taking it over in a dominant role in the ecological unit thus envisaged.

This construction remains, however, at a formal level, in so far as the ecological processes that explain the urban configuration observed (zones, sectors, nuclei, radii, etc.) are not themselves explained other than by reference to general economic laws. Now, a theory of urban structure must consider the laws by which different social contents are expressed through the processes described. The formulation of empirical observations on this or that urban reality do not enable one to advance in this way.

The 'neo-orthodox' school of human ecology has attempted a systematization of its researches, by codifying them in the terms of ecological complex or eco-system. In Duncan's (1959) formulation, the whole of an urban structure may be understood as the result of the interaction between four fundamental elements: the population (P), the environment (E), technology (T) and social organization (O), the last referring to the ensemble of institutions and social practices. Thus, for example, it tries to explain, with the help of these terms, the problem of air pollution in Los Angeles. (Duncan, 1961.) The whole analysis amounts to a formalization of the real processes observed, through their codification in these four elements. There is no transformation of the observations into concepts — let alone any establishment of relations between the elements — that accounts for the sequences observed. The only advantage, therefore, is to be able to sum up, under certain headings, certain empirical observations. Is this really an advantage? It is doubtful (as when, for example, transport is treated as the introduction of new industrial plant under the pretext that it is a question in both cases of technological progress). (For an extreme case of ecological technologism see the otherwise excellent work of Gibbs and Martin, 1959.)

On the other hand, the 'social organization' element is a veritable hold-all that allows one not to treat the precise articulations of the social structure, by merging them into an overall relation between the social and the natural (and the technological).

Gist and Fava (1964, 102–3) have tried to overcome this disadvantage by adding a fifth, cultural or psycho-sociological, element in order to differentiate the values of the institutions. But their analysis of the process of American suburbanization presents exactly the same characteristics as that of Duncan, and does not go beyond a mere formal categorization of the different 'factors', historically combined in the process of urban diffusion in the United States.

The insistence of the ecologists that the whole of the organization of space should be treated on the basis of interaction between members of the human species, the tools created by it and the natural environment, placed them in an extremely strong position, in so far as, in actual fact, these are the given elements of the problem and are sometimes apprehensible directly, even from the statistical point of view. (Duncan and Schnore, 1959.) But, because they did not try to theorize these relations, and presented them quite simply as factors in the universal process of the struggle for life, their crude biologism lent itself easily to the culturalist critique, in particular at a time when the social sciences were undergoing the expansion of psycho-sociology and when the problematic of values was being placed at the centre of research.

Thus, although the first detailed critiques, in particular those of Alihan (1938) and Gettys (1940) stressed above all the specificity of human behaviour, refusing to apply directly to communities the manifestations of natural determinism observed in the other species, a subsequent tendency openly inverted the terms of the question regarding space, on the basis of Walter Firey's study of Boston (1947), as shaped by the values and behaviour of the groups. For example, William Kolb (1955) formulates the cultural conditions necessary to urbanization (equivalent to the systems of values underlying industrialization, in the Weberian analysis) and proposes to interpret the composition of space according to the symbolic affinities of the social groups and the role they play in society.

Form (1954) has insisted on the spatial repercussions of the phenomena of social domination and a tradition of studies of historical and comparative geography, from Dickinson (1951) to Sjoberg (1960) and from Max Sorre (1952) to Pierre George, (1961), has demonstrated the social diversity of the spatial forms. Should one then infer, for all that, an organization of space, determined, essentially, by the action of men guided by cultural orientations?

Willhelm's (1964) critique attacks the problem at a deeper level, by showing how, under cover of ecological organicism, a fundamental feature of the human species is neglected, namely, the contradictory differentiation of social groups, the fact that the appropriation of space forms part of a process of struggle concerning the whole of the social product, and that this structure is not a matter of pure individual competition but that it sets in opposition the groups formed by the differential attribution of individuals to the various components of the social structure — whereas 'the ecological complex presents a distinction without showing a difference.' This theoretical bias is manifested very concretely in research, from the fact of using as basic material census data, which characterize a collectivity as a whole according to the categories of administrative practice but which cannot account for their internal dynamics, nor for the passage from social relations to the organization of space.

This is a new dimension and displaces somewhat the opposition between 'cultural factors' and 'natural factors'. For, in the culturalist problematic in the strict sense, one does not include the motive aspect of the appropriation of space in terms of social differentiation. Thus one recent formulation, that of Achille Ardigo (1967), regards the metropolis as a social system, by transposing the four Parsonian sub-systems into the urban area, and by showing how the different spatial settlements follow these processes of adaptation and exchange according to institutionalized values.

In fact, the problematic proper to any theory of space does not consist in opposing values and 'natural' factors but, on the epistemological plane, in discovering structural laws or the composition of historically given situations and, on the strictly theoretical plane, in establishing hypotheses as to the dominant factor of a structure in which, obviously, all schools include the totality of elements of social life. Their essential divergence concerns the status of each element and of the combinations of elements.

This juxtaposition of problematics explains the confusion, in the literature, of two types of criticism directed at the tradition of human ecology: that which replaces natural determination by a culturally based social arbitrariness and that which recalls the specificity of historical space, by introducing the division of society into classes, with the conflicts and strategies that results from it, into the social process of constituting a given space. Now, this theoretical common front against ecological naturalism was established on the right-wing (ideological) positions, that is to say, centred on the predominance of values in social explanation. This fusion is uniquely possible within a historicist perspective: men (social groups) create social forms (including space) through the sometimes contradictory production of values which, orientating behaviour and attitudes, and founding institutions, shape nature. One recognizes in this formulation the ultimate core of work as important as that of Lewis Mumford and Alessandro Pizzorno, among others, or of part of the thinking of Henri Lefebvre.

However, one may wonder whether this inversion of perspective does not lead to a purely voluntarist analysis of space, incapable of integrating the acquisitions of the ecological tradition, for which space is in relation with the material conditions of production and existence of each society. Thus, for example, when Leo Schnore (1966) treats the city as formed essentially by the connection between places of work and residential districts, with the functions and spaces derived from the dynamic elicited by these two poles, he opens up what could be a fruitful direction, on condition that one goes beyond the elementary character of this notion and develops the conceptual apparatus in terms of the complexity of specific research. (See also the work of the Centre for Demography and Ecology of the University of Wisconsin.)

Beyond any academic eclecticism, one must go further than the ideological opposition between the determination of space by nature and its shaping by culture, to unite these two terms in a problematic that recognizes the specificity of the humanly social, without seeing it as a deliberate creation which cannot be explained by laws. To the common ideological front of culturalism and historicism, we must oppose a theoretical front that integrates the ecological, materialist-based problematic in a sociological analysis whose central theme is the contradictory action of social agents (social classes), but whose foundation is the structural web that creates the problematic of any society — that is to say, the way in which a social formation fashions nature, and the mode of distribution and administration, and therefore of contradiction, that stems from it.

In this undertaking, the results obtained by ecology have more value for the establishing of a theory of space than a mass of socio-cultural correlations, for they reflect this primary determination by

the productive forces and the relations of production that stem
from them, which is not to be contradicted, but rather developed, by
articulating with its own effects on space, those produced by the
other agencies of social determination.

In a way, one may locate in this perspective the research of the
so-called Social Area Analysis school, founded by Shevky and Bell
(1955). They analyse urban space on the basis of the combination
of a series of socio-economic characteristics, broken down into three
main dimensions: 'social rank' (occupation, education, income);
'urbanization' (family characteristics); 'segregation' (ethnic differentiation in space). Although this kind of work, which has been taken
up enthusiastically by Duncan (Duncan and Duncan, 1955) and,
more recently, by the University of Wisconsin group, (Schnore,
1965) expresses the articulation between social differentiation and
the configurations of space, it cannot explain the production of
these forms. To do so, it would have to be related to the rest of the
elements structuring the form and rhythms of an urban area.

Raymond Ledrut (1967), on the other hand, tries to reconstruct
the whole, proceeding from an analysis of the differentiation and
composition of social space. After defining various forms of urban
units (the neighbourhood, the small town, the quarter, the city) by
relating them individually to a specificity of the processes of consumption, he analyses the city as a system of exchanges between
different sectors that occupy a place and fulfil a particular function
(this function, says Ledrut, is 'the role played by the sector in the
internal functioning of the city', p. 138). Hence the organization of
space according to the unifunctional or plurifunctional character of
its elements, and the type of articulation exerted by the *centres*,
nodes of communication and organs of hierarchization of the urban
structure. Having thus defined for each sector an interior and an
exterior (on the basis of its relation to the other sectors), after
having distinguished a series of urban functions, one may then
study the homogeneity and heterogeneity of each urban unit, and
follow the transformations caused in the circuit by the performance
of each activity.

This analysis, which represents considerable progress in the theory
of space, remains however somewhat formal, in so far as it is a
purely methodological scaffolding. Not that it lacks 'data', but the
reasoning proceeds by opposition or similarity; it does not involve
any precise theoretical content; we do not know which functions
are being discussed, nor what are the social and functional relations
between the different sectors. Now, to fill out these forms of
empirical operations can only lead to the description of a particular
mechanism, without any possibility of theoretical transcription.

For, between this systematic schema and a given reality, we must interpose a conceptual segmentation, which defines function and relations between functions, and which makes it possible to determine the historical content apprehended in concrete research.

More simply, it is not enough to think in terms of urban structure; we must define the elements of the urban structure and their relations before analysing the composition and differentiation of the spatial forms. Such a conclusion emerges easily from a reading of the account of the Journées de sociologie urbaine at Aix-en-Provence (1968).

What, then, are the perspectives, as far as a gradual elaboration of the theory of space is concerned? Let us look again at the elements that emerged in the discussion: it is a question of going beyond the description of mechanisms of interaction between locations and activities, in order to discover the structural laws of the production and functioning of the spatial forms studied; the opposition between the natural and cultural determinations of space must be superseded through an analysis of social structure, considered as a dialectical process of relation between two types of elements by means of social practices determined by their historical characteristics; the differentiation of a space, the distinction between functions and processes relating the various units, do not have signification if they are not related to theoretically significant elements that situate the content of space in the social structure as a whole.

This confirms our starting-point: there is no specific theory of space, but quite simply a deployment and specification of the theory of social structure, in order to account for the characteristics of the particular social form, space, and of its articulation with other, historically given, forms and processes.

This is, in fact, true of the theoretical tendencies to which we have referred, despite the particularly prominent place occupied by human ecology in the problematic of space. It is evolutionist organicism, inherited from Spencer, that is at the root of human ecology; it is psycho-sociology, disguised by Parson as the sociology of values, which directly influences the culturalist analyses; and it is historicism, of Weberian descent, that influences the voluntarist essays on the creation of space.

The cursory critiques that I have put forward are, therefore, strictly theoretical critiques, concerned with the very foundations of the point of view. They do not invalidate, even in such cases where this might be appropriate, the mass of studies and results obtained. For observations have been made, and the logic of social mechanisms exposed. But, in so far as these discoveries have been understood and analysed within an ideologically determined approach, they are difficult to transpose and only weakly cumulative.

Although we can indicate the limitations of this perspective, it is much more difficult to propose new elements that make possible a specific analysis, still unachieved, of the social organization of space. For it would be voluntarist pretension to seek to establish a new theory. My much more modest task is, while attempting a certain theoretical specification, to extend in the field of the analysis of space, the fundamental concepts of historical materialism, in so far as the Marxist problematic offers precisely a dialectical fusion of those different elements whose fragmentation in terms of 'factors' forbids, for the moment, the construction of a structural theory of space.

On the basis of the fundamental concepts of historical materialism, how can we grasp the specificity of the forms of social space? (For the general theoretical foundations see Poulantzas, 1968; Althusser and Balibar, 1970; Badiou, 1967. For points relating to urban problems, Castells, 1969; 170–90; Lojkine, 1970.)

Let us recall that any concrete society and therefore any social form (for example, space) may be understood in terms of the historical articulation of several modes of production. By mode of production I do not mean the type of productive activities, but the particular matrix of combinations of the fundamental instances (systems of practices) of the social structure: essentially the economic, the politico-institutional and the ideological. The economic, namely the way in which the 'worker', with the help of certain means of production, transforms nature (object of labour) in order to produce the commodities necessary for social existence, determines, in the final resort, a particular form of the matrix, that is to say, the laws of the mode of production. The combinations and transformations between the different systems and elements of a structure are brought about by the mediation of the social practices, that is to say, by the action of men, determined by their particular location in the structure thus defined.

This action, always contradictory, in so far as any social structure presents dislocations and engenders oppositions in its development, reacts on the structure itself. It is not simply a vehicle of structured effects: it produces new effects. However, these new effects proceed not from the consciousness of men, but from the specificity of the combinations of their practices, and this specificity is determined by the state of the structure. Thus one can explain that social relations are not simply an expression of metaphysical freedom, but retain the possibility of affecting, by their ever-renewed specificity, the structure that gave them form. This capacity for modification is never unlimited, however; it remains enclosed within the stages of deployment of a structure, although it may accelerate its rhythm and, consequently, modify considerably its historical content.

To analyse space as an expression of the social structure amounts, therefore, to studying its shaping by elements of the economic system, the political system and the ideological system, and by their combinations and the social practices that derive from them.

Each of these three systems is composed of a few interdependent fundamental elements, which determine the very realization of the objectives of the system (which consists, indeed, simply of its elements and the relations between them).

Thus, the economic system is organized around relations between the labour force, the means of production, and non-labour, which are combined according to two principal relations: the relation of property (the appropriation of the product) and the relation of 'real appropriation' (the technological labour process). The spatial expression of these elements may be found in the dialectic between two principal elements: *production* (= spatial expression of the means of production), *consumption* (= spatial expression of labour power) and a derived element, *exchange*, which results from the spatialization of the transferences between production and consumption, within production and within consumption. The *non-labour* element does not have a specific spatial expression; it is expressed in the way in which the two relations of property and appropriation are organized in relation to space, and in the form of spatialization of each element.

The concrete examples of what these elements signify in relation to space given below are extremely dangerous and have no other than an indicative value, for there is no congruence between a theoretical element and an empirical reality, which always contains everything at once. For example, housing is economic, political and ideological, although its essential contribution is placed on the level of the reproduction of labour power. For a more precise view of the different elements it would be better to refer to the first analyses attempted in this chapter.

P (Production)   : Ensemble of activities productive of goods, and information.
                      Example: industry, offices.
C (Consumption)   : Ensemble of activities relating to social, individual and collective appropriation of the product.
                      Example: housing, public amenities.

E (Exchange) : Exchanges produced between P and C, within
P and C.
Example: traffic, commerce.
A (Administration) : Process of regulating the relations between
P, C, A.
Example: municipal administration, urban
planning.

The articulation of the politico-institutional system with space
is organized around the two essential relations defining this system
(the relation of *domination-regulation* and the relation of
integration-repression) and the places thus determined. The spatial
expression of the institutional system, is, on the one hand, the segmentation of space (for example, *communes*, urban areas, etc.); on
the other, it is action on the economic organization of space,
through the regulation-domination that the institutions exert on the
elements of the economic system, including their spatial translation
(process of *administration*).

Lastly, the ideological system organizes space by marking it with
a network of signs, whose signifiers are made up of spatial forms
and whose signifieds are ideological contents, the efficacity of which
must be construed from their effects on the social structure as a
whole.

The social organization of space may be understood, therefore,
on the basis of the determination of spatial forms:

By each of the elements of the three instances (economic,
politico-juridical, ideological). These elements are always combined
with the other elements of their own instance.

By the combination of the three instances.

By the persistence of ecological spatial forms created by earlier
social structures. These forms are articulated with the new forms,
thus producing ever specific concrete situations.

By the differential action of individuals and social groups on their
environments; this action is determined by the social and spatial
membership of these groups, but may produce new effects, from
the fact of the specificity of the system of interactions.

An exposition of spatial structure would require, therefore, a
previous theorization of the different levels indicated (abstractions,
concrete realities) and of their modes of articulation. Then, concrete
analyses might be presented, realizing in a specific way the structural laws explored and thus demonstrating those laws.

Now, the theoretical situation in which we find ourselves is, as
we know, quite different. We must, therefore, abandon the order of
our exposition and even the order of our thought in favour of an

order of investigation, an order of tasks to be carried out, if we are to progress in our study.

I shall try, therefore, to make our problematic concrete, by dealing with the conditions of spatial expression of the principal elements of the social structure. On this basis, a first synthetic formulation, in conceptual terms, will become possible in relation to the problematic of space. Then, and only then, will we be able to come back to the conceptual delimitation of the urban, within a theory of space, itself a specification of a theory of social structure.

Let me say at once that it is not a question of setting out from data and then constructing the theory. For the concrete analyses already obey a certain theorization. But the analysis cannot really be made, if, in the study of one element, industry for example, one does not indicate the structural relations that unite it with other elements. Theoretically, we ought to begin by exposing the whole of the structure in order then to deduce the behaviour of each element, always caught up in a given combination. As long as a minimal definition of the spatial structure as a whole has not been acquired, we must carry out partial research the results of which ought, henceforth, to be theorized in concepts that can be related to the theoretical foundations that we have just exposed. This is a calculated risk based on the fruitfulness of historical materialism for the discovery of the laws of society in other spheres. It is clear that only our future ability to explain the forms and processes of space will bear out whether the attempt was justified or not.

Discussion of the theory of space, a summary of research carried out and attempts at explanation thus lead to a twofold result: on the one hand, they enable us to posit the conditions for a properly theoretical analysis of the organization of space, though they do not give us direct access to the conceptual tools necessary to its elaboration; on the other hand, they bring us partial discoveries, half-theorized results, that may serve as landmarks in observing the realization of certain social laws, through their effects on the structure of space.

Having *posed,* if not solved, the theoretical problem, we must now observe certain historical processes relating to space, which have been partly theorized, and which will enable us to advance in our research. The subsequent synthesis of the results and problems must not be a theoretical corpus closing in upon itself, but, on the contrary, an ever open series of working propositions, for a theoretical field does not evolve towards its closure, but towards its opening.

9

The Elements of the Urban Structure

I The articulation of the economic system in space

By the economic system, I mean the social process by which the worker, acting on the object of his labour (raw material) with the help of the means of production, obtains a certain product. This product is the basis of the social organization — that is to say, quite simply, of its mode of distribution and administration, and of the conditions of its reproduction. In fact, the product is not a different element, but only a moment of the labour process. It may always be broken down, in effect, into (re)production of the means of production and (re)production of labour power.

We call the *production* (P) element of the structure the ensemble of spatial realizations derived from the social process of reproducing the means of production and the object of labour. Marx shows, in *Capital* (178–9), the simple elements into which the labour process may be broken down: 1. the personal activity of the man actually at work; 2. the object on which labour acts; 3. the means by which it acts. 'The soil . . . in the virgin state in which it supplies man with necessaries or means of subsistence ready to hand, exists independently of him, and is the universal subject of human labour. . . . If, on the other hand, the subject of labour has, so to say, been filtered through previous labour, we call it raw material. . . . An instrument of labour is a thing, or complex of things, which the labourer interposes between himself and the subject of his labour, and which serves as the conductor of his activity.' It should be noted that the instruments or means of labour comprise, in a wider sense, all the material conditions which, without entering directly into its operations, are nevertheless indispensible or whose absence would render it defective. The means of labour of this category, already due to previous labour, are the workshops, the building sites, the canals, the roads, etc. If the means of labour and the subject of labour are distinct, 'if we examine the whole process from the point of view of its result, the product, it is plain that both the instrument and the subject of labour, are means of production'. (p. 181) Now it is the relation of the whole process to space that is at the centre of my analysis.

I call the *consumption* (C) element of the structure the ensemble of spatial realizations derived from the social process of reproducing labour power. 'Under this term, we must include the aggregate of the mental and physical capabilities existing in a human being, which he exercises whenever he produces a use-value of any description. (p. 167) This reproduction may be simple (for example, housing, minimum amenities) or extended (socio-cultural environments, etc.).

Lastly, a series of transfers (relations of circulation) operate between P and C within each of the elements. We call *exchange* (E) the spatial realization of these transfers. It should be noted that there will also be transfers between the elements of the economic system and the other systems and that, consequently, exchange will play the role of articulation in the space formed by these three systems. To each type of transfer will correspond, therefore, a distinct spatial expression, which can be understood not in itself, but in terms of the elements it connects.

These characteristics are too overall to lead to propositions that might explain real processes. Each element will have to be broken down into a series of sub-elements (expressed spatially) and these sub-elements will also be structured, that is to say, complex, a result of the differentiation of several levels and of the articulation of several roles or functions.

But the deployment and specification of the general theoretical framework will have a more precise meaning when we have attempted a first approach to a few essential elements of the spatial structure in its historical reality.

Production and space: the social logic of industrial location
Although the analysis of the relation between production and space includes not only industrial installations in the strict sense, but also the industrial and technological environment and the location of offices for organization and management, it is at the level of the productive unit (the industrial plant) that the fundamental determination of this relation may be grasped.

In a society in which the CMP (Capitalist Mode of Production) is dominant, the economic system is the dominant system of the social structure and, therefore, the production element is the basis of the organization of space. But this does not mean that the whole city is based on industry and that this industry shapes the space with no other logic than that of the economic system. For, as soon as one undertakes an analysis of a concrete situation, one must consider the interactions between the production element and the other elements and distinguish, within production, a diversity of tendencies resulting from the juxtaposition of the different industrial periods and of the refraction, within production, of the other elements and other systems.

Thus, it is obvious that the location policy of a capitalist industrial company will be governed by a tendency to increase its profit rate to the maximum. But this important affirmation remains too general, for between the search for the immediate profit necessary to the survival of the small engineering company and the normaliza- tion of long-term profits, derived from a strong situation on the market, there is a considerable difference as far as the organization of space is concerned.

Furthermore, the location problems are only one part of the problems dealt with by the company and an uncertain factor at that, since it occupies a place in an ensemble of technological and economic links. The dominance of profit, therefore, is not expressed in a direct way, in the location of plant, in terms of costs and selling price; instead, its logic must be reconstructed by observing the practices corresponding to the different technological, economic and social situations that define a plurality of forms of productive units.

I shall recall first a few of the main features of the spatial practice of companies in advanced capitalism and then proceed to an analysis of a specific social process, by studying the case of the Paris region.

a. *The tendencies in industrial location in monopoly capitalism* What strikes one on reading empirical studies of industrial location is the fact of an increasing freedom of location in relation to geographical constraints and therefore, essentially, of technological progress. Indeed, from the point of view of the means of production, we have witnessed a homogenization of space through energy, coal being replaced by electricity and the network of the distribution of energy having become increasingly dense. This evolution will be still more marked with the increased use of nuclear energy. Needs for raw materials have also undergone a considerable change since most of industry is based on synthetic raw materials and semi- finished products, thus reducing its direct contact with natural resources. Transport has been profoundly modified by the diffusion of the road network, by the rapidity and the increasing load capac- ity of the means used. The aeroplane plays an essential role in interpersonal contacts and, in certain cases, in the transport of goods or tools (for example, precision parts). Telex has increased the possibility of locating plant belonging to the same firm at greater distances, since it makes management at a distance possible.

On the other hand, mass consumption presupposes that, for the large companies, there are almost no irreplaceable specific markets. Each plant is located in a network of distribution that is governed not by the position of the buyer, but by the commercial policy of the company.

Thus P. S. Florence (1948; 1953), after a detailed analysis of British and American industry, declares that at the national level, out of twenty of the geographically most concentrated American industrial branches, only three were centred on raw materials and two depended on the location of the market. Out of twenty British industrial branches with a higher coefficient of geographical concentration, three were centred on raw materials and none on the market.

The British studies agree in considering that industrial mobility is fundamentally freed from constraints that are insurmountable on the level of functioning. For Luttrell, about two-thirds of British factories can successfully produce in any region of the country, by virtue of urban and industrial continuity. For Fogarty, the choice of location is determined above all by the nature of the relations that unite one branch to the mother-firm, that is to say, of the internal relations, and, furthermore, impediment and inertia are due essentially to the fear of not being able to reconstitute an industrial milieu. Loasby also observes this inertia of companies that tend not to move (except when forced to); in his opinion this inertia is not justified by any detrimental effects that might result from it for their activity. The reason for this inertia remains above all, for Eversley, in psychological resistances of two kinds: the fear of the unusual, which impedes removal, and the factor of social prestige, which governs the choice of location once the inertia is overcome. Noticeably different is the conclusion of an inquiry made by the University of Glasgow into decentralization, which finds as an important factor the presence of adequate and 'manageable' manpower and observes great freedom in the behaviour of the company, to the extent that the factors influencing the choice are presented much more as tendencies than as constraints.

Barnaud (1961) also concludes that there is an indeterminacy in the location of plant in France, since he affirms that the mobility of the companies studied is such that they seem able to be located viably in many different regions.

These facts show a tendency towards the homogenization of

space from the point of view of the natural conditions required by economic activity. Obviously, this homogenization is not absolute on a national scale. There exist regions that are geographically less favourable for industrial activity and vice versa. But the essence of the difference derives from earlier historical developments, from the weight of the past, in the urban and industrial milieux constituted in certain places. Increasingly, from the strictly technological point of view, space will be undifferentiated with regard to activity.

It is the passage from a natural milieu to a technological milieu that Georges Friedmann (1953) has described in another context. This transformation, which is simply a perspective in inter-regional comparison, is already an accepted fact for an industrial metropolis, as is the case for Paris or for the American megalopolis. The differences in resources and ease of functioning between the various points of the urban area are minimal; they are easily compensated for by movements over an ever denser transport network.

However, this homogenization of space in relation to the needs of companies for natural resources does not imply a freeing in the strict sense. New constraints specific to the technological milieu limit the choice of plant location.

To begin with, inter-company links assume considerable importance both for the outlet of products and for technological problems. The existence of a diversified industrial milieu is essential, both for the sub-contracting companies and for the large companies that have recourse to a whole milieu of integrated activity in their functioning. This is one of the obstacles that impedes the possibility of industrial decentralization on the basis of isolated acts. Thus the SODIC (1965) study of the industrial decentralization of a few Paris companies insists on the existence of a satisfactory industrial environment as the condition required by all the industrialists interviewed, whereas problems of transport and supply did not arise and financial cost is fixed without reference to a decision on location. According to Jean Rémy's (1966, 53) analyses, the central factors in the location of industry are those known as the urban-area economies, independent of the geographical position, since they are created anywhere, as soon as there is a sufficient area and a diversity of services — which increases the possibility of a voluntary policy of industrial location for the authorities, providing they realize they are creating an urban milieu.

Next, manpower appears as the fundamental constraint of modern industry (Isard, 1956) — whether it is a question of its level of skill, in the case of the technologically advanced industries, or of its abundance, in the case of traditional heavy industry. In France, Barnaud's (1961) report, which I have already mentioned, considers

that the most important factor in the location of the decentralized
companies is the availability of manpower on the spot, which seems
to justify Labasse's view that the inquiries recently carried out in
France reveal that the determining element in the location of industries is manpower in three-quarters of the cases. (Labasse, 1966.)
Barnaud believes that manpower has more effect in terms of quality
and quantity than in the cost of wages. The SODIC study of a few
Parisian companies also stresses the major problem of manpower.
The study of industrial movements in the Chicago region proposes
a model of concentric decentralization in accordance with the
growth of the city, which seems to be governed by two facts: the
relation between the need for space and the cost of land; and, above
all, manpower, which is the essential factor. It is on the basis of the
disposition of manpower in space, the technological characteristics
of the companies and the cost of setting up plant, that several zones
are defined and several modes of behaviour differentiated. (Department of City Planning, 1961.)

Manpower problems also play a large role in the location of the
industrial and commercial companies of the urban region of
Göteborg, according to an inquiry by a group of Danish researchers
into the activities of 842 companies. (Institute for Center-Planning,
1965.)

This importance of manpower in the choice of a location by the
company has wide-ranging consequences. Indeed, it is not only a
factor in production. It presupposes, on the one hand, a favourable
urban environment and, on the other, institutions capable of forming and recycling manpower whose degree of skill, not only in
purely professional terms, but in terms of initiative and understanding of the activity, tends to rise rapidly.

This introduces two kinds of consideration, which have become
classic among the most far-sighted specialists in urbanism. On the
one hand, the need for manpower leads the company to become
located in a favourable urban milieu. At the elementary level, the
workers will demand certain social and cultural amenities, schools
for the children, meeting-places, minimum comfort. Furthermore,
there will be a tendency to put higher value on places that are .
'pleasant' in terms of climate, landscape, surroundings. Pierre George
(1964, 219) points out the relevance of this point of view:

> ... Today concentration continues to work in favour of the activities of
> administration and the function of study, of research, of the creation of
> models of the large industrial companies. The rapid increase of productivity
> in the industrial domain and the reversal, in the calculation of profitability,
> of the proportions between supplies of energy and raw materials, on the
> one hand, and the remuneration of highly qualified services, the tying up

of very large investments and the setting up and equipping of the factories, on the other hand, *free the location of industries from earlier constraints.* The rates of respective increase correspond to new circumstances; certain cities, hitherto unattractive, are given new functions. Industries endowed with particularly good amenities or advantages relating to the site or position are taking the place of older activities (Annecy, Grenoble and even Nice, as well as Elbeuf and Montpellier in France). In Germany, Munich has inherited a good part of East Berlin, largely due to the proximity of the Alps.

At the same time, the importance of the training of manpower for industry, in particular for the technologically advanced companies, assigns an extraordinary role to the universities and training centres in the location of industrial plant. The setting up of IBM-France at Montpellier was due almost exclusively to the presence of the university. The most important French electronic and pharmaceutical companies stress the impossibility of removing far from the Parisian scientific milieu. Indeed, it is the combination of the value put on the spatial context and on a developed intellectual activity that characterizes the transformations of the most modernist zones (Grenoble and Nice in France, California in the United States).

This supports Rémy's thesis according to which the city, as the centre of the production of knowledge, is the milieu necessary to the development of modern industry. (See also *Prospective*, 1964.) The industrial urban areas undertake their own development, not only in terms of functioning and of factors, but also as nodal points for the exchange of information and possibilities of creation, the real base for modern industry.

Gottman (1961, 4–8) shows how the northeast coast of the United States, what he calls the megalopolis, has attained supremacy in the political, economic and cultural life of the United States, as an urban area, without possessing a sub-soil rich in minerals or any particular advantages in terms of energy supply or climate.

In the course of an interview, a senior executive responsible for the location of the plant of a very large French electronics company remarked that the fact of finding himself in the suburbs of Paris ten minutes by car from a hundred scientists and electronic specialists was an unparalleled advantage that made any other consideration in his decision quite irrelevant.

This is, therefore, a conception of location quite different to the classic theories of spatial economy, from Alfred Weber to M. L. Greenhut, centred on the calculation of profitability in terms of marginal use. This does not imply that this perspective does not bring any elucidation to the specific cases. The elements that have been quoted represent the constraints of functioning of a company in a rapidly evolving technological milieu. But if one analyses closely the results of the studies made, one finds another element of increasing importance for the company's choice of location. It is a question of the social value placed on the space as such.

Thus, for example, in the important inquiry of the Survey Research Center into the psycho-sociological aspects of industrial mobility, 51% of the industrialists questioned, constituting a representative sample of the industry of the State of Michigan, give answers classified as 'personal reasons': among these, in first place, come the preferences of the management and staff for a particular place, either because of the geographical origin of the members of the company or, above all, for reasons connected with climate, leisure activities, atmosphere, etc. (Survey Research Center, 1950.)

The same importance of personal factors and of the search for status is observed in the inquiry, already mentioned, into the Göteborg region. Now, when one speaks of the 'personal feelings' of the head of a company, of the need felt by middle management to live in a pleasant area, of the search by the company for proximity to decision-making centres, all this implies that, parallel with the separation of the company from space as physical reality, there is a social differentiation of space, especially for industries that are able to afford it. The appropriation of symbolic elements associated with a particular space play a certain role in the location of some categories of company.

The tendencies as regards location that have emerged are both too crude and too partial to allow us to construct an analytical framework. We have intentionally stressed factors that are innovatory in relation to classical economic theory. But it is clear that there are various systems of spatial constraints in relation to the location of companies, and that the diversity of economic relations to space will involve policies peculiar to the location.

The different types of constraint detected may be grouped according to Pierre Massé's, systematization: (Quoted in Labasse, 1966, 196).

Industries with induced location (through industrial and urban developments);
Industries with location linked to natural resources;
Industries with free location.

This classification, which broadly supports that of Florence, may serve as a basis for a typology of the constraints of economic space.

These constraints will be integrated in a different way by the various categories of company. It is certain, for example, that purely social factors will influence to a greater extent the large companies that are technologically freed from economic and functional constraints, whereas other more traditional factors will dominate the behaviour of more old-fashioned companies. To stress the innovatory and social behaviour of technologically advanced industry has the aim above all of breaking with the idea of a single rationality, that is, a rationality of objectives and not of values, one that must be applied to all types of company. Let us not lose ground by giving in to the temptation of a new undifferentiated interpretation in which technological progress has transformed the natural determinisms into a mere interplay of social forces.

We must still avoid separating on the one side spatial constraints and, on the other, the characteristics of the companies. These economico-spatial determinants are not a pure limit within which the company's location policy is situated. They are present in the company itself; they underlie its policy. The characterization of the company with regard to its location policy must result from connecting the company's type of activity and the type of economic relation it has with space.

These different tendencies in industrial location show a diversity of behaviour in space, corresponding to the diversity of the companies. Generally speaking, we can say that there is an evolution, on the basis of submission to natural conditions or to geographical position, towards a social value placed on space in the case of the freer companies. Another transformation operates in a parallel way: the passage from the necessary attachment to certain points in space to a functional location in a network of relations within a technological. milieu. There would, therefore, appear to be, in the locations observed, both a passage from the geographical to the social and an adaptation to the context of functional development.

The types of spatial constraints that have emerged do not correspond to these locations, which is logical enough, since it is a question not of a mechanical link between space and location policy, but of the social determination of the companies that underlies a particular policy.

b. *Specific analysis of the logic of industrial location in a large metropolis: the Paris region*   If these are the general tendencies observed, how can one explain the concrete social process by which a productive unit is established in a particular space? For it is the understanding of such a process that enables one to grasp the relation between the production element and the whole of the spatial structure in a given situation. The situation is, in this case, the Paris region, where I carried out an exhaustive study concerning all the *creations* of industrial plant, between 1962 and 1965. (Castells *et al.*, 1968; see also for a theortical development, Castells, 1967.)

The general hypothesis is that spatial location forms part of the company's policy, and that this policy is determined, fundamentally, by the position of the company in the production system. This position is expressed, essentially, on three levels: *technological, the economic link* specific to the problem dealt with (in this case, *space*) and *the relative position of the company* in relation to other production units.

For each of these three dimensions, I defined three fundamental situations in which the companies may be classified.

As far as the technological dimension is concerned (the technological conditions of production), I distinguished three types of company:

Type A: companies centred on the manufacture of one product and entirely subordinated, from the technological point of view, to other industrial sectors; for example, general engineering companies. They recall, in a way, the old factory.

Type B: companies centred on the organization of the manufacture of a product in series; this is the case of a large part of the processing industries, for example, food, motor-cars. It is, in general, large-scale industry.

Type C: companies centred on technological innovation, in the sense that their place on the market depends on their capacity to create new products, for example, electronics. These are 'leading' industries, as far as the development of the productive forces is concerned.

In relation to the *economic dimension*, I distinguished three types of link with space (according to the classification proposed by Pierre Massé and summing up the economic determination of the location).

Type 1: companies whose market is spatially determined.

Type 2: companies whose means of production have a rigid location.

Type 3: companies without spatial constraint from the point of view of their functioning, within the region considered.

Lastly, as far as their relative position is concerned, I differentiated the companies according to their *economic stratification* (financial capacity) into:

large-scale companies
medium-sized companies
small companies.

I cross-checked my first two dimensions and thus obtained a technico-economic typology of companies, with nine possibilities (A1, A2, . . . C2, C3). A second typology, with three cases, corresponding to economic stratification was also to intervene in the analysis.

I classified in these typologies the 940 companies studied. For this, the dimensions were transformed into variables on the basis of obtaining, for each type, a certain number of qualitative and quantitative indicators, which made it possible to characterize the company (a study of records). The list is as follows:

Technological variable

Type A: unit work or small-series work; the 'family' character of the company; the high proportion of skilled manual workers; the quality of the work; the unrepetitive character of the product.

Type B: high mechanization, in particular the existence of assembly lines; mass production; the standardized character of the product; high percentage of unskilled workers; and the use of Taylor's tradition of 'scientific management' — an important element in the functioning of the company.

Type C: the invention of new products; the presence of a research unit; a high proportion of technicians and engineers; advanced automation.

(It is clear that elements of the three types, A, B and C may be found together within the same plant. In that case, it is the elements that indicate a higher degree of technology that determine the definition of the company. Thus a C plant may also have B and A elements, but the reverse is not the case.)

Economico-spatial variable

Type 1: very small number of customers; sale in a limited zone of the Paris region; very limited delays in delivery; very frequent manufacturing contact with the customers, very high cost of transportation.

Type 2: connection with *localized supplies* (raw materials, water, energy, providers of special products used in manufacture), spatially localized manpower, a transport network; the important activity of geographical distribution.

Type 3: companies not classified in 1 or 2.

Economic stratification variable

Having found a good deal of difficulty in obtaining precise information as to the overall financial strength of the companies taken as a whole, I chose an indirect indicator, namely the quantitative size of the operation of the particular establishment, measured by the number of square metres of floor space constructed in the new plant (cost). The companies were divided into three levels, according to the relative size of the new surfaces.

Having defined and characterized the companies in this way, the next step in our research consisted in establishing a significant typology of their behaviour in relation to space. Three major tendencies were detected in recent industrial plant location in the Paris region, according to the precedence accorded to certain characteristics of space:

Location of type α: adaptation to the spontaneous growth of the urban area by an increase in the density of the urban tissue.

Location of type β: the solving of the company's problems of spatial functioning by the search for a good location on the transport network.

Location of type γ: the creation of a new industrial milieu by location in socially valued spaces.

Precise indicators served to define concretely, in the form of variables, the types of space thus constituted:

Indicator α: an index of urban density for the Paris region, constructed by INSEE from the combination of several factors.

Indicator β: an index of facilities in means of transport (constructed by the technical services of the IAURP).

Indicator γ: the social status of residential space, indicated by the proportion of middle management living in the *commune.*

These operations enable us to establish observable relations between the central variables of our analysis. Once again we must delimit theoretically significant hypotheses, formalize them in a coherent way and try to verify them.

In order to formalize our hypotheses, we will study the spatial behaviour of nine types of company defined in relation to three types of space α, β, γ. For each of these spaces, I have constructed a scale of adaptation, in three strata; thus we have: $\alpha - 1$, $\alpha - 2$, $\alpha - 3$, $\beta - 1$, $\beta - 2$, $\beta - 3$, $\gamma - 1$, $\gamma - 2$, $\gamma - 3$. (The 1 indicating the upper strata and 3 the lower.)

Each of the nine types of company will be given a value α, a value β, and a value γ, according to the hypotheses.

General propositions:

1. The technological level of the companies frees them from the constraints of the natural milieu, but subjects them to the demands of social prestige, in so far as they play a privileged role in the ideological delineation of space. As a result, all types with the C element will have a strong tendency to settle in space γ (a correspondence between C and $\gamma - 1$).

2. The economic link with a specific market is an extremely strong constraint, which places the company in a situation of dependence, whatever its technological level (a correspondence between companies of type 1 and spatial values $\alpha - 1$).

3. Companies centred on the organization of mass production and/or linked spatially with specific means of production will tend to favour, in their location of plant, problems of functional development, which amounts, in the modern urban region, to a good loca-

tion on the transport network (a correspondence between characteristics B and 2 of the companies, and the spatial values $\beta - 1$). This determination by B and 2, however, will be less strong than that exerted by C and 1, in so far as 1 establishes a dependence in relation to the city and C necessitates the company occupying a position in a network of strategic struggles, in which symbolic appropriation plays a decisive role. As a result, in the case of the mixed types (C2 or B1) it is the strong characteristic (C or 1) that will tend to define the company.

4. (*Complementary hypothesis* introduced after observation of the data.)

There exists a similarity between types of location α and γ, and an opposition between these two types and the type of location β. Indeed, it is a question of an opposition between urban space, socially defined, apprehended in α in its aspects of density and in γ in its socially valued spaces linked to 'quality' housing, and functional space, organized around the axes of transport, despoiled by major industry and extending into the periphery of the region. (Operationally, this means: companies that have values $\beta - 1$ will, at the same time, have values $\alpha - 3$ and $\gamma - 3$ and *vice versa;* on the other hand, companies having values $\gamma - 1$ will have values $\alpha - 2$ and *vice versa,* in terms of the similarity between behaviour α and behaviour γ.)

5. Lastly, two types of characteristics of the companies exert a limited determination: A, *qua* company with low technological requirements, and 3, *qua* absence of spatial constraints. These elements lead not to 'freedom of location', but to fluctuation of spatial policy. (Operationally, this means: characteristics A and 3 will always be dominated in their effects by the other characteristic defining the type of company; type A–3, being the most indeterminate, will occupy a middle position, value 2, in the three scales α, β, γ.

Thus one arrives at a set of twenty-seven empirical predictions forming a system consistent with the hypothesis formulated:

(For greater simplicity, I will introduce the variable *economic stratification* only after giving the first series of empirical results.)

In the light of these formalized hypotheses, we must now examine the statistical behaviour of the different types of company in their spatial locations.

For this, the method followed is extremely simple:

1. All the *communes* of the Paris region were classified in the three strata of the three scales α, β, γ, in terms of the values of the indicators used to define our three variables α, β, γ.

2. We calculated the frequency of location of each type of

Table 21

Prediction of the rank of the nine types of company in the scales of the three types of spatial location, α, β, γ

Types of company	Types of space		γ (Social prestige of space)
	α (urban milieu)	β (Transport)	
A_1	1	3	2
B_1	1	2	2
C_1	1	3	1
A_2	3	1	3
B_2	2	1	3
C_2	2	2	1
A_3	2	2	2
B_3	3	1	3
C_3	2	3	1

company in the *communes* of the first, second and third strata of the three scales.

3. We thus obtained, for each stratum of *communes,* an order of importance of the types of company. This order is compared with the hypothetical space. For example, in the first stratum of the *communes* classified according to the scale γ, companies C must come at the top of the list, followed by types 1, then by types B and 2. In the third stratum of scale γ, the reverse must occur, whereas, in the second stratum, it is those types of companies determined to an average degree by space γ that must occur most frequently.

Table 22 embodies these results.

The comparison for the first strata of the three scales, between the theoretical order and the observed order, makes it possible to verify all the hypotheses (a comparison to be made between Tables 21 and 23).

It now remains to introduce the third independent variable, inter-company economic stratification, into the schema thus constructed. We proceeded to a multivariate analysis with simultaneous cross-checking of the four variables, for which the figures are too complex to be presented in an abbreviated form. The highly significant results may be summed up thus:

1. *In locations of type* α, the economic characteristics of type 1 and the limited size of the company both play a part, reinforcing one another, but having an autonomous influence. This means that if a company is of type 1, even if it is large-scale, it tends to be integrated into the urban milieu. It also means, if a company is

Table 22

Frequency of locations (+) of the types of company in the communes of the Paris region classified in three strata (+++) according to the scales α, β, γ, 1962–1965. N_1 = 792, N_2 = 872, N_3 = 894

Types of company	Types of space									Total no. of plants located (N) (++)		
	Space of type α strata (1 > 3)			Space of type β (1 > 3)			Space of type γ (1 > 3)					
	1	2	3	1	2	3	1	2	3	for N_1	for N_2	for N_3
A_1	·53	·29	·18	·33	·36	·31	·32	·39	·29	264	264	264
B_1	·42	·42	·16	·38	·45	·17	·29	·49	·22	76	76	76
C_1	·47	·45	·08	·21	·42	·37	·48	·29	·23	51	60	66
A_2	·31	·35	·36	·45	·36	·19	·23	·39	·38	103	138	138
B_2	·19	·29	·52	·57	·26	·16	·23	·36	·41	84	112	112
C_2	·32	·42	·26	·31	·41	·28	·38	·36	·26	31	29	34
A_3	·30	·42	·28	·38	·36	·26	·31	·42	·27	103	103	103
B_3	·21	·33	·46	·55	·29	··16	·17	·48	·35	39	52	52
C_3	·36	·44	·20	·29	·34	·37	·45	·39	·16	41	38	49
Total companies ..	X^2 = 88·50 p < ·001			X^2 = 60·88 p < ·001			X^2 = 104·9 p < ·001			792	872	894

(+) Percentages calculated out of the total no. of companies of one type in the three strata.
(++) As a result of different adjustments made, the total number of companies varies slightly in the three cases, α, β, and γ.
(+++) N: number of companies analysed.

small, even if it is not of type 1, that it also follows the same tendency in its location.

2. On the other hand, *location of type β* is entirely determined by the technico-economic characteristics of the companies (B and 2), without their size having any influence.

3. Lastly, in *location of type γ* (prestige space), the multivariate analysis shows that a company must be both technologically advanced and of a certain size if it is to be located in such a space. A high degree of technological advancement is not in itself enough. It is the coincidence of a capacity for technological initiative and economic strength that is the basis of the formation of any new industrial space, linked to the social value placed on the context.

What is the theoretical significance of the discoveries of this research?

Table 23

Observed rank of the three types of company in the communes of the first stratum of the three scales: α, β, γ

	α	β	γ
A_1	1	2	2
B_1	1	2	2
C_1	1	3	1
A_2	2	1	3
B_2	3	1	3
C_2	2	3	1
A_3	3	2	2
B_3	3	1	3
C_3	2	3	1

Errors: α inversion $A_3 - A_2$ with 1 point gap.
β inversion $A_1 - C_2$ with 2 points gap.
γ none.

Let us remember that it is a study of the principal component (industry) of the production element, the dominant element of the spatial structure. Analysis has been directed not to the effects of this element on the urban structure, but to its internal organization, to its tendencies of development. Now, what is striking is the complexity within this element and, within each element, the way it breaks down, according to the refraction upon it of other elements of the urban structure, into three tendencies:

tendency α, which expresses the development of P according to the urban forms already constituted, in particular around the residential, that is to say, fundamental, milieu, according to the situation of element C (consumption);

tendency β, in which P follows, in its spatialization, element E (exchange), independently of any urban role it may play;

tendency γ, which expresses a preponderance of the ideological marking out of space (dominant social values) within P.

This breaking down of P into three tendencies operates not in an arbitrary way, but according to the technological, economic and financial characteristics of the productive units. Thus, the social structure is specified in the characteristics both of the companies and of the space, and the location practices observed are merely the concrete realization of the laws of relation between the technological, economic and social elements thus expressed.

We can guess the route thus sketched out. It is able to show on the one hand, the relation of specification operating in the relations thus organized between space and general social laws and, on the other hand, the establishment of a system of determinations and

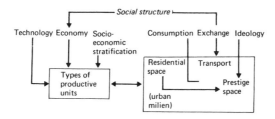

correspondences between the different elements of the structure of space.

It seems premature to advance further in this direction, simply on the basis of the results presented. The discussion of the concepts of the urban system (see below) will enable us to come back, if only in a very hesitant way, to these problems.

B *The space of consumption: the spatial process of the reproduction of labour power*

Under this heading, one may gather together a set of complex processes concerned with the simple and extended reproduction of labour power in its relation to space, for example, housing, but also green spaces, amenities and, on the level of social and ideological reproduction, the academic and socio-cultural apparatus.

In order not to overburden this account, I shall concentrate, in questions concerning residence, on the two aspects of the matter of housing and the constitution of residential space. Lastly, I shall briefly pose the problems raised by the connotation of the ensemble of the processes of social reproduction in space through the ideological theme of the environment.

a. *The housing question*

> *It cannot fail to be present in a society in which the great labouring masses are exclusively dependent upon wages, that is to say, upon the quantity of the means of subsistence necessary for their existence and for the propagation of their kind; in which improvements of the machinery, etc., continually throw masses of workers out of employment; in which violent and regularly recurring industrial fluctuations determine on the one hand the existence of a large reserve army of unemployed workers, and on the other hand drive the mass of the workers from time to time on to the streets unemployed; in which the workers are crowded together in masses in the big towns, at a quicker rate than dwellings come into existence for them under the prevailing conditions; in which, therefore, there must always be tenants even for the most infamous pigsties; and in which finally the*

house-owner in his capacity as capitalist has not only the right but, by reason of competition, to a certain extent also the duty of ruthlessly making as much out of his property in house rent as he possibly can. In such a society the housing shortage is no accident; it is a necessary institution and can be abolished together with all its effects on health, etc., only if the whole social order from which it springs is fundamentally refashioned.

(Karl Marx and Frederick Engels, *Selected Works*, vol. 2, pp. 326—327.)

The housing question is above all that of its crisis. Lack of comfort and amenities, over-crowding (despite the under-occupation of certain kinds of housing), old buildings, unhealthy conditions, make of this question an experience shared by a large section of the population: two French people out of five live in over-crowded housing (see, for France, Tables 24, 25, 26). What characterizes this crisis is that it affects other social strata than those at the bottom of the incomes scale and that it even reaches large sections of the middle strata better placed in other spheres of consumption, but unable to escape the housing shortage caused by urban concentration. This shortage is not an unavoidable condition of the process of urbanization, but corresponds to a relation between supply and demand, itself determined by the social conditions of production of the market commodity in question, that is to say, housing.

A relation between supply and demand, and therefore a market situation, not a relation of production. Indeed, we know that any assimilation of the tenant—landlord relation to the worker—capitalist relation is meaningless, and that if the crisis is a general one and affects other groups than the working class it is precisely because it does not derive from a relation of exploitation, but from a mechanism of distribution of a particular commodity. (See Engels, 1969, 326—7, for the theoretical basis of the arguments that follow.)

Hence the importance of the theme of speculation and the dependence of the housing question on the economic laws regulating the market. We should not conclude from this that the housing crisis is purely conjunctural and simply a matter of the balance between supply and demand. It is a case of a necessary disparity between the needs, socially defined, of the habitat and the production of housing and residential amenities. It is the structural determination of this disparity and its historical singularities that we wish to establish.

Housing, over and above its general scarcity, is a differentiated commodity, presenting a whole gamut of characteristics, in terms of

Table 24

Overcrowding and under-occupation of dwellings in France, 1968.
(proportion of households living in an overcrowded or under-occupied dwelling in relation to their overall socio-occupational category.)

	Not working	Farmers	Farm workers	Workers	Office workers	Middle manage-ment	Professional and upper manage-ment	Employers in industry and commerce
Overcrowded	22·4 %	13·7 %	18·4 %	7·6 %	9·8 %	15·8 %	2·1 %	6·7 %
Under-occupied	4·7 %	21·5 %	14·5 %	8·2 %	3·9 %		32·1 %	25·5 %

Source: G. Eberick et P. Barjac, *Le Logement, dossier noir de la France,* Paris: Dunod, 1970, 19.

its *quality* (amenities, comfort, type of construction, life-span etc.), its *form* (individual, collective, as architectural object, integration in the housing context as a whole and in the region) and its *institutional status* (without title-deeds, rented, owned, owned in common, etc.), which determine the *roles,* the *levels* and the *symbolic loyalties* of its occupants.

Table 25

Elements of comfort in housing, France, 1962

% of all housing	
Housing without running water	20·6 %
Housing without wash-basin	59·8 %
Housing without WC	39 %
Housing built before 1871	32 %

Source: Economie et Politique, Special Issue August—September 1965.

Table 26

Overall evaluation of annual construction needs, France, 1965, and no. of completed dwellings, 1965—1968

I. *EVALUATION*

Cause	No. of dwellings necessary
Increase in no. of households	140 000
Migration of French subjects to the towns	60 000
Foreign immigration	40 000
Rehousing of occupants of unsafe dwellings, in 5 years	120 000
Rehousing of repatriated subjects, in 5 years	20 000
Total elimination of over-crowding in 10 or 15 years	145 000 to 100 000
Elimination of critical over-crowding, in 5 or 10 years	170 000 to 85 000
Renewal of the housing area in 60 or 80 years	265 000 to 200 000
Total	815 000 to 665 000
Average	740 000 dwellings per year

(Evaluation by G. Mathieu.)

II. *NUMBER OF DWELLINGS CONSTRUCTED*

1965	....	411 599
1966	....	414 171
1967	....	422 878
1968	....	409 743

Too often one considers tastes, preferences, even sensitivity to certain mythical configurations, as determining the choice of housing and, consequently, the diversity of the forms of the habitat, their evolution, their profitability and, therefore, their mode of distribution. Although it is undeniable that the forms have a certain ideological and therefore material influence, they merely reinforce, and do not create, the mercantile organization of the unique commodity that housing is. The sociological problematic of housing must set out from a reversal of the usual psycho-social themes and centre itself on the analysis of the process of production of a certain durable commodity, in the diversity of its qualities, forms, status and in relation to the economic market and, consequently, its social context.

For this, we must set out from the characteristics specific to the commodity (housing), relying, as far as is possible, on the facts of a given historical reality, namely French society.[2]

Housing may be regarded, on the one hand, in relation to its place in the whole of the economic system and, on the other, as a product with specific characteristics.

Concerning the first point, housing is one of the essential elements of the reproduction of labour power. As such, it follows the movements of concentration, dispersal and distribution of the workers and also causes, in times of crisis, a considerable bottleneck in the production process. Historically, the housing crisis appears above all in the great urban areas suddenly taken over by industry. Indeed, where industry colonizes space, the housing of the necessary manpower must be organized for it, if only at the level of camping. On the other hand, by grafting itself on to an already constituted urban tissue, industrialization profits from the potential manpower that is already living on the spot and then causes a strong migratory movement whose dimensions go well beyond the building and amenity capacities of a city inherited from an earlier mode of production. Thus the shortage of housing, the lack of amenities and the unhealthy conditions of the residential space are a result of the sudden increase in urban concentration, in a process dominated by the logic of industrialization. (Huzard, 1965.) It is a question,

---

[2] The essential data may be found in the collection of *Immobilier* and of *Moniteur du Bâtiment et des Travaux Publics;* in addition, four works that are fundamental on account of the richness of their sources have been used: the excellent book by G. Matthieu (1963);. the special number on the housing crisis of the review *Economie et Politique,* August—September 1965; the recent work of liberal orientation by Eberik and Barjac (1970) and that of the Commissariat Général au Plan (1970). After writing this text, two documents appeared in 1971 that are indispensable for the housing question in France: 'Pour que le droit au logement devienne une realité' of the CNL and the work of the 'Logement' group of the *Secours Rouge.*

therefore, of a lack of balance in the population-element C (consumption) ratio, which results from a transformation of the urban structure under the dominant impulse of element P.

Thus the higher the rate of industrial (capitalist) growth, the more concentrated it is in the great urban areas and the greater the shortage of housing and the deterioration of existing housing.

Furthermore, one must take into account the multiplicatory mechanisms of the crisis: in a situation of shortage, speculation develops, prices rise, social hardships become greater (and it becomes much more difficult to meet the needs created). The difficulty of the problem slows down any attempt to solve it, thus making it worse and turning a vicious circle into a spiral.

Although the *production* mechanism of the housing crisis emerges clearly enough, the reasons for its *maintenance* are less immediate. Indeed, housing needs constitute an important demand on the market and, furthermore, the reproduction of labour power is impeded by this, with possible consequences both for labour itself and for social peace. If the response to this demand remains inadequate the reason for it must be sought in the social logic according to which this demand is treated. For the domination of element P operates not only on the rhythm of the urban structure, but also on the internal logic of each element (in this case, element C). In more concrete terms, housing depends, for its realization, on the characteristics and objectives of the construction industry. On a primary level, this means that, in the absence of public intervention, the only demand actually taken into account is solvent demand. Now, from a comparison between the incomes of households and the prices and rents of average apartments, one deduces the difficulty of solving the crisis simply by market mechanisms (Tables 27 and 28).

Given that in France, in 1965, 60% of urban families had an income under F 1600 per month, private building was not capable of offering a solution to the imbalance created. It is not, therefore, only a question of stratification in consumption, such as exists for all commodities in terms of social stratification, measured by purchase power, but, more directly, of a non-satisfaction of demand. The production of housing is such, in the historical situation studied, that left to itself, it would not be capable of housing most of the population of the cities. The study of the specificity of this process of production will help us to determine the reason for such a situation.

If one sets out from the idea that, on the private property market, housing is a commodity to be sold, that is to say, to produce a profit, one must ask oneself what are the particular characteristics

Table 27

Proportion of rent in household expenditure
(% of the table), France, 1968

Housing of good standard (kitchen, W.C., shower, central heating)	Rent	Disposable Income		
		2 000 F	3 000 F	5 000 F
Paris:				
2 rooms – 40 m²	620 F	31 %	21 %	12 %
4 rooms – 80 m²	1 250 F	62 %	41 %	25 %
Suburbs:				
2 rooms – 40 m²	270 F	13·5 %	9 %	5·4 %
4 rooms – 80 m²	640 F	32 %	21 %	13 %
Provinces:				
2 rooms – 40 m²	310 F	15 %	10 %	6 %
4 rooms – 80 m²	620 F	31 %	21 %	12 %

of realizing surplus value that determine a greater inability on the part of private industry to satisfy basic needs in this domain, more than in other sectors of individual consumption. The production of housing results from the articulation of three elements: the land on which one builds, materials and/or elements incorporated into the construction and the actual construction of the building, namely the application of labour power, in a given organization, to the basic materials, to produce housing. The characteristics of the three elements, their forms of articulation and their relation to the market determine a particular form of labour. Let us examine the specificity of the different phases.

In the first place, as is well known, one observes the very high dependence of construction on the availability and price of the land to be built on, and also on the speculation in land values that

Table 28

Distribution of the population
among the different income groups, France, 1965

Monthly income		Proportion of households	
less than 430 F	under 1 720 F	11 %	61 %
430–1 290 F		30 %	
1 290–1 720 F		20 %	
1 720–5 160 F		34 %	
above 5 160 F		5 %	

Source: Commission de l'habitation du Ve Plan.

results. It is a question of the articulation between ground rent and capitalist profit. But one cannot contrast, as has sometimes been done, the rationality of industrial profit with the pure speculation of the individual landowners. For, although a small section of the property market is still in the hands of small investors, most of the market, in the cities, is controlled by financial bodies that are very often already involved (in the holding companies that lend the money for building, for example). Underlying this speculative strategy there are two factors: 1. the shortage of housing, which ensures the possibility of realizing the land at an excessive profit in proportion to the increase in the shortage of housing (and, therefore, of land); 2. demand favouring certain locations, either for the social value placed on them and/or their functional desirability. This difference derives from the asymmetry of the structure of residential space (see below) and from the reinforcement of these tendencies by a 'passive' amenities policy (whereas it could lead to decentralization). The ground rent thus obtained is considerable: in 1950–65, a profit of 21% on initial capital (see Table 29). (See Gomez, 1965.)

The consequences for the production of housing are very serious: on the one hand, manufacturing costs rise, without any other justification, by as much as these speculative profits (thus, the price of land in France increased on average by 60% between 1962 and 1965; if one considers that this amounts to about 20% of the overall cost of an operation, we are dealing with an increase of 12% in the price of housing); (Cage *et al.*, 1970.) on the other hand, given the profit ratio on the investments, there is a tendency on the part of landowners not to sell, or to sell only at such prices as can be paid, often, only by companies that buy with an aim to super-speculation. This creates a scarcity of land and aggravates the crisis.

This being the case, the importance of land speculation derives, essentially, from the shortage of housing, which it helps to reinforce. Indeed, in a relatively balanced situation between the supply and demand of housing, speculation bears only on certain areas (the city centre, very high density zones, etc.), and not on the urban area as a whole, or even on its periphery. So, although from the point of view of a housing policy the first obstacle to be overcome is land speculation (for, once set in motion, its mechanism swallows up all the money for housing at one's disposal), *this is not the root of the enormous gap between building and housing needs.* The fundamental reasons for this gap must be sought in the process of production itself.

There is practically no private production of 'social' housing, whereas one finds industries manufacturing consumer goods

Table 29

Price per m² of land in the Paris region in 1962 and 1965,
appreciation on private land and annual rates of price increases between 1962 and 1965

Zones[1]	Price per m² 1962 in F 1962	1965 in F 1965	Appreciation on private land (millions of F 1965)	Annual rates of price increases between 1962 and 1965
A	1 500	2 200	6 800	1·15
B	800	1 300	3 100	1·18
C	550	850	7 500	1·16
1	95	200	7 550	1·24
2	200	425	12 650	1·29
3	65	125	2 800	1·24
4	150	350	2 250	1·33
5	125	225	2 600	1·22
All 8 zones			45 450	

[1]   *Zone A. B. C. :* Paris, Boulogne and Issy-les-Moulineaux.
  Zone 1: Saint-Germain-en-Laye, Maisons-Laffitte, Mesnil-le-Roi, Montesson, Sartrouville, Houilles, Le Vésinet, Chatou, Carrières-sur-Seine, Croisny, Bougival, Rueil-Malmaison, Vaucresson, Garches, Saint-Cloud, Marnes-la-Coquette, Ville-d'Avray, Sèvres, Chaville, Viroflay, Versailles, Meudon.
  Zone 2: Nanterre, Suresnes, Puteaux, Courbevoie, Levallois-Perret, Clichy, Saint-Ouen, Saint-Denis, Pierrefitte, Villeneuve, Montmagny, Deuil, Montmorency, Enghien-les-Bains, Eaubonne, Saint-Gratien, Sannois, Cormeilles-en-Parisis, Argenteuil, Bezons, Gennevilliers, Ile-Saint-Denis, Villeneuve-la-Garenne, Colombes, Asnières, Bois-Colombes, La Garenne-Colombes.
  Zone 3: Aubervilliers, Pantin, Pré-Saint-Gervais, Les Lilas, Bagnolet, Montreuil, Rosny-sous-Bois, Bondy, Villemonble, Gagny, Neuilly-sur-Marne, Neuilly-Plaisance, Le Perreux, Stains, Bry-sur-Marne, Champigny-sur-Marne.
  Zone 4: Maisons-Alfort, Ivry-sur-Seine, Kremlin-Bicêtre, Vitry-sur-Seine, Villejuif, Thiais, Choisy-le-Roi, Orly.
  Zone 5: Clamart, Vanves, Malakoff, Montrouge, Gentilly, Arcueil, Bagneux, Cachan, Châtillon, Clamart, Plessis-Robinson, Fontenay-aux-Roses, Chatenay-Malabry, Sceaux, Bourg-la-Reine, L'Hay-les-Roses, Chevilly-la-Rue, Fresnes.

intended for the whole range of incomes. If this is so, one may suppose that the profitability of capital in this sector is much less than in other industries — so much less, in fact, that investment is discouraged and it requires massive public intervention to limit the damage done. Indeed, the rate of rotation of capital invested in construction is particularly long, owing to the slowness of manufacture, the high price of the product bought, which limits the number of buyers and makes the owners fall back on renting, the length of the delay in obtaining profits from renting and, above all, the sensitivity of housing to social demands that can lead to frequent intervention by the state, with such measures as the rents freeze, which threaten the realization of profits. This fact leads to two others: the limited amount of private investment in this sector, and the search for a high rate of profit in as short a term as possible without the normalization of a moderate, long-term profit, as is the case for the great industrial trusts.

Such a situation, in interaction with the very characteristics of the labour process, which make less easy than elsewhere the mechanization and standardization of operations, gives rise to what is very often an archaic form of industrialization: activity split up between a multitude of small companies (see Table 30), a low rate of technological innovation, a low level of training among the workers and, above all, a low number of workers per company (in relation to other branches of industry), which limits proportionally the sources of surplus value, diminishes profit, increases costs and discourages investment. All these characteristics taken together lead to low productivity which, in turn, perpetuates the shortage, postpones any solution and, at the same time, requires a high immediate profit

Table 30

Composition of the construction industry in France by size of company

A) Distribution of building works (carried out in 1965) according to nature and size of companies.
(Total = 100 %)

Size of companies	New works		Upkeep and improvement
	Fabric	Finish	
(Number of persons)[1]			
From 1 to 5	2·1 %	8·4 %	6·3 %
From 6 to 20	4·7 %	10·4 %	5·5 %
From 21 to 100	9·9 %	13 %	3·7 %
Over 100	24·7 %	9·7 %	1·6 %

Source: Fédération Nationale du Bâtiment.

B) A movement of concentration is emerging within these companies, as is shown in the evolution of manpower:

	1955	1967
Private firms	144 000	147 000
Small companies	254 000	315 000
Medium-sized companies	217 000	318 000
Large companies	183 000	379 000

Source: F.N.B.

[1] Wage-earners and non-wage-earners.

on each operation, instead of spreading the profit ratio over a
future that, under these circumstances, is always uncertain (Table
31).

Table 31

*Evolution, in percentages, of the composition of the selling price of housing
in France, per m² of inhabitable surface*

Year	Land + charges	Construction	Various charges	Cost price	Profit margin	Selling price
1964	12·3%	63·4%	9·6%	85·3%	14·7%	100
1965	12·5%	60·9%	11·6%	85 %	15 %	100
1966	12·7%	61 %	13·1%	86·8%	13·2%	100
1967	14·9%	60·5%	13·6%	89 %	11 %	100
1968	13·9%	60·2%	16·7%	90·8%	9·2%	100

Source: Caisse de garantie immobilière de la F.N.B.

Progress has been made, beginning with the sector of least resistance, the manufacture of building materials, and a movement
towards the concentration and rationalization of the companies is
taking place (see Table 30). But such development has been made
possible only by the intervention of the state: creating a solvent
demand where there was none, it has made possible the realization
of profit and has attracted new capital, on the basis of the movement of concentration and the spread of prefabrication techniques.
The situation of scarcity thus created around an indispensible
commodity of use which is in a state of permanent imbalance sustained by the acceleration of urban concentration, has made
possible the multiplication of intermediaries and the organization
of a whole network of services whose sole end is to speculate on the
shortages and difficulties in the sector, by creating a solvent demand
where it did not exist and seeking to attract hesitant capital into
carefully planned operations. This is the case, in France, with
property development, which has expanded in a quite unregulated
way. (ADIRES, 1970.)[3] Originally, the developer was (up till 1963)
an intermediary, operating solely on the basis of the funds of possible acquirers, entrusted with the task of completing a property
transaction. After the slump in housing caused by excessive euphoria
in the creation of demand, property development became a veritable
enterprise, very often supported directly by a bank, which tried to

[3] When these lines were written (summer 1970) the research report of Christian Topalov
on property development in France (Centre de Sociologie Urbaine, Paris) had not yet
been distributed. This extraordinary study, which is the most complete that I know,
agrees with my analysis as a whole while developing and refining the same schema.

establish a construction market, by pre-fabricating demand according to well-known advertising techniques and playing on the insecurity sustained by the crisis in housing in those middle strata of the population that would have been capable of buying a home if credit mechanisms were set up.

This intervention of the developer plays a double role: first, it organizes activity, relates the different elements of the process and rationalizes the market, within the logic of profit; secondly, like every process of capitalist concentration-rationalization, it pushes this logic to the limit, systematically eliminating any other criterion except profitability, and is therefore addressed to that part of the population that can buy a home or pay a high rent undertaking the occasional social-housing project when the strategy of the public market requires it.

What is clear is that the developer's profit margin and various costs (consultants' fees, financial expenses, legal fees, management costs) represent 26% of the cost of a new home (1968), despite a recent lowering in the exorbitant profits of the developers (see Table 31).

The concrete result of this process is spectacular: between 1945 and 1964, in France, out of 3 628 000 apartments built, only 13·3% were built without any public or other aid and only 26·6% were moderately priced (F 6 per square metre). This means that 60% of the new apartments could not be moderately priced simply through the play of market forces! (Matthieu, 1963.)

The whole process may be summed up thus:

By taking as the centre of my analysis the question of housing in France, what I say is, obviously, based on a case in which the endemic crisis of housing is striking and which private enterprise proved quite incapable of solving. If this situation does tend to be the rule in most capitalist countries, there are, obviously, countries in which the housing crisis has been relatively contained and, above all, where it is confined to the 'lower' urban strata, instead of being generalized, as it is in France, Italy or Spain. (Blanc, J., 1966). My choice does not introduce bias into the analysis, for almost all the countries in which the overall situation of housing has improved (Great Britain, West Germany, Sweden, Canada) to the point of being able to allow to the private sector a considerable part of the present initiative, are countries in which public funds have facilitated a massive effort to overcome the deficiences of private building funds which, in Britain, make up as much as 85% of the financing of housing. (Ashworth, 1954.)

Thus, the process analysed in France has a general validity as far as the location of the problem is concerned and is different from

Production process of the housing crisis
in the capalist economy

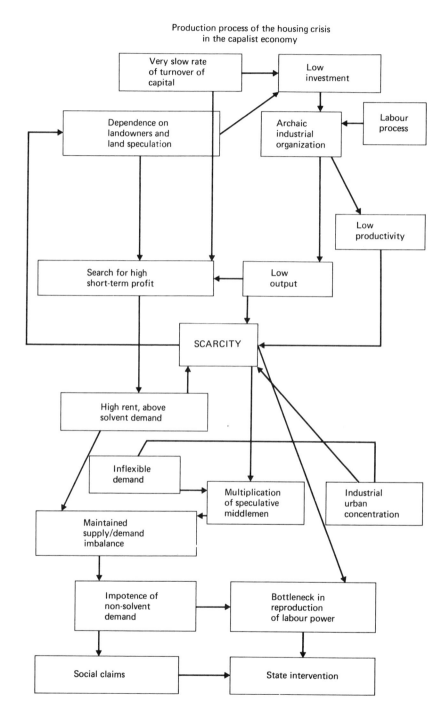

those of the countries mentioned only in the inability of the state
to resolve the situation. An analysis of the difference in efficiency
of public intervention requires a socio-political study of each
country, which would go beyond the limitations of this work. The
only country in which private enterprise has always provided most
of the residential buildings is the United States. This has well
known consequences in the poor quality of housing and in the discriminatory practices experienced by the 'poor whites', the blacks
and other ethnic minorities. (Fisher, 1959.)

Nevertheless, it is a fact that although public housing is extremely
undeveloped in the United States, the housing situation, for the mass
of the population, is markedly better than that in Europe. Several
factors, quite specific to America, have contributed to this process.
(Vernon, 1962.) Urbanization has scarcely had to graft itself upon
pre-industrial cities ill adapted to new spatial forms; the country
has not undergone successive destructions in war; industrial growth
has made possible a standardization of labour and a high development of prefabrication; the reign of the motor-car and urban dispersal have facilitated the acquisition of land and limited speculation; and, above all, the real high standard of living (due to American
power on the world market) has made possible both the creation
of a real solvent demand and the extension of the system of individual credit. We should be aware of what all these different factors
taken together represent and not forget how difficult it is to transpose into another country the capacity of the American construction industry.

The housing question in France is not an exception, but a typical
case, within the developed capitalist economy, at a certain phase in
its evolution.

The inability of the private economy to meet the minimum needs
in housing requires the permanent intervention of public bodies, at
both the local and the national level. This intervention is not unique,
but is part of state policy and, in particular, of its economic policy.
Thus different solutions and initiatives will be proposed, in relation
to the same problem, according to the variations in the historical
conjuncture. The forms of housing, the situation and the rhythms
of the property market will vary in accordance with them, but
always within certain limits defined by respect for the fundamental
rules of the capitalist economy, in particular as far as land ownership and the ceilings placed on rents and prices are concerned.

Since it is a question of establishing a balance in the situation of
a certain market commodity, public intervention can take place on
two levels: intervention in *demand*, with the creation of a solvent
demand, and intervention in *supply*, with the direct construction of

housing and the adoption of measures to facilitate building and to lower prices.

Action on demand is two-fold; first, it takes the form of a housing fund to assist families unable to pay too high a rent and, secondly, it involves credit for buying apartments, especially in public housing. The first formula is related, in fact, to social assistance and cannot be anything more than a contribution to alleviating extremely precarious situations. In 1964, 1 300 000 families benefitted from housing subsidies to the extent of 14 million new francs. But the scale of the subsidies, fixed by the state, was too low to alter the situation to any marked degree. And, furthermore, most of the financial burden fell on the funds set aside for family allowances, thus diminishing resources intended to alleviate other social problems.

The second possible mode of intervention is the granting of credit facilities for buying social housing or loans at a relatively low interest-rate to people belonging to organizations of the building-society kind. Here, too, the size of the initial contribution and of the interest to be repaid excludes a considerable mass of the population with low incomes, wheras members of high social strata profit from credit facilities to carry out speculative investment by buying apartments built as social housing.

It seems obvious that in any case public action on demand is too timid to create the solvent demand of which the property developers dream. (Matthieu, 1963, 68—70). This is, however, only natural, for a truly efficient system of housing subsidies would amount to a redistribution of income on a considerable scale, through the action of the taxation that would be involved to obtain the necessary funds. Though such a formula is not utopian, it is clear that it does not derive from the logic of the system, but from a certain power relation established by social protest movements. The development of credit for buying is, on the other hand, more feasible and, indeed, it is in this direction that French policy is moving, even if the limitations indicated must remain valid for a long time yet. But credit cannot of itself solve the situation if it is not based on a programme of public building that can be made profitable in this way. Indeed, public building offers the state, in its various forms, a possibility of effective intervention in economic activity and room for manoeuvre in the field of 'social action'. In fact, it is in the field of the construction, direct or indirect, of 'social' housing that public intervention has had a decisive effect (See Tables 32 and 33).

Since the Siegfried law (1894), which facilitated the construction of cheap housing, the French state has confidently intervened in

Table 32

Evolution of dwellings completed (in thousands), in France, 1943–1964

	1943 to 1954	1955	1956	1957	1958	1959	1960	1961	1962	1963	1964
Reconstruction	196·5	34·7	32·0	32·9	24·2	17·1	12·7	11·8	8·3	3·9	2·4
H L M. rented ..	67·8	36·0	30·4	54·5	68·7	82·8	77·0	70·8	68·3	78·9	92·6
H L M. owned ..	18·8	14·2	15·2	18·7	18·9	18·1	18·8	20·7	20·9	22·5	24·9
Logécos	12·2	34·6	51·7	67·4	74·0	86·6	89·1	98·9	103·3	112·7	102·9
Other subsidized housing	130·0	65·4	83·5	78·4	80·4	87·6	87·7	81·7	74·2	79·2	104·2
Non-subsidized housing	183·3	25·2	22·9	21·8	25·5	28·2	31·3	32·1	33·9	39·0	41·9
Total	608·6	210·1	235·7	273·7	291·7	320·4	316·6	316·0	308·9	336·2	368·9

Table 33

Distribution of overall budget for housing construction according to financial source, France, 1968 (in new francs)

Public bodies	10	thousand millions
Private firms	10·4	,,
Purchasers	10·8	,,
	31·2 thousand millions	

the financing of building of a social character, in particular, by
granting long-term loans at low interest-rates to public bodies entrusted with the construction and management of housing at
moderate rent (*'habitations à loyer modéré*, or HLM). (Guerrand,
1966) Other financial formulas were worked out involving higher
terms (*Logécos*) and others are in fact subsidies to stimulate private
building (ILN and private housing). The volume and forms of this
aid have varied according to the economic policy followed and,
sometimes, the social strategy of the dominant class. Thus, the first
third of the century was dominated by two parallel movements:
the beginning of the construction of cheap housing (*'habitations à
bon marché*, or HBMs) — it was not until 1921 that an overall decision was taken and until the Loucheur law of 1928 that a programme
was implemented — and the efflorescence of the *pavillon* development of the 1920s made possible by the Ribot law of 1908, encouraged by the Loucheur law and in perfect accordance with the
ideology of integration, which wished to bring the class struggle to
an end by making each worker an owner — outside his work, of
course.

This strategy came to an end, in so far as it was unable to achieve
more than the *form* of the housing (the detached house) and its
status (accession to ownership), but in such economic conditions
that it disintegrated the habitat by scattering it along the peripheries
of the urban areas and neglecting all the problems relating to amenities, communications and the environment in general. The result is
the failure of the enterprise as a whole and the constitution of a
strong pressure-group among the owners of the *pavillons*. (Raymond,
1966.) At the root of such a policy were the feebleness of the financial effort that the French state was prepared to make in this direction and the mainly ideological way, centred on 'social peace', of
treating the problem.

The economic crisis of the 1930s and the destructions of war
aggravated the crisis to such a point that social pressure became
threatening and the shortage of housing disruptive of the necessary
mobility of manpower. A massive public initiative became

indispensable: between 1945 and 1955 a whole range of measures (special loans, *Logécos*, HLM credits) alleviated the enormous gap that had occurred, in particular with the demographic explosion and urban concentration.

Thus, in 1967, 63% of housing was built with public funds. The form taken by this housing was the consequence of the mechanism that formed the base of the movement: it was necessary to act quickly, at accessible prices and therefore on land that was available and cheap, situated on the periphery of the urban areas; and it was necessary to build on a massive scale, if possible in series, whole flights of public housing. The result was the *grand ensemble*, or new large housing developments, which came to modify the French landscape and feed all the reactionary ideologies about the dehumanization of the city, based on the perfectly legitimate dissatisfaction of the cheaply housed residents, which blamed the form for what was attributable to inadequacies in amenities, and spatial deportation, directly determined by the necessity for low costs. (Chombard de Lauwe, 1959; 1960.)

This process also explains their social status. Thus, although Paul Clerc's (1967) inquiry shows the absence of any significant average differences between the *grands ensembles* and the large urban areas, a recent study by Chamboredon and Lemaire (1970) insists on the social specificity of the *grand ensemble*, cut off from the surrounding suburb and differentiated internally as to the temporary residents, belonging to the middle strata, and the permanent residents, mainly workers, who set the social tone of this ecological milieu, by constituting the few manifestations of social life within their residential unit.

However, once the extreme consequences of the crisis were overcome, the state tried to free itself of the financial burden of building, by trying to reintroduce profitability into the sector in order to attract private capital. Thus, in 1964, the proportion of public funds in the financing of housing was only 43% (Matthieu, 1963, 54) and only 33% in 1968. (Eberik, and Barjac, 1970, 78.) From 1955 to 1964, the proportion of HLMs in housing constantly decreased (see Table 34).

Such an evolution follows the tendency of intervention by the public sector in advanced capitalism: the direct resumption of responsibility for non-profitable needs, followed by an attempt to create conditions of profitability, after which, the sector is handed back to private capital. To attain this objective, one must first remedy the most pressing needs, those which, while providing grounds for protest movements, could not easily be transformed into a solvent demand for private building. Moreover, measures had

Table 34

	From 1955 to 1959	From 1960 to 1964	From 1955 to 1964
Number of dwellings built	1 331 600	1 646 600	2 978 200
Comprising: H L M (rented and available for purchase)	357 000	495 400	852 500
Logécos	314 000	506 900	821 200
Luxury dwellings (unsubsidized or subsidized at 6F per m²)	518 900	605 200	1 124 100

to be taken to make building more profitable. We must see from this standpoint the campaign for the unity of the property market, which involves raising the rents of old apartments, moving the low-income families living there, rehousing them elsewhere and thus creating a certain mobility between households. Given the lack of new cheap apartments, such a policy had the real effect of a levelling down and the creation of a profitable outlet for private property development, now assured of being able to obtain rents in step with the inflationary movement of the economy.

A second type of action on the profitability of building consists in intervening in land speculation and in the supply of building land. Having rejected nationalization of the land, the state had recourse to a freezing of land prices in certain *'zones à urbanisation prioritaire'* (ZUP), in which most of the building permits for communal amenities were concentrated; similarly, in the *'zones d'aménagement différé'* (ZAD), a right of pre-emption on the part of the state protects against speculative rises in land values. Once the land has been developed, the public body sells it to the builders at a price even lower than cost price. Consequently, the final objective of the reserve of building land thus constituted is not to limit speculation, but to bring it into line with capital invested in building, benefiting in this way from an excessive profit on the price of housing constructed in advantageous conditions, that is, without having to pay the increase in the price of land. The state, acting as an intermediary between landowners and developers, indirectly subsidizes the latter, without completely cutting short the manipulations of the former.

This perspective has become much clearer with the creation of the *'zones d'aménagement concerté'* (ZAC) with the 1967 law con-

concerning land development. These are zones urbanized jointly by the local authorities or public bodies and property companies. In exchange for a programme of construction being carried out in these zones, the administration takes responsibility for basic amenities, departs from the usual norms relating to building permits and annuls the land-occupation plan, which makes it possible, in particular, to increase the overall density of the housing built.

This formula, which constituted for the then minister of housing, M. Chalandon, the spearhead of land policy, confirms the decisive role of the state in the creation of the conditions of profitability necessary to the development of the private building industry. (See Bobroff *et al.*, 1970; also the interview with M. Chalendon in *Transport, Equipement, Logement, 38.*)

Still following the policy of providing building land for private enterprise, it was openly decided to attempt an 'American' solution, with the spreading of the urban areas along transport axes, thus dispersing the habitat and increasing the amount of land available. It is in keeping with this intention that the recent policy of the ministry of housing, in France, has put the emphasis on the development of motorways, usually built under concession by private firms, and of the spread of the individual habitat 'integrated into the countryside'. In both cases, public funds will be used to compensate for a possibly inadequate profitability — which is one way of ensuring private capital. This amounts to the application of a strictly economic reasoning, which sticks to facts without raising the general problem of urban organization; in any case, this problem definitively eludes the control of the planner, for the dynamism must come wholly from the initiative of the private companies.

Similarly, the state tries to encourage the process of economic concentration and technological rationalization within the construction industry and public works. For this, it depends on two series of measures; the organization of *tenders* for the execution of public building contracts and, in addition, the play of subsidies and fiscal and juridical advantages accorded for cooperation between the different parts of the production process. In particular, this system of tenders has helped to develop cooperation between the different groups, reinforcing at the same time the links between the public and private enterprises. Thus, among the winners of the contract for individual houses (1969), one of the most important initiatives of the Chalandon policy, five groups out of seven were formed expressly for the occasion. PROMOGIM, the only entirely private group to win, is composed of eight companies, including: the *Société chimique routière et d'entreprise générale*, the *Société des mines de bitume et d'asphalte du Centre*, the *Omnium d'entre-*

prise Dumesny et Chapelle. In 1968, these firms had a turnover in construction of 750 million francs.

Furthermore, the insistence on the one-family house also follows from the desire to encourage prefabricated industrial building. Not only the lightness of the structure so built makes it easier; above all, most of the patents for prefabricated units, of American origin, are intended for one-family houses, which have proved themselves in the gigantic process of the 'suburbanization' of the United States in the post-war period.

Lastly, in the policy as a whole, defined in this way, the housing question is treated under three complementary aspects:

1. The private company should now be capable of assuring part of the market constituted by solvent demand; for this, it depends on state aid in the creation of conditions of profitability and on the production of demand through advertising, using the commercial techniques already employed for other commodities of daily consumption. Housing is thus becoming, increasingly, an object. (Ion, 1970.)

2. For the fringe of the population that can be housed on credit, a new formula of private housing, with accession to ownership, has been envisaged, drawing on the oldest traditions of ideological integration and the petty-bourgeois myth of a home in the country. M. Chalandon's 'revolutionary urbanism' is presented as wishing to satisfy the aspiration of the average Frenchman to live in the country (while working in town, of course). As far as this is concerned, it is no longer possible to revive the unfortunate pre-war adventure of the suburban *pavillons*; an attempt is therefore made to construct houses (generally prefabricated) by grouping them in places provided with common amenities and served by roads. The amenities will be financed by public funds and the houses, built by those companies that win the contracts, will possess considerable advantages.

To whom is this new housing formula addressed? The brochure published by the ministry of housing describes him thus: he is younger than average (under 35); he agrees to save and accepts considerable financial sacrifice; he has a monthly income of F 1780; he is in middle management (31·1%), a white-collar worker (22·3%) or skilled worker (33·4%); 75% own a television set; 71% a car. It is addressed, as one can see by comparing the table of income distribution in France, to that fringe of the working population (middle management, white-collar workers or to a much lesser degree, skilled workers) capable of offering on the one hand a certain solvency and, on the other of appreciating the social integration offered by accession to home ownership, presented in

the form of the myth of the *pavillon*. Thus the ideology of the
individual house, which shapes in a certain form housing as a
commodity, shows in an exemplary way the complex play of social
determinations culminating in a particular form: based on the
failure to satisfy consumption, experienced in the compensatory
myth of a rediscovery of the peaceful country life, it results from a
combination of a dual need fundamental to the economic system
(extension of the urban area to be built, prefabrication, the relative
solvency of future acquirers) and of a political strategy aimed at
the reinforcement of the social basis of class domination, in the
politically fluctuating strata. For the credit system set up presupposes a stability of employment and regular, upward progress
in one's career.

3. Lastly, as the construction of HLMs for the strata of the
population still heavily affected by the crisis slows down, a programme of constructing sub-HLMs, the PLRs (*Programme à Loyer
Réduit*, Low-Rent Programme) and PSRs (*Programme Social de
Relogement*, Social Rehousing Programme), of very low quality is
being prepared: 'a solid, rustic conception', as M. Chalandon puts
it. (Ministère de la Construction, 1966) For example, they provide
no sewage-disposal units, no lifts, no central heating. Thus the law
of 14 June 1969 lowers the construction norms in terms of health
and quality.

Thus conceived, social housing openly takes the form of social
security and comes close to the image which, in many countries,
for example Canada, (Report of the Federal Ministry, 1969.) has
led the population to prefer any solution other than that of residential segregation. This, then, is the rationalization of the housing
question in the new perspective of French capitalism.

I have treated housing as a commodity, analysed the conditions
of its production and studied the causes and consequences of its
scarcity and of the differences in the social distribution of the
shortage. Should I add an analysis of the forms of housing, of the
roles and statuses it sets up, as I have indicated? No doubt I should,
but this analysis does not constitute the 'sociological' extension of
the previous 'economic' analysis; it follows logically from it, for to
study the production processes of a commodity amounts also to
studying its forms, if one accepts the hypothesis that they are an
ideological product (in the same way as art is) and that this ideology
justifies itself, and exists, in so far as it reinforces the social function
that has produced the commodity to which it gives form.

Thus as far as the status of housing is concerned, it is clear that,
since the rent is related to the situation, which amounts to paying a
higher price than its exchange value by using a commodity that one

does not own, there will be a general tendency to become owners. But such a status will be limited by the mechanisms of housing production that we have studied. The distribution of the roles of owner, co-owner, tenant, lodger, etc., follows the rules of the social distribution of commodities, as is shown by the analysis of the social categories in 'temporary' housing.

As to the form of the housing, one may combine the two essential characteristics concentrated — dispersed and individual — collective to obtain four fundamental types of habitat:

	concentrated	dispersed
individual	secondary urban areas II	Suburbs III (*pavillons*)
collective	City centre I	*Grands* IV *ensembles*

Each of these types is not the object of a 'choice'; it is produced by one of the processes described. Thus, as far as France is concerned, Type I becomes practically the prerogative of an élite and of official residences and its occupation is determined by an ability either to maintain a position of privilege (by the maintenance of the relative positions of the family), or by participation in the operations of urban restoration and development.

However, we should introduce here a third dimension that is not present in the table: that of social stratification. For Type I embraces three fundamental situations: the historically constituted bourgeois and middle-class quarters, the quarters invaded by urban renewal and quarters whose rent value is below the exchange value and in which, as a result, a process of deterioration has occurred, with under-occupation and refusal to renovate on the part of the owners in order to accelerate the process of obsolescence. Occupation of this type of habitat occurs in the first place through family position and/or milieu maintained; in the first and second, by enjoying an advantageous position in the social scale; in the third, by the fact of having lived in the place for a generation and having arrived in the city at the bottom of the social scale.

Type II has been brought about by the extension of the urban area with the absorption of the surrounding rural and semi-rural areas. Its occupation follows the rules of social distribution, in terms of functional advantages (in particular, ease of contact with the city centre) and of the pleasantness of the surroundings (which brings us back to its social status, see below).

Type III has been produced, as I have shown, by the successive

effects of the inter-war *pavillons,* property development directed
at a limited section of the population and the land policy now being
followed on account of the high cost of building land in urban areas.
The clientèle has varied accordingly, always wrapped up in the
same ideological discourse relating it to the countryside, but socially
differentiated, according to the mode of access to this individual
habitat.

Lastly, I have stressed the immediate social determinants of the
production of Type IV (the *grands ensembles*) and the concomitant
ideological condemnation parallel with this expedient to which the
bourgeois state saw itself *forced.*

In each case, demand is created by ideological pressure, in accordance with the form of housing made socially and economically
necessary. Thus, the ideology of the *pavillon* exalts good citizen-
ship, security, the feeling of being at home, privacy and the feeling
that one is away from it all; the ideology of the city exalts the pride
in consumption of the élite, which has become the master of the
spatial centre; the philosophy of social housing puts the accent on
the practical side, with an invitation to look back to the badly
housed and forward to a rural utopia, lived in a mythical way and
sustained as a bait for social mobility.

Housing is a world of signs, a world charged with drives and
frustrations, and the arrangement of its symbols is highly expressive
of the social role and the psychological evolution of its inhabitants.
(See the research of the Institute de Sociologie Urbaine, Paris.)

However, it is a pre-constructed context, the product of a general
socio-economic process and its occupation follows the laws of social
distribution. (Thus all inquiries into residential mobility show a
virtual absence of social 'choice': movements occur according to
the needs of the family, in particular its size, and on occasion its
financial possibilities, regulated by the rhythm of professional life.)
(See below, also Taisne-Plantevin, 1966.)

The quantity, the quality, the status and the form of housing
results from the conjunction of four systems: the system of production of housing as a durable commodity; the system of social distribution of this product; the system of social distribution of men
(the function of their place in production and administration); the
system of correspondence between the two systems of distribution.
(Berthaux, 1970.) The result thus obtained is articulated within
the ideological system (urbanistic utopias, architectural images,
etc.), which reinforces it and gives it coherence, through its constitution in material form and in residential myth.

The deeper signification of housing may thus be revealed on the
basis of an understanding of the social process that determines it.

Lastly, what happens when, in a situation of crisis, the state does not come to the aid of building or does so inadequately? The answer is clear: it is the invasion of available land by the homeless and the organization of a 'wild' habitat that obeys the cultural norms of its inhabitants, is equipped according to their own means, and develops in a struggle against police repression, legal threats and, sometimes, the criminal attacks of the property companies, whose plans have been thwarted. It is a massive phenomenon in the Latin American cities (*Espaces et Sociétés*, 1971), but it also forms part of the everyday life of the Western metropolises, as can be seen in the shantytowns of the Paris suburbs, inhabited mainly by immigrant workers.

The housing question is thus shown to be at the centre of the conflictual dialectic for the social appropriation of the product of labour.

b. *Urban segregation*

The distribution of housing in space produces its social differentiation and specifies the urban landscape, since the characteristics of the dwellings and of their residents are at the root of the type and level of amenities and functions that are attached to them.

The distribution of residential locations follows the general laws of the distribution of products and, consequently, brings about regroupings according to the social capacity of the subjects, that is to say, in the capitalist system, according to their income, their professional status, educational level, ethnic group, age group, etc. Consequently, one will speak of an *urban stratification,* corresponding to the system of social stratification (or system of distribution of products among individuals and groups) and, in cases in which social distance has a strong spatial expression, of *urban segregation.* By urban segregation, one means first the tendency to organize space into zones with a high internal social homogeneity and a strong social disparity between one another, this disparity being understood in terms not only of difference, but also of hierarchy.

If such is the general tendency it does not explain, in itself, the composition of the residential space of a particular urban area, nor even what is most significant about it. For, on the one hand, every city being an historical interweaving of several social structures, there are particular mixtures and combinations in the distribution of activities and statuses in space; on the other hand, every society contains contradictions and the general laws of the system are merely of the nature of tendencies, that is to say, they impose themselves on the logic of reproduction, if they are not counteracted by socially determined practices. This means, from our standpoint, that there is, on the one hand, an interaction between economic, political and ideological determinations in the composition of residential space and, on the other, a reinforcement of segregation, a spilling over of its expected limits or a modification of the factors of land occupation, according to the articulation of the class struggle in the place of residence, through the symbolic use of an urban zone, for example, or the reinforcement of the group community by ecological frontiers.

The complexity of such a determination of the social structure of space, made up of a network of interactions between elements with a different index of efficacity, may be sketched by going back to the analysis of a historical case that has often been studied, but seldom interpreted correctly, namely, the residential space of the North American cities, a terrain of inquiry privileged by a whole tradition of empirical sociology.

The analyses of American residential space, which were much influenced by the Social Area Analysis approach, are often limited to indicating the absence of the homogeneity of the space, from the point of view of the characteristics of its population. Thus the now classic study by O. D. Duncan and B. Duncan (1955) of Chicago leads to the following empirical results: the distribution in residential space of the different socio-occupational categories is strongly diversified, in such a way that, the greater the social distance between the groups, the greater the distance in their model of spatial settlement; this tendency is again confirmed by the fact that groups with a strong index of spatial segregation are the extreme groups (at the higher and at the lower level, in the scale of occupational stratification; thus, the lower one's socio-economic level, the more concentrated one is on the same space, and the more one occupies the central zone of the urban area.

The study of spatial stratification from this standpoint (extended and deepened, above all in the United States, by ethnic segregation) (Lieberson, 1963) rests on the linking of the following mechanisms:

1. Social characteristics tend to form spatial clusters. The closer these characteristics are, the more they tend to group together in space.

2. The essential principle that influences the distribution of housing in space is social prestige, the positive expression of which is social desirability (the preference for similar neighbours) and the negative expression social distance (rejection by different neighbours).

3. The differential distribution of income, an expression of the social sanction (positive or negative) of a given kind of work, determines accessibility to the residential space desired, since it is subject to the law of the market.

After organizing all the empirical data on residential location in the United States on these principles, Beshers (1962) finds a direct correspondence between the theory of social stratification and that of social urban composition.

However, certain of these data suggest new interpretations, which do not contradict this functionalist schema, but go beyond it. Thus, in the study by the Duncans already mentioned, one observes certain specificities of behaviour: white-collar workers are no more numerous than skilled workers in expensive residential zones, but they inhabit more often quarters that possess prestige in symbolic terms. An interesting inquiry by Lautmann and Guttman (1966) concerning fifty-five occupational groups shows the absence of any link between geographical proximity and occupational proximity.

There are innumerable examples to show a specificity of residential settlement of households, according to the differential articulation of the various social instances with the same subject or within the same class of subjects. (See Bell, 1968.)

Furthermore, singularities in relation to the general model have been observed, not only at the level of social groups, but at that of the structure's space as a whole. Thus Schnore's (1963) studies of the social characteristics of three hundred American suburbs have shown the hierarchy that exists between the residential suburbs and those dominated by a productive activity, through the systematically decreasing variations of thirteen indicators of socio-economic status over the fifteen analyses.

Another study, by Reynolds Farley (1964), is full of such examples. Farley shows the persistence of social characteristics in each type of suburb. Now, these results go against the general hypothesis concerning the existence, in the American urban structure, of a social hierarchy of city centres and suburbs, with the lower strata concentrated in the old urban nucleus.

In effect, a new study by Schnore (1963) of two hundred urbanized areas has shown that, in the oldest cities, the social status of the suburbs is higher, but that in the more recent zones, the opposite is the case, in so far as the buildings of the city centre are too recent to have deteriorated, and in so far as the new type of industrial location is less detrimental to the urban environment. We are confronted, then, with a social composition of space that varies according to the period (and therefore the conjuncture) of urbanization.

This is as much as to say that urban stratification and segregation are not the direct projection in space of the system of social stratification, but an effect of the distribution of the product among the subjects, and of the housing-product in space, and of the correspondence between these two systems of distribution. Such an approach requires, therefore, that we deduce the composition of residential space on the basis of the study of its process of production, both at the level of the urban forms and of the distribution among them of subjects.

Let us recall briefly the general tendencies that define this process in the United States. A dual feature characterizes post-war American urbanization: the acceleration of metropolitan concentration and the spatial diffusion of activities and populations, with a process of suburbanization that causes, in fact, a reduplication of each large city in a new zone, the warden of the essence of urban dynamism (see Table 35).

Table 35

*Growth of metropolitan areas in the United States,
by zones, 1900–1960*

	Total metro-politan areas	City centre	Suburbs
1900–1910	32·0	37·1	23·6
1910–1920	25·0	27·7	20·0
1920–1930	27·1	24·3	32·3
1930–1940	8·8	5·6	14·6
1940–1950	22·6	14·7	35·9
1950–1960	26·3	10·7	48·5

Source: US Census of Population, 1960: SMSA, PC (3) – 1D, table 1.

These transformations have had profound consequences for the spatial distribution of social characteristics. The shift towards the better suburbs, towards new houses and distant quarters, requiring a very advanced *individual* set of amenities and capacities for individual mobility, has been possible above all for the new middle strata; they benefit, in effect, from economic expansion and the creation of a whole mass of tertiary jobs opening up career possibilities and, therefore, making possible recourse to individual credit in the buying of a one-family house. Now, the dwellings thus abandoned have not been demolished, but reoccupied by a new population, made up of rural immigrants, particularly from the South (Table 36), and lower strata, at the bottom of the income scale and/or victims of ethnic discrimination, in particular, the Blacks (Table 37).

As the housing of the old urban nucleus is abandoned by its occupants, it is redeveloped by the owners and divided up into smaller apartments in order to obtain higher rents by increasing

Table 36

Net migration of non-whites 1950–1960 by region (individuals)	
North-east	+ 541 000
North-west	+ 558 000
West	+ 332 000
South	− 1 457 000

Source: HHFA, *Our Nonwhite Population*, p. 14.

the number of occupants. Furthermore, the landlord no longer carries out repairs, for it is actually to his advantage to accelerate the process of deterioration. There are two reasons for this: first, there is an increasing gap between the price of the building and the price of land, whose value is increasing on account of the increasing scarcity of central locations (in the suburbs, the reverse is true); secondly, given the fact that the new occupants have a limited choice, the landlord is always sure of finding a sufficient number of tenants among the new arrivals looking for work in the city (a reserve army at the housing level). (Greer, 1965.)

The strategy of the landlord is therefore simple: wait for the construction of new buildings or for urban redevelopment to bring him a profitable sale of the land and, meanwhile, obtain sufficient rent thanks to the particular conditions, socially defined, of the property market in which he operates.

This way of occupying and administering housing accelerates the process of the physical deterioration of the buildings. Furthermore, the phenomenon does not occur in isolation, but includes vast ecological units for, when lower strata and underprivileged ethnic groups begin to occupy a quarter, those families which had stayed though able to move out to the suburbs, now begin, in turn, to move. Particularly significant in this respect is the role of the schools. In view of the fact that they are organized and financed on a local basis, to remain in a community with a certain proportion of Blacks, for example, is equivalent to accepting racial integration in the schools, which many whites refuse to do. It is not only, however, a question of prejudice: any deterioration of the socio-economic level of a neighbourhood is accompanied by a diminution of the material means of the school, which is generally reinforced by the discriminatory practices of the administrations at a higher level — which has repercussions on the quality of the education. Similar processes occur with regard to other public services and more serious obstacles occur at the level of interpersonal relations.

The abandonment of a quarter by the 'middle class' and its replacement by the lower social and ethnic strata also leads to the

Table 37

Distribution of dwellings in the United States, according to criteria of quality and over-crowding, rural location, or inner urban or outer urban in the metropolitan areas, 1960
(in thousands of dwellings)

	United States	In the metropolises			Outside the metropolises	Urban	Rural
		Total	City centre	Suburb			
QUALITY							
Total	58 318	36 378	19 617	16 617	21 940	40 757	17 561
Suitable	47 727	32 535	17 406	15 130	15 192	36 490	11 238
Deteriorated	10 591	3 843	2 211	1 631	6 748	4 267	6 323
Percentage of the whole	100%	62%	34%	29%	38%	70%	30%
Percentage of all the deteriorated dwellings		36%	21%	15%	64%	40%	60%
OVER-CROWDING							
Total of occupied dwellings	53 024	34 000	18 506	15 494	19 024	38 320	14 704
One person per room or less	46 911	30 479	16 523	13 956	16 432	34 429	12 481
One person per room or more	6 113	3 521	1 983	1 538	2 592	3 891	2 223
Percentage of the whole	100%	64%	35%	29%	36%	72%	28%
Percentage of the total of overcrowded dwellings	100%	58%	32%	25%	42%	64%	36%

Source: Frank S. Kristof, Urban Housing Needs through the 1980's. *Research Report,* no. 10, National Commission on Urban Problems, Washington DC, 1968, p. 28.

disappearance of the pre-existing tertiary and its replacement by businesses and 'leisure activities' corresponding to the new population. Prices also rise: they now include risks of business location. (The best source of data for the whole development in the United States is the Report of the National Commission on Urban Problems, 1968.)

The result of this process is the occupation of the city centres of the great metropolises by a considerable proportion of 'poor' citizens and/or those belonging to ethnic minorities — underprivileged, in the market, from the economic, political and ideological point of view. (See Tables 38, 39 and 40.)

Table 38

Income level and location within metropolitan regions, United States, 1959 (in percentages of the whole population living in the same geographical conditions).

Families with an income of	Living in the city	Living in the suburbs
under 3000 per annum	17·6%	12·5%
over 10 000 per annum	16·5%	21·2%

Source: US Bureau of Census, Final Report, PC (3) — L.D

The movement thus established is bound to accelerate. According to the best projections (Hodge and Hauser, 1969), the city centres will lose, between 1960 and 1985, 5% of their white population and see an increase of 94% of their black population. It is true that we are speaking here of proportions and ratios. We must not forget that in absolute figures, this concentration remains in general a minority one, for the Blacks are only 12% of the American population and 'poor Whites' 10% of the white population. But, even in absolute figures, very large cities, such as Washington DC,

Table 39

Percentage of unemployed, by ethnic group and location of residence in the twenty largest metropolitan regions, United States, 1967

	Percentage of the whole active population		
	United States	City Centre	Suburbs
Total	3·8%	4·7%	3·3%
Whites	3·4%	3·7%	3·1%
Non-whites	7·4%	7·6%	7·0%

Table 40

*Ecological distribution by race and metropolitan region,
United States, 1960 and projection for 1985*

| | Millions of persons | | | |
| | 1960 | | 1985 | |
	City centres	Suburbs	City centres	Suburbs
Non-whites	10·4	2·8	20·1	6·8
Whites	47·9	51·8	45·4	105·7

Source: Hodge-Hauser, *op. cit.*

Newark (New Jersey) and Gary (Indiana), already have a black majority and the same situation is predicted for 1985, in such cities as New Orleans, Richmond, Chicago, Philadelphia, St Louis, Detroit, Cleveland, Baltimore, Oakland.

The main point is the social milieu that such a concentration gives rise to, the sub-culture it develops, the reactions of hostility that are set up between this community and the state apparatuses. For it is not in these urban zones that one finds the maximum poverty nor the most deteriorated housing, but rather in the rural zones of the United States or in the forgotten cities of the South. What is socially significant is not the fact of poverty or of discrimination in itself, but the fusion of certain social situations and a particular location in the urban structure. It is in this way that urban segregation is constituted as a specific phenomenon, and not simply as a reflection of general social stratification.

The city centre is, therefore, not uniquely a locus, an urban stratum placed at the botton of the scale. It becomes the ecological expression of the 'underdogs' in the society of opulence and, on this basis, the crystallization of a contradictory pole, a potential centre of conflict. It takes on a meaning that goes beyond mere inequality in the distribution of housing in space, from the moment when the fusion of social situations and spatial situations produces pertinent effects — that is to say, something new, specific to the spatial data — on class relations and, therefore, on the whole of the social dynamic.

However, if such is the general model of development of American residential space, each historical conjuncture specifies the forms of urbanization and segregation in space. Thus a new study by Leo F. Schnore of two hundred American urban areas (1964) has shown a diversity of possible types, which may be grouped together empirically in the following way:

1. The upper strata are over-represented in the city centre (for example, Tucson).

2. The élite and the social and ethnic minorities are simultaneously over-represented in the city centre. This type, the most striking example of which is Los Angeles, is the most frequent (seventy of the urban areas out of the two hundred studied).

3. The city centre is characterized by a concentration of the lower strata (for example, New York). This is what is called the 'classic model'.

4. No particular concentration of the lower strata in the city centre, whereas the socio-economic processes at work led to a prediction of a structure of type 3 (for example, Miami).

An analysis of the characteristics of the urban areas shows a few regularities in relation to each of the types thus differentiated:

The larger the urban area, the more its residential space conforms to the classic model (type 3).

The more recent the urbanization, the less the classic model explains the social stratification of its space.

The higher the growth rate, the more the social ecology of the city approaches type 2.

Furthermore, an examination of the data concerning non-white housing shows that, within the black minority, the segregating city centre/suburb model does not apply and that it must be replaced by a specific analysis of spatial segregation within the ghetto. Now, one finds that, in the North of the United States, the further away one's home is from the city centre (but still in the ghetto), the more one's socio-economic level rises. But the reverse phenomenon occurs in the ghettos in the south, south-west and west of the country. (Taueber and Taueber, 1965.)

That is to say, although one can observe a social differentiation of space, there is no possible general law in terms of geographical regularities, but always particular expressions of the articulation of class relations (economic, political, ideological) with the distribution of a product (housing) which includes among its qualities those of its spatial environment.

For example, the fact that the more recently urbanized cities should have a lower concentration of the lower strata in their central nucleus is, quite simply, the consequence of the lesser degree of importance accorded to the urban forms existing before the phenomenon of suburbanization. Not that segregation disappears, but it occurs sectorally; or, rather, it accompanies situations unfavourable in terms of the transport network, instead of being defined in relation to a rapidly disappearing centre. (Hoyt, 1964.)

Similarly, if the high rate of urban growth encourages

concentration in this centre of the two extremes of the social scale, it is because there is added to the phenomenon already described in relation to the lower strata, the creation of a new privilege: that of appropriating the last vestiges of 'urban-ness' and centrality that remain in a radically exploding city. Lastly, this superimposed play of two forms of segregation, the one social, the other ethnic, each interacting with the other, manifests the over-determination of the American class structure, in which the Blacks are both a proletariat and a reserve army for the white proletariat, with, in addition, specific effects in the domain of ideological armour (discrimination and racism), made necessary by the characteristics of primitive accumulation of American capitalism.

The process of formation of residential space, at once complex in its manifestations, and corresponding to extremely clear general tendencies, may also be apprehended at the level of the subjects, through a study of what is called residential mobility, that is to say, the movements of individuals in the residential space already produced. Despite the ideological bias of the majority of these studies (which set out from the 'preferences' of individuals, as if it were simply a market study), the empirical results already obtained are fairly revealing.

To begin with, Abu-Lughod and Fooley (1960) estimate that about 30% of the residential changes are 'involuntary': 10% are the result of the creation of new homes and 20% of the demolition of the earlier home or of an expulsion; 50% of the intra-urban mobility results, according to leading studies, from a change in housing needs, produced by a new stage of the life cycle (especially the birth or departure of children) (Goldstein, 1958; Lansing and Kish, 1957; Wilkinson and Merry, 1965); Rossi's classic study of Philadelphia shows the decisive importance of this variable. (Rossi, 1955.)

We must seek the principal cause of social mobility, therefore, in variations in the composition of the population (by immigration). The 'choice' of a new home involves, above all, the comfort and size of the home, as well as the social environment. The site and accessibility in relation to the rest of the urban area or the place of work scarcely feature. (Rossi, 1955, 85; Lapin, 1964.) The central factor in the decision, what determines whether it is taken or not, is the cost of the operation. This cost is determined by the income, the stage in the life cycle and the size of the family. But what is fundamental is the fact that the great majority of the movements take place towards urban zones with an equivalent social status. (Caplow, 1948–1949; Albig, 1932–1933.) Thus the very important study by Goldstein and Mayer (1961) of Rhode Island shows that 80% of the movements are towards 'pockets' classified in the same stratum or in a contiguous stratum (see Table 41). On the other hand, distance in relation to work generally increases with the move, since we are witnessing a growing extension of the urban area and it is easier to obtain a new home if one turns to the housing estates being constructed on the periphery. (Lapin, 1964; Duncan, 1964a.) And this applies despite the observed tendency to live as close as possible to the former place of residence.

Table 41

Residential mobility according to the social status of the residential zone, Rhode Island, USA, 1960
(in percentages of the total of the initial social stratum.)
Ultimate social stratum

Initial social stratum	I (high)	II	III	IV	V (low)
I (high)	63·8	12·0	11·3	8·2	4·8
II	8·2	51·0	20·6	13·3	6·8
III	6·1	18·8	50·4	16·7	8·1
IV	5·1	13·0	21·0	52·7	8·1
V (low)	4·1	13·2	17·3	17·4	48·1

Source: Goldstein and Mayer, 1961, p. 51.

This picture is significant enough. Although 20% of the American population moves every year, it is usually a question of adapting to a new familial situation, to new needs, rather than a redefinition of residential space on the basis of the individual's values. Just as the structure of the housing market produces its own demand, we observe that the individuals circulate biologically (according to the life cycle or the loss of their home) in a residential space (produced according to the process described) without changing their social characteristics, which depend on the distribution of the product among the classes and on the system of relations involved.

Urban segregation does not appear, therefore, as the distribution of the residences of the social groups in space according to a more or less graded scale, but as the expression, at the level of the reproduction of labour power, of the complex and changing relations that determine its modalities. Thus, there is no space privileged in advance, in functional terms; space is defined and redefined according to the conjuncture of the social dynamic.

In concrete terms, this means that the structure of residential space undergoes the following determinations:

At the *economic level*, it conforms to the distribution of the product among individuals and to the specific distribution of this product, that is to say, housing. This factor is at the root of the whole process.

Still at the economic level, the location of the places of production exerts only an indirect influence, that is to say, through the situation in the transport network. This forces us to consider segregation in a much more dynamic way, not simply as a difference of places, but as a capacity for movement and access in relation to the strategic points of the urban network. (Duncan, 1964b.)

At the *politico-institutional level,* 'local democracy' tends to reinforce the consequences of segregation, by practising a policy of amenities in terms of the interests of the dominant fraction of each administrative unit. In effect, since local resources depend on the economic level of the population, local autonomy perpetuates the inequality: the higher this level, the less public intervention in matters concerning public amenities is necessary. Therefore, the 'privileged' local communities will tend to close their frontiers, leaving to the responsibility of the federal state the subsidies necessary for the overwhelming needs of the underprivileged communities. Jeffersonianism, a fine egalitarian ideal, leads, therefore, in practice, to an increase in the inequality between the communities and an institutionalization of the barriers of social distance in space. (Long, 1966; 1968.)

At the *ideological level,* residential segregation is affected by two very different movements.

Firstly, the relative autonomy of the ideological symbols in relation to the places occupied in the relations of production produces interferences in the economic laws of distribution of the subjects among the types of housing and space, as has been observed, for example, in the case of the residence of white-collar workers. These specifications are situated, however, within certain economically determined limits.

Secondly, the correspondence between a social situation and a spatial location may reinforce tendencies towards the ideological autonomization of certain groups and lead to the constitution of ecologically delimited sub-cultures. Segregation may encourage the formation of communities which, on the one hand, will reinforce social and spatial distances even more and, on the other hand, will give them dynamic meaning, by transforming differences into contradiction.

Lastly, the *level of the class struggle* thus exerts an influence over the forms and rhythms of segregation:

1. Concerning the relations between the classes themselves, a situation of open struggle reinforces a spatial explosion that may even go so far as the formation of 'forbidden ghettos', foreshadow-

ing liberated zones. (Oppenheimer, 1969.) On the other hand, where there is total subordination and the domination of one class over another is accepted at every level, there may even be residential mixture in a sort of ecological paternalism, in which the dominant and dominated classes live in the same quarter, though in very different conditions. (McEntire, 1960.)

2. According to which strategy is adopted by the dominant class, one may see two possible interventions of the state apparatus: a *repressive* intervention, expressed, for example, in an urban blueprint that permits the control of and the maintenance of order in communities considered dangerous; (Hobsbawm, 1970) and *integrating* intervention, aimed at breaking up the community and dispersing it throughout the whole of a hostile residential space. (Rossi and Dentler, 1961.)

This, then, is the set of hierarchized determinations at work in the constitution of a residential space, as we have mapped them in the analysis of urban segregation in the United States.

An extremely detailed study of social segregation in the metropolitan area of Chicago may help us to show the explanatory capacity of the schema proposed. (De Vise, 1967).

Having isolated, with the help of a complex index of social and economic status, the ten highest and ten lowest communities in a scale of social stratification, a comparative study both between them and in relation to the different ecological sectors of the metropolitan area shows us the forces at work and their combined action in the process of segregation (see Table 42).

Table 42 shows the great extent to which the social differentiation of space is determined according to the place occupied in the relations of production and, consequently, in the distribution of the product: we have, on the one hand, those living off investment income, the liberal professions and senior executives and, on the other hand, workers, farmers, service workers and unemployed. This spatial distribution is overdetermined by the new ideologico—political cleavage of racial discrimination. Where there is an equality of socio—economic level, the blacks are the object of a particular segregation and they form the overwhelming majority (90%) of the ten most disadvantaged communities. The phenomenon is a general one: in 1960, 85% of the Blacks of Chicago lived in sectors in which over 75% of the population was black.

Such a spatial organization is reinforced, as we have shown, by the action of local institutions. Thus, for example, the tax assigned to school expenses depends on the rate of tax each community levies and it is a faithful reflection of the socio-economic asymmetry already established.

Table 42

Characteristics of socio-economic level in the Chicago metropolitan area, by geographical zone and administrative district comparing the extremes of the scale of urban stratification 1966

	Economic rank			Proportion of employment in different socio-occupational categories								Demographic characteristics		Quality of housing	
	Average income per household: dollars — per annum	Average value of the dwellings	Liberal professions and upper management	Office workers	Craftsmen workers	Farmers	Owners	Service	Number of unemployed workers	Percentage of unemployed	Percentage of blacks	Average number of children per family	Number of rooms	% constructed in last 20 years
Metropolitan area	9 400	19 910	21%	29%	36%	4%	1%	9%	137	2·2%	18%	1·4	4·8	32%
Chicago	8 100	19 800	17%	29%	37%	5%	1%	10%	123	2·7%	28%	1·2	4·4	15%
All suburbs	10 500	19 950	27%	27%	34%	3%	2%	7%	151	1·2%			5·2	53%
10 High status wards	22 027	40 846	54%	26%	8%	1%	7%	4%	169	0·7%			6·9	60%
10 Low status wards	4 810	—	5%	13%	45%	19%	—	17%	—	10 %	90%	2·2		

Source: P. De Vise, *Chicago's Widening Color Gap,* Inter University Social Research Committee, Report No 2, Chicago, December 1967.

This situation is the logical consequence of an extraordinary disparity in the means of labour and the qualifications of the teaching staff, revealed by every inquiry in this field.

Furthermore, the public services as a whole reveal the same picture.

The result, on the ideological plane, is the reinforcement of the ethnic sub-culture; at the level of the class struggle, we are witnessing attempts on the part of the state to disperse (Suttles, 1968) or to limit (Meyerson and Banfield, 1955) the ghetto and also the consolidation of these zones as a place for organizing revolt among the American ethnic minorities (see below, Part IV). (See also Rossi, 1955; Report of the National Advisory Commission, 1968.)

The situation described and analysed with regard to the United States reveals the general laws of the distribution of housing in space, while showing their historical specificity determined by the conjuncture and the rhythms of the racial composition studied. One has only to think of the organization of residential space in European or Latin American cities to realize the absurdity of a generalization of the concrete forms of the process in question. Furthermore, over the same North American continent, wherever class relations have different historical foundations, the principles of spatial distribution manifest themselves differently. A rapid comparison with the racial ecology of Montreal has enabled us to show the importance of the ethnic and cultural factor (English-speaking versus French-speaking) in the distribution of the population in space.

Through the diversity of the historical forms one rediscovers, however, the action of general laws of the distribution of dwellings in space and of the distribution of individuals in dwellings. Such laws have only a distant relation with the first impression of space — the reflection of social stratification — for they bring into play the complex totality of the determinations that characterize each social formation. Social segregation in space is, therefore, the specific expression of processes aimed at the simple reproduction of labour power, but these processes are always inseparably articulated with all the instances of the social structure.

c. *Social space and natural milieu: the urban environment*
If the process of reproducing labour power shapes space in a decisive way, we must specify what type of reproduction is involved, for such a level of generality does not enable us to approach an analysis of concrete situations.

A first criterion of differentiation might be the refraction, within the process of extended reproduction, of the different instances, economic, political, ideological, underlying a social formation.

Now, an extended reproduction in the economic sphere is the equivalent of a reinforcement of the potentialities of the labour force as a source of value. It is extremely difficult to give a concrete image of the processes at work in the enlargement of its capacities, for a whole set of elements comes into play, both of a biological and an intellectual order (acquisition of new skills, for example).

However, it is my hypothesis that part of the so-called problematic of the environment refers to this question, in so far as one covers, under this term, the relation between subjects and their environment, their conditions of everyday existence and the possibilities that are offered to them by a certain mode of organization of consumption. 'The environment,' one of the most eminent French ideologists in this field tells us, 'is whatever makes pleasant or unpleasant, healthy or unhealthy, the milieu in which we live, whether from the biological, psychical or visual point of view. This environment is collective, in contrast to the individual environment (within the home, the place of work). Thus, in a city, the environment is the quality of the water, the air, the food, the sound level, the urban landscape, the length of the journey to and from work, the presence or absence of green spaces, both for their role in the struggle against atmospheric pollution and for the contact with nature that they provide.' (Garnier, 1970.)

Although the psychologizing naivety and ideological confusion of this text prevent us from treating it other than as a symptom, it is a good expression both of the social process considered (the conditions of everyday existence of the subjects and therefore of the extended reproduction of labour force as such) and the overall ideological envelope in which it is enclosed (an almost natural, or naturally denatured 'living context' . . .).

Any sociological enquiry into the question thus connoted must, therefore, above all, establish a distinction between the different levels and themes that intersect in the problematic of the environment:

1. An overall ideology concerning social relations as a whole, apprehended as relations of the human species with the milieu in which it lives.

2. A set of questions, indicated by the term ecology, which refer, in the last resort, to the social use of natural resources. These questions concern, therefore, the general system of culture/nature relations, and not simply the 'urban' surroundings.

3. The contradictions caused by the extended reproduction of labour power in its biological dimension. It is in this sense that there is a link between such a process and problems concerning amenities and the organization of collective consumption within urban units:

it is a question here of the 'quality of life'.

The ideology of the environment is characterized precisely by the fusion it brings about between these three spheres, at least, by means of a dialogue concerning the conditions for achieving the well-being of man, in his eternal struggle against nature.

The argument is the same whether we are dealing with the semi-official American publication *The Environmental Handbook* (Bell, 1970) or the report of the French government. (*2000, 1970.*) Industrialization, urbanization, the deterioration of the environment and the 'social cost' are linked in terms both of deficiencies in consumption and of the social tension aroused. It is as if techno-logical progress, a blind and ineluctable force, was both the base of all the transformations of our societies and, at the same time, the source of all its problems, by bringing about a deterioration of the environment by means of the technological logic unleashed. The most salient factor of the ideology of the environment is this naturalization of social contradictions, this reduction of human history to a direct relation between Man, *qua* eternal and undif-ferentiated reality, and Nature, *qua* set of resources existing prior to him. Such a relation is governed by technology and one must therefore take care lest this domination is not more brutal than necessary and does not destroy one of the terms (or both) of the idealist dyad. In more concrete terms, the ideology of the environment is, as far as Nature is concerned, the equivalent of the ideology of alienation in relation to Man.

Indeed, in both cases, one is referring to an essence, to an earlier state that has been lost, that has deteriorated, that has been sullied by too narrow a subordination to technological imperatives, where-as one cannot bypass the continuous development of the productive forces. The ideological mechanism obviously consists in the reference to real phenomena, experienced as problematic by subjects, but which are explicable by a direct connection between ideal entities outside any social production and, in particular, outside any contradiction.

Furthermore, if an ideology is mapped by its internal structure, it is explicable above all by its social effect. The effect of the ideo-logy of the environment is obvious enough: it is a question of gathering together all the deficiencies of what is called 'everyday life', that is to say, the collective conditions for reproducing labour power, under a general label that presents them as a natural cala-mity against which one can only mobilize without exception 'men of good will', enlightened and supported by their government. 'Apolitical', humanitarian, universalist and scientist, the ideology of the environment transforms social inequality into physically harmful effects and merges social classes into a single army of boy scouts. In this way, it is the most complete expression (since it generalizes it) of the ideology of the urban (see Part II).

But this does not mean that the array of problems connoted by the thematic of the environment constitutes only a smokescreen to divert social struggles from their (necessarily social) objectives. On the contrary, extremely concrete questions are raised in this way and may be treated in other terms, providing one can recognize them for what they are in the prevailing fog.

Thus the social use of natural resources not only strikes the imagination through the extent of the ravages perpetrated on the ecological environment by a certain form of technological and social appropriation of these resources; it also strikes social groups, it effects the biological being in all its dimensions. Industrial smoke disturbs the respiratory system, DDT manifests a very high toxicity, noise has a direct influence on the nervous system, etc.; but these phenomena are not new. In particular, the working conditions of the industrial proletariat affect the biological being much more directly.

But if the question remains of the conditions of the social visibility of each type of problem (why now do we have problems of the 'environment'?), this is because we are dealing with typical elements in the living conditions of a given population. We should add others, which are less frequently brought up: when thousands of workers and students demonstrated at Nantes in May 1970 in order to reopen to the public the banks of the Erdre, a beautiful public river that had become the appurtenance of a few holiday villas; when in the summer French militants invaded some of the private beaches reserved for rich bourgeois, they demonstrated the link between the scarcity of certain resources (space, expanses of water, forest, sea) and the social determination of this scarcity. Or, to put in another way, that the use value is indissolubly linked, in capitalism, to an exchange value and follows its laws.

In the United States, seven million cars are thrown on the scrap-heap each year. It is enough to arouse apocalyptic images of cemeteries of cars, and for the organizers of the well-intentioned group 'Ecology Action' to enact a symbolic burial of a motor-car, at once the instrument of pollution and the producer of rubbish. Now, how derisory is the problem of this metal rubbish (even if unusable as scrap) at a time when one quite calmly and regularly deposits masses of radioactive waste throughout the world's oceans! And, above all, what is the social logic of the production of such 'harmful effects'? American left-wing militants have undertaken a systematic campaign to resituate the problems at their true level. To the abstract criticisms of modernity, they oppose an examination of a given social structure and its effects. (See *Ramparts,* 1970.) Thus, for example, an analysis of the California Water Plan, the realization of which is equivalent to the spread of the pollution of the water courses and the destruction of an impressive group of Californian natural sites, shows that it corresponds directly to the irrigation plan needed by the great Californian agricultural corporations.

Furthermore, the development of the protest movement around these themes has created an enormous market for the anti-pollution industry, whose expansion will inevitably accelerate in the near future. It goes without saying that the same industrial groups which, in the chemical industry in particular, contribute most to the pollution of the atmosphere and water, are in the forefront of production for this new market. The whole situation is directed and coordinated by what is already called the Eco-Establishment, under the patronage of the federal Secretary of State for the Interior.

Although the merit of the American critics is that they have demonstrated the logic of the social production of these 'harmful effects' — the logic of profit, which therefore uses technological progress in a certain way — they still remain within an ecological, that is to say, naturalizing, problematic. Even if one takes the ecology as determined by a social process, the same exteriority, implicit in the perspective, prevents its being understood. For, by separating once again the two terms (for example, the 'capitalist' social process and 'ecology') one falls necessarily either into a reification of Nature or into a simple application of the social structure. In both cases, one is prevented from grasping the social specificity of the questions considered.

But, in the last resort, what are these questions? The introductory report of the Armand Committee (1970), which the French government took as its basis in determining its 'hundred measures relative to the environment', lists the main ones:

1. The conservation of the biosphere (land, air, water) of the animal and vegetable species. This includes, therefore, all the effects of pollution.

2. The deterioration of the quality of the man-made environment ('the world of asphalt and concrete' . . .) or, in the words of the report, 'the biological and psychical milieu of the cities'.

3. The urban landscape.

4. Noise.

5. The waste produced by the large urban areas.

6. 'Open space', meaning both the rural landscape and green spaces.

Such a list confuses the three planes that have been distinguished (ideological, relation to nature, extended reproduction of labour power at the biological level), but it does specify certain points on which an analysis may be made: those that are usually included under the term harmful effects (noise, pollution, waste, lack of green spaces and, in general, lack of 'amenities'). These harmful effects are the 'concrete' anchorage-points of the general ideological package, those that make it possible to crystallize the diffuse anxiety felt by people on the subject of the environment. (See *2000*, 1969.)

Now, what does one find when one examines them more closely? Let us take noise, for example. Basically, there are perfectly mappable acoustical phenomena, a certain intensity of which produces effects on the nervous system and, as a result, on the physical system. But noise, as a social fact, depends on the relation established between emitter and receiver, that is to say, on the situation in which it is experienced. Hence:

1. Social differentiation of the subject-receivers, whose psychical conjunctures will be affected very differently and whose defence mechanisms or mechanisms of adjustment follow the social laws of the distribution of commodities (methods of sound-proofing, which are graded according to the 'standing' of the building);

2. Social differentiation of the production, of noise: it is usually said that almost 85% comes 'from the street'. But the street is whatever is not 'housing', and therefore activity in general. Noise comes from traffic? Indeed, but this is the view of the resident behind his window. And, furthermore, of the inhabitant of the city centre, who is becoming rarer and rarer. Industrial noise in the factories or the obsessional tapping of typewriters in offices reaches much higher levels (in boiler-making, 20% of the workers become markedly deaf). In the end, one begins to wonder who this strange resident is, shut up in his home in search of rest and invaded by so much noise from the outside. It is perhaps the unoccupied housewife, the rare possessor of the privilege of a silence undisturbed by children's cries? This brings us to the essential question of the rhythms of life, of the way one uses one's time; the invasion by noise is revealed in the form of a mythical enemy constantly disturbing a calm that one has almost attained.

3. For, in effect, there is still a social differentiation of the situations of noise emission — reception: noise as constraint, or noise as expansion. Is pop music not *noise*, even an infernal one, for certain cultural 'zombies'? For the young, who immerse themselves in it, it is a form of self-expression. Is the noise of machines that one must put up with the same noise, even physiologically speaking, as the throbbing noise of a crowded motorway during a weekend of imaginary freedom?

These remarks are elementary enough and are simply a way of saying: the social noise-factor does not exist, it does not have an individuality of its own, it is always a situation and, as such, it is distributed among several processes that redefine it and give it meaning.

One might make similar remarks for each of what are called the 'harmful effects'. Not that they do not exist, but their mode of social existence does not have the unity under which they are presented; they need to be redefined each time, made specific to each moment. The entity 'harmful effects' has no more than an ideological meaning, that is to say, in an imaginary—negative relation to the environment and, therefore, to the way of life. It is in this sense that the connection with the process of the extended reproduction of labour power as a whole is given. But, through the attempt to isolate the questions according to their false 'natural appearance' (pollution as a physical process, for example), they are emptied of social content and necessarily become those natural entities that can be linked to actual experience only in the positive/ negative mode. In more concrete terms, noise, pollution, etc., do not have the same social specificity as, for example, housing. Housing, by expressing all the instances of a society at once, has a relatively well defined place in the social structure, as a locus of the simple reproduction of labour power. However, these various 'harmful effects' refer to the whole process of enlarged reproduction, by dismembering it into physiological factors and by presenting it as a general and socially undifferentiated 'package' (the environment).

Disturbed by the divergence between the conclusions outlined in such an analysis and the expression of 'urban' experience, we carried out a brief inquiry into a test-case in the city of Paris.[4] Despite the limits of the inquiry, the results are fairly significant:

The press drew the attention of the public to the scandalous pollution caused by a large food factory in a working-class quarter on the outskirts of the city. The local inhabitants, in particular those living in a group of HLM apartment blocks near the factory, were being suffocated by the fumes and deafened by the noise. Petitions requesting the removal of the factory were handed in, but nothing could force the removal of the factory, since it had been established for a hundred and fifty years in a zone still classified as occupied by industry and warehousing. We carried out a direct investigation: first, the company expressed astonishment at this

[4] Inquiry carried out by Misses Cooper, Mehl, Obradors and Patriarca and by Mr Ferreiras, in 1971, at the Atelier de Sociologie Urbaine de l'Ecole Pratique des Hautes Etudes. See Castells *et al.*, 1977.

'campaign' and declared that the factory was not a source of pollution and had every intention of staying put; the workers, the overwhelming majority of whom were immigrants, lived near their work and seemed to find this an advantage. Indeed, neither the noise nor the pollution seemed excessive, except for a gas boiler, which is indispensable to the heating of the two thousand HLM housing units.

From our short technical report, it emerged that there was, in fact, no serious pollution of the atmosphere: the gas given off left no trace and the smells were limited to a very short period (twenty days in a year). When interviewed (a non-representative sample), the inhabitants of the housing estate declared that they had never suffered very much from their proximity to the factory (in fact, the noise of the traffic was much more disturbing than that of the factory), but expressed deep discontent about other aspects of their daily life — in particular, leisure amenities (especially for children), lack of crèches and the total absence of personal relations. Lastly, the tenants' association, which had formulated the demands against the factory, told us: 1) that they had great difficulty getting a collective position of this kind signed, whereas the other campaigns it wages usually get the support of the tenants; 2) that they became aware of the problem only after hearing a radio broadcast in which this particular factory was mentioned. They seized the opportunity in an attempt to obtain public amenities on the space left by a possible removal of the factory.

When the problem was put in this way, the question of noise proved to be almost imaginary. We still don't know *why* a press campaign was launched or whether the company would be greatly inconvenienced if it modernized its plant in the suburbs. Technically, removal would be quite feasible: the factory is situated in a quarter that has become more and more residential and compensation for the removal from a government with an eye to fine gestures in its crusade against pollution, in addition to the sale of the land, might almost cover the cost of a new factory.

But, more generally, it is clear that the concrete problem of pollution either has been experienced only from the outside (in terms of urban functionality) or has been apprehended as the materialization of a set of difficulties bound up with the daily organization of social life outside of work.

Although our brief investigation ran the risk of being a caricature, it certainly illustrates the ambiguity of the problematic at issue. Experienced as real, imaginary in its expression, it must be both delimited in terms of concrete practice and resituated in a context of significant social processes.

In order to pose the problem of the 'environment' in sociological terms, we must first distinguish between ideological discourse and the study of 'harmful effects', map historically each of these harmful effects, articulate them with different processes of the social structure, explain them in this way and, coming full circle, examine the forms of the link between the processes thus elucidated and the general discussion of the environment, in such a way as to understand this ideology as a whole through its social effects.

C The exchange element.

Inter-urban traffic: towards a sociological problematic of transport
Broad avenues inundated by roaring rivers of cars, suburban stations swarming with anxious faces, métro-corridors turned into slow-moving waiting rooms. . . . Beyond such striking images of the transport problem, it is generally agreed that circulation in an urban area should be regarded both as an expression of its flow patterns (and therefore of its structure) and as an essential element in determining its evolution. Indeed, the more the urban units increase in size and complexity (see Part I) the more important internal links become, for no sector can be self-sufficient, and the dynamic of the urban area is realized only at the level of its ensemble. This may explain why the theme lends itself easily to technicist utopias and why technological progress in transportation has often been regarded as the agent of new urban forms: thus, the motorcar is seen as the cause of the megalopolis, just as the tram was seen as the basis of the large industrial urban areas, while the helicopter and moving footpaths are seen as prefiguring the 'cities of tomorrow' (See *2000*, Special number, 1970).

Thus the study of the system of circulation is systematically transformed into a debate on the means of transportation. Now it is clear that to oppose the motorcar to public transport *in itself,* outside a given situation, is an ideological discussion directly determined by the economic interests involved. On the other hand, a sociological problematic of transportation must resituate the different technological means in a given social structure, from which they derive their meaning.

Indeed, an analysis of urban circulation must be understood as a specification of a more general theory of *exchange* between the components of the urban system, which means, in concrete terms, that one must establish the *content* of the traffic if one is to explain the mode of circulation. The content differs according to the type of *transfer,* that is to say, according to the elements of the urban structure between which it operates and according to the *direction, intensity and conjuncture,* that characterize it. That is to say, an analysis of circulation (and, on this basis, an analysis of *transporta-tion, defined as a means of circulation*) raises the question of the relations between the ensemble of the elements of the urban struc-ture; that is to say, it crowns and synthesizes such an effort rather than precedes it.

It is not a question here of developing so complex a framework, but of sketching the perspective in which one might formulate the classic problem of urban transport — a problem of great social importance but one ignored for the most part by sociological analysis. Rather than set out from transport, or even from the traffic system, we should, therefore, by reversing the perspective, consider methodically each of the possible transfers within the urban structure and show their different forms of spatial realiza-tion, according to the interaction between the structural content of each transfer, the historical specificity of the space in which it is realized and the social differentiation of the process in question.

Let us specify the path indicated by constructing a schema that we shall bring closer, by successive stages, to concrete situations. Setting out by distinguishing the elements of the urban structure as P elements (Production), C elements (Consumption), E elements (Exchange), A elements (Administration) and sub-elements defined within each of them, we have, at least, the following transfers, capable of coding theoretically the essential traffic flows:

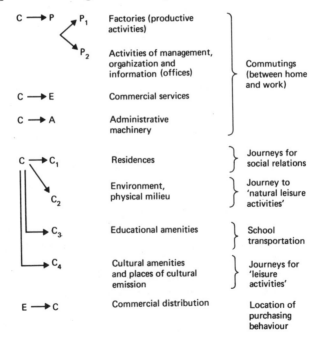

E $\longrightarrow$ E   Goods traffic

P $\longrightarrow$ E

P $\longrightarrow$ P

$P_1 \longrightarrow P_1$ Industrial traffic

$P_2 \longrightarrow P_1$ Industrial administration
                          (at a distance,
                          non-spatialization)

$P_2 \longrightarrow P_2$ Journeys on business

The usefulness of this schema is not limited to a certain systematization of the transfers considered and to the differentiation thus introduced into the analysis of circulation. It must, above all, make possible an explanation of the use of such means of circulation rather than any other, as well as the conditions of its realization, through the specification of the laws determining the elements that make up a transfer. Thus each of the transfers will have a series of requirements to be fulfilled as a priority, as far as the mode of its spatial realization is concerned. These 'requirements' express the laws of the social structure in question; they are more or less fulfilled according to the type of determinations. This point, though abstract, is essential and requires some explanation.

Allow me, simply by way of clarifying our ideas, to introduce a series of concrete 'factors' which, in the technologist tradition, characterize the different means of transport and make it possible to evaluate them. Let us say, for example, that a certain type of transport (means of circulation) must always combine, in a certain proportion, its *load* capacity, its *speed*, its *safety*, its *comfort* and its *cost* (let me say at once that the cost will result from the combination of the preceding factors). My line of analysis implies that each type of transfer combines these different factors with a specific weighting, and that these combinations are the concrete expression of the social laws governing the elements at the base of the transfer.

A combination of factors, realized in a certain spatial conjuncture and linked with the corresponding system of social differentiation, is expressed by a given means of circulation, that is to say, by a type of transport. On the other hand, what is called cost is constituted, once it is socially specified, as a mode of administering the means of circulation, that is to say, as an expression of the relations of production. In effect, by *mode of administration*, I do not mean the legal ownership of the means of circulation, but the logic of the functioning of traffic, for example, whether it corresponds to the search for budgetary profitability or assumes responsibility for this functioning, without a direct contribution by the users. We have, therefore, the following chain:

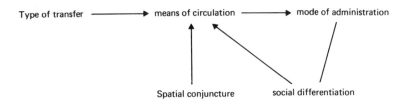

Without the introduction of a concrete spatial conjuncture, any precise determination of the means of circulation is impossible. Thus the motorcar/railways debate cannot be introduced at the level of the general table of relations between transfers and the combination of factors, for the respective speed, capacity and safety of each will depend on the viscosity of the historical space in which it must circulate.

For example if it is a question of a metropolis with zones of extremely diversified activity in which there is no predominance of the pre-industrial urban forms, the bus or even, with certain reservations, the motor-car offer greater flexibility; they may fulfil the conditions necessary to serve as a means of commuting; if the spatial situation is the opposite, the train or the underground train will have a greater range of possibilities. But I am not backtracking when I refer to the examination of each particular case. What is called 'spatial conjuncture' means, essentially, two things, which may be mapped perfectly easily from a theoretical point of view: 1) the persistence, in a social formation, of spatial forms linked to a previous mode of production (for example, the urban nuclei of the European cities); 2) the distribution of social activities and groups in space, according to the technological and social division of labour.

Similarly, the mode of administration of the means of circulation depends both on the means itself and on the type of social administration linked with it. In more concrete terms, if technological progress and urban evolution lead to an increasing socialization of the means of circulation, this does not lead necessarily to a collective realization and administration of exchange, for other social determinants (economic, political, ideological) are moving in the direction of a certain individualization of the means of exchange. This dual tendency lies at the root of the classic opposition between 'public' and 'private' transport, which may be characterized in the following way: for the first, there is socialization both of the conditions of exchange and of the exchange itself, whereas, for the second, there is a socialization of the conditions of circulation (production of the road network) and individualization of the tool of circulation (the private motor-car) — hence the distortion that follows. If there is spatial specification and determination of the mode of administration, there is also social differentiation, that is to say, an unequal distribution of the means of transport among the social groups (according, in the last analysis, to their place in the relations of production) and an unequal distribution of the means of transport in space, itself socially differentiated.

These remarks are enough to show that there is no necessary development from an adequate means of circulation to each type of transfer, since a complex, but well defined, network of social interaction is at work. However, a knowledge of the laws tending to favour particular types of transport, and the establishment of exceptions, of opposite effects, etc., in a given reality, make it possible to map the contradictions of the traffic system, thus leading up to the problematic of planning (which will try to resolve them) and of the social movements brought about by the immediate experience of such situations.

Having reached this point, the schema has not attained a sufficient degree of complexity for one to speak otherwise than on the basis of concrete situations. I shall now give a brief outline of these by way of illustration.

If one considers the Paris region, and takes as known the basic facts of its urban structure (see above), one may predict the scope, the frequency and the social importance of the journey for each type of transfer.

At a first level, the estimate of the proportional importance of each type of transfer led us to the following problematic: (See Merlin, 1967, for the essential data; also *Cahiers de l'IAURP*, 4&5 and FCUTCRP, 1970).

Table 43

Distribution of daily journeys in the Paris region
by type of transfer (purpose of journey), 1960

Purpose of journey	Number (in millions)	% of total journeys
Purchases and personal business	2·5	17%
Leisure	1·5	10%
Business journeys	1·1	8%
Accompanying a child to school, etc.	3·4	23%
Home — work (commuting)	6·0	40%
	14·5	

N.B. The table refers to working days only.

The only transfers taken into account by the statistics are those concerning people, excluding, for example, the exchange of commodities or industrial traffic. Thus, it is clear that the transfers between units of consumption (residences) and units of production and administration (work) represent the biggest number, and, by virtue of the fact of their concentration in time and space, will determine the structure of the circulation network. But from a mere estimate of the flows in the region, one will not be able to deduce the forms and rhythms of transport, their social signification. We must, therefore, return, in a methodical way, to the analytical schema proposed and try to show the specificity of the interaction between the various elements in the Paris region. One may, by cross-checking, obtain an approximate estimate of the flows, coded according to the typology of transportation by relating them, separately, to their social and spatial characteristics, for what is at stake is to obtain data that present these empirical combinations, in accordance with the type of analysis attempted.

Tables 44, 45, 46 provide a few indications of this sort, whereas information on other types of transport remains fragmentary.

Table 44

Transfers: C → P, C → E, C → A, according to social differentiation and relation to urban centrality.
Commuting (according to socio-occupational category, economic activity and sex, Paris region, 1960).

Category	Total	Non-commuters		Commuters crossing the Paris boundary		Commuters not crossing the Paris boundary	
		Number	%	Number	%	Number	%
Craftsmen, small tradesmen	290 900	224 940	77·3	20 400	7·0	45 560	15·7
Industrialists, Liberal professions	101 920	62 100	60·9	13 880	13·6	25 940	25·5
Upper management	276 180	59 240	21·4	93 260	33·8	123 680	44·8
Middle management	502 280	119 320	23·7	167 620	33·4	215 340	42·9
Office workers	691 920	136 820	19·8	250 840	36·2	304 260	44·0
Shop assistants	337 560	144 380	42·8	71 080	21·0	122 100	36·2
Army	67 740	16 820	24·8	19 980	29·5	30 940	45·7
Foremen, skilled workers	728 400	191 260	26·2	189 420	26·0	347 720	47·8
Semi-skilled, unskilled workers	735 960	264 320	35·9	139 300	18·9	332 340	45·2
Farmers	194 480	156 100	80·2	8 900	4·5	29 480	15·3
Others	4 740	660	13·9	1 760	37·1	2 320	49·0
Building and Public works	270 400	98 200	36·3	63 560	23·5	108 640	40·2
Engineering industries	673 280	156 520	23·2	160 240	23·8	356 520	53·0
Other processing industries	654 520	193 200	29·5	173 140	26·5	288 180	44·0
Transport	213 460	45 580	21·4	71 760	33·6	96 120	45·0
Retail commerce	330 080	157 780	47·8	66 020	20·0	106 280	32·2
Other commerce, etc.	472 100	124 260	26·3	158 200	33·5	189 640	40·2
Private services	558 380	297 580	53·3	102 420	18·3	158 380	28·4
Public services	533 300	150 000	28·1	154 440	29·0	228 860	42·9
Other activities, Undeclared	226 560	152 840	67·4	26 660	11·8	47 060	20·8
Men	2 357 200	746 260	31·7	606 340	25·7	1 004 600	42·6
Women	1 574 880	629 700	40·0	370 100	23·5	575 080	36·5
Married women	840 440	338 680	40·3	204 820	24·4	296 940	35·3
Total	3 932 080	1 375 960	35·0	976 440	24·8	1 579 680	40·2

Table 45

Level of spatial correspondence between C, P, E and A. Numbers according to place of residence and place of work, Paris region, 1960

Place of work / Place of residence	Paris	Urban belt Seine	Urban belt S.-et-O.	Suburban belt S.-et-M.	Suburban belt S.-et-O.	Zone of attraction S.-et-M.	Zone of attraction S.-et-O.	Outside the complex S.-et-M.	Outside the complex S.-et-O.	Total
Identical with place of residence[1]	441 240	476 400	127 560	8 740	90 420	8 280	55 800	95 980	71 540	1 375 900
Paris	764 120	484 000	105 800	8 860	111 620	6 060	24 780	10 300	10 440	1 525 940
Urban belt Seine	162 260	339 100	77 760	4 600	58 540	2 900	11 700	3 940	3 900	664 760
Urban belt S.-et-O.	12 220	24 660	38 640	1 020	15 520	140	5 220	200	2 720	100 340
Suburban belt S.-et-M.	180	420	420	2 020	420	560	0	360	0	4 350
Suburban belt S.-et-O.	5 600	10 060	6 280	580	27 440	300	3 400	500	2 580	56 740
Zone of attraction S.-et-M.	120	200	80	640	140	1 760	200	1 240	60	4 440
Zone of attraction S.-et-O.	4 420	6 460	5 000	80	5 080	100	17 260	240	7 420	46 060
Outside the complex S.-et-M.	1 160	1 060	280	220	680	620	200	36 540	600	41 360
Outside the complex S.-et-O.	1 440	1 500	1 020	20	2 580	100	5 380	740	26 220	39 000
Other départements	9 100	5 160	1 680	40	1 460	60	1 020	1 200	1 400	21 130
Undeclared	18 080	15 080	4 620	620	4 720	440	3 160	3 360	1 920	55 000
Total	1 419 940	1 364 100	369 140	27 440	318 620	21 320	128 120	154 600	128 800	3 932 000

[1] By place of work identical with place of residence, I mean people working in the commune (or quarter) in which they reside. It will be observed that only 15% of Parisians work outside Paris, while over 30% of residents of the suburbs work in Paris.

Table 46

Transfers C → C by geographical sector, Paris region, 1962, 1965
(Destinations of leisure journeys and various journeys)

Geographical area	Destination of leisure journeys (inquiry 1965)	Destination of various journeys (inquiry 1965)	Jobs (census 1962)	Resident population (census 1962)
Paris	48·6	37·0	50·8	32·8
Northwest suburbs	4·9	10·9	7·5	8·6
North suburbs	11·7	10·6	9·0	12·5
East suburbs	7·0	13·3	8·2	11·5
Southeast suburbs	8·2	9·5	5·9	9·3
West-southwest suburbs	0·6	6·6	8·5	10·6
Greater southwest suburbs (Saint-Rémy and Rambouillet lines)	9·5	0·8	1·0	1·7
Mantes Region	0·0	0·8	0·7	0·7
Greater west-northwest suburbs	0·9	2·8	1·4	1·9
Greater east suburbs	0·4	1·4	0·8	1·4
Greater southeast suburbs	2·2	2·3	1·1	1·3
Rest of the Paris region	5·0	3·7	5·1	7·7
Outside the Paris region	1·0	0·3	0·0	0·0
Total	100·0	100·0	100·0	100·0

However, we may, on the basis of general data concerning the Paris region, construct a table linking each type of transfer to the levels of adequate *capacity, speed, safety* and *comfort*, in the historical conjuncture considered. On the other hand, each of the combinations of these factors will be equivalent to a certain 'cost' on the basis of the mode of administration of the means of transport. In order to construct the table, we will give a score, +, 0, −, to each of the factors, according to the needs of each type of transfer, based on the known data for the Paris region. Naturally, the attribution of scores is largely arbitrary, since a true study in this direction has not been carried out. But I prefer to take the risk of a certain empirical margin of error in order to clarify the ideas in the perspective that I have indicated. The following table sums up roughly the results of such a characterization for the different transfers in the Paris region:

Transfer	Capacity	Speed	Safety	Comfort	Cost
$[C \rightarrow P_1]$ ——→	[+	+	+	−] ——→	[2]
$[C \rightarrow P_2]$ ——→	[+	+	+	0] ——→	[3]
$[C \rightarrow E]$ ——→	[0	+	+	0] ——→	[2]
$[C \rightarrow C_1]$ ——→	[−	+	−	+] ——→	[0]
$[C \rightarrow C_2]$ ——→	[−	+	−	+] ——→	[0]
$[C \rightarrow C_3]$ ——→	[+	+	+	0] ——→	[3]
$[C \rightarrow C_4]$ ——→	[+	0	0	+] ——→	[2]
$[E - C]$ ——→	[+	0	−	+] ——→	[2]
$[E - B]$ ——→	[+	+	+	−] ——→	[2]
$[P - E]$ ——→	[+	0	+	−] ——→	[1]
$[P_1 - P_1]$ ——→	[+	0	+	−] ——→	[1]
$[P_2 - P_2]$ ——→	[−	+	0	+] ——→	[2]

Under the heading of 'cost', I have introduced an estimate deriving from the net balance of the negative and positive scores for each factor, considering all the factors as equivalent: it is obvious that the inter-factor weighting appears as fundamental in the determination of the real cost. But the main idea that I am trying to introduce is that the cost of a means of circulation depends on the combination of factors, which are themselves dependent on the type of transfer (which is why I have used parentheses in the different terms of the table).

I will not justify each score in detail, for the important thing is to pursue the analysis, showing the adequation required between each of the situations considered and the use made of a means of circulation and a mode of administration. For this purpose, we must introduce the data relative to the spatial and social characteristics of each transfer, which are also present in the basic data. I shall limit myself to establishing the broad outlines.

Thus the spatial distribution of jobs and residences determines very considerable daily commuter flows between the centre of the urban area and the suburbs, for office jobs and for industrial jobs; and between different sectors of the suburbs, for a section of the industrial jobs. Given the concentration of activities, the dispersal of residences and the particular 'viscosity' of the centre of the Paris region, the appropriate means of transport is no doubt the railway (in its various forms). By way of comparison, for example, a railway train transports 50 000 passengers an hour in each direction, whereas a 3-lane motorway transports 6000 passengers at rush hours.

Such a means of transport must be *radial* and at the same time in the form of a *network*, in order to cover both types of movement observed. The *cost* is such that it can be realized only through an administration of the 'public utility' type, that is to say, by placing it at the service of socially dominant functions, without seeking a direct profit in the administration of the traffic network.

If we now examine another, very different type of transfer, $C_1 - C_2$ and $C_1 - C_4$ (that is, what are called 'leisure-based' journeys), one finds an even greater imbalance, since the centralization of 'cultural' leisure activities in Paris is total and since 'natural leisure activities' appear to involve much more sporadic journeys. The little time one can allocate to such journeys, its very unequal distribution among the different social strata, the ideology of the privatization of leisure and, above all, the distribution, in the annual time available to households, of the number of 'outings' call for, in the present social conditions, an individual means of circulation: the motorcar (see Table 47).

This being so, individual use is not equivalent to an individual administration of transport, for, as we have indicated, there is a dissociation between use and administration, the individualized tool of transport, and the production and administration of the conditions of circulation (the road network), the cost of which is even higher than that of the railways and which are therefore taken over by the state apparatus.

Table 47

Means of transport used for 'leisure' journeys (weekdays)

Car	43%
Taxi	1%
Two-wheeler	7%
Métro	21%
Urban bus	9%
Suburban bus	10%
Railway	9%

In the case of shopping expeditions (E → C) and personal journeys (A → C), which represent 17% of the total of the daily journeys, data are more difficult to come by, but one may formulate the hypothesis of a traffic flow similar to that of the tertiary job, as a result of the centralization of businesses and offices in Paris, and the lack of amenities in the suburbs. The *railway* and the *métro* seem to be a necessary response to such a movement, until the full effect is felt of the great commercial centres of the periphery, which are beginning to drain towards them currents of motor traffic — a means appropriate to a journey involving several stops and requiring an individualized load capacity (household shopping). The tendency, in this case, is towards an individualization not only of the tool of transport, but also of certain collective conditions for its use: the construction of car parks next to the large stores.

Rather than continue to deploy the internal logic of each type of transfer in the conjuncture of the Paris region (which, in order to be taken seriously, would require a series of specific analyses that are outside the scope of this present work) we must now introduce the historical conditions for the existence and functioning of the means of transport in Paris which, obviously, do not derive in a straight line solely from the logic of the traffic system, but also from a set of economico-political determinants. Furthermore, a sociological study of transportation is based on an analysis of the contradictions between the internal logic of a traffic system and the historical conditions of the means of transport through which it must be realized.

Lastly, these different contradictions are articulated with general social contradictions, by virtue of the fact that traffic takes place in a given social space, shaped above all by urban segregation.

If we link the logic of the traffic system in thc Paris region with the transportation situation, we can map, among others, the following contradictions:

1. Whereas we have observed the essential role that the urban railways must play in the concrete conditions of the traffic system of the Paris region, there is an obvious oversaturation of the capacity of these means of transport in relation to the flows:

The *métro* remains limited to the twenty *arrondissements,* no new line having been opened since 1939. Despite the intensive use of old material (which determines a fairly low speed of 21 km/h), the number of places offered per km has increased, between 1954 and 1960, by 10%, whereas the traffic has increased by 15%.

It has fallen, then, to the railways in the strict sense to make the link with the suburbs. Since the number of places offered by the SNCF (French Railways) has practically not varied between 1954 and 1960, the number of places per km has increased by only 11%, while the traffic has increased by 18%. Even more spectacular is the case of the Sceaux line, which is linked with the *métro* and serves the rapidly expanding southern suburbs; places increased by 8% and the traffic by 32%; on the other hand, the link with the *métro* network makes it necessary to change trains.

The bus was conceived as a supplementary means of transport, in order to make up for the many gaps in the *métro* network.

If, in this case, the oversaturation of capacity does not occur (+32% in places and +22% in traffic for the suburbs, −17% and −20% respectively for Paris), it has undergone a veritable paralysis, owing to the density of motor-car traffic and the absence of any urban road network reserved for buses (in 1953, the average speed was 13 km/h in Paris and 18 km/h in the suburbs; in 1970, 9 km/h and 12 km/h).

At a time when the concentration of jobs and activities is increasing and the rate of urbanization is accelerating, such a situation has as its logical consequence a diminution in comfort and speed, and a lengthening of the distances to be covered. In concrete terms, this means, for the commuters, an average of two hours travelling a day.

2. The network is strictly radial-concentric and it is interconnected only in Paris, through the *métro*. Given the importance of suburb–suburb commuting, especially for workers, we have, among others, the following consequences:

The need to change the means of transport, with the creation of much more costly and unpleasant broken journeys.

The gradual establishment of private (and much more expensive, since they are not subject to competition) transport companies, which already account for 5% of the traffic.

Use of the motor-car (1 400 000 suburb-to-suburb journeys out of 5 200 000 daily car journeys).

3. The French railways network follows the lines of social segregation in space and reinforces it. Thus, whereas working-class residence in the east of Paris is particularly high and the job/residence imbalance for all categories is more marked than elsewhere, the railway network in this zone is much less dense.

4. Given the oversaturation of public transport in relation to the transfers to which it must respond as a priority, it is practically non existent in the suburbs for the other transfers and, in particular, for those involving leisure, shopping, taking children out, etc. This partly explains the systematic expansion of the motor-car, itself encouraged by other lines of force (the motor-car industry, oil companies, not only as pressure groups, but in so far as they play a central role in the economy as a whole). Now, although, between 1954 and 1962, there was an increase of 150% in car parks, the

increase in the effective use was only 50%, for there could be no
metropolitan road network capable of receiving this flow of cars.
We are witnessing, then, a displacement of the difficulties of functioning of the traffic system to the individual level, without allowing
the use of individual initiative, for the simple reason that the car
cannot, in the Paris region, fulfil the conditions necessary to the
transfers that make up the commuter journeys.

5. Efforts to accommodate motor traffic are directed mainly to
the centre of Paris, which is threatened with paralysis (the average
speed is 16 km/h). The few data available seem to indicate that
there are two main types of car journey in Paris: shopping expeditions and business contacts (suburb—Paris journeys do not exceed
700 000 as against 2 400 000 for Paris—Paris). If the movement
towards the decentralization of commerce continues, the notorious
problem of Paris traffic will be, principally, one of business and
administrative journeys, replaced in the evening by 'leisure outings'
for which there are no means of public transport.

6. The car, like every commodity, is unequally distributed
throughout the different social groups and its use still more so.
Consequently, the more it makes up for the inadequacies of the
transport network, the more the gap widens between those who
live near their place of work, commerce and leisure, who are well
served and have more cars and are more able to use them, and those
who find themselves in the exactly opposite position.

Lastly, an analysis of the contradictions necessarily leads to a
study of the conditions of emergence of political interventions. The
conjuncture of the traffic system outlined here lies, in fact, at the
root of the attempts of the administration to control these contradictions, through, essentially, two types of measures:

1. Financial measures, aimed at making the system profitable,
which necessitates a constant increase of the fares paid by passengers
(between 1966 and 1970, the *métro* ticket increased by 17% a
year).

2. The creation of new means and, in particular, of a Regional
Express Network, the east—west line of which is now being built.
Jean Lojkine (1970) has shown the logic of such a choice, which
was preferred, for example to an extension of the *métro* system
into the inner suburbs, thus linking to the heart of the urban area
the very dense, working-class belt that surrounds it. The east—west
line corresponds, on the contrary, to an accentuation of the social
and functional logic already presented, which was in danger of
causing a paralysis of traffic, with no modification of the network.

It is, in effect, the displacement of tertiary activities towards the
west, around La Défense, and the increasing residential specializa-

tion of the south-east that has made this line urgent; its role, in effect, is to make the new pressure caused by a reinforcement of present tendencies in the commuter flows more bearable. But the effects of such a line, while making possible a certain type of economic functioning in the Paris region, reinforces the social contradictions, for, as Lojkine has shown, 'the reproduction of capital is improved (by the expansion of the labour market), while the reproduction of labour power is impaired (by the extension of the length of the journey).'

This set of contradictions does not give rise only to the intervention of planning: it is at the root of an increasing mobilization of the labour force to struggle against a certain transportation policy and to impose another kind of solution to the problems posed. Thus, in July 1970, a federation of passengers' committees of the Paris region was set up, grouping together about sixty local committees in the whole of the region. Meetings, information groups and demonstrations have since been organized. On 18 November 1970, a demonstration, involving several thousand people and supported by several left-wing organizations, paralysed the centre of Paris and revealed the emergence of a new protest movement on a question that had long been felt as something one could do nothing about. It remains to be seen whether this type of action and protest will adopt a role in the socio-ecological organization of the region, by trying to find a more adequate balance between the requirements of the different transfers and the means of circulation used, or whether there will be a shift from a critique of the deficiencies to a critique of the actual type of transfer, which would imply a challenge to the social organization of Paris space.

This question introduces, then, a problematic of social movements which goes beyond that of the urban structure, for other articulations with the social structure and class relations must be introduced (see below). But it is meaningful to show this indissoluble relation in a given historical situation: the urban structure is transformed through the interventions of the political apparatus and through social movements; these interventions cannot be understood (in relation to the urban units) without being seen against the structure of contradictions that give rise to them. It must be clear that the requirements of each type of transfer are not ahistorical, structural necessities, but requirements socially determined by the social content of the transfer, that is to say, by the mode of existence of the two poles of exchange. On the other hand, the means of transport are not determined solely by the transportation requirements, but, as we have seen in the case of Paris, by a set of influences to be specified in each case. The complexity of the schema and the specificity of the combination of the different elements might be apprehended through a comparative analysis of various societies which cannot be carried out at this level of generality. But one might remind the reader, by means of a few brief examples, of the essential role played by historical specificity in the analysis of a concrete situation.

Thus, in the United States (See Kain, 1968 for an excellent summary of research; also Mayer, 1968), although the volume of different transfers is comparable with that observed in Paris, with a greater proportion devoted to 'leisure' journeys (see Table 48), we know that we are confronted by a very different ecological organization (less concentration of industrial activities, decentralization of the tertiary, a higher social status enjoyed by the suburbs, one-family habitat and urban diffusion) and an unchallenged reign of the motor-car, which is due, above all, to the role played by car production in American industry, although it is coupled with a set of ideological elements relating to the way of life. It is true that, spatial organization being more diversified, the individual means is a more flexible instrument. But once the priority of the motor-car has been established, the means ultimately determines the system. Thus, in the great metropolises in which the concentration of activity approaches that of the European cities, like Chicago or New York, the subway (which is used for most everyday journeys) is duplicated by a complex of rapid thoroughfares for cars, linked to the suburbs by huge car parks in the periphery and, in the case of Chicago, in direct competition with a gigantic system of urban motorways leading right into the Loop.

Furthermore, the car acts not only on the traffic system, but also on the very volume of transfers. In a study based on data for Chicago, Detroit and Modesto, Shuldiner has established, as determinant variables of the number of journeys made, the size of the home and the ownership of a car, whereas the position in the urban network (distance from the central business district) seemed negligible. (Oi and Schuldiner, 1962.) Another significant element is the role of accessory to the car played by public transport in the great American urban areas. In Pittsburgh, although it is an old industrial city with a saturated business centre, one finds that over 85% of daily journeys in public transport are made by people who, on that particular day, did not have their car or who are unable to drive. (Pittsburgh Area Transportation Study, 1961.) In American society, the car thus plays a role that leads to the establishment of the transport flows and, therefore, of urban organization. That the instrument should create the function does not invalidate the schema of analysis presented, but invites us to consider the inter-

Table 48

Commuting in the USA
Journeys of urban residents according to purpose
Percentages of journeys going to:

Urban area (year of data)	Residence	Work	Business	Shopping	Leisure	School	Other	Total
Chicago (1956)	43·5	20·5	12·4	5·5	12·8	1·9	3·4	100·0
Detroit (1953)	39·5	23·5	6·9	8·2	12·1	3·0	6·8	100.0
Washington (1955)	41·7	23·4	6·6	8·2	7·1	4·4	8·6	100·0
Pittsburgh (1958)	43·4	21·0	13·5	8·4	7·9	5·8	0·0	100·0
St Louis (1957)	40·5	20·8	6·0	10·5	12·3	3·0	6·9	100·0
Houston (1953)	37·2	18·9	7·1	10·1	10·8	4·9	7·9	100·0
Kansas City (1957)	37·6	20·6	7·9	9·9	12·9	2·8	8·7	100·0
Phœnix (1957)	40·3	18·2	6·7	11·5	11·2	5·0	9·0	100·0
Nashville (1959)	38·4	19·1	6·5	10·5	13·6	3·3	9·4	100·0
Fort Lauderdale (1959)	38·6	17·2	11·7	13·8	12·9	0·4	5·4	100·0
Charlotte (1958)	36·6	21·9	7·5	9·0	12·8	2·8	9·4	100·0
Reno (1955)	38·6	16·9	11·2	10·4	14·3	0·3	8·3	100·0
% average	39·6	20·2	8·7	9·7	11·7	3·1	7·0	100·0

Source: Wilbur Smith and Associates, Future Highways and Urban Growth. New Haven, Connecticut, February 1961, p. 81.

action between the different elements according to a specific, historically determined logic.

II The institutional organization of space

Just as there is an economic reading of urban space, there is a possible reading of this space in terms of the institutional system, namely, the politico-juridical apparatus of the social formation under consideration. Thus, for example, the classic question of the lack of correspondence between the 'real' units of the organization of space (that is to say, economic units), such as the metropolitan regions, and the territorial units of administration, brings us to the dislocation of the two instances, the economic and political, in relation to the same space. Two problems are thus raised:

1. The administrative segmentation of space as the expression of the logic proper to the institutional system.

2. The social efficacity proper to such a segmentation which, once it is made, is articulated with the ensemble of economic and ideological effects and has a direct influence on the social processes and the political struggle (for example, directly determining the local political scene on the institutional plane).

That is to say, the institutional organization of space does not coincide with the study of that structural element which we have called administration, and which is the specific expression of the state apparatus at the level of an urban unit — which takes into consideration many other data that go beyond spatial organization (see Part IV).

It is a question of determining the organization produced by the politico-juridical apparatus in relation to the structure of urban space and, conversely, of specifying the effects of this segmentation on the processes of the organization of space derived from the other instances.

At a very general level, one may suppose that the institutional segmentation of space will follow the internal logic of the institutional system, that is to say, the ensemble of practices that this system assumed at the centre of a social formation. We know that the political-juridical system, expressed concretely through the whole of the state apparatus, can be understood only in relation to the class structure of a society and, in particular, to the dominant classes and their relation to the dominated classes. (Poulantzas, 1968.) These relations are bi-polar and, furthermore, have a different meaning according as they are seen from the point of view of the dominant classes or of the dominated classes. By bi-polarity, I mean that the state apparatus not only exercises class domination, but also strives, as far as possible, to regulate, the crises of the system, in order to preserve it.

It is in this sense that it may, sometimes, become reformist. Although reforms are always imposed by the class struggle and, therefore, from outside the state apparatus, they are no less real for that: their aim is to preserve and extend the existing context, thus consolidating the long-term interests of the dominant classes, even if it involves infringing their privileges to some extent in a particular conjuncture.

In a very broad way, one may express this double dialectic of the state apparatus thus:

The juridico-political apparatus tends to assure the domination of the dominant classes and the regulation of the contradictions that are manifested between them, and between the different divergent instances of a social formation (economic, political, ideological, vestiges of other modes of production, etc.); to do this, it deploys a whole series of channels of integration with relation to the dominated classes, while permanently exercising in relation to these classes a repression that is more or less overt depending on the conjuncture.

The institutional organization of space is determined, in the first instance, by the expression, at the level of the urban units, of the ensemble of processes of *integration,* of *repression*, of *domination* and of *regulation* emanating from the state apparatus.

Thus, for example, the double movement of *integration-repression* in relation to the dominated classes, is expressed, on the one hand, by communal autonomy and the division of space into locally-based collectivities enjoying a certain capacity for decision under the direct influence of the resident population (integration) and, on the other hand, by the administrative hierarchy of the territorial collectivities, their subordination to a set of instances ever more dependent on the institutional apparatus and the isolation of the different communities among themselves, with a firm limitation of horizontal relations and a preponderance of vertical links with centralized decision-making (repression).

Furthermore, the processes of *domination-regulation,* the expression of the ruling classes, organize space on the one hand by determining the norms of functioning for the whole of the segmented area and by retaining the possibility of central initiatives that directly transform the space of the local communities (domination) and, on the other hand, by intervening in order to adjust the social relation to space, where contradictory interests within the bloc in power and/or structural cleavages produced run the risk of worsening a situation or bringing it to crisis point: urban planning or the new administrative frontiers (such as metropolitan or regional government) are a good example (regulation).

Thus, when speaking of *institutional space,* one is not referring to the spatial seat of the state apparatus (for example, the location of the various administrations), but to the social processes which, on the basis of the politico-juridical apparatus, structure space. The spatial distribution of the apparatuses is merely one concrete expression among others of these processes, which are necessarily articulated with other instances in order, through social and political relations, to produce concrete space (and also, for example, this space of the administrative seats).

The problematic thus outlined is, once again, too vast and too abstract to be developed otherwise than through systematic concrete research. Simply by way of elucidation, I shall mention a few historical situations that become understandable in the light of the concepts proposed:

A The debate on the metropolitan governments in North America
The formation of vast metropolitan regions in North America, with the interpenetration of activities and social networks that result, has generally speaking come into contradiction with the Jeffersonian tradition of deeply-rooted local autonomy, for there is scarcely any possible decision concerning fundamental problems of urban amenities that does not involve the whole or an important part of the economico-spatial units, namely, the 'urban area'.

Thus Robert C. Wood (1967) has revealed the administrative jungle that is the basis of urban administration in the New York region, and we know that in 1967 the 228 metropolitan areas of the United States were administered by 20 745 local governments, that is to say, on average, 91 for each metropolitan area. There would seem to be, therefore, a preponderance of the space of integration over the space of regulation, in the sense that local autonomy is preserved, even at the cost of certain dysfunctions in urban development. This is the line taken, for example, by Scott Greer (1963) in his comparative analysis of the success of the establishment of a metropolitan government in Miami, in relation to the failure of the attempts in St Louis and Cleveland.

Several well synthesized studies, like the one by Norton E. Long, (1968) for example, have shown the social processes involved, beginning with the fundamental fact that space is differentiated socially and that, consequently, local institutions respond to the interests of the majority social groups. (See also Banfield, 1961.) Now, the gap existing in bourgeois democracy between juridical egalitarianism (the public domain) and the stratification of individuals in relation to consumption (the private domain) is being increasingly challenged by the growing socialization of consumption in the great urban areas, by virtue of the fact that it depends above all on the public amenities necessary to mass consumption. The maintenance of the system of stratification requires a separation of spaces, without which one would witness a real redistribution of incomes, the rich communities being forced to contribute to the financing of the public amenities that are especially necessary in the communities of the lower social strata, which are also the most deprived in terms of individual means of consumption. Particularly striking is the effect of this local financing on the level and orientation of the education apparatus, the essential instrument of the reproduction of inequality.

Thus, although the administrative fragmentation of the metro-politan space serves the interests of the better-off residential com-munities (this is the classic argument), which may thus fall back into their particularism, it also serves above all the process of social domination, assuring the reproduction of social relations, in particular through a strict differentiation of the educational and cultural apparatus. In these conditions, it is understandable that the different authorities are unable to work together. It must also ensure that the contradictions thus reinforced in the processes of integration and regulation are overcome, on the one hand, by drawing up plans for social assistance to be subsidised by the federal government, and, on the other hand, by creating *ad hoc* bodies of urban planning, as a response to the problems of regulation in functional terms, without redefining the dimensions of the local political apparatus as a whole.

In certain cases, the redefinition of the institutional space in-volves the organization or disorganization of the social groups on which political domination is based, thus producing a direct contra-diction between the processes of domination and regulation. For example, whereas Toronto has succeeded in giving itself a metro-politan government with fairly extensive powers, the Corporation of Metropolitan Montreal, created in March 1959, has come up against increasing difficulties and has been unable to achieve a genuine supra-communal institution. A rapid examination of the question[5] seems to indicate that the social basis of provincial power predetermines the outcome of the conflict. Whereas in Ontario, Toronto is the base of a provincial power largely acquired by the interests of industrial development, in Quebec, tertiary and industrial Montreal has always been in advance, socially, of the rest of the country, dominated by a coalition of agricultural notables and foreign capitalist interests. In these conditions, a powerful metropolitan Montreal in which protest movements were rapidly developing within the local administration, capable of affecting decisions, was in danger of giving political power to this vast social movement that had formed in recent years in Quebec. As a result, the provincial government skilfully held back any real attempt at this, while setting up administrative organs for the urban area of Quebec that was politically 'safer'. The collapse in the recent elections of the National Union and its replacement by the 'modernist' Liberal Party, scarcely alters the situation: having moved to the left, a metropolitan Montreal would provide a better

[5] Inquiry carried out under my direction by Miss La Roche of the University of Montreal in 1969.

base for the Quebec Party on the institutional plane and for FRAP, left-wing reformist in tendency, on the plane of mass mobilization (see Part IV).

The debate on metropolitan government in North America reveals directly the processes at work in the state apparatus and indicates the social and political issues that determine the institutional segmentation of space.

B   The difficulties of 'concerted city-planning' in the Grenoble urban area

In a different historical context, similar mechanisms are at work in the matter of redefining the administrative apparatus of intervention in space in an urban area with economic and demographic growth as rapid as that of Grenoble. An excellent sociological inquiry (Biarez *et al.* 1970) enables us to understand the process triggered off by the establishment of intercommunal study institutions (SIEPURG in 1967) and intercommunal development institutions (SIRG in 1968), which had been made necessary by the increasing complexity and collective character of the problems facing the local authorities. Indeed, the strong economic, social and, therefore, political differentiation of the thirty-one *communes* in the urban area gave rise to a plurality of situations, interests and strategies:

The urban centre, Grenoble, which raised its social level, took over the principal functions and set out to direct the development of the urban area as a whole.

The *communes* of the working-class suburbs, whose main problems were those of housing and public amenities, trying to retain their autonomy.

The residential *communes,* seeking to preserve a social *milieu* and to exert an influence over development as a whole by other channels than those of urban planning.

The small agricultural *communes,* playing on their particularism in terms of the constitution of land reserves and trailing behind the industrial growth of the urban area as a whole.

In view of this, it was easy to foresee that the intercommunal institutions would be a means of dialogue and of the expression of divergent interests, rather than bodies invested with real powers. But more interesting is the fact that, despite this diversity and apparent failure, the SIEPURG seems to be playing a more effective role in the redefinition of the capacities of urbanistic intervention. Indeed, being responsible for the initiatives of such technical bodies as the Agence d'agglomération (Agency for the Urban Area), it is, in fact, dominated by those locally responsible, especially those of the city of Grenoble; the opposing *communes* can do nothing but adopt a negative attitude towards them, thus paving the way for a hierarchical takeover, such as occurred after the failure of the discussions concerning the plan for modernization and amenities, which was settled, in the end, by the intervention of the prefect.

Thus, the specificity of the communal interests does not of itself resolve the problem of the reorganization of spatial responsibilities. We still have to know what these interests are and what is their relation to the central state apparatuses. In the case of Grenoble, the creation of intercommunal institutions proved to be incompatible with a social consensus, which was made impossible by urban segregation and its underlying class oppositions, but it contributed in a way to the creation of an urban-area space, by making possible certain central urbanistic interventions. The process of regulation is imposed on the requirements of integration (communal autonomy) in so far as it assures, in this conjuncture, the broadening of domination in the new conditions created by increased growth, recourse to hierarchy (repression) always remaining possible and acting in fact by a sort of implicit dissuasion.

C The battle of Dunkirk

Today, Dunkirk is more than a historic site. With the introduction of large-scale modern industrial plant (Usinor, Creusot-Loire, Vallourec, Air Liquide, etc., a refinery and naval dockyards) and a huge harbour under construction, it is one of the most formidable ventures on the part of French monopoly capitalism. It is expected that the urban area will increase by one third between 1965 and 1975, by way of replacing the dwindling mining activities in northeastern France. And already there is a massive influx of manpower, which is being parked in ZUPs such as that of Grande-Synthe, set up exclusively for the use of the Usinor workforce or, in the case of immigrants, in more or less disguised shantytowns.

Such a transformation could not leave unchanged the institutional segmentation of space. A complex process of redefining administrative responsibilities has been set in motion. And this process reveals the interaction of the two logics I have already indicated: that of the existing political apparatus and that of the social interests contained in each unit of social space.

To sum up the problem in broad terms,[6] four kinds of *commune*

---

[6] These observations are based on the first results of a systematic inquiry carried out from 1971 to 1973 into the production of the urban systems in the Dunkirk region. These pages were written in March 1971. For a complete development of this research, I would refer the reader to the book that later emerged from it. (Castells and Godard, 1974.)

make up the urban area of Dunkirk at the moment of the great economic take-off:

Communes in which the middle classes have considerable influence (even if they are very 'working-class' *communes*) and in which urban functions are relatively well established (Dunkirk, Rosendaël, with the addition of the only bourgeois residential *commune*, Malo-les-Bains).

Long-established working-class *communes* (for example, St-Pol-sur-mer).

Communes dominated by new industrial plant, in which there is increasingly concentrated an enormous new working-class population (Grande-Synthe).

Semi-rural *communes*, which constitute above all land reserves for the enormous urban complex now being set up.

This polarization must increase in the near future, for an increase of the tertiary at the centre, an extension of the residential zone along the eastern coastal strip and a vertiginous development of the harbour and of industries (with the construction of working-class estates) along the western coastal strip are being planned.

In treating the problems thus presented at the scale of the urban area, it was logical to think of a supra-communal body and Dunkirk is the only place in France in which an urban Community, comprising eighteen *communes*, was created (in 1968) at the request of the communes concerned. But this functional 'evidence' (process of regulation) is regarded in very different ways, according to the interests in question.

First, according to the logic of *domination*, one must ensure above all the establishment of a local apparatus which, while maintaining order, will not impede the expansion of a complex fundamental to the national plan. Now, the mechanism of the Community risks giving ever greater weight to the working-class *communes* that will develop to the west, and which might impose a policy of amenities and social control capable of impeding industrial development, in a zone in which the unchallenged reign of capital is one of the major attractions for investment. Since the electoral arithmetic confirms this tendency, the Gaullist majority, which controls the city of Dunkirk, tries to play down the Community, in the hope of setting up first of all a Greater Dunkirk, that is to say, the merging of the central *communes* of the urban area, in which the working-class minority would be subordinated to a structure comprising representatives of all classes, and whose weight would be enough to make it the driving force of a community that has thus become a harmonious partner and a force for integration in economic growth.

On the other hand, in the name of *autonomy*, some of the

working-class municipalities even refused to belong to the Community, and have sent in a counter-bill on the urban communities presented in the National Assembly by the Communist Party. In particular, this bill proposes a system of proportional representation and greater autonomy in relation to central government. Until they have at their disposal a true capacity for action, the working-class *communes* are afraid of being linked, in the name of common interest, to an arrangement worked out for the benefit of the industrial companies: they prefer to fall back on a particularist claim for amenities necessary to the people they represent, even if, for the moment, they form part of the Community, while remaining extremely distrustful of it.

Finally, the Community is defended by the majority of the *communes* in the urban area, thanks to the double electoral game of the Socialists: an alliance with the centre in the *communes* in which various classes coexist, and with the left in the working-class *communes*. This defence of the community follows the logic of *autonomy-integration,* which claims a minimum of distancing with regard to the economic programmes, without challenging them: in short, the Socialists are 'loyal' partners of the industrialists while representing the reasonable material interests of the working-class population (by 'reasonable' they mean those that the industrialists are ready to accept).

This 'centrist' strategy corresponds to the multi-class social base which determines this electoral tendency: not that there are no activist working-class *communes* that are not Socialist (for example, the new municipal council of Grande-Synthe is strongly active), but the overall tendency expressed by the chairmen of the urban Community is to represent the interests of the whole population in order to attenuate the social 'fall out', once it has been accepted that urban dynamism is to be governed by economic growth corresponding to a national strategy.

Thus Greater Dunkirk, communal autonomy and an urban Community are three distinct forms of the institutional organization of space; they correspond to the contradictory diversity of social interests, heightened by the effects of conjuncture expressed by the local political apparatuses.

An analysis of institutional space thus recalls the economic determination of the urban structure and brings us to the social dynamic, that is to say, to the political struggle which is at the centre of any concrete analysis of the transformation of a city.

III The urban symbolic

Space is charged with meaning. Its forms and its lay-out refer to one another and are articulated with one another in a symbolic structure whose efficacity for social practices is revealed by any concrete analysis. But this symbolic structure is not the equivalent of an urban text organized by the formal crystallization of social action. Indeed, under the influence of linguistics, we have seen emerge a dangerous tendency to develop a semiological analysis of urban space, according to which this space is the *signifier* of the *signified-social structure*; now, what we have here is either a reminder that space is a social fact (which refers quite simply to the whole of the structural analysis of urban space) or, more likely, a priority accorded to the analysis of forms and the apprehension of the urban phenomenon.

Indeed, as soon as one distinguishes signifier and signified, one posits a certain separation, tension and autonomy between the two terms, which has two important consequences: 1) there is an organization proper to *signifiers*, which is the organization of the urban; 2) the key to this organization is to be found in the relation to the social signified and the study of the urban is thus reduced to the laws of composition of those spatial signs, enabling us to discover, according to the wishes of Lévi-Strauss, the history of a society in the traces of its stones. However such an analysis is possible only if one reduces social action to a *language* and social relations to systems of communication. The ideological displacement carried out in this perspective consists in passing from one method of mapping traces of social practice through its effects on the organization of space to a principle of organization deduced from the formal expressions listed, as if social organization were a code and urban structure a set of myths. This perspective confronts us with a symbolic proper to spatial structure *qua form*.

Setting out from theoretical bases far removed from structuralism, Kevin Lynch (1960) arrives at the same results by separating the urban image from the 'observer' and by analysing its autonomous deployment as form. For Lynch, an *urban image* has a series of precise physical contents, which come together to form each particular image: it is composed of *paths, edges, districts, nodes,* and *landmarks* (pp. 47–8), which combine in such a way as to confer an *identity*, linked to a *structure* and possessing a *meaning* (p. 8). But, although the identity of an image and its possession of a structure may remain within a pure development of forms (referring to one another according to a code), the introduction of a *meaning* necessarily brings into play the process of production of these forms, their insertion in a *socially determined content*. There is thus, a contradiction between Lynch's approach which is 'designatory', implying an autonomous logic of forms, and the results of

his analyses, which refer constantly to a *social meaning* that is
always external and, consequently, largely arbitrary. It is curious
to rediscover, on this terrain, the classic dyad of all structuralist
semiology: structure (the reign of ahistorical necessity) and event
(the reign of chance and historical meaning).

And yet we have known since Bachelard (1957) that the image
is established in a cooperation of the real and the unreal, a meeting
of the function of the real and of the function of the unreal, and
that, 'if a house is a living value, it must integrate an element of
unreality. All values must remain vulnerable. A value that does
not remain vulnerable is dead'.

Every image is linked to a social practice. Not only because it is
produced socially but because it can exist ('remain vulnerable')
only in social relations, just as, ultimately, there is no language
without speech. It is in this respect that Raymond Ledrut (1970)
attempts to amend what Lynch has tried to do by studying the
image of the city on the basis of social practices, in particular on
the basis of the images that the city dwellers themselves have of
their city. In doing this, he reverses the problem without, however,
solving it, for the specificity of spatial forms and their relation to
social practice are replaced by the 'idea' that the inhabitants have
of the 'city', that is to say, by an analysis of the ideology of the
urban, rather than of the social effects of the forms of space. Now,
if images of the 'urban' deserve a detailed study (see Part II), the
urban symbolic derives its specificity precisely from the articulation
of the cultural forms of the spatial environment with the general
system of ideologies and, in particular, with their formal
expression.

This is the field of analysis that I wished to indicate, in delimiting
it by recalling a series of successive approaches to the theme of the
urban symbolic — approaches that have in common the rejection of
an articulated autonomy of the system of forms of space and of
the field of social practices. Now, if an analogy is to be made, we
must set out from a distinction between the natural language
(*langue*) and speech (*parole*), not forgetting that the first has
meaning and is transformed only in relation to the historically
given requirements of the second.

Let us take a closer look at the terms of the questions thus posed:
just as there is an efficacity proper to the economic or politico-
institutional through their spacial modulation and their place in the
urban units, so there is a certain specificity of the ideological
instance at the level of urban space. This ideological specificity is
manifested principally in two ways:

1. By the ideological component which, at the level of historical

reality, is present in every element of the urban structure. Thus, for example, every kind of housing or every means of transport is presented in a certain form, produced by the social characteristics of this element, but which, at the same time, reinforces them, for it possesses a certain margin of autonomy.

2. By the expression, through the forms and rhythms of an urban structure, of the ideological currents produced by social practice. It is at this level of mediation, through urban space, of the general ideological determinations, that one must situate the theme of the urban symbolic.

If we agree that spatial forms should be regarded as cultural forms and, consequently, as an expression of social ideologies, an analysis of these forms must therefore set out from the encounter between a general theory of ideologies and a consideration of the rhythm proper to the existing cultural forms. It is in this way that architecture has been understood by a whole tradition, as Panofsky has shown.

In order to advance in this domain, we must therefore apply to it the same principles of analysis as those concerning the ideological instance in general. Above all, we must bear in mind that an ideology is not to be defined by itself, but by its social effect, which enables us to understand, in turn, the contours of the ideological discourse itself.

This social effect may, despite its diversity, be summed up by the twofold dialectic of the effect of *legitimation* and of the effect of *communication*. (Althusser, 1970.) The first means that every ideology rationalizes certain interests in order to present their domination as the expression of the general interest. But what gives an ideological discourse its power is that it always constitutes a code on the basis of which communication between subjects becomes possible; language and the ensemble of expressive systems are always cultural processes, that is to say, constituted by a dominant ideological ensemble. It should also be observed that this communication is achieved by a process of *recognition*, between subjects (recognition of the possession of the same code) and that this *recognition* is also a *failure to recognize (méconnaissance)*, in so far as it is based on the code of a dominant ideology, which makes communication possible through a false apprehension of the situation experienced; thus, the 'citizen' may understand 'democracy' in so far as he apprehends himself as a formal juridical individuality beyond his class membership.

If ideology may be characterized by the social effect thus defined, ideological practices necessarily refer to a social process and any concrete analysis must be able to map the different places that one may occupy in this process. If one regards an ideological practice as a message, by analogy with information theory, one might distinguish the places of emitter, relay and receiver in the overall process of producing an ideological effect.

How do these remarks concerning the general theory of ideologies help us to understand the urban symbolic? Above all we must specify that it is not a question of purely ideological practices unconnected with spatial forms, nor of an effect derived simply from the formal structure of a space. There is an urban symbolic deriving from the use of spatial form as emitters, relays and receivers of general ideological practices. This means that there is no semiological reading of space that is simply a matter of decoding forms (the congealed trace of social action), but a study of the expressive mediation through which are realized ideological processes produced by social relations in a given conjuncture.

In this perspective, urban space is not an already written text, but a screen permanently structured by a symbolic that changes in accordance with the production of ideological content by the social practices that act in and on the urban unit. However, urban space is not simply a white page in which the ideological practices are inscribed. It has a certain consistency. But this consistency, if it is to be something other than a metaphysical entity, must be able to be broken down socially. Broadly speaking, one finds in it:

1. The effects of conjuncture, that is to say, already existing urban forms, the accumulated and socially combined historical product.

2. The symbolic charge proper to spatial forms, not in accordance with their place in the urban structure, but with their place in the cultural history of forms (for example, skyscrapers are the combination both of the symbolic that is attributed to them by ideological practices mediated through space and of the symbolic that they receive from the cultural conjuncture in which they are to be found (art, design, technology, materials, etc.).

The whole process of determining the urban symbolic might be schematized thus:

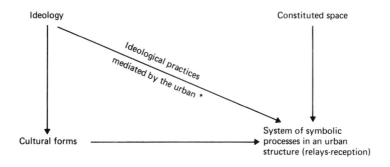

The above schema is excessively abstract and it is very difficult to attribute concrete forms to the places and functions indicated in relation to the ideological processes. However, one may, by way of somewhat distorting illustration, provide a few concrete images.

Thus a semiological analysis of the operations of urban renewal cannot set out from the overall symbolic structure of space, which refers to a matrix expanding to infinity; it must set out from the ideological content conveyed through the operation, itself derived from the effect of this operation of urbanism, both on the urban structure and on social relations. If we know these effects there will be a multiplicity of messages which, logically, must be emitted by the new urban forms: certain of these will be dominant, for example, technological modernity, social prestige, a high level of consumption, etc. Now, if the architectural forms (or their placing in the urban tissue) may play the role of emitter, things become considerably more complicated at the level of *reception*, for there are not only the buyers of the programme, there is the effect that spreads over the surrounding zone and, furthermore, there is the general symbolic effect directed at the entire population.

The content of the messages at the different levels depends on a series of correspondences or non-correspondences between the emitting forms and the receiving forms. But, it will be said, it is the subjects and not the forms that receive the message. Certainly, but this message has a spatial component and it is this component that we are dealing with. To put it more clearly, the 'formal' message is here the same for the inhabitants of the *grands ensembles,* for those of the suburban *pavillons* or for those of working-class quarters near districts affected by the redevelopment programme. Can differences of communication be explained entirely by distinctions in class membership? What is the margin of formal specificity of the 'urban receptors'?

As we proceed, we must obviously introduce the urban 'relays', namely, the symbolic mediations that make possible the translation of the codes or the fusion of several messages into a single message with a view to facilitating reception. For example, 'modernity' emitted through the redeveloped housing estates is relayed differently, according to whether one perceives them by car, on foot, or in terms of an everyday experience of public transport linked with the city centre.

Furthermore, one has always spoken of 'forms', but one may also argue in terms of flows, urban rhythms, empty spaces, space-budgets, etc.

Lastly, the processes, taken together, are neither 'wills', nor strategies, but necessary social effects on the ideology produced by a social relation to space. This means that, sometimes, the ideo-logical effects will contradict the economic effects of an operation, for there is no systematic control of the ensemble of effects. This also shows the limits of such a situation for the *tendential* law of the dominant logic tends to eliminate contradictory experiences, without ever succeeding in doing so.

The 'concrete' elements of such a process must be composed, found, by analysis. Now, these elementary observations of mine are aimed only at indicating a void, at delimiting a theoretical space to be filled, whose existence we have observed, negatively as it were, in the course of research in which these symbolic effects were materially identifiable by their refraction on other domains, but at the same time intellectually incomprehensible for lack of the tools of research.

In any case, the main thing in this domain is to overthrow structuralist semiology and to try to determine the symbolic charge of an urban structure on the basis of the social appropria-tion of space that is carried out by subjects. In a similar way, per-haps, to that used in the work of H. Raymond or K. Burlen. An approach setting out from ideological practices must not, however, fall into subjectivism, for the practices can be understood only in relation to the ideological content transmitted and to the place they occupy in the overall process. To set out from ideologico-spatial practices in order to discover the language of forms, by linking their relations to the ensemble of social relations of an urban unit — this is the complex, but well defined, perspective from which we must embark on this rich but unexplored theme.

IV Urban centrality

The problematic of centrality dominates the urbanistic utopias and theories of the city. It connotes the key question of the relations and articulations between the elements of the urban structure, but, entirely invested with ideology, it tends to become the surest indi-cator of the perception of the city/society relations underlying the analysis.

If we are to adopt a sociological perspective in the study of the urban centre, we must, even more than elsewhere, have worked out a series of conceptual and historical delimitations, without which one can make no progress over a terrain with so many ideological pitfalls.[7]

[7] For a theoretical discussion of recent sociological contributions to the study of the urban centre, including an account of some of the historical developments, see the impor-tant research report of C. Soucy, 1969: *La crise des centres.* (Centre de Sociologie Urbaine, Paris, roneo) — though he does not share my conception of the city centre.

Indeed, as frequently occurs in questions of urban sociology, the term urban centre designates both a geographical place and a social content. In fact, one may distinguish them quite easily, but the confusion really becomes a connotation; that is to say, even if they are theoretically separate, one supposes that, in practice, the social content thus defined will be located in one or several sites, which is equivalent to a fixation of the social content of urban centrality considered in itself, independent of any relation with the structure as a whole.

For the average urbanist (See, for example, Bardet, 1963; Choay, 1965), the centre is that part of the city which, spatially delimited — for example, situated at the confluence of a radial system of ways of communication — plays a role that is both *integrating* and *symbolic*. The centre is the space that makes possible, by the characteristics of its occupation, a coordination of urban activities, a symbolic and ordered identification of these activities and, therefore, the creation of the conditions necessary to communication between the actors. The classic image, in this perspective, is the square of the medieval city, dominated by the cathedral, the site of the buildings of local authority, and where the spontaneous and hierarchized gathering of citizens takes place at predetermined moments of ceremony or festival. (Mumford, 1961.)

This vision of the centre is not entirely a naive one. There is the idea of urban community, that is to say, a specific system of social relations and cultural values, a hierarchized, differentiated and integrated system. If, in fact, there is an urban community, and if society and space are necessarily in interaction, the ecological organization tends to express and reinforce this integration, through the centralization of the symbols and of a system of communication based on spatial participation in the values thus centralized. (Reiss, 1959.)

It would be dangerous to link too closely the idea of community centre with the historical type of the medieval city. Indeed, the centres that one tries to develop in the new housing estates in order to create a local *milieu* (Clerc, 1967), the civic centres of the British and Scandinavian new towns (see the report in Cahiers de l'IAURP, 7), the operations of urban renewal (Morris, 1963), are inspired by the idea of restoring a social unity around the centre of communication created by a central focus. Furthermore, the ideology that permeates town planning tends to attribute an essential role to the centre, precisely with a view to providing an integrating element. (See, for example Chombart de Lauwe (1965), who has often denounced such an ideology.) We might sum up the common denominator of the urbanistic ideology in the following proposition:

'To change the environment is to change social relations.' Now,
urban planning, which is usually based on a desire to impede
'urban social disorganization', is animated by a reforming, and
therefore integrating spirit. (Foley, 1960.) Where there is a break in
social relations or a weak interiorization of values, the aim is to
create an integrating, visible pole, arranged in terms of the urban
units that one wishes to integrate. The ecological characteristics
of such a centre are: a concentration of those activities intended
to encourage communication, accessibility for the whole of the
urban district of which it assumes the centrality, and an internal
differentiation of the central spaces.

Side by side with this conception of the centre, closely entwined
with that of the integrating centre, but clearly distinct from the
theoretical point of view, appears the interpretation of the centre
as a locus for the exchange and coordination of decentralized
activities. It is above all the current of urban ecology that has most
developed this perspective, as is only to be expected in a conception closely associated with the analysis of the processes of the
division of labour and of functional specialization, which characterize industrial predominance over urban organization. A particular
example of this is the ideology and research associated with the
Central Business District, which have helped to establish the now
classic image of the administrative and commercial heart of the
great urban areas. (Hawley, 1950; Quinn, 1955; Johnson, 1957;
Breese, 1964.) The fundamental activities gathered together in a
centre of this type are: commerce and business, financial and
political administration. There is, therefore, an exchange of goods
and services, a coordination and direction of decentralized
activities.

This type of centre is essentially functional in its dual aspect.
On the one hand, it represents the spatialization of the process of
the technological and social division of labour, with the centralized
administration of productive activities carried out in industrial
plant. On the other hand, it has been defined as the geographical
specialization of a certain type of units of consumption and services, what Labasse and Rochefort have called the 'upper tertiary'.
The centre is that part of the city in which are established services
aimed at the greatest number of consumers or specific users, spatial
proximity intervening in no way for the use of the services offered.
(Ledrut, 1968, 140.) It is easy to explain the introduction of these
activities into the centre, if one sees in the market economy the
regulator of the urban spatial system. One finds in this centre firms
whose centrality brings them sufficient profit to compensate for
the higher price of land and the problems of functional amenities

deriving from the congestion of this space. The activities attracted by the centre are, therefore, activities of a very general character, dependent both on their mutual proximity and on a certain equidistance, of a social rather than an ecological kind, in relation to the whole of the urban area. (Hawley, 1956.) This is equivalent to identifying, in terms of economic calculation, the same type of activities for which the ecological analysis of land occupation observed a central situation: exchange, distribution, administration, the emission of information. (Bartholomew, 1932.)

There remains one more characterization of the centre, the object of a whole semi-lyrical literature on the part of lovers of the urban landscape. This is the centre as a ludic nucleus, a concentration of leisure activities and the spatial location of the 'city lights'. It is not only a question of the directly functional aspect of shows and other kinds of entertainment, but of the sublimation of the urban ambiance itself, through a whole range of possible choices and the value placed on the accessibility of consumption in the wide sense of the term.

None of these three categories of centres, which are strongly charged with concrete expression, exists in itself, but as the result of a social process of organizing urban space. That is to say, the urban centre, like the city, is produced: consequently, it expresses the social forces in action and the structure of their internal dynamic. A sociological analysis ought to study the symbolic centre as the result of the process by which a society is organized in relation to the values expressed in space; the 'exchange centre', as expression of the process of urban expansion during the phase of industrialization, of the social division of labour, of functional specification and land occupation according to the law of the market; the ludic centre, as an expression of the process of formation of a society that places increasing value on consumption, with spatial differentiation of leisure activities in terms of the city/nature dichotomy, corresponding to a definite separation between home and work and to the horizontal organization of culture, which is both a highly private culture and a mass culture.

These hasty characterizations have no other aim but to show the extent of the divergence between the concentration of certain functions in space and the central role of a part of the city in relation to the urban structure as a whole. Just as it is now accepted that the urban centre has nothing to do with geographical centrality in an urban area, and that this central position, when it exists, is the result of a functional process, it should also be understood that the concentration of certain functions and their approximate equidistance in relation to the urban area, are merely the consequences of a specific process: that of accelerated urban expansion according to the law of the market. (George, 1964.)

The urban centre is not, therefore, a spatial entity defined once and for all, but a combination of certain functions or activities that provide communication between the elements of an urban structure. That is to say, one cannot simply posit the urban centre: it must be defined in relation to the whole of the urban structure. (See Breese 1964; 1969.) We should, therefore, make a clear distinction between the notion of the urban centre and the images of spatial occupation that it evokes, and give a definition of it deduced from its structural analysis.

In fact, the notion of the centre used by the urbanists is a sociological notion in so far as it expresses more a content than a form. But there is a systematic assimilation of content and form, as if each element of the urban structure had necessarily to have a direct material expression. We must, therefore, as everywhere in sociology, distinguish between concrete space and the 'centre' element of the urban structure. What the spatial forms of urban centrality in fact are, is a quite different question, a matter for research rather than for debate. Indeed, the great controversy *à la* Gutkind (to cite the most brilliant of the dreamers) on the disappearance of the centre, and therefore of the city, in the new forms of urbanization has no meaning without a specification of these terms. It is true that the concentration of certain activities of exchange on a space in symmetrical relation with the various urban zones is giving way to a multinuclear structure or to a sort of urban diffusion (see below). However, this does not imply that there is no longer any relation between the elements of the urban structure; it is simply that this new centrality may operate through other spatial forms.

To sum up we must:

1. Distinguish between the *centre* element defined in relation to the urban structure and what are called 'centres' or the 'centre' in an urban area;

2. Establish the levels of analysis of the urban structure and deduce the notion of centre for each of these levels;

3. Confirm the connection between each notion of *centre* in the different levels and its more or less mediated spatial expression. Or, in more concrete terms, show the exact meaning, in relation to an analytical breakdown of the urban structure, of spatial forms considered as centres in an urban area.

In order to resituate centrality at the different levels of a social structure specified in an urban unit, it is necessary, therefore, to define the processes connoted at each of these levels:

1. In relation to the economic level, centrality expresses a certain relation between the different economic elements of the urban structure (production, consumption, exchange) and of the relations internal to each element. It is a question, therefore, of an ensemble of processes included in the general problematic of transfers in the urban structure (see above).

It is easy to see in this definition of the urban centre the theoretical synthesis of the whole strictly ecological orientation, which situates the centre in relation to the metropolitan organism as a whole, the latter being determined from the spatial point of view by the extent of the centre itself. (Bogue, 1950.) Not because the centre defines the urban structure, but because its influence is taken as indicative of frontiers. A classic text by Johnson defines the centre as 'the area in which are situated highly specialized persons and institutions, which exercise a role of direction, coordination and influence over the market activities of the whole metropolitan region. Their location indicates the ecological centre, but not necessarily the geographical centre of the region. By metropolitan community, we mean a spatial and symbiotic schema, whose parts are dependent, when a city has reached the phase in which management of the companies, administrative tasks and financial control have become the dominant economic functions.' (Johnson, 1957; 248.)

What is debatable is the non-distinction between the function of the centre and the spatial contiguity necessary to the activities stated. Research in urban ecology has subsequently been orientated towards an understanding of the ecological centre as an ensemble of spatially diversified activities. (Horwood and Boyce, 1959; Ericksen, 1954; Schnore, 1965.) However, whatever the spatial translation into a particular historical form, one may retain a first fundamental notion of the centre as an organ of exchange between the processes of production and of consumption in the city or, to put it more simply, between the economic activity and social organization of the city. The process of urban exchange comprises both a system of flows, that is to say, circulation, and of 'turntables' of communication, that is to say, centres.

The centre as organ of urban exchange is, therefore, the spatial organization of the relays of exchange between the process of production and the process of consumption (in the sense of social organization) in an urban area.

2. In relation to the politico-institutional level, we must remember the connotation, by the problematic of centrality, of the idea of hierarchy, as expression of the social order and of its institutional transcription. Centre means distance (nearness–farness) and socio-

spatial ordering 'in relation to'. The spatial expression of such a centrality depends on the historical specificity of the state apparatuses and, in particular, on the respective importance of the local and national apparatuses, their direct influence on civil society and their character, which is more or less bound up with the expression of authority (for example, the spatialization of the Church apparatus sometimes plays a decisive role in the establishment of a centrality). In particular, we must distinguish carefully between this political centre, the symbolic centre, which is above all an emitter of values, and the 'decision-making' centres regarded as business centres, which belong to an analysis in terms of transfers within the economic system. Political centrality is defined rather by the establishment of urban forms, whose logic is to serve as relays for the processes internal to the institutional apparatus: these are, therefore, the centres that correspond to the institutional structure of urban space. When we speak of the political centre, we have in view the presidential palace, the ministries or the town halls, but as soon as one moves away from a concentrated image, politico-institutional centrality refers still more to the display of the strong points of the state apparatus: a repressive apparatus (network of police stations), an ideological apparatus (network of schools, youth clubs), an economic apparatus (ecological distribution of tax offices, etc.).

The politico-institutional centre is, therefore, the articulation of the strong points of the state apparatuses in relation to a given urban structure.

3. At the ideological level, as we have seen, a 'city' is not only a functional ensemble capable of controlling its own expansion; it is also 'a symbolic structure' (Lynch, 1960), an ensemble of signs, which makes possible a bridge between society and space and which links nature and culture. Not only does the plan of a city express with a greater or lesser degree of purity 'the urban unconscious', but above all the organization of space must stress the rhythms and activities, in order to permit the identification of the actors among themselves and in relation to their environment, in other words, the communication not of functions, but of representations. As soon as there is a city, there is, at the same time as urban functioning, an urban language. If the ecological system makes it possible to grasp the interrelation of the activities that make a city live, the semiological system makes comprehensible the communication of the actors among themselves, through their semantic situation in the diversity of the spatial context.

Seen in this way, the centre or centres of a city are the strong points of the semantic field of the urban area, representing, therefore, the spatialization of the signs that form the axis of the symbolic system. Now, these signs cannot be defined as such, but only in relation, once again, to the structure that gives rise to them. For example, the medieval cathedral is the symbolic centre only in a social and spatial structure that places religious values at the centre of the code of interaction, linking the interactions thus defined to a central place on the basis of which the community is integrated in relation to values and hierarchized according to norms. (Panofsky, 1970.)

There is more to the symbolic structure of a city than its public buildings. We must also, on the one hand, extend the urban signs to other forms than its 'historic buildings' and, on the other hand, determine the precise meaning of each building, not historically, but in its transcription according to the code of interactions that organizes social relations.

The symbolic centre, then, is the spatial organization of the points of intersection of the axes of the semantic field of the city, that is to say, the place (or places) that condenses in an intense way a value-laden charge in terms of which urban space is organized in a significatory way.

4. There is another domain connoted by the theme of the urban centre, which is articulated with different social instances: this is the centre as 'milieu of action and interaction' or, to put it another way, the articulation within the urban structure of different modes of social relations. Here, too, ideology largely dominates the analyses carried out from this point of view, for the centre becomes a space possessing a quasi-magical virtue of social innovation, the production of new types of relation, simply by interaction and density between heterogeneous individuals and groups. Without following such mystificatory ways, one may redefine this theme, within a problematic of urban social milieux, by enquiring into the nature of the link between the urban structure and the processes of *production* (but also and above all of *reproduction*) of social relations, other than by a mere description of the spatial facility of social interaction.

Thus *places* may be the amplified expression of a reproduction of gestures (for example, certain quarters that have suddenly become fashionable), but *places* may also broaden and concentrate the process of transformation of the dominant social relations (Nanterre and the Sorbonne in 1968, large factories at times of working-class struggle). Thus the centre, as a social milieu, is detached from a 'conformist' view of it as 'a space of freedom' (an urbanistic utopia that embraces 'freedom' as one more element in zoning) and is extended to the ensemble of situations (both of reproduction and of innovation) characterizing the articulations between urban structure and social relations.

The centre-social milieu appears, then, as the spatial organization of the processes of reproduction and transformation of the social relations of an urban structure, so that the interaction of the urban elements present adds a specific social content, qualitatively different from the mere addition of the social elements that compose it.

This brief theoretical definition of the problematic of centrality must make possible a systematic treatment of each of the social phenomena thus connoted. To begin with, it might be useful to suggest, briefly, a theoretical reading of the transformation of the urban centres in the great metropolises on condition that we regard it merely as a means of communicating our hypotheses rather than as the results of research that has not been carried out. (For the basic, especially American, data, see Green, 1964.)

To be very schematic, one might sum up the following characteristic features:

A The diffusion of the symbolic in urban space

The symbolic centre disappears as such, that is to say, as a place serving as relay for the identification of the urban language. There remain, of course, the 'historic buildings', but they no longer epitomize experienced expressions and must be reinterpreted as elements of the new system of spatial signs. On the other hand, the impressionistic assimilation of the skyscraper to the cathedral, as the expression of change in the system of values, may serve to encourage us to follow the path of semiological research, but not as a simple, direct transposition of one central form into another.

The system of signs tends to be an ensemble of relations, according to a reciprocal reference, between the layout of the city and the traffic flows. The metropolitan symbolic extends along the urban motorways and, rather than being concentrated on particular places, it is distributed throughout the green spaces. (Jacobs, 1961.) The only exception is provided by voluntary operations aimed at marking space at certain points, whether according to the signs of power (prestige projects) or as a tangible concretization of technocratic values (the modernistic housing estates, which are turned inwards rather than towards their relations with the urban structure).

B Deconcentration and decentralization of the commercial function

We are witnessing an increasing loss of the strictly commercial role of the centre as the city extends, as the mobility of the citizens increases and as other forms of buying than those of direct contact develop. (Horwood and Boyce, 1959; Hoover and Vernon, 1959; Sternlieb, 1963; Vernon, 1959; Labasse, 1966; Ardigo, 1967; see also the work of M. Boutilie, IAURP.) The day-time population of the business centre is no longer enough to maintain a concentration of the commercial function; if this kind of activity still remains characteristic of the ecological centres of the metropolitan areas, it is often a result more of inertia than of anything else, and is often financially supported by the turnover of the peripheric commercial centres. The commercial function of the centre is reduced to the maintenance of a few large stores, usually intended for a working-class public and, at the other extreme of the scale of stratification, to the location of shops specializing in the sale of products intended for a clientèle without any precise location.

From this point of view, the criterion for the definition of the centre proposed by R. Ledrut seems to me to suit the new, highly specialized type of exchange that is maintained there. However, in adopting this criterion, one runs the risk of continuing to place the function of exchange at the basis of the constitution of the centre, whereas this function is being decentralized, the old urban centre is being defined increasingly by its role of administration and information and the new centres are being characterized above all by the creation of social milieux.

The deconcentration of the commerical function leads to the creation of peripheric exchange-centres, serving particular urban areas, or benefiting from a situation in the network of daily traffic flows in the metropolis. Depending on whether these peripheric commercial centres are purely functional or are grafted on to the tissue of human relations, they may push urban development in two different directions. Shopping centres along a motorway, with parking facilities, represent one of the essential factors of urban diffusion. On the other hand, the introduction of commerce at a 'load-break' point of the daily urban flows (for example, interchange points between suburban trains and the underground railway system) gives rise to a nucleus of exchange and structures communication.

In either case, the geographical deconcentration of the commercial function merely expresses, at the level of location, the disappearance of the small shop and its replacement by chain stores, with a social and spatial technological division of administration and sale, a standardization of products and a division of space in terms of distribution.

C The creation of 'mini-centres' within the housing estates
The loss of the direct relation with the centre and the disappearance

of the quarters, with their local amenities, in the urban region lead at the same time to the organization of commercial centres linked to the zones of new urbanization.

The role of these 'mini-centres' has still been little studied, especially on the essential point of whether, beyond their function as amenity, they do not represent the condensation of a new social milieu characteristic of urban diffusion. In fact, they must be situated in relation to social relations in the great urban centres; indeed, an overall response to their role would be impressionistic, and we must consider the social structure of the residential milieu on which they are grafted.

From a few American inquiries (White, 1958), one might deduce that the greater the social homogeneity in the housing estate, the more the mini-centre may play a role of interaction. What is clear, in any case, is the considerable importance of an understanding of these centres for an analysis of the relations between the strong points of urban diffusion and the whole of the urban area.

D   The growing specialization of the old urban centre in the activities of administration

In so far as the symbolic role and the commercial function of the old urban centre have a growing tendency to spatial decentralization and in so far as residence has practically disappeared in this sector, the expression 'business centre' becomes the one most adequate to designate it, providing we realize that 'business' is understood in a sufficiently broad sense to include public and political administration. The centre becomes a milieu of decision-making, both by the desire to mark out a function by appropriating a certain space and, above all, by the existence of an informal network of relations, based not only on face-to-face contacts, but also on a certain spatial community in everyday existence.

This specialization of the centre in administration is not a matter of pure chance, but a consequence, first, of the spatial liberation of other activities in relation to the urban context, secondly, of the increasing link between decision-making technologies and the existence of a milieu of information and innovation and, thirdly, of a chain of non-reproduceable interrelations on the basis of a certain threshold of administrative complexity. The decision-making centre is not the spatial expression of bureaucratization but, on the contrary, the logical consequence, at the level of urban development, of the process of technocratization of highly industrialized societies. That is to say, what matters is not the distance between ministries and administered, but the proximity of the interdependent, decision-making nuclei, all equally dependent on the innovating function exercised by the milieu of information and knowledge production, constituted in the city centre through a long process of social exchanges.

In this evolution, it is normal that everything concerned with the production and emission of information, of whatever order — especially the mass media, publishing, etc. — which are largely dependent on the milieu of exchange of ideas and of the social content of the centre, as an expression of the urban ambiance, together with the decision-making activity, should have remained in the old centre.

E   The dissociation of the urban centre and leisure activities
Despite the commonly held view, there is no specialization of the centre of the urban area in the location of leisure activities. (Quin, 1965.) In order to establish what the new relations between space and leisure are, we must first analyse the relation between leisure and social evolution. (For France, see Dumazedier and Imbert, 1967; and the research of M. Maurel of IAURP.) But, as far as the centre is concerned, we must set out from a nature/technology or country/city dichotomy in leisure, which may easily correspond to the day/night dyad. In so far as 'natural' leisure is developing more and more, there is a loss of momentum in the attraction of the centre in leisure terms (Lamy, 1965), whereas 'cultural' leisure activity becomes a status symbol for certain social categories, rather than an urban function proper to the centre. (Lamy, 1967.)

The location of theatres and cinemas, etc., tends, logically enough, to follow the dispersal of residence in the urban areas as a whole. Although the American drive-ins are still very rare in France, in Paris, on the other hand, a fairly strange deconcentration of some of the best theatrical companies is taking place. In fact, there is a regrouping of entertainment, at several geographical and social levels, according to the means of transportation of the urban area and residential stratification — with, however, certain exceptional presentations and exhibitions reserved to the city centre, and particularly anything concerned with night-life.

In terms of leisure, the urban structure draws a distinction between the city and the suburbs, or, to put it another way, the urban atmosphere and urban residence. What is characteristic of the centre is not so much a particular type of entertainment, museum or landscape, as the possibility of the unexpected, choice in consumption, variety in social life. The urban centre then becomes the zone of the residue of the 'functional', an obligatory (and just as functional) counterpart of the spatial specialization of activities and residence. Since every activity has its context, one must also

establish the space preferred, in which the only common characteristic is a certain availability, a certain predominance of the
expressive over the instrumental. The centre is not, therefore, the
'leisure zone', but the space of action of possible leisure, to be
structured by the 'actors' according to general social determinants.

These characteristics are too descriptive to grasp the movement
of transformation of the whole structure connoted by the theme of
centrality. But they manifest a certain correspondence between
social tendencies and the instruments of interpretation that I have
proposed. To discover the 'urban centres' is not to set out from the
given ('the city centre'), but to retrace the lines of force of the
whole of an urban structure by revealing its articulations. If the
theme of centrality has such evocative power, it is because it has
precisely this quality of being both the condensed summary of an
urban structure and its ideological sublimation.

I O

From the Study of Space to the Analysis of the City

I   The theoretical delimitation of the urban

Although, through brief theoretical analyses and a few concrete examples, we have marked out a field of study of the structure of space, the delimitation of the urban remains ambiguous.

At a first level, one might judge such a problem to be purely academic and keep to an analysis of the structure and processes of the organization of space, whatever their content may be. Indeed, one might organize the whole thematic around the specific relation to space of a given social structure, whether this space be 'urban' or something else, once we have observed the vagueness and the historical relativity of the criteria concerning the urban. (See Castells, 1968; 1969.)

In fact, abandoning oneself to this common-sense pragmatism, one merely avoids the problem by hiding it behind false evidence: space. For what is space? Whatever theoretical perspective one adopts, one will have to accept that all space is constructed and that, consequently, the theoretical non-delimitation of the space being dealt with (for example, by calling it urban space or the space of exchange, etc.) amounts to accepting a culturally prescribed (and therefore ideological) segmentation. Since physical space is the deployment of matter as a whole, a study 'without *a priori*' of any 'spatial' form and manifestation will amount to establishing a history of matter. By this *reductio ad absurdum*, I am trying to explode the evidence of this 'space' and to recall the following elementary epistemological postulate: the necessary construction, whether theoretical or ideological (when it is 'given') of any object of analysis.

If this is the case, the supposedly 'spatial' specificity of the social structure is merely the 'evident' expression of a specificity relative to one of the fundamental instances of the social structure or to their relations. It is this theoretical question, connoted by the discussions on the definition of space or the delimitation of the 'urban', that must now be examined. Basically, it is not very different from the discussion of the delimitation of the social formation, for the political frontiers have never been enough to establish a criterion of specificty (for example, who, before 1962, would have seriously maintained that Algeria was part of the French 'social formation'?).

Lastly, by specificity, I do not mean a separate world, but the historically determined efficacity of a certain delimitation, with all the articulations and interactions to be established between such a sub-ensemble and the social structure in which it exists.

To pose the question of the specificity of a space, and in particular urban space, is equivalent to conceiving of relations between the elements of the social structure within a unit defined in one of the instances of the social structure. In more concrete terms, the delimitation 'urban' connotes a unit defined either in the ideological instance, or in the politico-juridical instance, or in the economic instance.

The ideological urban unit is the most generally widespread position and is summed up in the theses of urban culture and its variants. The city as a specific form of civilization provides a first foundation of delimitation, both social and spatial, whose lack of scientific basis and whose ideological foundations we are in a position to show (see Part II, The Urban Ideology).

The urban unit of the politico-juridical apparatus has, in fact, been the foundation of the existence of 'the city' in certain historical conjunctures, whether it be the Greek *polis* or the medieval cities centred on the juridical status of the burgesses. Even today the *commune,* or its equivalent, appears in certain societies, or in certain cases, as a segmentation possessing its own social density. However, in advanced capitalism and in particular in the metropolitan regions, we observe an almost complete lack of correspondence between these political frontiers and the specificity of their social content, this specificity being defined increasingly at the level of the economic. And this is no accident, for it is as if the spatial units were defined in each society according to the dominant instance, characteristic of the mode of production (politico-juridical in feudalism, economic in capitalism).

'The urban' as economic unit? Yes, but we must still ask ourselves whether the process connoted corresponds to the whole of the labour process or to one of its elements, and if so which one. Now, despite the brilliant analyses carried out by Jean Rémy (1966) in this direction, it does not seem that 'the city' or an 'urban region' is a significant segmentation at the level of the economic system as a whole: we are dealing, indeed, with a complex structure, in terms of monopolies (property relations) and sectors of production (technological relations) or, if one looks at it diachronically, in terms of cycles and phases.

Now, among the two fundamental elements of the economic process — the means of production and labour power — the search for a specificity of the first leads us much more to what are called regional problems, that is to say, to the arrangement of the different technological elements of production, taking into account natural and productive sources and movements of capital. The 'regional question' is situated, in my view, at the convergence of this specificity and the cracks left in a social formation by contradictions in the historical process of its constitution.

On the other hand, 'the urban' seems to me to connote directly the processes relating to labour power other than in its direct application to the production process (but not without relation to it, since its entire reproduction is marked by them!).

Urban space thus becomes space defined by a section of the labour force, delimited both by a job market and by the (relative) unity of its daily life. Imagine for example, the difficulty of establishing the unity of an urban region as a productive element, for the economic flows form a continuous network whereas the map of commuter flows usually serves to delimit an urban area. 'The urban', as a connotation of the process of the reproduction of labour power, and 'urban space', as a means of expressing the articulated units of such a process — these notions enable us, I think, to approach these questions in a theoretical way.

This being the case, these details only concern the theoretical bases on which the frontiers of the units studied should be established, without giving oneself up to the false spatial 'given'. Whatever this frontier may be, one finds, within the unit considered, all the elements of the social structure, specified in relation to their spatial deployment, and combined according to the general laws of the mode of production. But it is none the less important to know in relation to which instance this specification operates, for two closely linked problematics emerge:

1. The spatial distribution of each element of the social structure, forming part, at a very general level, of a theory of forms. Thus there will be an ideological space, an institutional space, a space of production, of exchange, of consumption (reproduction), all transforming one another constantly, through the class struggle.

2. The constitution of spatial units that combine in a specific way all the processes that we have mentioned, within a certain

process. I propose the following hypothesis: in advanced capitalist societies, the process that structures space is that which concerns the simple and extended reproduction of labour power; the ensemble of the so-called urban practices connotes the articulation of the process with the social structure as a whole.

Such a definition produces particular effects in the combination of the elements of the social structure, in the (spatial) units of such a process. The urban units thus seem to be to the process of reproduction what the companies are to the production process, though of course they must not be regarded solely as *loci*, but as being the origin of specific effects on the social structure (in the same way, for example, as the characteristics of the company – production unit – affect the expression and forms of the class relations that are manifested in them).

It is in order to examine these internal relations and their articulation with the structure as a whole that I propose the concept of the urban system.

II   The urban system

By urban system, I mean the specific articulation of the instances of a social structure within a (spatial) unit of the reproduction of labour power.

The urban system organizes the ensemble of relations already stated between the elements of the spatial structure. I shall briefly indicate these relations once again. The urban system is defined by:

1. The ensemble of the relations between the two fundamental elements of the economic system and the element that derives from them.

Element P (Production):   Specific means of production.
Element C (Consumption): Specific labour power.

The non-labour element appears as a necessary effect of the economic system in reproduction, which is divided into three products:

Reproduction of the means of production.

Reproduction of labour power.

Appropriation of the product by non-labour:

Social stratification at the level of the social organization (system of distribution);

Functioning of the institutions (political and ideological apparatuses);

At the level of the structures this may also amount to the reproduction of the means of production and/or of labour power.

Element E (Exchange) between P and C, within P, within C and with other instances.

2. Element A (Administration). I call *administration* the regulation of the relations between P, C and E in terms of the structural laws of the social formation, that is to say, in terms of the domination of one class. It is the urban specification of the political instance — which does not exhaust the relations between this instance and the urban system.

3. Element S (Symbolic), which expresses the specification of the ideological at the level of the spatial forms, without it being comprehensible in itself, but in its articulation with the whole of the urban system.

However, to say that the *consumption* element specifies the reproduction of labour power, or the production element the reproduction of the means of production at the level of the urban unit, refers to a problematic much too vast to be translated directly into explanatory propositions. We must, therefore, break down these elements, by establishing their internal structure.

The internal analysis of each element of the urban system must, if it is not to remain intuitive, apply one single principle. The specifications must not introduce new elements in relation to those already defined theoretically. I would say, therefore, that each element is broken down into sub-elements defined by the refraction on it of other elements (including itself) and/or other instances of the social structure. Things become clearer when we apply this principle and give, in each case, concrete examples (let us remember that examples only have an indicative value, for a concept never coincides with a reality).

A Consumption
The consumption element expresses, at the level of the urban unit, the process of the reproduction of labour power. We shall make a distinction, therefore, between simple and extended reproduction of labour power and we shall distinguish in extended reproduction the refraction of the three systems, economic, politico-juridical and ideological.

		Example
Simple reproduction of labour power.	C1	Housing and minimal material amenities (drains, lighting, roads, etc.).
Extended reproduction of labour power.		
• Extended within the economic system (biological reproduction).	C2	Green spaces, pollution, noise, etc. (environment).

• Extended to the institutional system (politico-juridical) (development of the capacities for socialization) (State Ideological Apparatuses).	C3	School amenities.
• Extended to the ideological system (outside the SIAs).	C4	Socio-cultural amenities.

B Production

There is a fundamental distinction to be made between the instruments of labour and the object of labour (in particular, raw material), on the one hand, and, on the other, the articulation of production with other instances.

		Example
Elements internal to the labour process	Instruments of work (P1)	Factories
	Object of work (P2)	Raw Materials
Relation between the labour process and the economic instance as a whole	(P3)	Industrial environment (technological milieu)
Relation between the labour process and other instances	(P4)	Administration, information (offices)

C Exchange

The exchange element, by definition, can be broken down into as many sub-elements as there are possible transfers within or between the elements and instances of the social structure in relation to a given urban unit:

Transfer	Sub-Elements	Example
Production → Consumption	E1	Commerce and distribution
Consumption → Production	E2	Commutings (urban transport)
Production → Production	E3	Goods transport (orders and administration)
Consumption → Consumption	E4	Circulation (residential mobility)
Consumption → Ideological	E5	Emission of information, shows, etc.
Production → Ideological	E6	Historic buildings
Consumption → Political	E7	Decision-making centres
Production → Political	E8	Business centres

D Administration
The administration element articulates the urban system with the political instance and governs the relations between the ensemble of its elements. It is defined, therefore, by its position in the double dichotomy global/local (representing the whole of the political system or linked to local conditions) and bears either on one of the elements of the urban system or on the whole of it (specific/general). This determines four possible sub-elements, derived from their systematic intersection.

E Symbolic
It is a question of the specification of the ideological instance at the level of the spatial forms of the unit of collective consumption (the expression 'forms' is understood in its widest sense).

The symbolic will take on particular configurations according to the relative importance of the different elements and places of the ideological instance. This instance is characterized by a double effect: at the level of practices, an effect of failure-to-recognize/ recognition/communication; at the level of the structural instances, an effect of legitimation (a marking out of space, for example, in the case with which we are dealing). On the other hand, the ideological instance, as productive of messages, involves places of emission, of reception and of relay. The combination of these two effects with these different places must make it possible to establish sub-elements of the symbolic more adequate to the apprehension of the formal complexity of any urban ensemble.

F Sub-elements and system of places
This internal breaking down of each element makes it possible to approach concrete situations in so far as one specifies analysis much more. But if one maps the *locus* of a contradiction, this contradiction must still be able to be expressed socially by the differential distribution of these elements in the support-agents. We must, therefore, define, within each sub-element, the places among which the supports will be distributed, according to their position in the social structure. It is this difference in places occupied by the support-agents that explains contradictory social practices and make possible transformations in the urban system, which must not only be broken down into sub-elements but differentiated, by specifying, within each sub-element, levels and roles.

Thus, for example, in C1 (Housing).

Levels   Luxury housing
          Social housing (+, −)
          Slums, etc.

Roles   Lodger
                  Tenant
                  Co-owner
                  Owner

or in P3 (Industrial Zone)

Levels   Well equipped
                  Badly equipped

Roles   Articulation of industry

with the: natural environment (water, space)
             communications (network of transportation)
             social milieu
             technology (industrial interdependencies).

The relations that obtain between these and with the social structure, the different sub-elements of the urban system, their roles and their levels, define the conjuncture of the urban system. The position of the support-agent in the structural web thus constituted will define urban social practices, the only significant realities for our research.

The rules of functioning of the urban system are easy to determine, for they merely specify the general rules of the mode of production. Thus, in capitalism, the urban system is a dominant system: it is, on the plane of the elements, the element P (means of production) and, on the plane of relations, the relation of ownership, rather than that of real appropriation. This being the case, the schema becomes complicated when we have to reproduce its logic at the level of the sub-elements and, above all, when we have to deal with not the functioning (reproduction) of the system, but its transformation. For we must then study the series of contradictions, that is to say, the passage from a partial dislocation to a condensation of the oppositions into a principal contradiction which, embodied in the confrontation of social practices, creates new structural rules that are impossible to deduce simply from the mechansim of functioning and of its extended reproduction.

Indeed, the urban system is only a concept and, as such, has no other use than that of elucidating social practices and concrete historical situations in order both to understand them and to discover their laws. Although our construction in terms of urban structure makes it possible to conceive of social situations, it cannot grasp the social process of their production without a theorization

242 The Urban Structure

of the practices through which these structural laws are realized; this requires the introduction of social agents and the specific link between the structural field that I have just outlined, the problematic of the social classes and that of the political scene, through an analysis both of the interventions of the institutional system and of its being called in question by social movements. Since there is no social structure without contradictions, that is to say, without a class struggle, the analysis of the structure of space prepares the way for and requires the study of urban politics.

IV Urban Politics

As soon as one approaches the analysis of a concrete situation, the essential axis of its interpretation derives above all from its location in the political process, that is to say, from its relation to power — providing we specify that power and politics are not confined in a preferential way to a particular instance of the social structure and that the problematic of power condenses and expresses the ensemble of social relations. We will define power relations as relations between social classes, and social classes as combinations of the contradictory places defined in the ensemble of the instances of the social structure, power then being the capacity of one class or section of a class to realize its objective interests at the expense of the contradictory classes or group of classes. (Poulantzas, 1968.)

Now, although at the level of the principles of structuring a society, the economic is, in the last resort, determinant, any conjuncture (present moment) is organized first around the class struggle and, particularly, around the political class struggle, that which has as its objective the preservation or the destruction-reconstruction of the state apparatus. It is at this level, consequently, that one may map the indices of change of a spatial formation, what is being transformed, what remains, what adopts new forms in accordance with the same social logic in order to deal with new problems.

It is normal, therefore, to posit that any sociological analysis should bear above all on the political processes. But two fundamental remarks should be made at once.

1. It is clear that the analysis of the political process does not exhaust a given reality, but it constitutes its first element, for it is politics that structures the whole of the field and determines its modes of transformation.

2. In order to be in a position to study the political process in an objective way, that is to say, otherwise than in relation to itself, it is necessary to make a detour by way of a structural analysis of

its elements and by way of the laws of its social matrix. For
example, in order to understand the proletarian political struggle,
we must begin by detecting the structure of the capitalist mode of
production and establish the laws of the structurally antagonistic
relations between the possessors of the means of production and
the supports of the labour force, without which social and political
movements, as a whole, become an utter rat race, an expression of
'the irrationality' of human beings. Most of the impasses in the
social sciences stem precisely from the separation between, on the
one side, the establishment of the laws of a structure (forgetting
that these laws are merely tendential, that they are always bent
and transformed by social policy) and, on the other, the direct
apprehension of social movements and political institutions, without any other reference than to their 'past' and their 'future' —
which provides no more than a simple chronicle of their birth and
death.

The methodological principle according to which only the structural (and dominant) matrix of a society renders it intelligible, but
according to which only an analysis of the political process makes
it possible to understand a concrete situation and its transformation, supersedes the ideological structure/event dyad and brings us
nearer a scientific study, following the classics of historical materialism from Lenin to Mao, by way of Gramsci.

The same goes for the urban question.

An analysis of urban structure, while elucidating historically
given spatial forms, in which is expressed the internal logic of the
reproduction of labour power, regularly comes to a halt whenever
it is a matter of apprehending the process of the production of
these forms and of these practices, whenever one wishes to establish its laws of development and transformation. Indeed, since the
structures exist only in practices, the specific organization of these
practices produces autonomous (though determined) effects that
are not all contained simply in the deployment of structural laws.

The heart of the sociological analysis of the urban question is
the study of urban politics, that is to say, of the specific articulation of the processes designated as 'urban' with the field of the
class struggle and, consequently, with the intervention of the
political instance (state apparatuses) — object and centre of the
political struggle and what is at issue in it.

The evolution of the thematics of urban sociology also bears this
out, as urban problems become overtly political problems, that is
to say, as, in the advanced capitalist societies, the contradictions
are bound more closely together and as class domination becomes
more visible in sectors (the world of consumption) in which it had

been marked by those effects of social inequality regarded as quasi-natural.

The field of study of urban politics results, therefore, both from necessity proper to any analysis in depth of the social and from the recent historical evolution in the industrial capitalist societies; it has gradually become structured in a contradictory development that has many lessons for us.

I I

The Emergence of the Theoretical Field of Urban Politics

In the sociological tradition, the theme of urban politics is closely bound up with that of local power, understood both as political process within a community and as the expression of the state apparatus at the local level. Now, such a fusion, historically determined by the autonomy of the North American local communities, has many consequences, in so far as it amounts to treating the administration of urban problems as essentially determined by the local political scene, itself regarded as the expression of a sort of micro-society, the 'community'. Thus, introducing one of the best collections of research papers on the theme, Morris Janowitz declares that 'the community produces an independent decision-making process . . . and can be conceptualized as an independent political decision-making system', and that 'in each study the urban community is the arena in which political power is exercised . . .. The intent has been not to use the community as a research site, but rather as an object of analysis.' (Janowitz, 1961, 14–15.)

It is through the successive development of the theoretical contradictions at which community studies have arrived that the field of urban politics has gradually revealed itself. (Schmidt, 1965.)

To begin with, there is the now classic debate to be found in all school textbooks between the theses of Hunter (1953) and Dahl (1961) on the structure of local power. (These theses, incidentally, are contained in their methodological approaches.) Let us remember that Hunter, on the basis of his research into Atlanta, regards local society as a pyramid of powers, at the summit of which one finds the élite, usually made up of the businessmen of the community, recognized as powerful by the whole community (the reputational approach). Dahl, on the other hand, sets out with the idea of a political plurality, the expression of divergent, but not necessarily, contradictory interests. On the basis of a study of New Haven, he shows how alliances are formed and broken off, how partners change, how strategies get different results according to the issue, the result being in no way determined in advance and the whole depending on the decision-making process (the decisional approach).

In fact, it is quite easy, as Nelson Polsby (1963) has done, to show the lack of any empirical and theoretical foundation in Hunter's thesis, for it is only in extreme situations that one witnesses a concentration of different powers in the hands of a concrete group of individuals. Hunter, therefore, reduces the problematic of class domination to the material 'usurpation' of the levers of power of the political apparatus. But the consequences he draws from it and, following him, the whole liberal intellectual current stemming from Robert Dahl, lead to the social indetermination of the political game, since everything is a function of the mechanisms of the process of decision, in particular, strategies, and these strategies are a matter of conjuncture. Even if one does not dare to deny the initial disparity of social roles in relation to the decision-making process, one assumes a large-scale rotation of jobs (with the help of social complexity) and one grants to the actors every latitude towards reversing their inferiority, on the basis of the range of possible alliances.

Such an autonomy of the political scene in relation to social content has been questioned within American community sociology itself by a number of works: for example, those of Robert Presthus (1964) who links the socio-economic specificity of the two communities studied with the political process detected; those of Robert C. Wood (1964) who, after studying 1467 political units in New York State, concludes that the different municipal strategies have little weight in relation to the determinant factor of economic growth, which is almost totally outside local control; or, lastly, the perspectives developed with great vigour by Robert T. Alford (1968), who concludes his analysis of the recent literature on the subject by summing up perfectly the theoretical problem in question in the following terms:

If a power structure is a set of persons, then finding different people involved in different issues might lead to the conclusion that a pluralistic power structure exists. If a power structure is a set of institutions, then it may be irrelevant whether or not the same individuals are involved in different situations. The point is not that individuals who have similar resources and institutional positions will always act in the same way. Rather, the two aspects must be considered separately and resources must not be simply viewed as attributes of individuals who choose whether or not to act on behalf of political ends in particular situations, but also as systematically allocated consequences of the institutional structure of the society and political system.

This debate, which in fact, is beginning to seem dated, has structured the field of study around two elements:

1. It is generally agreed that urban politics should be regarded as a *political process*, pitting social forces against specific interests or, in liberal terminology, actors seeking to realize their project by means of different strategies.

2. Although the local political scene is directly linked to the conflictual treatment of urban problems, these problems go well beyond the political scene and involve the ensemble of the determinations of the social structure.

In the first line of analysis, the difficulty was to apply the distinction, which is not always clear in research, between the local specificity of the general political process and the political treatment of urban issues at whatever level they may exist.

What Scott Greer and Peter Orleans call 'para-politics' (1968) revives the classic theme of voluntary associations, regarded from the point of view of their location, since this constitutes their principal organizational aspect. But their inquiry into St Louis shows very well the combined play of local and global political commitment in terms of the place occupied by individuals in a social structure, without the urban issues having any influence on the process, even if they are treated *en bloc* as 'local'.

This predominance of the local political scene in the treatment of urban politics appears particularly in the work of Edward Banfield, the most brilliant liberal political theorist of urban problems in the United States, for whom local government is the ultimate issue, in so far as it must combine the service function (administration of social problems) and the political function (the regulation of conflict at the local level in questions of public interest). But he conceives the orientation of this local government as the result of the interaction of different actors who are at the base of urban politics, in particular, the press, commercial companies (especially the large stores and property companies), the municipal administrations, the voluntary associations and the trade unions. (See Banfield and Wilson, 1963, especially Chapter 2.)

Robert C. Wood (1963), on the other hand, centres the terms of the problem by reversing them, that is to say, by considering *first* the urban issues, but then adding that they become socially significant only through the political process that is woven around them. One may generalize the schema that he later proposes by differentiating, in the literature and in reality, three broad ways in which urban problems emerge and can be treated politically:

1. The administration of these problems by the institutional system (national or local, general or specific). This may be gathered together under the theme of urban planning.

2. The emergence and expression of urban issues on the basis of the mobilization and conflict of the different social groups, that is to say (to confine ourselves to a simple designation for the moment), the urban political struggle (participation, protest, confrontation).

3. The two problematics thus outlined are brought together through a study of *local political institutions*, in so far as they are both the expression of the power relations on the local political scene and the locus of articulation of urban problems at the level of the institutional system.

Such a definition of the fields does not in itself imply the preponderance of one theoretical approach over another — which reinforces its analytical richness. Indeed, in research carried out on the three themes, one may find the same fundamental opposition between the two great intellectual currents that dominate the field: the liberal analysis and the analysis centred on the determinations of the social structure, in more or less Marxist versions. This debate (whose two poles sometimes meet at the heart of the same piece of concrete research) is the real theoretical debate that is at present taking place (1970) in the field of urban politics and, perhaps, in sociology as a whole.

As far as urban planning is concerned, although everyone agrees with Ledrut (1967, 43) in regarding it as 'a means of social control or urban order' and, consequently, as a political issue, there are deep divergences as to the social signification of this means. For the whole current of American liberal analysis,[8] urban planning is an instrument of mediation, based on the 'power of experts', or on the knowledge of the possible, between the different interests involved, the lowest common denominator between the particular aims of the actors and certain overall objectives generally shared to a greater or lesser degree (for example, economic growth or the struggle against pollution). There is planning in so far as there is prediction and a will to achieve certain objectives. But this prediction is possible in a pluralist society only if there is, on the one hand, agreement as to the very foundations of the system and the

---

[8] There is a bibliography as important as it is boring on the theme of urban planning in the United States. Perhaps the best synopsis and doubtless the most interesting of the texts is that of Gans (1968). See also Altshuller, (1965) and Eldredge, vol.2 (1967).

use of institutional means as the basis of planning and, on the
other hand, discussion, negotiation, cooperation and agreement
between the different actors, in such a way as to find objectives
that are generally shared, and if one can concentrate on the problems of means, which may be resolved rationally, since rationality
is defined (according to the famous Weberian dichotomy) as
adequation of means to objectives. The analysis of urban planning
thus becomes the study of the decision-making process involved in
an urban problem (for example, housing) on the occasion of administrative action. (Meyerson and Banfield, 1955.) It is often accompanied by an analysis of the planners, who consider that it is their
professional role and who insist in particular on their mediating
action. (Daland and Parker, 1962.)

The schema proposed by Michel Crozier (1965) for the study of
French economic planning sums up the perspective perfectly, while
raising its theoretical level. An adversary of what he considers to be
an 'ideological' debate on the ends of planning, he prefers to give
priority to the study of the means, mechanisms regarded as largely
autonomous in relation to the social content that they convey and
capable of arousing their own dynamism, which may even affect
the final outcome of the process (within the framework of the
limits of the system). This approach, which renews and extends
the 'decisional' analysis, is all the more attractive in that it corresponds to a certain intelligent realism, to a sort of historical
relativism: it takes what is given, the political conflicts or the
administrative decisions in question, and shows the tangled network
of interests involved. But it does more than merely describe a
mechanism: it systematizes its observations, composes processes
and gives them a meaning by constituting them as intentional
strategies. It sets out from observations of behaviour (propositions, conflicts, alliances, compromises) and attributes to them a
true immediate meaning, by taking them as so many attempts at
maximizing individual satisfaction (or, to put it another way, as
the success of a strategy). Sociology is becoming a vast
sociometry.

This perspective which, by virtue of the ease with which it
responds to the concrete problems that face the 'decision-makers',
is assuming increasing importance, in the steps of the analysis of a
'society at a standstill', rests entirely on an ideological base, for it
is based on a metaphysical postulate, without which it becomes
pure empirical description. This postulate is that 'ultimately one
must place the accent on the freedom of man, who remains, whatever his situation, an autonomous agent capable of negotiating his
cooperation'. (Crozier, 1965, 150.) It is in fact only from the

moment that one declares this irreducible individuality (individuals or groups) that one can conceive of social action as a network of strategies emitted from a multiplicity of autonomous centres. The entire theoretical construction rests on this first affirmation, which is a matter of belief.

For who are these 'actors'? Can they be defined in themselves, without reference to the social content that they express? Why does there seem to be a concrete reality that eludes the necessary labour of theoretical redefinition (the passage from the empirical objective to the theoretical objective) that any scientific research requires? 'But in the end one is dealing with men', it will be said. Yet, but apprehended in what way? As 'citizens', or as members of a social class or class section? In which of their different roles? Placed in what social contradiction? Subjected to what ideological communication? Engaged in what political process? How can one leap over this diversity in the modes of existence of these 'concrete men', and unify them in a single first entity, irreducible to any segmentation, the autonomous source of intentionality?

It is not possible to affirm a pure transcription of social structures in practices; it is by situating the elements of social structure in a prior theoretical context that one will succeed in making significant the practices concretely observed and then, and only then, can one rediscover this supposed 'autonomy' of the 'actors', that is to say, their determination at a second level, by virtue of the fact of the specific combination of the practices that are produced in a conjuncture. That is to say, the social meaning of the actors is rediscovered as the result of research, and not as the original source of a vital flow which, in spreading outwards, creates social forms.

Let us examine the problem in greater detail. The analysis that sets out from the concrete actors and their strategies necessarily ends up in an impasse: if these actors are simply empirical objects, the analysis becomes a mere description of particular situations; if they are first realities, therefore essences, the analysis is dependent on a metaphysics of freedom; if they are 'something other', therefore combinations of particular social situations, it is unthinkable to define them independently of the content of the social positions they occupy and, consequently, to analyse the processes that unfold between them as pure exchange, since this exchange will depend on the situation of the actors in the social structure and their 'message' on the information transmitted rather than on the code used.

The theoretical impasse of the liberal perspective has gradually oriented research towards an analysis in depth of the social determinants of urban planning as a process of regulation-domination

emanating from the political instance; this orientation is manifested
both in the English-language literature (for example, in the work of
Norton E. Long, Robert Alford or Herbert J. Gans) and in the
French literature, in particular, through such studies as those of
Alain Cottereau on the history of urban planning in the Paris
region, (1969; 1970) of Marina Melendres and Françoise Lentin on
the new towns in France (1970) or that of Jean Lojkine, Claude
Liscia, Francoise Orlic and Catherine Skoda on urban planning in
Paris and Lyon. (See Lojkine 1973a; 1974, also Lojkine and
Preteceille, 1970).

Thus, for example, after establishing that 'the contradictions of
capitalist urbanization have their sources in a contradiction between
the socialization of objects of property consumption and the frac-
tioned appropriation of the media-objects' (media-object: 'a use
value the unit of which is formed by the articulation of the material
supports of other use values'), Alain Cottereau — whose work is
becoming increasingly rich and pertinent as its author passes from
a perspective of the strategic type to an analysis in terms of social
structures — is in a position to define urban planning as 'an intervention of the political instance in the economic instance, with a
view to overcoming certain contradictions of capitalist urbanization,
by means of a collectivization of urban media-objects'; developing
his schema, he is able to propose a precise interpretation of the
social signification concealed in the Parisian planning of the *métro*
in the 1930s.

Thus, for example, 'what lay behind the decision in favour of a
local underground railway system was a desire to link the various
quarters of the city, to lower rents, to facilitate building in the outskirts and safeguard the centre. It was to bring about certain useful
effects of expansion and to collectivize their distribution, thanks
to the control of a new transportation amenity, thus superseding
the usual contradictions of the "industrial" concession of public
amenities.' (Cottereau, 1970, 385—6.)

The path covered is a long one and yet the theoretical conditions
for a sociological analysis of urban planning are barely sketched
out.

The same theoretical cleavage is present in the study of the processes of protest and mobilization with regard to urban problems,
even if the lack of research on the subject hardly enables one to
appreciate its extent. (See for America, Oppenheimer, 1969; Wilson,
1963; for France, Sauvage *et al.*, 1968; Antunes and Durand, 1970.)
By way of illustration, however, one may show the constant oscillation between the two problematics in one of the few recent
studies on this theme in France, that of Bernard Poupard (1970)

on La Rochelle. In seeking to encourage a concerted decision on traffic development in the city centre, the author is able to follow the discussion about the ensemble of urban issues. He sets out from three empirically defined groups: the 'local leaders', the 'technicians' and the 'users'. In the end, he finds three other groups, defined by their relation to the urban field and to decision-making, which do not coincide point for point with the first three: 'the doers', centred on short-term technical efficiency; the 'innovators', the advocates of participation, who want a very flexible and changing urban field; and the 'radicals', centred on the concrete use of their everyday space and opposed to the monopoly of a city by the groups in power. This leads the author to conclude that 'the role of certain specific groups appears to be determinant', and that one must concentrate above all on the images of the city emitted by the groups. But, on the other hand, one discovers that 'these groups have been detected in relation to decision-making', that they 'structure the problematic of decision-making and are structured by it' (p. 21), that there is a strong correspondence between social positions and the 'informal' groups and that the 'groups reflect the organizations and milieux that stand behind them'.

What is left of the autonomy of the groups in relation to the content of decision-making? Caught up in a profound contradiction, the author concludes by remarking, with great frankness, that 'the problem is not that of the modalities of decision-making, of the process that intervenes. The problem is that decisions are "taken", that they are a power in the hands of a few' (p. 38). Being unable to extricate itself from a definition of its object centred on the actors (the groups), this study, which is otherwise handled with great finesse, oscillates between a voluntarist apprehension of urban conflicts (the projects of groups) and a final return to a problematic of manipulation by 'occult powers' that is reminiscent of Hunter's theses. And yet, throughout this study, one may read the underlying structural contradictions in the positions taken up by these groups, which merely reinforce their objective position. This research shows, in an exemplary way, the emergence of a problematic of the socially determined conflict within a theoretical space still dominated by psychologism.

On the other hand, the question is grasped with much more clarity in certain texts of the Italian extreme left – in, for example, the analysis of the *Potere Operaio* of Pisa on 'political work in the working-class quarters'. This study sets out from the need felt by the established system to achieve the political isolation of the working-class quarters, in order to be able to conduct in them an unimpeded process of reproduction and consumption. Once the social signification of this urban situation has been detected, the text goes on to show the mechanisms (apparatuses) of production of this effect of isolation (the Church, social centres, the mass media, the decentralized administrations of working-class housing) and, on the other hand, the effect of the rupture of this isolation on certain political actions carried out in the quarters (alternative-education, underground-press, cinema) and, lastly, their relation to the struggles in the factories. Such a characterization then makes it possible to situate the interventions of the Student Movement in this domain and to bring out the scope of these interventions in relation to the political objectives of the movement. This is a true perspective, opened up by the rapid reflection that concrete practice has demanded of a few militants.

Lastly, the analysis of municipal politics approaches the two aspects of the urban political process, without however exhausting them, since, on the one hand, the other echelons of the state apparatus are also intervening increasingly in this domain and since, on the other hand, a good many of the protest struggles are developing outside the institutional framework.

This theme remains dominated, in general, by the analysis of a 'decisional' type, the best representative of which is Banfield (1961) despite a few isolated studies such as those of Schnore and Alford (1963). These authors demonstrate the determination of the mode of local government (more or less decentralized) by the socio-economic characteristics of the three hundred suburbs analysed; they verify the hypothesis according to which the higher the socio-economic status, the greater the concern for efficiency (the forms are therefore centralized and not elected); conversely, the more one is dealing with working-class suburbs, the more important are the problems of the representation of the citizens (in these cases, therefore, decentralized forms, elected by universal suffrage, are preferred). Terry N. Clark's (1968, 591) ambitious attempt is situated at the convergence of the three currents ('reputational', 'decisional', 'structural'), which he tries to synthesise.

Clark's aim is to go beyond a purely decisional study in terms of 'who governs' and to determine who governs where, when and with what effects. He is concerned above all with the differential results which, on the urban plane, are achieved through the processes of local decision-making. In the most important of his researches, he has studied fifty-one American communities (with an average of 250 000 inhabitants) and related three series of variables: 1. the 'structural' characteristics of the communities (economy, population, etc.), together with certain socio-political characteristics (voluntary associations, type of local government); 2. the characteristics of the process of decision-making and, in particular, its level of centralization/decentralization; 3. the urban 'outputs', among which the researcher chose to analyse general budget expenditure and the expenditure for urban renewal.

By means of an analysis of dependence, he establishes a series of correlations between the three series of variables (most of which are much weaker than a very affirmative text would lead one to believe). These results enable him to establish the following general formula: 'the greater the horizontal and vertical differentiation in a social system, the greater the differentiation between potential elites, the more decentralized the decision-making structure, which, without the establishment of integrative mechanisms, leads to less coordination between the sectors and a lower level of outputs.' Bearing in mind, of course, that for the expenditure of urban renewal the relation observed is the reverse of the one formulated.

But the main thing is the attempt to link the realities of the social situation of a community to the study of decision-making. However, in doing this, Clark proceeds to an extension of decisional reasoning without changing its orientation. Indeed, he explains the process of decision-making by the situation of the community, but, then, confers upon it an autonomous influence over outputs, in terms of formal characteristics (centralization/decentralization), without taking into account the specific direction of the process of decision according to the social content that is imposed upon it by the issues in question.

Clark's attempt goes as far as one can go in decisional analysis without fundamentally changing the problematic, although it integrates in a very intelligent way a certain number of the objections made to the work of Dahl. But it paves the way for the flowering, within this field, of the other great intellectual tendency that is emerging more and more clearly in the study of urban politics.

It is in this sense that it is fascinating to note the evolution of the best French team in this field, that of the IEP of Grenoble which, to begin with, in keeping with Clark's perspective and in direct collaboration with him, carried out research into the structure of local power in seventeen *communes* of the Rhône-Alpes region. (Kukawka *et al.*, 1969.) Using the typological method, they characterized the towns according to their economic activity, their situation in the urban structure and the predominance of social groups, on the one hand, and, on the other, according to the essential characteristics of the local political process, then relating the two together (see Diagram I). Very serious criticisms may be made with regard to the interpretation of certain variables: thus, the

Diagram I

Socio-economic structure and local political decision in 17 communes of the Rhône-Alpes region, 1969

	Social class relations	Size and situation	Power-base	Orientation of power	Logic of the development
1. *Diversified cities (Lyon, St.-Etienne)*	Reciprocal neutralization of the groups	extent of city centre	political arbiter	regulatory	development induced by the capitalist system. Importance of national political decisions for the regional metropolises.
2. *Diversified suburbs (Oullins, Bron, Bourg-les-Valence)*	Reciprocal neutralization of the groups	suburb	political arbiter	regulatory	development induced by the city centre
3. *Suburbs with middle- and upper-class majority (Tassin-Demi-Lune)*	dominant groups: office workers, middle and upper management, industrialists	suburb	administrative	expansionist	development induced by the city centre
4. *City centres with middle-class majority (Annecy, Valence)*	dominant groups: office workers, middle and upper management, industrialists	*Annecy:* central city outside the axis of development *Valence:* central city on the axis of development	administrative	Annecy: expansionist Valence: conservative	development based on local initiatives development induced by by the capitalist system

257

5. *Traditional, middle-class communes (Albertville, Montélimar)*	dominant groups: employers and craftsmen	autonomous	notables	expansionist	development based on local initiative
6. *Agricultural commune with sudden industrialization (Pierrelatte)*	dominant groups: farmers, employers and craftsmen	autonomous	notables	conservative	development induced by national political decision (CEA)
7. *Communes possessing old industrialization with conversion problems (Bourgoin, Villefranche)*	dominant group: workers	zone of influence of the Lyon urban area	administrators	expansionist	Contradiction between two tendencies: — development compromised by the capitalist system — local initiative
8. *Stagnant communes of the mining basin (Chambon-Firminy)*	dominant group: workers	mining basin of the Loire	*Chambon* notables	conservative	— development compromised by the capitalist system and local conservatism
9. *Communist suburbs (Fontaine, Vénissieux)*	dominant group: workers	suburbs	*Firminy* administrators	expansionist	— development based on local initiative
			administrators	expansionist	— development induced by the city centre — redistribution of resources as a result of local initiative

domination of a social class is interpreted according to the demographic weight of socio-occupational categories in the *commune*,
which, astonishing as it may seem, is logical if one sets out from an
empirical apprehension of social groups and if one centres political
relations (including class relations) at the level of the vote. But,
despite its interest, the whole research project stops short: indeed,
it limits its problematic to a differentiation of the formal mechanisms of the functioning of the institutional system and, in the last
resort, has recourse to a psychology of values expressed in terms of
the orientation of power (Diagram I).

Now, such a gap between the approach and the content of the
research necessarily results from the mixture of the two problematics, for Clark's analysis, so full of eclecticism, enriches the information at our disposal concerning the only problem that decisional
analysis is really interested in: how are decisions made, how does
an institutional system function. So any roundabout reintroduction
of a problematic in terms of social classes remains artificial and
amounts, more or less, to wondering what relation may exist between the level of proletarian consciousness and the place of the
municipal orchestra in the organigram of the town hall.

The theoretical contradiction contained in Clark's perspective
must necessarily be resolved in favour of one side or the other. But
this kind of overthrow is generally the work of outside researchers
who take up the work at the point at which criticism has already
illuminated the situation. Now, in the present case, the Grenoble
team, having shown extraordinary intellectual lucidity, carried out
its own critique and laid the theoretical and empirical bases necessary to launch a new programme of research into the nature and
role of communal institutions, in terms that seem to me to define
the question perfectly and, for the first time, to subject the local
political apparatuses to rigorous scientific analysis. Their research
project defines its objectives in the following way:

> The concrete determination of the nature and role of the communal institu-
> tions will be sought by relating the interventions of the communal institu-
> tions to the structural situation of the urban milieu studied and the state of
> social relations in these urban milieux.
>
> The production of urban space may be analysed as a series of processes
> that may be broken down by analysis, in order to reveal their underlying
> social logic.
>
> This analysis enables us to situate the signification of the intervention
> of social groups in these processes:
> (a) On the one hand, by the place that social groups do or do not take up
> in the process studied (this place is in effect determined by the structural
> analysis of the process);

(*b*) On the other hand, by the transformations that these interventions and the conflicts that may accompany them may bring to the initial structural content of the process.

The approach consists, therefore, in bringing to light the coherence of a process, on the basis of the existence of a relation between structural relations (elements and combinations defining the social structure) and social relations (or system of actors). It is in relation to these processes thus analysed, particularly bringing out the sectorial interests that are involved and the contradictions to be dealt with, that it becomes possible to study the signification of the interventions, direct or indirect, of the communal institutions in relation to these processes.

Each intervention resituated in relation to the process studied, will help therefore:

(*a*) To elucidate this very process, in so far as intervention throws light on the configuration of social relations determined by the particular issue, and reveals, by the support brought to certain interests, the domination of these interests.

(*b*) To specify the nature and role of the communal institution in its relations with social groups and the state.

These interventions on the part of the communal institution may be analysed as interventions of the political in the economic, or of the political in itself or in the ideological, it being understood that most of these interventions fulfil several roles at once. Thus, by way of example, the creation of an *Agence d'urbanisme d'agglomération* is both an economic intervention (development-planning), political intervention (institutionalization of relations within the urban area) and ideological intervention (for example, the affirmation of a technocractic ideology).

The problem, therefore, is to grasp them in their complexity while specifying their principal object.

The type of analysis proposed here will involve an awareness, in the study of the role of the communal institution in relation to the processes of production of urban space, of certain determinations external to the urban milieu considered: for example, the consequence of policies of national development, government policies concerning regional and urban institutions, local administrative areas, electoral systems or, again, land policies, housing policies, etc.

The theoretical frontiers thus outlined, which have slowly appeared through a contradictory deployment, within the ideological field, or the 'urban political science', mark a qualitative change that should now be consolidated and made fruitful.

I2

Theoretical Tools for the Study of Urban Politics

Let us now try to pinpoint more clearly the different theoretical elements that we have located, and make a first attempt to construct conceptual tools sufficiently specific to attempt concrete analyses.

I Delimitation of the theoretical field

The field of 'urban politics' refers to three theoretical specifications: the political, politics, 'the urban'. I have already indicated in what way one may reinterpret the ideological frontier represented by the urban (see Part III, The Urban Structure). Let me briefly recall the precise content of the other two axes that delimit this theoretical space:

— The *political* designates the instance by which a society deals with the contradictions and dislocations between the different instances that compose it, and reflects its structural laws, expanding them, thus assuring the realization of the interest of the dominant social class.

— *Politics* designates the system of power relations. The theoretical locus of the concept of power is that of class relations. By power I mean the capacity of one social class to realize its specific objective interest at the expense of others. By objective interests, I mean the predominance of the structural elements (which define by their combination, a class) over the other elements that are in contradiction with it.

Although the field of experience thus defined has a unity of its own, namely, the articulation of *power* and of the *urban*, it may be apprehended essentially in two complementary perspectives, depending on whether one places the stress on the structures or on the practices or, to put it more clearly, whether the analysis bears on a modification of the relations between the instances in the logic of social formation or on the processes of its transformation, namely, social relations as the direct or refracted expression of the class struggle.

Although this difference of perspective is essential in the concrete approach of an investigation, it must in the end take account of the whole process, whatever its starting point may be, for the structures are merely articulated practices and practices, relations between certain combinations of structural elements.

The study of urban politics breaks down, therefore, into two analytical fields indissolubly linked in social reality: *urban planning and policy* in its various forms and *urban social movements.*

There is, therefore, on the one hand, the study of the intervention of the state apparatuses, with all their variants, in the organization of space and in the social conditions of the reproduction of labour power. On the other hand, there is the study of the articulation of the class struggle, including the political struggle, within the field of social relations thus defined. The intervention of the state apparatuses thus being an expression of the class struggle, the theoretical unity of our field of studies is obvious, in this regard. However, it is much less obvious that we should link questions relating to the organization of space to those concerning processes of consumption. This link does exist, however, at present:

1. In social practice (spatialization of problems concerning 'amenities');

2. In the ideology of the environment and its derivatives (extending the tradition of 'urban society').

We have, therefore, reasons to suspect and reasons to study such an articulation. The horizon of our research, therefore, is a double one:

1. Knowledge of certain concrete social practices;

2. Theoretical redefinition of the ideological field, which is our initial object.

We may now, at a more general level, offer an initial definition of the two types of practices that concern our analysis:

1. The process of *planning*: the intervention of the political in the different instances of a social formation (including the political) and/or in their relations, with the aim of assuring the extended reproduction of the system, of regulating the non-antagonistic relations and of repressing the antagonistic contradictions, thus assuring the interests of the dominant social class and the structural reproduction of the dominant mode of production.

2. *Social movement*: the organization of the system of social agents (conjuncture of class relations) with the aim of producing a

qualitatively new effect on the social structure (relevant effect). By qualitatively new, I mean essentially two situations:

At the level of *structures*: a change in the structural law of the dominant instance (in the CMP — capitalist mode of production — the economic, as far as the property relation is concerned).

At the level of *practices*: a modification of the power relations, running counter to institutionalized social domination. The most characteristic index is a substantial modification of the system of authority (in the politico-legal apparatus) or in the organization of counter-domination (reinforcement of class organizations).

II The system of determination of urban political practices

Every 'urban problem' is defined structurally by its place in the conjuncture of a given urban system. Its social signification and its treatment in practice depend on this.

However, it is not solely defined by its place in the urban system; it is also defined by the simultaneous determination of:
Its place in the urban system.
Its place in the general social structure, especially:
   in the process of production;
   in ideology, in particular, in the state ideological apparatuses;
   in the politico-juridical, other than at the local level.
Its place in the social organization (social organization: historically given social forms resulting from the specific articulation of the structures and practices within a domain of the real: this is what are called *effects of conjuncture*) and notably its treatment by:
The system of distribution of the product among the support-agents
The organizational system (system of means).
The material forms specific to the domain treated (ecological forms in the case of urban problems).

The links between the different systems and between the different problems thus treated cannot be established by a structural link, but by the mediation of 'actor-supports', those men-who-make-their-history-in-particular-social-conditions. These 'actors', in so far as they do not exist of themselves, but through the elements that they convey, must also be defined in a way specific to the urban system in connection with the place that they occupy in the other instances of the social structure. There is, therefore, some purpose in defining a system of urban agents, by the differential appropriation of the places in each element of the urban system, and in articulating it with:

1. The places defined in the other instances.
2. Social practices bearing on distinct specific domains of the

'urban problems' that must be treated according to the same decoding (ensemble of class relations).

We can now define:

Urban planning: the intervention of the political in the specific articulation of the different instances of a social formation within a collective unit of reproduction of labour power with the aim of assuring its extended reproduction, of regulating the non-antagonistic contradictions, thus assuring the interests of this social class in the whole of the social formation and the reorganization of the urban system, in such a way as to assure the structural reproduction of the dominant mode of production.

The urban social movement: a system of practices resulting from the articulation of a conjuncture of the system of urban agents and of other social practices in such a way that its development tends objectively towards the structural transformation of the urban system or towards a substantial modification of the power relations in the class struggle, that is to say, in the last resort, in the power of the state.

It should be observed that 'social movements' and 'urban planning' are treated in the same terms and that there is no way of studying a policy structurally without passing through the field of practices. The distinction between the two themes derives, quite simply, from a difference of approach; it is not, however, without practical effect, in so far as one may be interested in the detailed mechanisms of the emergence of an urban social movement, without studying in depth the ensemble of its structural implications.

Even if we are still at too great a level of generality, one may attempt to sum up the ensemble of these articulations in the terms of Diagram II.

On this basis, we must establish precisely the ensemble of the determinations of the system of 'urban' practices by articulating urban system, general social structure and specific conjuncture, in relation to which the analysis of a concrete situation is carried out.

III The articulation of the urban system within the general social structure

The urban system is not external to the social structure; it specifies that social structure, it forms part of it. But in every concrete practice, account must be taken of its articulation with other levels than those specified in the urban system. This articulation comes about because the urban agents necessarily occupy a position in the system of economic, political and ideological places of the social structure and also in the different relations between the

Diagram II (*)

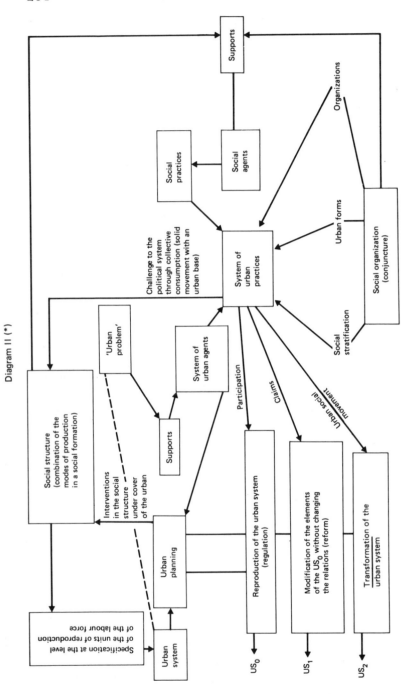

(*) **Important: the arrows do not indicate a sequential order. There is no 'triggering off' of the system, since the whole forms a complex unity continually 'in disequilibrium', because continually subject to the class struggle.**

places that define the systems in their internal structure.

In concrete terms, the urban agents will have a value (which may also be a negative value 0) in the three instances:

Places	Relations defined between *places*
Economic	
Means of production	— Relation of property
Non-labour	
Labour power	— Relation of real appropriation
Politico-juridical	
Dominant	— Regulation — integration
	(structures; practices)
Dominated	— Maintenance of order — domination (structures; practices)
Ideological	
Emission	— Communication — recognition — failure-to-recognize (practices)
Reception Transmission	— Legitimation (structures)

IV Articulation of the urban system with the social organization (Effects of conjuncture)

In every historically given society the structurally determined processes are linked with crystallized social forms, which form the specificity of each moment. 'Urban' practices emerge from the link between the articulated urban system and the general social structure, in social forms, on the basis of this triple determination of *actor-supports* and of the field of practices thus constituted.

Social organization suggests too many domains and refers to too many forms for one not to be forced to select certain particularly significant characteristics of the problem under discussion.

I have considered as fundamental in relation to our object the three dimensions of the *ecological forms* (or forms relative to the organization of space), the *social stratification* (distribution of the product among the supports) and the *organizational system*, the formal arrangement of the systems of specific means.

Places in the system of stratification

(income level; education, influence, etc.)

Lastly, the problem of *organization*, which really is central to our research if it is to be presented theoretically as a social form, requires, for its exposition, that one should have elucidated the articulation of the practices within the system of agents, for it is in relation to the fusion, the separation or the transformation of these bundles of practices that organization plays an essential role. I shall try, therefore, to specify this role after having sketched the general picture of the structural determinations of the agents and of their practices.

V The structural determination of urban practices

By urban practice I mean any social practice relative to the internal organization of the collective units of reproduction of labour power, or which, in relation to the general problems of collective consumption, takes as its field of action the urban units (because they are the units of these processes of consumption).

Places in the ecological forms

FUNCTIONS

	CONCENTRATION/ DISPERSION		Pluri-func- tionality		Mono-func- tionality

CENTRALITY	I centre	II exchangers		Produc- tion	Consump- tion	Exchange
PERIPHERY	new III towns	IV suburbs	I	1	5	9	13
		Urban types	II	2	6	10	14
			III	3	7	11	15
			IV	4	8	12	16

Urban practices form a system. But they do not, of themselves, have a signification. Their only signification is that of the structural elements that they combine. These combinations are realized by means of agents, on the basis of the determination and the multidimensional membership of these agent-supports. The field of urban practices is a system of combinations between given combinations of structural elements. It realizes and manifests, at one and the same time, the structural laws of the system, of its reproduction and of its transformation, of its organization and of its contradictions.

Diagram III summarizes the ensemble of possible determinations. Despite its complexity, it is only an outline and a social process may be read on different levels. There may, indeed, be a relating of practices, consequences and structural situations with a simple classification that combines a few fundamental elements or, conversely, an analysis of a particular process between the sub-elements. To each object of research corresponds an enlargement, contraction or particular arrangement of the field of practices and, consequently, a redefinition of the system of agent-supports. In short, everything depends on the 'problem' treated. One speaks of places and not of individuals.

What is the real contribution of this diagram?

Diagram III: System of places determining urban practices

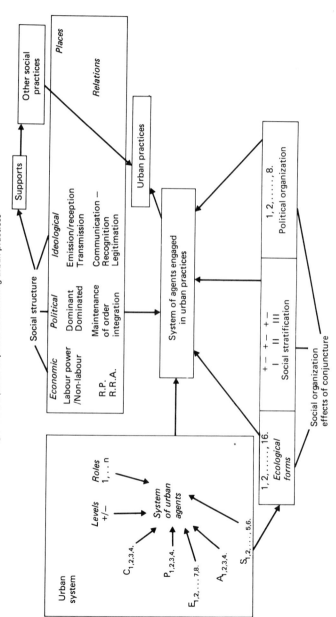

From the point of view of *structures* (the study of 'urban planning'), it enables us to study the input-output of each problem treated; or, in clearer terms, given a situation of dislocation or of contradiction in one of the processes, what are the consequences for the system, both as far as the regulation of its instances and the exercise of class domination are concerned?

From the point of view of practices, the diagram enables us both to detect the processes of formation of some of the practices (by an examination of the structural combinations on which they are based) and to define them not by their subjectivities but by their effects. By the same token, subjectivity itself is shown as playing a certain role in the social structure. Meaning has meaning only outside itself. But this outside can only be the production of a socially identifiable effect, and thus be within a predefined context.

In relation to an urban practice, one may, therefore:

Define the structural combination (manifested by the characteristics of the agents) that gave rise to it;

Name (or typologize) the practice, by an analysis of its *horizon* (structural consequences predictable in the logic of its development);

For example:

Reproduction of the urban system (regulation).

Modification of an element of the system (reform).

Reproduction, by means of the urban system, of another structural instance (maintenance of order).

Transformation of the structural law of the urban system (urban social movement).

Confrontation with the political instance (social movement with an urban base).

No effect, except the practice itself (demagogic movement).

Establish the natural history of each of these practices; hence the need to characterize the ensemble of practices that are articulated and oppose one another and to see to what extent their initial structural charge and their differential horizon make them disappear, subordinate themselves or impose themselves. The study of an urban social movement (defined by its determination and its horizon) then becomes the study of this ensemble of contradictory practices, realizing general laws, but being always unique, because conjunctural.

However, if this diagram makes a coding possible (which facilitates the collection and the correlation of the results of research, apart from their empirical diversity), it does not of itself guarantee a greater explanatory capacity and, above all, no hypotheses have been formulated as yet.

The only possible way of resolving this uncertainty is through concrete research. One may however have a certain confidence in the analytical force of the Marxist concepts that have, up to the present, increased the legibility of the social web, providing those concepts have been sufficiently specified in relation to the object in question. Now, this relative translation into urban problems has not yet been achieved.

To advance hypotheses on all the possible combinations in the table seems both excessively complicated and largely superfluous. Indeed, it is not a question of exhausting every possible situation, but of segmenting a reality with the help of these concepts and of obtaining both a testing of the general laws already known and the discovery of the new relations that show the differentiated deployment of the same logic.

For this reason I would say that there are no hypotheses relative to the diagram, but limits and operational rules. I shall provide only a few indications in order to make myself understood, though they will not have any demonstrative power — this can only come from later research. Once again, I shall distinguish two lines of reasoning, one centred on the *political* (study of planning), the other on *politics* (study of social movements).

VI Hypotheses for the study of urban planning

Let us recall that our study is centred on a society in which the capitalist mode of production is dominant. In saying that, one has not said everything (for, in particular, one must at least identify the period and conjuncture), but one has already laid down limits.

Indeed, the urban system is a dominant system, the dominant element being element P. Furthermore, the property relation cannot be fundamentally affected (at the level of the productive system, even if it is at a juridical level).

For example, if one turns to the determinations of the system with regard to urban planning in the capitalist mode of production (CMP) we know that there is a dislocation between the private control of labour power and of the means of production and the collective character of the (re)production of these two elements. · To refer concretely to our question at the level of the means of production, there is a contradiction between the highest profit obtained by a company that sets up in the already constituted industrial milieu of a large urban area, and the dysfunctioning caused by generalization, which is always subsequent to the social expression of the dislocation; it occurs as a factor accessory to the direct intervention of P in C; it expresses, in its form, the effect of the ideological on the economic; above all, it depends directly on the state of politics, that is to say, of the social pressure exerted by labour power. When the dislocation to be treated is based on a state of P, the intervention of A in P tends to occur through interventions in the other elements of the system, in particular in E.

In general, two contradictions are fundamental: that between labour power and non-labour and that between the property relation and the relation of real appropriation (productive forces). The urban problematic oscillates between two essential poles: element C (consumption) at the level of the property relation and element P at the level of the RRA. Thus, any dislocation of the system that favours consumption at RP level, runs the risk of going beyond it. Conversely, any dislocation deriving from a priority of P, at the level of RRA, runs the risk of unbalancing it by an excessive domination of element P affecting labour power.

Contradictions will be all the deeper:

as they affect the economic system;

as they affect the property relation (relations of production);

as they challenge the domination of element P (organization of the productive forces).

Any fundamental contradiction unregulated by the system leads finally to an overdetermined contradiction within the political system.

Lastly, contradictions are organized between the places of the different systems according to a content defined by the relation or relations that characterize the function of the system in the social structure (for example, for the political system, the function-relation of regulation-domination defines the places of the 'leaders-administrators' of the whole system and of the 'administered' centred on their particular interests); these places, occupied by different supports, define oppositions (contradictory situations), which are the deeper the more they are overdetermined by more general (ideologico-political) oppositions or even oppositions relative to the dominant instance (economic).

VII Hypotheses for the study of urban social movements

A social movement is born from the encounter of a certain structural combination, which contains several contradictions, with a certain type of organization. Any social movement causes, on the part of the system, a counter-movement, which is simply the expression of an intervention of the political apparatus (integration-repression) aiming at the maintenance of order.

(a) The plurality of contradictions occurs through the agents being in contradictory places within the same element of the urban system, social structure or social organization or different elements within the same relation (for example: the role of tenant or landlord within the Consumption element (housing); or labour power/non-labour within the property relation, or labour power/ means of production (C/P) within the relation of real appropriation).

One may offer the following rules:

The more contradictions have accumulated, the more there is a potentially mobilizing social charge.

The more the contradictions are in the economic or derived from contradictions in this instance, the more important they are. On the other hand, the more they are political or ideological, the more capable they are of being integrated into a regulation of the system.

The more the contradictions are divided up in their treatment, the less chance there is of confrontation and mobilization.

Direct confrontation between practices based on those structural combinations whose opposition derives from a fundamental contradiction can be resolved only by a regulation of the system or by an articulation with another contradiction. Thus, any unresolved contradiction, posed between complementary and opposed elements, leads to another contradiction. The sequence of contradictions (manifested by modifications in the system) leads to the locus of condensation of the contradictions of the system: *the political system.*

When there is lack of correspondence between the elements that define the 'actors' present, the contradictions may be expressed only through the articulation of these isolated elements in other fields of social practices.

The articulation of other practices with urban practices produces an increase of contradictions when they are defined by fundamental contradictions and vice versa.

The intervention of ideology has a particular importance at the level of the *forms* of expression of the movement: the intervention of the political, at the level of their historically given *content*; economic intervention at the level of their *dynamic* (structural horizon).

(b) The role of the *organization* (as a system of means specific to an objective) is fundamental, for, although the support-agent make possible the constitution of combinations between the structural elements, it is the organization that is the locus of fusion or articulation with the other social practices. When there is no organization, urban contradictions are expressed either in a refracted way, through other practices, or in a 'wild' way, a pure contradiction devoid of any structural horizon.

The genesis of the organization does not derive from an analysis of social movements, for only its effects are important. It is a crystallization of social practices and its characteristics will determine the consequences that it will have on certain structural combinations expressed in the system of actors.

An organization is defined, structurally, as an intervention, on the basis of a certain structural combination (*horizon of membership* defined as a combination of the characteristics of the agents of intervention) on another different structural combination that integrates it (*horizon of reference*: the sum of the combinations of the agents that compose it, if the objectives of the organization are realized).

The role of the organization in the formation of a social movement is to link the different contradictions present in the structural combinations with which they are dealing. The role of the organization in destroying the social movement is to *disperse* contradictions.

Furthermore, the organization may be born from the system of urban agents or be imported from other practices.

Fundamental hypothesis: if the organization is born from a mere relating of the elements contained in part of the system of urban agents, it does not qualitatively change the orientation and assures only the divided action determined by the different places. It is the level 0 or the organization (coordination of spontaneity) that cannot give rise to a social movement. Therefore, if the social movement is to exist, there must necessarily be the union of a sequence of contradictions in depth, which may be formed only by an organization imported from other practices. The solely 'urban' organization can only be, at most, an instrument of reform (see my typology of urban practices).

In all other cases, the organization, while intervening in the system of urban agents, has an external origin and can only be (by its own objectives, defined outside the urban system):

1. Instrument of domination
   Integration
   (class struggle in favour
   of the dominant class)

Instrument of confrontation
(class struggle in favour
of the dominated classes):

2. Economic confrontation
3. Political confrontation
4. Ideological confrontation
5. 2 + 3
6. 2 + 4
7. 3 + 4
8. 2 + 3 + 4

The organization is not the *deus ex machina* of the social movement. Its explanation eludes a specific analysis of the urban (in so
far as it is a crystallization of other practices). But the new organization, proper to the urban social movement, is perfectly analys-
able on the basis of the fusion of the characteristics of the
'imported' organization and of the structural combinations present
in the system of agents. There will be a social movement to the
extent that the practice and discourse of the organization link the
contradictions supported by the agents without loosening them in
a fragmented way (reformist ideology) and without merging them
in a single globalizing opposition (revolutionarist utopia).

There is an urban social movement when there is a correspondence between fundamental structural contradictions in the urban
system and a correct line on the part of an organization formed on
the basis of the crystallization of other practices. By correct line,
one may mean the political practice whose structural horizon corresponds to the objectives of the organization, themselves dependent on the class interests represented by the organization in a given
conjuncture.

VIII Putting research into practice

Although it is quite arbitrary to approach methodological problems
without previously delimiting a concrete object, one may at least
indicate the style of work, in order to link the theoretical preoccupation that we have been dealing with so far and the research
results that we hoped to obtain.

First, we can already specify where we should begin in the
study of urban social movements. Or, more specifically, we must
not begin where one usually begins, with organizations. It is a
question of mapping out contradictions ('problems') or indicating
the mobilizations specific to these problems. On this basis, we
must:

map the issue (or issues) and code them in structural terms;
map the social groups intervening in relation to each issue and
code them in the same terms, at different levels of depth, according to Diagram III;
characterize the organizations and determine their articulation
with the system of agent-supports.

We shall then proceed to the concrete analysis of the situation,
which will be at the same time the demonstration of a law, in so
far as the analysis realizes such a law in becoming intelligible
through the relating of the real elements subjected to our theoretical codification.

We shall have to overcome difficulties, classic in quantitative research, in applying the experimental method to a non-experimental situation. We will set out, therefore, from the hypothesis of a closed field, considering as constants all the elements not included in each specific analysis (the equivalent of the current procedures of control in quantitative research).

The technique of experimental verification that seems most adequate is that of a simulation model that functions as follows:

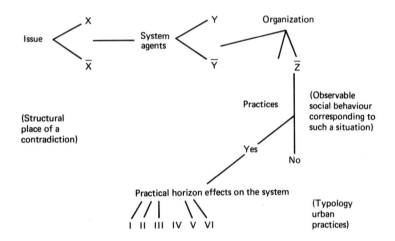

It is clear that this schema may be as complex or simple as one wishes:

in developing each element;

in changing the order of verification (one orders the model in relation to a type of practice, for example);

in combining issues.

But in any case, there are two fundamental operational rules:

1. Verification is carried out according to the presence/absence schema and according to the determination of each sequence by a single combination of elements.

2. The control procedure consists in seeing the differential organization of practices according to the distinct segmentation of the system of agents. For example, one distinguishes among different agents defined by their membership at a low level of the tenant role of C_1 — housing — by adding another criterion, refraction of the social structure at the level of the economic system (workers) and by comparing their behaviour in relation to the practice studied (for example, rent strikes).

Normally, since the situation is not an experimental one, since

it is a question of practices and not of responses to a question-
naire, it will be difficult to obtain all the controls. But, at least,
one will have at one's disposal several systems of practices, corresponding to different regroupings of the same actors and to the
treatment of various problems. On the basis of this diversity of
situations, one will have elements of comparison, and therefore of
explanation, for one will come very close to research situations
familiar to the sociologist.

The technical problems to be solved remain enormous, but we
can see our way to situating them and, consequently, in the long
term, to solving them.

If the difficulty of this course prevents us from being able to
present concrete demonstrations of its usefulness (for fundamental
links are missing and rectifications must be made), I still regard it
as valuable to present a few concrete analyses which, in their diversity, show both the difficulty of the task and the gleams of understanding that are already beginning to emerge here and there. It is
as an experiment, making possible a rectification, rather than as a
proof of our schema that I present them in order to make it
possible for the collective current that is emerging in this domain
to use our work in order to go beyond it, without, however abandoning the fruitful perspective in which we have been engaged.

13

Research on Urban Planning

On the basis of the preceding theoretical specifications, one may understand that urban planning has no univocal social signification (for the only meaning to be obtained from it in a uniform way seems to be the obligatory reference to a non-historical rationality), but that it must be interpreted on the basis of the social effect produced by the intervention of the political instance in the urban system and/or in the social structure.

A few case studies will help us to specify the extent of our analysis. In this respect, two important remarks must be made:

1. We should not identify urban planning with urbanistic plans, although the latter constitute the largest number of interventions of this kind. Indeed, very often, urbanistic plans, as documents merely expressing a doctrine or an urbanistic point of view, without obtaining means of realization, are above all ideological texts, which in no way deprives them of their social efficacity, but characterizes the intervention of the political as bearing not on the urban system, but on the general ideological instance. Our choice, in terms of the field of investigation, bears rather on operations that have been carried out or are in the course of being carried out, in so far as their effect is nonetheless more direct than in the case of master plans or white papers.

2. Furthermore, let us point out once again that, in a concrete analysis, the distinction between urban planning and social movements has no great meaning, for planning is also a form of class political practice, and social or confrontational movements directly affect the content and process of any urbanistic operation (if only by their absence, when they do not exist). In any case, our concrete studies of both themes will constantly show this link. Thus the distinction made has meaning only because our aim here is not so much to account in a very detailed way for a given

historical reality, as to test, very incompletely, certain theoretical tools that may in fact have specific features both in the political and in politics.

Lastly, it is clear that the case studies presented do not realize the whole of the schema worked out, especially as this schema was developed, reshaped, made more detailed, as our concrete research proceeded and as it is therefore in advance of that work in so far as we are trying above all, for the moment, to obtain working tools rather than to enclose ourselves in the alternative of blind description or a hasty rounding off of a theoretical model. However, they may show the concrete difficulties and the temporary contributions of the perspective outlined.

I The British New Towns

A halo continues to surround the experience of British urbanism, which is often presented as the supreme example of continuity in an urban project, from Howard's Garden Cities to the realization, in twenty years, of eighteen new towns, accommodating, in 1966, 650 000 people and providing a community environment (14 towns were started between 1946 and 1950).

Now, rather than plunging into a discussion of the town model thus elaborated, I have preferred to study it as a social process and to bring out the meaning of this urbanistic operation on the basis of an analysis of the contradictions underlying the intervention, and of the ensemble of the social, political and institutional relations that are linked together in such a situation. Since the British experience is widely known, I shall not spend too much time describing the historical and urban data, but will provide enough information to buttress my analysis of it.[9]

The new towns were above all a response to the urban (social and functional) crisis of the London region, resulting from excessive industrial concentration produced by the technological and economic evolution of British capitalism, according to the well known movement of the formation of the metropolitan regions. However, this concentration was particularly acute in Britain as a result of the transformations produced within the old industrial

[9] My analysis is based partly on a personal investigation carried out during the visit to the new English towns in 1956 and partly on historical and documentary research carried out in 1969 at the University of Montreal during a research seminar on urban planning. Miss Robitaille and Mr Leduc, under my direction, carried out a well documented study on which most of this section is based. For the basic data the following works of reference are worth citing: Ashworth (1954), Foley (1963), Rodwin (1956), Orleans (1962), Abercrombie (1959), Osborn and Whittick (1963), Nadge (1962), Mission d'etude de L'IAURP (1967), Merlin (1969).

base, centred on raw materials and on the conglomerates of traditional textiles. In the terms of our analysis of the tendencies of industrial location (see Part III), it might be said that one is witnessing a passage from a β dominance to a γ and α dominance combined, both centred on the urban, as market and as technological milieu.

This tendency, which is peculiar to industry, is duplicated, on the one hand, by the increasing 'tertiarization' of the productive system and the constitution of vast organizations and, on the other hand, by regional disparities, produced by the unequal development of capitalism. The particular interest of each company, seeking to maximize its profit, thus comes into contradiction with the balance of the whole, in the sense that such a spatial concentration of activity, if left to itself, produces a whole series of contradictions within the urban system of the London region, while accentuating the imbalance between the regions. In order not to weigh down my description with too much detail, I have summarized in Diagram IV the effects produced by this evolution of the productive system on the different elements of the urban system and the principal consequences that emerge from it. (For each of the processes indicated, I assume that the reader is familiar with the analyses in Part III of the social determination of the urban effects treated here; I shall content myself, therefore, with abbreviations and general formulations by way of reminders.)

This critical situation was maintained for a long time, worsening, it is true, more and more, but without arousing other reactions than those indispensable to the maintenance of order and to the reproduction of labour power. On the part of the institutional system, the only regulatory intervention at this level concerned housing; private enterprise proved quite incapable of responding to minimum needs, for lack of solvent demand: between 1919 and 1937, two-thirds of working-class housing was subsidized by the government. But apart from this, no regulatory agency was set up before the war. (The Greater London Regional Planning Committee, set up in 1927, was axed ten years later without having taken the slightest initiative.) As far as social forces were concerned, the experience of the industrial cities of the nineteenth century had already aroused the utopian reaction of the 'garden cities' movement, a very ambiguous movement in that it expressed a profoundly felt demand on the part of the working class, but in a backward-looking ideological envelope — Donald Foley (1960) has revealed the close links of this movement with the dominant values of the Establishment.

Why 1944, then? Why the Abercrombie Plan? And, above all,

279

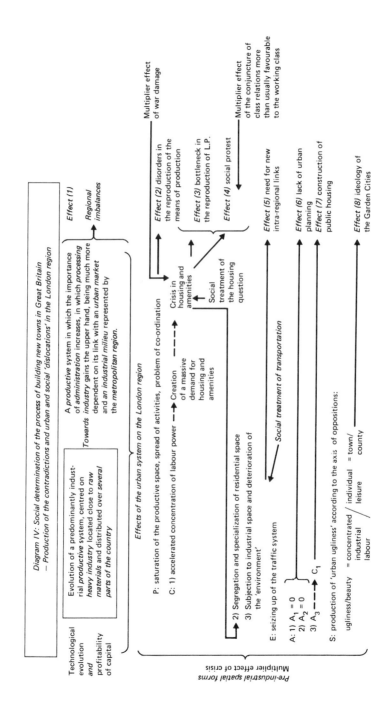

Diagram IV: Social determination of the process of building new towns in Great Britain – Production of the contradictions and urban and social 'dislocations' in the London region

Technological evolution and profitability of capital

Evolution of a predominantly industrial *productive* system, centred on *heavy* industry located close to *raw materials* and distributed over *several parts of the country*

Towards A *productive* system in which the importance of *administration* increases, in which *processing* industry gains the upper hand, being much more dependent on its link with an *urban market* and an *industrial milieu* represented by the *metropolitan region*.

Effect (1)

Regional imbalances

Effects of the urban system on the London region

P: saturation of the productive space, spread of activities, problem of co-ordination

C: 1) accelerated concentration of labour power ⟶ Creation of a massive demand for housing and amenities

Crisis in housing and amenities ⟵ Social treatment of the housing question

Effect (2) disorders in the reproduction of the means of production

Effect (3) bottleneck in the reproduction of L.P.

Effect (4) social protest

2) Segregation and specialization of residential space

3) Subjection to industrial space and deterioration of the 'environment'

E: seizing up of the traffic system

Social treatment of transportation

A: 1) $A_1 = 0$
2) $A_2 = 0$
3) $A_3 - - - ▶ C_1$

S: production of 'urban ugliness' according to the axis of oppositions:

ugliness/beauty = concentrated / individual = town/
                   industrial   leisure   county
                   labour

Effect (5) need for new intra-regional links

Effect (6) lack of urban planning

Effect (7) construction of public housing

Effect (8) ideology of the Garden Cities

Multiplier effect of war damage

Multiplier effect of the conjuncture of class relations more than usually favourable to the working class

Pre-industrial spatial forms
Multiplier effect of crisis

why was intervention carried out with such vigour after the passing
of the New Town Act of 1946? Certainly, the Barlow Report had
already posed the problem clearly enough in 1939 but, based above
all on industrial decentralization, it did not provide, of itself, an
instrument of effective intervention.

The destruction caused by the Nazis considerably aggravated the
housing crisis: in the County of London, nine houses out of ten
had been damaged. But the decisive element, without any doubt,
was the political conjuncture, with the upsurge of working-class
political awareness and the electoral triumph of the Labour Party,
which reinforced the pressure for change and required satisfaction
on the level of demand, in order not to radicalize the class struggle
(given the reformist outlook of the Labour Party). At the general
election of 1945, 98% of the Labour candidates and 84% of the
Conservatives mentioned the urban problem in their electoral
speeches.

However, the Abercrombie Plan went well beyond a mere programme of housing and collective amenities. Following in the path
of the Barlow Report, it aimed at decentralizing the activities of
the Greater London region, halting its growth and structuring it,
by means of a zoning in four concentric rings: 1) an urban belt,
corresponding to the zone already urbanized in 1944, whose
density had to be diminished; 2) a suburban belt, characterized by
dispersed low-density housing; 3) the green belt, made up of
agricultural land in which recreational facilities would be developed
and urban growth strictly controlled; 4) the outer belt, which was
to take the population from the centre of London and which
would be divided into eight new towns and existing towns which
were to be developed.

The new towns, then, were an additional element in a programme, the axis of which was decentralization and the constitution of urban ensembles, economically autonomous and socially
well equipped, in which the districts, based on single-family houses,
would provide both the countryside and a sense of community.

Now, it is obvious that such a reorganization of space which,
like most urbanistic documents, preserved an internal coherence
and envisaged a model of urban development, involved a direct
intervention in the productive system (A → P) essentially as far as
the relation of real appropriation was concerned, but also in the
property relation (meaning social control, not just legal ownership,
as in the case of nationalization). In essence, the Plan proposed:
1) that no new industry be admitted into the County of London
or into the surrounding counties and that regulations should
control the growth of already existing industries; 2) that several

industries be moved beyond the Green Belt. The following are the means actually used to intervene in P.

From 1945 onwards, companies wishing to extend the ground area they occupied by over 5000 square feet had to obtain special permission from the government (the ineffectiveness of the measure was discovered later and, in 1965, the limit was lowered to 1000 square feet for the southeast of England). After the war, the official policy of the government encouraged the location of industries in the new towns around London, that is to say, the Board of Trade suggested that companies should look for a new location. Today, more concrete methods of encouragement are used (but never coercion): companies who agree to set up plant in the new towns of Scotland (a 'development area') are given subsidies that represent 25% of the cost of constructing buildings, 10% of the cost of equipment and tax advantages in the form of shorter repayment periods. Furthermore, the 'development corporations' of the new towns carry out a propaganda campaign directed at the heads of companies, offering either standard factories and offices already built, or building land, with amenities, let by the corporation. But no legislative measure was taken to control the use of offices in London before 1964, while an accelerated growth and concentration in the activities of information and administration were taking place.

If, therefore, intervention was made in certain developments of the industrial environment (A → P$_3$) the essence of the movement of P and therefore of the whole of the urban system was not affected. It presents a specific realization, therefore, of the fundamental laws of capitalist urban planning: the difficulty of intervention in P and the dependence of any other intervention on this first.

As far as action on exchange is concerned, one may almost say that it has been non-existent. Indeed, in the minds of the planners, industrial and residential deconcentration was a necessary option to make it possible, indirectly, to regulate the problem of exchange by the ending of commuting into and out of London. The new towns, at an average distance of twenty-five miles from London, were conceived as autonomous centres thanks to the establishment of a balance in the employment/active population ratio. The Reith Commission (1945) recommended that the new towns should be situated along a railway (for commercial and industrial transportation and for people's occasional visits to the mother-city) and close to the great road junctions of the region, so that they might be connected as directly as possible. As we have seen, such a policy did not bring a direct answer to the problem since its solution depends on previous interventions in the sources of the intra-urban transfers.

So there remained intervention in consumption, housing and amenities, but also in the urban environment which, in fact, was now being brought into the extended programme of housing estates. However, the new towns did not result merely from an amenities programme: presented as the concrete realization of the old English utopia and expected to respond to the strong current of working-class demand, they express this utopia in the ecological form in which they have been realized.

They are characterized, first, by a concern to constitute 'complete' communities, that is to say, with adequate local employment; secondly, by their isolation, the almost intentional lack of links with the metropolis; and, thirdly, above all, by the mode of life that one wished to create: single-family houses constituting neighbourhood units, abundant green spaces, community centres, an almost total absence of places of entertainment (dance halls, cinemas), whereas there was a proliferation of churches and social centres. It represented a resumption of the old ideology of social reform through the modification of the environment. In any case such a form, and above all the type of industry attracted by such a situation, determined the nature of the resident population — middle managers, technicians and the upper reaches of the working class. It is this intervention in the urban symbolic that gave its stamp to the new towns, and this intervention must be understood as presenting the realization of the urban model proposed where there was merely an amenities programme.

These fundamental features of the new towns explain the institutional process of their realization. As it was a question both of the direct intervention of the state apparatus in consumption and an attempt to create an urban context appropriate to the ideological project, the initiative came from a sector of the apparatus concerned with consumption (the Ministry of Housing), but this apparatus, in accordance with the community project, delegated its powers to a state body at the local level (the Development Corporations), possessed of 'full powers' within the framework laid down (see the organigram of the institutional machinery in the new towns). Since local authorities have little weight and since it was a question of building a town, everything depended on a single centralized body, possessing financial and legal powers, supported by working-class organizations (since it was a response to their demands) and in no sense impeded by the companies, which were subjected to no constraint and which, on the contrary, were actually encouraged to establish themselves there. This explains the rapidity and efficiency of the realization of a programme combining the best conditions that a technocrat could dream of. It should be noted that these conditions, in turn, were such because of the precise urbanistic content that I have just established.

What remained, therefore, apart from the 'new towns, centres of new harmonious social relations'? Very little: the region of Greater London left to itself. The Abercrombie Plan had decided that it would increase no more. But this hypothesis depended on the realization of the conditions of urban control (A → P), implicit in the Plan. The theoretical error of the plan is socially determined: to be coherent with itself, it had to be incoherent in relation to a reality perceived as pure obstacle to change, without class interests. Now, the London region increased, between 1946 and 1956, by 1·7 million people, the new towns absorbing only 19% of this increase. All the problems remained as acute as ever. Faced with this disturbance in the reproduction of the means of production, a new rhythm of planning was established, based directly on economic functioning and intervening in P very indirectly, through action on transportation and on a complex system of incentives and developments. The most concrete expressions of this new orientation were the regional plan of the southeast region and the administrative reform of 1964, which tried to reform local institutions from a technical point of view (see Diagram V, which summarizes the essential determinations of the process).

The 'new towns' were swept up by this vast tide and have developed satellites, perhaps better endowed with amenities, which depend on other less 'new' urban areas.

First, on the work plane: in the best equipped towns (the first to be built, such as Harlow and Crawley), 20% of the population work elsewhere, for office jobs have not followed the demographic evolution; but in one of the newest communities, in Scotland, 50% of the population work outside. It is above all the weekend that sees the inhabitants of these new communities desert their boy-scout villages and seek the centre of the urban areas, in quest of the mirages that mass consumption could not fail to project on to these one-time new places: because of the lack of good public transport-links with the metropolis, the rate of individual motorization has reached extraordinary proportions. At last the habitat is beginning to feel the result.

The legend of British urbanism is diluted in the uniform everydayness of the residential suburbs of the great metropolis.

II Urban renewal in the United States

American urban renewal is one of the most enormous urban pro-

284

Administrative and Financial functioning of the new towns programme

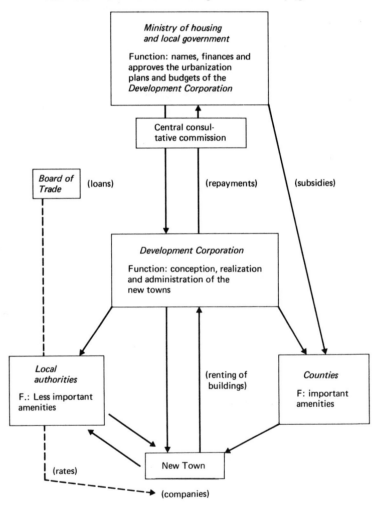

Ministry of housing
and local government

Function: names, finances and
approves the urbanization
plans and budgets of the
Development Corporation

Central consul-
tative commission

Board of
Trade   (loans)   (repayments)   (subsidies)

Development Corporation

Function: conception, realization
and administration of the
new towns

Local
authorities   (renting of   Counties
                              buildings)
F.: Less important   F: important
amenities   amenities

(rates)   New Town

(companies)

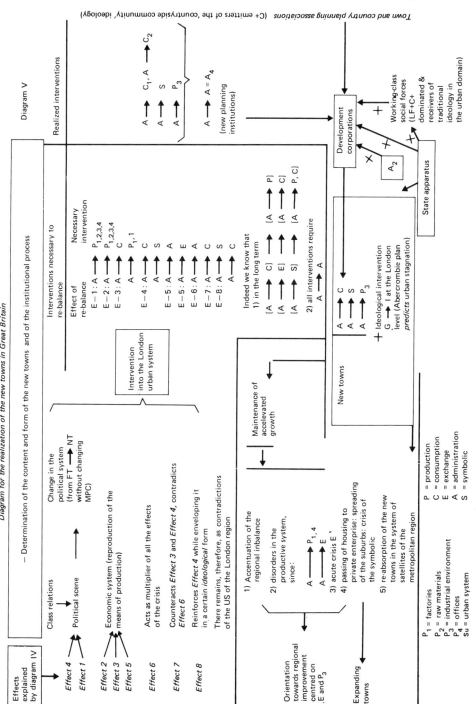

Diagram for the realization of the new towns in Great Britain

grammes that has ever been undertaken, even if its proportions seem more modest when compared to the power of the construction industry in the United States.[10] Nevertheless, between 1945 and 1968, over 7 thousand million dollars were handled by renewal bodies and 1946 projects were approved involving 912 municipalities.

But what is even more striking than its dimensions is the way in which this programme is a political issue for the White House, which for years has made it one of the themes of its pseudo-reformist propaganda; for 'honest reformers', who saw in it a means of fighting poverty and discrimination; and for the radical critics who have constantly denounced the enslavement of the programme to the interests of the construction companies.

[10] This analysis is based on an inquiry carried out in 1969 in the United States, with the help of the University of Chicago. Although I made several visits and had personal interviews, most of the work was provided by the mass of data and documents collected. Given the aims of the research (bringing out the main outlines of this phenomenon while developing a method of approach), I regarded a statistical treatment of the data presented here as being of relatively secondary importance.

The documentation on urban renewal in the United States is both very vast and inadequate. Indeed, innumerable studies, more of a technological than a sociological nature, have been devoted to particular operations, but it is difficult to establish comparisons on different definitions and, consequently, almost impossible to bring out the deeper tendencies on the basis of an accumulation of particular data. A first synthesis was attempted, in an extremely brilliant way, by M. Anderson, then a student at Harvard. His doctoral thesis (MIT Press, 1965) is a polemical presentation of the official data on urban renewal. Despite its conservative ideological bias (for it sets out to demonstrate that private enterprise is a better instrument for solving urban problems), it is the best source of data and references for the period studied, that is to say, up to 1962. Now, since then, a large number of new projects have been undertaken. For recent years, the basic document is a report that sets out to give an overall view of American urban problems This report embodies the conclusions of the National Commission on Urban Problems (NCUP, 1968) set up at the request of Congress and which is supposed to provide the basis of information and analysis for American urban policy. The best account of the analyses of urban renewal is the interdisciplinary work published under the editorship of J. Q. Wilson (1966). Another collective work that covers much the same ground as Wilson is Bellush and Hausknecht (1967). There are two other works intended as analytical syntheses of the programme of urban renewal. That of Greer (1965) is a clear and intelligent presentation of the essential features of the programme, with particular attention given to the social processes that condition the urbanistic content. I owe some of the main ideas of my analysis to this work. On the other hand, the work by Abrams (1965) is too general and 'balanced' an essay and contributes little in the way of new data. For a defense of the achievements of urban renewal from the side of the federal administration, see Slayton (1966) and Weaver (1966). For a relatively 'progressive' critique of the programme, see Gans (1965; 1968). A good journalistic account, full of data and references, is that of Lowe (1967). For official sources see *Journal of Housing* published by the federal services for urban renewal and housing, and *Housing and Planning references* published by the US Department of Housing and Urban Development. Finally, other information and references have been provided by the following: Wheston (1968) Stewart (1965), Doxiadis (1866) National Planning Association (1963), Schretter (1967), Rose (1968), Rapkin and Grigsby (1966). This analysis takes up the themes of my article (1970) in *Espaces et Sociétés* in a different and at once more condensed and more developed form on the theoretical plane.

What social contradictions justified such an accelerated effort throughout the years and made it so obviously a controversial matter? Indeed, other federal initiatives, like the programme of building freeways or the subsidies to agriculture, have been financially more important. And although it is obvious that renewal played a considerable ideological role in the image that Johnson wished to give to his Great Society, this was merely a secondary effect, soon dismissed as a gimmick to the profit of the Model Cities Program and frankly relegated to second place, in publicity terms, to the benefit of the pet theme of Nixon and Moynihan: the theme of the environmeht, of which urban renewal becomes a mere element. The programme itself has been profoundly transformed since its slow take-off with the Housing Act of 1949, giving increasing priority to the problems of the 'urban context' over those of housing, in particular, with the amendments of 1954 and 1961.

Although the text and speeches on this theme take up the whole urban problematic, one may centre the social efficacity of renewal by studying the characteristics of the space redeveloped and the social and functional content of the operations realized. However, these interventions are themselves determined by the present contradictions in the urban structure of the great American metropolises, whose model of development I have sketched elsewhere (see above, Parts I and III). Diagram VI recalls the principal processes at the root of these contradictions on the basis of the production of five 'social effects' which, running counter to the interests of the dominant classes and disturbing the functioning of the urban system, 'demanded' intervention, this 'demand' being conveyed by the institutions and social groups directly concerned in each case (see Diagram VII, which presents the whole process of renewal).

There are, therefore, three principal contradictions at the root of these renewal programmes:

1. The deterioration of the habitat in the city centres and the formation of slums.

2. The development of social conflict, particularly among the black community.

3. The crisis of what may be called urban centrality in the great metropolises (see Part III), with its various components.

Our research will consist in asking ourselves how these three contradictions have been treated by the programme of urban renewal, or rather, how this programme and the processes that are articulated around it have been determined by the nature of the questions that they raise. My arguments will operate at the level of the United States as a whole. Even if this procedure is crude, in view

288

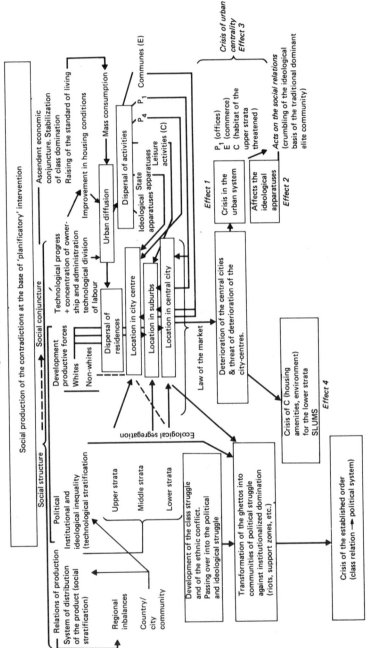

Diagram VI: URBAN RENEWAL USA

of the extraordinary variety of local situations, it is enough to bring out the profound social signification of renewal, even if it does not show in each case the specificity of the realization of this content.

A The struggle against the slums

If one really did wish to start a campaign to eliminate the deteriorated habitat, one would have to attack rural residences and the small towns rather than the metropolitan regions: 64% of deteriorated housing is outside the metropolitan zones, 60% is in rural localities.

However, the poor quarters of the large cities spread enough misery for honest folk to concern themselves with it. Is this one of the determinants of American urban renewal?

If it were a question of demolishing the slums, there would be no doubt: 400 000 homes have already been demolished; in 1963, 609 000 people were displaced by the renewal programme and the forecasts for 1973, according to the present programme, provide for 3800 dehoused occupants.

But, of course, these people have to be rehoused and in order to do this one must construct enough homes at rents that the dehoused can pay. Now, although the 400 000 demolished homes were obviously let at low rents, out of the 125 999 planned on the same sites, 62·3% could be of interest only to residents of middle and high income. Only 41 850 cheap homes were built. This means that only a little over 10% of the 400 000 homes with low rent demolished have been rebuilt in the same area.

It could not be otherwise, since the programme is intended to create such conditions that private initiative may revive the town centres (see below). Consequently, developers build, and not always then, only what they are forced to build on very favourable terms.[11]

But one cannot arrive at a conclusion as to the 'housing objectives' of renewal simply by considering the achievements defined in this institutional context alone. One might have thought, indeed, that the renewal programme was simply intended to reanimate the city and that it represented only a part of an overall plan, which,

[11] The housing act of 1968 tried to face this problem by laying down that half the housing built in the redeveloped areas should be used for low-rent or moderate-rent dwellings. The effects of this law should take some time to be felt, for it only concerns future projects and not those that have already been approved. The weakness of this arrangement is that it does not fix a number of dwellings to be built but makes this number dependent on the total volume of housing construction. In view of the growing proportion of non-residential installations in the redeveloped zones, one may well fear that this measure may encourage the tendency towards a diminution of the role of housing in renewal projects.

as far as the residential function was concerned, was rounded off by
the public housing programme. Thus, the displaced families would
be rehoused elsewhere, in more comfortable conditions. But the
public housing programme has fallen short of the scope that it
assigned itself. In 1949, Congress authorized the construction of
810 000 homes in six years. In fact, by 1967, only 480 000 had
been built. The reason for this failure must be sought essentially in
the opposition of 'middle-class' public opinion to this type of housing. With over 50% of the occupants black and a high concentration
of lower strata, it became the focus for every possible prejudice.
The accumulation of families in a 'deviant' situation in relation to
the dominant culture helped to discredit the only public programme
of help to the badly housed and irremediably slowed down its rate
of achievement. (Fisher, 1959; Lowe, 1967; Schnore, 1968.) Thus
the comparison, city by city, between low-rent housing demolished
and public housing constructed presents a balance-sheet which not
only is not positive, but is actually negative (see Table 49). If,
instead of taking into consideration, as the table does, the units
constructed before 1949, we compare the demolitions and constructions carried out during the implementation of the urban renewal programme (1949–1969), the debit balance, for the 73
towns analysed, amounts to 166 492 homes.

But, it will be said, was it necessary, then, to let people go on
living in wretched conditions? Obviously not, but that is not the
question. For once these houses are demolished, where are the
people supposed to go? Let us leave to one side the whole problem
of the destruction of 'community life', which is too often idealized
and ask ourselves, quite simply: where do they go? And it is here
that the second series of data tends to indicate the failure of urban
renewal from the point of view of its impact on the housing problem. I am speaking of a tendency, because an aura of mystery
surrounds the statistical data on the rehousing of persons displaced
by the projects of urban renewal.

In order to help the displaced, special payments are envisaged,
which may amount to as much as $200 per family. In reality, up
till 1967, the payments made were the following:

Table 50
Rehousing allowances (until 1967)

	Number of cases	*Removal expenses* (allowances paid)
Families	158 543	$95·32 (average for each family)
Individuals	64 114	$65·58 (average for each individual)

Source: Report of the National Commission..., 1968, p. 163.

The payments were well below the legal ceiling and did not involve all the displaced — and it is the only financial compensation received by tenants forced to move.

The data on the fate of the persons displaced are contradictory. The study carried out by the University of South California, in 1961, concerning 47 252 families from 41 towns showed that 25·9% moved into the housing recommended by the local authorities. Of these only 30% fell back into unhealthy housing. But among the 74·1% who found new homes for themselves, 90% were in deteriorated housing. (Reynolds, 1961.)

An examination of the data concerning several American towns leads Chester Hartman (1964) to conclude that a high proportion of the families displaced are now in deteriorated housing while paying higher rents; this is the case for 43% of those displaced in Chicago in 1957–58, 72% in Philadelphia, 18% in New York-Manhattan and 22% in Boston-West-End. (See also Meltzer, 1953.)

This is why the results of an official inquiry by the US Housing and Home Finance Agency (1966), carried out in 1964, into the fate of the rehoused was received with great scepticism.

In effect, according to the inquiry, based on a representative sample, 94% of the families were properly rehoused. The result is astonishing, for if, in fact, there were so many good homes available and accessible to families of modest income, why did these families remain in slums? One can only guess at the hypothesis underlying these figures: that there is a 'resistance to change' rather than a real problem.

Serious criticisms have been made of this inquiry, concerning in particular the number of households sampled who were not found (one-sixth of the sample), the fact of taking into account only families and not isolated individuals and, above all, the use of a 'generous' definition of proper housing. (Hartman, 1965; NCUP, 1966; Report of the NCUP, 1968, 93.)

In any case, where the figures are in agreement is on the fact of a considerable rise in rent for the families rehoused; rent represents, in effect, 28% of the family budget (instead of 25%) for the median of distribution.

Since public housing does not follow the rate of demolition (see Table 51), the people displaced have no other recourse than that provided by the market. Now, whereas a new home costs $150 a month, 50% of the families in the slums can pay only between $35 and $50, and the other half only between $65 and $110. (NCUP, 1968, 10.)

What are the chances on the market for the 13·3% of the 'poor' in the American population? We also know that certain families

Table 49

Comparison between public housing constructed and housing demolished by urban renewal in the United States
Data on 73 towns

Towns	Public housing constructed				Housing demolished		
	Planned 1949	Constructed 1949–67	Total 1967	Total dem. equivalent	Dem. by urb.–ren.	Total dem.	Surplus Deficit
New York, N.Y.	14 171	50 462	64 633	22 717	33 697	56 414	+ 8 219
Chicago, Ill.	8 483	24 477	32 960	5 338	26 058	31 396	+ 1 564
Los Angeles	3 468	5 819	9 287	1 689	4 641	6 330	+ 2 957
Philadelphia	3 248	12 471	15 719	6 280	15 856	22 136	− 6 417
Detroit, Mich.	4 879	3 301	8 180	847	11 216	12 063	− 3 883
Baltimore, Md	5 021	5 314	10 335	8 810	8 661	17 741	− 7 136
Houston, Tex.	2 251	348	2 599	2 210		2 210	+ 389
Cleveland, Ohio	5 179	2 279	7 458	3 977	5 095	9 072	− 1 614
Washington, D.C.	3 147	6 909	10 056	1 941	7 127	9 068	+ 988
St Louis, Mo	1 315	5 930	7 245	2 022	9 156	11 178	− 3 933
Milwaukee, Wis.	651	2 415	3 066	423	3 703	4 126	− 1 060
San Francisco	1 741	4 142	5 883	3 234	5 554	8 788	− 2 905
Boston, Mass.	5 102	5 871	10 973	8 480	8 906	17 386	− 6 413
Dallas, Tex.	1 750	4 622	6 372	946		946	+ 5 426
New Orleans	5 381	6 889	12 270	4 071	342	4 413	+ 7 857
Pittsburg	4 463	4 771	9 234	3 330	7 191	10 521	− 1 287
San Antonio	2 554	3 009	5 563	1 858	1 622	3 480	+ 2 083
San Diego	1 068	2 452	3 520	511	190	701	+ 2 819
Seattle, Wash.	2 571	1 799	4 370	1 800	2 715	4 515	− 145
Buffalo, N.Y.	3 818	2 404	6 222	3 084	9 012	12 096	− 5 874
Cincinnati, Ohio	3 305	1 740	5 045	1 928	3 233	5 161	− 116
Memphis, Tenn.							

293

City							
Denver, Colo.	770	2 826	3 596	3 030	852	3 882	− 286
Atlanta, Ga.	5 188	3 794	8 982	5 466	6 264	11 730	− 2 748
Minneapolis	464	2 825	3 289	305	.7.364		− 4 380
Indianapolis	748		748				− 748
Kansas City		2 383	2 383	1 171	3 173	4 344	+ 1 961
Columbus, Ohio	1 352	1 529	2 881	1 193	3 309	4 502	−11 621
Phoenix, Ariz.	604	1 000	1 604	733		733	+ 871
Newark, N.J.	2 711	8 180	10 891	3 517	5 486	9 003	+ 1 888
Louisville	3 005	1 957	4 962	4 182		10 638	− 5 676
Portland, Oreg.	400	1 059	1 459	51	6 456	1 705	− 246
Oakland, Calif.	922	1 094	2 016	920	1 654	2 594	− 578
Fort Worth	502	572	1 074	2 082	1 674	2 082	− 1 008
Long Beach							
Oklahoma City	354	464	818	2 423	368	368	+ 450
Rochester, N.Y.		256	256	356	767	767	− 511
Toledo, Ohio	1 440	513	1 953	1 280	943	3 366	− 1 413
St Paul, Minn.		2 354	2 354	1 347	2 107	2 463	− 109
Norfolk, Va.	730	2 990	3 720		4 763	6 043	− 2 323
Omaha, Nebr.	1 078	1 370	2 448	1 736		1 347	+ 1 101
Honolulu	361	2 149	2 510	442	1 842	1 842	+ 668
Miami, Flo.	1 318	3 140	4 458	772	959	2 695	+ 1 763
Akron, Ohio	550	219	769	3 095	1 201	1 643	− 874
El Paso, Tex.	660	990	1 650	2 037		722	+ 928
Jersey City	1 600	2 204	3 804	1 622	1 199	4 294	− 490
Tampa, Flo.	1 682	2 010	3 692		1 470	3 507	+ 185
Dayton, Ohio	1 191	1 143	2 334	837	3 359	4 981	− 2 647
Tulsa, Okla.		72	72		822	822	− 750
Camden, N.J.	1 102	932	2 034	917	713	1 550	+ 484
New Haven	1 035	1 092	2 127	1 228	3 801	4 718	− 2 591
Nashville	1 578	3 310	4 888	2 705	3 201	4 429	+ 459
Providence	1 056	1 916	2 972	642	3 245	5 950	+ 2 978
Syracuse	678	981	1 659		1 310	1 952	− 293

[cont'd over]

Towns	Public housing constructed			Housing demolished			
	Planned 1949	Constructed 1949–67	Total 1967	Total dem. equivalent	Dem. by urb–ren.	Total dem.	Surplus Deficit
Hartford	1 879	666	2 545	1 165	1 769	2 934	− 389
Paterson	300	1 990	2 290	896	1 280	2 176	+ 114
Scranton		888	888	490	1 251	1 741	− 853
Mobile	398	3 005	3 403	390	1 566	1 956	+ 1 447
White Plains					74	74	− 74
Little Rock	250	914	1 164	482	2 598	3 080	− 1 916
Winston Salem		1 538	1 538	149	2 400	2 549	− 1 011
Kansas City		554	554		1 849	1 849	− 1 295
Atlantic City	610	288	898	610	287	897	+ 1
Sacramento	478	282	760	767	1 087	1 854	− 1 094
Freno, Calif.	210	909	1 119	279	1 296	1 575	− 464
Springfield	340	392	392		1 411	1 411	− 1 019
New Britain	398	290	630	452	761	1 213	− 583
Stamford		429	827	717	459	1 176	− 349
Huntsville		1 555	466	271	1 284	1 555	+ 271
Worcester	264	939	939	711	534	1 245	− 306
Erie. Pa.	618	622	886	315	610	925	− 39
Cambridge	406	365	983	634	277	911	+ 72
McKeesport		598	1 004	717	550	1 267	− 263
Total 73 towns	126 496	230 795	357 291	142 021	255 266	397 287	− 40 004

Source: National Commission on Urban problems.

did not even have enough money to be accepted into public housing. (NCUP, 1968, 133.) Other obstacles are of a social order, thus until recently New York public housing did not accept women with illegitimate children.

Now, it so happens that the persons displaced by urban renewal are precisely those who are in the most unfavourable position in the market, in terms of income, education and ethnic membership.

Table 51
Estimate of the number of dwellings demolished in the United States as part of government programmes, up to 1967

Programme involving demolition	Period	No. of dwellings demolished (in thousands)
Urban renewal	1949–67	404
Freeways	1958–67	330
Construction of public housing	1937–67	177
'Equivalent demolitions'	1937–67	143
Local arrangements	1937–67	?
TOTAL		1054

Source: National Commission, 1968, p. 82.

Acting on the expression of poverty, but without altering its course, renewal displaces the problems in space, without resolving them; it makes the housing question more acute, therefore, as long as there is no public programme adequate to respond to housing needs.[12]

In the Commission's own words, 'it must be concluded that the main reason for the failure of this program [urban renewal], after eighteen years' experience, is that many local and federal civil servants, as well as a good many of its supporters, have not taken it seriously. Instead of being a great assault on the slums and deterioration, as an integral part of the campaign for proper housing and an adequate environment for every American family, renewal was regarded, and still is, as a possibility, financed by the government, of obtaining cheap land by a whole group of companies seeking profit or prestige'. (NCUP, 1965.)

[12] Recently the programme of public housing seems to have taken on a new life. Between September 1967 and October 1968, 74 859 new dwellings were built. The forecast for 1969 was to build 75 000 supplementary units; 130 000 for 1970 and 190 000 for 1971 (*Journal of Housing*, 1968, 454). However, let us remember that the report of the NCUP estimated housing needs at a minimum of two million a year, 500 000 of which would be needed by low-income families.

One conclusion that can obviously be drawn is the following: not only is American urban renewal not a housing programme, it has actually aggravated the shortage of cheap housing. It is not at all a reforming intervention responding to social demand in an anti-slum operation, since it is limited to displacing the problem in space, while making it more acute.

B Breaking up the ghettos

When slums have been demolished, it has not been a question of just any slums, but of those linked directly with the maintenance of a sub-culture, whose increasing opposition is endangering American society. That the project need not always be conscious does not make it any the less real. And even on an explicit level it is clear that, in American collective representations (for example, the mass media), large city, poverty, black ghetto, riot and renewal circulate on the same wavelength.

There can be no doubt that the operations of urban renewal were directed primarily at the black quarters. Indeed, according to Scott Greer, whereas blacks occupied about 25% of the deteriorated housing, almost 70% of the housing concerned in the programme of urban renewal was occupied by blacks.

Anderson gives the following figures concerning persons displaced by the operations in the urban centre.

Table 52

Proportion of Blacks and Puerto Ricans among, the persons removed by urban renewal

Year	Percentage
1957	76%
1959	71%
1960	68%
1961	66%

Source: Anderson, *op. cit.*, p. 65.

Thus the proportion of 'non-white' families, among those re-housed following the operation of urban renewal, oscillates between 62% in New York and almost 100% in Baltimore, Washington and Chicago. Throughout the whole country about 80% of the families rehoused were 'non-white'. (Marris, 1963; Duncan and Hauser, 1960, 85–6.) Let us remember that in 1960 the blacks made up only 10% of the American population.

This goes a long way to explaining the declaration of one of the best analysts of the black problem in the USA: 'The *Coup de grâce* came with the initiation of urban renewal. In city after city, this program has been utilized to clear slums and convert the land to heavier tax-bearing uses, typically removing low-income Negroes to make way for upper-income whites. The caustic slogan "Negro removal" has been well justified.' (Pettigrew, 1969, 59.)

But displacing the black quarters does not resolve the problem of racial tension. Although data on the ecological characteristics of the zones towards which the displaced persons were directed are very rare, it is practically certain that they are orientated towards similar urban areas, for the basic mechanisms of the process of segregation are not affected, in particular, the organization of the property market and the practices of racial discrimination. Despite federal policy, which proclaimed the need to apply the legal provisions against discrimination in housing, the study carried out in 1966 by the National Committee Against Discrimination in Housing concludes that these practices persist. For example, the low displacement of Blacks from Chicago towards the suburbs between 1950 and 1960 was directed towards the suburban ghettos in 63% of the cases. (Taueber and Taueber, 1965.) Even the White House recognized that urban renewal had contributed to reinforcing segregation rather than attenuating it. (White House Conference, 1966, 57–69.)

With the recent radicalization of the racial struggle, the administration, at its different levels, is trying to impede this process by encouraging the construction of public housing, occupied in the majority by Blacks, in white residential quarters. A recent provision (1969) has forced the Chicago local authority to implement such a location of housing projects. This is a case of a deliberate policy to counteract ecological polarization by trying, little by little, to break up the spatial basis of the ghetto. It remains to be seen what will become of such a provision, when we know the resistance encountered in Chicago itself by projects for locating this housing in quarters with a higher economic level. (Meyerson and Banfield, 1965.) Furthermore, the isolation of these 'small ghettos' in a white sea is not likely to be appreciated by a black community whose more politicized members demand autonomy rather than integration.

Lastly, one may doubt the effectiveness of this policy of ecological integration in terms of its objective of 'tension-management'. The excellent study carried out by Lieberson and Silverman (1965, 887–98) into seventy-six race riots between 1913 and 1963 shows the independence of these in relation to demographic characteristics and to the situation of housing in the towns involved, as well as their determination by the occupational structure and by the functioning of local institutions, in particular the police. (See also National Advisory Committee, 1968.)

Once again, ecological segregation merely expresses and reinforces social segregation. An urban policy cannot be substituted for a total policy. This means that despite some recent moves towards residential integration, urban renewal has acted above all defensively as far as the elimination of the ghettos is concerned. If in fact there was such a thing as 'Negro Removal', it was rather to establish barriers and to reinforce limits than to break up the ghetto.

Limits, yes, but in relation to what? Barriers against whom and to protect what?

C Urban centrality and the 'defence of civilization'
When urban renewal is presented as the means of relaunching the city, we should be careful to define our terms, for nobody seriously thinks of reoccupying the city centre or impeding the process of urban diffusion.

Since urban centrality has broken up and become decentred in new forms adapted to the metropolitan region and since population changes in the occupation of the city centre correspond to the profound social evolution of American society, urban renewal cannot, of itself, turn back the current, but it may carry out the necessary steps for the process not to provoke major upheavals.

Urban renewal is, in fact, the mechanism of adjustment intended to make possible in a social manner the passage between two urban forms, the large industrial city and the megalopolis.

What must be adjusted? It is a question, basically, of two sets of problems: handling the tensions produced by the accentuation of the process of segregation and the consolidation of vast slums; saving the remnants of 'urban civilization' and preserving what remains useful in the city centre for the whole of the megalopolis. This is to say, essentially, the city centre, both on its functional level and as a cultural emitter.

In order that the business centre may continue to play a role, in order that businesses which remain in the CBD (Central Business District), may continue to exist, their environment must be preserved from physical and social deterioration. The highly praised renewal of the Golden Triangle in Pittsburg is based on the concentration of the financial power of Pennsylvania in this sector. The need to maintain this milieu of decision and administration in which millions of people work is accompanied by the necessary care brought to this ambiance. Now, in effect, we know that most of the operations of urban renewal are concentrated on the city

centres, which, however, occupy a small surface and play a minor
role as far as housing is concerned. (Frieden, 1964.)

Thus, out of the 435 projects approved between 1966 and 1968,
65% concerned the city centre; furthermore, 9% of the projects
were situated in peripheric business centres.

This defence of the city centre against the social degradation of
its environment (of which the most visible indicator is the increase
in the number of underdogs, in particular Blacks) cannot be explained only in functional terms. The élitist attachment to the
values of urban culture is also involved. It is a defence of the groups
of the liberal intelligentsia, the seats of traditional cultural expression: theatres, concerts, museums, meeting-places, religious institutions, high-class commerce, high-class entertainment, etc. Let us be
quite clear about this: I am not claiming that this ensemble of
cultural expressions is the exclusive appurtenance of the élite, but,
quite simply, that a certain culture is expressed ecologically in the
old centre, whereas new, 'mass' expressions have found other locations (for example, drive-ins) or, simply no particular location (the
mass media, travelling libraries).

This over-consumption of cultural values, by an élite attached to
the city centre, is explained less in terms of accumulation of information than in terms of status, of membership symbol. The location of museums in the city centre is not a major problem for
the mass of people, who have few opportunities to visit them. And
it signifies almost nothing to the culturally excluded who live in
the city centre. But the preservation of these places for the traditional élite is a keypoint of the self-definition of this élite. The
luxury buildings that rise so full of pride in the place of the demolished slums would have no explanation without this analysis. They
reconstruct, at a very high level, the notion of community: members of the administrative class, over-consumers of urban cultural
values, which they have appropriated to themselves, these new
'urbanites' rediscover, beside their place of work, a lost *milieu* in
the tide of 'mass society' and are concerned only to erect protective
barriers against the black, moving waters that surround them.

Thus, having destroyed the old city, this society recreates a new
city for the élite, far from the anonymous suburbs, the right to
which is refused the new occupants of what was the industrial city.

The best illustration of this process is the set of urban renewal
projects directed by the universities. (Parsons, 1967.) Indeed, some
of the oldest and most important American universities have seen
themselves threatened by the deterioration of their environment,
as the part of the old city in which they are situated undergoes the
process described. Their very existence was in question, for it had

become difficult to maintain the notion of a campus in these conditions at a time when the liberal universities were discovering the difficulty of everyday liberalism, when this liberalism affected their status and their milieu of relations. Faced with this situation, and given an actual decline in the numbers of new students and an increasing number of resignations by the teaching staff, some universities had to choose between removal or a renewal of their environment. The most powerful of these opted for the second solution, strongly supported in this by the local residents, most of them linked to the university community, and by the local authorities, which saw in this enterprise an extraordinary ally to impede the flight of the higher strata towards the suburbs.

The most striking and most successful example is the renewal of the Hyde Park-Kenwood quarter, the seat of the University of Chicago since 1886 and a veritable pocket in the black ghetto. (Rossi and Dentler, 1961.) The urban renewal undertaken in 1949 and continued unremittingly right up to the present set out to eliminate the slums within a given perimeter and to construct a liberal community comprising a minority of middle-class Blacks. It worked through a powerful urbanism commission, supported by a very influential voluntary organization, 'The Hyde Park-Kenwood Community Conference', principally made up of professional people and university teachers, black and white. In eliminating the lower strata of residents, mainly blacks, the project succeeded in stabilizing the community, improving the quality of housing and services, developing the university installations and, on a middle-class base, allowing the survival of one of the few racially integrated quarters in the United States.

In other cases, the university took much less care with the social environment and tried, above all, to assure its own development. This was the case with Columbia University in New York City, with, as its result, a public protest in the district, the last echoes of which, some time ago, led left-wing students of the university to make this project one of their points of opposition to the administration.

The University of Pennsylvania which, in 1951, was considering transferring its installations from Philadelphia, reacted by organizing an institution, the 'West Philadelphia Corporation', which groups together several scientific establishments, and undertook the renewal and conservation of its environment.

In order to encourage this policy on the part of universities an amendment to the Housing Act (known as Section 112) was approved in 1959; it granted wide-ranging credit facilities to the programmes of renewal involving universities. In 1965, 75 projects of urban renewal had been approved, involving 70 million dollars and 198 university institutions.

Not only did 'urban' universities refuse to be moved; they also pr.ved to be an excellent instrument for penetrating the deteriorated zones and reanimating the city centres. The new campus of the University of Illinois in Chicago, situated on the edge of several ethnic ghettos and relatively near the Loop, spread its ultra-modern buildings right into the heart of the city and prepared itself to become a focus of urban reconquest. Here too there is a strong ambiguity in this process, which is both orientated towards social integration and confronted every day by the realities of the existence of ethnic and social minorities.

It is a question, therefore, not of saving the city, but of saving part of the heritage of the pre-existing urban forms, namely, certain functions that are still instrumental for the megalopolis and certain activities that are closely linked to the production of social values, to their social visibility and to their symbolic appropriation by certain social groups.

D The institutional and political process of American urban renewal

The elucidation of the social role actually played by urban renewal enables us to understand its institutional organization and its place in the political process. (Bellush and Hausknecht, 1967; Kaplan, 1963.)

On the institutional plane, one is aware of the administrative fragmentation of the American local collectivities (see Part III). The result is an accumulated inability on the part of the metropolitan city centres to assume responsibility for the expenditure necessary for their functioning. (Long, 1966.) Between 1945 and 1965, the expenditure of American municipalities increased by 571%, whereas the gross natural product increased by 'only' 259%. The municipalities of the city centres were particularly affected by this expenditure, 40% of which was allocated to education. Local taxes provided half the necessary income. The rest had to be sought from various sources. Now, it is in these city centres with a budget deficit that the problem of very costly renewal operations is posed.

This explains both why the federal government should offer its financial aid and why these municipalities should have an interest in getting approval for projects that improve the city centre and which represent a source of income for the future. It is logical therefore that it should be office buildings, stores and luxury apartment buildings that have priority in the new occupation of redeveloped land. Let us not forget that the initiative for the project came from the local authorities. It is in terms of this particular strategy that we must understand the urbanistic content of the operations proposed. (Weicher, 1968.)

The concrete functioning of a renewal project is as follows: the local authorities present a programme and submit it to the federal authorities which, if they approve it, assure by various means two-thirds of the financing. Thus armed with special powers and financially covered, the local authorities proceed to buy the land and buildings involved. They demolish the existing buildings and set about preparing the land surfaces thus freed. Once prepared, the land is sold to private promoters who build new structures and exploit it in the normal way, according to market forces. The selling price of the land is fixed, on average at approximately 30% of the total cost of its preparation. This loss is covered by the two-thirds provided by the federal government.

In fact, Anderson calculated that the promoter need spend only 3% of the funds necessary in cash.

The transformation of the urban zones was carried out, therefore, on the basis of land freed by public funds, with, as an essential item of expenditure, the sums paid to the owners of the deteriorated buildings (see Table 53).

Table 53
Itemized summary of the cost of urban renewal (up to 1967)

Chapter	% of the expenses incurred out of the total cost
Study and planning	1·8%
Buying and developing the site (including 60·5% for the purchase of buildings).	63·7%
Rehousing (not inc. removal allowances)	0·5%
Demolition	3·3%
Preparation of the site	10·6%
Installation of services	9·1%
Credit for expenses in public housing	2·1%
Education or health Interest	3·9%
Administration of the project	4·0%
Conservation and rehabilitation	0·3%
Various	0·7%

Source: NCUP *Final Report*, p. 162.

The growing importance of municipal elections in the opposition of the Blacks stems very largely from this fact: for the white majority to lose control of the city means abandoning the essential instrument of resistance to the ecological transformation of its everyday space.

Similarly, as far as 'participation' in urban renewal is concerned, the objective of the projects determines the direction of this participation, whatever its intensity or extent. (Wilson, 1963; Loring *et al.*, 1957.) Since it is a question of preserving a certain way of life or functions or institutions necessary to the whole of the urban area rather than to the residents of the zone, the organization of this participation is supported by middle-class groups able to remain in the redeveloped quarter, and by the institutions to be preserved. One seeks, therefore, class and, in many cases, ethnically homogeneous support in overcoming possible resistance from 'other citizens'.

Rossi and Dentler (1961, 292) have expressed the problem very clearly, in analysing the renewal of Hyde Park-Kenwood, the district of the University of Chicago: 'It seems likely that successful urban renewal in large cities — successful in the sense of widely accepted both within and without the neighborhoods under renewal — will come primarily either in neighborhoods that have an indigenous successful community organization or in neighborhoods in which some outside agency manages to create one. In the absence of such organizations physical renewal can be accomplished, but it seems likely that the neighborhood will lose whatever particular flavor it had through loss of essential population types.'

But what organization is involved? An association sufficiently powerful and locally rooted to represent and influence residents, but sufficiently in agreement with the urbanists not to oppose the operation in progress, that is to say, an organization that would act rather as a driving belt. 'These are the conditions to realize the plan with the people's consent, but without changing it.' The Hyde Park-Kenwood Community Conference was such an organization and its existence contributed to the success of the operation. But it is clear that this type of operation can exist only through an agreement as to the essential objectives between the participants and the renewal project. Now, when we know the change that generally occurs in the occupation of land, one may doubt the future of such a modality and one inclines rather to predict conflict rather than participation.

One finds confirmation of this analysis in the extreme difficulties encountered by the same body that carried out the renewal of Hyde Park-Kenwood when it tried to continue its work in the neighbouring sector of Woodlawn. (Parsons, 1967.) The population of this zone, mostly Blacks with low incomes, formed a federation of clubs and local organizations and opposed extremely vigorously the urbanistic projects of the University of Chicago. Very tough negotiations took place in 1965, with the result that substantial modifications in favour of the residents were made. This project and the consequent confrontations are still going on (1969). (For detailed information see Swenson, 1968.)

The same situation occurred in Newark (New Jersey) in 1967 and 1968, when the black community opposed the introduction of a medical school in the city centre that involved the displacement of residents. After a fairly violent conflict, which led to the riot of 1967, the surface envisaged was reduced by almost two-thirds, and rehousing facilities were granted. (Journal of Housing, 1968.)

The policy is closely tied up, therefore, with American racial politics and the so-called war on poverty. How can one move the slums of the minorities in order to permit the safeguarding of certain urban functions, without aggravating tensions, but also without prejudicing private enterprise, which is the key to the renewal programme? How can one control municipal institutions practising a policy opposed to the interests of a growing proportion of the city centres?

On what social base can this action rely? How can one maintain a balance between healthy ecological integration for the future and a respect for the market and, therefore, for the system of stratification and segregation?

While the new America of the residential suburbs mows its lawns on Sunday afternoons, the old urban America is trying to resolve its contradictions with bulldozers (see Diagram VII, which sums up the whole social process of American urban renewal).

III The reconquest of Paris[13]

The increased concentration of population and activities in the Paris region and the reinforcement of the centrality of the heart of the urban area have brought about important transformations in the old capital (see Part I, Chapter 2). Having become increasingly a city of offices (a fall of 200 000 industrial jobs and a rise of 300 000 office jobs is predicted for Paris by the year 2000), saturated with motor traffic, lacking amenities and green spaces and crushed by its double centrality (centre of a great metropolitan region itself concentrating the essential part of activity throughout the whole national territory), Paris has nevertheless been more or

[13] This section is based on the inquiry that I carried out with the Nanterre Urban Sociology groups in 1970. A first account of this is to be found in the article published in *Sociologie du Travail* 4, 1970 and a full account of the research (written by F. Godard) is to be found in the collective work *Renovation urbaine à Paris: structure urbaine et logique de classe* (1972) which also contains full information about the drawing up of the data, the bibliography and the carrying out of the inquiry.

Diagram VII: URBAN RENEWAL USA – Social production of the contradictions at the base 'planificatory' intervention.

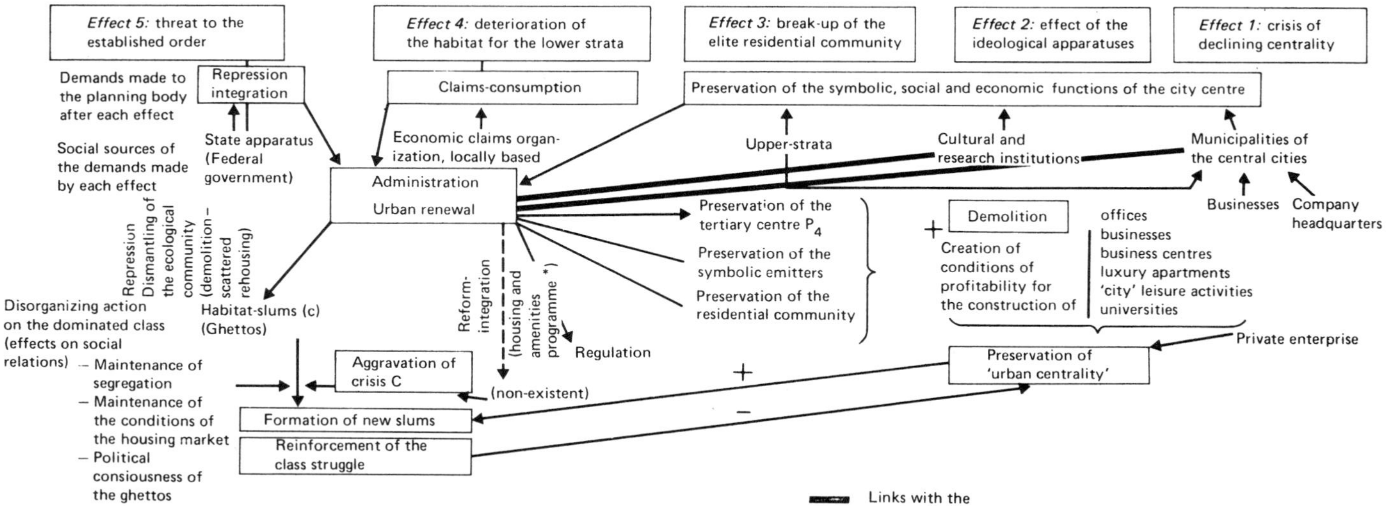

Effect 1: crisis of declining centrality

Effect 2: effect of the ideological apparatuses

Effect 3: break-up of the elite residential community

Effect 4: deterioration of the habitat for the lower strata

Effect 5: threat to the established order

Company headquarters

Businesses

Municipalities of the central cities

Private enterprise

Cultural and research institutions

Preservation of the symbolic, social and economic functions of the city centre

offices
businesses
business centres
luxury apartments
'city' leisure activities
universities

Demolition

Creation of conditions of profitability for the construction of

Preservation of 'urban centrality'

+

Upper-strata

Preservation of the tertiary centre P_4

Preservation of the symbolic emitters

Preservation of the residential community

Claims-consumption

Economic claims organ- ization, locally based

Administration

Urban renewal

Reform- integration

(housing and amenities programme[*]) (non-existent)

Regulation

Repression integration

State apparatus (Federal government)

Disorganizing action on the dominated class (effects on social relations)

Demands made to the planning body after each effect

Social sources of the demands made by each effect

Repression
Dismantling of the ecological community (demolition – scattered rehousing)

Habitat-slums (c) (Ghettos)

– Maintenance of social segregation
– Maintenance of the conditions of the housing market
– Political consiousness of the ghettos

Aggravation of crisis C

Formation of new slums

Reinforcement of the class struggle

+

–

Links with the institutional process

(*) . . . . . Intervention supposed to have taken place, but in fact did not

+, –: Production of an effect in the same or opposite direction

less abandoned to the dominant social tendencies, with scarcely
any regulating intervention on the part of the state apparatus
(especially where the development of traffic routes is concerned).
This is all the more significant in that the City of Paris, unlike
other French municipalities, is placed directly under the authority
of the Prefect and, through him, of the Prime Minister, without
the (elected) Paris Council being able to play a truly significant role.

This explains a great deal about the programme that the City of
Paris has called the 'Urban Reconquest of Paris', which consists of
a series of operations of conservation, rehabilitation and renewal;
this public initiative (both on the financial and the administrative
planes) is aimed at changing the occupation of space in a number
of Paris quarters. Being one of the new initiatives of any scope in
the urban planning of the City of Paris, and inspired directly by
the government, it makes it possible to establish both the social
content of French urban politics and the signification of Paris in
relation to the different economic, political and ideological issues.
For, despite its very modest proportions (31 operations undertaken
between 1955 and 1970, 381·6 hectares redeveloped, or in the process of being redeveloped, out of the 1500 hectares envisaged by
the Master Plan of the City of Paris), the spectacular character of
certain constructions and the ever greater eviction of former inhabitants of the working-class districts have given rise first to lively
controversy, then to social conflict (see below). The 'Reconquest
of Paris', which was intended as a historical successor to the work
of Haussmann has come close to being so on every level and, in
particular, also, on the strictly political level.

To decide on the social signification of a programme so charged
ideologically, which claims, of course, to be both the new grandeur
of Paris and the remedy for the acute problems arising on the level
of collective consumption, one must, once again, stand back in
order to see the subjectivity of the urbanistic projects and social
forces involved. Since there is action on an already constituted
space, we will examine first the characteristics of this space — why
such a space rather than another? Then we shall establish the social
content of the renewal operations, seeing what the modifications
brought by each element of the urban structure are. A comparison
of the spaces to be redeveloped and the content of the operations
(redeveloped future space) will enable us to establish the social
logic at work in the operation. On this basis, the institutional process of the programme will become understandable since we will
know what interests are involved; lastly, we will be able to establish the link between this intervention in the urban and the conjuncture of social relations in French society.

Such a reading of the transformations of space obviously necessitates a theoretical grid that will be provided for us by the construction in terms of an urban system. But we should make it clear to begin with that this urban system refers to an urban unit (in the sense of a unit of collective reproduction of labour power), whereas in the case of the City of Paris, we are dealing with only a part of the unit represented by the Paris region. We must take into account, therefore, the character of this part, which varies according to different elements of the urban structure. To study urban renewal in Paris is to study the transformation of all the elements of the urban structure of the region, at the level of one of the poles of the social process apprehended.

A The space one wishes to efface

Although the first renewal operations (1955–1958), linked to a very modest slum clearance programme, could be directed at a few unhealthy pockets, most of this programme (and it is this that constitutes its strength) did not involve assistance to the deteriorated Paris quarters. Indeed, a comparison between the map of unhealthy pockets and that of the renewal operation shows how little they correspond. What, then, is the specificity of this space whose use one wishes to change?

It may be established by studying the place occupied in the different elements of the Paris urban structure by the redeveloped sectors. Or, to put it another way, in operational terms, how great is the divergence, in relation to the Paris average, of the different variables that express each of the structural elements? The greater this divergence, the more these variables specify the sector and the more these elements or sub-elements must form the base of the process of renewal, that is to say, provide the reason for it.

Thus, the consumption element (reproduction of labour power, that is to say, housing and social characteristics of residential space) must play a preponderant role in the renewal programme, for it provides it with a pretext. But the essential question is: which of the two sets of variables (deterioration of the environment or social composition of space) acts more strongly on the transformation of land occupation? Or, in other words, is it a question of an intervention at the level of amenities or at the social level of the resident population.

In order to provide an answer, I have compared the values in percentages of a certain number of variables that could be known, both for the whole of Paris and for all the sectors redeveloped before *renewal* (mostly in 1962; for a few, in 1954). On the basis of these data, I have established an index of differentiation for urban renewal (IDUR) constructed as follows:

$$\text{IDUR} = \frac{\begin{array}{c}\text{Value of the variable (in percentage) in}\\ \text{the ensemble of sectors redeveloped}\end{array}}{\begin{array}{c}\text{Value of the variable (in percentage)}\\ \text{in the whole of the City of Paris}\end{array}} - 1$$

(The calculations were carried out for 23 of the 30 renewal operations, for which data by census tract area were available. It is obvious that the value 0 of the index corresponds to the absence of specificity for the sectors redeveloped.)

The classification of variables thus obtained indicates, from the highest value to the lowest, the influence, positive or negative, of each variable on the operations of urban renewal. (It should be remembered that this was an exhaustive study bearing on all the operations completed or in progress.)

Table 54
Specificity of Parisian space affected by urban renewal 1954 to 1962

Variable	Index of differentiation (IDUR)
Proportion of Algerians in the population	+1·529
Proportion of upper management and liberal professions	+0·575
Dwellings without water	+0·590
Proportion of semi-skilled and unskilled workers	−0·602
Overcrowding in the dwellings	+0·504
Dwellings without WC	+0·380
Proportion of foreigners	−0·259
Proportion of persons over 65	−0·189
Rate of women's activity	−0·070
Proportion of craftsmen and tradesmen	+0·056
Proportion of persons under 19	−0·055
Rate of activity of the population	+0·052

This index presents, therefore, the specificity of the sectors of the Paris space affected by urban renewal. They are sectors in which the housing has deteriorated, of course, but they are also sectors strongly marked by the presence of immigrant and unskilled workers, and by the absence of the upper strata of the population.

I have tried, then, to evaluate the association between each variable and the importance of the operation. For this, I have calculated a coefficient of the correlation of rank (the Spearman test), for twenty-three renewal operations studied, between their classification in order of size (in hectares redeveloped) and their classification in relation to the set of variables already indicated. The results

(see Table 55) indicate that the operation was all the more important in that it concerned old people, semi-skilled and unskilled
workers, foreigners, working women and Algerians. And, on the
other hand, there was a low, but inverse relation with the variables
concerning the deterioration of the housing.

Table 55
*Correlation of rank between the size of the operations of urban
renewal and the variables of housing and of the social composition
of the population
Paris, 1954 and 1962 (Spearman Test)*

·50 :	
·36 :	Over 65
·24 :	Proportion of semi-skilled and unskilled workers
·23 :	Foreigners, plus active women
·20 :	Algerian Muslims
·17 :	Craftsmen
·16 :	Management and liberal professions
0	
—·07 :	Overcrowding
—·14 :	Active population
—·16 :	Dwellings without water
—·19 :	Dwellings without W. C.
—·31 :	Under 19
—·50 :	

These tendencies make it possible, then, to formulate the hypothesis that it is change in the social occupation of space rather than
the bad state of housing that seems to be at the base of renewal
operations. Not that this housing was not in a state of deterioration, but it was no more so than in other quarters that had been
spared renewal.

As far as the production element is concerned, the central question was to envisage a link between the renewal programme and
the transformation then in progress of industrial Paris into Paris as
the centre of management and organization. For this, I have classified the renewal operations in a space differentiated by:

1. The importance of industrial occupation prior to renewal,
considering the number of productive industrial wage-earners by
arrondissement (wage-earners at place of work, not at place of
residence).

2. The importance of the removals of industrial plant, considering the figures for demolition of industrial plant in the period
1960–1966 inclusive.

3. The importance of the introduction of offices, by the supply
of offices in 1962, in floor area.

4. The rate of increase in the introduction of offices, by the increase in the supply of offices between 1962–1968.

Lastly, in relation to the exchange element,[14] I studied commerce and urban flows. The average number of wage-earners per place of work supplied a convenient indicator of the size of businesses.

For the spatial concentration of businesses, I ascertained the number of streets in which there were more than 15 businesses per hundred metres.

I calculated the distribution of businesses by the number of wage-earners per 1000 consumers, and the type of business, and the proportion of exceptional and occasional businesses. For the study of urban flows, I calculated the number of lines calling at each station. For the total of operations for an *arrondissement*, I took the number of stations, weighted by the number of lines: this constituted the indicator I called 'Area Served by *Métro*'. To conclude, I listed the number of parking places offered per *arrondissement*, in order to calculate their parking capacity.

In every case, it was a question of classifying sectors, quarters and *arrondissements* according to a strong and weak value for each variable and of observing the percentage of hectares redeveloped in each of the spaces thus differentiated (see Table 56).

The major tendencies may be summarized as follows:

Urban renewal accompanies the transition from industrial space to space with a high concentration of offices, where this was formerly not the case.

It operates on a space with a high density of small, fairly dispersed businesses, directed towards daily consumption; on the other hand, there were scarcely any large commercial surfaces. It is, therefore, an instrument of concentration for the commercial sector.

It has rarely (19%) occurred in *arrondissements* that are well served by the *Métro*. This would seem to indicate that the privileged links in the traffic flows are not those of interregional daily commuting, but those of the internal milieu (business centre) and those with the field of action of administrative centes (the provinces: close to railway stations, acting as structuring poles).

On the other hand, parking space is virtually non-existent in the surrounding area, hence a new bottle-neck, which may offer promoters an interesting outlet for future operations connected with urban renewal.

Finally, two remarks concerning the institutional and symbolic content of the space concerned in renewal.

---

[14] An analysis of the institutional and financial process of removal would overburden this already complex account of its social signification and must be ommitted. The reader is referred to the works cited.

Table 56

Urban Structure — Classification of renewal operations, weighted by their surface, in the Paris urban structure (figures: number of hectares renewed or under renewal, % calculated out of the total of hectares renewed or under renewal) (*)

Value of the variable	Industrial space	Industrial movement	Establishment of offices in 1962	New establishments of offices	Commerce size	Commerce Type (daily or not)	Commerce spatial concentration	Commerce distribution
−	0 / 0	0 / 0	323·2 / 751	144·9 / 381	381·6 / 1 001	355·2 / 931	381·6 / 100%	381·6 / 100%
=	135·3 / 35·5%	76·9 / 20·1%	0 / 0	58·4 / 151	0 / 0	26·4 / 7%	0 / 0	0 / 0
+	246·3 / 64·51	304·7 / 79·9%	58·4 / 15%	178·3 / 47%	0 / 0	0 / 0	0 / 0	0 / 0
TOTAL	381·6 / 100²%	381·6 / 100²%	381·6 / 100%	381·6 / 100%	381·6 / 100%	381·6 / 100%	381·6 / 100%	381·6 / 100%

Value of the variable	Area served by métro		Parking places	
−	50·5	·13%	335·9	88%
=	259	68%	45·7	12%
+	72·1	19%	0	
TOTAL	381·6	100%	381·6	100%

(*) *Arrondissements* and sectors renewed, classified into three groups according to the value of the variable indicated in the column.

Since the field of intervention is defined within the frontiers of the City of Paris, and the different *arrondissements* have no autonomy, there is no possible institutional specificity of Paris space. This does not mean that there is no strict relation between urban renewal and the institutional system, as we shall see. But this relation does not exist via the administrative segmentation of space.

On the other hand, it is certain that there are noticeable differences between the spaces redeveloped and other quarters of Paris on the level of the urban symbolic. Although I have not specified these, I could say that they are expressed along two axes: 'bourgeois Paris/working-class Paris' and 'historic/suburban Paris'. Renewal seems to be concerned above all with the working-class and more modern quarters, whereas, for the historic quarters like the Marais, one finds either rehabilitation operations obeying a specific logic or *ad hoc* operations centred much more on the direct expression of state power (Les Halles), or operations sufficiently profitable to allow the individual initiative of redevelopers. This explains perhaps why some *arrondissements* of Paris that are more deteriorated than others (for example the 3rd and 4th *arrondissements*) are scarcely affected by renewal.

B   The space one constructs
What is the point of changing Parisian space? Urban renewal is not, in any case, a re-housing programme: the demolition of 29 059 homes and the construction of 36 495 homes was envisaged, whereas, in a private enterprise context, between 1954 and 1964, 6000 demolished homes were replaced by 52 500; at the same time, 41 000 others were constructed without prior demolition.

Since it is not possible to establish the specificity of the new space after renewal (for most of it is still in the course of construction or has scarcely been begun in 1970), it is possible to outline the direction of the transformation by analysing the content of the renewal programmes, proceeding to a whole series of corrections and calculations. Obviously, we must preserve the same reading grid as for the pre-renewal space, in order to establish the expected changes.

The key-question concerning consumption is always whether it is a matter of amenities, aimed at re-establishing balance in collective consumption or of the social level of space. Indeed, we have seen that the space involved was that of the lower social level. But there is nothing to lead us to believe that it remains at this level. Since there are still very limited data on the change of social categories in space, I will estimate future changes according to the percentage of public housing (HLM) in the renewal programmes (for all other types of housing seems to be beyond the means of the vast majority of the former residents):

Table 57
Distribution of the operations, by number of hectares renewed, according to the proportion of HLM dwellings to be constructed out of the total of dwellings constructed in the operation

	under 30% HLMs	from 30% to 50% HLMs	over 50% HLMs	Total
No. of hectares renewed	245·3 ha 66%	65·8 ha 17·5%	60·1 ha 16·5%	371·2 100 %

Now it should be added that a large number of residents do not have enough money to rent HLMs (20%, 33%, 50% in the different pockets) and that, furthermore, an essential part of the programme is not geared to housing. It can be said, therefore, that the tendency is toward the eviction of most of the former residents and occupation of the new space by social categories of higher status.

Is this, perhaps, the price to be paid to obtain better amenities? Indeed, the guiding schema for Paris fixed as its objective: 'to carry out a policy of reconstruction of the quarters deprived of amenities and with badly utilized surfaces'.

An analysis of some of the amenities on which we were able to obtain reliable data (educational amenities, crèches, green spaces) shows that:

Renewal does not bring new educational facilities, since it confines itself to covering, on average, the needs of the new population. In certain cases (13th and 19th *arrondissements*), it even benefited from the existing facilities, which were slightly more generously provided than elsewhere, in order to saturate them at the same level as in the rest of Paris.

56% of the redeveloped surface is below the Paris average for green space area (0·8 square metres per inhabitant), 21% are above the average, but without reaching the minimum objectives laid down by the plan itself.

Thus renewal is no longer an operation aimed at improving amenities.

Must we find the reason for this in the functional development of the new conditions of production?

It seems, indeed, that the building of new office blocks is one of the essential axes of the programme: 62·6% of the hectares redeveloped expect a concentration of offices higher than the Paris average. Now, this datum coincides perfectly with the logic of residential stratification, for 'an increase in office space and an increase in the number of better-class quarters go hand in hand' (see the master plan for Paris), as does the play of the property market.

On the other hand, industrial activity in the strict sense is erased from the map as far as companies are concerned and highly limited for small craftsmen: 56·8% of the surface redeveloped makes no provision for craftsmen and the remainder expects far-reaching changes among the craftsmen already established (becoming, for example, service workers for the new buildings).

Further, the transformation seems significant: 95% of the area redeveloped integrates commercial installations, but, which is more to the point, for 71·3% of this area it is a matter of large-scale commerce, previously entirely absent, or of the creation of 'local centres', which may play the role of secondary centres for Paris in relation to the urban area as a whole. This restructuring character of the social centres seems to be one of the major options of the programme, thus extending and developing the predominance of the City of Paris over the region.

Lastly, at the level of the urban symbolic, important modifications as yet little recognized have been introduced by the programme. The importance accorded to tower blocks and the insistence on 'functional' materials and the style of certain buildings seem inevitably to mark the space with a certain technocratic modernity, centred on the spread of the technological performance of high construction, with little concern for empty or fragmented spaces left all around. On the other hand, the large paved pedestrian areas and the striving for 'de luxe' effects in the shopping precincts seem to prefigure symbolic consumption, centred on the spectacle of possible purchase and which, obviously, is in no way in contradiction with the first. However, it is clear that what we have here is a break with the pre-existing symbolic centred on the street, work and small businesses, dominated therefore by the imagery of the quarter (though we are unable to say anything definite about the persistance of the sense of community in the quarter, which has been heavily eroded by the diffusion of social relations).

C The meaning of the 'reconquest' of Paris in relation to the urban system: the renewal-reproduction of a space
Our data may be grouped in the form of a table of probabilities, combining the characteristics of space before renewal and the urbanistic content of the programme in progress in relation to the different elements revealed. In fact, we know how many redeveloped hectares correspond to each section of the whole programme in relation to the different variables treated. From the 'marginal'

numbers for each table (those at the end of each line and column), we can reconstruct each square and, by standardizing in accordance with the total of hectares redeveloped, obtain the proportion of area redeveloped that presents both characteristics. Comparing the various probabilities with one another, we can deduce the differential quantitative influence of each element in relation to renewal, which enables us to elucidate the meaning of the marginal probabilities, thus summarizing the differentiation that each variable introduces into the renewal programme. One may thus compare the respective influence of each factor (Table 58).

Thus, for example, let i be the characteristic 'high proportion of Algerians in the space before renewal' (with its complementary ī) and j̄ the characteristic 'high proportion of HLMs in the programme' (with its complementary j̄). Dichotomizing them and crossing them, we obtain:

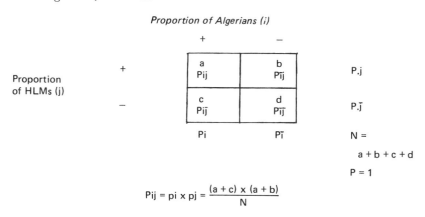

$$P_{ij} = p_i \times p_j = \frac{(a+c) \times (a+b)}{N}$$

It is clear that these 'probabilities' merely extrapolate tendencies in progress and are not ineluctable. They serve however to specify the relative importance of renewal in relation to the different elements studied. Table 58 summarizes these results.

I shall not comment on it in detail, but confine myself to indicating the social signification that emerges from it.

What strikes one above all is the systematic tendency of the renewal process to reinforce the 'spontaneous' (that is to say, determined according to the general line of social evolution) tendency of the urban system of the Paris region, even at the level of all its elements.

Thus it develops and accentuates residential segregation, extending the occupation of the City of Paris by the upper strata and squeezing out the working-class strata towards the under-equipped suburbs. This model of urban segregation, linked to the cultural, historical and functional charge of Paris as capital tends to relegate more and more to a secondary level the historical cleavages between the East and the West.

More important still is the role of renewal at the level of the extended reproduction of the specialization of productive space, the mechanisms of which I have already established (see Part I). The constant increase in the setting up of offices in Paris, which has become a gigantic tertiary centre, although above all the expression of the division of labour and the constitution of the great organizations of monopoly capitalism, also finds considerable reinforcement in the action of the renewal bodies.

Since we are witnessing, therefore, the consecration and extension of Parisian centrality, which now extends to the whole of the city and which is exerted both over its own region and over France, with an eye to Europe as a whole, some regulation becomes necessary in the channels of functional exchange, urban flows and commercial centres. Since the transportation programme at district level is charged with the first aspect, it falls to renewal to launch these new commercial centres which are at the same time meant to be cultural emitters rooted in the values of consumption (the whole, as always, in line with the current social tendencies; that is to say, according to the spatial logic of the most dynamic sectors of international monopoly capitalism).

Lastly, the few elements at our disposal concerning the urban symbolic are also in line with the reproduction of social tendencies at the level of urban forms, with, however, the important proviso that these be the most advanced tendencies within the dominant logic; thus, for example, the tower blocks, an expression of the forms most strongly imbued with technocratic values (modernity, efficiency, rationality) will be given preference over purely conservative forms (for example, buildings built of stone).

The 'reconquest of Paris' is, therefore, without any doubt, an intervention of the state apparatus in space; its aim is the extended reproduction of the urban system of the Paris region, from the point of view of its centrality, at the higher level of the productive apparatus and of urban stratification.

One must, then, ask why state intervention was needed to extend the development of social tendencies whose strength we have already established. Although it is true that the overconcentration of the central functions necessitates regulatory intervention, urban renewal appears rather as an accelerator of the process. Rather than a response to a crisis in the urban sytem, it appears as an initiative emanating first from the state apparatus and one that must be understood on the basis of the internal logic of the political.

D *The politico-ideological determination of the 'reconquest of Paris'*
Since any intervention of the state apparatus may be understood through its effects on the economic, the politico-institutional (that is to say, itself), the ideological or, directly, on social relations, it is in the link between urban renewal and the different instances that its full signification is revealed.

Now, the relation of the state apparatus to the economic is simply what has been described above: the reproduction of a central space in the wake of the process of regional and urban concentration of the Parisian urban area, itself produced by the evolution of the productive system. Since renewal adds no new effects at this level, an interpretation that keeps to the economic instance would limit itself to seeing in the renewal programme simply the manipulation of the organs of urban administration, in order to create opportunities for profit for redevelopers, which is in line with the logic of the system. But although facts of this kind certainly exist, they seem to me rather the result of the social role of renewal, determined in relation to other instances.

Table 59
Distribution, in hectares, of the operations of urban renewal in the quarters and arrondissements of Paris, classified according to voting in the municipal elections of 1965 and the legislative elections of 1967.

	Left list No. % Ha.		Establishment of the PCF No. % Ha.		Electoral situation of the UNR *	No. Ha.	%
Sectors with high figure (+)	238·7	66·5	263·7	73·4	High (+)	109·0	30
					Average (=)	26·2	6·7
Sectors with low figure (−)	120·2	33·5 100 %	95·2	26·6 100 %	Low (−)	223·7	62·3 100 %
	358·9		358·9			358·9	

Thus, on the institutional plane, one may wonder what interest the state has in changing the functions and social occupation of Parisian space. One answer that comes immediately to mind is — in order to change the electorate. Indeed, if we correlate some of the significant voting results with the importance of the operations of urban renewal (Table 59), we see the following:

1. Urban renewal is aimed above all at left-wing and, in particular, Communist sectors of the electorate. This is logical enough, given the social strata living in these sectors. But the fact of establishing a correlation with another variable does not remove the significance

of the political fact in itself. Changing this population means changing the political tendency of the sector.

2. Urban renewal is strong where the electoral tradition of the parliamentary 'majority' is weak, which is the obverse of the previous result. But the space least effected by renewal is not that in which the Gaullists are well established, but that in which their dominance is uncertain. This seems to derive from a triple movement: (*a*) changing the left-wing sectors; (*b*) launching prestige operations in the sectors in which the right is consolidated; (*c*) altering zones that are at the moment indecisive.

Although this is so, it would not seem of itself to account for the strategy of the state apparatus, for we still have to explain why it had to occupy electorally the space of the City of Paris.

Things become clearer when one brings into the analysis the role played by prestige operations in Paris on the ideological plane. Not only as regards the urban symbolic, but ideological emission in general. The mythology of French *grandeur* and the affirmation of the new values of the great international companies seem to combine to launch a far-reaching campaign to make Paris-the-capital the shop-window of a certain kind of prosperity and efficiency in public affairs. In addition to the renewal projects, which are imbued above all with the values of advanced capitalism, the state would leave its mark on the centre of Paris, from the redevelopment of Les Halles to the creation of the business centre of La Défense, offered by the state apparatus to the monopolies of the year 2000.

Thus the contradiction French bourgeoisie (de Gaulle)/international capitalism (Pompidou) seems to be superseded in a new phase, which, on the urban plane, would consecrate the articulation of the Paris region at the European economic axis and the role of Paris as the business centre and emitter on a continental scale.

However, the ideological marking out of a space is never an end in itself, in so far as any ideological emission exists only by virtue of the effect it produces at its reception. This means that not only the intervention in the Parisian electoral base but also the effect of ideological demonstration seem to be aimed at social relations of power, or, to be more precise, seem to be moving in the direction of a profound transformation of the class content of the City of Paris. And this, not in the ordinary sense of social stratification (a change in the social occupation of space), but in the profound sense, affecting all the instances, of the articulation of space with the class struggle. This is no more than hypothesis, of course, but all the analyses seem to converge towards this point, which is much more difficult to grasp than the data so far established. Indeed, why would the class struggle find expression in the occupation of a certain space? Why is it significant that the Gaullists control the City of Paris, rather than the suburbs or the provinces?

I have sketched out two hypotheses:

The first concerns the conjuncture of the political struggle in France, namely the attempt on the part of the upper bourgeoisie, since 1958 and under cover of a powerful leader, to obtain for itself a large hegemonic party, unconditionally attached to the orientations of monopoly capitalism and solidly rooted in the electorate. Now, if an electoral base has been obtained through subtle combinations, taking advantage of elements in the conjuncture, the party very obviously lacks solidity and is not rooted in all social strata; once it has lost its leader, it runs the risk of breaking up into the various sections of the bourgeoisie, which will no longer recognize it as a relatively autonomous political instrument. This popular base, especially at the level of local institutions, is in the hands either of working-class forces or of the traditional bourgeois and petty-bourgeois forces. The Gaullists are trying desperately to move in this direction, to constitute a local administrative base that would give them a structure of 'local leaders', on which to base a party that will not be subject to the hazards of political circumstances. Since the large provincial cities, generally speaking, are held firmly by other forces, Paris presents a privileged case, in which, depending directly on the government, a long-term plan may be implemented that will gradually transform its social and political conditions until the moment comes to give it, tentatively, the status of local autonomy and to make of it the base of popular support for the great neo-capitalist party.

For one can hardly underestimate the role played by Paris in the history of the class struggle in France. One thinks, of course, of the Commune, but the movement of May 1968 also had Paris as axis and stage: the support of the Paris population was an element of primary importance in the concrete process of the struggle that had begun. Why this importance? one may ask. Why, for example, did the struggles in the factories need to be expressed in Paris? On this matter, it is impossible to give any definite answer. But one might think (and this is my second hypothesis) that this importance derives from the concrete conditions of political organization in contemporary France. Indeed, if the struggles in the factories or in the universities are to have any real political import, they must be related to the problematic of the seizure of power, even if it is at a very low level. This requires, obviously, an organized expression or, to put it another way, in the broad sense, a party. Now, we know that the movement of May '68 and the revolutionary tendencies that have been developing in France for a certain time are charac-

terized precisely by the absence of any organized expression of
such a movement (or, to put it another way, by the proliferation
of small political groups). The only point of unity, the only mode
of organized political expression of this movement, both in 1968
and in 1970 is the street. 'Power is in the street', was not merely an
'anarchistic' slogan; it was a reference to the only organized link
which, above purely ideological conflicts, held the movement of
revolt together.

A bourgeois Paris is a Paris cut off from possible confrontational
expressions, which will have to oscillate between the dispersed
struggles in separate schools, factories, etc., and the direct confrontation with repression in the political isolation of the streets of
Paris.

It is obvious that there is no conscious plan on the part of the
bourgeoisie that is so clear-sighted, but it seems to me that renewal
does have this effect and is, consequently, seen as positive, in other
forms, sometimes veiled by the ideology of those very people who
have an interest in it. But if the representatives of a social class do
not always know how to recognize themselves, the class itself
knows its own interests, in the sense that its unconscious logic
tends to sweep away whatever does not serve its interests.

Furthermore, renewal is not only that. It is, above all, the extended reproduction of the urban system of the Paris region, in the
sense described and in this sense it realizes the social logic at the
base of the structure of the Paris region. But what requires explanation is why there is a direct correspondence between economic
class interests, directly expressed in space, and the logic proper to
the state apparatus, to which I attribute a relative autonomy. And
I believe that one might be able to explain this coincidence and
this mutual reinforcement through the impact of renewal on social
relations, with its effects redoubled on the economic, the politico-
institutional and the ideological (see Diagram VIII).

Lastly, it is true that there is a great distance between the modest
proportions of the renewal programme and the scope of the implicit
objectives that are attributed to it. But this programme plays a
pilot role, opening a breach in the working-class quarters and creating the condition for private enterprise to pursue and multiply
activities in this direction. This is how we must understand the increasingly marked tendency to give way to private renewal and the
development of procedures of concerted action.

Looked at from this point of view, the 'urban reconquest of
Paris' seems to acquire a more precise signification. It is the reconquest of working-class Paris by the bourgeoisie at the level both of
activities and of residence. The great dream of the Versaillais would

321

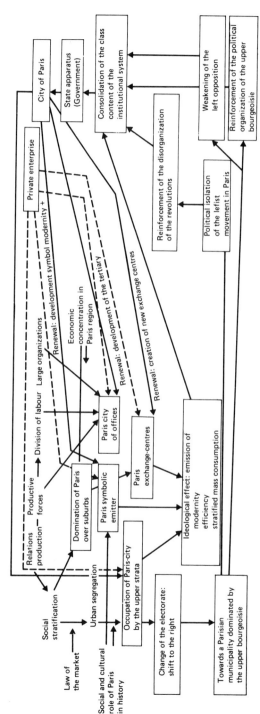

Diagram VIII: Social logic at work in the urban reconquest of Paris

Renewal: action on residence

seem to be realized. Cut off from its historical roots, emptied of its
social foundation the Commune would seem to be dead, at last!

IV A few general conclusions on urban planning as a social process

The research presented brings out a problematic, rather than leading
to a vigorous demonstration. However, on the basis of this research,
certain results may be stated in a provisionally general form, in
such a way as to rectify them or to develop them through an examination of the specificity of other concrete situations. By way of
example, I shall mention a few.

The operations of urban planning studied develop the capitalist
structural logic and respect the limits thus imposed. This affirmation does not exhaust analysis, since we must still see specifically
in what way this logic is deployed. But if it does not tell us everything about it — far from it — it does say a great deal, in particular,
about the capacity for intervention of A in P, at the level of the
urban system, as we have indicated in the general hypotheses.

The mere existence of a crisis situation in the urban system does
not necessarily trigger off the intervention of the planner: it must
be expressed socially at first, then it is transcribed into the terms
of the political apparatus, which always begins by organizing itself
at the level of the urban system (constitution or reorganization of A).

On the other hand, there may be interventions on the part of
the urban planner, without a strictly urban crisis, in terms of the
internal logic of the state apparatus.

Any intervention required by a manifest but unrealized contradiction (as a result of a structural law forbidding it, or because
of the conjuncture of power relations) is replaced by a corresponding intervention in the ideological.

The priority accorded to interventions derives from the power
relations existing at the level of class relations. Thus, if it is a question above all of dealing with working-class claims (Great Britain),
action will bear essentially on consumption; if it is a question of an
offensive on the part of the dominant class ('Reconquest of Paris'),
the ensemble of elements will be the object of the regulating intervention.

It appears, in concrete research, that one must devote particular
attention to the production of linked social efforts and that the
social signification of an intervention may come not from the intervention observed, but from the extent of this intervention in
relation to another domain of the social (for example, American
urban renewal as a means of political struggle against black militants).

The social barriers, produced by the permanence of crystallized forms inherited from other modes of production and periods (for example, the pre-industrial town) act above all as multipliers of dislocations and contradictions in the dominant structure rather than being their source.

The institutional process has a relative autonomy, in the sense that it is not the direct and mechanical transcription of the social effects of intervention by planning. But it in no way depends either on chance or on the freedom of the actors. It is determined, at a second remove, in the sense that the specificity of its logic is explained by the analysis of the social content of the interventions.

When, at the base of the operation, there is a protest movement, there is a strong chance of finding a correspondence between the ideology of the protest and the urban forms created, rather than between their respective social contents (the British new towns).

Propositions of this kind might be organized into an axiomatic system, combined among themselves, from which one might deduce new propositions, etc. The material base of concrete research is still lacking to begin such an enterprise, but the way is marked out.

14

Research on Urban Social Movements

Important observation

If, between the few theoretical elements proposed by way of orientating our task and the first research into urban planning, there is a certain gap, one finds oneself nevertheless in the same conceptual universe in which concrete analysis answers, partly at least, the theoretical questions and the theoretical tools succeed in elucidating certain processes.

The situation is quite different where urban social movements are concerned.

Indeed, we can only see the reflection of this problematic, that is to say, it has been mapped out, on the one hand, in ideology (the expression of political conflicts in 'urban' terms), and on the other hand, by a theoretical analysis, in the sense that one may predict a certain specificity in the articulation of the urban problematic with the different domains of the class struggle. Now, the lack of research in this field (from the point of view of the study of social movements, as opposed to that of local participation) necessitates extreme prudence when undertaking concrete research. The tactical problems of research dominate those of the theoretical perspective. For it is necessary, above all, to know what one is talking about, that is to say, to learn to recognize 'urban social movements', to put a little flesh, that is to say concrete history, on to what is still only a badly delimited theoretical space or a generalizing ideological reference.

Before carrying out demonstrative, or even illustrative, analyses of the theoretical perspective outlined, we must circumscribe our concrete object through a long exploratory phase. But this does not mean falling back into empiricism, limiting oneself to mere

observation which, of itself, can never be other than an accumulation of incidents. It means treating phenomena that are supposedly
charged with contradictions from the point of view of the emergence
of social claims and political mobilizations, as one seeks the laws
of their articulation with the class struggle in general. But this
apprehension must be made in such terms that, while being closer
to the concrete than the theoretical schema presented, one pre-
serves the thematic, the modes of articulation, the type of reasoning. I have clung, therefore, to the elaboration of tools capable of
apprehending more directly a political process, without having to
reconstruct the ensemble of underlying structural combinations, as
they are presented in the general theoretical schema. The tools are
rather descriptive and are intended to show the articulations of a
given process in such a way as to bring out structural laws. They
do not represent, therefore, a change of content in relation to the
theoretical perspective. They are adequate at an exploratory phase,
situated at a semi-descriptive level, but impregnated with the problematic described earlier. For there is nothing wrong in admitting
that at the moment of writing these lines (January 1971), we have
not solved the practical problems posed by the development of the
overall schema in terms of concrete research. We are striving to do
so, by approaching all the necessary mediations. The exploratory
phase, with its specific conceptual tools, is an essential phase. That
is why, in a text that is intended above all as a communication of
experiences and perspectives rather than a completed exposition, I
insist on presenting the first steps in this direction.

It is also why, rather than accumulating a series of cases on
which our research has so far yielded results (if only exploratory
ones), I have preferred to deploy the overall process of a single
struggle, located in one Paris quarter, in order to show the successive mappings through which we are trying to grasp the birth of a
new reality. The fact that it involves an opposition to the project
of urban renewal whose logic I have just analysed may help our
understanding of it.

Lastly, in the articulation between 'urban' struggle and political
struggle, it is very risky to limit oneself to studying the relation in
one direction, for there is a strong chance of finding the maximum
movement of transformation where the political class struggle is
the central element of the 'urban' mobilization, and thus duplicated
in its expression. That is why, through very fragmentary evidence,
we will try to pose the problem of their relation by referring to
two highly instructive historical processes, the Quebec 'citizens'
committees' and the movement of the *'pobladores'* in Chile during
the Popular Unity.

I The challenge to the urban reconquest of Paris: the struggle for rehousing in the 'Cité du Peuple'[15]

An old quarter of Paris, with a high proportion of working-class residents and a strong concentration of ethnic communities and immigrant workers. However, contrary to popular belief, the deterioration of the old buildings is no greater than that of the Paris average, although overcrowding is noticeably more pronounced, on account of the characteristics of the population rather than those of the quarter (see Table 60).

Table 60
Socio-economic characteristics and conditions of residence in the
Cité du Peuple in relation to the Paris average

	(Value in percentage in the Cité du Peuple/Value in percentage for the whole of the City of Paris) – 1
% of the population over 65	–0·22
% of the population under 19	+0·09
% of Algerian Muslims	+0·90
% of foreigners	–0·11
% of semi-skilled and unskilled workers	+0·34
% of upper management and liberal professions	–0·50
% of craftsmen and small tradesmen	–0·24
% of the active population	+0·01
% of active women	–0·09
% of persons living in overcrowded conditions	+0·36
% of dwellings without water	0
% of dwellings without WC	+0·08

The site has considerable advantages for a possible luxury apartment block and the proximity of the expanding business quarters creates basic conditions for an operation of 'urban reconquest' aimed at physical, social, functional and symbolic change in the occupation of the land.

Two types of urban renewal followed one another: the first, beginning slowly in 1958, concentrated on the demolition of a few unsanitary, extremely run-down pockets. The second movement, which accelerated about 1965–66, and which is at present in full

[15] The elements of this analysis derive from research in progress that I am carrying out into urban social movements in the Paris region with Ms F. Lentin (CNRS). Since the research, both in conception and execution, is being carried out in common, it is obviously impossible to dissociate here the contribution made by Ms Lentin. However, I wish to thank her for allowing me to present our work in this text. I have intentionally omitted any concrete indication so that the research may remain a pure element in the understanding of the internal dynamic of a social movement and give no opportunity to operations of urban pacification. It is enough to know that we are dealing with a quarter of Paris-*inter-muros* and that the inquiry was carried out in 1970.

swing, concerns above all the transformations of space typical of the operations of 'urban reconquest'.

The accentuation of this orientation and that, consequently, of the rhythm of work have caused a displacement of the preoccupations and demands of the population concerned. The demand for decent housing at affordable rents and convenient to the place of work has been relegated to second place before the threat of eviction, before the great fear of finding oneself without any housing at all or reduced to a transit estate.

Out of the spontaneous reactions to the interventions organized, of a protest and/or political kind, a certain mobilization took place around the question of being able to remain in one's dwelling as long as one was not given a satisfactory offer in terms of size, comfort, price and locality. The issue, therefore, is one common to the different actions carried out in the *'Cité du Peuple'*, a contradiction between, on the one hand, the housing conditions of the population concerned and, on the other, the project of the urban renewal of Paris (on the social, functional and symbolic planes) articulated with the profit of the property developers. This being the case, the first pole, (concerning the population) covers a diversity of situations (tenant, lodger, owner, co-owner, tradesman, etc.) and may possibly be broken down into terms of internal contradiction (for example, between owner and tenant).

In relation to the same objective issue, the particularities of the social base concerned in each sector and the type of intervention giving rise to the process of mobilization produce a variety of forms of struggle and lead to a wide spectrum of political situations and urban structures. It is this ensemble of specific processes that I am trying to explain, with the help, in particular, of the analysis of two quarters of the *Cité du Peuple*, in which mobilization was more marked than elsewhere and in which a variety of orientations was subjected to the test of practice.

But first we must retrace the evolution of the claims actions carried out on the housing front in the whole of the sector.

A Claims actions for the building of social housing
When the threats linked to the process of renewal became clear, there was a development of claims action among the workers and small tradesmen who constituted the dynamic element of the district. The origin of these actions is to be found in the initiative of the national tenants' organization, which was very strong in the locality and had solid political support, though declaring itself to be apolitical in its statutes and trying in fact to be so in practice. The national policy of this organization, placing the accent essen-

tially on the increase in public housing, found a particularly favourable response in the *Cité du Peuple*, in so far as the inhabitants were being directly subjected to both the experience of slums and the threat of having no home.

In 1965, in the context of an overall campaign aimed at relaunching the construction of HLMs in Paris — in which 430 homes had been built (whereas there were 100 000 families on the badly housed list and only 7000 homes could be begun on available land belonging to the Paris HLM organization) — a vast mobilization took place in the *Cité du Peuple* with a view to obtaining the construction of a large HLM block on the site of former industrial plant.

The claim was brought to the attention of the City of Paris and of the Prefecture of Police, in order to get first an allocation of the land for the construction of housing; it was then brought before the HLM organization, in order to obtain the necessary funds. The renewal of a whole pocket and the threat of a direct eviction of its residents accelerated the movement. Petitions were signed, meetings organized, speeches made at the market on Sunday mornings.

The Prefecture put forward contrary arguments: first it suggested the creation of an industrial zone, then it alleged an excess of noise in this quarter.

A large street demonstration was organized in front of the gates of the disused factory that still occupied the site, the object of the claim. Tension mounted and the police exerted various pressures on the known militants. The demonstration took place peacefully, however, and with the participation of several hundred local residents.

The land was finally allocated to the construction of HLMs, with the agreement of the City of Paris. Furthermore, a certain percentage of HLMs was granted as part of the renewal operation in progress in the most affected sector. The claims pressure was kept up, however, to obtain the definite construction of homes. This was the situation, as presented in a statement handed out after this initial victory:

> — We have got the site allocated for the building of HLM apartments despite the many rejections of the scheme by the authorities.
> — Square Gaieté, in spite of all our setbacks . . . HLMs have been promised that could be started immediately, if the necessary credits were granted.
> This is a success and we should congratulate ourselves on it. BUT THE ALLOCATION OF THE SITE IS NOT YET A BUILDING. In fact, the ceiling cost of building imposed at the HLM Office, and above which the government will not agree to credits, does not allow building to start, since no company

will agree to take on the building at that price. Consequently, for two years, no HLM has been built in our *arrondissement*, while many sites are available.

The pernicious policy of the government as far as housing is concerned encourages under-cutting and thus facilitates private building by the big property companies to the detriment of public building.

As a result, at the present time, in Paris, 35 000 homes at exorbitant rents are empty, while thousands of families are housed in slums or threatened with eviction.

This situation is becoming more and more critical and we must carry out this common action, in order:

— That there should be no eviction without rehousing.
— That the ceiling price of building imposed by the HLM Office of the City of Paris should correspond to the cost price of the building and that the necessary credits should be allocated.
— That speculation on building land should be rapidly brought to an end.
— That half the employers' 1% contribution should be paid to the HLM Office, in order to allow the workers of companies to be rehoused in HLMs and not in very expensive rented apartments.
— That public building in our *arrondissement* should be instrumented and correspond to the needs of the population of our quarters, with rents that can be paid by ordinary families.
— That by means of a piecemeal operation the following should be rehoused:

  — the residents of the pockets to be redeveloped,
  — the badly housed who live in slums, hotels, etc.,
  — young couples who cannot find homes and who, often, live with parents or will soon find themselves in overcrowding, with three generations in the same home, with all the difficulties that this involves, etc.

— That homes should be planned for old workers corresponding to their needs and abilities.
— The limitation and control of present rents, the form and extension of housing allocations.
— That social and cultural amenities, schools, crèches, youth clubs, playgrounds, etc., should be planned and completed at the same time as the building of the apartment blocks.
— The maintenance and modernization of old buildings in good repair.

At the present time, the HLMs have been built and occupied on the site provided. At first sight, this is a success for a broad claims action for the construction of public housing, setting out from an essentially working-class mobilization and confronting the public bodies (Prefect, City of Paris, the HLM Office), with the responsibility of providing housing and amenities, as a result of a process of urban renewal. For us, it is a question of establishing the meaning of such an action as a social process and, consequently, of measuring its effects in relation to the actors themselves and to the whole of the social dynamic involved.

In fact, the essential fact is the following: HLMs were actually built (half those demanded during the claims campaign), but the overwhelming majority of the threatened population of the quarter, at the base of the mobilization, has not been rehoused there. The reason is simple enough; it concerns the administrative mechanism of the allocation of public housing, which is tied to a waiting list common to the whole department. Consequently, the housing obtained by the struggle of the residents of the *Cité du Peuple* was allocated to badly housed families who had been waiting for years in the whole of Paris. There is a lack of correspondence, therefore, between the base of the mobilization and the possible response to this claim, since the administration cannot override the arrangements for allocation. Now, although it is clear that one may envisage local action bearing on an overall policy (just as the workers of a factory may strike in order to stop the implementation of a stabilization plan at the national level), let us remember that it was a question of providing homes for people threatened with eviction. And this situation was the basis of their ability to mobilize.

There was, however, one claim capable of reestablishing the link between the situation at the origin of the problem and the objective to be obtained; the need for piecemeal operations in the context of each renewal programme, that is to say, the building prior to demolition and in the same area, of housing in which the evicted families would be rehoused at reasonable rents. But such a claim runs counter to the very foundation of the renewal operation, which is aimed above all at the social transformation of the quarter and at the introduction of a high dynamic of consumption (which requires therefore a higher purchase ability) and a symbolic marking out (linked to the social status of the residents). This, therefore, is an issue that puts the residents in danger of eviction directly in the hands of the powerful machine of the urban renewal programme in Paris.

This demand certainly figures in the claims programme of the campaign that we have described. But since its nature is very different from the simple demand for the construction of HLMs (which scarcely effects the renewal programme itself), the level of struggle necessary in order to achieve it was higher. Was it unrealizable? In any case, a new problematic, which is at the centre of our analysis, begins to emerge: what happens to this mass claims movement that suddenly finds itself without a *raison d'être*?

I shall reconstruct the effects of this process on the basis of the analysis (carried out in 1970) of two sectors that are very important both on the level of the renewal-operation and on that of effective mobilization.

We should examine briefly, therefore, an action of a different style, which, though not particularly remarkable in itself, suggests, in the context of the whole process, a few interesting hypotheses.

B The conditions of anti-speculative action
A pocket of handsome buildings in the middle of the quarter. Built about 1905, in stone, with balconies, they are divided into apartments and rented to office workers, middle management, etc. Nothing would lead one to suspect the threat that hung over this sector. Indeed, nothing would justify it from an urbanistic point of view. Yet the proximity of a park and the high status enjoyed by this part of the quarter in relation to others created the possibility for a speculative operation aimed at buying the buildings, demolishing them and building high-rise luxury apartment blocks. The renewal body bought the buildings and promised the tenants, now greatly disturbed by the new situation, new homes . . . in the outer suburbs!

Faced with this threat, tenants rushed to the offices of their association and a committee was formed on the spot, leading to meetings in the whole of the pocket. A campaign was launched to alert public opinion: press conferences, letters to deputies and municipal councillors, protests to the administration.

The administration responded (though its response, was not, of course, made public!). The association's delegate in the building was summoned by an official body and offered a fine apartment on very advantageous terms. She refused.

Having thus alerted public opinion as to the purely speculative character of an operation concerning buildings whose condition was well above the average, the committee obtained full satisfaction. The property company, which was no longer interested in the matter from the moment the demolition was set aside, resold the buildings to another company, which itself resold to the tenants at very advantageous prices, and all the lower because their attitude has been tough during the protest period. Certain tenants, who were unable to buy, had to move, but were given very high compensation. The buildings were not touched.

With a middle-class basis, and at the end of an action centred on institutional approaches and the alerting of public opinion, the association was therefore able to counter totally what was presented as a single purely speculative operation. But it is significant that it was only the conjunction of the three elements that gave force to the campaign carried out:

1. The individual character of the situation enabled a localized opposition to form, without challenging a wider complex of forces representing considerable interests.

2. Since it was pure speculation, it was difficult to bring in the public procedures of expropriation. This shows the concrete importance of the fusion between the theme of slum renewal and conquest-renewal, the first serving, in most cases, as a screen for the second.

3. But, in any case, the action was able to succeed, because it was based on a fairly special social base that had the social and economic capacity to oppose a limited intervention. In concrete terms, since the apartments had been sold for between eight and fifteen million old francs, there was no change in occupation in so far as the inhabitants could find such sums.

Thus, the case of an action centred on public opinion and on institutional approaches that obtained complete success is such a special one that it leads one to reflect. Is there, perhaps, a correspondence between the type of action generally carried out in the quarter and the defence of the housing of the middle strata? Does this type of action collapse when confronted by a large programme such as urban renewal?

C The cônfrontation with renewal

If mobilization took place in the quarter, it was not so much because of the bad housing conditions that reigned there (in this respect it did not differ from other Paris quarters), as because of the renewal programme, undertaken with the support of the administration, and which presented the residents with the constant threat of eviction.

At its Paris conference, the national tenants' association decided to carry out a vigorous campaign against renewal and to set up defence committees to oppose dehousing in any conditions.

This position was expressed with great clarity in the resolution of the Conference on Urban Renewal, which I reproduce here:

RENEWAL

On the problem of renewal itself, everybody agreed that it should take place, that slums should give place to proper housing.

But all members were equally agreed that renewal should be carried out in certain conditions that should form part of the Federation's programme. For example:

— *Rehousing in the same place or nearby* in new buildings, under HLM control with regulated rents, related to the income of the inhabitants.

— *Exchange facilities*, notably for the elderly and those with low incomes (with a lowering of rent through the allocation of compensation).

— *The rehousing of all residents*, including those living in hotels (whether or not unmarried), concierges, etc.

— *Reasonable compensation* enabling tradesmen and craftsmen to reestablish their businesses, it being understood that factories that are not environmentally harmful will be retained in the quarters.

— *An acceptable formula* envisaged for co-owners and the owners of small detached houses;

— *In order to facilitate these public renewal programmes*, the Commission demands *a limitation on the price of building land, whether or not it has been built on*, and *priority of purchase accorded to the City of Paris* for its HLM Office or for property companies, as has occurred in the operation of the avenue d'Italie and the Hauts-de-Belleville.

Of course, the practice of such a method in renewal will not come about of itself. Such claims will be achieved only by a grouping together of all interested categories living in the unsanitary pockets marked out for renewal. Unceasing action, including the signing of petitions, the publishing of bulletins or appeals, the detection of available land, delegations to elected representatives and public bodies and the organization of meetings, must be carried out in a rational way. Not forgetting the setting up of a small headquarters with regular hours of opening and the constitution of committees building by building.

For this, the constitution of a defence committee in these pockets is indispensable.

This was the second point, the principal point examined by members of the Commission, the one that above all motivated the creation of the said commission.

The discussion was very useful and showed how necessary it was and, consequently, how necessary it is also to warn our local militants.

In fact, so much was said to these militants about social housing, about construction, about renewal, about committees of this or that, that a certain confusion may have taken root in the minds of certain of our militants.

The discussion was very valuable, therefore, and resulted in something that should not be forgotten.

Social construction, with the constitution of very broad Committees calling on the very diverse associations formed on the initiative of our sections, is to be encouraged and developed. But that is one thing.

The Defense Committees are something quite different. Of course, they must also be very broad, constituted apart from any other consideration than renewal, but, essentially, they must also depend on our sections (and be represented on the executive commission) and include only our members — at least as far as the tenants are concerned. We must not leave to other much less representative organizations the task of setting up these committees.

In these committees, at a general assembly of the interested parties, will be appointed the members of the Bureau and an appeal will be made to representatives of the co-owners, tradesmen and craftsmen. Since, as a body, we cannot issue the organization's membership cards to co-owners, we shall, at the formation of the committee, call on the assistance of a delegate from the National Association of Co-owners. It will be left to him to issue cards, as required. Co-owners of good faith, living in their own property, will be able to follow our work, participate in it closely and if important delegations take place, the representatives of the National

Association of Co-owners may accompany us. Special meetings will be arranged for the tradesmen and craftsmen.

Although the term, '*operation-tiroir*' (the piecemeal method of renewal, by which only small residential areas are developed one at a time), is not used, the formula proposed amounts to the same thing in practice. In any case, as the report says, this formula is fundamentally opposed to the logic of the renewal programme and could be imposed only by the struggle of the defence committees. Indeed, the preoccupation with a strict control of the activity of these committees explains the feeling that very tough battles, with political implications, might occur around this question.

I have been able to reconstruct the action carried out in this perspective in two very important sectors within the *Cité du Peuple*: the Square Gaieté and the Presqu'ile.

Table 61

Socio-economic and housing characteristics in the Gaieté and Presqu'île sectors. Comparisons with the Cité du Peuple and between the two sectors, 1962

Characteristics	Presqu'île		Square Gaieté	
	Average value	Comparison : $\dfrac{Presqu'île}{Cité\ du\ Peuple} - 1$	Average value	Comparison : $\dfrac{Sq.\ Gaieté}{Cité\ du\ Peuple} - 1$
	%		%	
+ 65	11·2	0	+0·13	12·5
− 19	22·0	−0·09	−0·11	21·5
Algerians	3·3	+0·10	−0·77	0·7
Foreigners	9·2	+0·61	−0·13	5·0
Semi-skilled and un-skilled workers	24·0	+0·14	−0·13	16·2
Upp. man.	1·5	−0·30	−0·06	4·7
Lib. profs.	8·0	0	+0·30	10·0
Craftsmen, tradesmen	50·0	−0·10	+0·07	58·0
Active population Active women	42·4	0	0	42·9
Overcrowding	40·0	0·76	+0·30	31·3
Dwellings without water	14·3	+0·58	+0·44	4·0
Dwellings without WC	80·0	+0·75	−0·10	43·0

a. *The Square Gaieté* at the centre of one of the most important renewal operations, has for several years been the focus of protest movements in the quarter. As the table shows, it is characterized by a deterioration of the habitat, distinctly more pronounced than for the quarter as a whole (in particular, the most telling indication of this is the proportion of dwellings without water), but by a social level distinctly above the average in the quarter, fewer skilled and unskilled workers, far fewer Algerians and above all an over-representation of craftsmen and tradesmen.

This sector was in the forefront of the mobilization described, which led to the building of the HLMs. But given the outcome of these events (the systematic non-rehousing of local residents in the buildings thus obtained), 'a certain hesitation crept in' (an interview with militants). As the renewal operation advanced and eviction became more pronounced, rehousing overshadowed any other question. And since no collective solution could be envisaged in the context of the renewal programme the association was reduced to the role of intermediary and adviser in a whole series of individual and fragmented negotiations which, it is said, succeeded in rehousing a large number of the evicted residents: some of them in HLMs built as part of the programme, others in Paris, others in the suburbs. In any case, it was a process of individual rehousing, with or without the support of the association, and without opposing an overall rejection of evictions, since there could be no question of defending the slums. Most of the militants in the association were rehoused and the new members, in the years 1968–70, were recruited rather among the new arrivals in the HLM estate, with fairly specific claims, far removed from the problem of the eviction.

After this process of filtering and rehousing, and when most of the renewal programme was underway, there remained a rump at the Square Gaieté – people who had not left, either because they could not, or because they did not feel directly threatened, or because they had decided to 'benefit' to the end from the low rent, at the risk of being rehoused hastily when finally evicted by the authorities.

On to this rump, of which the Impasse Philippe is one of the best examples, was grafted a new mobilizing intervention, when the National Tenants' Association had left the field.

The origin of this intervention was a combination of agitation in the university and a group of students who decided to make a systematic study of the *Cité du Peuple*, attempting both to arrive at a concrete appreciation of a social situation and to initiate a political process among the residents of the quarter. There was street agitation; there were addresses to the crowd in the market denouncing the grip of the developers on renewal; the movement looked around for a focus of attention. The students thought they had found it in a defence of the residents who were threatened with eviction by force. They carried out an investigation. The most dramatic case was that of the *concierges*, who had no right to rehousing – the renewal body does not hand out presents. When there is no legal obstacle, it works quite simply by force. And so a protest action was started, as described in the bulletin of the anti-renewal committee:

> In order not to pay compensation to two old people left alone, the renewal body is ready to demolish their house over their heads.
>
> They hoped to demoralize these two old *concierges* who lived on the ground floor by demolishing the roof of the building. When it rained, water dripped into their apartment; demolition next door caused water and gas leaks; these urban renewal scoundrels were in no hurry to rehouse them and waited for them to leave or for the house to collapse on top of them.
>
> Disabled and with no resources, the two old people remained; the company then sent in the bulldozers. A hoist was attached to the corner of the building, the whole edifice shook, stones hit the doorstep.
>
> At the request of a few comrades who had been told of what was happening, the workers went off and resumed their work further on. But later, the man in charge of the site intervened and declared that there was no danger and that the demolition should be resumed.
>
> Faced with these unscrupulous monsters, ready to risk killing two old people, some comrades went to the company offices to demand the immediate rehousing of the old people. They were ordered to leave: the police were called. Six comrades were taken to the police station, then released, after the police had recognized the scandal in the street.
>
> Confronted by this mobilization, the company retreated and rehoused the old people two days later.
>
> But this was only a half victory, for the renewal body had rehoused the old couple in another slum from which they would certainly be evicted again within six months. Our mobilization had not been big enough: the renewal is once again beginning to throw residents into the street. A larger part of the population must be mobilized; faced with our unity and determination, the company will give in.

Starting from the effect that this issue had in the quarter (generally speaking, it was welcomed, since the affair of the *concierges* was regarded as scandalous), they undertook a systematic campaign, in particular on an ecologically well defined unit, the Impasse Philippe, just on the edge of the renewal sites, where a few dozen households remained, under direct threat of eviction. When the letters granting a delay arrived, before eviction was proceeded with, the Anti-Renewal Committee intervened, stuck posters on the walls of the street and militants went from door to door trying to get a collective petition signed that demanded detailed facts from the renewal body as to the date and methods of the dehousing-rehousing intended. 'We made this proposition because we realized that the common concern of all the residents in the Impasse was to know exactly how the renewal body intended dealing with them, and this body had left them in complete ignorance in order to

weaken their resistance' (internal report of the AC). But meanwhile the company had sent a letter to each of the tenants, making
him a number of very detailed propositions, specifically aimed at
each case. The individualization of the problem deprived the collective letter of any interest. This letter was signed only by ten tenants
who, indeed, had never been able to meet. Each household treated
its problem separately and the AC lost contact and in the end its
action was weakened. The direct and almost exhaustive inquiry
being carried out among the residents of the Impasse who were still
there three months later showed that there was practically no trace
of this intervention either in the memory or in the practice of the
tenants, who spoke of it only in terms of 'leftists I had shown the
door to'.

The fragmentation of this action can be explained largely by
conjunctural elements: the external character of the AC in relation to the quarter, amateurism, the lack of regular office opening
times. More important still, the intervention had occurred at the
end of the process: when the chips were down, the most militant
had left, the base was weak and the operation was drawing to a
close. However, it might also be claimed that the conjuncture was
favourable for the organization of a new style of resistance to eviction. Now, what seems to me characteristic is precisely the existence of a very concrete claim and a style of institutional action on
the part of the tenants (petitions, etc.), coupled with an overtly
ideological language and spectacular but irrelevant action. There
was alternation between rather than a combination of the brilliant
attack on injustice and law-abiding protest action such as had been
previously practised by the tenants' association.

The protest was not locally rooted and the population emerged
from a protest experience that had been resolved by the individualization of the problems. Thereafter, a protest action with weak
means at its disposal, juxtaposed with an ideological challenge open
to external minority actions, was, by its very nature, exposed to
repression and, above all, to indifference. The complete disintegration of the AC followed relatively logically.

Those who remained in the Impasse Philippe — the blind old
man who knew nothing but this street doomed to demolition, the
many families who were awaiting their transfer to transit estates,
the house-owners who tried to extract profit up to the last
moment — all these formed part of a different world, the world of
deportation, the underside of the new Paris.

b. *The Presqu'île.* Here the situation was much the same, but the
issue became more dramatic. First, from the point of view of the

population, which was characterized by a marked predominance of workers (semi-skilled and unskilled), immigrant workers and ethnic communities. Secondly, the degree of deterioration of the habitat was much higher than in the *Cité du Peuple* as a whole (see Table 61). And yet, the renewal programme was markedly less advanced than in the Square Gaieté. Was this due to the increased resistance of the population? Partly, since this sector had for many years been in the forefront of the protest movement in the *Cité* as a whole. A committee of the badly housed had been formed in the area that was linked to the National Tenants' Association, but centred on the specificity of the situation: the committee linked resistance to eviction with the demand for decent housing.

Here renewal as such was not disliked, providing it was carried out for the benefit of the residents; it should be said that these residents belonged to the poorer strata and were particularly sensitive to the discrimination that might be practised against them in a future environment over which they would have no control. So the appropriate claim was for a piece meal operation in phases (for example, the rehousing of part of the population within the *arrondissement*, if it could not be done locally, and the construction of a home for the elderly, etc.). There was a fairly intense mobilization for this objective on the part of a section of the residents (the immigrants and ethnic communities — Jews, North Africans — remaining outside). Meetings took place over a long period, residents stood up to the threats of eviction (like the old woman who had lived for a year in a bit of building under a rubbish dump on a building site until she was rehoused), petitions were signed by an overwhelming number of residents (700 signatures were counted in a single morning). Delegations presented these demands to the City of Paris and to the Prefecture. But, in fact, the answer was to come, on the one hand, from the HLM office and, on the other hand, from the renewal body. The former, however, had no legal obligation to give preference to the residents of the Presqu'île by housing them in the HLMs of the *arrondissement*. As far as the renewal body was concerned, the solution could only be by re-housing elsewhere. Only 150 HLMs were to be built on the site. This is all that was achieved by this mobilization, whereas it was a matter of replacing 2500 homes.

Furthermore, the 150 HLMs were far from being guaranteed. They did not come high on the list of priorities and, furthermore, they were planned on the site of an existing chapel, which would have to be demolished — against the opposition of the archdiocese. This arrangement of the general plan verged on Machiavellianism. It had already caused a religious split within the Committee, the lay majority preferring to accept this promise rather than nothing and the Catholic minority refusing the demolition of the chapel, which was indispensable, within the renewal time-table, to the realization of this mini-piecemeal operation.

The result was confrontation: the residents having decided to remain, for the moment at least, and the renewal body pulling out all the stops to reduce the only serious resistance in the *arrondissement* as a whole.

There is little point in enumerating the panoply of measures of intimidation used: windows walled up as soon as anyone was forced to leave, frequent burglaries (or attempted burglaries), inadequate maintenance of the public thoroughfares (except for drastic reclamation), threats about the increasing difficulty of satisfactory rehousing, etc. And above all a piecemeal operation aimed at splitting one case from another and reducing opposition by distributing it in time and space.

The conflict was too acute for the protest to succeed easily. Despite the multiplicity of the institutional approaches, this type of action did not have sufficient weight on this occasion. The account, in June 1970, of the last interviews with those responsible is an admission of failure:

> At the end of our magnificent New Year evening, which brought together over a hundred people, our Committee decided to go and see our elected representatives and to explain our problems to them. What we wanted was:
> the immediate construction of the 150 HLMs that had long since been promised us;
> the allocation of dwellings for the residents of the quarter out of the 1789 that had already been constructed on the site of the former factory;
> the immediate construction of homes for the elderly.
> Our first approach was to the elected representatives of the area. To begin with, we saw the municipal councillors, of which Mr S. was the representative.
> Mr S. was well acquainted with the preoccupations of the quarter (his speeches at council meetings were evidence of this). He concluded by expressing his regret that views expressed in speeches were very often ignored, owing to the fact that the councillors favourable to our claims were not in a majority on the council.
> Our second approach was made the same day to M., our deputy. Having listened to our claims, he declared that all this did not come into his field, but into that of the municipal council. However, he promised to do all he could to help us.
> Thus we eventually found ourselves in the office of Mr A., an assistant to Mr V.
> Both passed responsibility for decisions on to the town hall and blamed

the 'compartmentalization of government'. In the course of this interview, M. told us that he had gone to see the prefect to explain our grievances to him and that the prefect 'became angry, banged his fist on the table and flung in front of him the building plans of our 150 HLMs'.

We were received by Mr P., an assistant to the prefect, to whom we had brought our grievances.

As far as the 150 HLMs to be built were concerned, Mr P. told us, contrary to Mr R., that the building permit would be granted only after approval of the overall plan proposed by the renewal body. Now, at the present time, this is the fourth project to be examined — the first three having been rejected by the town planning services on the grounds of inadequacy in the provision of social amenities.

Mr P. also declared that the HLM organization had no obligation to rehouse the company's tenants in the buildings constructed on the site of the old factory.

He told us, on the other hand, that an old people's home would soon be started (80 rooms with shared amenities), and a further 80 rooms, in the sector . . . . But in the latter case, plans have not yet been accepted.

In fact, except for a home of 80 rooms and the 150 HLMs, which had been promised from the outset, nothing has been gained.

The exodus began. In a few months, over 1000 homes were vacated, with individual arrangements, sometimes negotiated with the moral and legal support of the committee, but always in unfavourable conditions. Those who remained were either those who did not yet believe themselves to be in immediate danger (this was the case with a whole section of the quarter belonging to the second stage of the operation) or the few rare militants and those who could not move and whose situation was desperate. This was the case, for example, of this household (account of a visit):

Furnished room: a very dilapidated building in which very few residents remained.

A *working-class* household (the father a building worker), five children (one to eight years old), living in a single room.

The children live either in the beds, or sitting on a bench (things are better since they have started going to school). The only time they can play is on Thursdays — a school holiday — when they go to a day nursery. There they can run around. The effects of this situation are as follows: a dyslexic child, a child with personality disorders (the doctor at the dispensary says that this child needs a room to himself). The health of the husband has suffered — he has difficulty in breathing, which is nervous in origin.

Reaction to eviction: the wife (very calm, well dressed, well organized) makes constant attempts to get an HLM; one of these attempts almost succeeded; they visited the apartment, but the husband was off work, sick — the apartment was refused them.

The reason given was the insecurity that the obligation to pay rent

would bring to this family (they themselves believe that with sickness benefit and family allowances, not to mention a possible housing grant, they
would have quite enough to live on). The second approach was a file drawn
up with the help of the social worker. This file was returned to the prefecture because one item had arrived late — it was thought that they had
given up their application. The wife went to the prefecture and asked for
her file back and, incidentally, succeeded in getting her children competently treated (speech therapy, etc.).

The husband was angry and desperate: 'They won't get me out of here
until they give me a decent home. They can send the police if they like —
I've got two bottles of butane gas.'

He was a member of the Association, but is so no longer, because he has
refused to pay his rent, 'ever since there has been no running water on this
floor'.

The leader of the committee, a devoted militant, who is very
well known in the quarter, admits that he is discouraged at the
local level, but is resuming the struggle in the *arrondissement* as a
whole.

In these desperate conditons, a new kind of intervention arose,
the clearest example of which is the evolution of the struggle in
one of the zones of the Presqu'île, the rue de la Boue.

The rue de la Boue is a slum inhabited, for the most part, by unskilled workers, immigrants or North African Jews!

The Committee of the Badly Housed has not taken root in the
area, particularly on account of the cultural barrier. Yet the living
conditions are worse than anywhere else: in particular, there is a
strong risk of buildings collapsing and hygienic conditions are well
below the minimum norms (there are rats everywhere, for example).
And yet the residents are directly threatened with eviction. They
want to leave. How could they do otherwise, having lived in these
conditions for ten, fifteen or twenty years? But, except in very few
cases, they have refused to leave on just any conditions. They want
to remain in Paris and in the case of the Jewish community, they
wish to remain together. These Jews are natives of Tunisia and
regard it as essential to remain in a district in which employment
and residence keep Jews together (the employers belong for the
most part to the Ashkenazy community, which has been established
here for thirty years) and in which the links within the group may
be preserved. Now, since they have very little money, they are in a
worse position than anybody to refuse removal to the suburbs. So
they remain. Like the old people, like the families of the Yugoslav
unskilled workers, like the large families of handicapped semi-
skilled workers, living on top of one another and being refused
housing in an HLM because the inquiry shows 'that they are not
clean'.

This terrain gave rise to the intervention of a new organization, directly centred on political confrontation, and which presented itself as such to the residents. It was made up of young workers and proletarianized students living in the quarter, and it set out above all to establish day-to-day relations with the residents. For example, they helped to carry out repairs; they organized games for the children, who proved to be the best propagandists for the committee; they offered to convert a muddy wasteland into a playing field. On the basis of this contact, kept up by constant door-to-door encounters, and by a daily presence, they organized a tenants' defence committee, the aim of which was to get the residents rehoused in the same quarter and at rents they could afford. Meanwhile, they offered to carry out repairs for the residents, to create amenities on the spot (in a nearby quarter, they occupied a garden square and tried to organize a crèche) and to resist eviction and intimidation. They immediately linked their claims to the general political struggle:

What does renewal mean?
It means: building expensive apartment blocks near the park.
And the poor who live there in old crumbling buildings will be removed to the suburbs.
But, faced with the anger of the residents, they propose to build a few HLMs (2500 evicted families, 35 HLMs to be built). They will pile in as many people as possible to the square metre, because the higher 'the co-efficient of land occupation', the higher the developers' profit.
And what about health? What about air pollution?
And the crèches? And the green spaces?
And the sports fields?
No, it's always money that decides everything!
Thousands of foreign workers brought into France by the employers are piled into old, dirty homes in shantytowns, because they are over-exploited for starvation wages or reduced to unemployment.
We cannot stand for it!
Let us organize to make sure that the *Cité du Peuple* remains a working-class quarter with new housing and air to breathe.   .
In the struggle and through the struggle we shall break our chains.
TOGETHER WE SHALL BRING THE BOURGEOISIE DOWN!

The renewal body stepped up its activity in the rue de la Boue. It allowed squatters, Yugoslav workers who had just arrived and whose presence terrorized the neighbours, into the few empty apartments. One day, workmen arrived to cut off the water. There was a general mobilization. The militants were there. But all the housewives in the street were there too. And the children refused to get off the streets. The water would not be cut off. The police gave up the idea of intervening.
A direct investigation among the tenants showed the support

and sympathy enjoyed by members of the Committee, 'despite' their overtly expressed political allegiances. Although the local people did not take the activity of the Committee in hand completely, they felt supported by this action, in the midst of the abandonment and general hostility of the government bodies and services that dealt with them.

But the claim of the Committee (renewal to the benefit of the residents of the quarter) was disproportionate in relation to the weakness of the pocket of resistance thus constituted. Little by little, people's energy ebbed away. A meeting called to revive action (and approved by the tenants on their doorsteps) failed because of low attendance. The children were directly threatened by the police ('You'll go to prison for the rest of your life if you play with those people'). Partial collapses of buildings began to occur. Anxiety spread. More and more people left. In the short term, removal on an individual basis (on the renewal body's terms) was inevitable.

The militants knew this. But, for them, it was not a question of winning a claims battle whose scope exceeded their strength. 'The main thing is to bring about a change in people's heads.' The failure of the claims action thus led to political radicalization. Is this true?

On this basis, the Committee had to spread the struggle throughout the *Cité du Peuple*, to broaden the action. A demonstration took place in the market place, with posters, placards and speeches. The process began again. And the renewal programme continued on its way, without much modification to its plans. The political struggle, in the strict sense, took the upper hand. Although for the dominant class, urban renewal seems to be a means of killing the Commune, for the militants, the defence of the residents is part of a perspective directly opposed to that; a hundred years after 1871, a manifesto handed out in those quarters of Paris in which resistance to renewal was being organized bore a significant title: *Living Commune*.

D The struggle for rehousing as a social process
Although the articulated exposition of the principal protest movements revealed a certain logic on occasion, it is clear that the description of a mechanism cannot take the place of explanation. Since my aim is to map out the conditions of emergence of social movements in the 'urban' domain rather than to dwell on a given conjuncture, we shall try to establish, briefly, the principal elements of each of the actions (or ensemble of actions linked around an objective and a mode of intervention) and to determine their interrelations, in particular in relation to the type of effects

Diagram IX
Process of struggle for rehousing in the 'Cité du Peuple'

Issue	Social base	Organization	Social force	Adversary	Claim	Action	Urban effects Political effects
(1) Square Gaieté	Developer's profit + Renewal programme (Housing of residents)	•Several classes *except* upper management •Importance of craftsmen and tradesman	•An active Tenants' Association with national influence and strong local roots	Workers with support of tradesmen	Prefecture of City of Paris HLM Mixed renewal body	Construction of HLMs + Rehousing	•Propaganda •Petitions •Delegation •Meeting •Street demonstration	1) Construction of HLMs, but without rehousing the population there 2) Rehousing of part, negotiated individually 3) A rump left to be expelled 4) Demobilization
(2) Presqu'île	+ No repairs conditions housing + Developer's profit + Renewal programme	•Clear preponderance of semi-skilled and unskilled workers, immigrants and foreigners	•National Tenants' Association	Unskilled workers	Prefecture of City of Paris HLM Mixed renewal body	+ *Opération* tiroir	+ Tenants' refusal to leave + Constant meetings and office with regular opening hours	1) = 1 ⎫ for Square 2) = 2 ⎬ Gaieté 3) 150 HLMs ⎭ promised to re house *on the spot* part of the population 4) A large proportion left to be re-housed. 5) Discouragement Intervention maintained

(3) Impasse Philippe	Same issue as Square Gaieté	• More working class, older, with more immigrants than Square Gaieté	• Action committee outside the quarter: *uniting economic claims with ideological contestation*	Students external to the quarter	Mixed renewal body	• Rehousing on the spot with equivalent rents • Resistance to eviction	• Occupation of offices (Police confrontation) • Agit-Prop. • Petition to be signed by tenants	1) Temporary re-housing of an old evicted couple 2) Rejection of collective petition from most residents 3) Decline, then extinction of the Action Committee (in existence for 10 months) 4) Individual stampede by families that remained
(4) Rue de la Boue	Same issue as Presqu'île	• Clear preponderance of North African Jews and unskilled workers	*Local* Action Committee that linked economic claims + political contestation + ideological contestation	• Tradesmen + some proletarianized students living in the quarter	Mixed renewal body	• Amenities on the spot • Equivalent rehousing near place of residence • Resistance to eviction	• Agitation • Daily help and material help • Collective resistance to workers cutting off water, etc • Petitions • Meetings and door-by-door interviews	1) Withdrawals of the renewal body on postponed evictions 2) In the short term, de-housing 3) Support of the population for resistance against eviction 4) A certain political radicalization

produced on the urban structure and/or on the conjuncture of social relations.

We shall propose, with all due precautions, a semi-theoretical, semi-descriptive classification of the elements of each action in Diagram IX.

We are not in a position to interpret systematically the connections that appear in this diagram. Too many links are missing. One may, however, bring out a few of these connections, first *analytically*, between the different elements, then, *synthetically*, by reconstructing the course of an action.

a. *The relations between the elements of a claims action*
The more a general issue (threat of eviction) is reinforced by a specific issue (housing conditions), the tougher the confrontation and the more intense the mobilization.

The *social force* mobilized is always a specification of the *social base*. They do not intersect. This specification derives directly from the type of organization (and, consequently, of the claims made).

The relation between *social* base and type of *organization*: The more the base is *working-class* and ethnically French, the more deeply rooted is the national claims organization. The more the base is *socially low*, the more revolutionary politics can take root (with the indispensable condition that this must be locally based). Any *external intervention* remains cut off from the social base whatever it may be.

The more diversified and general the *adversary*, the more chances there are for a certain claim to succeed. But chances do not vary as far as claims concerning the renewal programme are concerned. Let us say that chances of success increase if the claim avoids this area.

The closer the correspondence between the immediate interests of the social base and the *claim*, the more *intense* the action is. This correspondence, which is brought about by the organization, must be understood as an immediate *material* response to the situation from which this claim derives.

The *urban* effect depends directly on the *issue* and on the *level of mobilization*. But one may summarize the mechanism in the following way:

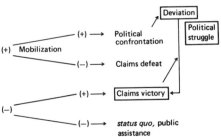

The *political* effect depends on the *urban* effect, on the *level* of *mobilization* and on the type of organization. One may analyse the relation between the elements according to the following schema:

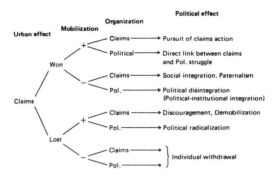

b. *The social determination of actions*
We are confronted with four actions, which we shall deal with in the order in which they occur in Diagram IX.

In the first case, there was a correspondence between social base, organization, level of mobilization and claim, but the political confrontation that resulted from it was *diverted* (transformed claim) and there was therefore, on this basis, a gap between claim and issue, which consequently, caused demobilization.

In the second case, the correspondence remained throughout and it was reinforced by a *defeat*, due to the limits of a purely claims-orientated mobilization.

In the third case, apart from the particularly unfavourable conjuncture, the type of organization (external to the social base and lacking in local roots) seems to have conditioned the *non-fusion* of elements characteristic of this failure.

Lastly, in the fourth case, social base, organization and claim correspond, but the process seems to end with a claims defeat (power relations involved), which might lead to a political radicalization.

It should be pointed out that the whole of the analysis took place against the background of a total inability to penetrate the level of institutional political struggle, owing to the unique functioning of the Municipal Council and of the opposition, on the part of the majority, to any initiative that ran counter to the renewal plans. In such conditions, each claims defeat that is not politicized in the direction of a radicalization is also a political defeat, since the passage on to the institutional stage cannot take place.

These brief analyses, which we shall not develop here, given the extremely limited character of the terrains observed, nevertheless enable us to begin to establish systems for the detection of social movements, which, we know, is the major problem of our research.

II The relation between urban struggle and political struggle: the Quebec and Chilean experiences[16]

If a social movement is to be distinguished by its pertinent effects in the power relations, it is clear that the problematic of the urban social movements has as its axis the forms of articulation between 'urban' struggles and 'political' struggles, that is to say, the conditions in which an urban claim becomes a political issue and the way in which each specific process leads to a distinct political treatment; or, in other words, which contradictions and mobilization are repressed, which are integrated, which manage to create a new situation in political class relations, which do not succeed in becoming clearly articulated with other levels of social relations.

I shall try to pose this problem through the discussion, necessarily summary and schematic, of two historical experiences, which, on this plane, are of exceptional interest.

A   Urban claims and political action in the Montreal citizens' committees:[17] *From social work to protest*
Perhaps it was a long march from footpath maintenance to the transformation of society, with public joy and civic goodwill uniting in a common attack upon the power of evil and money.

The *citizens' committees* which developed in Quebec and especially in Montreal from 1963 onwards, based upon the problems of daily life in various districts, were, in fact, at their inception, a per-

---

[16] This section re-written in 1972 and includes material additional to that in the French edition.
[17] The information upon which this analysis is based comes from several sources: personal experience, especially in the *Mouvement d'action politique municipale* during my stay in Montreal in 1969; the work of Quebec students in my urban politics seminars at Montreal University in 1969 and at the University of Paris in 1970 and 1971; long conversations with one of the leaders of the *Front d'action politique* (FRAP) in 1971; discussions with Evelyne Dumas, author of a series of articles on this theme in the *Montreal Star;* continual exchange of information and ideas with Ginette Truesdell, a Quebec sociologist who has written a study on this theme; bulletins, tracts, publications and internal reports of FRAP and Montreal citizens' committees. It goes without saying that none of these people or sources are responsible for errors or statements I may have made. On the other hand, they count for a great deal in the information and analyses given. In this chapter I did not censor place names or circumstances since, as a result of Quebec's particular characteristics, these have all been published. Finally, I have abstained from any political judgement of this experience in the strict sense: It is up to the people of Quebec and their militants to judge.

fect expression of that strange and fascinating phenomenon, Quebec society, rooted in the old Christian community spirt and the political naivety of North American liberalism, via social work, and in the mobilization capacity of 'decent people' when they are faced with flagrant injustice.

The historical roots of one of the most important urban struggles of recent years were in old, dilapidated districts with residents dependent upon social assistance and battling against unemployment, sickness and the lack of communal facilities as a result of the liberal logic of *laissez-faire*; social workers paid by the City of Montreal (*Conseil des Oeuvres*) to manipulate needs, trying to get to the root of the problems, and some members of the *Compagnie des Jeunes Canadiens*, an organization that assisted the federal government and passed gradually from institutional help to political awareness.

The scene was set for a vast Christmas tale, complete with snow. But the development of urban claims was part of a general process; the radicalization of structural issues and the emergence of social movements in Quebec after the 'quiet revolution',[18] the passage into a new economic phase characterized by the increased involvement of Quebec in the economic network of large American firms. Thus it was that the citizens' committees had to face various new issues in the course of their action:

The crisis of the Quebec petty bourgeoisie and its political radicalization, expressed in the development of the nationalist, separatist movement, with all its variations, from individual acts of terrorism to the pro-American separatism of the leaders of the large *Parti québecois* formed as the result of an absorption process among the different bourgeois and petty-bourgeois groups which had been set up under cover of the nationalist revival.

The growing political awareness of the student world, and the establishment within it of nationalist and Marxist tendencies at the same time as its numerical significance was increasing and its professional outlets decreasing.

The 'left-wing' orientation of Quebec trade unions, notably of the former Christian union (*Confédération des syndicats nationaux* − CSN), but equally of the FTQ − *Fédération des travailleurs du Québec*, the Quebec branch of the AFL−CIO − a consequence both of the general political crisis and of a stagnant economy which

[18] The 'quiet revolution' was the name given to the 1960 electoral victory of the Liberal Party, representing the interests of the Anglo-Canadian bourgeoisie, over the Union Nationale, the party of the dictator Duplessis, who, with the support of the rural petty bourgeoisie, had given Quebec over to American mining companies. For a brief, but fairly clear analysis of the major features of the socio-political situation, see Racine and Denis (1971).

was leading to increasing unemployment. This evolution is demonstrated concretely in the CSN by the introduction of a 'second front' on the questions of consumption and lifestyle, and by the increased number of professional party politicians who, supported by the powerful union machinery, brought about the possibility for the first time in Quebec, of the emergence of militant, politically committed workers outside a purely electoral context.

Part of this general movement, the citizens' committees moved from social help to involvement in claims, and their staff became gradually transformed, both in terms of recruitment (there were more and more politically committed students who wanted to 'reach the people') and from the point of view of their orientation: they saw politics as a logical sequence of the partial local struggles.

This turnabout gave rise first of all to an 'experience coordination' movement: on 19 May 1968, the representatives of twenty citizens' committees from all over Quebec met in Montreal and instigated the process of passage from localized claims to a generalization and politicization of their action. As far as the fights themselves were concerned, the same trend was emerging: at the beginning of 1969, the campaign by residents of the Petite-Bourgogne district against the urban redevelopment that was causing them to be evicted and not rehoused, came to a climax in a massive uproar when the Canadian Prime Minister visited the redeveloped sector.

The scandal of Montreal City   This hardening of positions was determined not only by the mounting social tension in Quebec, but also by the actual conditions surrounding the urban claims in Montreal itself. In fact the situation as far as housing and communal facilities were concerned had been steadily worsening: over one quarter of the city's housing was slums, and one third of families badly housed; 75% of Montreal residents were tenants, whereas in Toronto this proportion fell to 33%. These tenants devoted 25% of their family budget to rent, one of the highest levels in the world. Along with this situation, not only was there no public housing worth speaking of (housing represented 0·4% of the city budget), but at the same time 2000 homes were being demolished each year, for the urban renewal programme, and replaced only by luxury apartment blocks. Furthermore, there was no health service in the working-class districts of Montreal, and only 10% of schoolchildren enjoyed adequate medical services (the health budget represented 1·5% of the municipal budget). There was a total neglect of public transport in favour of cars and the launching of the underground had been little more than a publicity stunt; the network had not been extended and the fares had increased by 66% in two years.

On the other hand, the city council was indulging in a grandiloquent policy of publicity operations, including the organization in 1967 of the World Fair, in close cooperation with large financial companies. Firmly controlled for years by the local leader Jean Drapeau and his *Parti Civique* (a mere electoral clique in the service of its leader), the city of Montreal had become a simple technical instrument of the interests of the Montreal upper bourgeosie, with no possibility of opposition within the city council and a terrorist policy against any show of local resistance. This is seen, for example, in the way the city's executive committee denounced the federal social assistance organ *Compagnie des Jeunes Canadiens*, in autumn 1969, as a tool of revolutionary subversion!

Municipal politicization: the FRAP and its ambiguities   This attitude of systematic indifference, apart from a few paternalistic gestures (the appointment of sports instructors for children from poor districts, for example) considerably assisted the radicalization of the citizens' committees in that no negotiation was possible. Thus it was that the residents of poor districts began to support the most radical positions of the 'social workers', starting from a very low level of political involvement, and began to consider how they could impose their demands. But for the issue in hand (the total transformation of the entire communal consumption policy of the city) they needed sufficient means to be able to face up to both financial interests and the municipal bureaucratic machine. They therefore conceived the idea of reinforcing the coordination between the citizens' committees and extending the urban struggles at the level of municipal politics, under cover of the vast nationalist mobilization and the social agitation at the end of 1969.

The municipal elections were approaching: they were fixed for autumn 1970 and offered an opportunity to start a popularization campaign for the struggles which until that time had been uncoordinated. The occasion was still more favourable in that the trade unions — which had originally scorned the committees, too often linked with 'lumpen' elements — had decided to give their second front a truly organic structure, and they were looking favourably upon the sharing of its work by the production and the politico-consumption fronts, the latter directing possible 'leftist' inclinations from their traditional field of intervention. So in 1970 the FRAP (*Front d'action politique*) was formed by the regrouping of the main citizens' committees and the political militants from the unions. This gave rise from the start to a basic ambiguity between several socio-political intentions:

the social base, i.e., the citizens' committees and a certain number of social workers, were conerned with gaining a tool to satisfy their claims by putting a permanent form of pressure on the authorities;

for the unions, the FRAP was *both* a beginning of syndicalism in the field of consumption and an experiment for a possible future labour party which would be an institutional expression of the specific interests of employees;

a few militants, mainly students, along with a minority of the citizens' committee members, felt that the FRAP should provide the possibility of establishing a mass movement within which a revolutionary current, independent of petty-bourgeois nationalism, could be created and developed.

These generally recognized ambiguities were expressed directly in the objectives and unfolding of the electoral campaign. For the first tendency, the objective was to gain an electoral victory by taking advantage of the separatists' progress to get social candidates elected in the 1970 provincial elections. For the most politically involved, the first aim was to take advantage of the campaign and develop politico-ideological agitation by pointing out a connection between the 'misdeeds' of daily life and structural capitalist logic, and the necessity for all the Quebec political parties — thus considered as bourgeois — to submit to this logic. The FRAP's electoral programme (FRAP, 1970) expressed this double tendency: it drew upon a pitiless condemnation of living conditions in the different districts of Montreal and established a link between them and the mechanisms of capitalist exploitation very well, only to propose remedies arising from — a new programme of city administration! At the same time the organizational structure which the movement had adopted had two sides: it was based on the political action committees (CAP) in the various districts and supported localist trends and the immediate claims of the citizens' committees, but at the same time its central machinery was organized with several commissions and a permanent secretariat whose task was coordination and the instigation of certain central political moves. There was a certain split between the two levels and a permanent state of tension between the secretariat and the local CAPs, which bore witness throughout the existence of the FRAP to the delicate balance between requirements which were sometimes simply divergent and sometimes downright contradictory.

And yet, during the early period of its influence, agreement was possible through an identical practical application of the different tendencies, in that the establishment of a genuine popular movement had to be undertaken from an extremely weak level of resis-

tance and political awareness, this in spite of the fighting spirit
revealed during occasional local struggles: the fight against private
property development in Milton Park, the demand for the building
of a hospital at Saint-Henri, the fight for a community centre at
Maisonneuve, etc.

The political crisis in Quebec and the popular movement   The
serious political crisis that shook Quebec in autumn 1970 entirely
transformed the conditions of electoral intervention and forced the
FRAP to define its position openly as one of opposition to the
established social order.[19] After a television speech by the mayor,
Drapeau, threatening the population with a situation 'where the
streets would run with blood' if the FRAP won the elections, and
after a campaign in which FRAP candidates were openly followed
by police cars during their local door-to-door canvassing, the elections, held in this atmosphere of terror, saw the collapse of the
FRAP, which obtained, on average, only 17% of the votes in the
districts where it presented candidates. With the exception of two
or three districts, notably at Saint-Jacques were social help had
long had a strong influence, the FRAP's popular support melted
away with the sudden politicization of the issue. Caught in its own
trap of municipal action for respectable citizens and nothing else,
the FRAP was unable to reply with a different form of political
argument, and saw its work of electoral organization and the objective beginnings of a common fighting front for the different tendencies, undone in a few days.

The crisis within the FRAP after its electoral defeat was grave:
the president (who in fact represented the workers' unions) resigned
in protest against the 'leftist' nature of the politicization; the
various district committees brought their action to a halt, without
knowing what to think as far as general orientation was concerned;
the secretariat spent its time finding organizational compromises
that might preserve this fragile machinery, without touching the
basic problems at all. In fact the FRAP went into hibernation, and
it was not until the 'Reorientation Congress' in March 1971 that
any clarity or decisions on new actions appeared.

Although the electoral failure can be explained by the repressive

---

[19] Here is a reminder of the main features of the crisis: members of the FLQ (*Front
de Libération de Quebec*) kidnapped an English civil servant and a Quebec minister to
obtain the liberation of political prisoners. In the face of government intransigence, the
Labour minister was executed. A state of war was declared in Quebec. The army
occupied Montreal. Hundreds of people were arrested, all the working-class organizations
attacked and press censorship was set up. The mayor of Montreal took advantage of the
crisis to accuse the FRAP of supporting the FLQ and, after a campaign of manipulation,
obtained a 'great electoral victory'. See *Quebec Occupé, Partis Pris* (Montreal, 1971).

circumstances that arose quite unfortunately, it is less easy to
understand why the organization itself was affected, at a time when
nobody had been seriously considering the possibility of really
taking over municipal power. (Ipola, 1971.) The reason for the
political crisis within the FRAP and in the relationship between
the committees and the local residents is that ambiguities had existed from the start within the FRAP's strategy over the question of
whether to use the urban claims and the electoral platform as a
means of political agitation or as ends in themselves. This political
opportunism turned against the committees from the moment
when the general political context began to raise unavoidable questions. In fact it would seem that the direct expression of urban
claims on a political level, without any qualitative transformation
of these claims into objectives of struggle properly speaking, leads
to a sort of 'consumer trade-unionism', sometimes even to the
actual existence of a pressure group which has no chance of success
unless it relies at once upon organizations and officials directly
orientated to the defence of communal facilities only. The link
between urban claims and political struggle does not form spontaneously; organized intervention is necessary to unite them in mass
political action. But in the citizens' committees, the politico-urban
link was never made in practice. It was more or less expressed, in
the constitution of an organization, the FRAP, but all this organization did was to assemble the urban claims in the form of a
political programme without linking them in a strategy for taking
power. In fact the objective presented was that of establishing an
institutional agency capable of applying pressure for the solution
of these 'concrete daily problems'. The urban question — expressed
on the institutional political level in terms of claims and not of
issues capable of bringing about mass political involvement — thus
became the objective base around which was formed a pressure
group seeking to obtain better living conditions for the victims of
the established social system. It is solely in this perspective, which
corresponds to the process of the FRAP's formation, that the question of municipal politics becomes a central theme. This of course
clashed with the subjectivity and the ideology of the most active
militants who, having experienced a process of radicalization during
the powerful popular struggles of previous years, and who were
therefore seeking to secure popular bases for the development of
an extreme left-wing movement centred on the working class. When
the crisis forced the FRAP to abandon its short-term thinking and
draw up a strategy, conflict broke out not only between the tendencies within the organization, but also between the various forms
of struggle in the different districts. When this happens, the prob-

lem is to determine how the urban struggle and the political struggle were joined — or separated — and also what effects the predominance of one form of action over another had on the degree of mobilization and power gained by the local residents.

From Charity to Ideology   When they were forced to define their political action in terms of social class objectives, the political action committees and the citizens' councils reacted in diametrically opposed ways: the one moved backwards, limiting itself to immediate objectives, defending local living conditions and attempting to do this efficiently; the other leapt forwards, setting itself an unambiguous long-term revolutionary task and initiating to this end an in-depth ideological education campaign. The first tendency is best illustrated by the evolution of the Sainte-Anne CAP and the second one by the Saint-Jacques district committee. We consider an analysis of their action to be useful, since they both reveal aspects of the politico-urban dialectic.

The preferred action area of the Sainte-Anne CAP was an old working-class district along the St Lawrence (La Pointe Saint-Charles), inhabited to a large extent by people on social assistance (40%) and seasonally unemployed (20%) in real slums. It had always been one of the privileged districts for social help and all sorts of committees flourished there (for housing, facilities, health, etc.). The ground had been well prepared for the CAP organization. Furthermore, the election results had not been too disappointing. But after the 'crisis' its militants were no longer accepted in the public activities of the district unless they associated themselves with undertakings outside their jurisdiction and strictly apolitical in nature: local intermediaries of the public assistance organs, loan societies, production co-operatives, etc. The militants tried to fit in locally, but a discrepancy soon became apparent between the 'locals' solely concerned with problems of facilities and the militant 'outsiders' (who sometimes lived a kilometre away), who wanted above all to bring politics into every action. This gulf cut across that between the original base of the citizens' committees and the political militants who had belonged directly to the FRAP. Under these conditions no lasting independent action was taken: the CAP devoted itself to the discussion of ideas, to the preparation of the FRAP congress, then to the discussion of the new orientations. After a year's work the committee disintegrated completely and vanished. Yet citizens' committees continued to exist, conducting day-to-day skirmishes as 'pressure groups for the poor'.

According to the Sainte-Anne CAP's analysis 'the failure was due to a transition between the non-structured citizens' committees,

pursuing very precise aims, and a broader, more highly structured
workers' organization, whose aims were more political.' If this is
the problem, we should be asking ourselves why it was not possible
to make this transition in order to unite the two elements (militants
and local population) necessary to any mobilization process. The
answer seems to be twofold: on the one hand, the social base,
lower-proletarian, was a favourite area for charitable organizations
and had a long way to go before political awareness could emerge
from daily oppression; on the other hand it was partly a consequence of the characteristics of that district; the issues were seen
in the context of social assistance and the balance of power was
never questioned. All in all, the CAP (led by former social workers)
seems to have suffered from the lack of a consistent line; it wavered
between supporting all claims without discussion because they
'came from the people' and putting aside any work which was not
directly political. The result was that in Pointe Saint-Charles the good
citizens kept themselves to themselves whereas the surviving militants attempted to create a general coordination organ (district
council) to prepare an 'intermediary between the citizens' committees and a more highly structured workers' organization' . . . if
this ever came into being.

In the Saint-Jacques district, the social characteristics were the
same (40% unemployed) and the problematic involved identical to
that of Pointe Saint-Charles, but the orientation and political
action which it brought about were fundamentally different. Originally the Saint-Jacques CAP was concerned with social work and
for once it was pretty efficient: by the organization, first, of a cooperative, then of a local clinic administered by the citizens themselves, the committee had managed to win the respect of a large
section of the population, which led to a relatively good electoral
performance (almost 30% of the votes) and a fairly large number
of local militants. But it was more politically-orientated than the
other CAPs in the FRAP, had existed for a long time and was less
influenced by the Christian social workers, and it at once became
the political conscience of the FRAP (some would say 'the guilty
conscience') and viewed the 1970 crisis as the perfect example of
the weakness of a position undefined from the political point of
view. The CAP advocated a rigorous Marxist line and militants
trained accordingly, and decided to centre its energies upon the
formation of a 'qualitative rather than quantitative' core, prefiguring in its line of thought and its organization a true revolutionary
party, whose essential work was to be with the working class. They
wanted therefore to take advantage of the local base obtained
through urban claim actions to develop a core of *avant-garde* mili-

tants. Under these circumstances, the two main demands made by the Saint-Jacques CAP on the FRAP are understandable; the complete independence of local CAPs, since the secretariat was seen as the driving force of the social-democrat tendency, and emphasis upon the training of militants and action to spread ideological propaganda — the past stage was analysed as a preparatory phase. Thus the Saint-Jacques CAP became an ideological core, extremely solid and dynamic, even in the concrete task of surveys and propaganda, but neglecting urban claims in their action insofar as their strength was concentrated upon the major conflict (workers' struggle) and upon the principal aspect of this conflict (the construction of an ideological *avant-garde* for the whole of Quebec society, starting with the Saint-Jacques district committee).

The link between urban struggle and political struggle   By different routes these two experiences both had as their conclusion the negation of the FRAP's initial plan for a people's party built upon the local experiences of urban struggle. It is therefore quite natural that the other local committees had to define themselves in terms of the same polemic, and that some of them attempted to revert to an action which combined both claims and political elements in day-to-day experience. This experiment was carried out with particular enthusiasm in the case of two other experiences which have much to teach us.

The Côtes-des-Neiges CAP, with a high degree of political involvement, but lacking the previous experience of a citizens' committee (in that it was largely composed of students and professors from Montreal university) had to deal with an extremely petty-bourgeois district. At the outset it tried to remain close to the local level of awareness, without becoming discouraged, and viewed its long-term work as dependent upon an initial campaign of very concrete demands. They led two 'battles' the themes of which were selected entirely in accordance with the social characteristics of the district. The first was the democratization of the administration of a savings bank and the second the establishment of the district's first tenants' association. Now it must be admitted that the distance between the revolutionary subjectivity of the militants and intervention in the general assembly of a savings bank to ensure the shareholders' rights was too great for the two to come together. Similarly for the tenants' association; the CAPs desire to be concrete and efficient led to its using up its energies in the organization of a very heavy administrative service, which functioned like a legal council, complete with consultations by telephone. The result was that when the committee had succeeded in getting a certain audience and had

gathered together several dozen tenants, the latter ('the people')
refused to take over the association or even to elect representatives
to its bureau — what was the point, since these young people had
given their (free!) services so competently? The Côte-des-Neiges
CAP's disillusionment turned into self-criticism; they decided that
all interventions must be politicized from the start, but without
neglecting the concrete issues involved. But then the CAP found
itself out of line with its local base, an upwardly mobile petty-
bourgeoisie. The new style of work involved delocalization and
intervention in accordance with the FRAP's central coordination.
The temporary failure of one action opened the door to the following basic conclusion; urban struggle, workers' struggle and political
struggle must be united, by interventions centralized as far as
strategy was concerned, but always concrete and localized, in the
places and the issues relevant in the circumstances.

     In fact it was just such a situation that arose during the CAP-led
mobilization in the Hochenlaga-Maisonneuve district against the
proposed east-west motorway which would require the demolition
of thousands of homes. There was a combination of all the elements
necessary for the desired unification of struggles: a majority of the
local residents were workers, a number of whom were unionized —
a popular and dynamic district; there had been a citizens' committee for a long time and this had won a considerable audience by its
long, hard fight for the creation of a community centre, a plan
which had finally met the fate of final rejection by the authorities.
The local residents were therefore both socially mobilized and fore-
warned of the social paternalism of urban institutions.

     The issue for which the committee had been formed was equally
exemplary; it directly concerned the population (houses, pollution
affecting a large sector of the city); it questioned the ingenious
financial arrangements between the provincial government in
Quebec and the federal Canadian government; the proposed route
was useful only within the framework of an urban planning scheme
which deliberately ignored public transport. The campaign was
launched at the beginning of 1971 and was carried out very seriously both in the district itself and throughout Montreal. A combined
front of organizations, unions and working-class organizations, was
formed and obtained the support of the *Parte québecois* in the
provincial parliament. Information sheets were circulated, meetings
held, a petition taken from door to door and signed by thousands
of people; mass demonstrations were organized, including one
where the demonstrators drove along the proposed motorway
route.

     And yet the plan was retained, support dwindled and the local population lost interest; finally the committee alone remained and had a difficult job to oppose the vast underlying financial and political machinery and the 'rationality of urban transport'. They refused to abandon their slogans, but, as the machines slowly started turning again, they were forced to admit the total failure of the campaign. Why should this have been the outcome, given all the conditions described above? Precisely because of the importance of the issue. Faced with interests so powerful, although it was entirely correct to engage in a fight which of necessity turned from an urban claim into a political combat, considerable means were needed. Only the committee (through the FRAP) was prepared for this combat, apart from a few more or less respectful opposition groups. The FRAP was in the throes of an internal crisis; with its diverging tendencies on the one hand and its social objectives on the other, things were almost at breaking point. Thus the weakness of the central organization, brought about by errors in local intervention, rebounded upon local conflicts, preventing the mass struggle from developing to a higher political level, despite the otherwise excellent conditions, including an issue involving basic points of conflict. Thus the inevitable dialectical link between the centralization of strength and the local concentration of combats, which actually had a general political significance, was demonstrated in practice. But awareness of this was gained only at the price of a new defeat. All they could do was put it down as experience and start afresh.

Weakened by the left-wing split of the Saint-Jacques CAP, by the split in the opposite direction of the 'social worker' tendency and by the disintegration of several CAPs after these failures, the FRAP had to transform itself.

The 1971 *Congrès de réorientation* had been little more than a consecration of local autonomy and a step towards disintegration. At the beginning of 1972 the FRAP attempted to bring about a total transformation upon the ruins of the former CAPs, based on a highly-structured central initiative and with the objective of building a popular party for which urban matters would be only one of the protest issues. Emphasizing the necessity of having a political working-class organization as an indispensable tool in the fight against the capitalist class 'with the idea that it is towards the state and state power that this organization should be turned' (FRAP, 1972), there was a new FRAP trying to emerge. Within this new perspective, new initiatives were set in motion at the beginning of 1972, notably the formation of a front composed of political and union organizations, the *Conseil Ouvrier des Transports* (Workers' Transport Council), under the direction of the FRAP, to oppose the new urban transport law by demanding the reorganization of public transport and rejecting the hold of financial groups on public services, especially on taxis. The first successes recorded during this rigorous campaign seem to reveal a consistent line of action on the part of militants hardened by the successive crises they had experienced in the political action committees.

But in its attempt to revive the combat, this new organization is taking into account past failures in attempts to link urban protest and political mobilization. And its militants know by now (1972) that the area of intervention and the concrete conditions of liaison with the masses in combat must not be confused with the political basis for the foundation of an organization. Put more simply, they know that if they try to build a revolutionary party by direct extrapolation of urban protest movements, they run the risk of achieving a municipal revolution and nothing more.

B   Urban struggle and revolutionary struggle in the Pobladores movement in Chile[20]
Santiago de Chile, 1971. The revolution was rumbling at the foot of the Andes, the old world of oligarchies, superimposed by successive periods of economic dependence and political oppression, was beginning to crumble, not without resistance, not without suffering, certainly not without violence. The Chilean popular movement, by a combination of revolutionary struggle and institutional political struggle, had made a breach, indeed a serious one, in the system of domination by the Chilean bourgeoisie and the new imperialism, with the electoral victory of the Popular Unity in September 1970. But everyone knew that the ability of the reforms introduced into the economic structures since the Left had come

[20] The information on which my analysis is based comes from personal experience during visits to Chile lasting several months, in 1968, 1970 and 1971, and especially through contacts with left-wing militants and repeated visits to the camps; collaboration with the research group on this theme at the Latin American social science faculty in Santiago; above all, the systematic survey which we carried out between July and October 1971 in the 25 most important encampments in Santiago. This survey was carried out by the research team on social movements from the CIDU (Inter-disciplinary Centre for Urban Development) in collaboration with Popular Unity militants within the *pobladores* movement. We reconstructed the political history and analysed the social characteristics of each of these camps from prolonged observation and systematic talks with the leaders, the militants and the residents. The survey and the analysis were the collective work of the entire CIDU Urban Politics Research Team, M. Castells, H. T. Chadwick, R. Cheetham, A. Hirane, S. Quevado, T. Rodriguez, G. Rejas, J. Rejas, F. Vanderschueren. A report presenting the complete results of this investigation is in preparation (1972). Given the burning political topicality of the theme, we have omitted all information that might allow the identification of places, people and organizations, except in the case of historically known social facts. (*Pobladores* does not simply mean squatters. The term has another political connotation. Our analysis will attempt to determine exactly what this is.)

to power to open the way to genuine social transformation depended upon the balance of political power it could manage to establish.
This balance of power was conditional both upon the degree to
which the class alliance could be extended under the direction of
the working class and upon the existence of a correct political line
that would be able to unite the different struggles and concentrate
them in a systematic attack upon the exploiters' machinery of
domination. A single working-class front, alliance with the poor
peasants, liaison with the petty bourgeoisie, co-ordination with the
student movement — so many political battles which would condition the outcome of the ultimate confrontation with the political
machinery of the oligarchy and the classes on which this relied.
But in Chile a new element came on to the scene, a necessary component of the revolutionary movement; this was the existence of a
large mass of people characterized first by their illegal establishment of an unofficial residential milieu and secondly by their
political expression through a movement organized on the basis of
urban protest: the *pobladores* movement. Several tendencies co-
existed within this movement, corresponding to the broad political
currents in Chile, from the Christian Democracy, via the Popular
Unity, to the revolutionary left wing. It must be made clear at
once that in Chile it was not simply a question of that well known
phenomenon, the formation of vast shantytowns, as in the metropolises of dependent capitalist countries; the originality and the
importance of this process arose from its direct link with the question of power. The invasion of urban sites to build homes which
could not be found elsewhere, with the participation of working-
class organizations, had taken place in other countries (Peru,
Colombia, Venezuela, etc.) from time to time, but what was
characteristic of Chile was the directly political role of these
actions and, conversely, the determination of the political composition of these camps by the conditions under which they came into
existence and by the orientation and strategy of the political forces
that lay at the root of their formation.

In fact, although the starting point of this illegal occupation of
urban sites and the building of genuine working-class districts
(called *campamentos*) outside of the established order (or rather,
against it) was the structural housing crisis,[21] these actions cannot

[21] In 1960 Chile was 490 000 homes short for its population of 7 300 000 and in
1970 it was 600 000 short for 9 300 000. Apart from this, the state of deterioration of
housing in the city centre and the total lack of facilities in the outskirts, would justify
talk of a general housing crisis. This crisis is not linked with 'underdevelopment' but with
the structure of housing production in Chile — building companies make immense profits
and have always been one of the most influential pressure groups. See Santos and Seelen-
berger (1968) and Cheetham, (1971).

be considered as an automatic reaction to a lack — it is a *social process*, closely bound up with the relations between social forces and very much dependent upon the repression-integration dialectic of the state. Thus, in the final analysis, the social significance of the invasion of sites and the construction of camps arises from their connection with class relations and political strategy. This is why the *pobladores* movement in Chile provides the clearest example of a concrete historical experience of the social conditions surrounding the linking of the urban, the political and the revolutionary, i.e., the emergence of an urban social movement. In order to grasp these conditions, it would be better perhaps to have a brief sketch of the evolution of the class struggle and political strategy in recent years.

Class conflict, political conjuncture and occupation of urban land. It is well known that the collapse of the political system of the old Chilean oligarchy and the electoral victory of the Christian Democrats in 1964 were the starting-point for an ambitious attempt at popular reform on the basis of an alliance between the most dynamic portion of the Chilean bourgeoisie, linked with international capital, and broad working-class sectors, under the hegemony of the bourgeoisie. This was put into concrete form with agrarian reform and the launching of a programme of social assistance and local participation in housing and urban problems. This initiative was not simply aimed at the lumpen-proletariat (baptised 'marginal' by a new ideology), but also at the lower levels of society affected by the housing crisis, including labourers, salaried workers and even lower civil servants. This urban reform programme was intended for the workers, not as such, but as 'badly-housed people'. They were therefore mobilized for a secondary issue with which the state was trying to deal while it waited to create profitable conditions in this sector.

In the early days the programme raised great hopes. Sites were given to the homeless and building materials delivered to them. But the limits of such an undertaking soon became evident — it did not attack the mechanisms that had brought about the crisis, and had not the necessary resources to deal with unsatisfied needs. In particular, no organization was set up to build public housing, an indispensable element of any true reform programme. Hope soon turned into impatience. The 1967 municipal elections provided a suitable opportunity to draw attention to the government's inefficiency in this matter, by concrete action: several sites on the outskirts of Santiago were invaded and occupied; huts and tents were installed there. Now this occupation was an illegal act that

challenged the government's land policy and the relationship they
were seeking with the property groups. Incapable of absorbing this
social protest, the Christian Democrats (DC) replied with police
repression. A temporary halt was brought to the movement. But
the terms of the conflict process had been defined: the failure of
the emergency housing programme (*'operacion Sitio'*) and the continued fall in the building of homes only served to reinforce the
protest movement, which was to find itself up against repression
machinery that was there to compensate for the shortcomings of
the social integration machinery.

Into the breach opened up by this came two different political
trends, both opposed to the plan. On the one hand the workers'
parties (Communist Party and Socialist Party) attempted to fight
the political battle on the same battlefield as the DC, demonstrating the government's inability to resolve the problems and thus
paving the way for the 1970 electoral campaign. On the other hand
the revolutionary left wing embarked upon armed struggle, finding
in the existing explosive situation confirmation of its own theses
and the opportunity for a mass confrontation with the repressive
machinery of the bourgeoisie.

Under this dual impulse, the occupations of urban sites increased
and encampments were formed. Whatever the political tendency,
the process of formation of an encampment was always the same:
a political organization (sometimes linked with a union group or a
definite cultural *milieu*) would organize a committee for the badly
housed based either on a district, a profession or a workplace, for
a certain length of time. Once the illegal occupation of a site to
build homes had been decided upon, several committees with
similar political tendencies were brought together and an action
group designated to prepare the occupation and divert the attention of the police. One night the word was given, the families
assembled with their possessions, a circle of tents was set up, a
boundary sketched out and the Chilean flag hoisted while the militants confronted the police and, in some cases, while left-wing
political figures attempted to negotiate with the 'special intervention brigades' that had come rushing to the scene. If the occupation was successful, the following day saw the arrival of new
families — as many as the camp committee, formed immediately,
was prepared to accept. After a few weeks a new working-class
habitat was in existence.

Thus the urban question became one of the pivots of the social
struggle in Chile during the period that preceded the 1970 elections,
sometimes reaching a higher degree of significance than the
workers' struggle. This paradox can be explained by the tactical

convergence of the three principal political tendencies, making this secondary issue into a major and immediate one. But this convergence conceals quite different reasons in each case.

As we have already remarked, the DC needed an objective that was popular, able to bring about mobilization and affecting several classes, such as the housing question; the Popular Unity[22] for its part was also interested in the development of a claim that did not directly question capitalism (i.e., centred around the method of distributing what was produced rather than on the method of production) insofar as its strategy was to 'take over government' by means of the elections, in order to change the structural economic relationships afterwards. The revolutionary left wing was concerned above all with building its party and saw a tactical advantage in an urban issue that opened up for it a means of penetration into the working class, facilitated both by the organic weakness of the *pobladores* movement and by the violence of the social situation that had arisen.

The first wave of site occupations in 1969 met with very strong institutional resistance: on 9 March at Puerto Montt in the south, the police massacred with machine guns a group of families who had first set up an encampment. This aroused general indignation and the repression was moderated. The first mass occupations in Santiago at the beginning of 1970 were accompanied by extremely violent confrontations between revolutionary militants and special brigades of police. But the electoral campaign was under way, and the Christian Democrats, abandoned by the bourgeoisie, were playing their left-wing hand to a lower-class electorate; this was incompatible with the ferocious repression of an increasingly widespread movement and, after a further incident in July 1970, the government renounced any action that might tarnish its image. During the months that preceded the September 1970 elections, tens of thousands of people occupied sites in Santiago. The DC itself organized occupations in a bid not to lose its working-class base entirely. The two months between the left-wing victory and the official investiture of the new president saw further acceleration of the movement.

Finally, although the Popular Unity movement brought a halt to the occupations in Santiago by launching a public housing programme, it authorized the maintenance of the status quo by legalizing the existence of the encampments.

Thus it was that at the beginning of 1971 some 300 000 people

[22] Popular Unity (UP): left-wing coalition (communist, socialist and radical parties, MAPU and independents) that won the 1970 presidential elections with their support for Allende against the DC and the right wing.

had organized camps at Santiago, 10% of the population. But the social and political importance of these groups was greater still because of the concentration of the process in time and in space and also by virtue of its close connection with a revolutionary situation.

A new world had been born, a world of earth and wood, a world of popular militia and workers' brigades, of discussions between civil servants and children smiling in the rain.

To question this world and determine the significance of its existence means answering two groups of questions: was there a new way of life in the camps and, if so, what? What everyday social innovations were made? And above all, what is the relation between this and the other movements that arose from this life and death struggle; with the workers' struggle and the political struggle? In the last resort, what we want to know is what specific effect an urban social movement has upon power relations between the classes and therefore what its revolutionary potential is.

Social organization in the camps and the transformation of life-style The conditions under which the encampments were formed placed them from the start in a position of opposition to the social order and forced their inhabitants to face up to the various problems of daily life on their own. On the other hand, insofar as they were the expression of a protest relating to housing and community facilities, they evolved towards a social 'normalization' as the social claims were genuinely satisfied by the left-wing government. There was therefore no micro-society 'outside' the general social organization. Nevertheless, it is possible to imagine, during the transition period when the camp still had a certain independence, the appearance of new forms of struggle, from the point of view of content and organization, forms that could even be a glimpse of the future transformation of social relations as revolutionary processes develop.

Were there in fact any experimental innovations? And what were the factors determining them?

According to our survey, the most significant changes as far as general social organization was concerned were in relation to questions of security, discipline and justice, because the illegal position of the camps had the effect, especially in the early days, of bringing about the establishment of a defence system against police repression. This situation also led to the organization of an independent system for the prevention and repression of delinquency and a judiciary system to deal with problems of communal life. 'Popular militia' and 'surveillance committees' were created at the start, and gradually disbanded after the arrival of the Popular Unity, since the left-wing parties maintained that it was better to rely on the 'police of the popular government'. But the inadequacy of this police force in fighting delinquency and its hostile attitude towards the squatters brought about a revival of the autonomous organiza- tion of security services in the encampments, especially at night. Nevertheless the existence of these forces did not make a profound difference to the communal activity of the camp; it was even found that in some cases they could become instruments of oppression in the service of a small group. Conversely, they became organs of popular power if they were linked with an autonomous legal machine whose decisions they enforced, and *vice versa*; the local popular justice, to be respected, needed an instrument to ensure the application of its decisions while it waited for the gradual development of a higher level of awareness on the part of the large majority of squatters.

This *popular justice* was an experiment limited to a few camps, and therefore showed very different degrees of organization and stability, ranging from arbitration by the camp's source of moral authority (a responsible leader or committee) to local tribunals, often composed of the population itself.

The determining factor for the existence of an efficient system of popular justice seemed to be the degree of mobilization and political organization independent of individual political views, whether this mobilization arose from the importance and coherence of the political group that formed the encampment or from the experiences of conflict with the repressive machinery that marked the beginnings of this new habitat. Another factor with a distinct influence was revealed by the fact that a local popular justice out- side the institutional sytem existed in camps distinguished by a high proportion of workers with employment, except when the sub-proletariat was predominant.

These experiments with popular justice were characterized not only by the creation of new 'institutions' but also, in some cases, by the new content given to justice: protection of communal values and consideration of matters ignored by bourgeois law. For exam- ple, absence from meetings or disorderly behaviour during the assemblies was considered a fault and behaviour within the family was closely watched. Drunkenness was severely reproved: alcoholic drinks were banned in several camps and shelters were set up at the entrance where residents who returned a little too merry could sleep it off. These measures were completed by a re-education pro- gramme and an attempt to attack the social roots of alcoholism.

The difficulties of elaborating a new type of sanctions were much greater, given the small range of possible activity in this field at the disposal of the camp, and the necessity of a transformation in social relations before a non-repressive justice could be effective. Although self-criticism was pretty widespread and although sanctions sometimes took the form of reflection upon revolutionary texts, there were also arrests, fines and sometimes physical repression. The gravest punishment was expulsion from the camp. Finally, methods of re-education were worked out. Nevertheless, even the most advanced experiments reached a point where they could go no further; they could not develop locally without a generalization that implied a qualitative change in the state apparatus — and this was dependent upon the correlation of the social forces present.

Another field in which the encampments gave rise to new experiences was unemployment, the permanent scourge of most of their inhabitants. Depending on the degree of mobilization committees were formed for the unemployed, for the allocation of communal tasks within the camp, work that was paid for by the residents who had jobs, and even the formation of 'workers' brigades' — groups of unemployed men who undertook the building of public housing with state funds, thus unofficially short-circuiting the private monopoly of building. One fact is important — the camps where these experiments were tried had the same characteristics as those where popular justice functioned. Here there was a mutual reinforcement of connected activities, determined by the underlying general political capacity and controlled by some sort of local government.

In fact, almost everywhere where there were camp authorities with real powers, who acted as intermediaries between outside agencies (state institutions, political organizations) and the treatment of daily problems in the camp. These organs of local government could take several forms: elected leaders and an assembly; leaders and an assembly linked with the old committees for the homeless who had remained organized within the camp; and, finally, in the most developed cases, there was an organization in each block, alongside organizations for each task ('workers' front', health, education, cleaning, etc.) with delegates to an elected, revocable authority.

One characteristic common to these different types of 'local democracy' is that the coherence and stability of the authorities and their influence on the residents were dependent above all upon their ability to resolve concrete problems. This was how the influence of a political line could be extended or weakened — starting from the militant core within the camp. The organization mobilized the residents on certain issues and, if they were successful, won a degree of support that allowed them to take longer-term initiatives.

Having said this, however, even if the capacity to solve problems of collective consumption (health, education, housing, facilities, etc.) depended solely, at an early stage, upon the degree of mobilization and organization of the squatters, with the change of government and the application of the Popular Unity's programme, it was the efficiency of the state intervention that became the determining element, in combination, of course, with the local auto-organization.

This change of circumstances explains the virtual non-existence of experimental innovations in these fields. In fact the essentially collective treatment of the problems reduced the camps' ability to develop an organization any different from that which corresponded to the socialization process in the country as a whole. Thus in the case of education the adult programmes never took root; the experiment of self-management in a school was first and foremost an instrument to put pressure upon the government; attempts to control the traditional ideological content of certain programmes brought about the resignation of some teachers, forcing the *pobladores'* leaders to back down, etc. In fact the real change was the decision taken by the government to set up permanent schools all over the country, using old houses converted into classrooms. It was therefore the state, with its new policy, that raised the level of education.

In the same way, as far as *health* was concerned, the 'health brigades' formed early on in the camps, were only efficient in places where the National Health Service (i.e. the state) had established a permanent service, with a dispensary. Furthermore there was a connection between the presence of local 'health brigades' and the good functioning of the public health services, which would seem to show that the latter were organized not so much where there was a need for them, but rather as a result of the capacity of each camp to make social claims.

In the building of *homes* and *land use*, the initial phase of uncoordinated initiatives on the part of the squatters, largely the carrying out of odd jobs necessary at the time, was replaced by the massive intervention of the Popular Unity's emergency plan; in 1971 'Operation Winter' was launched — the construction of standardized huts and the establishment of a minimum of urban services in most camps. This initiative substantially improved living conditions, despite the fact that the integration of this plan into the general programme of economic measures taken at the time, and the urgency of the procedure, resulted in a very small participation of the camp residents in the drawing up of the architectural plans and the planning of either the temporary or the permanent buildings. Nevertheless, wherever initiative from the residents was made possible it only took the form of altering details, without introducing any new ideas as far as the suggested forms of habitat were concerned. Everyone wanted individual homes (to the point of regarding being housed in a block as punishment), they wanted to be separated from their neighbours, with each house on its own plot of land . . . all of which only serves to confirm the inevitable lag of cultural innovations behind economic claims and political mobilization.

In fact it was in the realm of *cultural and leisure activities* that the least dynamism was observed, along with a great inertia inherited from the practices learned within the framework of the dominant ideology; these activities were reduced to traditional sports contests and the no less traditional feminine tasks in the 'Housewives' Centres'. There was only one exception: a revolutionary encampment where a popular theatre group produced plays about contemporary workers' struggles and took part in mobilizations against the bastions of Chilean cultural conservatism. In fact the 'cultural revolution' seems to demand both a high degree of political mobilization and a series of profound social changes, beyond the narrow limits of the world of the camps.

Nevertheless, even if the camps were not centres of cultural innovation in the proper sense of the term, they did represent sources of social change in some cases, and in some fields. To put it in more concrete terms, this occurred in those cases where there was a solid working-class social base within which a determined, coherent revolutionary line was expressed, regardless of which revolutionary tendency was expressed.

Social innovation was not generalized: it occurred in those fields where a significant issue appeared in the social order — and insofar as the state machinery did not take over the treatment of the problem completely. It is this last point that explains why, during the movement's first phase, before Chile's left-wing government, socially innovatory practices were much more frequent than after the elections. After Allende's succession to the presidency there was no real mobilization except when the government had not sufficient power to overthrow the structural logic: in legal institutions and house-building (still the private monopoly of the Chilean Building Chamber).

Thus we reach a first significant conclusion. Experimental innovations in the social organization of the camps arose from the interaction of three basic elements; the structural importance of the issue in question; the small power of intervention by the state in this field; the presence of a coherent and organized political line

orientated towards social change. Thus the squatters' movement
was linked on the one hand with the Popular Unity government's
policy aimed at satisfying communal needs, and on the other to
the social mobilization necessary to conquer the centres of power
which were in conflict with the social order of which the camps
were a precursor.

*The link between the squatters' protest action and social issues
as a whole*   The form and the intensity of the relation between
the social process of the camps and the processes based on other
issues of social structure reveal the capacity for transforming the
relations between the classes as a whole through practice, or, in
other words, *its* efficiency as a social movement — not from the
point of view of the influence the camps can have on the individual
mobilization of its residents, but rather with regard to the convergence between the squatters' movement and social struggles arising
from other social and political problems.

In order to carry out this analysis clearly, we are going to consider the various aspects of the social structure in succession, in
order to pick out in each of them the connection that exists between them and the squatters' movement, and the factors that
determine this:

1. As far as issues in the sphere of *production* are concerned, the
connection between the squatters' movement and workers' struggles
is generally weak or non-existent, with the exception of two camps
with a left-wing, revolutionary orientation, especially one of them
voluntarily set up within an industrial zone in order to connect it
with struggles in the factories, which was in fact done. In both
cases the political animators of the camp led and supported factory
occupations, considering that the role of squatters is directly involved with all revolutionary action. Also in these camps there was
a permanent organic link with the workers' struggle in the form of
squatters workers' co-ordination committees, based on geographical areas.

So the following conclusions can be drawn:

(a) The encampments as such have no tendency to participate
in workers' struggles without the intervention of a political organization.

(b) For the workers' parties, the co-ordination between squatters'
movements and union movements is achieved at the level of their
respective authorities, under the hegemony of the union movement,
or else in a day-to-day political action with a constant fusion of the
two movements within the party.

(c) The revolutionary left-wing, for whom the camps were a

means of penetrating among the workers, attempted to create the conditions for a direct link between the squatters' struggle and the workers' struggle, both in organization and in action.

2. In the field of collective consumption (housing, facilities, health, etc.) the camps revealed a great capacity for participation in external protest action, even in the case of camps where the political awareness was not very high, which shows the correspondence between a link with an urban protest movement and the capacity for spontaneous mobilization within this combat front.

For example there was a high degree of participation by the camps in mobilizations on the subject of housing, including the occupation of empty houses and the blocking of roads. It should be pointed out that the nature of the camps most active in these struggles changed completely with the political conjuncture: under the popular government it was the camps directed by the Christian Democrats, whereas the left-wing squatters gave the government a respite to enable it to organize its public housing programme.

On the other hand, in a different type of action on the same combat front (collective consumption), revolutionary and moderate camps were found side by side, even under the popular government. This was in the protests against bureaucratic delays and against the malfunctioning of public services: occupation of hospitals, invasion of administrative offices, tipping of garbage in the reception rooms of town councils neglectful of the camps' problems, etc.

Such a potential for protest mobilization on the part of the squatters is really worthy of note, especially at a time when the popular government was making a great effort to improve public services, and when as a result the left-wing leaders, a majority in the movement, were reducing mass actions. In other words the level of fight achieved by the squatters, as far as collective consumption is concerned, was extremely high. It also shows that there was a link between the grouping of people in camps and mobilization over issues of collective facilities.

3. On the other hand the encampments' contribution to the transformation of *individual consumption*, especially by control over shopkeepers and the formation of consumer committees, was much less evident. Whereas price-watching committees were formed in other popular quarters of Santiago, nothing of the sort existed in the camps and attempts to create cooperatives failed. The only measure successfully applied was a control on retail prices within the camp, by a regular inspection by all the camp authorities. In fact the slight degree of mobilization in this field is merely a reflection of the absence of a militant tradition in the realm of consump-

tion in Chile, something quite logical for a country where, until
quite recently, the problem of a majority of the people was not
the mode of consumption but simply that of access to a minimum
amount of products to consume.

4. The camp's links with the *political struggle* properly speaking
would seem to be the key to its revolutionary potential. The analysis of the various experiences compels us to introduce a distinction
between two dimensions of political struggle: that which could be
called *dominantly institutional political struggle*, e.g., participation
in electoral campaigns, vote orientation, etc., and that which we
shall call *extra-institutional*, in which other means are used to
express the political struggle (offensive demonstrations, occupations, self-defence, etc.).

Thus a whole typology of the political behaviour of the camps,
closely linked with a series of determining factors, can be observed:

I Camps with a *low political participation*: those which are
dominated by a local *cadi* rather than by a political party.
It should be noticed that in this group there were moderate
camps and revolutionary camps, coming from various levels
of society, so the key factor appears to be the style of
political leadership.

II Camps with a moderate degree of *institutional political participation*: those which were dominated by a conflict between
different political tendencies.

III Camps with a *high degree of institutional political participation*: both those directed by the PU's political opponents.

IV Camps with a *low degree of institutional political participation* (e.g. rejection of elections) and with a *high degree
of extra-institutional political action*: all the revolutionary
left-wing camps *and only them.*

V Camps with a *high degree of participation in both types of
action.* In this case there was only one camp, the only one
which was directed by the Popular Unity and dominated by
a left-wing revolutionary orientation.

These observations are sufficiently systematic for the conclusion
to be drawn that the type and strength of links between the camps
and political struggle depend directly upon the characteristics of
the dominant political organization in the camp. This does not
mean that the party is the *deus ex machina,* for its influence and
efficiency should be explained too. But although the party is not a
sufficiently important factor in itself for the political development
of the camp, its presence is absolutely necessary and the orientation
of the struggle bears its stamp.

5. Finally the link with *ideological transformation* appeared to

be extremely weak, with the exception of a few left-wing revolutionary camps where the dominant political organism attempted at first to diffuse a new system of values throughout the community. But once the situation was stabilized, daily tasks became more important, and the participation in general ideological transformation seemed to be limited to the development of popular folklore and an increased dissemination of Marxist authors. This said, the basic weakness on this point does not seem to come from the camps themselves, but from the virtual non-existence in Chile of a movement of ideological revolutionization with which they could unite.

Thus the links with the student movement, ideological agent par excellence, seemed sporadic and centred mainly around 'voluntary work' campaigns; if they had any ideological effect it was on the students rather than the squatters.

From our analyses, throughout the different types of social issue, the fundamental role of political forces as far as the orientation of the movement within each camp is concerned, can be appreciated. This conclusion, which reinforces the similar remarks made about the social organization of the camps, leads to a questioning of the social conditions that help or hinder the development of each of the political lines — an element of classification that should be studied in its turn.

The social factors affecting the success of the different political lines in the squatters' movement   The social organization of the camps and the method of liaison with general social conflicts seemed to be largely determined by the dominant political strategy in each camp. The origin of the various strategies is clear: given the formation process of the camps, there was always, at the base of each, political machinery with an established line. But the central question is this; what determines whether a particular line was adopted and applied by the camp residents on their own account? Our survey shows in fact that there were considerable differences between camps with the same political tendency; whether the proposed political line was applied or not in mass action depended upon the social conditions and the type of process involved.

Three broad types of political line can be determined in a most schematic way; we prefer to describe rather than name them, so as to avoid any value connotations:

Line I is characterized by a desire to radicalize the process politically, turning the occupation of urban sites into a direct confrontation with bourgeois legality and attempting subsequently to transform the camps into agitation bases — action linked with the workers' struggle and revolutionary politics.

Line II attempts to mobilize the squatters to obtain both satisfaction of housing claims and an institutional political victory; once this was achieved, the aim was to create the right conditions for a rapid solution to the concrete problems in the camps, by a planned intervention on the part of the Popular State. In the transition phase, while waiting for the definitive integration of the camps into the public building programme, the political organization took in hand the functioning of daily life in the camp. Based on this, a strong institutional political mobilization developed. In other cases, liaison with the trade union movement, under the direction of this mobilization, was proposed.

Line III is characterized alternatively by *paternalism* or by *claims and corporation*, according to whether or not it brought the public social aid institutions to bear in different political conjunctures. Thus when it was in power, its concern was to ensure an electoral audience by making concessions in the realm of town planning; when it was in opposition, it demanded housing for these same people, without general social mobilization outside of the electoral support which it hoped to obtain in this way. These three broad lines do not cover the entire range of political organizations represented in the squatters' movement, but are the basic elements which, in combination, produce the concretely expressed lines of each organization. Thus a particular workers' party may have a line that is in fact a constant oscillation between types I and II as described by us.

So what are the factors affecting the development of each of these lines? The importance of the nature of the camps must be pointed out. In fact if the camps that followed line I and those that adopted line II are compared, the split is not between sub-proletariat and proletariat, but between two distinct functions of the working class. Line II is supported by those camps where the workers have a higher general level of income and education or where there is a small proportion of unemployed. Line I, on the other hand, is closely followed by camps characterized by a social base ravaged by unemployment. This is quite different from a lumpen-proletariat base with no part in the productive sytems, for the camps which corresponded largely to this last characteristic usually ended up in a state of social disintegration and political confusion.

These observations seem to be directly linked with the classic theses on the relation between workers' aristocracy and trade-unionism, misery and depoliticization, and a working class with experience of crisis and class consciousness.

To this determination by the social base can be added factors specific to the type of political intervention. Thus line I is favoured by the existence of leaders from the ranks of the squatters themselves; by the internal organization of the camp according to combat fronts; by a strong social and ideological cohesion in the method of recruiting the camps' residents. In the same way, line II is reinforced where the political leadership has developed from the committees for the homeless rather than from the organization itself; where concern with efficiency in action outweighs electoral strategy; where there is no interaction with the various political machines.

Finally line III, corporatist and paternalist, is facilitated by a social base very high (relatively) or very low in the social scale, i.e. by a petty-bourgeoisie (salaried workers, civil servants, etc.) in search of individual comfort and concerned only with this objective, or by a sub-proletarian base prepared to perpetuate the traditions of charitable paternalism. The other factor that seems relevant for this line is the type of relation maintained with the state machinery; given the opportunism of the social base supporting line III, claims very easily give way to integration (and vice versa) according to the satisfaction obtained.

The revelation of these constants observed in the development of political lines does not, of course, explain the matter entirely. It does at least enable us to determine which organizational strategies immediately seem to be decisive. It is the *relation* between political line and the masses that is in fact in the forefront of processes of social change.

The reality of the 1971 Chilean squatters' camps is therefore a diverse reality. Side by side with the social disorganization observed in certain cases, highly mobilized communities can also be observed, in the same way that paternalism allows for social innovation in some fields. But we have tried to establish the social sources of transformation in urban protest action rather than remaining in this relativism. In this sense it seems clear that the social significance of the camps varies with the conjuncture and that its political content is determined by three basic elements: the objective structural content of each claim; the social base; the political line practised, this depending in turn upon a series of specific factors in each case. We see therefore a changing structure, in constant interaction with the general conflicts in Chilean society. This is why the life of the camps depended less upon their individual evolution than on the general dynamic of the Chilean class struggle, of which they were a component.

III The conclusion is in the streets

New social issues are at the root of new forms of conflict and also
of new methods of the collective creation of everyday life. The
urban social movements are the most striking expression of this.
The further urban struggles develop, the greater their influence on
political processes and the greater the need to determine precisely
the social composition of the phenomenon and the concrete effects
it brings about.

Working with a few selected examples of urban mobilization
under the new social conditions, we have been able to perceive the
internal structure of these processes of change and conflict, the
conditions for their link with other social and political processes
and the factors governing this set of dialectical relations.

A few provisional conclusions can be drawn from this cursory
look at a theme scarcely considered by the 'social sciences' and no
more so by Marxism, despite the fact that it is making headlines in
the mass media and affects everyday political action.

First, it is evident that we cannot speak of 'urban' struggle in
general, for this term combines and confuses widely differing problems in which the ability to question the structural laws of a society
is quite different according to the content of the claim which is
given the name of 'urban'. Thus it is that the social significance of
the problem and the terms of the issue are completely different in
the cases of public transport and the installation of letterboxes in
blocks of flats. This means that we must not speak of 'urban
struggles' but break this false unity and carry out a structural analysis of the basic problem in order to identify the social content of
the issue by replacing it in its economic and political context. In
fact indiscriminate unification of 'urban struggles', which places
them all on the same level, leads directly to the ideological view of
urban problems as those that affect the 'framework' of our life,
forgetting that life is not a 'framework' but a practice; and, above
all, forgetting that these problems take on a very different meaning
according to our social position. Thus, to be understood, each
'urban struggle' must have its structural content specified, and be
considered in terms of the role it plays *vis-à-vis* the various social
classes involved. Then and only then will we know what we are
talking about.

This said, it does seem that whatever the level and the content
of the various 'urban issues' they can all be characterized as secondary structural issues, that is to say, ones not directly challenging
the production methods of a society nor the political domination
of the ruling classes. In this sense, to make urban issues the princi-

pal issue, and urban social movements the new revolutionary force
is the same as accepting a prophetism of modernity that limits the
thematic of the workers' movement to a capitalist society that
today is considered anachronistic. Now our analyses have shown
the extreme degree of dependence of urban struggle upon other
social struggles, and even their inability to develop without linking
with the political conflicts still dominated essentially by the
current forms of the capital-labour confrontation. But this does
not mean that urban struggles are necessarily relegated to the world
of administrative reformism. Quite the reverse; their decisive
importance in certain political conjunctures has been determined,
for a structurally secondary issue can be a conjuncturally principal
one. This means that the political importance of an urban movement can only be judged by relating it to the effects it has upon
the power relations between social classes in a concrete situation.

We have been able to establish that these effects upon class
relations are determined above all by the way in which the urban
issues are linked with other issues in the social structure. Thus the
urban movements become social movements insofar as they become
one component of some political movement challenging the social
order, for example the workers' struggle. The emergence of a consumer unionism based on claims linked directly to the method of
distributing communal resources must therefore be distinguished
from the development of class conflict out of these issues. And just
as there is a close link between unionism and the revolutionary
workers' movement, there is also a constant interaction between
urban protest and the questioning of our way of life. Furthermore,
insofar as communal consumption is directed more and more by
the state apparatus (at a general and a local level), urban movements tend to question the social administration of our way of life,
concretely illustrated, through public intervention, in the basic
facilities of daily life. So the more or less revolutionary side of
urban movements will depend to a large extent upon the ability of
the state apparatus to integrate, that is to say, upon the mass of
resources it can devote to integration, as well as upon the balance
of power between classes, which lies at the root of the form and
orientation of the administration of public resources.

This link between struggles and political struggle, this progressive passage from one sphere of the social structure to another, is
the basic point in the dynamic of change that can be aroused by
urban social movements. But this successive concatenation does
not only depend upon the objective issue represented by one problem or another in a given social situation. It also depends upon the
actual process of the urban struggle, the agents that intervene, and

their nature and the forms taken by the conflict. Our survey has revealed the orientation and evolution of an urban social move- ment — whether it seeks to link urban issues to general social issues, or whether it seeks to separate them by pursuing specific, limited objectives. In the first case the urban movement becomes a source of social change; in the second it becomes an instrument of partici- pation within general, dominantly institutional objectives. The characteristics of the organization and its line of action are them- selves subject to specific social factors in the same way as are their success or failure in leading social mobilization. One of the essential tasks of research is therefore to explain the social conditions sur- rounding the different lines of action. But in every case it is in this interaction between the position of the urban issue in the social structure, the position of the social group in the class relation and the politico-ideological characteristics of the intervening organiza- tions that the ultimate secret of urban social movements lies.

Thus we can begin to understand how the city changes not under the pressure of city-planning technicians but under that of the conflict process in social groups, and also how the new ques- tions posed by the urban problematic are expressed in action that reopens the roads to revolution in our societies by linking other forms of conflict with those arising from the productive system and from political struggle.

This explains why the last word on this issue is outside of this text, why it does not lie with us. For the urban social movements are not simply a subject for research. They have their birth and development in everyday facts, posing new problems and issuing new challenges, in a cry of life and conflict that drowns the techno- cratic myths of urban rationality. A cry that is a strong reminder that urban power, too, lies in the streets.

Thus the field of urban politics that is gradually emerging in research and in social practice may be redefined through the con- tradictory dialectic between policy and social movements, itself determined by the structural charge of the issues that define each historical conjuncture.

V The Urban Process

The Interaction Between Urban Structure and Urban Politics

The case of the urban crisis in the United States (*)

The analysis of the urban structure allows us to understand the particular arrangement of a social structure around the urban *issues*, as we have defined the term. The study of urban politics is the key to understanding the dialectics between maintenance and transformation with regard to the urban system. Therefore, any empirical research must link very closely both levels of analysis to embrace the complex reality which we have to deconstruct and reconstruct in order to establish its social meaning. What people perceive in everyday life, that is, *the urban process,* is produced through the interaction between the elements of urban structure and the variations of urban politics. We would like to show the empirical usefulness of the whole theoretical discussion through the analysis of a concrete historical process: the development of the urban crisis in the United States. It should be clear that this analysis, as presented here, does not use systematically and explicitly the whole conceptual apparatus that we have presented. Nevertheless, it is rooted in the same intellectual perspective and takes into consideration the same theoretical and methodological foundations in the analysis of the urban contradictions. We are not yet in a position to present a systematic account of a whole urban process in a form which could follow exactly the terms of our definition. But we can propose, at a lower level of formalization, some historically grounded analysis that fits with the more general premises of our theory. Because we accept the law of uneven development in the process of research, we think that it could be useful to attempt a first degree of articulation between two elements of our thinking: the analysis of *each level* of the social reality by itself

(*) This part was written in 1975 in the United States. It is published for the first time in the English edition. I am particularly grateful to David Harvey for his help, comments and in-depth revision of the manuscript.

and the explanation of a historical process which necessarily includes *all levels* of a complex reality. In this respect, the development of the urban crisis in the United States is a very meaningful example of the interaction between urban structure and urban politics as the underlying framework of the urban process.

15

Beyond the Myths of the Urban Crisis: the US Model

'There was an urban crisis at one time,' said William Dilley 3rd, Deputy Assistant Secretary of Policy Development at the Department of Housing and Urban Development. (Holsandolph, 1975.) But in 1975, as proclaimed by President Ford's aides, 'the urban crisis of the 60s is over.' They simply neglected to say that the urban crisis of the 1970s was exploding.

In fact what the official wanted to express very frankly was that the black ghettos were under control in spite of the recession. As right-wing ideologist Daniel Moynihan declared in Congress, there is not an urban problem but a Negro problem. (Jones and Hoppe, 1969.)

Is that really true? Is the urban crisis just the ideological expression used by the ruling class to naturalize (through an implicit ecological causation) the current social contradictions? (Castells, 1975.)

This is, without any doubt the most current view among the political élite. So, Senator Ribicoff, opening the Congressional Hearings on urban problems in 1966 put it in unambiguous terms (NCUP, 1966, 25):

> To say that the city is the central problem of American life is simply to know that increasingly the cities are American life; just as urban living is becoming the condition of man across the world. . . . The city is not just housing and stores. It is not just education and employment, parks and theaters, banks and shops. It is a place where men should be able to live in dignity and security and harmony, where the great achievements of modern civilization and the ageless pleasures afforded by natural beauty should be available to all.

Similar wood existed in the public opinion. A survey conducted by Wilson and Banfield on a sample of homeowners in Boston in 1967 in order to identify what the 'urban problems' were for the people, concluded that:

> The conventional urban problems — housing, transportation, pollution, urban renewal and the like — were a major concern of only eighteen percent of those questioned and these were expressed disproportionately by the wealthier, better educated respondents. . . . The issue which concerned more respondents than any other was variously stated — crime, violence, rebellious youth, racial tension, public immorality, delinquency. However stated, the common theme seemed to be a concern for improper behaviour in public places. (Wilson, 1968, 26–7.)

Nevertheless, while the urban crisis of the 60s remained largely confined to the situations of poverty and racial discrimination and to the social programs designed to control blacks and unemployed, during the 70s, the urban crisis has progressively adopted rather different connotations:

The urban crisis has been used to speak of *the crisis of some key urban services*, like housing, transportation, welfare, health, education, etc., characterized by an advanced degree of socialized management and a decisive role of state intervention. (Gartner and Reissman,`1974; Jacobs, 1966.)

The urban crisis is also *the fiscal crisis of the cities*, the inability of the local governments to provide enough resources to cover the required public facilities because of the increasing gap between the fiscal resources and the public needs and demands. (Fusfeld, 1968; Bergeman, 1969.)

The urban crisis is, at another level, the development of *urban movements and conflicts* arising from the grass-roots community organizations and directed towards urban issues, that is towards the delivery and management of particular means of socialized consumption. (Mollenkopf, 1973; Connery, 1969; Lipsky, 1968.)

And, currently, the urban crisis is also the impact of the *structural and economic crisis* on the organization of the cities and on the evolution of social services. (San Francisco Socialist Coalition, 1975.)

So, is the multiplicity of meanings of the urban crisis an ideological effect? Certain it is if by this we mean that the roots of the different levels of crisis that we have cited are produced by a particular form of the spatial organization. But if the crude use of the term 'the urban crisis' is an ideological artifact, the association between the different levels and problems connoted by the term is not an arbitrary one. It is a biased reading of actual connections experienced in social practice.

In fact, our hypothesis is that the US urban crisis is the crisis of a particular form of urban structure that plays a major role in the

US process of capitalist accumulation, in the organization of socialized consumption and in the reproduction of the social order. Since this function is performed at multiple levels so is the crisis, its connections and its effects. This is the unifying perspective that will underlie our exploration of the multidimensionality of the urban crisis.

The story is currently well known. (See Schnore, 1965; Duncan and Lieberson, 1970; Favagist, 1975; Goodall, 1968; Hawley and Zimmer, 1970; Hadden and Borgatta, 1965; Glaab, 1963.) The specificity of the US urban structure since World War II — underlying the crisis of American cities — results from the historical articulation of the processes of *Metropolitanization, suburbanization,* and *social-political fragmentation.*

I Metropolitanization[23]

Concentration of the population and activities in some major areas at an accelerated rate. Metropolitanization follows from the process of uneven development and from the concentration of capital, means of production and labour in the monopolistic stage of capitalism. Regional economies and agriculture are devastated/restructured by the penetration of market forces and the transformation of production under the hegemony of financial capital. Mass migration follows. On the other hand, the combined effect of positive externalities, agglomeration economies, the focusing of

[23] This process is obviously *differential* in the sense that each metropolitan area grew up at a different time and is the expression of, first, a particular form of capitalist production and distribution, and later, of a particular mode of succession and combination of the different activities. For this crucial point regarding the urban analysis of the US see the forthcoming paper by David Gordon, Toward a Critique of Capitalopolis: Capitalism and Urban Development in the US', which I was able to discuss personally with the author. Given the level of generality of our analysis and its particular focus on the social breakdowns emerging in the largest metropolitan areas, we will not differentiate the types of metropolitan areas. But any attempt to explain the particular spatial pattern or economic structure of American cities should deal with this problem to avoid generalizing all the aspects of the urban crisis to all large cities. Here we deal with the 'cities in crisis,' namely the largest and oldest metropolitan areas. The Californian and Southern large metropolitan areas will share *some* of the problems analysed here (particularly racial discrimination and its consequences as well as the crisis of 'social services') but the interplay between these contradictions and the urban structure will follow only partially the analysis presented here. Instead of complicating our synthesis excessively we prefer: a) to outline a general historical model that seems empirically valid for the oldest metropolises; b) to leave as an open question the validity of the analysis for the newest metropolises, particularly Los Angeles, Houston and Atlanta (the specificity of Los Angeles can be better understood by the perceptive monograph by Fogelson (1967)); c) to point, nevertheless, to the fact that major elements of the general model described (for instance, the social-political fragmentation, the distribution of sources, etc.) would apply *also* to these situations; d) to suggest the urgent need for some analyses that, in addition to the work of typologizing the cities, could relate the variations in the urban structure to the specific forms of 'urban crisis' existing there.

transportation networks, the concentration of metropolitan markets, economies of scale in management and in the institutions of circulation of capital, is to bring together workers, means of production, means of consumption and organizational structure, in a few large cities. These form the so-called metropolitan areas and are an expression of dominance over the 'hinterland', that is, over the entire society.

II   Suburbanization

(See Masotti & Hadden, 1973; Schiltz & Moffitt, 1971; E. Sclar of Brandeis University is finishing an important book on the subject, which we were able to discuss.) The process of selective decentralization and spatial sprawl of population and activities within the metropolitan areas, begun as early as the 1890s, and renewed in the 1920s, suddenly accelerated in the period after 1945 and has remained essentially unchecked until the present. This is a selective process in the sense that the population which migrates to the suburbs is not random, but has a higher social status. For employment, there is a double differentiation: on the one hand, business activities and major administrative services remain in the urban core while manufacturing and retail trade tend to decentralize their location. On the other hand, within the industrial and commercial sectors, large-scale monopolistic plants and shopping centres go to the suburbs, leaving in the central cities two very different types of firms: a small number of technologically advanced activities and luxury shops; the mainstream of industrial and service activities of the so-called 'competitive sectors' (a sector characterized by low-labour productivity, mass-union, low-wage labour, comprising primarily retail and small business functions) as well as the marginal activities known as the 'irregular economy', (much of which is illegal).

This process, which is a major trend of the US urban structure (Harrison, 1974) with very decisive consequences, is a self-reinforcing one. The immigration of poor blacks expelled from the agricultural South concentrates them in the inner cities. (Katznelson, 1973.) The exodus of the upper and middle income groups draws service activities to the suburbs. The location of jobs relates in part to patterns of housing opportunities for different segments of the labour force — the 'competitive sector' with its demand for loss wage labour, for example, locates in the central city where it has access to ghetto labour. The distribution of jobs is also sensitive to the transportation system — suburban residents commute to downtown or use the system of 'beltways' and 'freeways' to reach suburban industrial and service jobs. The ecological patterns of residence become increasingly differentiated: (Schnore, 1972) suburban single family houses on two acre lots contrast with increasingly obsolete inner city apartment dwellings. Differences in cultural style, rooted mostly in social class and family practices, will be symbolically reinforced by the social–spatial distance and by the environmental imagery. The two worlds of the suburb and the inner city increasingly ignore each other except insofar as they develop reciprocal fears, myths and prejudices, often articulated as racial and class barriers. (Gans, 1962a; 1962b; 1967.)The segregated school system becomes a major instrument and symbol of self-definition and perpetuation of the two separate and hierarchically organized universes. (Farley & Taueber, 1972.)

The suburbanization process has been facilitated by major technological changes in transportation, in the mass production of housing and in the increasing spatial freedom of the industrial plants and services as their locational requirements have become less restrictive. But suburbanization cannot be attributed simply to technologied charges (such as those associated with the automobile). On the contrary, the massive auto-highway transportation system and the new locational patterns of residence and activities express a new stage of capitalist accumulation and have been made possible primarily by the policies of the state designed to serve this purpose. (Haveman and Hamrin, 1973; Smerk, 1965.) Let us summarize briefly the specific connections between capital accumulation, state policies, and suburbanization.

The recovery of US capitalism after the Great Depression of the thirties was made possible by the war and by the development, in its aftermath, of three major economic trends:[24] a) the internationalization of capital and the increase in the rate of exploitation on a world scale under the US hegemony, as a direct consequence of the economic and political situation of each country after World War II. b) The rapid expansion of new profitable outlets through the development of mass consumption. c) The decisive structural intervention of the state in the process of accumulation, in the creation of general conditions for capitalist production and in the socialization of costs of both social investment, such as education and health, and the reproduction of labour power. At the same time, as a result and as a major causal factor of this accelerated capitalist growth, the stability of the social relationships of exploitation was

---

[24] I will be necessarily schematic here on this major topic. Someday my analysis and references on the post-war development of US capitalism will be available, contained in my draft paper 'The Graying of America. The World Economic Crisis and US Society.' (University of Wisconsin, August 1975). I prefer not to repeat here the whole set of data.

maintained through a combination of economic cooptation and political repression of most of the working class.

How do these trends relate to suburbanization? The increasing profits of monopoly capital allowed the expansion of material production. On the one hand, the investment in new technology and transportation facilities led to the decentralization of larger plants; on the other hand, economic growth although it allowed a less than proportional rise of the workers' wages, gave to some of them the prospect of job stability, increased purchasing power and access to consumer credit. The need to find massive new outlets was met just in time by the sudden expansion of mass production of new housing, highway-auto transportation and associated public facilities. America practically built up in twenty years a new set of cities, contiguous to the preexisting metropolises.

Suburbanization occurred in part because the land was much cheaper on the urban fringe and in part because the mass production of housing with light building materials generated a strong multiplier effect on the economy as a whole, particularly if we consider the implied necessity of a decentralized individualized transportation system (for an outline of this interaction, see Harvey, 1975.) Under these conditions of production and relying on a system of easy installment credit, the construction and auto industry could draw into their market a substantial proportion of the middle-class American families, opening the way to the inclusion of a sector of the working class into the world of 'middle-class consumption'.

Nevertheless, the decisive element in the feasibility of this economic, social, and spatial strategy was the role of the state, particularly of the federal government, which introduced key mechanisms for the production of housing and highways in a form entirely subordinate to the interests of monopoly capital. In the case of housing, as the most recent US government's report on housing states (See US Government Report, 1973, the most important source of data on housing in the US):

> In the 1930s, Congress made two fundamental policy decisions which remain basically intact to this day. The first was the complete restructuring of the private home financing system through the creation of the Federal Housing Administration (mortgage insurance); the Federal Home Loan Bank Board and Bank System (savings and loan industry); institutions like the Federal Deposit Insurance Corporation and the Federal Savings and Loan Insurance Corporation (insurance on deposits of commercial banks, mutual savings banks, and savings and loan associations); and finally, the Federal National Mortgage Association (secondary mortgage market). Creation of these institutions, resulting in the acceptability of the long-term, low down

payment, fully amortizing mortgage and a system to provide a large flow of capital into the mortgage market, are probably the most significant achievements of the Federal Government in the housing area.

With the provision of a risk-free mortgage system for financial capital, the state overcame the major obstacle to the profitable mass production of housing within capitalism: the absence of a reliable home-ownership market. Once the government under-wrote the risk of mortgage foreclosures, many working-class families could afford to enter the home-ownership housing market; starting the process that allowed the relative modernization of the building industry and the lowering of costs which further enlarged the suburban market. In addition to these basic mechanisms, the government implemented during the past forty years a number of fiscal measures to protect real estate investors and to favour home ownership. (See Starr, 1975.)

Concerning the development of the *highway—auto transportation system,* three elements have to be considered: [25] a) the deliberate destruction by the auto corporations (with the acquiescence of the state and federal authorities) of alternative means of transportation, namely by acquiring the streetcar and railway companies and dismantling them. (Yago, 1974.) b) The launching by the federal government of a huge programme of highway construction (called inter-state highways but with a major emphasis on intra-metropolitan highways); a crucial element in this policy was the Federal Aid Highway Act of 1956, but in fact the initiatives were at all levels, including the organization of autonomous state-based agencies. The Federal government paid 90% of the cost of highway construction and had spent, by 1973, 60 times more in this sector than for urban mass transportation. (Smerk, 1965; 1973.) c) Obviously, residential and industrial sprawl were necessarily connected to the highway-auto transportation system, and in this sense capitalist interests and state policies created a set of mutually reinforcing trends: the auto, and therefore the highway, became a need.

The role of suburbanization in the process of capitalist accumulation was not limited to the capital directly invested in the production of housing, highways and public facilities. The whole suburban social form became an extremely effective apparatus of individualized commodity consumption.

---

[25] We are looking forward to the development of the current research by Glen Yago (Sociology Department, University of Wisconsin) on State Policy, corporate planning and transportation needs: the development of the US urban ground transportation system. We have learned many things about US transportation through our discussions.

The shopping centres and the supermarkets were made possible by suburban sprawl, as were the new leisure activities (from the drive-in restaurant or cinema to the private swimming pool). But even more important was the role of the single-family house in the suburb as the perfect design for maximizing capitalist consumption. Every household had to be self-sufficient, from the refrigerator to the TV, including the garden machinery, the do-it-yourself instruments, the electro-domestic equipment, etc.

At the same time the suburban model of consumption had a very clear impact on the reproduction of the dominant social relationships. At the most elementary level, this whole domestic world was built on borrowed money and the chronic indebtedness tied individuals into the job market and into society in general in a most repressive way. Any major deviation or failure of individuals to conform could immediately be countered by withdrawal of access to consumer credit. Mass consumption also meant mass dependency upon the economic and cultural rules of the financial institutions.

The social relationships in the suburban neighbourhood also expressed the values of individualism, conformism and social integration, reducing the world to the nuclear family and social desires to the maximization of individual (family) consumption.

We will not discuss here the alternative hypotheses about the suburbs being produced by the combination of technological possibilities and subjective values towards suburbanism. This would require a whole critique of the ideological assumptions of current theory. However, we will make just three remarks:

a) People's consciousness and values are produced by their practices and experiences and these are mostly determined by their place within the social rela.ionships of production and consumption. (Godard, 1972; Preteceille, 1975.)

b) There is a 'return to Nature' dream linked to the myth of recovering, at least in the evening, the autonomy of the petty commodity and peasant production from which salaried labour was historically drawn.

In the United States this 'myth' *appears* peculiarly important in part because of a pervasive ideology drawn from images of rural Jeffersonian democracy and in part because of the continued significance of the 'rural economy' in American life until recently. The distinctive function of this myth is to persuade the mass of wage workers that a degrading relation to nature experienced in the industrial work process can be compensated for by a satisfying relation to nature in 'the community'. One of the consequences of this pervasive mythology and the ideology which accompanies it, is that work-based discontents are registered in the community as protests about 'the quality of life and environment'. The ecology and the suburban 'no-growth' movements of the late 1960s had this as their basis.

c) This myth is as strong in Europe as in the US yet the response has not been the construction of suburbs. In this sense the US is unique in the world, in spite of the incredible ethnocentrism of many American urbanists. Obviously the suburbs have grown everywhere with the expansion of the metropolitan areas, but the pattern of social segregation is not the same. In fact, the inner cities in Europe frequently have a higher social status on the average. Suburban privately owned housing is much less common and the automobile is not, by and large, the major mode of urban transportation. This is not to be interpreted either as a matter of an 'inferior level of development': the 'suburban-like-US pattern' has been steady in Paris in the last ten years after having increased to some extent in the early sixties. (Freyssinet and Regazzola, 1970; Topalov, 1974.) This point is made not to stress the absolute specificity of each society but to show how the process of US suburbanization was determined and shaped by a particular pattern of capitalist development at a particular critical stage characterized by the decisive intervention of the state. (Leo Schnore has frequently stressed this dependence. For a re-assessment of this perspective see Schnore, 1975.)

  The other face of the process of suburbanization was the new role played by the inner cities in the process of accumulation and in the reproduction of labour power. We must differentiate here between the Central Business District and the inner cities at large. (For data and references, see Congressional Research Service, 1973; see also Tabb, 1970.) The former kept the major directional and organizational economic functions, as well as a number of luxurious commercial activities and several major cultural institutions, while it lost a large proportion of the retail trade. The inner cities lost jobs and activities (especially in large-size manufacturing plants), and a significant proportion of the middle-class and workers in the high-wage monopoly sector industries. At the same, the inner cities received increasing numbers of black and poor-white immigrants, mostly from the southern depressed areas and Appalachia, as a consequence of the mechanization of agriculture and of the destruction of the backward regional economies. (Taueber and Taueber, 1965.) They became simultaneously the location of 'competitive sector' activities employing low skilled and low-paid labour, making use of the surplus population (unemployed and underemployed) often made up of the discriminated-against ethnic and racial minorities.

The inner cities also comprised forms of organization and consumption which were entirely different to those found in the suburbs. The housing market, in particular, was supposed to work according to the 'filtering down' theory. Namely, the upper strata of inner city residents (excluding the top elite who are mostly concentrated in well-defended 'high society ghettos') left their urban dwellings for new suburban homes. This supposedly allowed the middle strata to jump into the vacated houses, in turn freeing their standard housing for the lower income groups whose slum housing could be left for the newcomers. In fact such a theory never corresponded to the realities since it assumed that the whole population could be upwardly mobile. (Congressional Research Service, 1973, 103.) Instead, we observe a distinct process of uneven development between the suburbs and the inner cities. Some neighbourhoods in the inner city were well-maintained relative to incomes, usually where home-ownership prevailed and was supported by white, ethnic, neighbourhood savings and loan associations. (Masters, 1972.) But by and large the low- and middle-income strata were not able to afford the level of rents or mortgage payments necessary to move into the superior housing coming on to the market. Before they could move in, therefore, the housing had to be 'devalued' and brought into a state of deterioration which the different income groups could afford. In addition, racial discrimination barred minority groups from access to equal housing opportunities, imposing a 'race over price'. (Harvey, 1975.) The result in the inner city was that the housing stock was acquired by landlords, since home ownership was beyond the means of the poor and credit was denied to racial minorities even when they had adequate incomes. In order to keep respectable levels of profit, the landlords combined lower rents per head with over-crowding and lack of maintenance. The housing stock in these areas rapidly deteriorated.

The fixed assets of the inner city were, as a result of these general processes, reduced in value. What was occasion for profit for capital in the suburbs was cause for impoverishment of people in the inner city. The increasing indebtedness of the suburban middle-class was paralleled by accelerated deterioration of living conditions for the slum dwellers. The reduction in value of the tax base in the inner city led to a decline in tax revenues and consequently to the decline in services, particularly those needed by the social groups that could not afford to purchase commodities in the market. Thus, the process of suburban expansion was, at the same time, the process of inner city decay. Put another way, a high rate of investment in the suburbs was structurally related to a high rate of disinvestment in the inner cities. Both were produced by the domination of the capitalist interests which affected differentially the various segments of the social classes. (See Boulding *et al.*, 1973, part 1.)

III The political fragmentation of the local governments

The specific model of post-war US urban development can be completed by considering this third major trend; their considerable relative autonomy and the role that this autonomy plays in the maintenance of social residential segregation and of the corresponding organization of consumption.[26]

'Separate and unequal', the communities of the metropolitan areas have transformed the Jeffersonian ideal of grass-roots local democracy into a barbed-wire wall of municipal regulations built up to preserve regressive mechanisms of redistribution of income through the public delivery of goods and services. (Long, 1967.) An interesting analysis by Richard Child Hill (1974) of a large number of metropolitan areas shows a close relationship between the level of income inequality and social status on the one hand, and the inequality in the distribution of local resources among local governments. This inequality reflects primarily the major cleavage between city centres and the suburbs, but it also directly affects the intra-suburban stratification. The more consumption ought to be socialized because the lower income of the residents prevents them from meeting their needs through the market, the less the local government has the resources to meet the needs and demands. Thus, not only are the more exploited and oppressed people trapped in the low-wage labour market and in commodity consumption, but, in addition, the public institutions are structurally regressive when the mechanisms of redistribution are concerned. Furthermore, the political fragmentation becomes a social and racial barrier through the connection of the cultural prejudices with the real-estate interests and with the protection of private property. The school system plays a major role in creating inter-generational mobility chances for each stratum within the population, at the same time as it serves to reproduce the whole system, economically and ideologically. (Campbell & Meranto, 1967; Coleman *et al.*, 1966.) The wage-earner population is, thus, split up into a patchwork quilt of residential areas which crystallize each social position into a spatial configuration with differential access to services, different organizational networks and local institutions. As a consequence,

[26] I have borrowed several interesting ideas from a paper by Ann Markusenn (Economics Department, University of Colorado). Since she does not want to be quoted, I do not quote the paper.

conflict is channelled towards competition among the almost-
equally exploited residents for a 'never-enough-for-all' pie. The
suburban local governments exacerbate this situation through all
kinds of discriminatory land-use regulations: large-lot zoning,
minimum house-size requirements, exclusion of multiple dwellings,
restrictive building codes, and the like.

Thus, the dual structure of inner city and suburb, which arises
from uneven capitalist development, is ultimately preserved and
reinforced by the state through the institutional arrangement of
local governments and the class-determined fragmentation of the
metropolitan areas.

Urban development in the United States has been accomplished
through promoting individualization of the consumption of commodities produced for profit and, simultaneously, increasing deterioration of non-profitable socialized consumption. At the same time,
institutional mechanisms have been developed for the preservation
of social order, and for the reproduction of the social structure.

The coherence and the elegance of this model appeared as neat,
well ordered, and impeccable as were the uniforms of the guards
behind the smiling screen of the advertising society.

The new metropolitan world seemed able to go on and on.

16

The Social Contradictions of the Model of Urban Development and the Attempts at Regulation through Urban Policies

The new dynamic stability of the capitalist model of suburban growth did not last very long. Several important contradictions, structurally implicit within the model, became increasingly more apparent. Some were manifest very early on, as early as the 1950s. Others have yet to mature and will be aggravated by the mass discontent of some sectors of the American people and by the specific policies designed to control the situation. (See David and Peterson, 1973; J. Wilson, 1968.)

The first generation of urban crises arose around two major problems: a) the concern of corporate business and political élites with some aspects of the decay of the city centres; b) the increasing loss of social control over the minorities and the lower working class of the inner city.

The first point refers essentially to three major consequences of the process which were highly dysfunctional for the dominant interests: 1) The deterioration of services and of the social environment threatened the existence and activities of the Central Business District. The preservation of the CBD was essential as some directional functions needed to be concentrated there because the value of fixed capital investments and real estate holdings of large corporations was threatened. 2) Some important central city functions at the level of symbolic dominance, cultural institutions and élite residential and leisure activities, were also threatened. 3) The influence of 'machine politics' (as in Chicago) over a large proportion of the oldest working class in the ethnic-based neighbourhoods had to be maintained as a base of institutional power and this required the city to provide a minimum level of services and jobs.

To avoid a worsening of the situation on these three dimensions, the deteriorating fiscal balance generated by an increasing gap between shrinking revenues (mostly from property taxes) and an

expanding budget had to be checked. This implied stemming the
flight to the suburbs of additional businesses and jobs and encouraging the location of profitable activities and of some middle-class
groups in central areas of the city. Most of the inner city was in fact
abandoned but the corporate interests tried to concentrate their
response in the form of a programme of *downtown redevelopment,*
combining urban renewal, real estate initiatives and easy connections with the wealthy outer ring of the suburbs through new highways reaching the urban core over the roofs of the blighted ghettos.
This strategy required the mobilization of the dominant social and
political forces of the largest cities around a programme which articulated the interests of specific capitalists, local political élites and
the federal government. Thus there were formed what Mollenkopf
(1975) calls, in his key paper, the 'pro-growth coalitions', which
elected during the 50s several mayors who became local bosses in
order to implement and to legitimize these redevelopment programmes: (Daley in Chicago, Alioto in San Francisco, Lindsay in
New York, White in Boston, etc.).

Nevertheless, the success of this strategy relied entirely upon the
development of a gigantic programme of urban reveval which, using
the provisions of the 1949 Housing Act, was launched in the fifties
and accelerated in the sixties, two-thirds of which was financed by
the federal government. This programme, that transformed entirely
the downtown areas of cities like Boston, Newark, Baltimore, or Los
Angeles, and large parts of all big city centres, was wholly directed
towards the attraction of commercial and business interests in
order to increase the tax base, to preserve the centrality functions,
and to protect the CBD against the surrounding ghettos. Diagram X
summarizes the underlying social logic of the programme.) The
programme, with a cost to date of $8·2 billion in direct outlays and
$22·5 billion in bonded debt, *for the public authorities,* has dis-
placed, together with the highway programme, over 250 000 *families
each year.* These families were generally not relocated and received
compensatory payments averaging $80, that is less than one
percentage of the direct federal outlays. The results are, as usual,
twofold: on the one hand, the downtown districts have been partially
'saved,' the deterioration of the municipal budgets was slowed and
some central functions (for instance, some urban universities) were
preserved. On the other hand, a number of communities were disrupted, a mass of sound housing stock was destroyed, without
equivalent replacement either for it or for the bulldozed slums, the
displaced families went through very serious difficulties and the
general situation for housing and services, in the inner city as a
whole, worsened. (Friedland, 1975; Castells, 1970.)

No wonder that urban renewal came under attack from grass-roots movements and that a number of urban struggles started as a reaction against the programme. (Hartman, 1974; Mollenkopf, 1976.) In that sense, the partial economic benefits that corporate and élite interests received from the pro-growth policies were offset by increasing difficulties in the maintenance of the social order. This was exacerbated by the emergence of another parallel set of contradictions.

The inner-city residents were subjected not only to the urban bulldozer but to the impact of increasing unemployment and inflation both of which seriously affect their living conditions. 'Poverty' became suddenly a reality that nobody could ignore in spite of the image of affluent America. The very serious depression of 1957—58, once the economic stimuli of the Korean War were left behind, stuck particularly at wages and jobs in the 'competitive sector' and thus most seriously affected the newcomers in the large cities. Without any possibility of mounting a collective response to their situation, many inner city dwellers, particularly the youth, started to react individually in growing numbers. The so-called 'crime in the streets' rose dramatically, the neighbourhood gangs spread in the ghetto. The social order was seriously threatened in the inner cities. (President's Commission, 1968.)

At the same time the civil rights movements, launched by black people in the South with white liberal support in the northeastern cities, had started to transform the consciousness of the uprooted black immigrants expelled from agriculture. The ghetto organizations became more and more militant.

These tendencies contributed to a new strategy of the federal political élite on behalf of the ruling class. The late fifties (particularly the 1957—58 depression and the Soviet sputnik) focused the attention of the American dominant interests on the need to introduce some new social regulatory mechanisms to match the pattern of accumulation. The labour unions reacted to the 1957—58 depression by threatening to withdraw their support for the use of labour-saving technological improvements. This was a serious matter. While a fraction of American capital, and most of the political personnel, wanted to pursue the trend that had been so successful during the 1950s, adding, if necessary, more repression, the most enlightened fraction of the establishment supported a new reformist strategy. They sought to handle the situation by introducing compensatory mechanisms which would help to preserve the most precious advantage of US capital: the stability of the exploitative social order. They thought that this 'new frontier' was not only useful but also could be reached without losing positions of power.

Internally, the McCarthy period had eliminated any possible alternative from the Left. The socialist forces had been isolated, dis-
credited and dismantled. The unions had been either coopted or
repressed. The ideological order had been secured through the
combined effect of the cold war, of the hot (Korean) war and of
the rapidity of economic development. Externally, nuclear equili-
brium had set a limit to the possibility of defeating the Soviet
Union: the period of 'pacific coexistence' that followed allowed a
large field of manoeuvre and rendered superfluous the continuous
mobilization of the conservative myths. In summary, in the late
fifties the most enlightened sector of the ruling class realized that
the model of development required social reforms and that they
had the political strength to carry these reforms out without any
trouble. The purpose: to enlarge their social base, to increase their
political and ideological legitimization, to modernize the economy
by rectifying mechanisms of over-exploitation that were only required by backward sectors of capital. One of the major targets of
this reformist strategy was to provide mechanisms of integration of
the Blacks into American society, or at least to give symbolic
channels that could prevent a mass-based organized revolt. Furthermore, the specific political instruments that had to be used by the
reformist wing required a mobilization of the black vote (particularly
in the northern cities) in order to compensate for the loss of the
right-wing democratic vote in the South. (Piven, 1974.) In fact,
Kennedy won the key vote of Chicago in 1960 by relying on the
black vote. If it is true that the ghettos traditionally voted demo-
crat, what was new in 1960 was the exceptional turn-out of Blacks
voting for Kennedy. Yet, the whole rationality of this strategy did
not convince a significant proportion of the American rulers, and
the implementation of their policies was not a 'structural necessity'
but the result of a political struggle (the 1960 Nixon-Kennedy
election) that gave a narrow victory to the man who was at the same
time the candidate of the Establishment and the hope of the over-
exploited against short-sighted 'middle America'.

The 'New frontier policies' and the 'Great Society' programmes
were aimed at two major targets: a) the implementation of the 'civil
rights,' particularly against legal discrimination in the South and
against restrictions on labour mobility; b) the reduction of the
consequences of uneven development by establishing special services
and benefits for 'the poor', trying at the same time to maintain the
social order and to relegitimize the 'American Way of Life'. For both
reasons, the inner cities became the natural battleground of the new
reformers. A pioneer programme, New York's East Side's Mobilization for Youth, 'discovered' that the best way to prevent juvenile

delinquency was to organize the young people in order to mobilize their collective demands for jobs, services, and revenues. The only trouble being that the programme became increasingly contradictory to the social order that had generated it. Also, the set of programmes comprising the War on Poverty, through the Office for Economic Opportunity, had to be complemented, at the grass-roots level, with the Community Action Program which tried to organize and to mobilize neighbourhood residents to put pressure on the bureaucracies in order to obtain the required services. (Morris and Rein, 1970; Moynihan, 1969; Piven and Cloward, 1974; Watten *et al.*, 1974.) How is it possible that the bureaucracies were pushing the bureaucracies? Because they were different bureaucracies: it was clear, at the *federal level,* that all efforts at even modest social reform would be absorbed by the interests vested in the *local government bureaucracies* unless some grass-roots pressure were organized under control. The real problem was that such control was eventually lost. But not because of the naive idealism of the reformers (as some conservative bureaucrats think (Moynihan, 1969) but because of contradictions, internal and external, within the reformist programmes. Consider, first, the internal contradictions: how to mobilize people without convincing them? And how to convince and to be trusted by people without engaging in some actual economic or institutional reform? And how to do this without hurting the local particular interests of the established cliques? The external contradictions were of another sort. The expansion of the Great Society programmes was historically connected to five major disruptive trends in the crucial period of the 1960s: 1) The militancy of black people and the development of the Black movements. 2) The Vietnam War which absorbed more and more public resources, and which prevented the Federal government from meeting the expectations raised by the social programmes. 3) The revolt of the students and major breakdowns in capitalist ideology with the emergence of the counter-culture, both of which were a symptom of a 'legitimacy crisis' in American Government (a crisis that has reached its nadir with Watergate). 4) The development of the neighbourhood struggles that more and more opposed the 'pro-growth coalition' both in the inner cities and, ultimately, in the suburbs also. 5) The inflationary process that lowered standards of living and contributed to undermining faith in the market mechanisms, turning people's attention towards the issue of service delivery.

The interaction of the 'urban programmes,' designed to improve social peace, with these various trends, turned them, initially, into so many disruptive mechanisms. In a second phase, this outcome determined their dismantlement (started by Johnson in 1967—68

398

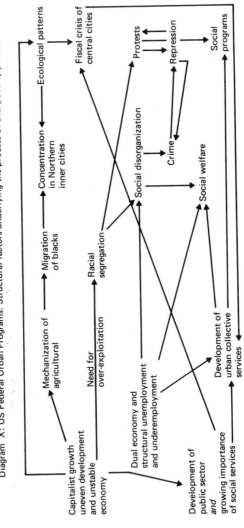

Diagram X: US Federal Urban Programs: Structural factors underlying the process of anti-poverty policies

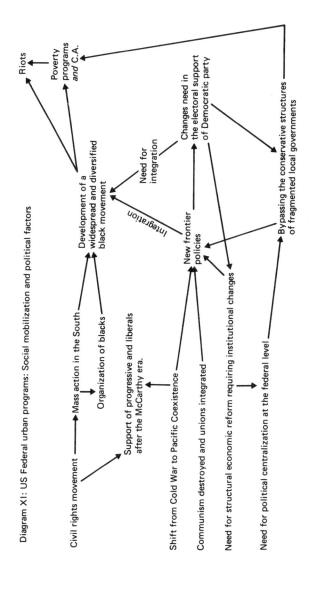

Diagram XI: US Federal urban programs: Social mobilization and political factors

400

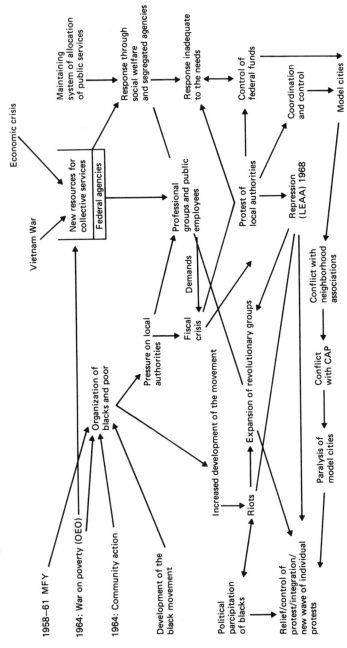

Diagram XII: US Federal Urban Programs: The process of anti-poverty and community action policies in the 1960's and accelerated by Nixon) and the use of massive repression in the inner city, under the reinforced control of local bureaucracies.

In order not to expand this analysis excessively we have summarized the whole process of the 'urban programmes' in Diagrams X, XI and XII, which should be considered as different interrelated dimensions of a single historical process, as presented in Diagram XIII (see below, p. 404).

Thus, both urban renewal and the urban social programmes, policies designed to improve the economic situation and the social stability of the decaying inner city, served only to deepen the contradictions and accelerate the amount of social conflict as expressed by community mobilization in the neighbourhoods and by mass disruptions in the ghettos. These events, together with the problems arising within the structure of public service provision led to a new and more dangerous form of urban crisis that exploded in the 1970s.

17

Dimensions and Processes of the US Urban Crisis in the 1970s

The failure of urban policies aimed at handling the problems generated by the uneven urban—suburban development and the maturation of the contradictions underlying the production and delivery of services, precipitated a multidimensional crisis in the 1960s which violently shook the model of urban development and endangered its crucial function in the process of accumulation and segregated consumption. This crisis developed along several different lines that, although interrelated, will be better understood if considered separately.

I The breakdown of social order in the inner city

The most direct and most disruptive expression of the urban crisis was the series of events which clearly threatened, in radical fashion, the reproduction of the social order. These events cannot be explained away 'ecologically' by referring simply to the conditions in and location of the inner city (as some sociologists have attempted to do by focussing on 'density and congestion'. They had their roots in the social structure of exploitation and in the political and ideological experiences of oppression. Nevertheless, since the inner city was, on the one hand both physically and socially a material expression of the repressive social order constructed on behalf of capital, and on the other hand, a form of organization of the 'reserve army' of labour power and of employment in the stagnant economic sector, the revolt of the over-exploited against the conditions of labour took the form of a rebellion against the symbols and practices of the rulers, as these were experienced in everyday life in the inner city.

This major disruption of the dominant social order took several forms that, without by any means being equivalent to each other, all expressed the rejection of a given situation and produced a similar impact on the functioning and structure of the city centre. The most important forms taken by the breakdown of social control were rapidly rising crime rates, burgeoning urban protest movements over a wide variety of issues, and the urban riots. We will consider each of these briefly in turn.

A. The rapid increase in so-called crime and particularly in 'crime in the streets' was clearly linked to an individual reaction against the situation of structural oppression coupled with the absence of a stable mass-based political alternative. (See Erlanger, 1974.) 'Crime' is not explained solely by 'deprivation'. Diagram XIII shows, for example, that in the depression during the 1930s crime rates actually went down and it was only in the late 1950s and early 1960s that a sharp upward trend occurred. In the current depression the rates of crime are even higher (+20 per cent in 1974/ 1975). What this implies is that the collective movement that during the 1930s forced the government to launch the New Deal was viewed by most urban dwellers as an adequate response to oppressive conditions. The lack of a broad collective movement leads individuals to seek personal solutions to social problems. Today, at the same time, the inner city contains much more structural unemployment. No effective channel for mass action seems likely in the immediate future. But we observe also that the most rapid increase in crime was during the 1960s, when in fact the economic situation was improving on average, at least until 1966. So it seems that the major factor has been the collapse of the system of social control operating through the family, the school, and other community institutions. In addition, the strong urban to inner-city migration, forced for economic reasons, led to the disruption of many social and institutional arrangements which gave stability to the social order. Not only was urban crime a challenge to that order but it became a way of living, economically and culturally, for a large sector of inner-city youth who had no chance outside of the 'irregular economy', to which some forms of so-called crime are structurally connected.

B. On a totally different plane, another form of challenge to the established social–spatial division of labour and consumption was the development of community organizations and urban protest movements. These confronted the logic and function of the delivery of specific services as well as the legitimacy of the power exercised by traditional local authorities. (Fainstein and Fainstein, 1974; Mollenkopf, 1973.) The most widespread urban movements in the inner cities were mobilizations against urban renewal in order to protect the neighbourhood from demolition or to obtain adequate

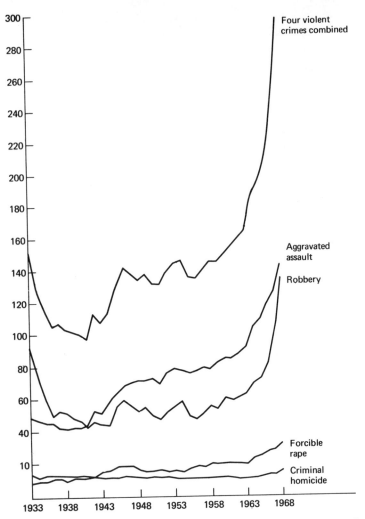

Diagram XIII. *Variation in reported UCR Index offense rates for the four major violent crimes. 1933–68 [rates per 100,000 national population.]*

Note. – The levels and trends up to 1967 are readjusted by FBI according to the methods of app. I. (FBI unpublished data.)

Source: National Commission on Causes and Prevention of Violence, Washington DC, 1969.

relocation and compensation. Given the security of the threat represented by urban renewal programmes, the mobilizations were simultaneously relatively easy to develop but defensive and limited in their scope. Nevertheless, after several years of experience, the movements shifted their demands from parochialist objectives towards a demand for comprehensive neighbourhood planning, thereby forcing a new approach to urban redevelopment.

The *rent strikes,* as analysed by Michael Lipsky (1970) particularly in New York, in St Louis, in Philadelphia, in Chicago, etc., also marked a new period when the 'filtering down' process was blocked by legislative actions requiring adequate repairs and controlling rents according to some public standards instead of the landlord's will. (Mollenkopf and Pynees, 1972.) All the services (health and education in particular) as well as the level of social welfare payments became the subject of confrontation and complaints on the part of inner-city residents, which effectively presented the progressive deterioration in market allowances and public sector resources. Frances Piven and Richard Cloward (1971) have shown how, in fact, the spectacular increase in the welfare rolls during the 1960s was not due to the increasing *needs* (which already plainly existed) but to the increasing *demands*. All of this cannot simply be seen as part of some vaguely defined 'urbanization process'. Pressures from the grass-roots arising out of the internal contradictions implicit in the provision of urban services and out of the generalized unrest in American society, led to collective forms of action which forced an adjustment to the dualistic structure of collective consumption.

The mobilization extended even to middle-class groups, and the poor and Blacks were paralleled by a reinforcement of the Alinsky-type of community organizations trying to develop citizens' participation and control over the local governments and social services. Bailey (1972) has shown how this very moderate populist approach developed mostly where middle-class groups found 'poor-people types of problems' that is when the inner-city crisis struck the remaining middle-class dwellers. Thus, in spite of their ideological conservatism and pragmatic approach, the Alinsky experiences were a real threat (contrary to the opinion expressed by Bailey) to the social order, since they were channelling towards protest, groups that were generally supportive of the local institutions. Certainly, their localism and economicism kept them within the mainstream of the consumers movement, but their growing influence was a revealing factor in the direction of a pluri-class movement that could have been developed on a broader and more conflictual base in a different political context. In summary, while limited, localistic and strictly economic, the urban movements spreading during the 1960s draw a line clearly sharing the limits of the over-exploitation implicit in the until-then predominant pattern of urban development.

C. Nevertheless, the most significant factor in the breakdown of social order in the cities during the sixties were the *riots*, mostly in the black ghettos. After the explosions of Harlem (1964) and Watts (1965) they became general and widespread in the famous 'hot summer' of 1967, in 1968 as a mass response to the murder of Martin Luther King, and followed in 1969, 1970 and 1971 in a

number of very important but less publicized riots. (Feagin and
Hahn, 1973; Surkin, 1975.) Certainly, the riots were not 'urban
movements' in the sense that they were not exclusively a protest
against living conditions in the inner city. They were a part of a
general protest and struggle by the black people against the general
conditions of their oppression. After many debates and massive
empirical research on the course of riots, the best systematic
statistical analysis, carried out by Spilerman (1970; 1971), gives as
the only significant variables correlated with the occurrence and
intensity of riots the size of the black population in the city (the
larger the black population, the more riots, and the region (the
northern cities have higher probabilities). Clearly this means that,
statistically speaking, the riots were strongly linked to the large
inner-city ghettos of the largest metropolitan areas. This can be
interpreted either in organizational terms (the ghettos formed the
largest possible base for sustained mass organization) or in terms of
the specific effects of the segregated organization of work, services
and everyday life, as expressed in the largest ghettos. Both hypotheses can be supported from various case-studies and from documentation on the riots and on the Black movement. The hypotheses
should be viewed also as complementary to each other. The riots
were mass protests against the racism of society, and included as
one of its dimensions, the specific pattern of racial segregation in
the ghetto and its effects on job opportunities and on the provision
of services.[27]

Even though the Black movement, in its various manifestations,
could not overcome its isolation, and although much of its radical
component was destroyed by repression, the struggles of the sixties
nevertheless forced the state, at the federal and at the local level,
to undertake a major reexamination of the use of inner cities as a
reservation for the ethnic and racial minorities. Access of Blacks to
local governments and to the state agencies was given increasing
emphasis, more and better services began to be distributed (at least
for a period) and more public jobs were made available for inner-
city residents. Very often this was a part of a general policy of
cooptation of the community leaders in an attempt to disorganize
the grass-roots. Nevertheless the overall effect was to produce a
decisive breach in the social logic dominating the provision of urban
services and the political orientation of local governments. So, the

---

[27] The connection between the black movement as a social protest movement and
the open housing movement as a service-reform movement has been shown in detail by a
case study on Milwaukee carried out by a working-group of the University of Wisconsin's
seminar on urban politics: Ron Blascoe, Kim Burns, David Gillespie, Greg Martin, and
Linda Wills, 'Milwaukee open housing and the grass roots', August 1975.

mobilization and protest from the grass-roots, at the same time as it was met by cooptation, obtained tangible social benefits, challenged the structural logic and eventually precipitated a crisis in the provision of urban services.

II The crisis in the system of production and distribution of the means of collective consumption

The crisis of the post-war pattern of urban development does not concern only the social breakdown: it arises also out of the increasing difficulty of keeping the basic mechanisms for accomplishing the segregated provision of urban services functioning smoothly. While the same problems emerged in relation to almost all kinds of social services, we will consider only the most significant examples: housing, transportation and education. (Gordon, 1971; Pynees *et al.*, 1973.)

A. The crisis of the housing market was particularly acute in the inner cities of the large metropolitan areas. It resulted mostly from a total failure of the 'filtering down' theory. Pre-existing structural problems in the housing market were exacerbated in the 1960s, by inflationary pressures, the relative deterioration of the resources of the poor, rapidly rising property taxes and costs of maintenance, as well as the accelerating economic depreciation of the housing stock by the overall decay of the city and by overcrowding and lack of maintenance.

In fact, there was a progressive diminution of effective demand for housing on the part of low-income groups and a decline of profitability for the landlords. (Congressional Research Service, 1973, I§6.)

The Bureau of Labor Statistics calculate that it would take, at the minimum, $1178 per annum for an urban family of four to obtain 'adequate housing' in 1971. Assuming that 20% of family income was allocated to rent, 24% of city centre families had lower incomes than required, and therefore were unable to pay rents high enough for landlords to find proper maintenance profitable. This led to three major alternative consequences: a) Several families were crowded into small dwellings, accelerating the rate of deterioration and making any maintenance impossible. b) Families abandoned housing units not to 'go up' as the classic theory proposes but to 'go down' in search of cheaper housing. c) The tenants launched rent strikes and then either they were evicted (the house being then emptied) or the landlord kept the house vacant since the last possibility for him was to force deterioration and subsequent renewal and compensation.

On the other hand, many inner city landlords were also trapped by the process. (Sternlieb and Burchell, 1973.) They could not sell their stock because of the absence of buyers or because of tenants' resistance. They faced increasing costs and property taxes and they could not obtain higher rents because of the low income of the tenants. So they stopped all repairs and maintenance and, later on, they stopped even paying the property taxes, obtaining thus some super-profit for a few years, before the moment when the city could legally take over the house. Many inner-city landlords deliberately abandoned their housing and did so in increasing numbers. Some-times rehabilitation programmes funded by the cities with federal assistance allowed a new landlord to acquire the newly fixed up house at a low cost in order to re-start the same process, often under the control of the same network of landlords. But, the rate of deterioration was so great that city government was incapable of assuming the massive rehabilitation costs and the housing units were simply abandoned. Since the cost of demolition was high and with-out profitable purpose, the houses remained empty, sometimes to be occupied by squatters, sometimes by drug addicts, and inner city gangs and always by the rats. Violence, prejudice, actual assaults, and wide-spread fear contributed to the abandonment of entire sections of the city, spreading like a contagious epidemic which left behind a derelict no-man's land in large parts of the inner cities. This trend is developing very fast in the US. Some official figures for 1973 (Congressional Research Service, 1973, 107) estimated ('consecutively') 100 000 units abandoned in New York City, 30 000 in Philadelphia, 12 000 in Baltimore, 10 000 in St Louis, etc. These figures are probably underestimated. The process of abandon-ment has been going on in New York for the last eight years at a rate of 50 000 housing units each year, which (allowing for demoli-tion and previously abandoned stock) gives an estimate of between 400 000 and 450 000 abandoned apartments.

The process of residential abandonment in the largest US city centres allows us to speak of the collapse of the urban system in the most literal sense.

B. Furthermore, this crisis in the housing stock of city centres is paralleled by another very deep, although entirely different, crisis in the mechanisms of production and distribution of suburban housing. On the one hand, the increasing density of development in the suburbs and the increasing demand for single-family owned houses (stimulated and subsidized by federal tax policies) triggered a process of land speculation that raised land prices and checked profits. In order to minimise the cost of land, developers turned in the late sixties to apartment and condominium construction in the suburbs as an alternative. Federal tax arrangements further stimulated this new housing market. The traditional image of the typical suburb underwent a rapid transformation as a result.

But the most important contradiction that has been growing in recent years is the impact on suburban housing of creeping inflation and instability in financial markets. (Harvey, 1975.) Financial intermediaries and access to credit are decisive in the family's ability to purchase a home. Very briefly, the major contradiction concerns the increasing indebtedness of the individual, of the corporations, and of the state, in general, in the US economy, and in particular with respect to residential debt. Actually, the residential mortgage debt as a proportion of total debt rose from 9·5% in 1947 to 23·7% in 1972. What this means is that more and more resources have to be devoted to paying interest and amortization on the past debt. With skyrocketing interest rates and with the stagnation of real income of Americans between 1965 and 1972 (and its deterioration since then) new suburban housing has been caught between rising costs and falling effective demand. This meant a major threat of a collapse that could start an explosive chain reaction. The sustained action of the federal government avoided these pending dangers for years (providing, for instance, in 1972, as much as 7·8 billion in direct and mostly indirect help to the middle and upper income housing market. But the investments are becoming more and more risky and therefore leading financial institutions are tending to withdraw from the mortgage market. Let us examine the evolution of the share of the private residential mortgage market held by the different financial institutions:

Institutions	Share of outstanding home mortgage held		
	31/12/68	30/6/74	% change
Federal agencies	5·3%	9·9%	+87%
Commercial Banks	15·4%	17·8%	+16%
Savings and Loan Associations	43·9%	49·1%	+12%
Mutual Saving Banks	13·9%	11·0%	−21%
Individuals	9·9%	6·6%	−33%
Life Insurance Companies	11·5%	5·4%	−53% (66)

These shifts indicate that the residential mortgage market was becoming less attractive to some of the major institutions (particularly the life insurance companies) while the rapid rise in federal holding of the mortgage debt — something which had occurred once before in the great depression of the 1930s — indicates that many institutions were probably unloading their 'devalued' or high risk mortgages onto the broad shoulders of the federal government. In the period after 1945 the federal government had been continuously involved in promoting the demand for new housing, particularly in the suburbs. From 1968 onwards it seems that the federal government has also become involved in solving the 'devaluation' problems arising in the inner cities. So the federal government is now instrumental in promoting the high rate of suburban investment and absorbing the costs of the concomitant high rate of disinvestment in the inner cities.

There was, in fact, a substantial boom in the housing market, affecting both the turnover of old properties and new construction in the period 1969—73. This boom was based on a period of 'easy money' in which there seemed to be a great deal of idle money in the American economy looking for productive forms of investment. From the standpoint of the individual, apart from the subsidy given to home ownership via tax concessions, home ownership made sense in a period of rapid inflation because inflation reduces the value of the debt in real terms. In effect, much of the debt is 'monetized away' through inflation, which implies a redistribution of income from creditors (savers) to debtors. It was 'rational', therefore, to go into debt rather than to save.

But there are two major unsolved contradictions linked to this process. Either the interest rates grow faster than the inflation (which is impossible in the United States since mortgages are taken out at a fixed interest rate, at least until very recently) or as inflation gathers pace so the financial institutions increasingly withdraw from the mortgage market. In either case the financing of residential construction would collapse, as it did towards the end of 1973 when a tight-money policy combined with a high rate of inflation led financial institutions to withdraw from real-estate investment on a large scale. The construction industry has been plunged, as a consequence, into a serious depression as the number of housing starts was halved from nearly 2·4 million in 1973 to 1·2 million in 1975. The financial institutions engaged in real-estate investment activity have been seriously hurt. The federal government could, of course, intervene. But intervention becomes increasingly difficult as the state struggles to contain inflation by cutting back its own expenditures and reducing its own indebtedness. And, clearly, housing has low priority compared to military expenditures. In the spring of 1975, for example, President Ford vetoed a congressional bill providing more insurance for mortgage funds to stimulate the suburban housing market. The veto was justified as 'anti-inflationary' but critics pointed out that unless something could be done to revive suburban housing construction, not only would unemployment in the construction industry continue to rise and the demand for all kinds of other products fall off rather rapidly, but severe instability could emerge in financial markets if the real-estate investment process could not be stabilized. With prices of new and old single-family housing going up very rapidly and the housing market in its worst depression since 1945, America began to wonder if the 'suburban dream' was turning into a tension-filled nightmare.

C. *The evolving pattern of transportation* in the dual model of urban-suburban structure also exhibited several contradictions which grew in importance during the sixties. (Owen, 1966.) The most important was the differential speed of residential sprawl on one hand and decentralization of activities and job opportunities from the inner city on the other. As a consequence, millions of workers, mostly in the expanding service sector, had to commute at the same time. The much neglected public transportation network became increasingly overcrowded and deteriorated while the new urban highways were not sufficient, by and large, to handle the peak-hour commuter traffic. In general, the inner city was unable to handle the rush of city workers living in the suburbs. Congestion became more and more serious. An increasing proportion of central land was devoted to parking lots and the downtown streets were more and more clogged by traffic. The federally backed trend towards the automobile precluded large scale investment in mass transit so that the suburban railroads and metropolitan subway systems were in permanent financial difficulty that reinforced the downgrading of the services, forcing even more commuters on to the highways. (Danielson, 1965.) The consequence was that, by the late 1960s, in all the largest cities excepting New York and Boston, more than 40% of trips to work in the downtown area were by automobile. This tend provoked major protests from two main sectors: a) The downtown—redevelopment interests that required renewed public support for mass transit in order to make the facilities that they were building more accessible. b) The inner-city residents, many of whom could not afford automobiles, who suffered maximally from the congestion and from the deterioration in the public transit systems and who were increasingly isolated from new job opportunities opening up in the suburbs. As a response, the federal government started a new programme, funding up to 80% of the costs of city projects for mass-transit development. (Veatch, 1975.) The most important initiative under this new provision was the BART system in the San Francisco Bay Area. But as several analysts have shown (particularly Peter Marcuse) this experience, as well as the general trend in other on-going mass-transit programmes, has been more effective in serving the suburban residents (and particularly those of higher socio-economic status) going to work in the central business district than they have been in overcoming the increasing isolation of inner-city residents or even in serving the mass of workers commuting from the working-class suburbs to the more dispersed industrial job opportunities. This initiative represented an attempt to overcome the increasing absurdity of a mass rush by private car from the suburbs at the peak hours together with diminishing metropolitan accessibility for inner-city dwellers.

Even from the standpoint of the suburban dweller the model of development appeared less and less satisfactory. The whole structure of job opportunities and service provision in relation to household location made two cars almost a necessity for the average suburban family. Not only did this mean increasing congestion and pollution problems in suburbs, which were supposed to preserve the image of 'closeness to nature' and to provide a 'high quality life'. But the whole system made immense demands upon energy resources and took for granted very cheap and almost unlimited quantities of gasoline. The 'gas-crisis' of 1973 quickly demonstrated to all suburbanites how vulnerable their way of life was, and how fragile the suburban dream could be. At the same time as the pace of development built into the whole post-war suburbanization process was swamping the suburbs to the point that even the suburbanite could see that 'the developer was boss', so the suburbanite was forced to recognize the inherent irrationality of a transportation system which presupposed the necessity and the ability to drive hundreds of miles every week to gain access to jobs and basic services. Increasing congestion and a mandatory 55 mile-per-hour speed limit imposed to save gasoline, to say nothing of the long queues for gasoline during the 'gas crisis', are the kinds of experiences which must surely make the suburbanite wonder if the transport system still makes sense.

The American way of life has been built around an American mode of transportation. At this juncture most forms of mass public transportation are deteriorated or obsolete and the individualized, high-energy-consuming automobile system is increasingly being called in question. These are the symptomatic problems in the transportation sector which stem from the post-war model of urban development in the United States.

D. Another key mechanism in the class model of urban structure that is currently crumbling is the school system. We will not refer here to the whole complex set of contradictions concerning education as a major form of social investment for capitalist growth, but exclusively to its role in the reproduction of the system of class structure and urban segregation through 'separate and unequal' provision. The autonomy of the school districts with regard to the functioning of the schools has come under attack both from the

grass-roots and from the ruling class at the same time. The neighbourhood movements, particularly in the minority sectors of the city,
have campaigned for community control over the schools, in order
to improve the quality of education by mobilizing the resources of
parents, and to break down the differential class logic of the educational bureaucracies in the inner city school system. Without challenging segregation, this movement attempts to counter the effects
of segregation on the quality of education thus threatening the
structural inequality in the distribution of public resources. (Fainstein and Fainstein, 1974.) At the same time, the failure of the
manpower training programmes in the early 1960s demonstrated to
capitalists the need to improve education for the 'reserve army'
elements in the inner city if they were to be effectively mobilized
as part of the labour force.

The impact of the mass protest and of the pressures mounted by
liberal politicians on behalf of enlightened capitalists led to a potentially explosive solution: the busing of school children among
different school districts in order to keep a racial balance, to avoid
segregation and to improve educational quality.[28] This is effectively
a one way measure designed to bypass the vicious circle of social
status determined by the quality of education on the one hand and
quality of education determined, through residential segregation,
by social status on the other hand. But because it touches the system of stratified fragmentation in the population that is so deeply
rooted in the system, busing began to be enforced only during the
1970s and only after the civil rights organizations won some
important cases in the Courts. Starting with the 1971 *Swanson* v.
Charlotte-Mecklenburg Board of Education case, some cities, and
particularly Boston, have court-ordered two-way busing in order to
improve integration in the schools. While the upper and middle-
classes do not care too much, being 'protected' in the suburbs (because court cases brought to enforce metropolitan-wide busing
failed) or having the possibility of sending their children to private
schools, the white working-class neighbourhoods have reacted
strongly (rioting and demonstrating in Boston, Louisville, etc.)
against what they consider a threat to the social chances of their
children or even to their physical security.

Another technique devised to overcome the rigidity of the
locally-based schools has been (under the initiative of the élite this
time) to allocate 'educational vouchers' to families, who can use

[28] I have relied on the very detailed summary research paper done by a working group
of my seminar on urban politics (Wisconsin): Mary A. Evans, Alfonzo Thurman, Anthony
Edoh and August Figueroa, 'Busing and urban segregation: the continuing struggle.'
August, 1975.

them in the school of their choice, each school receiving funding proportionate to the demand. This is, to some extent, an attempt to make the schools work through a kind of market mechanism. The experience of this, particularly in California, does not seem very convincing either in terms of efficiency or equality since the mechanisms of reciprocal selection by schools and parents work to keep the same social recruitment patterns consistent with the pre-existing social structure.

These tensions and contradictions within the educational system in the United States indicate that the mechanisms of reproduction of social structure within the overall model of urban development are not functioning well. The processes of accumulation and replication of social structure became increasingly inconsistent with each other during the sixties.

E. Similar problems appear in most of the other basic public services, such as health, garbage-collection, welfare, etc. An analysis of these would provide additional evidence about the general breakdown in the organization of the means of collective consumption, the expansion of which was fundamental to the development of American capitalism after World War II.

The most striking effect of all of these trends was undoubtedly the growing abandonment and physical destruction of large sectors of the inner cities, particularly in the ghettos. Baltimore's Pennsylvania Avenue, Boston's Columbia Point, St Louis' Pruitt-Igoe, etc., are symbols of the potentially massive destruction that could happen unless some new elements enter to reverse the current pattern. The most famous example is the South Bronx District in New York, where 600 000 people live. The process of abandonment, the deterioration of real estate values, and the loss of control by the system, have induced the landlords to 'arrange' fires in order to obtain some payment from the insurance companies. They pay children to start the fires: $3 to $10 each. There were 12 300 fires in South Bronx in 1974, that is ten every night, with more than one-third proved intentional. And this is not a unique district: Brownsville-Brooklyn, Bushwick, etc. are also burning. Zones of New York appear as if they had been bombed. And among the ruins, the unemployed and kids without schools sit and chat waiting to see what might turn up.

The crisis of urban services and the breakdown of the social order at the individual and at the collective level finally had a major impact on the management of the urban system itself, ultimately striking at the heart of the state apparatus and its operations: this is what emerged openly as the urban crisis of the 1970s. (Greenstone and Peterson, 1973.)

III The crisis of local governments in the large inner cities

The most visible impact of the urban contradictions and conflicts on the state apparatus is in the form of a *fiscal crisis of inner city* governments. (See Hill, 1975; Friedland, 1975.) This is the direct culmination of the different processes we have already described. If the city budget was merely required to provide the services needed by downtown business, the city would have been able to handle the problem once the urban renewal program was started, in spite of the shrinking tax base which resulted from deterioration in the rest of the inner city. But, in addition to the satisfaction of the business demand, local governments had to accept the responsibility for expanding services and municipal jobs as well as for satisfying the demands of increasingly militant consumers and workers. Consequently, the local governments began to move into budgetary deficit on current (as opposed to capital) account. In many cases current account deficits are forbidden by law in the US (precisely in order to prevent an 'excessive' use of local autonomy to favour residents). In fact, the fiscal crisis of the inner cities was a particularly acute expression of the overall fiscal crisis of the state, that is of the increasing budgetary gap created in public finance in advanced capitalist countries because of the historical process of socialization of costs and privatization of profits. The crisis is even more acute for the local governments of large inner cities because they express the contradictory expansion of the 'service sector'. (Baumol, 1967; Sternlieb, 1971; Ganz, 1973; Wilson, 1975.) On the one hand, corporate capital needs to build directional centres which require concentration of service workers and public facilities downtown. On the other hand, if social order is to be maintained, the state has to absorb the surplus population and to provide welfare and public services to the large unemployed and underemployed population concentrated in the inner cities. During the 1950s, the accumulation requirements had top priority and local finance was able to cope. During the 1960s, the mass protest in the inner cities forced, as we have seen, some level of redistribution through social expenditures as well as through the provision of jobs. But the process did not stop there. The necessary expansion in the number of municipal workers (to administer and provide these services) triggered a process of escalating wage-demands and economic struggles that was exacerbated by the absence of established bargaining patterns in the public sector. Teachers, municipal service workers, public health workers, sanitation men and finally fireman and policemen, have been among the most militant sectors of American labour. Municipal workers unionized rapidly and strikes and slow-

downs became quite common in many cities. They have improved
their position substantially even if they are yet behind the level of
wages in the private monopoly sector. The entire set of labour relationships has been disrupted in the public sector, creating inflationary pressures on the cost of provision of these labour-intensive
services. The city did not react by raising new taxes on the corporations, which were the most expensive municipal-service consumers,
but by taxing the inner-city residents more and trying simultaneously
to appease the tax-payers, the welfare consumers, the low-wage
labour force and the municipal workers. In spite of the renewed
fiscal effort and of higher public service charges, the city had to
resort increasingly to debt financing, issuing municipal bonds,
counting on expected future revenues in order to balance the budget. Deficit-financed capital expenditures could be mixed with
current accounts illegally to conceal budgetary deficits. And default
on the debt as a means of handling the crisis emerged as a possibility. This is what happened to New York City in 1974–75, provoking a world famous fiscal crisis that became a test of the capacity of
the US government to handle the economic crisis in general.[29]

   During the 1950s the New York City budget expanded at an
annual rate of approximately 6%. Since 1965, as pressures from
communities and workers mounted, the budget increased at an
annual rate of 15%. Under the reformist Lindsay administration,
(for the link between reformism and the corporate interests, see
Gordon, 1973). New York accentuated its trend as the city
distributing more public services than any other city in the US,
partly because of the continuous immigration of structurally
unemployed: one-eighth of the New Yorkers were on welfare in
1974. New York maintains the largest system of public hospitals,
of subsidized mass transit, of welfare payments, of cultural facilities,
a tuition-free university, etc., largely as a consequence also of its
history as one of the most politicized places in the country, with
well-organized grass-roots communites.

   Table 62 shows the difference between New York and the other
cities. Nevertheless, the 'bankruptcy' of New York City is not a
consequence of the 'excessive' services and jobs distributed, as the
élite have tried to argue. It is the combined result of the refusal by
corporate interests to pay more taxes to support social services
and, even more important, by the decision of the financial community to discipline the New York City social welfare policy. In

---

[29] I have used, besides reading the *New York Times* and speaking with some friends
in New York (particularly Marvin Surkin, Allan Wolfe, Robert Cohen, Bill Tabb, Ron
Lawson etc.) the well documented paper done by one of my students at the University
of Wisconsin: Joel Devine, 'Working paper on the urban fiscal crisis, a case study; New
York City.' August 1975.

Table 62

City	Police and fire	Health and hospitals	Education	Public welfare	Debt interest	Pension fund	Other	Total
New York	100	151	295	316	66	88	430	1446
Chicago	69	30	260	21	24	14	297	715
Detroit	70	60	241	26	25	5	266	693
Los Angeles	75	51	260	144	15	21	309	875
Philadelphia	91	48	217	18	41	22	294	731

Source: US Dept. of Commerce, Bureau of Census

fact, the fiscal crisis that exploded in April–May 1975 was a two-fold crisis: there was a $1 billion cash flow crisis for May and June 1975 and, secondly a $641 million anticipated deficit for the fiscal year 1975–76. The State Legislature (with a majority of Republicans), the White House, and financial circles decided not to help the city in the short term unless there were major cuts in the budget for 1975–76 in order to put it in balance. Since the budget was already an austerity budget this implied massive lay-offs of municipal workers, drastic cuts in services, wage-freezes in the municipal sector and rising charges for public services.

Business interests forced Mayor Beame to accept this policy by: 1) Refusing any new credit to the city; 2) Establishing a New York State-Sponsored Municipal Assistance Corporation (called 'Big Mac') that would be in charge of selling the City's municipal bonds in the financial markets and, at the same time, supervising the City finances in order to ensure the reliability of the City bonds; 3) Controlling 'Big Mac' closely in order not to allow any doubt (the Governor appointed as chairman of the finance committee Mr. Felix G. Rohytyn, vice-president of Lazard Freres Co. and member of the board of ITT). 4) Requiring from the City an immediate action programme, including thousands of lay-offs, tuition charges in the University, higher public fares, reduction of all kinds of services, a wage-freeze; etc. 5) Once the 'fiscal responsibility' of the City was restored, providing assistance to find buyers for the bonds in financial markets.

Since this strategy was backed by the federal government, the City had to surrender. The measures were applied provoking initially a massive, although unorganized, response of municipal workers, who went on strike, demonstrated, and even, in the case of the police, started using some disruptive tactics. The sanitation men launched a one week wildcat strike which threatened health in the city and the government threatened to bring in the National Guard to provide services. Finally, with the help of the unions (which advanced money out of their pension funds in order to pay workers) the situation was temporarily controlled. Most of the unions agreed to a schedule of retirements and lay-offs, but in September 1975 thousands of teachers went on strike to challenge the lay-offs and again reversed, temporarily, the trend towards a rapid reduction in city services. But strong pressures were brought to bear via the financial community and the federal government which again forced the city close to the brink of bankruptcy. In the face of these pressures organized labour — the unions— curbed their opposition and acceded to a programme of lay-offs and wage reductions. The unions became the tools for disciplining labour. By the end of 1975 some 67 000 municipal employees had been laid off, including some 50 000 teachers, and a new round of lay-offs had been scheduled to take place during 1976. With the 'disciplining process' almost completely effective and encountering only scattered grass-roots community and 'wildcat' resistance, the Federal Government intervened with direct loans to help New York out of its financial difficulties in December 1975. Federal assistance did not prevent, however, a 'technical default' on the payment of some of the City's debts, a large portion of which was held by small middle-class savers, the large institutions having, for the most part, divested themselves of New York debts and obligations some time before. Nevertheless, the fact that some 50 banks in the United States had more than 50% of their net worth invested in New York City obligations obviously played an important part in encouraging federal government intervention. Clearly, the stability of the financial system and the stability of capital markets would be seriously threatened by an all-out default. The problem for the federal government and for the ruling financial élite, was to use the threat of bankruptcy in a 'brinkmanship' policy to discipline New York's municipal labour force and effectively to reduce the provision of services which had been established in response to political demands, without, at the same time, plunging the whole financial system into chaos.

The case of New York City is perhaps the most extreme example of the tendency implicit in the whole evolution of the urban contradictions in the United States. Most inner cities face similar problems. In Cleveland, the ratio of the city's debt service to its current budget expenditures is 17·9%, even higher than in New York. In Milwaukee, this ratio (an indicator of potential imbalance) is 15·2% in spite of very high local taxes. Detroit also has a structural deficit and laid off 15% of the municipal workers in 1975. Buffalo has a deficit of $17 million over its $229 million budget. Boston reduced the municipal workers by 10% in 1975, particularly in the health sector. San Francisco faced in September 1975 a strike of firemen and policemen that forced the Mayor to keep their jobs and to raise their salaries, provoking the indignation of the financial community and eliciting bitter attacks on the Mayor from the City's Board of Supervisors. In the annual Conference of City Mayors held in Boston, all the large cities, excepting Houston, appeared to be on the road towards very serious fiscal crises that will almost certainly be handled differently than in New York, depending upon the political process.

The potential consequences of the urban fiscal crisis are very serious because they could threaten the already unstable political legitimacy of local governments as well as their financial viability. Let us explain this important point.

The municipal reformers of the progressive era of the 1890s, when much of the present structure of American local government was set up, attempted to give legitimacy to local government by replacing the pork-barrel and patronage policies of the political machines by the urban development schemes of the city managers. They risked the loss of the person-to-person ties on which the control of the inner-city neighbourhoods by the political apparatuses was founded. Successive and periodic waves of urban reform gradually replaced 'patronage politics' by city governments dedicated to efficiency in the provision of urban services. The pressures from the grass-roots during the 1960s forced local bureaucracies to open up to the poor and to the ethnic minorities. These pressures even led to changes in the political personnel as shown by the number of black mayors (actually in ninety-six cities, including such cities as Detroit, Cleveland, Gary, Atlanta, and Los Angeles) and by the progressive orientation of a number of new elected officials. This enlarged the base of popular support in the inner cities and broke the power of some entrenched interest groups in local government. If, before the new patterns of political support can be consolidated, a new orientation toward 'all out business' policies becomes necessary, the local governments of the largest cities are going to become increasingly isolated from the interests they represent and are going to lose all the past sources of legitimacy, either in terms of clientele, in terms of management or in terms of specific interests being served. As the focus of the revision of social policies in the sixties, the cities are actually now under the cross-fire of business interests clamouring for restraint and efficiency and the workers and consumers refusing to carry the burden of a crisis which is not theirs. Thus the state apparatus in the inner cities, besides exhibiting increasing contradictions in terms of fiscal policies and being shaken by demands for services, jobs, and wages, is also losing political control over the social conflicts growing out of urban issues.

IV The crisis of the model of urban development

Whatever happens in the future, it is clear that the post-war pattern of urban development itself is now in question. The converging trends of social conflicts, the crisis of service provision, the emergence of the fiscal crisis and the economic and political crackdown of government have brought into question the urban—suburban structure that emerged as a powerful force in the process of capitalist accumulation and segregated commodity consumption. Actually, even the trend of metropolitanization is now being reversed. For the first time in US urban history, between 1970 and 1973 the population of five of the eight major metropolitan areas has declined rather than increased. That is, not only were the inner cities losing population (as they did during the sixties) but also the metropolitan areas as a whole. The New York metropolitan area had a net decrease of 305 000 inhabitants. For the Chicago area, the decrease was 124 000; for Philadelphia 75 000; for Detroit 114 000; Los Angeles, which during the sixties had a net immigration of 1·2 million, in 1972—73 showed a net out-migration of 119 000. Boston (+0·4% and San Francisco (+0·5%) remained stable after their growth during the 1960s. Only Washington grew by 1%, largely because of expanding federal government employment.

These changes suggest that the large metropolitan areas have started to be dysfunctional, in their present state, both for capital and for people. But now, a new and even deeper contradiction arises. If the flight of activities and residences continues towards the non-metropolitan areas (which gained 4·2% in population in 1970—73) the deterioration of the large cities will accelerate. Yet the large metropolitan areas still represent an organizational form of major economic and political significance to the ruling class. They are also the dwelling place of a large proportion of the American people. The new urban form emerging from the current crisis will be largely determined by urban policies arrived at as the outcomes of urban social movements and political conflicts.

18

Policies for the Urban Crisis, Grass-Roots Movements and the Political Process

There appears to be no alternative model to the crumbling pattern of urban—suburban development within the structural parameters set by the unrestricted dominance of corporate capitalist interests. The almost perfect functionality of this urban form, for the accumulation of capital, for the organization of corporate centralized management, the stimulation of commodity consumption, the differential reproduction of labour power and the maintenance of the social order, explains why the dominant capitalist interests will strive, no matter what the circumstances, to respond to the multilevel crises by mechanisms that, ultimately, will reestablish the already-proven model with slight modifications. There has been some speculation about the lack of interest of corporate capital in maintaining the inner cities, since most people there do not work for it, nor do they consume its commodities in great quantities. So, why not simply abandon these obsolete areas?

This is pure science fiction. As Roger Friedland (1975) says 'such a scenario is highly unlikely, given the importance of the big-city vote for national elections, the continued concentration of corporate and financial headquarters in the major central cities, and the economic imperative of maintaining the value of public infrastructure and private construction in the central cities. . . . The value of central city properties is the bedrock upon which the residential, commercial, and municipal loans are based. Thus the viability of the financial institutions of this country and ultimately the nation's capital market itself are dependent on maintaining the value of central city properties'.

But then the problem arises: how to handle, from the perspective of corporate interests, the growing set of contradictions demonstrated in our analysis? The virtue — and the shortcoming — of US capitalism is its pragmatism. Instead of devising big national pro-

jects — '*à la francaise*' — urban policies have traditionally emerged
as specific solutions to particular problems depending upon when
and where these problems appear. The trouble with this piecemeal
approach is that eventually it triggers new contradictions and
conflicts less and less susceptible to control.

Thus, the opposition to urban renewal did not stop the programme;
it was, rather, expanded during the seventies under new forces and
actually was accelerated in some cities, for instance, Los Angeles.
The failure of the Great Society programmes to control the social
order led to a total revision of the strategy and a progressive dismantling of these programmes after 1968, at the same time as new laws
were approved and massive funds were devoted to bolster repressive
police and 'crime' enforcement policies. The Model Cities programme,
for instance, was a transitional measure in which emphasis was given
to the problems of coordination and the idea of autonomous community mobilization was specifically rejected so that the whole thing
was put under the supervision of the local authorities, whose power
was restored. With Nixon's revenue-sharing policy, in 1972, the
change of direction, in social and political terms, was complete. By
cutting off the funding of the special programmes and by replacing
them by a distribution of federal tax funds to the states and local
governments, the dominant interests succeeded, in a single move in
by-passing the excessively reformist-minded federal agencies, in
reducing considerably social welfare expenditures and the costs of
distributing services, and in putting the burden of political responsibility on to the shoulders of the local authorities. This analysis
assumes that in the US most local authorities are in fact more
socially conservative than the federal government, since they are
almost entirely responsive to the socially dominant interests in
each city and rarely representative of the grass-roots. As analysis of
the two first years of the revenue-sharing programme shows that in
half of the cases the money was not spent but used to reduce local
taxes. Concerning the funds actually used, the two most important
items were law enforcement (police) and education, which is the
usual responsibility of local authorities. Less than 3% was spent
on welfare or on some kind of special social programme. In most
of the large cities there were no expenditures at all on activities
to replace the cancelled federal programmes. Using repression
more than integration and cooptation in handling the inner city
problem, the next step was to improve the productivity of
services in the public sector and to coordinate more effectively
at the technical and economic level the socially and politically
fragmented metropolis. But in order to increase productivity
and to mobilize resources to improve the functioning of the metro-

polis without affecting either the major privileges of the corporations (with respect, for example, to taxation) or the established political network, a number of things had first to be done: the surplus labour absorbed by local government had to be purged from the employment roles, the social services had to be heavily cut, the real wages of municipal workers reduced and charges for services increased. That is, the policies of the sixties were denied and the model of metropolitan accumulation re-shaped to incorporate tougher policies and tighten controls.

The implementation of this hard-line policy in the urban sphere is not going to be easy since the heritage of the sixties was not only more services and higher public wages but also more experience of struggle and organization at the grass-roots level. Consequently, the future evolution of urban structure and of urban services in the US will depend upon the outcome of an escalating conflict between the capitalist-oriented hard-line urban policies and the mass response and political alternative that could emerge from the city dwellers.

There are some indications that the shortcomings of the community movements during the 1960s may be overcome. (Katznelson, 1975.) These movements were checked by two major problems which were almost inevitable in the early period of development: a) their localism, defining themselves more in terms of their neighbourhood and/or race and ethnicity rather than in regard to specific issues. b) Partly as a consequence of the first difficulty, their *social* and *political isolation*, both with respect to other groups and in relation to the political system as a whole.

Making alliances (and then winning allies) and penetrating the political system (and then winning positions in the network of power) seem to be the major requirements for a shift from grass-roots pressure to grass-roots power in the shaping of urban policies. Contrary to what the perceptive analyses by Cloward and Piven suggest, the problem with the 1960s protest movements was not their integration into the system and their inadequate spontaneous base, but, on the contrary, their insufficient level of organization and their role as political outsiders. Thus, the results were the absence of any cumulative mass movement, an inability to sustain the advantages obtained in urban services, and political isolation. All of these opened the way to repression and dismantling of the grass-roots movements.

The lessons were well learned. The urban movement of the 1970s grew up mostly around particular issues. Large sectors of people were organized not on the grounds of their spatial togetherness but on the basis of their common interests and from the standpoint of their long-term interests: tenants' unions, mass-transit riders' com-

mittees, schools' parents and teachers, public-utilities users, etc.,
spread all over the country. In the process, step by step, a huge
decentralized network of protest-oriented mass organizations and
activities was created which has the potentiality to coalesce into
some major social movement in the future.[30]

Yet the movement is extremely diversified. On the one hand, the
neighbourhood-based movements not only have not disappeared
but, on the contrary, there is a proliferation of self-help activities
at the level of the community: co-ops, health centres, independent
schools, community radio stations, local construction cooperatives,
local agricultural and industrial production (obviously on a very
small scale), and, even black cooperative capitalism in some ghettos.
This community-based movement is becoming more and more distinct from the grass-roots protest organizations and is a far cry from
political struggles pursuing the dream of a new metropolitan utopia.

At a second level, defensive movements of resistance against the
consequences of urban policy for people (i.e., to stop urban renewal
or new highway systems) or to fight back against the attack on the
quality or level of services (i.e., protests against the reduction of
hospital facilities in San Francisco, unrest in the New York subway
to oppose the increase in subway fares, etc.), have become quite
general in all large metropolitan areas.

At a third level, some of these movements are trying to recover
the initiative to shape urban policy along two major lines of
development:

1) The transformation of initial reactions into specific demands
which can then be translated into a progressive movement in pursuit
of a new social content to urban policies. Perhaps the best example
is the evolution of the tenants' movement combatting the process
of residential abandonment in New York. After having realized that
most attempts to launch a rent strike led to abandonment by the
landlords, many tenants' committees stopped their action in order
to avoid any deterioration in their current situation. But after verifying that some abandoned houses had been rehabilitated by the
city and sold at a low price to another landlord, they evolved a new
tactic. They triggered rent strikes, forced the landlords into abandonment and then applied to the city to obtain a rehabilitation
grant for themselves as cooperative owners, eventually using the
rents saved through the strike to pay for repairs. The implacable
logic of urban decay is, thus, reversed not by the urban planners
but by the people combining to fashion an urban movement.

[30] I have trusted (and perhaps misunderstood) information provided personally by
John Mollenkopf, Roger Friedland, Janice Perlman, Ira Katznelson, Marvin Surkin and
Ron Lawson. Also, I have done in some cases a bit of 'tourist participant observation'.

2) The other developing line is the emergence of public facilities consumer-unions that try to respond to the deterioration in social services and to the growing impact on family budgets by sustained economic action focusing on the production, distribution, and management of collective goods and services. An example is the nation-wide campaign launched in 1975 against the rise in electricity rates by several thousand members of a movement significantly called 'Just Economics'.

Finally, in conclusion, we can note that for the first time in the last thirty years, real alternatives for urban policy are being posed at both local and state government level. We see not only social welfare programmes reflecting the interests of corporate capital, but policies emerging out of actual priorities dictated by the immediate interests of grass-roots movements combined with the search for an increase in the rationality of urban management. Proposals to muni- cipalize urban land or electricity companies, to expand the public system of urban transportation, to develop community control over schools and hospitals, etc. are widespread now in cities such as Madison (Wisconsin), Berkeley (California), and Austin (Texas) which are run by progressive coalitions elected with strong grass- roots support and where a clear social-democratic trend has devel- oped in urban policies. Certainly, these cities are a-typical (because they contain major universities) but the first conference on 'Alter- native State and Local Public Policies' sponsored by the Institute of Policy Studies, gathered in Madison in June 1975, was attended by nearly 200 elected public officials from all over the country, in order to define a 'populist' tendency to control the public sector and to establish a permanent system of exchange of experiences and resources. Even if this trend is not yet so visible in the large cities; it represents nevertheless the mobilization of a growing organized force that could eventually link up with the relatively progressive black mayors of some big cities.

This trend towards a populist-oriented new urban politics must obviously connect with the national political process. And herein lies one of the most significant potential effects of US urban move- ments on the general system of class relationships. As Roger Friedland (1975) writes 'By transforming urban daily life into national partisan issues, the large number of poor and working class people who have no meaningful connection or place in the national electoral system could be given choices that make a difference.'

Now, if we consider these developing trends from both sides (that is, on the one hand, from the point of view of monopoly capital and the big city bureaucracies, and on the other hand, from the point of view of a multi-class populist front made up of grass-roots movements) then a major social clash over urban policies appears a distinct possibility in the near future.

The exploitative and increasingly contradictory model of urban– suburban expansion that dominated metropolitan America in the last thirty years will be transformed only if the people's forces take decisive steps in the approaching battles. This would mean, however, an almost intolerable setback for corporate interests. This explains why the Establishment has been so violent in repressing the relatively progressive stand of New York City and also why the dominant emphasis in current local policies is given to the development of a repressive apparatus. In January, 1975, Los Angeles police prac- tised 'food-riot control training'; special élite units are being deve- loped in all metropolitan police forces; the aftermath of the sixties led to the provision of an incredible mass of sophisticated weaponry for repressing mass protests in the large cities, in addition to the formation of anti-riot squads. Since it has become clear now that the costly desperate riots have been replaced by long-term oriented, permanent mass movements, the FBI and military organizations have renewed their attempts to infiltrate grass-roots organizations. Emergency procedures and day-to-day repression (often using ghetto gangs) have been now developed to pave the way for a new edition of the monopoly capital pattern of urban development. The stake is important, so 'they' are ready to pay a high price, even in terms of political legitimacy. Watergate and the revelations of illegality on the part of the FBI, CIA and other 'police' organiza- tions appeared to force a pause. Yet at the same time a wide-ranging criminal justice bill, known as SI, with incredibly repressive and restrictive law-and-order provisions came before Congress and appeared to have a good chance of passing. Revelations of illegality and the attack on police power were, apparently, to be countered by measures to make the repression legal.

So, unless the progressive forces of the US are able to develop a major movement, with enough social and political support to rec- tify the dominant trend in the forthcoming urban policies, what could emerge from the current urban crisis is a simplified and heightened version of the exploitative metropolitan model with the addition of massive police repression and control exercised in a rapidly deteriorating economic setting. The suburbs will remain fragmented and isolated, the single-family homes closed off, the families keeping to themselves, the shopping centres more expen- sive, the highways less well-maintained but people forced to drive further to reach jobs and to obtain services, the central districts still crowded during the office hours but deserted and curfewed after 5 p.m., the city services increasingly crumbling, the public facilities less and less public, the surplus population more and more visible, the drug culture and individual violence necessarily expanding, gang society and high society ruling the bottom and the top in order to keep a 'top and bottom' social order intact, urban movements repressed and discouraged and the urban planners eventually attending more international conferences in the outer, safer world. What could emerge if the urban movements fail to undertake their political tasks is, perhaps, a new and sinister urban form: the Wild City.

Conclusion

Exploratory Theses on the Urban Question

The theoretical work carried out has not yet reached the stage of discoveries; however, it does make possible a reformulation of the questions posed in a perspective that should help us to create the conditions for their scientific treatment and their social supersession by means of a correct political practice. That is why one may speak of exploration, of groupings, of the production of a dynamic of research, rather than of 'results' which, in their positivity, might in fact be no more than a juxtaposition of description and formalism.

However, a theoretical product may be relatively finite, without acquiring the force of a piece of knowledge. It may be situated at a certain level in the development of research in such a way as to pave the way for discovery in the strict sense. What is this level that has been reached in our practice? How far have we got in this exploratory phase? We may gather together in the form of 'theses', by way of clarifying our ideas, a few essential points that one may deduce directly from the analyses carried out. But it is in the dynamic to which they may give rise that we must judge their relevance.

1. The urban question, as it has been formulated in social practice and in sociological and urbanistic 'theories', is an ideological question, in the precise sense that it confuses in the same discourse the problematic of spatial forms, that which concerns the process of the reproduction of labour power and that of the cultural specificity of 'modern society'.

2. Such an ideology is defined by a twofold social effect:

a) On the level of the production of knowledge (and non-knowledge), it assimilates a given historical form of reproduction of labour power to the 'culture' of the society as a whole and makes the latter dependent on a process of increasing complexification of its territorial site; in doing so, the dominant culture masks its class character for, on the one hand, it is presented as general for all members of this society and, on the other hand, it seems to result from an almost necessary evolution, since it is determined by the mode of relation to nature.

b) On the level of social relations it naturalizes the social contradictions in the process of reproduction of labour power and interprets as a dissociation between 'Nature' and 'Culture' what is the effect of a particular social matrix, determined by the dominant relations of production. This ideology displaces, therefore, the axis of the contradictions towards a general mobilization of 'society' to make up for the misdeeds of its technological progress, misdeeds which, elsewhere, appear as unavoidable; in so far as this shift occurs, social integration is reinforced.

3. The social base that allows the urban ideology to take root is formed by the contradictions, experienced every day by individuals and social groups, as far as the process of simple and extended reproduction of their material and of the social relations attached to it are concerned.

Owing to the increasing importance of the processes external to the productive act itself in advanced capitalism, the development of these contradictions reinforces in an extraordinary way the capacity for diffusion of this ideology, without in any essential way altering its contours.

4. The unmasking of such an ideology cannot derive simply from a denunciation. It requires the development of a properly theoretical study of each of the questions that are fused, and confused, in this problematic: the social forms of space, the conditions for the realization of the reproduction of labour power, the relation of the first two elements to the cultural systems of each social formation.

5. It is scarcely more possible to make an analysis of space 'in itself' than it is to make one of time. Space, as a social product, is always specified by a definite relation between the different instances of a social structure, the economic, the political, the ideological, and the conjuncture of social relations that result from them. Space, therefore, is always an historical conjuncture and a social form that derives its meaning from the social processes that are expressed through it. Space is capable of producing, on the other hand, specific effects on other domains of the social conjuncture, by virtue of the particular form of articulation of the structural instances that are constituted by it.

6. The understanding of the spatial structure proceeds via its characterization, its decomposition and its articulation, in the terms proper to the general theory of social formations. Thus one must analyse economic, politico-juridical, ideological space, while pre-

cisely specifying these categories in relation to the domain in question, and deduce from them the forms (spatial conjunctures) on the basis of the elements referred to.

7. The theme of 'the urban' seems to connote the processes of simple and extended reproduction of labour power, while emphasizing the particular conditions of their realization. In more concrete terms, in the advanced capitalist societies, we are witnessing an increasing collectivization of the conditions underlying these processes, since there is a technico-social interpenetration of the productions and activities necessary to it and since the concentration of the means of production and their administration involve a parallel concentration of the means of consumption. In such a situation, the urban refers not only to a spatial form, but expresses the social organization of the process of reproduction.

8. The link, in social practice, between 'the urban' and 'space' is not a mere ideological effect. It derives from the social nature of the delimitation of space in advanced capitalism and from the internal structure of the process of reproduction of labour power. There are urban units in so far as there are units of this process of reproduction defined on the basis of a certain everyday space of labour power. The urban unit is to the process of production what the company is to the process of production: a specific unit articulated with other units that form the process as a whole. Such a specificity of the urban is historical: it derives from the domination of the economic instance in the social structure — the space of production being regional space and that of reproduction being called urban space.

9. The link between space, the urban and a certain system of behaviour regarded as typical of 'urban culture' has no other foundation than an ideological one: it is a question of an ideology of modernity, aimed at masking and naturalizing social contradictions. On the other hand, the relation between urban space and specific social milieux is an object of legitimate research, capable of elucidating the emergence and efficacity of specific sub-cultures. However, in order to be able to pose the problem of the articulation between these two elements, it is necessary first to define them precisely, which, on the level of the urban, requires an adequate theorization of urban structure.

10. An understanding of urban units at the different levels requires their articulated segmentation in terms of urban structure, a *concept* that specifies the articulation of the fundamental instances of the social structure within the urban units considered. Thus the economic instance, the political-juridical instance and the ideological instance specify at least five fundamental elements of the urban

structure (Production, Consumption, Exchange, Administration, Symbolic), which constitute it in their relations and only in their relations.

11. Since the urban structure is a concept, it paves the way for an analysis of a concrete situation, but is not capable of accounting for it, in so far as any concrete situation is made up of systems of practices, defined by their position in the structure, but whose secondary effects express a relative autonomy, capable of redefining the situation beyond their structural charge. These practices are structured essentially around practices that condense and summarize the system as a whole, namely, political practices. By political practices, I mean those which, more or less directly, have as their object class relations and as their objective the state. They are defined, therefore, for the dominant class, above all through the interventions of the politico-juridical apparatus and for the dominated classes through the political class struggle. As far as the urban problematic is concerned, the theoretical field that corresponds to the intervention of the state may be called 'urban planning', that relative to its articulation with the political class struggle, 'Urban social movements'. Thus the field of 'urban politics' is at the heart of any analysis of the urban phenomenon, just as the study of the political processes is at the base of the science of social formations.

12. By urban planning, I mean more precisely the intervention of the political in the specific articulation of the different instances of a social formation within a collective state of reproduction of labour power, with the intention of assuring its extended reproduction, of regulating the non-antagonistic contradictions that have arisen and of repressing the antagonistic contradictions, thus assuring the interests of the dominant social class in the whole of the social formation and the organization of the urban system, in such a way as to ensure the structural reproduction of the dominant mode of production.

13. By urban social movement, I mean a system of practices resulting from the articulation of the particular conjuncture, both by the insertion of the support-agents in the urban structure and in the social structure, and such that its development tends objectively towards structural transformation of the urban system or towards a substantial modification of the power relations in the class struggle, that is to say, in the last resort, in the state power.

14. 'Urban' social contradictions are characterized above all by two fundamental features:

a) They are of a 'pluri-class' nature, in the sense that the cleavages they effect do not correspond to the structural opposition between the two fundamental classes, but rather distribute the classes and fractions in a relation whose opposing terms vary widely according to the conjuncture. It is deduced from this that 'urban politics' is an essential element in the formation of class alliances, in particular in relation to the petty bourgeoisie.

b) Structurally, they are secondary contradictions, in the sense that they do not involve directly the fundamental laws of the mode of production and that, consequently, their articulation with a process aimed at the conquest of state power traverses an ensemble of mediations. This being so, it may be that there are conjunctures in which this articulation becomes crucial as far as the criterion for the development of the seizure of power are concerned. These are the conjunctures in which the crystallization taking place around them makes it possible to make a decisive step forward in the constitution of an offensive of the dominated classes (for example, facilitating an indispensible class alliance or permitting an ideological self-definition of the exploited class).

15. It follows from this that the precise definition of an urban problem poses as an essential question its articulation with the structural contradictions and with the articulation of the different practices involved in the class struggle. The result will, therefore, be very different according to the definition, in terms of urban structure, of the 'problem' treated.

16. A few consequences of these theses for a political practice with regard to 'the urban' may be sketched out, providing we remember that:

1. We must begin by exploding the false unity of the problematic thus stated and by identifying the place of each question in the contradictions of the social structure.
2. The more important the class alliance in a particular conjuncture, the more essential is the relation to the urban.
3. Conversely, the more the construction of proletarian autonomy is involved, the less important this theme is.
4. In any case, there is a need to dissociate political intervention in the urban from the question of organization on a district basis. Although they may coincide in practice, they are two theoretically autonomous processes.
5. Intervention in relation to an operation of urban planning must be determined, in objectives and in intensity, by at least three considerations:
   a) The place it occupies in the general system of social contradictions;
   b) Its meaning as regulation of the interests proper to the dominant classes;
   c) Its meaning as an expression of class domination;

d) The articulation of a contradiction proper to the urban structure with other economic, political and ideological contradictions. Thus, for example, the contradiction existing at the level of urban transport is directly bound up with the capital/labour contradiction; the contradiction that is expressed increasingly at the level of the spatial organization of educational amenities is related to the movements of revolt among the young, etc.

6. The ideological community at the base of an urban unit derives from a certain overlap between the economic, political, and ideological specificity and the territorial segmentation. It may be reinforced or broken down on the basis of a specific intervention aimed, through it, at the realization of particular social objectives. Such an enumeration might be extended indefinitely.

The examples cited serve to illustrate the almost immediate correspondence between these analyses and the concrete problems posed by political practice.

17. Among the consequences for theoretical practice with regard to the urban that result from this, one may mention:

1. Any specific analysis in this domain must begin by a previous delimitation of the theoretical field studied, in order to carry out an initial purification of the ideological discourse that invades the whole of the problematic, while explaining this ideology *qua* social process, without, however, using it as the definition of the tasks of investigation.

2. One must specify the structural instances in relation to the urban unit or to the space that is the object of analysis. One must then show their internal articulation with the different instances in the social structure as a whole, which presupposes confronting the theoretical question of the transition from a line of thought concerned with the level of the mode of production to an analysis of social formations.

3. These structural articulations are expressed in terms of relations and exist historically only in practices. This means that the central theoretical problem to be resolved is that which consists in analysing social practices without changing perspective, but while taking into account the specificity produced by the distribution of 'social agents' in the different structural places.

4. Lastly, there is a relative autonomy of the system of practices. An autonomy, because the organization of practices, dominated in particular by the principle of contradiction in the context of a class society, produces new effects, in relation to

the structural charge conveyed and, in particular, is even capable of changing the laws of the structure. Relative, because this production of new effects is itself subjected to laws that depend on the structural determination at the base of the practices that occur.

5. Any concrete analysis of an 'urban problem' necessarily involves all the theoretical questions indicated, for, in social practice, there is a simultaneous presence of the structural instances, social relations and effects of conjuncture, even if there exists a hierarchy of dominance between the different elements. Or rather, there is no other possibility of advancing towards a solution of these theoretical questions than the realization of concrete analyses that make it possible to progress on three levels at once: the production of knowledge, which is always partial, about certain historically given social practices; the production of concepts and modes of articulation of concepts capable of elucidating in a specific way a certain domain of the social, which necessarily requires its articulation with the processes of society as a whole; the production of a certain practical research experience, which makes it possible to resolve gradually the considerable methodological problems that are proposed in relation to the experimental apparatuses required by such a theoretical perspective.

18. We are now in a position to understand the *raison d'être* of this book. It simply expresses a problematic and offers theoretical ways for its gradual elucidation. For one must first pose the problems before one can resolve them. In concrete research practice this is almost never the case — it was not so in our case either. These theoretical ways are discovered gradually, as one tries to carry out analyses that constantly refer back to a series of unresolved questions. But progress in theoretical practice (which depends in the last resort on social conditions, and therefore on political practice) can never be the result of an individual (individual or group) 'project'. It is from the constant resumption and rectification by different 'theoretical subjects' defining themselves in relation to a diversity of concrete situations that new ways may emerge, within the limits of the historical situation of the production of knowledge. This, therefore, is a powerful reason for communicating the emergence of a problematic bearing on the very bases of the analysis in relation to the urban question. As a product of experience, the act of communication makes possible its own supersession, by merging it in a movement of contradictory rectification that might lead, on the one hand, to a better understanding of these 'urban' practices misconstrued/recognized by ideology and known/unknown by the

subjects and, on the other hand, to its own supersession through an ever stronger articulation with other areas of historical materialism.

The long theoretical detours, the mediations necessary to unblock concrete research in a predominantly ideological field, must not move too far from the ultimate aim of the tasks undertaken: to destroy the technocratic and/or utopist myths about 'the urban' and to show the precise ways in which the practices thus connoted are articulated with social relations, that is to say, with the class struggle.

Afterword 1975

This book, written in 1970—71, was intended as a work tool — as a tool of theoretical work, of scientific research work and also, through numerous mediations, as a tool of political work. But, produced as it was in given historical circumstances, it had (and has) in relation to its aim, serious limitations and theoretical errors. Despite an awareness of the problems implicit in the work carried out, I believed that its publication, by marking a certain stage in my thinking, would help to supersede some of these difficulties through collective practice. That is why I said that 'this text merely communicates certain experiences of work aimed at producing a research dynamic rather than establishing a demonstration that would be unrealizable in the present theoretical conjuncture.' To some extent, these objectives are beginning to be reached in so far as the criticisms and suggestions expressed form part of a broad current of thought, research and practice on 'urban problems', a current that has developed in several countries in recent years. But, at the same time, it has undergone, like so many other works, a certain process of fetishization that has crystallized into theoretical principles what were merely stammerings emerging from a phase of work centred above all on the critique of the ideologies of the urban and on the recognition of the historical terrain. Furthermore, the progress made by Marxist urban research enables us today to rectify certain confused, or, quite simply, useless conceptions that were developed in this book. Such a rectification must not take the scholastic form of a rewriting of the text.

The book is what it is and it must remain an historically dated product. But since an opportunity to prepare a new edition has been offered, it might be useful to give the reader a few orientation points as to the present state (1975) of the questions discussed, while leaving the text, for the most part, in its original form. These rectifications are expressed in new theoretical work that, I along with many other working colleagues have produced since the publication of the book. I shall try, then, to provide a brief account of these analyses and a few references to new research in the field.

A few rectifications and theoretical remarks
  a) With the perspective given not by time but by practice, perhaps the most serious difficulties of this book derive from too rapid a leap from a theoretical critique to an extremely formalized theoretical system. In particular, the theoretical construction in terms of the urban system, with elements and sub-elements, was merely a classification grid, and not a tool of the production of knowledge in the full sense of the term. Not that it was 'wrong' to speak of the urban system or that the elements defined are not 'right'. In fact, such a construction proved useful enough in organizing our information throughout our inquiries. (See Castells and Godard, 1974)
  The problem is not so much that of its correctness as that of its usefulness. In fact, the 'urban system' with its elements and relations is a formal construction the essence of which, that is to say, the dynamism of its articulations, is produced by laws of historical development and social organization of which this 'theory of the urban' does not take account. The most important task, from the point of view of the present phase of theoretical work, is not, therefore, to define elements and to formalize their structure, but to detect the historical laws at work, in the so-called 'urban' contradictions and practices. It is premature at the moment to try to reach the level of structural formalization proposed, for historical laws determine the forms of the structure rather than the reverse.
  From this point of view, my work was influenced by a certain interpretation of Althusser (rather than by the work of Althusser himself) with a view to constructing a coded and formalized theoretical ensemble before moving towards concrete research, which necessarily led to a juxtaposition of formalism and empiricism and therefore leads to an impasse. What is involved is the very style of the theoretical work, the epistemological approach in question. One must choose between on the one hand, the idea of a 'Great Theory' (even a Marxist one), which one then verifies empirically, and, on the other hand, the proposition of a theoretical work that produces concepts and their historical relations within a process of discovery of the laws of society given in their specific modes of existence. It is not only a question of 'carrying out empirical research'. It is a question rather of the fact that 'theory' is not produced outside a process of concrete knowledge. Such is the

experience of historical materialism and such is the lesson that I should have taken into account more rigorously. Certainly, there are mediations and theoretical moments in which one must pause to discuss certain concepts. But one must never sever the umbilical cord between these elaborations and the historical laws of social practice. In more concrete terms, the translation of urban problems into terms of the reproduction of labour power and their formalization by means of the urban system is useful only in so far as it is a step towards expressing the forms of articulation between classes, production, consumption, the state and the urban. The fundamental point, therefore, is not that of a transformation of language (which may become, at most, a pure symbol of membership of an 'intellectual family'), but that of the historical content of the relations thus formalized. Having said this, one must reject strenuously the attacks of those who criticize a 'jargon', only to oppose it by another (a functionalist one, for example) or to replace it by 'everyday language', that is to say, by an ideological code that suits them for structural reasons. The epistemological distinction between everyday perception and theoretical concepts is more necessary than ever in the urban domain, which is so strongly organized by ideology. What is necessary is to implement this distinction and this production of concepts in a process of theoretical work and not simply in a formal ordering that can only be a subsequent and secondary technical operation. Now, for the moment, the urban system as defined in this book is not a concept, but a formal tool. It will be what one makes of it in terms of concrete research producing both historical knowledge and the conceptual medium for this knowledge. And it must be used only if it helps in the development of this research.

b) Another problem that raised a lot of confusion and misunderstanding was the terminological displacement carried out, in particular, the definition of the urban in terms of collective reproduction of labour power and of the city in terms of a unit of this process of reproduction. 'Why should a city be only that?' people ask. In a city, there are also factories, offices, activities of every kind. Furthermore, the process of capital accumulation, the production of commodities, the administration of society take place, for the most part, in cities and shape urban problems in a decisive way.

Of course!

The misunderstanding derives from the difficulty of the epistemological reversal that I must carry out. For it is a question of:

Showing that the ensemble of so-called 'urban' problems is apprehended through the categories of a certain ideology (the urban ideology), which, both prevents an understanding of them and realizes the social interests of the dominant classes.

Recognizing that the growing importance of this ideological problematic does not derive from mere manipulation, from the fact that it organizes symbolically, in a certain way, the problems experienced by people in their everyday practice. It is a question, then, of identifying these problems in empirical terms, of treating them theoretically by means of an adequate set of tools and, lastly, of explaining the social roots of the development of the ideology of the urban. The fundamental moment of the analysis is, however, the concrete analysis of these 'new problems' or of the new place of these old problems in the present phase of the capitalist mode of production.

It is in this sense that I say that the essential problems regarded as urban are in fact bound up with the processes of 'collective consumption', or what Marxists call the organization of the collective means of reproduction of labour power. That is to say, means of consumption objectively socialized, which, for specific historical reasons, are essentially dependent for their production, distribution and administration on the intervention of the state. This is no arbitrary definition. It is a working hypothesis that may be verified by the concrete analysis of advanced capitalist societies — and this is what I have set out to do.

This being said, the confusion created by my 'definition of the urban' (which is not a definition at all) is such that both a remark and a long explanation are required.

A remark: a concrete city (or an urban area, or a given spatial unit) is not only a unit of consumption. It is, of course, made up of a very great diversity of practices and functions. It expresses, in fact, society as a whole, though through the specific historical forms that it represents. Therefore, whoever wishes to study a city (or series of cities) must also study capital, production, distribution, politics, ideology, etc. Furthermore, one cannot understand the process of consumption without linking it to the accumulation of capital and to the political relations between the classes. The problem still remains of deciding the specificity of this process of reproducing labour power and the relations that exist between the collective reproduction of labour power and the urban problematic.

It is here that a long explanation seems to be necessary to rectify certain unfortunate theoretical effects produced by a certain reading of my work. Let us examine, step by step, how the problem of the theoretical redefinition of the 'urban field' in relation to the declared objectives is posed.

In urban research, we are prisoners of notions (and, consequently, of a certain coding of the real), which corresponds to the terms of everyday language, usually dominated, as far as we are concerned, by the ideology of the urban. So, as soon as we try to set out from other theoretical foundations, we are forced to employ a different language, made up of concepts that belong not to a specific field of experience, but are common to social science in general. This is what I am now trying to do in undertaking an analysis of collective consumption on the basis of the mode of production and by examining in turn the theoretical problems raised in a study first of the infrastructure of the capitalist mode of production, then of the superstructure. From a logical point of view, such an approach is self-sufficient. The only problem — and it is the essential one — is to link this conceptual development with concrete historical practices in such a way as to establish social laws that account for the phenomena observed, while superseding purely formal constructions. But from the point of view of scientific vocabulary I could well do without, at the present moment, certain currently used notions, certain terms of social practice ('language', therefore ideology), as 'urban', 'city', 'region', 'space', etc. From this point of view, the problem of the definition (or redefinition) of the urban does not even arise. Such terms as 'urban', charged with a precise ideological content (and not only because they are ideological) are entirely alien to my approach. This having been said, the theoretical work does not take place in a social void; it must be articulated, in the state of knowledge/ignorance, with the practices observed; it must take into account the conjuncture and constitute a veritable tactic of investigation. Thus the more invested, the more constituted by the dominant ideology, a domain of the social is, the more one must both distance oneself as far as the production of conceptual tools for its analysis is concerned and establish links between the theoretical conceptualization and the ideological apprehension of these practices. In other words, it is a schizophrenic process that is being established, an incommunicability between the experience of the masses and scientific work.

But let there by no misunderstanding. It is not a question of changing one term for another by bringing it closer to a language that is more familiar or more sympathetic (in terms of ideological affinity). It is a question of ensuring, in a parallel way, the development of certain concepts (and therefore not of 'words', but of tools of theoretical work always referring back necessarily to a certain place in a certain theoretical field) and the intelligibility of these concepts in relation to everyday experience, by showing the community as a real object of reference between a particular concept and a particular ideological notion. Of course, such a term-by-term correspondence cannot exist: one notion involves in fact a whole process; another may be a pure ideological artefact without any direct correspondence with a real practice. However, I set out·from the hypothesis that certain ideologically constructed (delimited) domains rest on a certain unity, specificity, of practical experience. It is by basing itself on this homogeneity of experienced practice that an ideology may grow social roots, displacing everyday experience towards a field of interpretation created by the dominant ideology. That is, the ideology of the urban rests on a certain specificity of the urban as a domain of experience, but since this 'urban' is comprehensible only in the fantasies of a certain ideology, we must both elucidate the reality thus connoted and take into account its specificity.

Let us begin, then, with *space*. This is something material enough, an indispensable element in all human activity. And yet this very obviousness deprives it of any specificity and prevents it from being used directly as a category in the analysis of social relations. In fact, *space*, like *time*, is a physical quantity that tells us nothing, in itself, about the social relation expressed or as to its role in the determination of the mediation of social practice. A 'sociology of space' can only be an analysis of social practices given in a certain space, and therefore in a historical conjuncture. Just as in speaking of the nineteenth century (itself, one might remark, a questionable expression), one is not referring to a chronological segmentation, but to a certain state of social formations, so in speaking of France, the Auvergne, the quarter of Ménilmontant, the Matto Grosso or the Watts district, one is referring to a certain social situation, to a certain *conjuncture*. Of course, there is the 'site', the 'geographical' conditions, but they concern analysis only as the support of a certain web of social relations, the spatial characteristics producing extremely divergent social effects depending on the historical situation. From the social point of view, therefore, there is no space (a physical quantity, yet an abstract entity *qua* practice), but an historically defined *space-time*, a space constructed, worked, practised by social relations. Does it not, in turn, have an effect on the said social relations? Is there not a spatial determination of the social? Yes. But not *qua* 'space' — rather as a certain efficacity of the social activity expressed in a certain spatial form. A 'mountain' space does not determine a way of life: the discomforts of the physical milieu are mediatized, worked, transformed by social conditions. In fact, there is nothing to choose between the 'natural' and the 'cultural' in social determination, for the two terms are indissolubly unified in the single material reality of the social point of view: *historical practice*. Indeed, all the 'theories of space' that have been produced are theories of society or specifications of these theories. (See on this point the detailed analyses carried out in Part III, Chapter 8.) Socially speaking, space, like time, is a conjuncture, that is to say, the articulation of concrete historical practices.

Something fundamental for my analysis emerges from this: the social signification of the different forms and types of space, the significative segmentation of space, the spatial units, do not have meaning outside the segmentation of the social structure in scientific terms, therefore in terms of the mode of production and of social formations. That is to say, each mode of production and, at most, each stage in the mode of production implies another segmentation of space, not only in theoretical terms, but also in terms of the real relations established between the different spaces. Let us say, in a very general way, that the specificity of these types of space will correspond, essentially, to the instance not only determining, but dominating, a mode of production — in the case of capitalism, the economic. Furthermore, any space will be constructed conjuncturally, and therefore in terms of social formation, and therefore in terms of the articulation of modes of production, in such a way that the dominance will be expressed against a background of the historically crystallized forms of space.

What does a segmentation of space mean, under the dominance of the capitalist mode of production, in terms of economic segmentation? It means an organization of space specific for each of the elements of the process of immediate production, on the one hand (labour power and reproduction of labour power; means of production and reproduction of the means of production) and, on the other hand, an organization of space specific to the administration of the labour process; lastly, the space of the process of circulation of capital.

I present the fact that, at least as far as the monopoly stage of the capitalist mode of production is concerned, the last two processes, concerning the administration and circulation of capital, are characterized by their de-localization, their movement on the world scale. It is a question of the tendential elimination of space as a source of specificity. Whereas time, on the other hand, becomes increasingly central to the process, fragmenting it into specific operations according to the differential speed of realization. This, of course, has still to be shown. The consequence of these statements are considerable for any new 'theory of space' (and it will be necessary, in time, to undertake a systematic examination of these areas of research).

The spatial specificity of the processes of reproduction of labour power and of the processes of reproduction of the means of production introduce my problematic much more directly.

In fact, I think that the means of production are not organized on the spatial plane at the company level in an economy so complex as that of advanced capitalism. The milieu of technological inter-dependences, common resources, 'external economies', as the mar-ginalists say, are realized on a much broader scale. On the scale of an urban area, then? Not always. For although certain urban areas possess a specificity at the level of the organization of the produc-tion apparatus (within, of course, a generalized interdependence), other residential units (urban areas) are no more than an entirely heteronomous cog in the process of production and distribution. The organization of space into specific, articulated units, according to the arrangements and rhythms of the means of production, seems to me to refer back to distinctions of practice in terms of region. In fact, if we consider, for example, the regional question, expressed in terms of economic imbalances within the same country, the reality immediately connoted is what the Marxist tradition treats as the effects of the unequal development of capital-ism, that is to say, unequal development of the productive forces and specificity in the organization of the means of production according to a differential rhythm linked to the interests of capital. Unequal development of the economic sectors, the unequal value placed on natural resources, the concentration of the means of prod-uction in the most favourable conditions, the creation of productive milieux or 'complex units of production' — these are the economic bases of what are called the regions and regional disparities. (There does exist, of course, an historical and cultural specificity of the regions as a survival of another segmentation, political or ideologi-cal, of space, in other modes of production. Regionalism is ex-pressed, however, as a social movement on the basis of the articula-tion of these survivals of the contradictions grounded in the economic.)

The spatial organization of the reproduction of labour power seems, on the other hand, to lead to very familiar geographico-social realities, namely, the urban areas, in the banal statistical sense of the term. What is an 'urban area'? A production unit? Not at all, in so far as the production units are placed on another scale (on a regional one, at least). An institutional unit? Certainly not, since we are aware of the almost total lack of overlap between the 'real' urban units and the administrative segmentation of space. An ideological unit, in terms of a way of life proper to a 'city' or to a spatial form? This is meaningless as soon as one rejects the cultura-list hypothesis of the production of ideology by the spatial context. There is no 'Parisian bourgeoisie' except in terms of semi-folkloric details. There is international capital and a French ruling class (in so far as there is the specificity of a state apparatus); there are *regional* (not city) ideologies in terms of spatial specificity in the organization in the means of production. But there is no cultural specificity of the city as a spatial form or of a particular form of residential space. (I would refer to Part II, Chapter 7, for a discussion of this point.)

What is, then, what is called an urban unit? Or, more generally, an urban area? This term of social and administrative practice designates rather — it would be easy enough to agree — a certain residential unit, an ensemble of dwellings with corresponding 'services'. An urban unit is not a unit in terms of production. On the other hand, it possesses a certain specificity in terms of residence, in terms of 'everydayness'. It is, in short, the everyday space of a delimited fraction of the labour force. This is not very different from the definition, current among geographers and economists, of an urban area on the basis of the map of commutings. But what does this represent from the point of view of segmentation in terms of mode of production? Well, it is a question of the process of reproduction of labour power: that is the precise definition in terms of Marxist economics of what is called 'everyday life'. On condition, of course, that we understand it in the terms explicitated, namely, by articulating with it the reproduction of social relations and pacing it according to the dialectic of the class struggle.

However, we must differentiate between two broad types of process in the reproduction of labour power: collective consumption and individual consumption. Which of the two structures space? Around which are the urban areas organized? It goes without saying that both processes are articulated in practice; consequently, the one that dominates the process as a whole will structure the other. Now, the organization of a process will be all the more concentrated and centralized, and therefore structuring, as the degree of objective socialization of the process is advanced, as the concentration of the means of consumption and their interdependence is greater, as the administrative unity of the process is more developed. It is at the level of collective consumption that these features are most obvious and it is therefore around this process that the ensemble of consumption/reproduction of labour power/reproduction of social relations is structured.

We can, therefore, retranslate in terms of the collective reproduction (objectively socialized) of labour power most of the realities connoted by the term urban and analyse the urban units and processes linked with them as units of the collective reproduction of labour power in the capitalist mode of production.

Indeed, an intuitive allusion to the problems treated as 'urban' in practice is enough to observe the overlap (we have only to think of the structural meaning in the mode of production of such questions as housing, collective amenities, transportation, etc.).

But what, then, is a city? In its present sense, it may be only a generic connotation of urban units, of different sorts of units.

But what, then, are we to make of the difference between town and country, between rural and urban? Are not villages units of the reproduction of labour power?

Of course they are, and in the sense that we must replace the rural/urban dichotomy by a discontinuous diversity of spatial forms and by a differentiated plurality of units of reproduction of labour power, the place occupied by the unit in this process and, above all, the specific mould of labour power that is being produced.

At the level of spatial forms, the difference between 'town' and 'village' is not the only one to be established. There is, rather, a great diversity of forms (village, 'borough', 'medium-sized town', 'regional capital', 'large urban area', 'metropolis', 'megalopolis' and other terms used by geographers), which refer to a differentiation of spatial forms and therefore to a plurality of 'spatial' units, units of collective consumption, irreducible to a pure dichotomy in terms of rural/urban. (See on this subject the works of Bernard Kayser and his team on the relation between rural space and urban space.) Why is the 'medium-sized town' closer to the village than to the metropolis? Or is the reverse the case? It is quite simply something else. But this something else is not to be established in impressionistic, typological, descriptive terms, but in terms of a specific place in the process of collective consumption.

But is there not, then, to be any separation between 'town' and 'country'? Is it a matter of 'generalized urbanization'? In reality, this problematic has no meaning (other than an ideological one) as such, posed in the terms in which it is generally posed. For it already presupposes the distinction and even the contradiction between rural and urban, an opposition and a contradiction that have little meaning in capitalism. The spaces of production and consumption in the monopoly phase of capitalism are strongly interpenetrated, overlapped, according to the organization and unequal development of the means of production and the means of consumption and are not frozen as definite spaces only in one of the poles of the social and technological division of labour. When we speak of the 'urbanization of the countryside' (through tourism in particular) or of the 'ruralization of the towns' (the extension of the residential suburbs), we have symptoms of an inapplicability of the problematic that become explicit even within ideology. This being said, such an overlap does not signify the end of the social contradictions expressed *through* and by *mediation* of the spatial forms, but only the non-reducibility to a dichotomic opposition between town and country as principal contradiction.

On the other hand, one can explain the persistence of this problematic and the diffusion of this theme, which Marx and Engels took up in *The German Ideology*. In fact, the contradictions between 'town and country' expressed, in the analysis of Marx and Engels, the social contradiction between the direct producers working the land and the administrators of the product whose existence was based on the appropriation of the agricultural surplus. Historically, the possibility of 'towns', that is to say, of residential concentrations not living off an agricultural product directly and locally obtained by working the land, emerged when there was an agricultural surplus and an appropriation of this surplus by a class of non-workers. Thus, as long as the essential base of the economy was the agrarian economy, the labour of the peasants, under different forms of social relation, the 'towns' were the spatial form and the social organization expressing both the administration— domination of the exploiting class and the place of residence (and of consumption) of this class and its apparatuses and services, whereas the 'country' was the world in which the 'fundamental mass' (see Mao on the concept of 'fundamental mass') of the exploited lived and worked. The contradiction between town and country, identified almost completely with the separation between manual labour and intellectual labour and expressing the bipolarity of the principle contradictions between exploiters and exploited, had, therefore, a profound meaning. On the other hand, as soon as there was a displacement of the principle contradiction, with the dominance of the capitalist mode of production, the town/country contradiction lost the univocity of its meaning. For there is no contradiction between peasant-workers and urban proletariat, as long as an identity of social interests is created between industrial capital and agricultural capital in a rural economy increasingly dominated by monopoly capital. The so-called town/country contradictions become, then, secondary contradictions between productive sectors, between fractions of capital. What we have here is the dialectic of unequal development that we sketched out under the heading of 'regional problems', but there is no longer a univocal contradictory bipolarity, as was the case in slave-owning society, Asiatic-despotic society or feudal society or, even, in the opposition between the feudal and seigneuries and the bourgeois cities during the transition to capitalism. Of course, there are specificities, economic and ideological, in the situation of the peasant working his own strip of land and the agricultural worker, in relation to other exploited classes and strata. But such specificites are treated in a broader web of social relations as the spatial forms of human activity become diversified, in such a way that the rural/urban dichotomy, even when expressed in the classic terms of the opposition between town and country, is merely a material support of the reactionary culturalist ideology of the evolution from 'traditional society' to 'modern society'.

This has an immediate effect on our approach, namely, that the 'theoretical translation' of the urban problematic into terms of collective consumption and that the treatment of 'spatial units' as units of reproduction of labour power has only a historical meaning and that therefore such an analysis is specific to the capitalist mode of production and cannot be applied to the 'towns' of other modes of production. (Thus, for example, the politico-administrative autonomy of the cities of the Renaissance, linked to the rise of the mercantile bourgeoisie in opposition to the feudal lords, is at the base of the specificity of the European 'cities', the memory of which is at the base, even today, of the ideal type of city.)

Furthermore, it is very doubtful whether the urban problematic connotes the same dimension of the social structure in societies placed in a different or even opposite situation, in the articulated chain of social formations that constitute the world imperialist system. In particular, this is the case of the dependent societies, in which, 'urban problems' usually refer to the so-called problematic of 'marginality', that is to say, of the lack of any demand, from the point of view of capital, to reproduce a large section of the population that is structurally outside the labour force and whose role is not even required as a reserve army. (Castells, 1973; 1975.) A direct transposition of my analyses on to advanced capitalism in such situations, instead of using a similar style in reasoning, may have quite paralysing intellectual effects.

This having been said, in advanced capitalist societies, what is to be done, it will be asked, with so many 'urban' themes that do not deal directly with the reproduction of labour power? Must we, for example, leave to one side such important themes as the place occupied by urban growth in capital investment and financial speculation? Is not the occupation of the urban centres by the skyscrapers of company headquarters an urban theme?

There are a number of things that need to be said on this matter:

1. The social specificity of a process (that of the reproduction of labour power) and the units that derive from it should not be confused with the social production of this process and of these units, of their internal structure, of their development and their crisis. Thus when one speaks of the role played by capital through ground

rent in the 'urban', it is not a question of setting aside the subject because it does not deal directly with the reproduction of labour power, but rather of treating them as being realized in this process of reproduction. Similarly, the production of the 'urban centre' is a matter of capital and of the political apparatus, but we do not know what this 'urban centre' is as long as we have not decoded it theoretically. Therefore, it is in knowing that this production of the 'urban centre' is the structural place of the product envisaged that we will be able to understand the specific form of realization of the interests of capital in its production.

2. The analysis of the spatial elements is not, of itself, an analysis of the processes of reproduction of labour power, it is not an urban analysis and, consequently (for this is the important point), it does not correspond to the particular rules discovered in the domain of the urban. But this is so very often because of the segmentation of space into specific units on the basis of the process of reproduction of labour power. The 'urban centre' is urban because the spatial form and the social relations that are expressed in it are an element of the functioning and of the change of the units of collective reproduction of labour power, 'urban' units.

3. The fundamental point is this: the fact that the process of reproduction of labour power should have a certain specificity, deriving from the relative autonomy of 'the urban' and of 'urban units', does not mean that it is independent of the social structure as a whole. Furthermore, it is itself structured (as is every social process) by a specific combination, organized by the principal contradiction between the classes, fundamental elements of the social structure. It is this internal structuring of the process of collective reproduction of labour power that we call 'urban structure'. It is made up of the specific articulation of the economic, political and ideological instances of the modes of production in the social formation, within the process of collective reproduction of labour power. This, which looks horribly complicated and abstract, is nevertheless the mode of reasoning currently used by Marxists in other regions of the social structure: the difficulty derives rather from the confusion caused by the fog of the ideology of the urban.

In fact, everybody agrees in 'situating' a factory structurally at the level of the economic and more precisely in the process of reproduction of the means of production. And yet the factory is not 'just that'. But it is first of all that. Inside it processes of reproduction of ideological social relations are realized, political relations of domination are practised, and also, in a certain sense, processes assisting the reproduction of labour power occur (for example, safety measures in work). However, this ensemble of processes is realized within an immediate process of production and the articulation of the elements of the social structure here is specific, in the sense that it corresponds to modern rules, different, for example, from those that articulate the social structure within the state apparatus. (The reader would do well to detach himself from the empiricist immediacy of the analysis in 'factory' terms, in the example used and to extend the reasoning to the process of production as a whole.)

Thus the same internal structuring of the whole of the social structure at the level of cities is realized in a specific way by the process of collective consumption. It is not unimportant to know which process specifies this structuring, for the historical practices rooted in such a process will bear its mark.

It is important, furthermore, to remember that it is not a question here of pure 'formal combinations' of structural elements, but of historically determined articulations, specifying, in a particular form, the contradiction between capital and labour (and therefore the class struggle) and the contradictions that derive from it.

But what is the use of all this? And how can one justify it?

It serves to develop scientific research into the problems connoted (and therefore to orientate the corresponding social practice) and is justified only by the fecundity of the research results acquired as a result of these new bases.

Thus, for example, if one sets out from a culturalist analysis of the urban, one will try to establish and compare different 'lifestyles' according to the forms of space and to detect the underlying links of causality. If one sets out from the contradictions between 'town' and 'country', one will establish the characteristics of these two terms and will go on to show the particular effects of these geographical and economic characteristics on the social relations that derive from them. If one remains within an analysis of the production of space, one will choose a particular economic or political process and go on to show the results to which they lead as far as spatial form is concerned (from the pleasantness of the context to the functionality of the arrangement of the volumes constructed).

If one sets out from the analysis that I have carried out, one will centre above all on the analysis of the collective means of consumption, studying consumption in a differential way according to the moulds of labour power, that must be reproduced and the class contradictions that are expressed in it in a specific way.

If such hypotheses are justified, a concrete analysis of these processes of collective consumption must illuminate, in the end, the essence of the problems usually referred to as 'urban'. This is the only possible demonstration (in terms of social efficacity) of the validity of our point of departure, beyond logical reasonings and recourse to the moral authority of classic authors.

What, for example, are the concrete problems through which the growing importance of the urban over the last twenty years has been expressed?

1. Growing urban concentration, that is to say, the concentration of the population in ever more enormous urban areas, with all that derives from that.

2. The massive intervention of the state in the production and distribution of public amenities and in urban development.

3. The development of 'urban struggles', new forms of social conflicts.

4. The vertiginous development of talk about the urban, of the attention paid to this by the official institutional apparatuses.

An analysis of these historical phenomena in terms of collective consumption would tend to show the correspondence and causality between these 'realities' and the fundamental structural tendencies of monopoly state capitalism:

1. The objective socialization of the reproduction of labour power and the concentration of the means of consumption as a result of the concentration and centralization of the means of production and of their administration.

2. The necessary and permanent intervention of the state apparatus in order to mitigate the consequences of the differential profitability of the production sectors of the means of consumption and to ensure the functioning of an increasingly complex and interdependent process.

3. The claim of the dominated classes for more and more 'indirect wages' in so far as this is assuming an increasing place in their process of simple and extended reproduction.

4. The treatment of this ensemble of new problems by the dominant ideology, by displacing them, naturalizing them and spatializing them: the development of the ideology of the urban that is universalized in the form of the ideology of the environment.

It goes without saying that this series of remarks cannot be regarded as having proved anything. But it will serve to show the way in which I intend to set the urban problematic, which is dominated in our time by culturalist idealism or by spatial empiricism, on its feet again. *Hic Rhodus, hic salta!*

c) A last, very important, theoretical rectification concerning the analyses made in this book is that which refers to the study of urban social movements.

The great danger of the perspective that I developed in the final pages of *The Urban Question* is that of subjectivism in the analysis of the practices that seem to have been coupled with a certain structuralism in the analysis of the urban system. In fact, as Jordi Borja (1974) wrote in one of the best texts on these themes:

> The analysis of the urban phenomenon suffers, in its theoretical formations, from a particular difficulty in explaining *both* the urban structure and the urban movements . . . The rupture, idealist in origin, between structures and practices paralyses dialectical analysis and develops an analytical dichotomy between a *theory of reproduction* ('the city of capital') and a *theory of change* of a historicist type (the city transformed by 'urban social movements'). The dialectical analysis conceives any structure as a contradictory reality in continuous change. These objective contradictions give rise to social conflicts that appear as *immediate agents* of change. There are no structures that are not something other than an ensemble of contradictory and conflictual social relations, more or less crystallized, but always in a process of change. And there are no urban movements, in which all the social classes participate to different degrees, that are not situated within structures, expressing them and modifying them constantly.

I could not put it better myself!

Now, from this point of view, although I do not think the analyses in this book can be accused of being structuralist (for they constantly draw attention to the fact that structures exist only in practices and that the 'urban structure' is merely a theoretical construct through which analysis necessarily passes by means of a study of urban politics), they do lend themselves to subjectivist deviations as far as the urban social movements are concerned. More precisely, my grid of analysis for urban movements, as presented in the book, takes into consideration only the internal characteristics of the movement and their impact on the social structure. In fact, a study of urban movements can be carried out only by observing the interaction between the structural interests and the social agents that constitute the movement and the interests and social agents that are opposed to it. This means that the grid of analysis of the urban movements must consider at least four planes in constant interaction:

1. The *issue* of the movement, defined by the structural content of the problem treated.

2. The internal structure of the movement and the interests and actors that are presented in it.

3. The structural interests opposed to the movement, the organizational expression of these interests, the concrete practices of this opposition.

4. The effects of the movement on the urban structure and on political and ideological relations.

My work on these themes over the last three years has put this methodology into practice with rather encouraging results. (Castells *et al.*, 1977.)

Moreover, one must delimit more clearly the difference between the study of the *urban struggles* (as historical practice) and the discovery of the *urban social movements* (as transforming historical practice). I studied the first in order to discover the elements capable of developing the social movements, that is to say, systems of practices capable of transforming the structurally dominant logic. And one of my central hypotheses, which must be recalled yet again, is that there is no qualitative transformation of the urban structure that is not produced by an articulation of the urban movements with other movements, in particular (in our societies) with the working-class movement and with the political class struggle. In this sense, I do not claim that urban movements are the only sources of urban change. (Pickvance, 1975.) I say rather that the mass movements (including urban movements) produce in the urban organization qualitative transformations, in the broad sense of the term, through a change, local or global, of the correlation of forces among the classes. And this passes, necessarily, through a modification, local or global, of the political power relations, generally expressed in the composition and orientation of the political institutions.

The three rectifications that I have made do not in the least exhaust the problems posed in relation to the questions dealt with in this book. But I do not inend to revise everything; merely to indicate the principal points that may have led to confusion and to comment on the present development, not only of my own work, but of the much broader current of Marxist research that is now being developed on urban problems.

However, the essential point is not to be constantly going over the conceptual delimitations necessary to undertake the work, but to test the movement as we proceed — by making progress in the specific analysis of the problems referred to in advanced capitalism as 'urban', that is to say, in the study of the new contradictions linked to the processes of collective consumption and to the capitalist organization of the national territory. Although there is no question here of undertaking such a study — in annotations to an earlier stage in my work — I should like to indicate the direction of my thinking on this matter, in order to articulate this book all the better, such as it is, with the development of the work that derived from it.

*On the theory of collective consumption in advanced capitalism
and its relation to urban political contradictions*

Perhaps the source of the principal theoretical problems encountered in developing the theses stated in *The Urban Question* is the
fact that it adopts a general approach that is against the stream.
That is to say, instead of setting out from particular theoretical
bases (those of Marxism) and defining its own criteria (the social
logic underlying the means of consumption and/or the social organization of space), it skims over the urban problematic, separating
itself gradually from the implicit ideology, through a movement
that combines criticism, concrete research and the hesitant promul-
gation of new concepts. One could not have proceeded differently,
for every new theoretical field emerges from the contradictions that
develop out of pre-existing limitations.

Once the essence of the criticism has been developed, one must
reverse the intellectual approach. One must set out from a new,
theoretical and historical definition of the problems and proceed to
the inquiry. In reality, one of the greatest problems encountered by
the development of Marxist research applied to our period is that
Marxist intellectuals take up too much time trying to justify the
fact of being Marxists. It is much more important to get down to
the tasks of research, of elaboration and inquiry that await us. The
fruit of our work is the development of a scientific practice and a
mass political practice. The force of our analyses must come from
their explicative capacity and not from their polemical skill. That
is why *The Urban Question* is only a preparation for research, a
clearing of the ground obscured by sociological idealism. On this
basis, a new approach must be developed (and is, in fact, being
developed) in an autonomous way, posing its own questions.

That is why in this text, which has the aim of articulating an
already written book with a movement that is ulterior to it, I
should like to propose a few ideas on the materialist analysis of
the processes of consumption and in particular of collective consumption in advanced capitalism, for they seem to me to be at the
base of the issues recognized/ignored by the urban problematic.
(Castells, 1976.)

Social classes and the process of consumption

By *consumption,* I mean the social process of appropriation of the
product by people, that is to say, social classes. But the *product* is
broken down into reproduction of the means of production, reproduction of labour power and surplus value. This *surplus value* is
broken down into: extended reproduction of the means of produc-

tion (or productive consumption, in Marx's terms), extended reproduction of labour power (or, for Marx, 'individual consumption')
and what Marx himself calls, in a rather imprecise term, 'individual
luxury consumption', by which he means the consumption by
individuals beyond simple and extended reproduction according to
historically defined needs. Moreover, it ought to be made clear that
in the simple and extended reproduction of the means of production
and of labour power, one must include all the social 'costs' that
derive from the institutional superstructure (in particular, state
apparatuses) necessary to the said reproduction.

If such is the process of consumption from the point of view of
the mode of production, considering the economic in the strict
sense, there is a specificity of consumer goods as constituting one
of the two large sections (Section II in the analysis in *Capital*) into
which production may be divided. This involves a certain number
of particular rules.

From the point of view of social classes, consumption is both an
expression and a *means,* that is to say, a social practice, which is
realized according to a certain (ideological) content and which
concretizes at the level of the relations of distribution the oppositions and struggles determined by the relations of production.

Like any social process, consumption is determined by the
general rules of the mode of production, by the social matrix in
which it is inscribed. But this determination occurs at different
levels and with specific effects if one takes into account the diversity of the social significations of consumption: *appropriation of
the product,* for the social classes; *reproduction of labour power,*
as far as the production process is concerned; *reproduction of social
relations* as far as the mode of production as a whole is concerned.

Furthermore, the material realization of the process of consumption involves the relating of *products* (or consumer goods) with
agent-consumers, according to a relatively autonomous social determination. The link between these two determinations and the
direct determination of the process of consumption are at the base
of the rules (or mode of consumption) underlying the social practices in this domain.

These practices of consumption must be apprehended at the
three levels indicated, that is to say, as processes of reproduction
of labour power, as the expression of class relations at the level of
the relations of distribution and as reproduction of the social relations inherent in the mode of production. Any unilateral analysis
of one of these three planes leads to deviations that may be termed
successively 'economism', 'politicism' and 'ideologism'. In order to
advance in this direction, we must elucidate a few of the elements

of the historical evolution of consumption in capitalism, attempting in this way to try out the conceptual tools that we are forging.

The transformation of the process of consumption in advanced capitalism

We know that the capitalist mode of production, at the present time, is characterized by three fundamental features:

1. An unprecedented increase in the mass of surplus value, but, at the same time, the central role of the struggle against the tendency of profit rates to fall, resulting from the ever accelerating increase of the organic composition of capital.

2. The accelerating, though unequal and contradictory, development of the productive forces.

3. The unequal and contradictory, but always rising development of the class struggle.

Through these three fundamental features, what emerges is not a stagnant capitalism, but a capitalism that is developing in a contradictory, accelerating and uninterrupted way, undergoing new phases within the monopoly stage, developing extensively (on a world scale), both in relation to itself (in such a way that the most advanced phases penetrate and dissolve the relations of production of the less advanced capitalist phases) and in relation to other modes of production (pre-capitalist or archeo-capitalist). Such an evolution does not imply the historical eternity of the capitalist mode of production, for with this gigantic development, these contradictions deepen, spread throughout the whole world, become interdependent on a world scale and lead to a generalized crisis. But this means that one must avoid any mechanistic vision of the collapse of a mode of production simply through the dynamic of its internal crises. The contradictions thus produced always pose the terms of a historical alternative, but the principal aspect of the contradiction always results from a given historical process — dependent on the class struggle and on its political expression.

This analysis of the contradictory expansive tendencies of the capitalist mode of production of the last two decades enables us to situate more clearly the role played by the process of consumption.

In fact, the three great tendencies indicated determine three specific effects at the base of the transformations in the consumption sector:

1. Monopoly capital, in search of new investment outlets, occupies and transforms new sectors of the economy, hitherto less advanced on account of a lower profit rate. In particular, this is the

case of the production of means of consumption, from agriculture to electrical household goods. It is clear that this transformation results from the interest of capital invested rather than from social demand — hence the need for advertising, the development of credit and other systems of directing demand in order to adjust it to supply.

2. By transforming the power relations between the classes, the development of the class struggle and the growing power of the working-class movement open up breaches in the dominant logic along the line of least resistance, thus affecting the relations of distribution rather than the relations of production. There is, therefore, a historical need for a rise in the level of consumption by the lower classes, a need which the system may respond to without seeing its logic collapse, even if it involves great battles (1936 in France, for example; 1960 in Italy; 1959—61 in Belgium, etc.) in order to contain it. All the more so in that, in a way, this popular demand may be used by capital in search of new sectors, providing it can direct sufficiently closely the type of means of consumption to be produced: we can glimpse here the constitution of a new contradictory issue between the interests of capital and those of the lower classes as a whole (and not only the proletariat).

3. *The development and growing socialization of the productive forces,* both require and permit the development of the mass of the means of consumption and of the strategic role they play in the economy. In fact, the more production is on a large scale and interdependent, the more the reproduction of labour power is both complex and important. *Complex:* because it has to ensure the adjustment of an enormous mass of workers to needs and ever more precise and indispensable planning. *Important:* because in a process of production dependent on normalized, long-term profit on a world scale, the important thing is the smooth, regular functioning of the least predictable and controllable element: labour power. Given the constantly increasing mass of 'crystallized labour' that living labour must develop, the more the organic composition of capital increases, the more the remaining fraction of living labour becomes strategically central.

Furthermore, the development of the productive force, together with the increase of productivity that it represents, permits the rise in the level of consumption in the advanced countries and sectors within the unequal development of the capitalist mode of production on a world scale (it should be remembered that two-thirds of the human race remains below the level of biological reproduction).

Given these basic tendencies one can understand the transformations that occur in the process of consumption:

On the one hand, the penetration of monopoly capitalism has
brought about the destruction of archeo-capitalist relations that
are particularly important in the production of the means of consumption intended for the lower classes and in the distribution
sector.

From the agriculture of big capital, through the sometimes futile
mechanization of housework, to the supermarkets, we are witnessing what is experienced as 'mass consumption'. It is clear that it is
not the most 'useful' objects (in terms of use value) that are produced in this way, but those that are the most profitable. But, at
the same time, the backward-looking criticism of 'consumer society'
tends to regret 'loss of quality', while forgetting that this so-called
quality was always the preserve of an élite. No serious criticism of
consumption can be made without relating it to historically determined class practices, otherwise we fall back into variations on the
theme of the eternal tragedy of an abstract Man at grips with the
forces of Evil.

On the other hand, the process of consumption acquires a decisive place in the reproduction of the mode of production as a whole
in its present phase:

At the economic level, it is essential both to the reproduction of
labour power and to the mode of realization of surplus value. It
becomes essential for the skilled labour force, necessary to the
smooth functioning of the interdependent mass of the unskilled
labour force. From the point of view of the realization of surplus
value, although the relation between sector I and sector II has
always been at the root of the crises of overproduction in capitalism, the more the mass of means of production (sector I) increases
exponentially, the more the balance between the sectors becomes
susceptible to the slightest variations of the realization in Sector II.

At the political level, consumption assumes an ever more important place in the process of claims-integration, in so far as the tactic
of 'conflictual participation' linked with neo-capitalism deflects the
conflict to the level of the relations of distribution. But this also
means that any defects in the integrating mechanism (consumption)
broadens the bases of opposition to the system in so far as the basis
of claims at this level is recognized as legitimate and practised by
all classes, fractions and strata.

At the ideological level, consumption is, it is true, the expression
of class practice and of level in the hierarchy of social stratification.
But it is also a mercantile consumption of signs, this exchange value
of the sign having extended still further the sphere of capitalist
production, which not only has penetrated the production of the
means of consumption, but also that of the symbolic that is bound

up with them and develops according to a relatively autonomous logic. It is important, therefore, to recognize this dimension of consumption and to assign it a place in the analysis, without however making it the privileged axis of the expansion of the mode of production thus attributing to it the exorbitant role of condenser of new class contradictions (as the semiological ideology tends to do).

Furthermore, the specificity of the phase of state monopoly capitalism is expressed through the following phenomena:

1. The monopolies organize and rationalize consumption as a whole in every domain. Thus the relative autonomy of this process in relation to the dominant monopoly logic is abolished and one may speak of veritable rhythms of consumption. This is expressed at the level of experience by a growing oppression in everyday life and the imposition of an entirely heteronomous rhythm in activity outside work.

2. The state apparatus intervenes in a massive, systematic, permanent and structurally necessary way in the process of consumption, and in different forms:

a) Direct aid, to the capitalist monopolies, in order to facilitate their takeover of certain sectors (example: a tax system that favours the distribution chains against the small tradesmen).

b) 'Filling in the gaps' left by big capital in certain sectors of consumption. Thus we shall witness a takeover by the state of vast sectors of the production of means essential to the reproduction of labour power: health education, housing, collective amenities, etc. It is here that the 'urban problematic' sends down its roots.

c) Since the state is taking charge of a considerable, and objectively socialized, part of the process of consumption, since it intervenes in direct aid to the large economic groups that dominate that process, since consumption is becoming a central cog in the economic, political and ideological levels, whereas no centralized regulation of the process is being set up in the economic, the state becomes the veritable arranger of the processes of consumption as a whole: this is at the root of so-called 'urban politics'.

Collective consumption

I have referred to Marx's classic distinction between *productive consumption* (contributing to the reproduction of the means of production), *individual consumption* (contributing to the production of labour power) and *luxury consumption* (individual consumption exceeding needs, historically determined by the reproduction of labour power).

'Productive consumption' is not taken into account by current language in the 'process of consumption'. Moreover, even if from the theoretical point of view it really is consumption ('social appropriation of the product'), we exclude it for the moment from our field of analysis in order to simplify our already highly complex task.

Furthermore, the distinction between 'luxury consumption' and 'non-luxury consumption' seems to me highly debatable, since it refers in fact to a naturalistic theory of needs, however one interprets the words used. Therefore, I shall leave it in abeyance until we have carried the analysis further.

On the other hand, Marx's analysis seems to me to omit a fundamental difference in the process of consumption today, a difference, it is true, whose importance is much greater today than at the competitive stage of capitalism analysed by Marx.

This is the distinction between individual consumption and collective consumption, the second being consumption whose economic and social treatment, while remaining capitalist, takes place not through the market but through the state apparatus. 'Collective commodities', say the marginalist economists, are those that have no market price. This is obvious enough. The distinction between individual and collective consumption has been challenged in general because of the criteria used in the characterization of the latter, based as it is on some supposedly 'natural' character of certain commodities (for example, the indivisibility of such commodities as air, water, etc.). Now, we have only to think of the process of privatization of natural resources to be aware that nothing can escape big capital; within a dominant capitalist logic everything, absolutely everything, may become a commodity.

Everything except commodities whose process of production refers to a lower than average profit rate. Everything, except those commodities and services of which the state must have a monopoly in order to ensure the interest of the capitalist class as a whole (schools, police, etc., according to the historical situations).

This collective consumption is, therefore, consumption of commodities whose production is not assured by capital, not because of some intrinsic quality, but because of the specific and general interests of capital: thus the same product (housing, for example) will be treated both by the market and by the state, and will therefore be alternately a product of individual or collective consumption, according to the criteria, which will change according to the historical situation. Thus I would distinguish my approach from that of an empiricism that consists in identifying a different social given (collective consumption) and a material product (housing as use value). On the other hand, these 'collective consumer goods' seem to be those that are necessary to the reproduction of labour power and/or to the reproduction of social relations, without which they would not be products, despite their lack of interest for the production of profit.

Above all, this production of collective consumption (with a very weak or non-existent profit rate) plays a fundamental role in the struggle of capital against the tendency of the profit rate to fall. Indeed, by devaluing part of social capital by unprofitable investments, the state helps to raise proportionately the rate of profit attributed to social capital as a whole. So, even if this mechanism is not capital's main weapon against the TPRF (tendency of the profit rate to fall), the intensification of exploitation and its development on a world scale being its essential weapon, the intervention of the state in consumption is nevertheless one of the principal cogs of monopoly capitalism, and not only for the reproduction of capital.

If this is the determination of the process of collective consumption, we must distinguish between *the production of the means of consumption* and *the process of consumption* itself, although the second depends upon the first and bears its mark. However, although such an approach is appropriate from the point of view of historical causality, from the point of view of the order of thought, we must theorize the process of consumption in itself, for it is impossible to know what are the specific effects of a cause on an effect of which we know little.

With this in view, I shall take account of three fundamental points:

1. Collective consumption mainly concerns the process of reproduction of labour power and the process of reproduction of social relations, but as articulated with the reproduction of labour power (and therefore obeying specific rhythms). This reproduction may be simple or extended. Extended reproduction should always be defined according to a historical specification and constitute one of the strong points of the analysis and one of those that presents the most difficulty.

2. Like every social process, collective consumption is made up of elements that may be defined only in their relations. Indeed, it is nothing but relations, historically determined between these elements. What are these elements? The same as those of the process of production: Labour Power, Means of Production, Non-Labour, but organized differently. In the structural organization of the

contradictions specific to this process resides the ultimate secret of collective consumption. (This sybilline sentence scarcely tries to conceal the embryonic and provisional state of our research on this point of the analysis.)

3. Any process of consumption defines units of realization of this process. These units, articulating collective means of consumption, constitute the material base of the urban units. That is why the urban problematic is linked fairly directly to the relations between social classes and the consumption process.

The politicization of the urban in state monopoly capitalism: some historical tendencies

The politicization of 'urban problems' in state monopoly capitalism is directly determined by the transformation of class contradictions in the new phase of the capitalist mode of production and, in terms of practical politics, involves specific effects at the level of power relations.

Thus, to begin with, from the point of view of a transformation of the urban processes (that is to say, those concerning collective consumption), we are witnessing the emergence of a whole series of structural features that are at the root of new social and political conflicts, namely:

The growing importance of the predictability of the behaviour of labour power in a complex and interdependent production process requires increasing attention to the collective treatment of the processes and its reproduction. This tendency is reinforced by the increasing demands of the masses of workers gradually extending their claims from the area of wages to that of the overall conditions of their reproduction. These two features are at the root of the urban protest movement, in one direction, and of the movements of integration and participation in the opposite direction.

The existence of veritable rhythms of consumption in everyday life, through the objective socialization of the process combined with its subordination to the interests of capital, is at the root:

On the one hand, of ever more violent and sudden revolts, very often of an entirely spontaneous kind, which spring up by concentrating collectively the individual aggressiveness that has become normal in conditions of existence imposed by the great units of reproduction of labour power.

On the other hand, of an increasing demand for regulation of the urban system according to the logic of the dominant class. This demand paves the way for the development of the practice and ideology of urban planning.

The permanent and ever extending intervention of the state apparatus in the area of the processes and units of consumption makes it the real source of order in everyday life. This intervention of the state apparatus, which we call urban planning in the broad sense, involves an almost immediate politicization of the whole urban problematic, since the administrator and interlocuter of the social claims and demand tends to be, in the final analysis, the political apparatus of the dominant classes. However, the politicization thus established is not necessarily a source of conflict or change, for it may also be a mechanism of integration and participation: everything depends on the articulation of the contradictions and practices or, to put it another way, on the dialectic between the state apparatus and urban social movement.

The generalization and globalization of the urban problematic is at the root of the vertiginous development of the ideology of the urban, which attributes to the 'environment' a capacity to produce or transform social relations. Such a tendency helps to reinforce the strategic role of urbanism, as a political ideology and as a professional practice. Basing itself on the objective socialization of the consumption process, on the structural demand for the intervention of the state and on the ideological spatialization of new contradictions, urbanism (and therefore the urbanist) becomes a discipline in the strict sense of the term, that is to say, the political capacity to impose a certain model of social relations under cover of an arrangement of space. This explains the sudden proliferation of critical utopias, which misconstrue the ideology of official urbanism by opposing to it another, 'human' urbanism, which remains nevertheless on the displaced ground on which class conflicts have been transformed into conflicts of space.

If, instead of observing the process of politicalization of the urban from the point of view of the structural transformations of collective consumption, we now observe it from the position of the new forms of political struggle and of the tendencies characteristic of the political scene in advanced capitalism, we may also make a few fundamental points:

From the point of view of the dominant class (big capital), although it is true that the urban problematic is entirely the expression of the dominant ideology, which is increasingly diffusing and globalizing it, its development is at the same time bound up with the emergence of new structural contradictions at the level of collective consumption, manifested, for example, in political discussion and economic claims that have more and more to do with 'collective

amenities'. So much so that there is a growing contradiction between the diffusion of the ideology of the urban by the dominant
class and the political effects intended as the economic contradictions that it connotes deepen.

From the point of view of the new tendencies of petty-bourgeois
revolt, based essentially on a counter-culture (one that is perfectly
adapted both to the economic bases and to the ideological expressions of the urban problematic): indeed, they question the consumption model and 'everyday life' more than the relations of production
and political domination. Their opposition is based on a humanist
critique of the totalitarian and global 'environment' that is well
suited to the naturalist registers of the ideology of the environment,
taking its bearings in the communal utopia of the past and of the
future rather than a certain contradictory place in the structure of
class relations. In a sense, it might be said that the petty-bourgeois
cultural revolt provides the principal militant mass of the movements based on the urban ideology. A quite different problem is
that of knowing in what conditions they become an element of the
urban social movements, acting as a challenge to class power.

From the point of view of the tendencies of reformist opposition,
an expression of the immediate interests of the dominated classes,
while releasing them from their historical interests, and therefore
making claims and modifying the relations of distribution and administration without changing the relations of production, 'urban
problems' appear as the privileged domain of reform. In fact, they
are profoundly felt; they appear at first sight as an element condi-
tioning the workers' living conditions; in varying degrees, they concern all social classes; they refer to consumption, and therefore do
not directly challenge the relations of production or political domination; above all, the occupation of certain positions at different
levels of the state apparatus makes it possible to possess certain
apparatuses of regulation and intervention in the domain. One may
expect, therefore, an unprecedented development of the reformist
tendencies of a 'social municipalism', trying to make socializing
experiments in this field. Already in Japan 'urban reform' is at the
base of important political victories won by the parliamentary left,
in particular, the conquest of the municipalities of all the large
cities.

From the point of view of the revolutionary political opposition
(that aiming at the destruction of the bourgeois state apparatus and
the creation of political conditions that will allow the beginning of
a transition to socialism), the place of urban contradictions, and of
the struggles that derive from them, in overall strategy, depends on
its judgement of the conjuncture of the class struggle and on the

characteristics of the economic and political organizations of the dominated classes.

In fact, if one believes that revolutionary parties exist, that they are solidly established among the masses and that, therefore, the working class is organized for the main task, the key of the problem is then to unite the broader masses around an anti-monopoly political programme, that is to say, to construct the historical bloc of the dominated classes under the hegemony of the proletariat. Urban problems then play a privileged role in the construction of the class alliance based on protest (not only political), on account of their 'pluriclassism' and their character as secondary contradiction, but one directly at grips with the state apparatus.

On the other hand, if one sets out from the idea that proletarian autonomy is still to be constructed, politically, ideologicaly, organizationally, then urban issues are relatively secondary in relation to the workers' struggle and to directly political conflicts.

If we now think of the importance of the political tendencies that converge in an increased interest in the urban question (the dominant class, petty-bourgeois revolt, reformism, revolutionary tactics in the class alliance phase), one will be able to explain the growing importance of this problematic: not only does it express certain new structural tendencies at the level of the economic, but the specifically political dynamic of most of the main currents on the political scene of advanced capitalism leads them to make them a privileged issue in their strategy. This explains the scope and ambiguity of the urban question, which is both a terrain booby-trapped with ideology and a source of political conflicts, in the precise sense that I have just established.

The new tendencies in urban research

The most important transformation to occur in the intellectual field treated by *The Urban Question* since it was written is, without any doubt, the accelerated development of a current of empirical research that asks adequate questions and tries both to deal with them rigorously and to link them to social and political practice. The idea, expressed by some ill-informed commentators, that this book is at the root of the current that has developed, is quite unacceptable to me. Not only because such an affirmation would be absurdly pretentious, but because it is entirely false. Rather the opposite is the case. This book forms part of an overall current that has developed, unequally, in several countries at a given historical moment because it corresponded to a need to understand new so-called social contradictions that were at the centre of the practice of the dominated classes and dominant classes. Because of a particularly favourable conjunction of political, intellectual and institutional conditions, this current of research gained considerable influence in France, even attaining a certain hegemony within the academic world and in the research bodies on account of the quality and interest of the studies carried out. But, in different and varied forms, a similar current has developed in Italy, in Spain, in Latin America and, more recently, in Britain and the United States. In speaking of such a current, I do not mean that there is a theoretical agreement or even that it is a question in all cases of Marxist research, even if Marxist theory is the most common identifying feature. But, given its diversity, it is research that asks similar questions, concerning the relations between the classes, power and urban problems, and which tries to advance in their treatment through concrete analyses of concrete situations. Certainly, enormous problems appear in the development of such research and much of it is hesitant, ill constructed, extremely biased from the ideological point of view. This does not matter. The main thing is the reversal of perspective that it has brought about. Gradually, as a result of practice, it is refining its methods, becoming more patient, more rigorous, better articulated with the problems that are posed in social practice. We must not, however, be over-optimistic, for we are still (and how!) in the prehistory of the social sciences. Nevertheless, substantial progress has been made and relevant, systematic and accumulative research is clearing a way through the field of social practices connoted by the 'Urban Question'.

That is why this book would be dated today if there were no reference, however brief, to some of the examples of research work carried out in the last few years. For it is this current that is now to be enriched and improved in as animated and open a discussion as possible. My aim here is not to provide even a brief bibliography by way of completing the one that already exists in the book and which goes, more or less, up to 1970. My aim here is more limited and more precise; I wish to provide examples of a new type of research that scarcely existed in 1970 and which represents a fundamental transformation of the analysis of urban contradictions by the social sciences. I hope, therefore, to draw attention to this research and to facilitate communication between workers who are sufficiently close to be able to help each other in their work.

To begin with, very significant progress has been made in the sphere of the functioning of capital in the production and distribution of goods and urban services. I would mention, in particular, the work of Topalov (1973; 1974) on the builders and on urban land ownership, those of Asher on the production of built environment (Asher and Lucas, 1972) and on housing (Asher and Levy, 1973; Asher and Lucas, 1974) that of Duclos (1973) on the role of capital in Urban Renewal, that of Preteceille (1973) on the production of the large housing developments, that of Théret and Dechervois (1975), on the one hand, and that of Alain Lipietz (1974), on the other, on land rent, that of Pottier (1975) on the public financing of urbanization, etc. Generally speaking, the Centre de Sociologie Urbaine (Paris) has produced a whole series of monographs concerning the analysis of capital in the urban domain.

But perhaps the most important progress concerns the analysis of the urban politics of the dominant classes through a direct observation of state intervention in the urban services and in the organization of space. In this field, we should mention the work of Lojkine on Paris and Lyon (1973a; 1973b; 1974; 1976), of Cottereau on Paris (1969; 1970), of Godard on urban renewal in Paris (1973), of Rendu and Preteceille on urban planning (in progress), of Suzanne Magri on housing policies (in Biarez, 1974), of the CERAT team at Grenoble on the communal institution, of Castells and Godard (1974) on relations between the state and the corporations in relation to the urban, of Amiot (1972) and Ion (1973) on the policy of cultural amenities, and also the research, unfortunately unpublished, of Henri Coing on urban politics in several towns and the work of François d'Arcy, on the one hand, and of Mesnard, on the other, on the relations between law, politics, and urbanism.

Research has begun into the urban social movements both at the Centre d'Étude des Mouvements Sociaux (Castells *et al.*, 1976; and current research) and at the Centre de Sociologie Urbaine (especially by Freyssinet) and by a group of urban researchers at Rennes (Huet, 1973). Although some work on this subject has already been published (Castells, 1973; and the periodical *Espaces et Sociétés*), it is one of the terrains, and an extremely significant one, in which new urban research is still to develop a true analysis, going beyond lyrical commentary or political polemics.

Somewhat outside this current, and sharing neither its problematic nor its orientations, new important work has been produced in France, in particular, a general theory of space developed by Henri Lefebvre (1972; 1974) out of his personal readings of the Marxist classics in relation to the city. A rather original current is developing in a para-psychoanalytic orientation, in the work of the group centred around CERFI. (*Recherches*, 1973.) The work of Alain Medam (1972; NGP) is trying to form a bridge between this 'subjectivist' current and the Marxist tradition. Other recent research in urban sociology has been that of Raymond Ledrut (1973), Jean-Claude Thoenig (1974), Jean Rémy and Liliane Voyé. (1974.)

Taking all this work as a whole two things remain more and more obviously lacking:

1. Serious work on the role of ideology in urban contradictions and on the ideology of the urban itself. In particular, the materialist analysis of architecture does not seem to be developing at the same rate, despite the useful inquiry of Raymonde Moulin (1973) and other work, little of which has been published, that is beginning to come to grips with the question.[31]

2. A systematic reflection, based on an analysis of historical development, on the relation between urban contradictions and means of collective consumption, in particular, by studying the interactions between the state and urban movements. Given that this seems to me to be at the root of all the problems mentioned, it is to this research task that I have been devoting most of my efforts for some time — with extremely slow results, for the difficulties are considerable.[32]

I said above that research tendencies close to work that I have just mentioned (in theme and in orientation) are developing in several countries. It might be useful to the reader to have a few references with regard to these tendencies, though of course these can be neither exhaustive nor systematic and could have been much longer.

No doubt the most advanced country in these research orientations is Italy. With the same institutional means that are available in France, the Italian researchers seem to have produced much more advanced work, for the practical (essentially political) conditions of this reflection are excellent. One must refer in particular to the economists, sociologists, urbanists, militants, centred on the review *Città-Classe*, which links theory with practice, stimulating discussion in the unions and in the neighbourhood committees: Paolo Ceccarelli, Francesco Indovina, Maurizio Marcelloni, Bernardo Secchi, etc. are among the researcher-practitioners who have made most progress in Marxist urban research in Italy. (See Indovina, 1973; and the journals *Città-Classe* and *Archividi Studi Urbani e regionali*). Close to this current are sociologists, who have developed analyses of urban movements, such as Andreina Daolio (1974) and

[31] The most interesting works, no doubt, are those of Manfredo Tafuri. See also the work of Katherine Burlen, Bernard Dubord, Henri Raymond and Marion Segaud. A very fruitful discussion is introduced by the two articles by Manfredo Tafuri and Diana Agrest on the New York skyscrapers in the special number in the USA of *L'Architecture d'Aujourd'hui*, March–April, 1975.

[32] I am now trying to develop a comparative analysis between France, the United States and Italy in order to present the differential effects of the forms of state intervention and of the level reached by the class struggle on the organization of urban services and their relation to the consumption process.

Giuliano Della Pergola. (1974.) In other areas of the Italian left, we must situate such important work as that of Enzo Mingione, (1976) Mario Boffi and his team, (1972) Marcella Della Donne (1973) and, above all, Franco Ferrarotti (1970; 1974.)

In Spain, the particular conditions of intellectual repression have made the public expression of the very important urban research that has been developing there, particularly in Barcelona, rather difficult. I should mention above all the work of Jordi Borja and the Centro d'Estudis Urbans of Barcelona; the work of the CIDUR group of Madrid; the work of Manuel Campo (Barcelona) on urban movements; the unpublished theses of Maria-Josa Olives on the production of the *grands ensembles* in Barcelona; and, in a different perspective, the inquiry of Mario Gavira (Madrid) on tourism in Spain. Even in the socialist countries a very important renewal of urban research has developed recently, especially through the work of Ivan Szeleny (Hungary) and Jiri Musil (Czechoslovakia).

In Latin America, the CIDU group in Chile had become an exemplary experience of the articulation between mass work, research work and theoretical work. Its review *EURE* was, until number 8 (September 1973), the meeting-point of a new critical and analytical current in urban research in Latin America. The terrorist repression of the Chilean Junta dispersed the group and 'reorganized' CIDU. *EURE* 'changed direction', while waiting to be published in another Latin American country and finding once again its role as an intellectual stimulus of urban reform. Work groups are being formed and are developing here and there (São Paulo, Quito, Costa Rica, Mexico City, Buenos Aires) though they have not yet been able to establish the exemplary relation between theory and practice that characterized CIDU. Centres like the CEUR of Buenos Aires or CENDES of Caracas tried to construct a research programme that asks the basic question in the specific situation of Latin America.

Researchers such as Rosamond Cheethan (at the Universidad Metropolitana, Mexico City): Lucio Kowarick and Paul Singer (CEBRAP, São Paolo): Emilio Pradilla (Bogota); Martha Steinghart (El Colegio de Mexico); Alejandro Rofman, José Luis Coraggio, Jorge E. Hardoy, Oscar Moreno (CEUR-Buenos Aires); Anibal Quijano (Lima), among many others, are trying, in difficult conditions, to think of urban and regional questions in a new way, articulating the analysis of space with class relations, economic exploitation and political domination.

Also, in the English-speaking tradition, so long impermeable not only to Marxist theory, but to any analysis in terms of class, there has been a rapid development of a new tendency which, without calling itself Marxist in most cases, places the problem of power and its relation to the economy at the centre of its reflection on space and the urban. In England, one thinks of such researchers as Tom Davis (London), Michael Harloe (CES, London), Ray Pahl (Kent), Chris Pickvance (Kent), etc. The Conference of Urban Sociologists of Great Britain which met in York in January 1975, was dominated by discussions and research that were extremely close (from the point of view of problematic) to those that have been developing in France in the last few years.

In the United States, a current of extremely vigorous research is developing on urban problems among the Union of Radical Political Economists[33], though such exemplary Marxist work as that of David Harvey (1973; 1974; 1975; and above all his next book on the relation between capitalist accumulation and territorial organization) is still an exception.

Works of Marxist economics, in particular those of David Gordon (1971) and William Tabb (1970) are beginning to be influential. In urban sociology and the sociology of communities, works such as those of Robert Alford (1975; Alford and Friedland, 1976) are significantly celebrated by the new generation of sociologists and the books that have been most commented upon in recent years in the subject of urban politics have been those of Francis F. Piven and Richard Cloward (1971, 1974), who are developing a class analysis of the urban programmes in the large American cities. Although it is true that such a tendency is far from being so hegemonic in the United States as it is in France, it is making its impact felt on researchers as a whole and many of the more influential of them are beginning to break the empiricist yoke under the double effect of new intellectual stimulus and of the crisis of legitimacy of the American Way of Life.

This avalanche of references on urban research is not intended as a bibliographical updating of *The Urban Question*. For many names and titles, which are very significant from the point of view of urban research in general, are missing. My references are intended quite simply to dispel the assumptions that were at the root of this book when it was written, in a much broader, much more collective, intellectual movement, in which the theory-practice relation becomes the essential problem, on the basis of the experience accumu-

---

[33] In February, 1975, at New York, they organized a conference on the theme of the Marxist analysis of the city. The contribution to this colloquium, which were generally very interesting, will be published in 1976. I would also like to mention the works of John Mollenkopf and Richard Hill.

lated and in terms of objectives that are now beginning to emerge more clearly.

My main aim is to make this book obsolete through its supersession in practice.

Madison, Wisconsin, June 1975

References

Abaydoulla, Housagen, 1966: Le nouveau Sin Kiang. *Chine en Construction*, January.

Abercrombie, P. 1959: *Town and country planning*. London: OUP.

Abrams, C. 1965: *The city is the frontier*. New York: Harper & Row.

Abu-Lughod, J. and Fooley, M. M. 1960: Consumer strategies. In Foote, Nelson, N. editor: *Housing choice and housing constraints*, New York.

ADIRES, 1970: Contribution à la connaissance de la promotion immobilière privée. Paris (roneo).

Albig, W., 1932–33, The Mobility of Urban Population. *Social forces*, 11, 351–67.

Alexandersson, G. 1956: *The industrial structure of American cities*. Stockholm: Almquist & Wiksell.

Alford, R. R. 1968: The comparative study of urban politics. In Schnore, Leo F. editor, *q.v.* 263–302.

1975: *Health care politics*. Chicago: U. of Chicago Press.

Alford, R. R. and Friedland, Roger, 1976: Political participation. Madison, Wis.: U of Wisconsin (roneo).

Alihan, M. A. 1938: *Social ecology*. New York: Columbia UP.

Althusser, L. 1968: *For Marx*. London: New Left Books.

1970: Les appareils ideologiques d'état. *La Pensée*, June.

Althusser, L. and Balibar, E. 1970: *Reading 'Capital'*. London: New Left Books.

Altshuler, A. 1965: *The city planning process*. Ithaca, N.Y.: Cornell UP.

Amin, S. 1970: *L'Accumulation du capital à l'échelle mondiale*. Paris: Anthropos. (1972: *Accumulation on a world scale: a critique of the theory of underdevelopment*. Monthly Review Press)

Amiot, Michel,1972: *Politique municipale et equipements culturels*. Paris: Ministère de l'èquipment.

Anderson, N. 1959: Urbanism and urbanization. *American Journal of Sociology* 65, 68.

1962: The urban way of life. *International journal of Comparative Sociology* 3 (2), 175–288.

1965: *The federal bulldozer, a critical analysis of urban renewal 1949–1962*. Cambridge Press: MIT Press.

Anderson, T. R. and Egeland, J. A. 1961: Spatial aspects of social area analysis. *American Sociological Review* 26, 392–8.

Antunes, A., Durand, C., 1970: Paris: ministère de l'équipement: *Contribution à une sociologie des groupes sociaux.*

Aravena, Maria Eugenia, 1968: Dependencia Y urbanizacion en America Latina: el periodo colonial. Saniago de Chile: FLACSO (mimeo).

L'Architecture Aujord'hui, 1975, special number on USA.

Ardigo, A. 1967: *La diffusione urbana.* Rome: AVE.

Armand Committee, 1970: Report to the Council of Ministers. Paris.

Asher, Françoise and Levy, Daniel, 1973: Logement et construction. *Economie et Politique,* May.

Asher, Françoise and Lucas, Chantal, 1974: L'Industrie du batiment: les forces productives à libérer. *Economie et Politique,* March.

Ashworth, W. 1954: *The genesis of modern British town planning.* London: Routledge.

Axelrod, M. 1956: Urban structure and social participation. *American Sociological Review,* February.

Bachelard, G. 1957: *La poétique de l'éspace.* Paris: PUF. (1964: trs Maria Jolas, Orion Press).

Badiou, A. 1967: Le (re)commencement du matérialisme dialectique. *Critique,* May.

Bailey, Robert Jr. 1974: *Radicals in urban politics. The Alinsky approach.* Chicago: U. of Chicago Press.

Balibar, E. 1970: The basic concepts of historical materialism. In Althusser, L. and Balibar, E. *q.v.* 199–308.

Banfield, E. editor, 1961: *Urban government.* Glencoe, Ill.: The Free Press.

Banfield, E. and Wilson, J. Q. 1963: *City Politics.* Harvard U.P.

Baran, P. A. 1953: *Political economy of growth.* Monthly Review Press.

Bardet, G. 1963: *L'Urbanisme.* Paris: PUF.

Barnaud, 1961: *Rapport sur les motivations determinantes dans la choix de la localisation des établissements industrielles.* Prais: Ministère de la Construction.

Barraclough, S. 1968: *Notas sobre tenencia de la tierra en America Latina.* Santiago de Chile: ICIRA.

Bartholomew, H. 1932: *Urban land uses.* Cambridge Press: Harvard UP.

Bastié, J. 1964: *La croissance de la banlieue parisienne.* Paris: PUF.

Baumol, William, J. 1967: Macroeconomics of unbalanced growth – the anatomy of the urban crisis. *American Sociological Review,* June.

Beaujeu-Garnier, J. and Bastié, J. 1967: *Atlas de Paris et de la région parisienne.* Paris: Berger-Levrault.

Beaujeu-Garnier, J. and Chabot, G. 1963: *Traité de géographie urbaine.* Paris: A. Colin. (1967: *Urban Geography,* London: Longman.)

Bell, W. 1958: Social choice, life styles and suburban residence. In Dobriner, W. *q.v.*

— 1968: The city, the suburbs and the theory of social choice. In Greer, S. *et al., q.v.*

— 1969: Urban neighborhoods and individual behaviour. In Meadows, P. and Mizburchi, Ephraim H. *q.v.* 120–46.

Bell, W. and Forge, T. 1957: Urban neighborhood types and participation in formal associations. *American Sociological Review* 21, 25–34.

Bellush, J. and Hausknecht, M. editors, 1967: *Urban renewal: people, politics and planning.* New York: Anchor Books.

Bergel, E. 1955: *Urban sociology.* New York.

Bergeman, Barbara, 1969: The urban crisis. *American Economic Review,* September.

474   *References*

Berger, B. M. 1960: *Working class suburb. Study of autoworkers in suburbia.* Berkeley: U. of California Press.

Bernstein, T, P. 1967: Leadership and mass mobilization in the Soviet and Chinese collectivization campaigns of 1929–30 and 1953–56, a comparison. *The China Quarterly*, July, 1–47.

Berry, Brian J. L. 1962: Some relations of urbanization and basic patterns of economic development. University of Oregon (unpublished paper).

Berthaux, D. 1970: Nouvelles perspectives sur la mobilité sociale. Varna: 8th world congress of sociology (paper).

Beshers, J. M. 1962: *Urban social structure.* Glencoe, Ill.: The Free Press.

Bettelheim, C. 1967: *Planification et croissance accélérée.* Paris: Maspero.

Biarez, S., Kukawka, P., Mingasson, C. 1970: Les élus locaux et l'aménagement urbain dans l'agglomération grenobloise. U. of Grenoble (roneo).

Biarez, S., Boisberanger, G., Bouchet, C. and Mingassa, C. 1974: *Institution communale et pouvoir politique.* Paris: Mouton.

Blanc, Jordi., 1966: La agravacion del problema de la vivienda en Espana. *Cuadernos Ruedo Iberico* 5, February.

Blumenfeld, H. 1965: The modern metropolis. *Scientific American*, Sept. 64–74.

Bobroff, J., Novatin, A., Toussaint, R. 1970: Étude de la politique du ministre de l'équipement et du logement, M. Albin Chalandon. Nanterre: Groupe de Sociologie Urbaine, Faculté des Lettres (roneo).

Boffi, M., Cofini, S., Giasanti, A., Mingione, E. 1973: *Città e conflitto sociale.* Milan: Feltrinelli.

Boggs, S. L. 1964: Urban crime patterns. *American Sociological Review* 4, 522–9.

Bogue, D. J. 1950: *The structure of the metropolitan community. A study of dominance and subdominance.* Ann Arbor: U. of Michigan.

Bogue, D. J. and Hauser, P. M. 1963: Population distribution, urbanism and internal migration. World Population Conference (roneo).

Bollens, J. and Schmand, H. 1965: *The metropolis: its people, politics and economic life.* New York: Harper & Row; 2 rev. edn 1970.

Borja, Jordi, 1974: Estructura urbana y movieientos urbanos. Universidad Autonoma de Barcelona, Dept. of Geography.

Bose, Nirmal Kumar, 1965: Calcutta: A premature metropolis. *Scientific American*, September 91–102.

Boskoff, A. 1962: *The sociology of urban regions.* New York: Appleton Century Crofts.

Boulding, Kenneth E., Pfaff, Martin, Pfaff, Anita, 1973: *Transfers in an urbanized economy, the grants economics of income distribution.* Belmont, Ca.: Wadsworth.

Boulet, Boulakia, 1965: L'industrialisation de la banlieue nord-ouest de Paris. Paris: CREDOC-IAURP (roneo).

Bowers, R. V. 1939: Ecological patterning of Rochester, New York. *American Sociological Review* 4, 180–9.

Braddwood, R. J. and Willey, G. R. editors, 1962: *Courses towards urban life: Archeological considerations of some cultural alternates.* Chicago.

Breese, G. editor, 1969: *The city in newly developing countries.* Englewood Cliffs: Prentice Hall.
    1964: The daytime population of the central business district. In Burgess, E. W. and Bogue, D. J., editors, *q.v.* 112–28.

Browning, H. L. 1958: Recent trends in Latin American urbanization. *The*

References   475

Annals of the American Academy of Moral and Political Sciences, March, 111–26.

Burgess, E. 1925: *The growth of the city*. In Park *et al. q.v.*

Burgess, E. W. and Bogue, D. J. editors, 1964: *Contributions to Urban sociology*. Chicago: U. of Chicago Press.

Cage, B., Granelle, J. J., Valette, E. 1970: *Sur la formation de l'offre par la promotion immobilière privée*. Paris: ADIRES.

Cahiers de l'IAURP 4, 5: *Les Transports dans la région parisienne*. 7: *Les Experiences des villes non valles*.

Campbell, Alan K. and Meranto, Philip, 1967: The metropolitan education dilemma: matching resources to needs. In Gittell, Marilyn, editor, *Educating an urban population*. Beverly Hills: Sage Publications.

Caplow, T. 1932–33: Incidence and direction of residential mobility in a Minneapolis sample. *Social Forces* 11, 351–67.

Cardoso, F. H. 1968: *Cuestiones sociologia del desarrollo en America Latina*. Santiago de Chile: Editorial Universitario.

Cardoso, F. H. and Faletto, E. 1970: *Desarrollo y dependencia en America Latina*. Mexico City: Siglo XXI.

Castells, M. 1967: Les politiques d'implantation des entreprises industrielles dans la région de Paris. Paris, unpublished doctoral thesis in sociology, University of Paris.

1968: Y-a-t-il une sociologie urbaine? *Sociologie du Travail* 1, 1968.

1969a: Théorie et ideologie en sociologie urbaine. *Sociologie et Sociétés* 1, (2) 171–91.

1969b: Entreprise industrielle et développement. *Synopsis*, Oct. 67–75.

1970: La rénovation urbaine aux Etats-Unies. *Espaces et Sociétés* 1.

editor, 1973: *Imperialis mo y urbanizacion en America Latina*. Barcelona: Gustavo Gille.

1973: *Luttes urbaines*. Paris: Maspero.

editor, 1974: *Estructura de clases y politica urbana en America Latina*, vol. 1. Buenos Aires: SIAP.

1975a: Urban sociology and urban politics. *Comparative urban research*, 6.

1975b: Collective consumption and urban contradictions in advanced capitalism. In Lindberg, L. editor, *Stress and Contradiction in Modern Capitalism*. Lexington: Heath. (See *Il Mulino*, 1, 1974 for an earlier version.)

Castells, M., Ahtike, V., Touraine, A., Zygel, S. 1968: La mobilité des entreprises industrielles dans la région parisienne. *Cahiers de l'IAURP*, 11.

Castells, M. and Godard, Francis, 1974: *Monopolville: l'enterprise, l'état, l'urbain*. Paris: Mouton. London: Macmillan, forthcoming.

Castells, M., Cherki, E., Godard, F., Mehl, D. 1977: *Crise du logement et mouvements sociaux. Enquête sur la région parisienne*. Paris: Mouton.

CEGS, 1964–65; L'attraction de Paris sur sa banlieue, observations complementaires. Paris (roneo).

CEPAL, 1963: *El desarrollo social de America Latina en la postguerra*. Buenos Aires: Solar-Hachette.

Chamboredon, J. C. and Lemaire, M. 1970: Proximité spatiale et distance sociale dans les grands ensembles. *Revue Française de Sociologie*, January, 3–73.

Chambre, H. 1964: *Urbanisation et crossanu économique en URSS*. *Economie Appliquée*, 17 (1) 5–109.

1965: L'urbanisation en URSS. In Carrier, H. and Laurent, P. *Le phenomène urbain*. Paris: Aubier-Montaigne.

Cheetham, R. 1971: La Camara Chilena de la construccion. EURE 3.
Chevalier, L. 1950: *La formation de la population parisienne au xixe siècle.*
Paris: PUF. (1973: trs F. Jellen etc. Labouring Classes and dangerous classes
in Paris during the first half of the nineteenth century, London: Routledge.)
Childe, V. G. 1960: The urban revolution. *Town Planning Review,* April.
Chi-Ming How 1968: Sources of agricultural growth in communist China.
Journal of Asian Studies, August, 721–39.
Choay, F. 1965: *L'urbanisme: Utopies et realités.* Paris: Seuil.
Chombard de Lauwe, P. H. 1950: *Paris et l'agglomération parisienne,* vol. 1.
Paris: PUF; vol. 2, 1952.
   1960: *Famille et habitation.* Paris: CNRS 1.
   1963: *Des hommes et des villes.* Paris: Payot.
   1965: *Paris, essais de sociologie 1952–1964.* Paris: Les Editions Ouvrières.
CIDU, 1972: Campamentos de Santiago. *Revista Latinoamericaine de Estudios
Urbanos y Repiondes 5.*
Clark, Terry, N. 1968: Community structure, decision making, budget ex-
penditures and urban renewal in 51 American cities. *American Sociological
Review 33,* August. p. 591 ff.
Clerc, P. 1967: *Grands ensembles, banlieues nouvelles.* Paris: PUF.
Clinard, M. B., 1960: A cross-cultural replication of the relations of urbanism
to criminal behaviour. *American Sociological Review,* April, 253–257.
Cloward, Richard A. and Piven, Frances F. 1974: *The politics of turmoil.* New
York: Pantheon.
CNL, 1971: Pour que le droit au logement devienne une realité. (pamphlet.)
Coing, H. 1966: *Rénovation urbaine et changement social.* Paris: Les Editions
Ouvrières.
Cole, J. P. 1965: *Latin America, and economic and social geography.* London:
Butterworth.
Coleman, James S. *et al.* 1966: Equality and educational opportunity. Wash-
ington: US Government Printing Office. (mimeo)
Commissariat Général au Plan, 1970a: *Les villes: la société urbaine.* Paris:
A. Colin.
   1970b: *Le logement.* Paris: A. Colin.
Conde, R., Cortes, and Gallo, E. 1967: *La formacion de la Argentina moderna.*
Buenos Aires: Paidos.
Congressional Research Service, 1973: *The central city problems and urban
renewable policy.* Washington, Study prepared for the subcommittee on
housing and urban affairs, 93rd Congress: US Government Printing
Office.
Connery, Robert H., editor, 1969: *Urban riots: violence and social change.*
New York: Vintage Books.
Cornuau, C., Imbert, M., Lamy, B., Reudu, P., Retel, J. O. 1965: *L'attraction
de Paris sur sa banlieue.* Paris: Les Editions Ouvrières.
Cottereau, A., 1969: L'apparition de l'urbanisme comme action collective:
L'agglomeration parisienne au début du siècle. *Sociologie du Travail 4.*
   1970: Les débuts de la planification urbaine dans l'agglomeration paris-
ienne: le mouvement principal parisien. *Sociologie de Travail 4.*
Crozier, M. 1965: Pour une analyse sociologique de la planification française.
Revue Française de Sociologie 6, 147–63.
Dahl, R. A. 1961: *Who governs?* Newhaven, Conn.: Yale UP.
Daland, R. T. and Parker, S. A. 1962: The role of the planner in urban devel-
opment. In Chapin, F. Stuart, and Weiss, S. F., *Urban growth dynamics,*
New York: John Wiley, 182–223.

Danielson, Michael N., 1965: *Federal-metropolitan politics and the commuter crisis.* New York: Columbia UP.

Daolio, Adreina, editor, 1974: *La lotte par la casa Italia.* Milan: Feltrinelli.

David, Stephen M., and Paterson, Paul E., editors, 1973: *Urban politics and public policy: the city in crisis.* New York: Praeger.

Davis, K. 1965: The urbanization of urban population. *Scientific American,* September (Cities).

Davis, K. and Golden, Hilda H. 1954: Urbanization and the development of pre-industrial areas. *Economic Development and Cultural Change 3,* October 6–26.

de Bell, D. editor, 1970: *The environmental handbook.* New York: Ballentine.

Délégation Générale du District de la Région de Paris, 1963: *Avant-projet de programme duodécennal pour la région de Paris.*

della Pergola, Guiliano, 1974: *Diritto alla città e lette urbana.* Milan: Feltrinelli.

della Donne, Marcella, 1973: *La questione edilizia.* Bari: De Denato.

Department of City Planning, 1961: *Industrial movements and expansion 1947–1957, City of Chicago.* Chicago.

Devine, Joel, 1975: Working paper on the urban fiscal crisis, a case study: New York City. Madison, W.S.: U. of Wisconsin.

De Vise, P. 1967: Chicago's widening colour gap. Inter-university Social Research Committee, report no. 2. Chicago.

Dewey, R. 1960: The rural-urban continuum: real but relatively unimportant. *American Journal of Sociology* 66, (1) 60–67.

Dhooge, J. 1961: Tendances actuelles en sociologie urbaine. *Social Compass* 8 (3) 199–209.

Dickenson, R. 1951: *The West European city.* London: Routledge.

Dobriner, W. H. 1958: Local and cosmopolitan as contemporary suburban character types. In Dobriner, W. H. editor, *The suburban community.* New York: Putnams.

Dorselaer, J. and Gregory, A. 1962: *La urbanizacion en America Latina.* Fribourg-Bogotà: FERES-CRSR, 2 vols.

Doxiadis, K. A. 1966: *Urban renewal and the future of American city.* Chicago: Public Administration Service.

Dragan, J. 1970: Rhythme de l'urbanisation et intégration urbaine des migrateurs d'origine rurale. Communication au Congrès mondial de sociologie, Varna.

Duclos, Denis, 1973: *Propriété foncière et processus d'urbanisation.* Paris: CSU.

Dumazedier, J. and Imbert, M. 1967: *Espaces et Loisirs,* vol. 2. Paris: CRU.

Duncan, B. 1964a: Intra-urban population movement. In Hatt, R. K. and Reiss, A. J., editors, *Cities and society,* Glencoe, Ill.: The Free Press, 279–309.
1964b: Variables in urban morphology. In Burgess, E. and Bogue, D. *q.v.* 17–31.

Duncan, B. and Hauser, P. 1960: *Housing a metropolis.* Glencoe, Ill.: The Free Press.

Duncan, B. and Lieberson, S. 1970: *Metropolis and region in transition.* Beverly Hills: Sage Publications.

Duncan, O. D., 1959: Human ecology and population studies. In Hauser, P. M. and Duncan, O. D., editors, *The study of population,* Chicago: U. of Chicago Press, 681–4.
1961: From social system to ecosystem. *Sociological Inquiry* 31 (2) 140–49.

478   *References*

Duncan, O. D. and Duncan, B. 1955: Residential distribution and occupational stratification. *American Journal of Sociology* 60, 493–503.
Duncan, O. D. and Reiss, A. J. 1956: *Social characteristics of urban and rural communities.* New York: John Wiley.
Duncan, O. D. and Schnore, L. F. 1959: Cultural, behavioral and ecological perspectives in the study of social organization. *American Journal of Sociology* 65, 132–146.
Duncan, O. D. *et al.* 1960: *Metropolis and region.* Baltimore: Johns Hopkins Press.
Durand, J. D. and Pelaez, A. 1965: Patterns of urbanization in Latin America. *Millbank Memorial Fund Quarterly* 43 (4) 166–96.
Eberik, G. and Barjac, P. 1970: *Le logement: dossier noir de la France.* Paris: Dunod.
Economie et Politique, 1965. special number on the Housing Crisis, August-September.
Eldredge, H. Wentworth, editor, 1967: *Taming megalopolis.* Vol. i: *What is and what could be.* Vol. 2: *How to manage an urbanized world.* New York: Anchor Books.
Eldridge, H. T. M. 1956: The process of urbanization. In Spengler, J. and Duncan, O. D., editors, *Demographic analysis.* Glenco, Ill.: The Free Press.
Emmanuel, A. 1969: *L'Échange inégal.* Paris: Maspero.
1972: trs. by B. Pearce, *Unequal Exchange.* London: New Left Books.
Engels, F. and Marx, K. 1969: *Selected Works.* Moscow: Progress Publishers. (London: Laurence & Wishart.)
Ericksen, E. G. 1954: *Urban behaviour.* New York: Macmillan.
Erlanger, Howard S. 1974: Interpersonal violence. U. of Wisconsin (typed paper).
Espaces et Sociétés, special number, Imperialisme et urbanisme en Amérique Latine. 1971.
Evans, Mary A., Thurman, Alfonzo, Edoh, Anthony, Figueroa, Augusto, 1975: Busing and urban segregation: the continuing struggle. U. of Wisconsin (paper).
Fainstein, Norman and Fainstein, Susan, 1974a: *Urban political movements: the search for power by minority groups in American cities.* Englewood Cliffs, N.J.: Prentice Hall.
1974b: The future of community control. Columbia (mimeo).
Faris, R. E. L. and Dunham, H. W. 1939: *Mental disorders in urban areas.* Chicago: U. of Chicago Press.
Farley, R., 1964: Suburban persistence. *American Sociological Review* 1, 38–47.
Farley, R. and Taueber, Alma, 1972: Racial segregation in the public schools. U. of Wisconsin (mimeo).
Fava, S. F. 1956: Suburbanism as a way of life. *American Sociological Review* 21, 34–37.
1958: Contrast in neighbouring: New York City and a suburban community. In Dobriner, W., editor, *q.v.*
Fava, S. F. and Gist, Noel P. 1975: *Urban society.* New York: Thomas Crowell.
FCUTCRP, 1970: *Livre noir des transports parisiens.* Paris.
Feagin, Joe R. and Hahn, Harlan, 1973: *Ghetto revolts, the politics of violence in American cities.* New York: Macmillan.
Ferrarotti, F. 1970: *Roma da capitale a pereferia.* Rome: Laterza.
1974: *Vita dei baraccati.* Rome: Laterza.
Firey, W. 1947: *Land use in central Boston.* Harvard UP.
Fisher, R. M. 1959: *Twenty years of public housing.* New York: Harper & Row.

Florence, P. Sargant, 1953: *The logic of British and American industry.* London: Routledge.

1948: *Investment, location and size of plant.* London Cambridge UP.

Fogelson, Robert M. 1968: *The fragmented metropolis,* Los Angeles 1850–1930. Cambridge Press: Harvard UP.

Foley, D. L. 1960: British town planning: one ideology or three? *British Journal of Sociology* 11, 211–231.

1963: *Controlling London's growth.* Berkeley: U. of California Press.

Form, W. H. 1954: The place of social structure in the determination of land use. *Social Forces,* 32, 317–323.

Frank, A. G. 1967: *Capitalism and underdevelopment in Latin America.* London: Monthly Review Press.

Frank, A. Gunder, Pereira, L., Germani, G., Graciarena, J. 1969: *Urbanizacao e subdesinvolvimento.* Rio de Janeiro: Zahar Editores.

Frankenberg, R. 1966: *Communities in Britain.* London: Penguin.

FRAP, 1970: Les salairés au pouvoir. Montreal (pamphlet).

1972: Document de travail pour le développement de l'unité des militants. Montreal.

Freyssinet, M. and Regazzola, 1970: Segregation urbaine et déplacements sociaux. Paris: Centre de Sociologies Urbaine.

Frieden, B. J. 1964: *The future of old neighbourhoods.* Cambridge Press.: MIT Press.

Friedland, Roger: 1975: Corporate Power and Urban Renewal in the US. PhD thesis, U. of Wisconsin.

1975: Big apple and the urban orchard. Berkeley (paper).

Friedmann, G. 1953: *Villes et campagnes.* Paris: A. Colin.

Furtado, C. 1965: Obstaculos politicos, ao crescimento economico do Brasil. *Revista Civilizacao Brasiliera* 1 (1) 133–41.

Fusfeld, Daniel R. 1968: The basic economies of the urban and racial crises. Conference paper of the Union for Radical Political Economics.

Gans, H. J. 1967: *The Levittowners, ways of life and politics in a new suburban community.* New York: Pantheon. London: Allen Lane.

1962: Urbanism and suburbanism as ways of life. In Rose, Arnold M., editor, *Human behaviour and social processes.* Boston: Houghton Mifflin.

Gans, Herbert J. 1962: *The urban villagers: group and class in the life of Italian Americans.* Glencoe, Ill.: The Free Press.

1965: The failure of urban renewal. *Commentary,* April, 29–37.

1968: *People and plans.* New York: Basic Books.

Ganz, Alexander, 1973: The city-sandbox, reservation or dynamo? *Public Policy* 21.

Garcia,Vasquez, F. J. 1968: *Aspectos del planeamiento y de la vivienda en Cuba.* Buenos Aires: Jorge Alvarez.

Garnier, C. 1970: Des progrès contre nature. *Le Nouvel Observateur,* 18 May.

Garnier, P. P. 1973: *Une ville et une révolution: La Havane.* Paris: Anthropos.

Gartner, Alan and Riessman, Frank 1974: *The service society and the consumer vanguard.* New York: Harper & Row.

Gaviria, M. *et al.,* 1968: Gran San Blas. *Revista de Arquitectura,* Madrid.

George, P. 1950: *La ville.* Paris: PUF.

1961: *Précis de géographie urbaine.* Paris: PUF.

1962: *L'URSS.* Paris: PUF.

George, P. and Randet, P. 1964: *La région parisienne.* Paris: PUF. (w.J. Bastié).

Gettys, W. E. 1940: Human ecology and social theory. *Social Forces* 18, 469–76.

Gibbs, J. P. and Martin, W. T. 1959: Toward a theoretical system of human ecology. *Pacific Sociological Review*, 2, 29–36.
1962: Urbanization, technology and the division of labour: international patterns. *American Sociological Review*, 27, 667–77.
Gillmore, H. 1953: *Transportation and the growth of cities.* Glencoe, Ill.: The Free Press.
Gilmore, H. W. 1944: The old New Orleans and the new: a case for ecology. *American Sociological Review* 385–94.
Gist, N. P. 1957: The ecology of Bangalore, India: an east-west comparison. *Social Forces* 35, 356–65.
Gist, N. P. and Fava, S. F. 1964: *Urban society.* New York: Thomas Crowell.
Glaab, Charles N. 1963: *The American city. A documentary history.* Homewood, Ill.: The Dorsey Press.
Godard, Francis, 1972: De la notion de besoin au concept pratique de classe. *La Pensée*, 166.
Godard, Francis, Castells, M. *et al.* 1973: *La rénovation urbaine à Paris: structure urbaine et logique de classe.* Paris: Mouton.
Goldstein, S. 1958: *Patterns of mobility 1910–1950.* Philadelphia.
Goldstein, S. and Mayer, K. B. 1961: *Metropolitanization and population change in Rhode Island.* Providence.
Gomez, P. 1965: La spéculation foncière. *Economie et Politique,* August, 77–84.
Goodall, Leonard E. 1968: *The American metropolis.* Columbus: Charles E. Merrill.
Goodson, David, editor, 1971: *Problems in political economy: an urban perspective.* Lexington: Heath.
nyp. *Towards a critique of capitalopolis: capitalism and urban development in the US.*
Gordon, Diana R. 1973: *City limits. Barriers to change in urban government.* New York: Charterhouse.
Gottmann, J. 1961: *Megalopolis. The urbanized northeastern seaboard of the United States.* Cambridge, Mass.: MIT Press.
1967: The skyscraper amid the sprawl. In Gottmann, J., editor, *Metropolis on the move,* New York: John Wiley, 123–51.
Graciarena, J. 1967: *Poder y clases sociales en el desarrollo de America Latina.* Buenos Aires: Paidos.
Green, Constance McLaughlin, 1965: *The rise of urban America.* New York; Harper & Row, 1966: London: Hutchinson.
Green, V. 1964: *The heart of cities.* New York: Simon & Schuster.
Greenstone, J. David and Peterson, Paul E. 1973: *Race and authority in urban politics. Community participation and the war on poverty.* New York: Russell Sage Foundation.
Greer, S. 1962: *The emerging city.* Glencoe, Ill. The Free Press.
Greer, S. 1963: *Metropolitics.* New York: John Wiley.
1965: *Urban renewal and American cities.* Indianapolis: Bobbs Merrill.
Greer, S. and Orleans, P. 1962: The mass society and the parapolitical structure. *American Sociological Review,* 27, 634–46.
Greer, Scott, McElrath, Dennis L., Minar, David W., Orleans, Peter, editors, 1968: *The new urbanization.* New York: St Martin's Press.
Groupe de Sociologie Urbaine de Nanterre, 1970: Reconquîte urbaine et rénovation diportation. *Sociologie de Travail* 4.
Guerrand, R. H. 1966: *Les origines du logement social en France.* Paris: Les Editions Ouvrières.

Guillermaz, J. 1967: *La Chine populaire*. Paris: PUF.
Guterman, Stanley S. 1969: In defense of Wirth's urbanism as a way of life. *American Journal of Sociology*, 74, 492–99.
Gutkind, P. C. W. 1966: African urban family life and the urban system. *Journal of Asian and African Studies*, 1, 35–42.
Hadden, Jeffrey K. and Borgatta, Edgar F. 1965: *American cities: their social characteristics*. Chicago: Rand McNally.
Hall, Peter, 1966: *World Cities*. London: World University Library.
Halperin, M. 1968: Growth and crisis in Latin American Economy. In Petras J. and Zeitlin, editors, q.v. 44–76.
Handbook of political economy. Moscow: Foreign Language publishing house.
Handlin, O. and Burchard, J., editors, 1963: *The Historian and the city*. Cambridge, Mass.: MIT Press.
Harloe, M., editor, 1976: *Captive cities*. London: John Wiley.
Harris, C. D. and Ullman, E. L. 1945: The nature of cities. *The Annals of the American Academy of Moral and Political Sciences*, 242, 7–17.
Harrison, Bennett, 1974: *Urban economic development: suburbanization, minority opportunity and the condition of the central city*. Washington, DC: The Urban Institute.
1964: The housing of relocated families. *Journal of the American Institute of Planners* 30 (4) 226–86.
1965: A comment of HHFA study of relocation. *Journal of the American Institute of Planners*, November.
Hartman, Chester, 1974: Yerba Buena.
Harvey, David, 1973: *Social justice and the city*. London: Edward Arnold.
1974: Class-monopoly rent, finance capital and the urban revolution. *Regional Studies* 8.
1975: The political economy of urbanization in the advanced capitalist countries: the case of the US. *Urban Affairs Annual Review*, Beverly Hills: Sage Publications.
Hatt, P. 1946: The concept of natural area. *American Sociological Review* 11, 423–7.
Hauser, P. M., editor, 1961: *L'Urbanisation en Amérique Latine*. Paris: UNESCO.
Hauser, P. and Schnore, Leo F., editors, 1965: *The study of urbanization*. New York: John Wiley.
Hautreux, P. Lecourt, D and Rochefort, M., 1963: Le niveau supérieur de l'armature urbane française. Rapport au Commissariat Général du Plan, Paris (roneo).
Haveman, Robert H. and Hamrin, Robert D., editors, 1973: *The political economy of federal policy*. New York: Harper & Row.
Hawley, A. H. and Zimmer, Basil G. 1970: *The metropolitan community*, Beverly Hills: Sage Publications.
Hawley, Amos H. 1950: *Human ecology*. New York: Ronald Press.
1956: *The changing shape of metropolitan America*. Glencoe Ill.: The Free Press.
1963: Human ecology, definition and history, Ann Arbor, Michigan (unpublished lecture notes).
Hill, Richard Child, 1974: Separate and unequal: governmental inequality in the metropolis. *American Political Science Review*, December.
1975: Black struggle and the urban fiscal crisis. New York: Conference on urban political economy (mimeo).

The History of the CPSU. Foreign Language publishing house, Moscow.

Hobsbawm, E. 1970: La ville et l'insurrection. *Espaces et Sociétés* 1, 137–49.

Hodge, P. L. and Hauser, P. M. 1969: *The challenge of America's population Outlook,* 1960–1985. New York: Praeger.

L'Homme et la Ville, special number, October 1960: Recherches Internationales à la lumière de marxisme.

Hoover, E. M. and Vernon, R. 1959: *Anatomy of a metropolis.* New York: Doubleday.

Horwood, and Boyce, 1959: *Studies of the central business district and urban freeway development.* Seattle: U. of Washington Press.

Hoselitz, B. F. 1953: The role of cities in the economic growth of underdeveloped countries. *Journal of Political Economy* 61, 195–203.
    1957: Urbanization and economic growth in Asia. *Economic development and Cultural Change* 6 (1) 42–54.

Howe, C. 1968: The supply of urban housing in mainland China: the case of Shanghai. *The China Quarterly,* January, 73–97.

Hoyt, H. 1939: The structure and growth of residential neighbourhoods in American cities. Washington DC: Federal Housing Administration.
    1964: Recent distortions of the classic models of urban structure. *Land Economics* 40, 199–212.

Huet, Armet *et al.* 1973: Le role idéologique et politique des comités de quartier. Paris: Ministère de l'Equipement.

Hunter, F. 1953: *Community power structure.* Chapel Hill: U. of N. Carolina Press.

Huzard, A. 1965: Un siècle de crise. *Economie et Politique,* August, 31–8.

Imbert, M. 1965: Aspects comparés de la vie de loisir à Paris et en banlieue. CEGS.

Indovina, Francesco, editor, 1973: *Lo spreco edilizio.* Padua: Marsilio.

INSEE (D.R. de Paris) 1961: Délimitation de l'agglomération parisienne. Paris.

Institute for Center-Planning, 1965: *Motivations de localisation des établissements dans la région urbaine de Göteborg* (Trans. by IAURP from Danish.)

International Urban Research (Berkeley) 1959: *The world's metropolitan areas.* Berkeley: U. of California Press.

Ion, J. 1970: La promotion immobilière: du logement à l'habitat. *Sociologie du Travail* 4, 416–426.

Ion, J. *et al.* 1973: Les Equipements socio-culturels et la ville. Paris: Ministère de l'Equipement.

Ipola, Emilio, 1971: Le FRAP devant la crise. *Québec Occupé,* Montreal.

Isard, W. 1956: *Location and space economy—A general theory relating to industrial location, market areas, land use, trade and urban structure,* Cambridge Press.: MIT press.

Jacobs, Jane, 1961: *The death and life of great American cities.* New York: Random House. 1972. London: Penguin.

Jacobs, Paul, 1965: *Prelude to riot. A view of urban America from the bottom.* New York: Vintage Books.

Jalée, P. 1969: *L'Impérialisme en 1970.* Paris: Maspero.

Janowitz, M. editor, 1961: *Community political systems.* Glencoe. Ill.: The Free Press.

Johnson, E. S. 1957: The function of the central business district in the metropolitan community. In Hatt & Reiss, *Cities and Society,* Glencoe, Ill.: The Free Press, 248–59.

Joly, J. 1970: Le recensement de la population française de 1968: les premiers résultats. In L'Institut d'Etudes Politiques de Grenoble, *Amenagement du territoire et développement regional*, Grenoble, 385—440.

Jones, Charles O. and Hoppe, Layne D. 1969: *The urban crisis in America.* Washington DC: National Academy of Sciences.

Journées de Sociologie Urbaine d'Aix-en-Provence, 1968: Les fonctions urbaines et la structure de la ville. Aix (roneo).

Kahl, J. A. 1959: Some social concomitants of industrialization and urbaniz-ation: A research review. *Human Organization*, 18 (2) 53—74.

Kain, J. F. 1968: Urban travel behaviour. In L. Schnore, editor, *Social Science and the city.* New York: Praeger, 161—192.

Kaplan, H. 1963: *Urban renewal politics: slum clearance in Newark.* Columbia UP.

Katz, D. and Hill, T., 1958: Residential propinquity and marital selection. *Marriage and Family Living*, 20, 27—35.

Katznelson, Ira, 1973: *Black men, white cities, race politics and migration in the United States and Britain 1948—68.* London: OUP.

1975: Community conflict and capitalist development. Paper given at the annual meeting of the American Political Science Association, San Francisco.

Keller, S. 1968: *The urban neighbourhood: a sociological perspective.* New York: Random House.

Keyfitz, N. 1965: Political Economic Aspects of urbanization in south and southeast Asia. In Hauser and Schnore, editors, *q.v.* 265—311.

Kin-Ki, 1966: Partout fleurit l'esprit de Tatchai. *La Chine* 2.

Kolb, W. L., 1954—55. The social structure and functions of cities. *Economic Development and Cultural Change* 3, 30—46.

Konstantinov, A. D. 1960: Some conclusions about the geography of cities and the urban population of the USSR based on the results of the 1959 census. *Soviet Geography* 7.

Kopp, A. 1967: *Ville et révolution.* Paris: Anthropos (1970: *Town and revolution.* London: Thames and Hudson.)

Kuan-I-Chen, 1960: *World population growth and living standard.* New Haven: Yale UP.

Kukawka, P., Mingasson, C., Roig, C. 1969: Récherche sur la structure du pouvoir local en milieu urbain. Grenoble: Institute d'études politiques (mimeo).

Labasse, J. 1966: *L'Organisation de l'espace.* Paris: Hermann.

Lagneau, G. 1959: Chine en chantier. *Cahiers Franco-Chinois* 88—103.

Lampard, E. 1955: The history of cities in the economically advanced areas. *Economic Development and Cultural Change* 3, 90—104.

1965: Historical aspects of urbanization. In Hauser and Schnore, *q.v.* 519—54.

Lamy, B. 1967: La fréquentation du centre-ville par les diferentes catégories sociales. *Sociologie du Travail* 2. 164—79.

Lansing, J. B., and Kish, L. 1957: Family life cycle as an independent vari-able. *American Sociological Review* 22, 512—519.

Lapin. H. S. 1964: *Structuring the journey to work.* Philadelphia.

Lautmann, E. O. and Guttman, L. 1966: The relative associational contiguity of occupations in an urban setting. *American Sociological Review* 31 (2) 169—78.

Lavedan, P. 1960: *Histoire de Paris.* Paris: PUF.

Ledrut, R. 1967: *Sociologie urbaine.* Paris: PUF.

1968: *L'espace social de la ville.* Paris: Anthropos.

1973: *Les images de la ville*—Paris: Anthropos.
1970: L'Image de la ville. *Espaces et Sociétes*, 1.
Lefebvre, H. 1967: Quartier et vie de quartier, Paris: *Cahiers de l'IAURP* 7.
1968: *Le droit à la ville.* Paris: Anthropos.
1970a: *Du rural et de l'urbain.* Paris: Anthropos.
1970b: *La révolution urbaine.* Paris: Gallimard.
1972: *La pensée marxiste et la ville.* Paris: Castermann.
1974: *La production de l'espace.* Paris: Anthropos.
1971: La ville et l'urbain. *Espaces et Sociétes* 2.
Lerner, D. 1965: *The passing of traditional society.* Glencoe, Ill.: The Free Press.
Leron, R. 1970: Eléments pour une conparaison Paris-province. In Institut d'Etudes Politiques de Grenoble, *L'Aménagement du territoire et développement régional,* Grenoble, 441—65.
Lewis, J. W. 1966: Political aspects of mobility in China's urban development. *The American Political Science Review,* Dec. 899—912.
Lewis, O. 1953: Tepoztlan restudied: a critique of the folk-urban conceptualization of social changes. *Rural Sociology* 18, 121—38.
Lieberman, S. 1963: *Ethnic patterns in American cities.* Glencoe, Ill.: The Free Press.
Lieberman, S. and Silverman, A. R. 1965: The precipitants and underlying conditions of race riots. *American Sociological Review* 30 (6), 887—98.
Linsky, A. S. 1965: Some generalizations concerning primate cities. *The Annals of the Association of American Geographers* 55, 506—13.
Lipietz, Alain, 1874: *Le tribut foncier urbain.* Paris: Maspero.
Lipsky, Michel, 1968: Protest as a political resource. *American Political Science Review* 62 (4).
1970: *Protest in city politics, rent strikes, housing and the power of the poor.* Chicago: Rand McNally.
Lojkine, J. 1970a: Eléments pour une théorie scientifique de l'urbanisation capitaliste. Laboratoire de Sociologie Industrielle (roneo).
1970b: La création de l'axe ouest-est de RER Saint Germain-Boissy-St Léger. Unpublished report (roneo).
1973a: *La politique urbaine dans la région parisienne, 1945—1972.* Paris: Mouton.
1973b: Contribution à une théorie marxiste de l'urbanisation capitaliste. *Cahiers Internationaux de Sociologie* 1.
1974: *La politique urbaine dans la région Lyonnaise 1945—1972.* Paris: Mouton.
1976: Urban policies and urban social movements. In Harloe, Michael, editor, *Captive Cities,* London: John Wiley.
Lojkine, J. and Preteceille, E. 1970: Politique urbaine et stratégie de classe. *Espaces et Sociétes* 1.
Long, N. E. 1966: Local government and renewal politics. In Wilson, J. Q. editor, *q.v.* 422—34.
1968: Political science and the city. In Schnore, L. F., editor, *q.v.,* 243—62.
Loring, W. C., Sweetser, F. L. and Ernst, C. F. 1957: *Community organization for citizen participation in urban renewal.* Cambridge Mass.: Harvard UP.
Lowe, J. R. 1967: *Cities in a race with time; progress and poverty in American renewing cities.* New York: Random House.
Luttrell, W. F. 1962: *Factory location and industrial movement.* Cambridge.
Lynch, K. 1960: *The image of the city.* Cambridge, Mass.: MIT Press.
McAdams, Robert C. 1966: *The evolution of urban society.* Chicago: Aldine.

McElrath, D. E. 1962: The social areas of Rome. *American Sociological Review* 27 June, 389–90.

McEntire, D. 1960: *Residence and race.*

McKelvey, Blake, 1963: *The urbanization of America 1860–1915.* New Brunswick: Rutgers UP.

McKenzie, R. D. 1933: *The metropolitan community.* New York: McGraw Hill.

1926: The scope of human ecology. *Publications of the American Sociological Society* 20, 141–54.

Mann, P. H. 1965: *An approach to urban sociology.* London: Routledge.

Marris, P. 1963: A report on urban renewal in the United States. In Dhul, L. J., editor, *The Urban condition,* New York: Basic Books, 113–34.

Marris, Peter and Rein, Martin, 1972: *Dilemmas of social reform,* 2nd. edn. London: Routledge.

Martin, W. T. 1958: The structuring of social relationships engendered by suburban residence. In Dobriner, W., editor, *The Surban community,* New York: Putnams.

Marx, K., 1970: *Capital,* vol. 1. Moscow: Foreign Language Publishing House; London: Lawrence & Wishart.

Masotti, Louis H., and Hadden, Jeffrey K., editors, 1973: The urbanization of the suburbs, *Urban Affairs Annual Review.* Beverly Hills: Sage publications.

Masters, Stanley H. 1972: The effect of housing segregation on black-white income differentials. Institute for Research on Poverty, U. of Wisconsin (mimeo).

Matthieu, G. 1963: *Peut-on loger les Français?* Paris: Seuil.

Mayerson, C. L. 1965: *Two blocks apart.* New York: Holt, Rinehart & Winston.

Meadows, P. 1967: The city, technology and history. *Social Forces* 36: 141–7.

Meadows, P. and Mizuchi, E. H., editors, 1969: *Urbanism, urbanisation and change.* Reading, Mass.: Addison-Wesley.

Medam, Alain, 1972: *La ville censure.* Paris: Anthropos.

nyp: *Les sens de la ville.*

Melendres-Subirats, M. and Lentin, F. 1970: La planification urbaine face au marché du logement: trois projets de villes nouvelles en France. *Sociologie du Travail* 4.

Meltzer, J. 1953: Relocation of families displaced in urban redevelopment. Experience of Chicago. In Colemen Woodbury, editor, *Urban redevelopment: problems and practice.* Chicago: U of Chicago Press.

Merlin, P. 1967: *Les transports parisiennes.* Paris: Masson.

1969: *Les villes nouvelles.* Paris: PUF.

Meyer, J. R. 1968: Urban transportation. In Wilson, J. Q., editor. *The Metropolitan enigma.* Cambridge Mass.: Harvard UP, 44–76.

Meyerson, M. and Banfield, E. 1955: *Politics, planning and the public interest.* Glencoe, Ill.: The Free Press.

Miner, H. 1952: The folk-urban continuum. *American Sociological Review* 17, 529–537.

Mingione, Enzo, 1976: Sociological Approach to regional and urban development: some theoretical and methodological issues. In Harloe, M *q.v.*

Ministère de la Construction, 1966: Circulaire no. 61–38, 7 August.

Miro, C. A. 1964: The population of Latin America. *Demography* 1, 15–41.

Mission de l'Etude de l'IAURP, 1967a: Villes nouvelles en Grande-Bretagne.

1967b: Urbanisme en region de Londres. *Cahiers de l'IAURP* 8.

1973: On the causes and consequences of neighbourhood political mobilization. Paper delivered at the Meeting of American Political Science Association, New Orleans.

nyp: Growth defied: Community organization and the struggle over urban development in America. PhD thesis, Harvard.

nyp: The post-war politics of urban development. *Politics and Society* and *Espaces et Sociétés.*

Mollenkopf, J. and Pynees, Jon, 1972: Property, politics and local housing policy. *Politics and Society,* 2 (4).

Morse, R. M. 1962: Some characteristics of Latin American urban history. *American Historical Review* 67, (2) 317–338.

1965: Urbanization in Latin America. *Latin American Research Review,* Autumn (consulted in Spanish edition, with enlarged bibliography, U. of Texas, 1968).

Moulin, Raymonde, 1973: *Les architectes.* Paris: Calmann-Lévy.

Moynihan, Daniel P. 1969: *Maximum feasible misunderstanding.* Glencoe, Ill.: The Free Press.

Mumford, Lewis, 1956: *Man's Role in changing the face of the earth.* Chicago. 1961: *The city in History.* New York: Harcourt Brace; London: Secker and Warburg.

Munizaga, G. and Bourdon, C. 1970: *Sector Manuel Rodriguez: Estudio de un sector habitacional popular en Santiago de Chile.* Santiago de Chile: CIDU.

Nadge, J. 1962: The new towns program in Britain. *Journal of the American Institute of Planners* 28.

National Commission on Urban Problems 1966: the *Ribicoff Hearings:* report of the NCUP.'

National Planning Association, 1963: The scope and financing of urban renewal and development. Washington.

Norton, G. and Ginsburg, S. 1965: Urban geography and non-western areas. In Hauser and Schnore, editors, *q.v.* 311–47.

O'Brien, R. W. 1941: Beatle Street Memphis, a study in ecological succession. *Sociology and Social Research,* 26, 439–36 (sic!).

OEA, 1970: Situacion demografica de America Latina. Washington.

Oi, Walter, and Schuldiner, P. 1962: *An analysis of urban transportation demands.* Evanston, Ill.: Northwestern U.P.

Oppenheimer, M. 1969: *The urban guerrillas.* Chicago: Quadrangle Books.

Orleans, H. 1952: *Stevenage: a sociological study of a new town.* London: Routledge.

Orleans, L. A. 1959: The recent growth of China's urban population. *Geographical Review,* June, 43–57.

1966: China's population: reflections and speculations. In Adams, Ruth, editor, *Contemporary China,* New York: Pantheon.

Osborn, F. J., and Whittick, A. 1963: *The new towns: the answer to megalopolis.* New York: McGraw Hill.

Owen, Wilfred, 1966: *The metropolitan transportation problem.* New York: Anchor books.

Pahl, R. E. 1970: *Patterns of urban life.* London: Longmans.

Panofsky, Edwin, 1970: Architecture gothique at pensée scolastique. Paris: Miniert.

Park, R. E. 1925: The city: suggestions for the investigation of human behaviour in the urban environment. In Park, R. E., Burgess, E. W., McKenzie, R. D. *The City,* Chicago: U of Chicago Press.

Parsons, K. C. 1967: The role of universities in city renewal. In Eldredge, editor, vol. 2, *q.v.* 979–1002.

Pchelintsev, O. S. 1966: Problems of the development of the large cities. *Soviet Sociology* 5 (2).

Pekin Information, 1969: Les jeunes gens instruits progressent dans la voie révolutionnaire. February.

1969b: La pensée de Mao-Tse-Toung nous guide dans la lutte pour dompter la nature. 24 November.

Pekin Revolutionary Committee, 1969: La voie de l'industrialisation socialiste en Chine. *Pekin Information*, 27 October.

Perkins, D. H. 1967: Economic growth in China and the cultural revolution: 1960. *The China Quarterly*, April, 33–48.

Perspective, 1964: Special number on Urbanization, June.

Petras, J. and Zeitlin, M., editors, 1968: *Latin America: Reform or revolution?* Greenwich, Conn.: Fawcett Publications.

Pettigrew, T. F. 1969: Racial issues in urban America. In Friedan, B. J. and Nash, W., editors, *Shaping an urban future*, Cambridge Mass.: MIT Press.

Pickvance, C. 1975: On the study or urban social movements. *The Sociological Review* 23 (1).

Pinto, A. 1962: *Chile: un caso de desarrollo frustrado.* Santiago: Editorial Universitairea.

Pirenne, H. 1927: *Les villes de moyen-Age.* Brussells.

Pittsburgh Area Transportation Study, 1961: *Study Findings*, vol. 1. Pittsburgh.

Piven, Frances, F. and Cloward, A. 1971: *Regulating the poor.* New York: Vintage; London: Tavistock.

1974: The great society as political strategy. In Cloward, A. and Piven, F. *The politics of turmoil*, New York: Pantheon.

Pizzorno, A. 1962: Développement économique et urbanisation. Actes du vᵉ congrès mondiale de Sociologie.

Polsby, N. 1963: *Community power and political theory.* New Haven, Conn.: Yale UP.

Popenoe, D. 1963: On the meaning of urban in urban studies. *Urban Affairs Quarterly* 6. 1969 in Meadows and Mizuchi, editors, *q.v.* 64–76.

Potere Operaio, 1970: Pour un travail politique dans les quartiers populaires (mimeo).

Pottier, Claude, 1975: *La logique du financement public de l'urbanisation.* Paris: Mouton.

Poulantzas, N. 1968: *Pouvoir politique et classes sociales de l'état capitaliste.* Paris: Maspero.

1973: *Political power and social classes* trs. O'Hagan, London: New Left Books.

Poupard, B. 1970: Contribution à une sociologie de la politique urbaine. Paris: Ministère de l'Equipement et du Logement (mimeo).

Préfecture de Paris, 1968: Communication au Conseil de Paris sur la rénovation urbaine. Paris.

President's Commission on law enforcement and administration of justice, 1968: *The challenge of crime in a free society.* New York: Avon Books.

Pressat, R. 1958: La population de Chine et son économie. *Population*, Oct. 569–90.

Presthus, R. 1964: *Men at the top: a study in community power.* New York: OUP.

Preteceille, Edmund, 1973: *La production des grands ensembles.* Paris: Mouton.

1975: Besoins sociaux et socialisation de la consommation. *La Pensée,*

180.
Pynoca, J., Schafer, R., Hartman, C. editors, 1973: *Housing urban America.*
Chicago: Aldine.
Quijano, A. 1967a: Dependance, cambio social y urbanizacion en Latino
America. CEPAL (mimeo).
1967b: Tendencias de cambio en la sociedad peruana. Universidad de
Chile, (mimeo).
Quin, J. A. 1940: The Burgess zonal hypothesis and its critics. *American
Sociological Review*, 5, 210—218.
1955: *Urban Sociology.*
Racine, Luc, and Roch, Denis, 1971: La conjoncture politique québecoise
depuis 1960. *Socialisme Québecoise* 21—2.
Ramparts, 1970: Special number, May.
Rapkin, C. and Grigsby, W. C. 1960: *Residential renewal in the urban core.*
Philadelphia: U. of Pennsylvania Press.
Raymond, M. G. 1966: *La politique pavillionnaire.* Paris: CRU.
Reiss, A. J. Jr., 1959: The sociological study of communities. *Rural Sociology*
24.
Recherches, 1973: Special number. Les Equipement Collectifs. Paris: CFRFI.
Redfield, R. 1941: *The folk culture of Yucatan.* U. of Chicago Press.
1947: The folk society. *American Journal of Sociology* 3 (4) 293—308.
1954: The cultural role of cities. *Economic Development and Cultural
Change* 4.
Remy, J. 1966: *La ville, phenomène économique.* Brussells: Les Editions
Ouvrières.
Remy, J. and Voyé, Liliane, 1974: *La ville et l'urbanisation.* Brussells: Duculot.
Report of the Federal Housing Ministery, 1969: *Le logement au Canada.*
Ottawa.
Report of the National Advisory Commission of Civil Disorders 1968
Washington.
Report of the National Commission on Urban Problems to the Congress and to
the President of the United States, 1968: *Building the American City.* 91st
Congress, 1st session, house document 91—34.
Retel, J. O. 1965: Quelques aspects des relations sociales dans l'agglomera-
tion parisienne. In Cornuau, C. *et al. q.v.*
Reynolds, D., 1961: What do we know about our experience with relocation?
Journal of Inter-Groups Relations 342.
Riessmann, L. 1964: *The urban process.* Glencoe, Ill: The Free Press.
Rochefort, M., Bidault, C., Petit, M. 1970: *Aménager la territoire.* Paris:
Seuil.
Rodwin, L. 1956: *The British new towns policy.* Cambridge Press: Harvard UP.
Rose, A. 1968: The crisis in urban renewal. *Habitat* 11 (3) 2—8.
Ross, H. L. 1965: Uptown and downtown: a study of middle-class residential
areas. *American Sociological Review* 30 (2).
Rossi, P. H. 1955: *Why families move.* Glencoe, Ill.: The Free Press.
Rossi, P. K. and Dentler, R. A. 1961: *The politics of urban renewal.* Glencoe,
Ill.: The Free Press.
Rostov, W. W. 1960: *The stages of economic growth. A non-communist mani-
festo.* London: Cambridge UP.
Salaff, G. Janet, 1967: The urban communes and anti-city experiments in
Communist China. *The China Quarterly*, Jan. 82—109.
Santos, E. and Sielenberger, S. 1968: *Problematica estructural del sector
vivienda.* Universidad Catolica de Chile.

Sautter, Gabrielle, 1963: Naissance de la vie sociale dans un nouveau quartier (Pontoise). Paris (roneo).

Sauvage, A., Bolle, P., Burlen, C. *et al.*, 1968: L'information, l'éducation et la participation des citoyens dens les processus de developpement urbain. Paris. Ministère de l'Equipement (roneo).

Schiltz, Timothy and Moffitt, William, 1971: Inner city — outer city relationships in metropolitan areas: a bibliographical essay. *Urban Affairs Quarterly* 7 (1).

Schmidt, Catherine, 1965: Quelques recherches récentes sur le problem du pouvoir dans les communautés locales. *Sociologie du Travail, 2.*

1961: Transportation systems, socio-economic systems and the individual. Transportation Design Considerations, 841, Washington: National Research Council.

1963a: Characteristics of American suburbs. *Sociological Quarterly* 4, 122–34.

1963b: The socio-economic status of cities and suburbs. *American Sociological Review* 28: 76–85.

1964: Urban structure and suburban selectivity. *Demography*: 1, 164–78.

Schnore, Leo F. 1965a: *The urban scene.* Glencoe, Ill. The Free Press.

1965: On the spatial structure of cities in the two Americas. In Hauser and Schnore, editors. *q.v.*

1966: The city as a social organism. *Urban Affairs Quarterly* 1 (3) 58–69.

editor 1968: *Social Science and the City.* New York: Praeger.

1972: *Class and race in cities and suburbs.* Chicago: Markham.

editor 1975: *The new urban history.* New York: John Wiley.

Schnore, L. F. and Alford, R. R. 1963: Forms of government and socio-economic characteristics of suburbs. *Administrative Science Quarterly* 8 (1).

Schorr, L. 1968: How the poor are housed in the US. In Fava, S. F., editor, *Urbanism in world perspective.* New York: Thomas Crowell, 485–96.

Schretter, H. A. 1967: Downtown revitalization. U. of Georgia, Institute of Community and Area Development.

Segré, R. 1970: Urbanisme, architecture et révolution: l'apport de Cuba. *Espaces et Sociétés* 1, Paris: Anthropos.

Shevky, E. and Bell, W. 1955: *Social area analysis.* Stanford: Stanford UP.

Simmel, G. 1950: The metropolis and mental life. In K. Wolff, editor, *The sociology of Georg Simmel,* Glencoe, Ill.: The Free Press.

Sirjamaki, J. 1961: *The sociology of cities.* New York: Random House.

Sjoberg, G. 1960: *The pre-industrial city: past and present.* Glencoe, Ill.: The Free Press.

1965: Cities in developing and in industrial societies: a cross-cultural analysis. In P. Hauser and L. F. Schnore, editors, *q.v.* 213–65.

Slayton, W. L. 1966: The operations and achievements of the urban renewal program. In Wilson, J. Q., editor, *q.v.*

Smerk, George, M. 1965: Urban transportation in the federal role. Bloomington: Indiana UP. 1973: The politics of transportation. In David. S. M. and Peterson, P. E., editors, *Urban politics and public policy: the city in crisis.* New York: Praeger.

Smith, T. Lynn, 1964: Why the cities? Observation on urbanization in Latin America. In Astuto, P. L. and Leal, R. A. *Latin American problems.* New York: St John's UP.

Soares, G. A. D. n.d.: Congruence and Incongruency among indicators of economic development. Berkeley: Institute of International Studies.

SODIC-IAURP, 1965: Examen concert de cas de deserrement industriel. Paris (roneo).

Solari, A. 1965: *Sociologia rural latino americana.* Buenos Aires: Paidos.

Sorlin, P. 1964: *La société soviétique.* Paris: A. Colin.

Sorokin, P. A. and Zimmerman, C. C. 1929: *Principles of rural-urban sociology.* New York.

Sorre, M. 1952: *Les fondements de la géographie humaine.* Paris: A. Colin.

Soucy, C. 1969: La crise des centres. Paris: Centre de Sociologie Urbaine (roneo).

Sovani, N. V. 1964: The analysis of over-urbanization. *Economic Development and Cultural Change* 12 (2) 113—22.

Spengler, O. 1928: *The Decline of the West,* vol. 2. London: Allen & Unwin.

Spilerman, Seymour, 1970: The causes of racial disturbances: a comparison of alternative explanations. *American Sociological Review* 35.

1971: The causes of racial disturbances: tests of an explanation. *American Sociological Review.* June.

Stalin, J. n.d.: The bases of Leninism. Moscow: Foreign Language Publishing House.

Starr, Roger, 1975: *Housing and the money market.* New York: Basic Books.

Sternlieb, G. 1963: The future of retailing in the downtown core. *Journal of the American Institute of Planners* 29, 102—12.

1971: The city as a box. *The Public Interest,* autumn.

Sternlieb, G. and Burchell, Robert W. 1973: *Residential abandonment, the tenement landlord revisited.* Rutgers: Center for Urban Policy Research.

Stewart, M. S. 1965: Can we save our cities? The story of urban renewal. New York: Public Affairs Committee.

Surkin, Marvin, 1975: *I do mind dying. A study on urban revolution.* New York: St Martin's Press.

Survey Research Centre, 1950: Industrial mobility in Michigan. Ann Arbor: U. of Michigan: ISR.

Suttles, G. D. 1968: *The social order of the slum.* Chicago: U. of Chicago Press.

Svetlichnyi, B. 1967: Some problems of the long range development of cities. *Soviet Sociology,* summer.

Swenson, W. 1968: The continuing colloquium on University of Chicago demonstration projects in Woodlawn. Aspects of a major university's committment to an inner-city ghetto. U. of Chicago: Center for Urban Studies. (roneo).

Tabb, William, 1970: *The political economy of the black ghetto.* New York.

Taisne, Plantevin, C. 1966: Typologie des communes dans la région parisienne. *Cahiers de l'IAURP* 3.

Taueber, K. E. and Taueber, A. F. 1964: White migration and socio-economic differences between cities and suburbs. *American Sociological Review* 5, 718—29.

1965: *Negroes in cities: residential segregation and neighbourhood change.* Chicago: Aldine.

Tchen-ta-Louen, 1968: Les petits usines jouent un grand role. *Chine en Construction,* June.

Theodorson, G. A., editor, 1961: *Studies in human ecology.* Evanston, Ill.: P. Row, Peterson & Co.

Theret, Brunot and Dechervois, Miguel, 1976: *Contribution à l'étude de la rente foncière capitaliste.* Paris: Mouton.

Thoenig, Jean-Claude, 1974: *L'ère des technocrates.* Paris: Dunod.

Topalov, Christian, 1973: Capital et propriété foncière, Paris: Centre de Sociologie Urbaine.

1974a: *Les promoteurs immobiliers.* Paris: Mouton.

1974b: Politique monopoliste et propriété du logement. *Economie et Politique*, March.

Touraine, A. 1961: *Ouvriers d'origine agricole.* Paris: Seuil.

Ullmann, M. B. 1961: *Cities of mainland China: 1953–1959.* Washington: US Bureau of Census.

US Department of Housing and Urban Development. *Journal of Housing: Housing and Planning References.*

US Census of Population, 1961: 1960 Number of inhabitants, United States, summary. Final Report, P.C. (1)-1A.

US Government Report 1973: Housing in the seventies. Hearings on housing and community development legislation 1973, part 3. House of Representatives subcommittee on Banking and Currency. 93rd Congress, first session. Washington: Government Printing Office.

US Housing and Home Finance Agency, 1966: The housing of relocated families: summaries on a census bureau survey. In Wilson, J.Q., editor, *q.v.*

Utopie, 1970: *Urbaniser la lutte de classes.* Paris.

Vernon, R. 1960: *Metropolis 1975.* Cambridge, Mass.: Harvard UP.

1959: The changing economic function of the central city. New York: Committee for Economic Development.

1962: *The myth and the reality of our urban problems.* Cambridge, Mass.: MIT Press.

Veatch, James, F. 1975: Federal and local urban transportation policy. *Urban Affairs Quarterly* 10 (4).

Weaver, R. C. 1966: *The urban complex.* New York: Doubleday.

Weber, M. C. and Weber, C. C. 1967: *Culture, territoriality and the elastic middle.* In Eldredge and Wentworth, *q.v.*

Weber, Max, 1905: *The City.* (1966) Glencoe, Ill.: The Free Press.

Weicher, J. C. 1968: Municipal services and urban renewal. U. of Chicago, PhD thesis.

Weisslitz, J. 1969: *Les migrations au Pérou.* Paris: Sorbonne.

Wheston, W. L. C. 1968: Housing, renewal and development bibliography. U. of California, Dept. of City and Regional Planning.

White, W. H. 1956: *The organization man.* New York: Simon & Schuster.

White House Conference, 1966: To fulfil these rights.

Whyte, W. H. 1958: Urban Sprawl in The Editors of Fortune, *The exploding metropolis,* New York: Doubleday, 115–39.

Wilkinson, R. and Merry, D. M. 1965: A statistical analysis of attitudes to moving. *Urban Studies,* 2, 1–14.

Willhelm, S. M. 1964: The concept of the ecological complex a critique. *American Journal of Economics and Sociology,* 23, 241–8.

Willmott, P. and Young, M. 1960a: *Family and kinship in east London.* London: Routledge.

1960b: *Family and class in a London suburb.* London: Routledge.

Wilson, J. Q. editor. 1968: *The metropolitan enigma.* Cambridge, Mass.: Harvard UP.

1966: editor, *Urban Renewal, the record and the controversy.* Cambridge, Mass.:

1963: Planning and politics. Citizen participation in urban renewal. *Journal of the American Institute of Planners* 29 (4) 242–9.

1968: editor, *City politics and public policy.* New York: John Wiley.

1968b: The Urban unease. *The Public Interest,* summer, 26–7.

Wilson, Franklin D. 1975: The organizational components of expanding metropolitan systems. U. of Wisconsin: Center for Demography and Ecology.

Wirth, L. 1938: Urbanism as a way of life. *American Journal of Sociology*, July.
    1964: *On cities and social life*. Chicago: U. of Chicago Press.
Wood, R. C. 1964: *1400 governments*, New York: Anchor Books.
    1963: The contributions of political science to Urban form. In Hirsch, Werner, Z., editor, *Urban life and form*, New York: Holt, Rinehart and Winston, 99–129.
Wooley, L. 1957: The urbanization of society. *Journal of World History*, 4.
Wu-Yuan-Li, 1967: *The spatial economy of communist China; a study on industrial location and transportation*. Stanford: Hoover Institution.
Yago, Glenn, 1974: How did we get to the way we are going? General motors and public transportation. U. of Wisconsin (mimeo).
2000, 1969. Revue de l'aménagement du Territoire, special number, Pour une politique de l'environnement.
2000, 1969: Special number, *L'environnement*. December.
2000, 1970: Special number, *Les transports*, October.

Index

500   *Index*

socialism and industrialization in, 65
urban expansion in, 65, 66
Spanish Civil War, 110
Spain, urban research in, 469
Spencer, Herbert, 124
Spengler, O., 76
Spilerman, S., 406
Springfield, 294
Stamford, 294
Starr, R., 387
state intervention, x
in urban housing, 158, 159
in consumption, 459, 463
statistical empiricism, and concept of the
urban, 10
Sternlieb, G., 230, 415
and Burchell, R. W., 408
Stewart, M. S., 286n
suburbanization, 384
and capitalist accumulation, 385, 421,
426
and fragmentation of government, 391
and housing, 408
and inner cities, 389, 402
and residence patterns, 385
and residence segregation in, 391 –
and role of state, 385, 410
and social relations of, 388
and transport problems of, 411
Surkin, M., 406, 416, 424n
Survey Research Center, 22, 136
Suttles, G. D., 108, 183
Svetlichnyi, B., 65
Swenson, 304
Syracuse, 293

Tabb, W., 389, 416, 478
Taisne-Plantevin, C., 36, 168
Tampa, 293
Taueber, K. E. and A. F., 103, 177, 297,
389
Tchen-ta-Louen, 71
technology, as basis of the metropolis, 21,
22, 23
as basis of spatial regrouping of
activities, 22
as basis of urbanization, 40, 46
of communications, 21
and ideology of environment, 185, 187
and industrial location, 137
and specialized urban centres, 231
and technocracy, 23
and technologism, 120, 231
Theodorson, G. A., 116
Theret, B. and Dechervois, M., 467
Thoenig, J., 467
Toledo, Ohio, 293
Tonka, Hubert, 94
Topalov, Christian, 155, 389, 466
Toronto, 211
Touraine, A., 61
Toynbee, Arnold, 76
Toulouse, 100, 102, 107

Truesdell, Ginette, 348n
Tucson, 177
Tulsa, Oklahoma, 293

Ullmann, M. B., 69
'underdevelopment', 40–3
and dependence, 44, 47
United States, contradictions of, 422
and McCarthy period, 396
and metropolitanization in, 383
and 'New Frontier' policies, 396
suburbanization in, 384
urban crisis in, 379, 402
urban research in, 470
United States Census of Population, 10,
172
University of Glasgow, enquiry into
decentralization of industry, 132
University of Pennsylvania, 300
Uruguay, 60
'urban', definition of, 9, 10, 17, 234, 431,
445
development of, 88
dichotomies associated with, 15, 23,
24, 31, 47, 78, 447, 453
and 'environment', 186, 451
and extended reproduction of labour
power, 237, 431
as economic unit, 235, 236
as ideological unit, 235
ideology of, 186, 235, 431, 463, 468
in Lefebvre, 89, 90, 94
as politico-juridical unit, 235
and problem of freedom, 90
and socialism and capitalism, 91
and statistical empiricism, 10
urban areas, definition of, 444
American, 210
accelerated growth of, 46
French, economic power of, 31
institutional organization of, 210
segmentation of space and, 127, 444
urban colonization, and Roman Empire, 12
and Russia, 65
urban culture, 9, 15, 431
and capitalist-socialist dichotomy, 80–4
formulations of, 76, 77, 78, 80, 81, 82,
83, 431
and industrialization, 82
and sub-cultures, 97, 431
and population density, 80, 84
and urban centrality, 299, 316
and urban ideology, 73, 74, 83, 84, 85
86, 186, 430
urbanization, definition of, 9, 10, 15
acceleration of, x, 15, 18
culturalist tendencies in analysis, of, 9
dependant, 47, 48, 50
and industrialization, 9, 14, 40, 41, 42,
45, 88
Lefebvre's interpretation of, 88, 93
and level of articulation of system of
economic development, 40, 129
and migration, 61, 62

behaviour patterns in, 97, 98, 107, 108
in East London, 98, 106
ethnic, 183
formed by cultural systems, 109, 110
in France, 103
and habitat, 96, 97
Madrid, 110
neighbourhoods of, 102
neighbouring in, 97
social life in, 97, 98, 99, 109
and spatial organization of, 97, 101,
102, 104, 108
suburban, 98, 99, 100
in United States, 103, 106, 109
Urban transport systems
bus, 203
car, 203, 204, 206
commuting, 195, 207, 411
contradictions in, 411, 434
factors in cost of, 196
in La Rochelle, 253
and location of places of production,
180
in metropolitan region, 21, 24, 25, 27,
133, 192, 383
métro. 202, 203, 204, 252, 310
in New Towns, 281
of Paris, 35, 36, 37, 131, 195, 196, 197,
198, 199, 200, 253. 310
passenger committees and protest, 205
private, 24, 194, 210
public, 195, 203
in Quebec, 358, 359
railways, 202, 203
social determinants of, 194, 195, 200
sociological problematic of, 191
in United States, 206, 424

and United States suburbs, 383, 387
'Utopie' group, 94, 95

Valence, 256
Veatch, J. F., 411
Vernon, R., 21. 118, 158, 230
Voyé, Liliane, 467

Washington, DC, 26, 27, 175, 207, 296,
297, 420
Weaver, R. C., 286n
Weber, Alfred, 135
Weber, Max, 13, 76, 80, 120, 124, 250
Weber, M. and C., 109
Weicher, J. C., 302
Weisslitz, J., 57, 61
Western Siberia, 67
Wheston, W. L. C., 286n
White House Conference, (1966), 297
White, W. H., 20, 107, 231
White Plains, 294
Wilkinson and Merry, 178
Willmott and Young, M., 98, 106
Wilson, F. and Banfield, E., 383
Wilson, J. Q., 20, 27, 252, 286, 303, 393,
415
Winston Salem, 294
Wirth, Louis, 77, 78, 80. 90, 105, 118
Wood, R. C., 210, 247, 248
Wooley, L., 7
Worcester, 294
Wu-Han, 71
Wu-Yuan-Li, 69

Yago, G., 387